American Music

American Music

A

Panorama

Daniel Kingman

SCHIRMER BOOKS
A Division of Macmillan Publishing Co., Inc.
NEW YORK

Collier Macmillan Publishers
LONDON

Schirmer Books
A Division of Macmillan Publishing Co., Inc.
866 Third Avenue, New York, N.Y. 10022

Collier Macmillan Canada, Ltd.

Library of Congress Catalog Card Number: 78–22782

Printed in the United States of America

printing number

3 4 5 6 7 8 9 10

Library of Congress Cataloging in Publication Data

Kingman, Daniel.
    American music.

    Includes bibliographies and index.
    1. Music, American--History and criticism.
I. Title.
ML200.K55   781.7'73   78-22782
ISBN 0-02-871260-9

To Louise

The *panorama* was a popular form of didactic art in the larger frontier cities of America in the mid-1800s. It was an exhibition of the painter's art done on a mammoth scale. A huge canvas, twenty feet high or more, would slowly pass before the assembled audience, moving, scroll-like, from one large roll to another. The paying spectators would in this way have unrolled before their eyes vast scenes, in a sort of primitive motion picture—battle scenes, or the entire course of the Mississippi River between two points. Often this was done to the accompaniment of music.

Contents

cumstances; the music of the spirituals—contemporary accounts of the singing, musical derivations; the survival of the folk spiritual—the vocal quartet, the later addition of instrumental accompaniment as the beginnings of gospel music; SECULAR FOLK MUSIC, 42: Cries, calls, and hollers—the embryonic blues scale in the field holler; folk blues—social changes that spawned them, blues texts and subjects, blues form, the music of the blues; work songs and ballads; FURTHER READING, 54; LISTENING, 59; PROJECTS, 60.

PART TWO: SACRED MUSIC IN THE POSSESSION OF THE FOLK   119

CHAPTER FIVE: RELIGIOUS MUSIC OF EARLY AMERICA 121

PSALMODY IN AMERICA, 122: Calvinism and the psalms; psalm tunes and psalters—the Geneva Psalter, the Ainsworth Psalter, the Bay Psalm Book; two divergent "ways"—the folk (oral) manner of performance and the written manner; reform and instruction; THE SINGING SCHOOL TRADITION, 128: How the singing schools worked; William Billings (composer of *Chester*) and the other Yankee singing masters; Yankee tune-books by the hundreds—their music (including *When Jesus Wept*); the end of an era; MUSIC AMONG OUR SMALLER INDEPENDENT SECTS, 135: The Moravians; the Shakers—and two Shaker songs; FURTHER READING, 141; LISTENING, 144; PROJECTS, 145.

CHAPTER SIX: NATIVE RELIGIOUS MUSIC DURING AND AFTER THE TIME OF EXPANSION   148

NATIVE TRADITION SUPPRESSED IN THE URBAN EAST, 149; THE FRONTIER, 150: The "long boys" move west; the shape notes; infusion of the folk element—*Amazing Grace, Captain Kidd* and *Wondrous Love*; revivalism and the camp meeting—the turbulent Kentucky and Great revivals; the revival spiritual—transformations of "On Jordan's stormy banks I stand"; parallel traditions of the white and black spiritual; THE CITY, 165: urban hymn collections—Lowell Mason; white gospel song—Ira Sankey; black gospel song—Thomas A. Dorsey, the Sanctified Church; popular religious song today; FURTHER READING, 171; LISTENING, 173; PROJECTS, 176.

PART THREE: THREE PRODIGIOUS OFFSPRING OF THE RURAL SOUTH   179

CHAPTER SEVEN: COUNTRY MUSIC   181

ENDURING CHARACTERISTICS OF THE MUSIC, 181: The instruments; the style of singing; melody and harmony; ENDURING CHARACTERISTICS OF THE WORDS, 185: Fundamental attitudes; perennial themes—love, death, religion, nostalgia, trains, and event songs with their ballad legacy; dialect; A SURVEY OF THE MUSIC'S TIMES AND STYLES, 188: Pre-"discovery" professionalism and the medicine show; commercial beginnings—early recordings and radio, Uncle Dave

CHAPTER SEVENTEEN: EXPLORATION AND EXPERIMENT: TECHNOLOGY AND NEW ESTHETIC CONCEPTS   510

Illustrations, Captions, and Credits

The following captions and credits refer to illustrations on the cover and at the opening of each chapter:

COVER. Courtesy The Metropolitan Museum of Art, Gift of Mrs. Russell Sage, 1908.

CHAPTER 1. The homegrown music of the rural fiddler has become a characteristically American sound. (Lenox, Ga. John R. Griffin, 80, plays "Love My Sweetheart Good As Anybody" while his brother, Arthur, in his 70's, "beats the straws," adding a staccato rhythmic drone by striking the violin strings with a broomstraw. American Folklife Center, Library of Congress, photo by Carl Fleischhauer.)

CHAPTER 2. The spiritual, a vital folk tradition, lives on in the praise songs of today. (Holiness Church service near Marion, Alabama. Photo by Frederic Ramsey, Jr., from *Been Here and Gone*, Rutgers University Press.)

CHAPTER 3. An ancient Hopi Indian dance, in which the music is inseparable from the rite. (C. 1912. Courtesy of the American Museum of Natural History.)

CHAPTER 4. Folk music as a propaganda weapon. (Almanac singers [left to right], Sis Cunningham, Millard Lampell, and Pete Seeger. Greenwich Village community flat, July, 1942. Courtesy of Culver Pictures, photo by Morris Gordon.)

CHAPTER 5. In many religious communities, music had an integral function in daily life. (The Moravians in Salem, N.C., celebrate the 4th of July, 1783. Painting by John Clymer, reprinted with the permission of the American Cyanamid Company.)

CHAPTER 6. An outdoor Methodist camp meeting about 1837. (Courtesy of The New-York Historical Society, New York City.)

CHAPTER 7. Country-Western, originally a rural, regional music, adapts to a wider, popular audience. (Willie Nelson and Waylon Jennings. Photo by Michael Putland/Retna.)

CHAPTER 8. The heir to a long line of down-and-outers, the urban blues singer. (Photo by Charles Sawyer.)

CHAPTER 9. The rock group and its mass audience. (Members of the Jefferson Starship at the Great American Music Fair in Syracuse, N.Y., 1975.)

CHAPTER 10. The great era of popular make-believe. (Helen Morgan, popular torch singer, c. 1935, best known for her role in "Show Boat." Courtesy of Culver Pictures.)

CHAPTER 11. The minstrel show, a popular genre of caricature, parody, earthy humor, and music. (Early sheet music cover, c. 1847.)

CHAPTER 12. The art of the jazz performer at its optimum in the small combo. (Bebop musicians, Charlie Parker on alto saxophone and Miles Davis on trumpet, N.Y.C. 1940s. Photo by William P. Gottlieb [Edward J. Gottlieb collection].)

CHAPTER 13. Cartoonists' conceptions of two popular composer/performers. (Pianist Louis Moreau Gottschalk in 1869. Bandleader John Philip Sousa in 1906. Courtesy of the New York Public Library at Lincoln Center, Performing Arts Research Center.)

CHAPTER 14. The American West on the ballet stage. (Omnibus-TV production of Aaron Copland's "Billy The Kid," 1953. Courtesy of Roy Stevens, photographer.)

CHAPTER 15. The composer and his interpreter, both indispensable to the musical experience. (Leonard Bernstein and Elliott Carter, 1969. Photo by Bert Bial. Courtesy of the New York Philharmonic.)

CHAPTER 16. Two Yankee innovators, George Ives in bandmaster's uniform c. 1892 and his son, Charles Ives, composer/insurance executive, c. 1913 in Battery Park. (Photographs courtesy of the John Herrick Jackson Music Library, Yale University.)

CHAPTER 17. Two hallmarks of the avant-garde, electronic technology and multi-media. (Performance of *Variations* V in 1965 with music by John Cage [left foreground followed by David Tudor and Gordon Mumma], choreography by Merce Cunningham [partially hidden in center], and electronics by Robert Moog and Billy Klüver. Photo by Hervé Gloaguen, courtesy of the Cunningham Dance Foundation.)

Foreword

by Virgil Thomson

One of the many virtues of this course-book on American music is that the subject is not treated chronologically. Histories of governments, of reigns and dynasties, of kings and presidents, can with some justice be pegged to a list of dates. But art, music, and poetry, though they may reflect the stylistic variants that we call "periods," do not constitute at all a continued story or a stream. In fact these very "periods," though they can be lined out on calendars, do not follow in their structural evolution any pattern of growth resembling what we observe casually as "current events." The most remarkable flowerings in these domains—the Greek or the Elizabethan theater, the Viennese symphonic expansion from Haydn through Schubert, Impressionist painting in France, or Cubism—are likely to encompass at most fifty years, often, as with Cubist painting, far less. And if between these shining moments something vaguely derivative or even promising seems to go on, pinning that to the concept of "influences" or likening it to a flow gives no more a true picture of what happens in art than it would in genetic variation, which proceeds, as we know, by the most astonishing and unexpected jumps, and not always forward either.

Kingman has, moreover, not assumed that producing the "classical" is music's main business. Actually his book is already more than half over when he gets around to enumerating our classical composers, that family of all-pretty-much-alike purveyors of composition to the concert and operatic platforms, just occasionally accompanying worthy efforts (read "serious") in dance, ballet, or films.

That family runs roughly from 1875 to now, beginning with John Knowles Paine, who started at Harvard our first university department of music, as an academic subject (learned composition after European models taught by learned composers who had learned their skills in Europe). We are a tiresome lot, we classical composers, and lots of books have been written about us. Our music gets played by the standard ensembles, with some luck published and recorded. Lots of people like it too and listen to it on radio, buy recordings, go to concerts. There is nothing wrong with it, any more than there is with Beethoven or Bach or Mozart or Schumann or Debussy. What is tiresome about us is that our music, exactly like that of our European masters, is so thoroughly explained already in books and program-notes, and that every ten years or so a batch of new books brings everybody up to date about us.

This part of Kingman's book, the finale, is lively to read because he perceives differences, and he writes about us without getting quarrelsome. This advantage comes from his natural gift for judgment, a rare one among laymen. But he is not a layman anyway, he is a composer. He knows what music is about. He even knows what most of us are about; so he doesn't have to get angry at us, as laymen tend to do when they encounter music they are not prepared to encompass. Nevertheless, this part of his book is not the most vibrant, from the simple fact that there are already plenty of books on the subject, though few in its class.

There are also lots of books about jazz. This is a rich vein for musical analysis, as well as for human interest stories that cut through the social strata. The sociology of jazz has been laid wide open, like its aesthetics. Its economics remain obscure, like the enormously secret sources of its inspiration and its integrity. Jazz has been for fifty years now a self-conscious and proud, though persecuted, chamber-music with such power to reject impurities that even our vast commercial machine has never been able to take it over, simplify it, standardize it, and distribute it for mass consumption.

Our other rich veins for musical mining have been the religious (both black and white), the rhythmic for dancing (both black and Creole, by which I mean French and Hispanic), and the poetic (especially the ancient balladry of white Anglo-Saxons and the black blues of our Negro brethren). The pop music of our commercial establishment, moreover, is vastly powerful and vies for world favor, dollar for dollar about fifty percent, with the only other really strong pop music, which is the Hispanic. And it is quite possible that these two dominant strains, both of them far more sophisticated than anything else of their kind now existing, may dominate the receptivity of their peoples to the detriment of the classical product. Something of the kind seems to have weighed upon Ireland in the eighteenth century and Hungary in the nineteenth. The popular there outgrew the classical and pushed it aside. Whereas in England, Germany, Italy, and France the classical dominated, even in religion, show biz, singing, and social dancing, with little refuge left for the popular spirit save children's games, or quietly sinking underground.

Music-making anywhere—folk, pop, or classical—is not merely a matter of inspiration. It also has its methods. For carrying meaning it has melody and rhythm, the one mainly vocal, the other instrumental. It has structures that are the same as everywhere—harmony and form, the things we learned from our German music teachers. Melody speaks either in words or like them, and rhythm not only makes you move around but tells you when to move and how. Tunes produce emotional relief, and their words define or channelize that relief. But they also play games with rhythm. And instruments, whether they imitate singing or dancing, also make like speech. They "talk," as in the perpetual motion of a fast fiddle-piece or in the harsh "dirty" sounds of a jazz saxophone or trumpet.

And out of it all comes counterpoint, a multiplicity of tunes and rhythms that leads us through complexities of form and texture right into classical, or fine-art, music. Because the difference between straight music—pop balladry, dance, blues, or worship—and art music is the difference between simple meanings and multiple ones. And concealing a simple meaning under layers of more meanings—simultaneously heard, in succession, or both—is the device that produces in classical music (and in good jazz) the phenomenon sometimes referred to as "absolute" music, the illusion that there is no meaning at all, at least none you could sing about or dance to, but merely an ecstasy.

We do have that kind of music in jazz and in our concert-and-theater styles. Whether the technological imposition of constant presence—junk music or any other—may be putting all music in danger is something musicians like to worry about. It has already produced a certain inattention, but music is still around, all kinds of it. And all those kinds are the subject of Kingman's present study and of his teaching. I like him for his penetrating sociology of the musical function. For that I can even read with pleasure another book that pays serious attention to what might be called irreverently the classical dodge.

Preface

An author usually finds himself living with a rather clear and persistent image of the reader for whom he is writing a book. I have always envisioned the ideal reader of this book as a person who has somewhere picked up a lively interest in some kind of American music—be it blues or bluegrass, Cage, Coltrane, or Copland—and whose desire to find out more about *that* has led to engagement, bit by bit, through the interconnectedness of things, in the whole subject. The reader I have in mind need not be a musician or musically trained; an active, open mind and an inquiring spirit—these I have regarded throughout as the only essentials.

This work had its genesis, many years ago, in little more than an awakened enthusiasm for the music of my native land, an enthusiasm that manifested itself modestly enough at first in the inclusion of a few lectures on American music in the context of a general introductory course. My involvement came, by progressive stages, to embrace all of our varied musics, with the growing conviction that no aspect of our music should or *could* be excluded without maiming our perception of the whole teeming panorama. By this time an entire course had evolved, at a time when few such courses were offered, and when writing on the subject was, with few exceptions, rather narrow, and uninformed by a sense of the vastness, variety, and grandeur of the scene to be surveyed.

It is interesting to note some of the landmarks along the path of a lengthening perspective of American music. Looking over my very early notes, for example, I find Charles Ives and John Alden Carpenter treated together. It made a certain sense at the time; they were nearly exact contemporaries, and both were businessmen-composers—heirs, it seemed, of a distinctly American tradition of amateur composers who earned their daily bread in some occupation entirely apart from music. The tradition can be traced all the way back to William Billings and his fellow Yankee tunesmiths; it exists no more. It does not diminish Carpenter's place in American music to see at this vantage point that he was a talented mannerist with a rather narrow range, while Ives, with all the unevenness of his vast output, was a true pioneer and something of a giant.

Similar siftings and reassessments go on continuously; in another twenty years, no doubt, longer perspective will suggest—even demand—other realignments. A new skyline will have emerged by then. But I am now ready, as Charles Ives said about one of his publications, to "clean house" and to offer the fruits of my labors in the form of this modest guidebook.

The present work is not a history of American music—though a thorough perusal of it would furnish, it is hoped, a reliable historical framework upon which the results of further investigation by the reader would fit into place. Rather, this work is a panoramic survey, which directs the eye first to one and then another of the more or less parallel streams of American music.

The reader will naturally want to know how I have gone about distinguishing and identifying these streams. This is indeed the most immediate problem facing any writer who would survey and map for his readers such an extensive landscape.

Traditional distinctions, based on differences in kind and function, have been of some help. There is a triangular relationship between what are basically three kinds of art in the modern world—a relationship that perceptive observers have rather consistently noted. Carl Belz, for one, has presented a lucid exposition of this in his book *The Story of Rock*. At one apex of the triangle is *folk art*. This art is the homemade product of the nonspecialist—created to satisfy the perhaps unconscious expressive or esthetic urge of the individual, or in former times to meet the similar needs of a community more or less isolated and self-sufficient culturally, as in other ways. At the second apex of the triangle is what is best described as *fine art*. This is the custom-made product of the specialist—the artist. It is not divorced from reality, but it presents reality as seen through a lens, the temperament and technique of the artist.

Both these kinds of art are self-sustaining; they are not dependent upon popularity for their existence, although the products of either may be popular at any given time. At the third apex of the triangle is *popular art*, the very existence of which is predicated upon its popularity. It is the mass-produced product of the craftsman-entrepreneur, made to satisfy the demands of a community large enough to support the industry needed for its production and distribution. While popular art must be self-sustaining economically, it tends not to be self-sustaining artistically, but rather to imitate either folk art or fine art.

It will be noticed that folk art, at one apex, is the subject of the first part of the book, and fine art the subject of the last. Everything in between may be thought of as lying along the continuum of folk art to fine art, via a detour to popular art—this third apex consisting in America, until fairly recently, of the "Broadway galaxy." I have no intention of laboring this point as a rationale for my arrangement, despite the attractive simplicity of the generalizations implied.

While recognizing the validity of the distinctions inherent in this triangular concept, I confess I am more comfortable with the metaphor already alluded to—that of American music as comprised of several streams, more or less parallel, some narrow, some broad, some at times nearly drying up, some at times overflowing their banks, spilling into one another, interpenetrating, merging, diverging again.

From where I am now standing I think I can make out six such streams. Folk music, vastly varied and constantly changing, flowing from many sources, may well be occupying a channel nearly dry now, its waters having entered many other streams. Our native religious music has been amply fed from the stream of folk music, but it may also be in a dry season in terms of inherent vitality, with its future at least uncertain. Music having its source in the rural South constitutes a third stream consisting of three large branches—country music, blues, and rock. These have each become, in fact, mighty rivers, and have all nearly completely flowed over into commercial entertainment music (the fourth stream), changing it drastically. The two last streams are those of art music. Jazz, the unique American music of the performer, is relatively new. Having flowed mightily for a time, it is now somewhat reduced in volume, but in spite of threatened engulfment by the swelling currents of rock it has maintained much of its purity and force. The sixth stream, labeled fine art, is not large in volume, but is ever vigorous, mirroring the other streams from time to time on its varied surface and lending them its substance without itself becoming diminished. It has an enormous capacity for assimilating the waters of other streams without being diverted from its course or losing its essential character.

This view gives us six intermingling and mutually influential streams to observe. Whatever reservations one may have about this way of mapping the terrain (and I freely confess to some of my own), it can at least be said that each stream consists of a considerable and important body of music waiting to be known. Once the enthusiast has gotten to know the music, he can discard the categories or rearrange the music into his own. Nor are the boundaries always sharp. There are ambivalent composers and ambivalent pieces that could fit almost as well in one category as in another. Was John Philip Sousa primarily an entertainer, or a "serious" musician? William Billings was one of a "school" of composers and his contemporaries wrote almost nothing but sacred music. Yet he is sometimes regarded as our first popular composer; his *Chester*, at least, was indisputably the hit song of the American Revolution. And what of

Leadbelly's *Goodnight, Irene?* Leadbelly himself came into prominence as a folk singer, but this song—certainly not traditional—made the hit parade as a popular song. The thoughtful student can add many more examples. Rather than being exceptions, they prove the rule that American music is broadly interrelated, unpredictable, and defiant of categories.

My decision to abandon the traditional chronological-historical approach in the overall organization, in favor of the separate treatment of distinct but interrelated streams, was part of the basic plan of the work from the very beginning and reflects my views as to its essential nature. My purpose has been to put into the hands of both teacher and student a substantial but flexible guide to the *whole* of American music.

The work is substantial in that there is an ample treatment of each of the main streams, in a carefully designed succession of chapters. If its proportions are generous, so, it must be said, are those of the subject. It is my conviction and experience (a conviction fully shared by the publisher) that the skeletal outline approach is hardly adequate to convey anything of the substance of the subject, in its exuberant variety and detail.

The work is flexible in that it allows both teacher and student to use any of the six parts as a point of departure for the exploration of the whole subject. For example, those who feel most at home with folk music, or hold the view that this is the key to our musical culture, will naturally begin with part 1 but will be able to go on from there to explore our folk-based popular music in part 3, trace the folk influence in our native religious music in part 2, and then observe its use as a basis for much of our art music in parts 5 and 6.

But the study of American music could begin equally well with jazz (part 5), then proceed to a treatment of its roots in the first three parts, and then trace its relation to the rest of our art music in part 6.

Religion has played an important role in the formation of American character and culture. A study of our native religious music in part 2, and in chapter 2 of part 1, could be followed by a study of both its echo and its antithesis as observable in blues, country music, and rock (part 3) and in jazz (part 5); its influence on other art music could be traced in part 6.

The music of the "Broadway galaxy" (Broadway, Hollywood, and Tin Pan Alley) has been for many their first contact with American music, and could well serve as a point of departure, as could also our vigorous tradition of fine-art music, which has produced many works of wide appeal. Wherever one should choose to begin, in other words, one can find, if my intentions have been to any degree realized, not only a substantial treatment of that subject but also an invitation to relate it to all other parts of the whole.

Fine-art music in particular is often felt by many to be somewhat forbidding. The organization of part 6 is designed to overcome this barrier by a logical succession of stages. The music of chapter 14 ("Music with Film, Dance, Drama, and Poetry") constitutes an admirable introduction, in my experience, to our mature art music. All of it has reference to something outside music itself, and to something at the same time significant in most instances in American culture or history—a film, a dance, or a drama on an American subject, or poetry by an American such as Walt Whitman or James Agee. Chapter 15 follows this with music that has no overt extramusical associations. But the progression here is from very accessible pieces (the Gershwin Preludes or the Barber *Excursions for the Piano*), via chamber and orchestral music, to a work as complex as the Double Concerto of Elliott Carter. After this, the student is introduced to our more distinctly and consciously innovative tradition, going backwards chronologically to George and Charles Ives and forward to the avant-garde composers of the 1970s. The chapter on the "pioneers," with its emphasis on individual figures of the past, may be taken up either at the beginning or at the end.

Musical examples have been used rather profusely in certain chapters, where they seem to be practical and particularly essential. They should enhance the text for the individual reader who can read music; in the lecture hall or classroom the teacher may play or sing such examples as are relevant. Songs and song excerpts have been pitched for comfortable singing.

It is not usual to call special attention to notes, but I have reasons for most earnestly advising readers that they are in this case far from perfunctory. In addition to the usual and necessary documentation of bibliographical references, they serve two further and even more important functions: First, they furnish references to recorded examples that are the nearly indispensable illustrations of the points being made; second, they provide additional background, references, and relevant "asides," beyond what it was possible to incorporate into the text itself, opening up avenues of further exploration for the interested reader.

The reading lists, which I feel it is more useful to have at the conclusion of each chapter rather than all together at the end of the book, are quite selective, and include only those works that are apt to be readily available, are important to any further investigation of the topic in question, and are eminently readable in their own right. A basic collection of books on American music is recommended for access as a reference library in connection with this book. These books, representing a further degree of selectivity, are marked with an asterisk in the reading lists for the individual chapters.

Listening to as much of the music as possible is, of course, indispensable. Live performances are best, but records are a nearly obligatory substitute for immediate first acquaintance. Discography dates rapidly, is unnecessary in some areas, and more or less arbitrary in others. For the individual chapters, the lists of suggested recordings are as extensive as it seems useful to have them. In addition, a basic reference library of anthologies or single albums currently in print and/or available to libraries and schools is suggested; these items are indicated by an asterisk in the lists at the ends of the chapters. Of particular value is the *Recorded Anthology of American Music*, a collection of a hundred albums covering nearly every aspect of the subject. Issued by New World Records (3 East 54th St., New York, N.Y. 10022), a nonprofit recording company created through a grant from the Rockefeller Foundation, it is being distributed without cost, worldwide, to about seven thousand educational institutions with significant music departments, to public libraries, and to other qualifying institutions. Because of its broad range and its wide availability, many of the musical examples have been deliberately keyed to this collection, for the convenience of teacher and student.

An earlier series of recordings, *Music in America*, was issued by the Society for the Preservation of the American Musical Heritage. It is no longer in print, but many music department libraries have sets.

Since this book is an open-ended introduction to the subject, the suggestions for projects at the end of each chapter are to be considered an integral part of it. They are intended to give the student an opportunity to investigate further, on his or her own, many different aspects of American music. Even a tiny scrap of knowledge that one discovers, with a little effort, for oneself becomes a cherished corner of the whole subject—forever one's own, in a sense. It will be seen that the projects vary rather widely in the extent of work they involve and in the amount of musical background they presuppose, although the number of those calling for some knowledge of music has been kept to a minimum. This range is designed to allow for as much flexibility as possible in the use of individual projects. Furthermore, they are merely suggestions; the imaginative teacher and the inventive student can come up with many more, along similar or different lines. It will be noted that in nature and format the projects are by no means confined to the conventional "paper." I remember with pleasure how one student learned a group of sixteenth-century psalm tunes, set words from the Bay Psalm Book to them, added a simple, tasteful modal guitar accompaniment, and sang them for the class. The historical anachronism involved was a minor consideration as compared with the value of experiencing these old tunes as living music. (Needless to say, a similar project found its way into a list in this book.) I would be pleased to hear from students and teachers who have been innovative in this regard. The substance of what this book attempts to offer is not confined to the material in the chapters themselves. For the reader with the curiosity of an inquiring mind, the suggestions for projects, supported in many cases by the suggestions for further reading, offer many more avenues of approach to American music. It is for precisely that sort of reader, whether he or she happens to answer to the name of student, teacher, or simply enthusiast, that I like to feel this work was written.

Looking back over the long period of the book's gestation, it is heartening to recall, and a distinct pleasure to be able to acknowledge at last, the assistance and guidance of those friends and colleagues so knowledgeable in their particular fields who so graciously contributed their suggestions: Kenneth Owens in American Indian music, Joaquin Fernandez in Mexican-American music, Stanley Lunetta and Ken Horton in rock, and Herb Harrison in jazz. Frederick Westphal, during the entire project, never failed to give encouragement and to share willingly his knowledge, experience, and wisdom. I feel privileged indeed to have had, at various stages of the book's development, the perceptive and astute counsel of Virgil Thomson. And it would be difficult to imagine more discriminating yet warmly encouraging editors than Ken Stuart and Abbie Meyer, whose enthusiasm often helped to keep my own alive.

ACKNOWLEDGMENTS

I would like to thank the following people and organizations for material reprinted in the book:
I wish especially to thank Moses Asch, of Folkways Records, for generously granting permission to reprint from its vast and important issues of American music numerous lines of text, to be found in chapters 1 and 7.

Chapter 1

Yale University Press, *British Ballads from Maine*, Barry, Eckstrom, and Smyth, for tune and words of *The False-Hearted Knight*.

xxx   ACKNOWLEDGMENTS

David Seneff McIntosh, for tune and text of *Black Jack Davie*, ballad version, as found in M.A. thesis, "Some Representative Illinois Folk-Songs," by David Seneff McIntosh, Iowa State University, 1935.

Chapter 3

Recorded Anthology of American Music, Inc., for text of Rabbit Dance, from the notes of its album *Songs of Earth, Water, Fire, and Sky*, by Charlotte Heth. RAAM: NW–246.

Arhoolie Records, for text and music of *El Corrido Gregorio Cortez*.

Ramms Music, for music and lyrics of *La Muerte de Martin Luther King*, by Rafael Ramírez.

Chapter 4

University of Pennsylvania Press, *American Folksongs of Protest*, by John Greenway, for various song texts.

One line from *Birmingham Sunday*, by Richard Farina; copyright © 1964 by Ryerson Music Publishers, Inc. Assigned copyright © 1977 to Silkie Music Publishers, A Division of Vanguard Recording Society, Inc. Used by permission. All rights reserved.

One line from *Warm and Freedom Love*, by Rev. Frederick Douglass Kirkpatrick; copyright © 1968 by Rev. F. D. Kirkpatrick, 1978 by Sanga Music, Inc. Used by permission. All rights reserved.

Two lines from *Revolution* (John Lennon and Paul McCartney), copyright © 1968 by Northern Songs Limited. All rights for the U.S.A., Canada, Mexico, and the Philippines assigned to Maclen Music, Inc., c/o ATV Music Corp. Used by permission. All rights reserved.

Chapter 6

J. J. Augustin Incorporated Publisher, for extract from *Down-East Spirituals*.

Chapter 14

Harcourt Brace Jovanovich, Inc., for excerpt from *I Ride an Old Paint*, from *The American Songbag*, edited by Carl Sandburg.

D.K.

Part One
Folk Music

A scanning of the vast panorama of American music can begin nowhere more logically than with folk music. The very name is one to conjure with in our time of complexity yearning for simplicity, of rootlessness yearning for tradition, and of sophistication yearning for renewed contact with things of the soil. It is also true that America's music, throughout its broad spectrum, is so relatively new as to have remained closer to folk sources for its sustenance than is the case with any other country. What might be termed the "professional sector" of American musical life has never gone for very long periods without returning to refresh and revitalize itself at the fount of folk culture. Masterpieces as diverse as Porgy and Bess and Appalachian Spring *bear witness to this, as well as large amounts of music perennially in popular culture, from Dan Emmett to Paul Simon.

Yet this very indebtedness of our musical culture to its roots in folk music is attended by a paradox: There is probably no other country in the world in which the soil of folk culture as traditionally known has been so profoundly broken up, and either eroded away or rendered sterile. Not only have the all-pervasive media spread commercial urban music thoroughly, but they have put music largely into the hands of the professional entertainer and homogenized it. Continuous and extensive migration has broken down isolation and regionalism. And affluence, widespread in relation to the rest of the world, has put the mass-produced products and paraphernalia of the media into the hands of virtually everyone, so that the need or desire to make one's own music has apparently disappeared. For the time being, the most indispensable motivation for the cultivation of folk music seems to have been lost.

So it would appear that the humus of folklore has provided us with rich nourishment but proved to be fragile as well. Given the impact of mobility and change on our people, André Malraux's dictum that "folk art has ceased to exist because the folk have ceased to exist" may be nowhere more applicable than in America. Or if the folk have not ceased to exist, it may at least be true that we can no longer say with much certainty who they are. Some recent attempts to redefine the folk are described in chapter 4; the most noteworthy thing about them has been their failure.

What, then, is the state of folk music in the modern world? There are two views. The first is held by those (Charles Seeger has called them "structuralists") who regard folk music as a series of reservoirs, their currents forever stilled, that contain within their stable confines many valuable and cherished items. In this view the last reservoir was completed and filled at least half a century ago—before the spread of the mass media— and all that we call folk music today is either the preserved fragmentary relics of the past or an intellectual abstraction useful to those who want to make either money or propaganda.

The other view is held by those (whom Seeger has called "functionalists") who regard folk music as a flowing stream, ever changing and *adapting, and accepting whatever it can use from wherever it may find it. In this view folk music lives on, in ever-mutating form, in spite of all. Indeed, oral tradition has survived in the space age, and a visit to the local coffeehouse or college campus will incline one to the view of the functionalist rather than that of the structuralist. The phoenix of authentic folk music—not quite the same bird we thought we knew from the venerable old collections, to be sure—may be rising from the ashes of the fire set by an already outmoded modernism.*

Chapter One

The Anglo-American Folk Tradition

AMERICAN CULTURE, by virtue of its very genesis, has enjoyed a greater variety of folk influences than the culture of any other country. An ethnic music existed among the sparse inhabitants of the continent before the transoceanic migrations of historic times began. With these migrations have come folk traditions from three other continents, in continuing waves. This chapter and the next will treat the two dominant strains of American folk music—those whose preeminent influence in our culture is undeniable. These are the ones whose origins can be found in the British Isles and in black Africa.

The Anglo-American strain is best epitomized in the ballad. There are songs, hymns, and dance tunes as well, of course, and these will be dealt with. But it is the ballad that has been the main vehicle of the tradition, that most typifies it, and that has attracted the most serious attention, both from scholars and folk singers.

Because ballad singing has been virtually continuous among English-speaking peoples since that language emerged, we are not dealing with a phenomenon that can be limited to any single historical period. Ballads may be very old; some bear clear traces of medieval origin, while some hint of origins still older. Or they may be very young; on the fair assumption that ballad making is not dead, it is possible that today, somewhere, there is being fashioned or refashioned a piece that will eventually be recognized as a traditional ballad, or a variant of one.

As an introduction to this vast body of folk literature, you might try to hear several different versions of a single traditional ballad. *Barbara Allen*, the most popular in America (possibly because it was printed in so many songbooks in the nineteenth century), would be a good one to start looking for. You might be fortunate enough to hear the song in person from several singers: professionals, amateur folk enthusiasts, or just friends or acquaintances. This is the folk way. But if this is not possible, there is the medium of recordings.[1]

Barbara Allen has traveled far and wide. The Library of Congress Archive of American Folk Song contained, as of 1962, 243 notations of this ballad, picked up from twenty-seven states, from Maine to Florida to California. In addition to a wide geographical range, you will become aware of a wide range in styles of presentation. Your search might yield versions that range all the way from a field recording of the unadorned performance of a solitary singer, who learned the song from oral tradition, to a full commercial production number with studio orchestra and choral background. You will thus acquire a sense of both the pervasiveness and the durability of the traditional ballad. This done, it will be time to examine more closely some of its characteristics.

SOME MARKS OF THE BALLAD

A good story well told is one of the delights of human intercourse. If we add to this the power of a good tune to fix story and mood in the memory, and to this the hand-rubbed luster that any well-worn object has received from loving generations of its possessors, we have the essential ingredients of the ballad.

A story sung—preferably from memory; this will do as the beginning of a definition. It is also metered and rhymed, though with innocent inexactitude. The casualness of the traditional ballad in both meter and rhyme is illustrated in the following charmingly wayward stanza:

> They gave to her the nutmeg,
>   And they gave to her the ginger;
> But she gave to them a far better thing,
>   The seven gold rings off her fingers.

We must not expect of the true ballad of the folk the discipline of literary poetry. By way of rounding off the definition, we can note as an unvarying feature of the ballad that all its many verses (each usually four lines in length) are sung to the same tune.

The ballad has roots, many of which go deep. When we hear Pete Seeger sing of the plucky girl who cleverly turns the tables on a habitual murderer and pushes *him* into the sea to drown, we are hearing a tale that has been sung in varying versions by the Danish, Swedish, Norwegian, Icelandic, German, Polish, Magyar, Italian, Spanish, and Portuguese folk, and a tale that has its analogy in a story from Hebrew scripture. When Woody Guthrie sings *The Gypsy Davy,*[2] his version sounds very much at home on the western plains, but this ballad is at least as old as the attempt by king and parliament to expel the gypsies from Scotland about the time of Shakespeare.

What the ballad offers us is drama—drama as unfolded by a solitary singer. It is drama often of extraordinary terseness and condensation. The main points of the mournful tale of *Barbara Allen,* for example, may be set out in eight or nine verses. Usually the characters are not given any introduction, or it may be a very cursory one ("a lady in the North Countrie"; "a wooer out of the West"), and time and place are described in barest terms ("'Twas in the lovely month of May"; "the land where the grass grows green"). Prior events leading up to the climactic action are rarely set forth. The poet Thomas Gray characterized this terseness by saying that the ballad "begins in the fifth act of the play."

Description is lean, or lacking entirely. Occasionally it may be very telling, as:

> She glistened and glittered and proudly she walked
> The streets on the banks of the sea.

Often, however, it is rendered in the conventionalized language of the cliché phrase ("milk-white steed"; "lily-white hand"). These phrases may wander freely from one ballad to another.

Altogether, the way of the ballad is to leave a great deal to the imagination of the hearer, who is thus free to fill in scenes and events with extraordinary vividness. Jean Ritchie, a well-known folk singer from the Appalachians, tells of the impression made on her as a child by these scenes, which were fleshed out in her imagination as she heard the ballads:

> The song itself seemed unreal and far, far away, telling dreamily of Fair Ellender and Lord Thomas and courts and processions, love and death, but the people my half-closed eyes saw were alive and beautiful. Fair Ellender rode slowly by on her snow-white horse, her hair like long strands of

silver and her face like milk in the moonlight. Then came her waiting maids, dressed all in green, and holding their heads high and proud. There was Lord Thomas, tall and brave with his sword shining in his hand, there the wedding folk around the table.[3]

ORAL TRADITION AND THE BALLAD TEXTS

A folk song is an organic whole, consisting of words, a tune, and a way of singing. It is incomplete without any one of the three. For purposes of further study, however, we must consider each element in turn. We shall begin with that element which first attracted the attention of literary men and scholars, and which can most easily be grasped by the general reader—the words.

It is an accepted criterion of folk music that it not rely on print, but be transmitted and preserved simply by being sung or played. This is what is meant by oral tradition, and it has a significance, when we think about it, far beyond that of simply a technical definition. What is committed to the reservoir of memory is intimate to us, and has importance in our lives. Most of us can remember the strong impression made on us in childhood by a song that someone close to us sang from memory. "By heart" is not a gratuitous or accidental phrase. We don't properly sing a folk song until we have lived with it long, handled its imagery, and allowed its meaning to resonate within us. By this time memorizing has become incidental. Only then do we project it fully. Charles Seeger mentions the "luminous quality" that characterizes true ballad singing, which is often possessed not only by the exceptionally talented but even by ordinary carriers of the tradition.[4]

The Forces of Change

It is generally agreed that traditional folk singers do not intentionally alter a song. But there are many things about oral transmission that make changes inevitable—that lead, in other words, to the production of variants. Since the processes as well as the products of oral change may be fascinating, let us look at just a few. Simple forgetting is a constant factor. The change it works may be minor, and not affect the ballad to any essential degree, since something almost equally suitable may be substituted for what is forgotten. If from one singer we hear "When the flowers they were blooming" and from another "When red buds they were swellin'," the precise image has changed but the general evocation of spring remains. Or if some element is left out entirely, it may be very incidental and sufficiently far removed from what has been called the "emotional core," or very essence, of the ballad to make no great difference. But when major portions—the entire ending or the whole narrative context, for example— are forgotten, the whole point of the ballad may be changed.

The tendency to "localize" both the place names and the names of characters in the narratives is another obvious source of change. The "Oxford girl" easily becomes the "Knoxville girl" or even the "Waco girl." [5] Similarly, conventionalized descriptions may change; the "milk-white steed" becomes, more appropriately in the West, the "buckskin horse."

A misunderstanding of elements of language as the ballad ages is an interesting source of change. Difficult or ambiguous words, or words and phrases no longer in current usage, are very vulnerable to change. An older version of *The Gypsy Laddie*, still retaining aspects of the super-natural, says of the gypsy band that as they saw the lady "They coost their glamourie owre her." A presumably later and obviously garbled version says of the gypsies at this point that "They called their grandmother over"! Not only has the word *glamourie* ("glamour") been misunder-stood, but its older meaning as an actual spell to be cast over someone has been lost, to the impoverishment of the ballad.

Misunderstanding of older words and phrases has produced especially interesting results in the refrains, or burdens, of the ballads. "Juniper, gentian, and rosemary"; "Savory, sage, rosemary, and thyme"—in this age of renewed interest in the use of herbs it is surprising that these names should ever have been misunderstood or forgotten. But behold what the loss of their meaning has wrought with the passage of time. The first phrase appears transmuted into girls' names—"Jennifer gentle, and Rose-maree"—and the second has undergone a bewildering array of transforma-tions. Some of these, gleaned from Bronson's fifty-five versions of this ballad (known variously as *The Elfin Knight*, *Scarborough Fair*, or *The Lovers' Tasks*, among other names),[6] are here arranged in approximate order of increasing distance from the pure "plant" refrain:

Save rosemary and thyme.

Rose Mary in time.

Rose de Marian Time.

Every rose grows merry in time.

Every leaf grows many a time.

So sav'ry was said come marry in time.

Whilst every grove rings with a merry antine.

Green grows the merry antine.[7]

In each of these one can sense an attempt to be faithful to the *sound* of that which was heard but not understood, and at the same time in many cases to make some kind of new sense out of it.

Refrains make a particularly interesting study in themselves. It may be that some refrains which now consist completely of nonsense syllables are descended from phrases that once had meaning, even as incantations of some sort. But this is speculative. In any case, even if they have lost all "meaning" in the usual sense (if they ever had any), or any direct connection with the story, they cannot be eliminated without damaging the ballads artistically. This sense of their effect on both the mood and the pace of the narrative has kept them an integral part of many ballads. The effect of the refrain is cumulative, evocative, almost hypnotic. As Evelyn Wells has written: "One's interest is held by a singer who, with every other line, pauses for the refrain; the tale is dignified by the interruptions. Suspense mounts, and mounts rhythmically, with the regular recurrences of the refrain. The tempo of the tale is steadied, its stride evened." [8]

Finally, a kind of censorship, conscious or unconscious, may operate to make changes in the ballad. Folk singers will naturally be selective in the themes, images, or elements of the story that they "remember" according to their own moral or esthetic standards or those of their society, and whether or not this is done at a conscious level is not of great significance. In certain instances sexual themes are muted, or avoided entirely, as are references to nakedness, but this is not very common. Far more consistent and interesting are the changes that reflect an altered framework of reality as the legacy is passed to succeeding generations. References to the supernatural are very common in the old versions. These tend to disappear in more recent ones, especially in the transplantation to the New World. This often impoverishes the ballad from a poetic or imaginative standpoint, for the loss of the supernatural dimension is not usually compensated for by a corresponding gain in depth of insight from the standpoint of human nature.[9]

What happens to old ballads, then, is very like what happens to old buildings. None survive the passage of time intact. Some, of exceptional strength, may have only a few stones replaced here and there. In some, a ruined or lost wing may be replaced by an entirely new part, so that the outlines of the whole are drastically altered. Of others, only a wall or piece of foundation remains—an inscrutable fragment that no longer makes sense in our world and has to be relegated to fantasy. Still others may become dismantled entirely, and their stones scattered; later the keen observer may happen to notice a cornerstone, or a piece of an arch, that has been appropriated by builders of a later age, so that out of their new work bits of the old project curiously here and there as strange and unaccountable anachronisms.

Print and the Ballad

The oral tradition—human memory as the reservoir and the human voice as the "publisher"—has been stressed here at some length. But how would most of us know of the ballads today if they had not been written down? In our print-oriented society of course we would not. And it is a fact that traditional ballads have been appearing in print from time to time for centuries. What happens to them then? Are they no longer items of genuine folklore? Fortunately, we can leave this last question to the specialists. But the influence of print on the ballad is indisputable. We cannot trace here the fascinating interactions that take place between the written and oral traditions, but we can note that print is the *still* medium which freezes the ballad in some particular pose, protecting it but also ossifying it, while oral tradition is the medium in which *motion* and evolution occur—change, growth, decay, even unto death and dissolution.

ORAL TRADITION AND THE MUSIC OF THE BALLADS

It is somewhat unfortunate that the early attention given the ballads was directed almost exclusively to their texts. Early collectors and scholars were, for the most part, not musicians, and neither sensitive to the tunes nor equipped to record or study them. Indeed, "the ballad as literature" is still a dominant theme, and in fact has been more prevalent in America than in England. The imbalance of this one-sided approach is being restored, and it should be a function of a book on American music to lend a hand in this restoration.

To be sure, for the person not skilled in music and just becoming interested in ballads, the words are certainly their most approachable element. The story, and its embodiment in language, is the very core of the ballad. Most folk music the world over is closely wedded to words. But it is also true that it is simply not possible to gain any true idea of a ballad separated from its music. The words alone, abstracted in print as we find them in books, can impart only the dimmest notion of the effect of the same ballad sung—just as a reprint in black and white must fail to convey the depth, color, nuances, and mood of the original oil painting. Many traditional singers, it is interesting to note, find themselves unable to recall either the words apart from the music or the music apart from the words of a folk song.

Tune Variation

Tunes are subject to the same organic processes of change wrought by oral tradition that operate on the words, and these also produce tune variants—sometimes in great numbers. How does the tune of *Barbara Allen* go? It all depends on who is singing it. Here are two versions, recovered from traditional singing. They are quite different. Each is representative of a large group of tunes that has dozens of variants. The first was recorded in West Liberty, Kentucky, in 1937.

(Transcription by the author)

It was early in the month of May,
   When the May-buds they were a–swelling,
Sweet William on his death-bed lay
   For the love of Barbara Allen.

The second is from Tennessee, as sung for the Library of Congress Archive collection in 1936.

(Transcription by the author)

'Twas in the lovely month of May
The flowers all were bloomin'.
Sweet William on his death-bed lay
For the love of Barbry Allen.[10]

Interestingly enough, the most commonly printed tune in popular collections, and thus the one most frequently encountered in commercial arrangements and professional performances, is not to be found in traditional sources at all. It apparently derives from a version of the ballad first printed in England in 1839.

In Scarlet town where I was born,
There was a fair maid dwelling,
Made every youth cry, Well away,
And her name was Barb'ra Allen.

As must be clear by now, it is not that folk singers try to be different, or original. But time, memory, and geography operate on music as well as on words, and no ballad is apt to have only a single tune indissolubly wedded to it. Yet neither is any given tune always exclusively associated with only one ballad. Charles Seeger puts it both accurately and colorfully when he writes that "both spouses are frequently unfaithful to their common-law kind of union." Yet he does attest to "a permanence of a sort not lightly to be regarded." [11]

Tune Sources

Where do the tunes come from? In folk music this is usually very difficult to answer with certainty. It is easier in the cases in which a tune from a known source, or by a known composer, goes over into the oral tradition for a long enough period to acquire the characteristics of folk music, including the production of variants. But this takes a long time, and it happens very rarely. Most tunes associated with the ballads can be definitely traced only as far back as the nineteenth century, though a few are traceable as far as the seventeenth. This is not to say, however, that some do not exhibit characteristics of far greater antiquity. Paying attention to tune *characteristics*, rather than note-for-note identity, makes it possible to trace a tune's family back much farther. Bertrand Bronson [12] has shown in a number of cases, for example, the relation between tunes of the traditional ballads and sections of medieval plain-chant. While it is not possible to claim on the basis of this relation that the ballad tunes were derived directly from the chants of the Roman Catholic church that were in use during the Middle Ages, it does show that certain tune prototypes, or tune *shapes*, have been a part of our musical heritage for a thousand years or more. Some tune types have proven to be extremely durable, with the ability to travel far and outlive any number of different word settings.

Tune Scales

Whether the tunes of many of the ballads as we know them are really very old or not, many of them sound archaic, particularly those coming from the Appalachians. Their antique flavor is based in part on a free concept of rhythm; they don't appear to us to keep "strict time," and of course this is related to the fact that traditionally they are sung without accompaniment. But a good deal of this antique flavor can be attributed to the scales on which they are based. Many use five-tone or six-tone scales, or else seven-tone scales that conform to the older *modes* instead of to our more modern major and minor scales. The modes were assigned their present Greek names during the Middle Ages, and you may encounter them in descriptions of folk tunes: Dorian, Phrygian, Lydian, Mixolydian, Aeolian, and Ionian. These modal scales are also being used currently in some of the more esoteric and folk-influenced jazz and rock. A full explanation of the use of five-tone, six-tone, and modal seven-tone scales in folk music is beyond the scope of this book,[13] but if you have access to any keyboard you can acquire a rudimentary knowledge of the scale material of Anglo-American folk music (and, indeed, most of the world's folk music) by some exploratory playing using the white keys only. Resist the gravitational attraction that more conventional music has given to the note C (you will have to know or learn the letter names of the keys), and you will begin to get the feel of the greater freedom of choice as regards a *final* tone that is characteristic of folk music. A fairly common mode in this music, for example, is the Dorian, which, on the white notes, uses the following scale, with D as final:

Here is a ballad tune collected in Maine that is in the Dorian mode:

I'll tell you of a false-hearted knight
    Who courted a lady gay,
And all that he wanted of this pretty fair maid
    Was to take her sweet life away.

The finals of the other modes (still using just the white notes) are: Phrygian, E; Lydian, F; Mixolydian, G; Aeolian (our natural minor scale), A; Ionian (identical in material, if not in its usage, with our familiar major scale), C. Not all these modes, however, are used in Anglo-American folk music with anything like equal frequency; the Lydian and Phrygian are very rare indeed.

Very common in folk music are various hexatonic (six-tone) and pentatonic (five-tone) scales. These scales can also be played on the white notes alone; indeed their sound, as used in folk music, is very similar to that of the full seven-tone modal scales, with the omission of one or two tones. The first two versions of *Barbara Allen* quoted above are both pentatonic. The first uses this scale:

Final

(The duplications do not add new tones to the scale, but merely extend the range.) The second uses this one:

Final

It can be shown that these scales are both versions of the same prototypical pentatonic scale. This scale (which can also be produced by playing just the *black* keys on the keyboard) is extremely widespread in its use. The number and geographical distribution of tunes that are pentatonic (or very nearly so) is surprising. Our music has received this legacy from many sources: native American Indian tunes, tunes from central Europe, from Scotland, and from the Orient. It has also been adopted, perhaps unconsciously, by writers of popular songs when they are composing in a vernacular or quasi-folk idiom. As an example, the first two phrases of two of Stephen Foster's best-known songs, *Old Folks at Home* and *Oh, Susannah*, are pure pentatonic.

Instruments and Ballad Singing

Today we seldom hear folk songs unaccompanied, and it may be surprising to learn that traditionally they were usually sung without accompanying instruments. In the southern highlands, for example, there was both an instrumental and a vocal tradition, but they were apparently kept separate for the most part. The fiddle was the most common instrument originally in most parts of rural America, but very seldom was it used to accompany folk songs; its usual role, as we shall see, was to provide music for dancing. Three instruments that have since become associated with folk songs, in the approximate order in which they were introduced into tradition, are the dulcimer, the banjo, and the guitar.

The addition of instrumental accompaniment to the medium of purely vocal folk music operates to change that music in very fundamental ways. In the first place, all instruments except the winds (which are the most closely related to the human voice) lend themselves to a manner of playing that is rather strongly marked rhythmically—that is, there is usually a very discernible "beat." This tends to make more rhythmic, but at the same time more rigid, the formerly free-flowing vocal line. Accompaniment also has a strong impact on harmony. Instruments like the guitar tend to become, especially in the hands of the modestly skilled, fundamentally harmonic—that is, used to produce chords only. Furthermore, the number of chords at the command of the casual player is not great, so that the accompaniment comes to consist of those very few chords (basically three) that have become fundamental to Western cultivated music since the dissolution of the old modes. This has naturally tended to force the old tunes into a new and rather limited harmonic mold—or to force the replacement of the old tunes by newer ones conceived in the new mold. The result has been the suppression, almost to the point of extinction, of the older tunes, with their rich, varied, and strange-sounding modality.[14]

Singing Style as an Integral Part of Folk Song

Finally, we cannot turn from the music of the ballads without treating the third vital ingredient of the ballad as mentioned earlier: a *way* of singing. Just as the printed text of a ballad is deficient without the music, so even the addition of printed music fails to convey the whole of the ballad, in that it cannot indicate the manner in which it is sung. Musical notation is a highly useful convention, but it is most useful in dealing with that music which has evolved around a written tradition (such as fine-art music), and which has only one authoritative version—that of the composer. Notation is least adequate when dealing with music highly dependent upon oral tradition. Of the six American musics dealt with in the six parts of this book, the one in which print bears the least relationship to the actuality of the sound is folk music. The tone quality and inflections of the voice, the way a singer embellishes a tune, the way rhythm and pitch are subtly varied—these are all part of the song.[15] There is here, as in the case of words and notes alone, much latitude for individual variation, but there are also rather widely accepted conventions of singing style within folk communities.[16] Sound recordings have become indispensable for the preservation, propagation, and study of this aspect of folk song.

Folk Music in the Hands of the Professional Singer

How has folk music fared in the hands of the professional singer or entertainer? It depends, of course, upon your point of view. A short answer would probably be, Not as badly as might be thought. But to understand the situation more fully, we must at least consider briefly the distinction between the traditional folk singer and the professional. The traditional singer is himself part of the tradition: He has learned the songs from it, his memory constitutes the reservoir of this tradition, and through his singing it is not only enjoyed by his community but transmitted to others of that community and thus preserved. The traditional singer may happen to *become* a professional, if he is sufficiently talented, but the role of the professional is quite different. The professional, for whom singing becomes a livelihood, must reach a larger audience—a vastly larger audience, in fact, if he is to survive—and must of course please and entertain that audience. He must therefore make his song as attractive as he can to those who do not belong to its tradition, and who may know little or nothing about that tradition. In doing so he may find it necessary to make changes, large or small, that compromise the tradition somewhat. It has been said that the professional must think not only of *what* he is singing but of *how* he is singing it. Personal traits, interpretive or "expressive" idiosyncrasies that may help him put the piece "across," become trademarks of his style, so that we may be hearing more of the singer than the song. But the professional has definite positive contributions to make as well. He may stimulate interest in, and thus help to preserve, traditional music that would otherwise be lost. He brings to his performance a proved degree of musical talent which is bound to be inherently greater than that of the average "carrier" of the tradition. At best knowledgeable in the field of ballads and sensitive to their values, he will seek out many different versions, listen to many traditional singers, and choose and collate from the versions those elements of text and music that are artistically the most satisfying. And since he is a professional, his renditions are not going to be marred by the lapses of memory that mutilate many a ballad in the hands of traditional singers. All in all, it should be appreciated that the contributions of both the traditional singer and the professional are significant, but that their roles are distinct, and that this distinction should be kept in mind in listening to either one.

The Ballad Today and Its Contributions

Some students speak of the fifteenth century as the ideal "ballad age." Others point to a flowering of the ballad in the eighteenth century. Certainly it cannot be said that our time is in any sense a golden age of the ballad. Yet we now know that the ballad lives, whereas a short time ago it was thought to be dying. Not only does it live, but it has managed to color the music and poetry of our own time. The revival of the cultivation of folk music over the past quarter-century has not only kept the ballad from disappearing forever but has allowed its style and outlook to permeate our popular musical-poetic life—resulting in the creation of a whole new genre of popular song, vast and uneven in quality, to be sure, but reflecting at its best the common touch, the poignancy, the unflinching observation of life, and the touches of poetic realism that place it far above the trite mediocrity of the run-of-the-mill popular song of a generation ago. This new enrichment bears witness in no small measure to the influence of the traditional ballad and those qualities that have given it such a long life.

LYRICAL SONGS, PLAY-PARTY GAMES, AND FIDDLE TUNES

Following the paths of the ballad takes us far and wide, and offers ample material for a fascinating study in and of itself, but if we are to gain a fuller picture of Anglo-American folk music as a whole, it will need some rounding out.

First of all, it may naturally be asked whether there are not other folk songs besides the ballads. Indeed, there are. In fact, the term "folk song" is sometimes used in *contradistinction* to the term "ballad." That is, a song which is *not* narrative, but primarily lyrical, is often what is meant, strictly, by a folk song. The distinction, of course, is not always easy to make. Among the most strikingly beautiful lyrical folk songs are the love songs, such as *Black Is the Color of My True Love's Hair*.

Another type of Anglo-American folk song occupies a peculiar kind of ground somewhere between the ballad and the fiddle tune (discussed next). These are songs that became widely used for a form of organized dancing called the *play-party*, and so became known as play-party games or play-party songs. They have their origin in the prohibition among the stricter folk against dancing as such, but especially against the use of the fiddle, considered a sinful instrument of the devil. At the play-party, originally, there was neither fiddle nor orchestra, so that the participants made their own music by singing, with spectators clapping hands and stomping feet.[17] Among the more familiar play-party songs are: *Skip to My Lou* ("Lou," from Scotch usage, is a word used to mean "love" or "sweetheart"); *Going to Boston*; *Charlie's Sweet* (the Scotch heritage is found here again in the reference to Bonnie Prince Charlie and the eighteenth-century Stuart uprising); *Loupy Lou* (or *Looby Lou*); and *Get Along Home, Cindy*. Some of these songs, such as *Old Dan Tucker* and *Buffalo Gals*, show an interesting derivation from blackface minstrel songs.

Many of the play-party songs are also found as fiddle tunes: *Old Joe Clark*; *Sally Goodin*; and *Old Dan Tucker*, for example. There is considerable overlapping of the vocal and instrumental tradition with this type of song. It may be treated as a song with instrumental accompani-

ment or a dance tune to which verses of the song are simply sung intermittently.[18] Many phrases of the texts make it clear that the songs, regardless of their origin, have for a long time been associated with dancing:

> One hand in the hopper and the other in the sack,
> Ladies step forward and the gents fall back.

> Corn-stalk fiddle and shoe-string bow,
> Come down gals on Cotton Eyed Joe.

> Blackeyed Susie, sitting in a corner,
>   She's a pretty girl, 'pon my honor.
> Hey pretty little blackeyed Susie,
>   Hop up, pretty little blackeyed Susie.

> Shake that little foot, Sally Ann. . . .

> Fly all around, my pretty little Pink. . . .[19]

Finally, we come to the fiddle tunes themselves. There is probably no
form of rural, homespun music as indelibly associated in the popular mind
with the American folk scene as the familiar "hoedown." The fiddle, in
spite of religious prejudices against it in some quarters, was long the
dominant instrument in the "country" music of rural white America. Indeed, the violin as an instrument to accompany dancing has had a long
history in Europe, where it retains its popularity and dominance in folk
dance to this day, especially in Scandinavia. "Violin" and "fiddle" are
usually used as contrasting terms to describe the contrasting uses to which
the same instrument is put in the fine-art and folk traditions, respectively.
Interestingly enough, both words come from the same root.

Fiddle Tune Types and Sources

What kinds of tunes are found in the repertory of the country fiddler?
Most typical, of course, are the "hoedowns," or "breakdowns"—rapid
dance tunes in duple meter, relatives of the reels and hornpipes of the
British Isles. The names and tunes of the most popular breakdowns are
well known to any square-dance enthusiast or frequenter of fiddlers' con-
tests: *Soldier's Joy*; *Devil's Dream*; *Leather Britches*; *Wag'ner* (*Wagoner*);
Old Joe Clark; *Lost Indian*; *Give the Fiddler a Dram*; *Natchez Under the
Hill*; *Sourwood Mountain*; and so on.[20] The term breakdown is yet

another illustration of the frequent exchange between the often-parallel musical traditions of blacks and whites that is characteristic of American music. It was a name used in the nineteenth century for any dance in Negro style, but especially those popular with the white boatmen on the Ohio and Mississippi.[21]

The jigs are there, too (called in some areas quadrilles)—lively tunes in 6/8 time like *The Irish Washerwoman*—but these are not actually very common. The waltz, a seemingly unlikely transplant from central Europe, has a somewhat surprising currency among country fiddlers. Less surprising are the occasional schottisches, with their characteristic dotted rhythms like those of the Scotch strathspey. More recently the fiddler's repertory, especially in the lowlands and in the West, has even come to include a few rags and blues.

The tunes come from a variety of sources. Since we earlier considered the ballads at some length, it would be appropriate to ask first whether there are any traditional ballad tunes that have been transformed into fiddle tunes. The answer is, Very few. One interesting example, shown below, is an adaptation of a tune to *The Gypsy Laddie* (Child 200). The fiddle tune, as heard in Oklahoma, is given first, followed by the ballad tune in a variant recovered in Illinois (from "Some Representative Illinois Folk-Songs" by David Seneff McIntosh), but belonging to a group of such tunes prevalent from North Carolina to the lower Midwest. Both ballad and fiddle tune go by the common name of *Black Jack Davy* (or *Davie*).

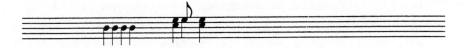

From *The Fiddle Book* by Marion Thede. Copyright © 1967 Oak Publications Division of Embassy Music Corporation, New York. Reprinted by permission of Oak Publications.

Black Jack Davie came ridin' through the plain,
He sang so loud and clearly.
He made the green-wood around him sing,
To charm the heart of a lady,
To charm the heart of a lady.

The play-party songs as fiddle tunes have already been mentioned. Neither the ballad nor the folk song repertory has furnished the bulk of Anglo-American fiddle tunes, however; these have come more or less directly from the thriving body of reels and hornpipes used for dancing in the British Isles, and especially in Scotland.

Some individual tunes not in any of these categories may have interesting histories. For example, both *Jordan Is a Hard Road to Travel* and *Old Dan Tucker* (the latter already mentioned as a play-party song) were written by Dan Emmett for the professional minstrel stage. And the famous *Bonaparte's Retreat* is a kind of reminiscence of the battle of Waterloo—no doubt, as the solemn drone indicates, having reached the fiddle repertory by way of a bagpipe air.

Fiddle Tune Variants

The fiddle tunes, as circulated among the folk musicians, were occasionally written down by individual fiddlers as a jog to memory or in response to some collector's instinct. And a few collections were published from time to time. In the main, however, it is safe to say that oral tradition operated here as fully as in the case of the ballads. Most tunes, though they may have existed in print here and there, were apparently almost never *learned* from print, but simply by listening to the playing of others—and the fiddler added a certain amount of creative improvisation until he got it the way he liked. Marion Thede writes perceptively, and from a good deal of personal observation, about this process:

> I am inclined to the belief that fiddlers pick up a tune by hearing the general structure and then supplying a whole set of notes to their own fancy. After repeated tries, there finally emerges a fixed version only used by this

one fiddler and perhaps his immediate family; even that is doubtful. Even in the same community, each fiddler comes out with his own personal way of playing a tune.[22]

The variants, therefore, even of very common tunes were staggeringly numerous, and apt to differ so widely from each other as to constitute in some cases different tunes altogether. The detailed study of fiddle tunes and their variants has never been undertaken to the degree that it has been with the ballads, and probably it is too late now, in spite of the revivals, to study the traditional tunes to any extent. From phonograph recordings, however, and from the few really careful written transcriptions, we can form some idea of the process, and the profusion of variants in existence. Here is an example in the form of three versions of an old reel called *Tom and Jerry*. The first is from an old printed collection, and is no doubt closest to the Scotch prototype. The second is transcribed from a recording of 1951, and the third from the live performance of a fiddler in Oklahoma. It must be pointed out that these versions are closer together than many variants that share a common title.

1. From *One Thousand Fiddle Tunes* (Chicago: M. M. Cole Publishing Co., 1940–1967), p. 45; transposed with note values halved, for purposes of comparison.
2. Reprinted from *The Old-Time Fiddler's Repertory: 245 Traditional Tunes*, edited by R. P. Christeson, by permission of the editor and the University of Missouri Press. Copyright 1973 by the Curators of the University of Missouri.
3. From *The Fiddle Book* by Marion Thede. Copyright © 1967 Oak Publications, Division of Embassy Music Corporation, New York. Reprinted by permission of Oak Publications.

The Instruments

We have implied that although the violin and the "fiddle" are quite different instruments as far as usage is concerned, they are at least physically the same instrument. Even this is not strictly true. The fiddler's instrument may be "store-bought," possibly from a mail-order house. (An old catalog lists "Our Amati Model Violin" for $7.25, while the "Special Stradivarius Model" sells for $9.25, the latter including bow, case, an extra set of strings, an instruction book, and a fingerboard chart.) [23] On the other hand, fiddles were often entirely homemade, out of any well-seasoned wood that was available, or they were in some cases reconstructed from parts of damaged violins.

The standard violin tuning in perfect fifths was used, but so were a number of variants as well, and for various reasons. To secure a low "drone" string, the G string was sometimes tuned down to an E or even a D; open strings were sometimes duplicated for resonance in a given key (the standard tuning for *Bonaparte's Retreat*, for example, uses three D strings!); or more fourths, or even thirds, were introduced into the tuning to make possible the sounding of two strings in unison in a technique requiring very little shifting of the hand, and for the most part, not using the little finger at all.

Such were (and are) the marvelous eccentricities and nonconformities of country fiddles and fiddlers. We can say "are" with a degree of assurance that would have seemed unfounded optimism two decades ago. The old-timers are leaving the scene, to be sure. But there is currently enough interest among younger performers to inspire reasonable confidence that the highly social and contagiously joyous art of country fiddling will not perish for some time to come.

FURTHER READING

General Song Collections, with Expository Notes

* LOMAX, ALAN. *The Folk Songs of North America*. Garden City, N.Y.: Doubleday & Co., 1960.

    This excellent broad collection surveys the entire field of American folk songs in the English language. The introduction and notes are especially valuable.

---

* Items thus marked are part of the suggested reference library to be available in connection with this book.

* SANDBURG, CARL. *The American Songbag.* New York: Harcourt, Brace & World, 1927.

> An early landmark collection by an American writer famous for his enthusiasm for folklore, song, and poetry. The notes have the Sandburg touch, and make good reading.

Specialized or Regional Song Collections, Mostly with Expository Notes

BARRY, PHILLIPS; ECKSTROM, FANNIE H.; and SMYTH, MARY W. *British Ballads from Maine.* New Haven: Yale University Press, 1929.

BELDEN, HENRY MARVIN. *Ballads and Songs Collected by the Missouri Folk-Lore Society.* 2d ed. Columbia, Mo.: University of Missouri Press, 1955.

COX, JOHN HARRINGTON. *Folk-Songs of the South.* Cambridge, Mass.: Harvard University Press, 1925.

DAVIS, ARTHUR KYLE, JR. *Traditional Ballads of Virginia.* Cambridge, Mass.: Harvard University Press, 1929.

EDDY, MARY O. *Ballads and Songs from Ohio.* New York: J. J. Augustin, 1939.

LOMAX, JOHN A. *Cowboy Songs and Other Frontier Ballads.* 2d ed. New York: Macmillan Co., 1916.

NILES, JOHN JACOB. *The Ballad Book of John Jacob Niles.* Boston, 1961. Paperback reprint, New York: Dover Publications, 1970.

RANDOLPH, VANCE, and SHOEMAKER, FLOYD C. *Ozark Folksongs.* 4 vols. Columbia, Mo.: The State Historical Society of Missouri, 1946–1950.

RITCHIE, JEAN. *Singing Family of the Cumberlands.* New York: Oak Publications, 1963.

* SHARP, CECIL. *English Folk-Songs from the Southern Appalachians.* 2 vols. Edited by Maude Karpeles. London: Oxford University Press, 1932.

> Not only is the collection a rich source of ballads and their variants in pure form from oral tradition, but the introduction is a valuable essay on both the folk and their songs.

Primarily Studies, with Some Complete Ballads

* ABRAHAMS, ROGER D., and FOSS, GEORGE. *Anglo-American Folksong Style.* Englewood Cliffs, N.J.: Prentice-Hall, 1968.

> A brief but comprehensive study dealing technically but lucidly and interestingly with all aspects of the subject.

* WELLS, EVELYN KENDRICK. *The Ballad Tree.* New York: Ronald Press Co., 1950.

> A broad and well-written study, ranging in scope through such topics as the supernatural elements in the ballads, the ballad's influence on

literature, theories of the origins of the ballads, and biographical studies of Child and Sharp.

Studies of the Ballads

Bronson, Bertrand Harris. *The Ballad as Song*. Berkeley and Los Angeles: University of California Press, 1969.

Coffin, Tristram. *The British Traditional Ballad in North America*. Philadelphia: American Folklore Society, 1950.

Laws, G. Malcolm, Jr. *American Balladry from British Broadsides*. Philadelphia: American Folklore Society, 1957.

* ———. *Native American Balladry*. Philadelphia: American Folklore Society, 1964.
    A significant study of native balladry outside the Child canon, it deals with an area of American folk song indispensable to a comprehensive picture.

Wilgus, D. K. *Anglo-American Folksong Scholarship Since 1898*. New Brunswick, N.J.: Rutgers University Press, 1959.
    Indispensable for anyone interested in what has been going on in the study of the ballads here since Professor Child published the last volume of his crucially important collection.

Extensive, Basic Reference Works on the Ballads

Bronson, Bertrand Harris. *The Traditional Tunes of the Child Ballads*. 4 vols. Princeton, N.J.: Princeton University Press, 1959–1972.

Child, Francis James. *The English and Scottish Popular Ballads*. 5 vols. Boston, 1882–1898. Paperback reprint, New York: Dover Publications, 1965.

Fiddle Tune Collections, Some with Expository Material

Bayard, Samuel P. *Hill Country Tunes*. Harrisburg: University of Pennsylvania Press, 1944.

Christeson, R. P. *The Old-Time Fiddler's Repertory*. Columbia, Mo.: University of Missouri Press, 1973.
    A finely printed practical collection of 245 tunes, collected (some from recordings, apparently) mostly in Missouri. Some expository material.

Ford, Ira. *Traditional Music of America*. New York: E. P. Dutton & Co., 1940.

* Thede, Marion. *The Fiddle Book*. New York: Oak Publications, n.d.
    This excellent collection also contains a wealth of information, set forth in an interesting manner, and some fine pictures.

One Thousand Fiddle Tunes. Chicago: M. M. Cole Publishing Co., 1940–1967.

> A huge collection of tunes, which looks like a reprint of an older collection, emphasizing mostly Scotch and Irish forms. Its major drawback is the almost complete lack of information as to sources. Some tunes include directions as to dance steps.

LISTENING

General

FROM THE *Recorded Anthology of American Music* (RAAM)

* *Oh, My Little Darling: Folk Song Types.* RAAM: NW-245.

> This collection "focuses on the rural Southeast," with excellent introductory notes on the various song types by Jon Pankake.

* *Brave Boys: New England Traditions in Folk Music.* RAAM: NW-239.

> Complementing the above, this collection, with notes by Sandy Paton, constitutes a valuable survey of the lesser-known folk traditions of the Northeast.

Ballads

FROM THE LIBRARY OF CONGRESS ARCHIVE OF AMERICAN FOLK SONG (AAFS)

* *Anglo-American Ballads,* ed. Alan Lomax. AAFS: L-1.

Anglo-American Ballads, ed. B. A. Botkin. AAFS: L-7.

Anglo-American Songs and Ballads, ed. Duncan B. M. Emrich. AAFS: L-12, 14, 20, 21.

The Ballad Hunter, John A. Lomax (lectures with music examples). L-49–53.

Versions and Variants of Barbara Allen, ed. Charles Seeger. AAFS: L-54.

* *Child Ballads Traditional in the United States,* ed. Bertrand H. Bronson. L-57, 58.

> These selected reproductions are available for public purchase from The Library of Congress, Music Division, Recorded Sound Section, Washington, D.C. 20540. Traditional singers perform their versions of Anglo-American ballads; most are field recordings.

OTHER

* *Anthology of American Folk Music,* vol. 1, *Ballads.* Folkways: 2951.

> These re-pressings from early commercial recordings demonstrate the breadth of American ballad tradition. The notes include bibliographical material.

The Long Harvest. Argo: (Z) DA-66–75.

Ten records including 44 ballads in numerous variants, sung by Ewan MacColl and Peggy Seeger, two eminent authorities very close to the ballad tradition. The extensive notes that accompany the complete printed texts are very valuable. The recording is of excellent studio quality.

Joan Baez, Joan Baez, vol. 2, Joan Baez in Concert. Vanguard: VSD-2077, 2097, 2122.

Useful as examples of the approach of the enlightened professional folk singer to the ballads. Many more could be cited. These, which include the singing of eight Child ballads and several native ballads, are typical of the best.

Fiddle Tunes: Current Authentic Performances

* *Anthology of American Folk Music,* vol. 2, *Social Music,* bands 28, 29, 30. Folkways: 2952.

* *Mountain Music of Kentucky.* Folkways: 2317.

Includes four standard fiddle tunes.

Mountain Music Bluegrass Style. Folkways: 2318.

This re-creation of traditional styles by younger performers includes two "standards" on the fiddle.

Old-Time Country Music, Mike Seeger. Folkways: 2325.

Includes *Bonaparte's Retreat.*

Anglo-American Shanties, Lyric Songs, Dance Tunes, and Spirituals, side B. AAFS: L-2.

Play and Dance Songs and Tunes. AAFS: L-9.

Contains a wealth of traditional tunes, played on dulcimer and banjo as well as fiddle.

PROJECTS

1. Find an example of a traditional ballad sung by a present-day professional singer, and compare it with a version in a printed collection (either words or music, or both).
2. Find, by way of comparing recordings, an instance in which a professional singer has modeled his or her version of a traditional ballad on the performance of a traditional singer.
3. Find examples of popular music, especially folk-rock, which in your opinion show the influence of the ballad, and define this influence.
4. Find some traditional ballads in collections of folk music from your own region. (A few outstanding regional collections are listed

in the "Further Reading" section accompanying this chapter. Libraries in your region will emphasize local collections.)

5. Make a collection and comparison of ballad refrains, noting the presence or absence of meaningless syllables, words, or phrases.

6. Find and record some piece of folklore (song, poem, story) that your family, friends, or acquaintances know from oral tradition.

7. Investigate the *localization* of names and places that occurs when ballads travel. If you have access to the services of a large library you might consult a doctoral thesis by W. Edson Richmond, "Place Names in the English and Scottish Popular Ballads and Their American Variants" (Ohio State University, 1947).

8. If you are familiar with another language and its culture, find an example of one of the traditional ballads (many of which are international) in this other language.

9. If you perform folk music, learn a traditional ballad and add it to your repertoire. You may feel it desirable to collate a version from several sources, as is common with professionals, but invent or change *on your own* as little as possible.

10. If you are a musician familiar with the dulcimer and have access to one, use it to demonstrate the older modal scales by means of its various tunings. Useful in this regard is *The Dulcimer Book*, by Jean Ritchie (New York: Oak Publications, 1963).

Chapter Two

The Afro-American Folk Tradition

THE FOLK MUSIC of the blacks in America has been not only a richly cultivated tradition in itself but one whose influence on American music generally has been both pervasive and critical. There is very little of our music, especially in popular tradition, that has not been at least touched by it. Since it was really the first native music to be "discovered" and made known to Americans (and to the world) at large, it was for a time, during our first important wave of musical nationalism, considered to be almost our *only* folk music.

So vast and varied is Afro-American folk music that no single image is adequate to embrace it all. Instead, various separate and vivid pictures are apt to flash before us, distinct and yet sometimes blurring one into another. There is the picture of the slave at work, in the field or at the oars of a boat—and we think of the field hollers or the rhythmic chanting of the work songs. There is the picture of the slave at rare moments of play—the slave quarters ringing with the sound of singing and dancing, to the accompaniment of homemade fiddles and banjos, and of clapping and stomping—and we think of the breakdowns, the banjo tunes, the cake-walks. There is the picture of black folk improvising praise songs with deep meaning out of remembered strains of Dr. Watts's hymns, and pouring forth a "torrent of sacred harmony" in the meeting house or at the out-doors revival—and we think of the spirituals. There is the picture of the strange, fierce, voodoo-flavored dances in Congo Square, New Orleans—and we think of *La Bamboula*, and other Creole songs. In contrast, some-what removed from folk music, is the picture of the black musician as the accomplished professional, much in demand as a fiddler at dances—and we think of the "Negro jigs" published in early collections. At a later time there is the picture of his rural heir, the itinerant minstrel with his most prized possession, his guitar, his "easy rider," slung around his neck, some-times playing and singing for all-night parties for a few dollars—and we think of the blues. All, and more, are part of the panorama, and we cannot fuse them into a single convenient image.

AFRICAN MUSIC AND ITS RELATION TO BLACK MUSIC IN AMERICA

The fact that black people came to this continent from Africa in more or less continuous waves of forced migration over a period of some two hundred years raises a profound first question with regard to our black music: To what extent is it African? This question is not new; it does not belong only to the heightened racial consciousness that has marked the third quarter of our century. It has fascinated students since the Civil War.[1]

There is a broad disparity in the relative strength and distribution of African survivals in the New World. These survivals are found to be most intact in South America and the Caribbean—the Caribbean including, culturally, French-dominated New Orleans until this century. In the southern United States African traits tended to die out or become amalga-mated with traits of the white culture. This had to do with such causes as the size of the plantations, the degree of direct white supervision, the degree to which the whites attempted to convert the slaves to Christianity or otherwise change their religious beliefs and practices—and even with the matter of whether or not the use of drums was prohibited.[2] It should be noted that Africanisms were suppressed by many blacks themselves; there was a time when even the term "African" was felt by many to be an insult.

One interesting exception to the relatively greater absorption and elimination of African survivals in the United States itself, outside of New Orleans, is found on the Sea Islands off the coast of Georgia and South

Carolina. Here, in relative isolation, numbers of black people, often in extreme poverty, retained Africanisms in music, speech, and customs well into this century. This area has been a rich mine for folklorists and anthropologists.[3]

While it is beyond the scope of this book to include a treatment of African music in any detail, certain outstanding traits which have marked correspondences with black music in America can be noted. Most obvious, and of the greatest importance, is the dominance of *rhythm*, manifested in a number of ways: (1) a high development of what has been called the "metronome sense"—the sense of an inexorably steady pulse governing the music; [4] (2) the active enjoyment of a high degree of rhythmic complexity and diversity for its own sake; (3) the perception of music as largely a *kinetic* experience, practically inseparable from some form of bodily motion such as dancing; and (4) the corresponding dominance of percussion instruments. Other traits, having to do with musical form, are the use of short vocal phrases, repeated and varied, against a continuous rhythmic background, and the often-cited use of the call-and-response pattern.

To sum up the question of African influence, one could do worse than simply listen to two examples in juxtaposition. From many you might choose first a piece of music in praise of a Yoruban chief, recorded in Nigeria, and then the famous and oft-mentioned ring-shout *Run, Old Jeremiah*, recorded in Louisiana.[5] You will not only hear embodied many of the traits previously mentioned, but will deepen your appreciation of African influence by direct experience and feeling.

RELIGIOUS FOLK MUSIC: THE SPIRITUALS

The birth and life of the spiritual in the nearly two and a half centuries before the Civil War is cloaked in an obscurity unrelieved except for a few fragmentary contemporary observations, now treasured and quoted over and over. That the black folk adopted and sang psalms and hymns is clear. Much evidence is inferential, but a few direct observations, all by ministers, have been gleaned.[6] They attest to religious instruction, which would at that time have included singing instruction.

From New York in 1745:

> I have got our Clark to raise a Psalm when their instruction is over, and I can scarce express the satisfaction I have in seeing 200 Negroes and White Persons with heart and voice glorifying their Maker.
>
> —Rev. Richard Charlton

From the southern colonies in the 1760s:

> My landlord tells me . . . they heard the Slaves at worship in their lodge, singing Psalms and Hymns in the evening, and again in the Morning, long

before break of day. They are excellent singers, and long to get some of Dr. Watt's [sic] Psalms and Hymns, which I encourage them to hope for.

—Rev. Wright

Again from the southern colonies, no date:

I can hardly express the pleasure it affords me to turn to that part of the Gallery where they [the slaves] sit, and see so many of them with their Psalm or Hymn Books, turning to the part then sung, and assisting their fellows who are beginners, to find the place; and then all breaking out in a torrent of sacred harmony, enough to bear away the whole congregation to heaven.

—Rev. Samuel Davies

We can be sure, then, that at least a certain number of the blacks knew and sang the Protestant metric psalms and hymns. But the old psalm tunes seem to have had no appreciable survivals in any of the spirituals we know of. In the case of the later hymns, the situation is quite different and definite correspondences have been found, as we shall see.

Dissemination and Adaptation of the Spirituals

Though antebellum accounts of Negro singing hinted at the existence of a large body of song, mostly but by no means exclusively religious in character, these songs did not become known to the outside world generally until after the Civil War. Then it was among the liberal whites in the North that the most interest was generated. Their "discovery" can be traced to circumstances under which northern abolitionists came into direct contact with slaves and former slaves. Thomas Wentworth Higginson, a Unitarian minister, commanded the first Civil War regiment made up of former slaves; James Miller McKim, a former Presbyterian minister, visited the South Carolina Sea Islands as agent for the Port Royal Relief Society; his daughter Lucy, later married to a son of William Lloyd Garrison, took part with her father in the Underground Railroad; Henry George Spaulding, a Unitarian minister, was a member of the United States Sanitary Commission, which visited the Sea Islands of South Carolina during the War; William Eleazer Barton, later a Congregational minister, taught school as a young man in Tennessee. All of them, and ultimately many others, collected or at least wrote about what they called variously Negro "songs," "spirituals," "camp-meeting melodies," or "plantation hymns." Articles about these songs, including in some cases transcriptions of the music, began to appear in northern periodicals even before the end of the war. Finally, in 1867, the first collection in book form appeared, entitled *Slave Songs of the United States.* This justly famous collection includes a number of spirituals well known today, albeit some are more familiar in later variants. These include *Roll, Jordan, Roll*; *Michael, Row the Boat Ashore*; *Nobody Knows the Trouble I've Had*; and *Good News, Member*. There were also a number of secular songs, among them work songs ("Heave away, Heave away! I'd rather court a yellow gal than work for Henry Clay"—a song that later appeared frequently as an American fiddle tune, *Run, Nigger, Run*) and a number of Louisiana Creole songs in patois French. Altogether a rather broad collection!

After the Civil War a number of schools and colleges were established in the South, under the auspices of the Freedmen's Bureau and various church and missionary groups, to begin the great task of educating the newly freed blacks. One of the first of these was Fisk University, in Nashville, Tennessee, founded by the American Missionary Association in 1866. Early on, the inevitable financial problems arose. George L. White, the school's treasurer and music instructor, formed a chorus from the many fine singers among the students. After a period of intense training and some successful local concerts, he took the singers on a daring tour of the northern states to raise money for the school. Although their programs consisted of a variety of songs (which at first did not even include spirituals), they soon found that it was the spirituals which were the most enthusiastically received, and which ultimately won over audiences. Even though most of their programs were given in churches, it was a long and hard struggle for them to escape the image and expectations set up in the popular mind by the minstrel show. When the group, which had by then adopted the famous name Jubilee Singers, sang in Henry Ward Beecher's Plymouth Church in Brooklyn, New York, the headline in the *New York Herald* read: "Beecher's Negro Minstrels: The Great Plymouth Preacher as an 'End Man'—a Full Troupe of Real Live Darkies in the Tabernacle of the Lord—Rollicking Choruses, but no Sand Shaking or Jig Dancing." Not all critical comment was as demeaning, however, for the singers and their songs were winning audiences and critics alike, and the Brooklyn concerts, under Beecher's aegis, proved to be a turning point. They went on for a successful tour of New England, and sang in Washington, D.C., where they were greeted by President Grant. Subsequently a group of eight of the singers toured Europe with tremendous success. By the time the original group disbanded in Hamburg in 1878, the Jubilee Singers had, in seven years' work, raised $150,000 for Fisk University, and still more importantly, had pioneered in making the Negro spiritual widely known by musicians and public alike in this country and in Europe.

Of course the Fisk Jubilee Singers were not alone in this work. In 1873 the famous Hampton Singers, of the Hampton Institute in Virginia, were formed and began to tour. The tradition spread, and in this century, in addition to the continuing work of Fisk and Hampton, the choirs of Howard University and the Tuskegee Institute have become well known. In 1925 the first Hall Johnson Choir was formed; as professional choirs, these groups have also furthered the tradition of choral spiritual singing.

Solo singers also performed the spirituals. Although white soloists began including them in their programs in the 1920s, it was great black artists such as Roland Hayes, Paul Robeson, and Marian Anderson who sang them with the greatest effectiveness and meaning, and established their stature in the repertoire of solo song.

Thus the spiritual, in what might be termed its concert phase, was launched. It began almost at once to diverge from its folk phase. The concert spiritual, like the ballad in the hands of the professional folk singer, who was faced with the task of popularizing a folk form in a cultural milieu outside the original folk community, inevitably underwent adaptation and change. It was written down, harmonized, arranged, and usually (especially for the solo singer) provided with a piano accompaniment—all of these more or less in keeping with the character of the original song, depending upon the talent, background, and intent of the arranger. That the results *did* so often preserve the spirit of the original is attested by the impact which the arranged spirituals continued to have when well performed, and is a tribute to the skill and integrity of such musicians as J. Rosamund Johnson, Hall Johnson, and R. Nathaniel Dett. The concert spiritual is, of course, perfectly valid music. The point to be aware of is that it should not be confused with Negro religious folk song as it originally existed, or as it has continued to exist down to our own time, in the backwoods churches and camp meetings of the South.

The Words of the Spirituals

Not all Negro folk music is religious. Firm distinctions are made by many black people. And while we may consider the condemnation of the blues as sinful to reflect a particular tradition of religious orthodoxy, we can also recognize that between the broad epic and moral connotations of *Go Down, Moses* and the self-centered eroticism of the *Black Snake Moan* there is indeed a considerable gulf fixed. Nevertheless, the lines of demarcation between sacred and secular are far from rigid. The Biblical imagery so pervasive in the totality of Negro folk music may appear in the work song:

Well, God told Norah.
  Hammer, ring.
Well, God told Norah.
  Hammer, ring.
You is a-goin' in the timber.
  Hammer, ring.
You is a-goin' in the timber.
  Hammer, ring.

It may even occasionally crop up in the blues:

> I went down in Death Valley, nothin' but the
>   tombstones and dry bones,
> I went down in Death Valley, nothin' but the
>   tombstones and dry bones,
> That's where a poor man be, Lord, when I'm dead
>   and gone.

Of greater significance is the all-encompassing view expressed in those songs commonly regarded as "spirituals." No image was either too humble or too intimately connected with daily life to be used.

> Cryin' what kind o' shoes am dose you wear, . . .
> Cryin' dese shoes I wear am de Gospel shoes, . . .

> Mind out brother how you walk de cross,
>   Wan'ta go to heaben when I die.
> Yo' foot might slip-a an' yo' soul get-a los',
>   O, wan'ta go to heaben when I die.

> I know my robe's gwinter fit me well,
>   I'm gwinter lay down my heavy load,
> I tried it on at de gates of hell,
>   I'm gwinter lay down my heavy load.

> Loose horse in the valley
> Aye
> Who goin' t' ride 'im
> Aye
> Nothin' but the righteous
> Aye, Lord
> Time's a drawin' nigh.

If it be true—to quote another spiritual—that "he's got the whole world in his hands," then nothing in the whole range of human feeling is beyond inclusion. Of the wheel of Ezekial it was sung:

> There's 'ligion in the wheel
>   Oh, my soul! . . .
> There's moanin' in the wheel
>   Oh, my soul! . . .

There's prayin' in the wheel
   Oh, my soul! . . .
There's shoutin' in the wheel
   Oh, my soul! . . .
There's cryin' in the wheel
   Oh, my soul! . . .
There's laughin' in the wheel
   Oh, my soul! . . .

The spirituals, as we know, have drawn deeply upon a thorough acquaintance with Biblical narrative and symbol, as dramatized through the generations by many a gifted and anonymous backwoods preacher. So immense is their number and range that they constitute *in toto* an epic re-creation, in folk fashion, of virtually the entire Bible, from Genesis:

He made the sun an' moon an' stars,
   To rule both day an' night;
He placed them in the firmament,
   An' told them to give light.
My God He is a Man—a Man of War,
My God He is a Man—a Man of War,
My God He is a Man—a Man of War,
   An' de Lawd God is His name.

to Revelation:

De Lord spoke to Gabriel,
   Fare you well, Fare you well;
Go look behin' de altar,
   Fare you well, Fare you well.
Take down de silvah trumpet,
   Fare you well, Fare you well.
Blow yo' trumpet Gabriel;
   Fare you well, Fare you well.

Instances abound of the vivid pictorial imagery brought to their subjects by the anonymous black poets:

Dark clouds a-risin'!
Thunder-bolts a-bustin'!
Master Jesus comes a-ridin' by
With a rainbow on his shoulder.

It should be noted that the anonymity generally assumed was not universal; the existence of individual Negro "bards" in the late nineteenth century has been documented. James Weldon Johnson, in his preface to *The Books of American Negro Spirituals*, describes "Singing" Johnson, who went from church to church, making up, singing, and teaching new songs to the congregations.

No consideration of the texts of the spirituals can be considered complete that fails to treat the question of their relation to contemporary circumstances among the black people. A once-common concept is that the spirituals represented solely an otherworldly view; that they expressed the consolation for intolerable worldly conditions which the blacks found in religion, and that the promises and hopes referred only to the life hereafter. There is considerable evidence to refute this concept, however, and arguments for a contrasting view, a view of the spirituals' concrete relationship to contemporary conditions, began to be put forward a century ago by abolitionist writers and others.[7] In this view the spirituals express (or cloak) in Biblical terms not only the intolerability of slavery, but hopes and plans for an escape from its bondage in this life. This could come about either through northern intervention (thus "de Lord" could stand for a collective embodiment as "de Yankees") or through escape ("Steal away") to the North ("heab'n") or to Canada ("Canaan"). The secret meetings to which the faithful were called ("Go down in de lonesome valley") kept hope and morale alive, spread news, and laid plans. The yearning for a "home" encouraged by the colonization projects could be expressed as a reliance on the "old ship of Zion" that would "take us all home"—or even as the hope for a Moses who would smite and divide the broad waters ("Deep river") so that the blacks could miraculously pass over—back to Africa. The figure of Moses was quite naturally a very central one. The Israelites were the slaves, longing for deliverance; Pharaoh represented the slave owners; Egypt (or alternatively, Babylon) was the South and slavery. The famous *Go Down, Moses* hardly needs "translation" to see its relevance to the black people in slavery.

> When Israel was in Egypt's land,
>   Let my people go;
> Oppressed so hard they could not stand,
>   Let my people go;
>
> Go down, Moses,
>   'Way down in Egypt's land;
> Tell ole Pharaoh
>   Let my people go.

There is evidence, indeed, that this interpretation of the spiritual was not lost on the slave owners, especially in the uneasy years between the bloody Nat Turner revolt in Virginia in 1831 (Nat Turner himself, it should be remembered, had been a preacher) and the Civil War a generation later. References to freedom, and especially to escape and to vengeance on the slave beaters and betrayers had to be more carefully veiled than ever. In South Carolina in 1862 slaves were jailed for singing *We'll Soon Be Free*—it was then quite evident that the freedom sought was not just in the life *after* death.

The Music of the Spirituals

When we come to a description of the music of the spirituals, it is well to keep in mind that we are dealing with folk music, and that what we see in print cannot convey anything like the total effect of the music as sung. To quote William Francis Allen, writing in 1867:

The best we can do, however, with paper and types, or even with voices, will convey but a faint shadow of the original. The voices of the colored people have a peculiar quality that nothing can imitate; and the intonations and delicate variations of even one singer cannot be reproduced on paper. And I despair of conveying any notion of the effect of a number singing together, especially in a complicated shout, like "I can't stay behind, my Lord," or "Turn, sinner, turn O!" There is no singing in *parts*, as we understand it, and yet no two appear to be singing the same thing—the leading singer starts the words of each verse, often improvising, and the others, who "base" him, as it is called, strike in with the refrain, or even join in the solo, when the words are familiar. When the "base" begins, the leader often stops, leaving the rest of his words to be guessed at, or it may be they are taken up by one of the other singers. And the "basers" themselves seem to follow their own whims, beginning when they please and leaving off when they please, striking an octave above or below (in case they have pitched the tune too low or too high), or hitting some other note that chords, so as to produce the effect of a marvelous complication and variety, and yet with the most perfect time, and rarely with any discord. And what makes it all the harder to unravel a thread of melody out of this strange network is that, like birds, they seem not infrequently to strike sounds that cannot be precisely represented by the gamut, and abound in "slides from one note to another, and turns and cadences not in articulated notes." [8]

This description tells us quite a lot about the singing, in fact. At least four distinct points are confirmed that will serve as an introductory description to the music as actually performed. First, the subtlety and variety of vocal delivery is noted: the "intonations and delicate variations," the "sounds that cannot be precisely represented by the gamut," the "slides from one note to another." Second, we are definitely reminded that this is communal singing; unlike the more solitary blues, it calls for the participation, the interaction, of a closely knit society of singers, all feeling the same impulsion to break into song. Third, though it is choral singing, there is usually a leader to whom the rest of the group responds, although these responses do not have the drilled rhythmic precision we are used to in performances of spirituals by trained choirs. And fourth, we are reminded of the important role of improvisation—the spur-of-the-moment variations wrought spontaneously by the singers. This is a trait particularly associated with black music. "No two African performances are identical," says A. M. Jones, and the description applies equally to American blues, American jazz, and the Negro spiritual, though we are not as accustomed to thinking of the latter in these terms.

Only one further observation, implicit in early descriptions, needs to be added to round out a fairly accurate picture of early spiritual singing in its folk phase. This is that there was in most cases no accompaniment by instruments. The use of piano, guitar, tambourine—even in some cases trumpet or trombone—was a later addition belonging more to the gospel songs.

In terms of where the music of the spirituals comes from, we are probably as close to a realistic view of its sources as we can get if we realize that by the 1920s (a period which saw the publication of a number of important collections) the music of the spiritual was a remarkable *medley*, as Miles Mark Fisher has expressed it. No doubt, much was original within the folk community. In some of the tunes, there are references to African correspondences.[9] That there is also evidence of derivation from Anglo-American hymn tunes, and even from secular ballads, is undeniable, and is recognized in some degree at least by all writers.[10] Indeed, it would be strange if this were not so, though the whole process might be more accurately described as one of *interaction*. The editors of the 1867 *Slave Songs* rejected some songs sung by the blacks that were found in Methodist hymn books, but variants of these were later included in collections of spirituals. The well-known *Go Down, Moses* is an interesting example of interaction. The Negro tune was first published in 1872 in the first edition of *Jubilee Songs*. Of course it had been in oral tradition before this. The tune of a song called *There Is a Rest Remains*, of which the first half is nearly identical with *Go Down, Moses*, was published in 1868 in Troy, New York, also as recovered from oral tradition among Methodists in upstate New York and New England. The first halves of these two songs [11] are given below.

Go Down, Moses

There is a Rest Remains

Since both published versions came from oral tradition, it cannot definitely be established which way the borrowing took place. The altered *leading tone,* however (in this case an a sharp), a note found neither in the natural minor nor in the majority of other spiritual tunes in the minor mode, is an integral part of every variant of this tune, and points rather strongly to European white influence.

The Survival of the Folk Spiritual

"The black masses have preserved the spirituals. Acculturated Negroes have generally neglected them unless they were edited." So wrote Miles Mark Fisher in 1953. We have already referred to the cleavage between the folk and the concert spiritual that began with the spread and popularization of Negro religious folk music after the Civil War. The folk spirituals, as preserved by the black masses, have indeed survived, and the description deduced from Allen's observation of 1867, quoted earlier, may be reviewed as a quite accurate description of rural spiritual singing as it has survived into our own time. Fortunately some of this old-style singing was recorded in the 1930s and 1940s. It is probably best epitomized in the spirituals sung by Dock Reed and Vera Hall of Alabama. In *Look How They Done My Lord* and *Handwriting on the Wall*, for example, we hear variants of traditional spirituals, which have been reproduced in printed collections, sung in a living folk context.[12] Call-and-response, in which the responder finishes the line begun by the caller (a practice described by Allen over a century ago) is beautifully illustrated, as is the rhythmic impulse, or metronome sense. We also hear in their singing the use of the "neutral" third and seventh degrees of the scale, a practice that does not belong exclusively to the blues.[13] *Move, Members, Move* and *My Name Has Been Written Down*, by a family of singers, furnish fine examples of communal singing in the old style, with hand clapping emphasizing the rhythmic pulse and drive of this music.[14]

To be aware of the larger context of the spiritual, you should experience an actual religious service, especially the sermon, during which members of the congregation, in their role as responders, become actual participants. Often then the intensity of feeling and participation finds outlet in musically intoned sounds, and the tones gradually accumulate into a kind of choral background. The preacher himself may break into song. If this cannot be experienced in person, the next best thing is to listen to recordings. A number of these sermons with responses were re-corded and sold in the 1920s and have been reissued in anthologies.[15]

The spiritual, as one of our richest and most perennial funds of folk music, has provided material and inspiration for many subsequent forms. Though it is still cultivated to some extent in the old style as a folk form, it was inevitable, given changing social and cultural patterns, and par-ticularly the growth of popular music and a popular-music industry, that the religious music of the blacks should reflect these changes. The story of the emergence of gospel music, both black and white, as an enterprise in itself belongs elsewhere. But from our present vantage point of folk music, it is possible and instructive to trace the gradual replacement of the older spiritual, the successive imprints of currently popular sounds on Negro religious music, and the trend (in the sacred music of both races) toward professionalism and commercialism in this century.

First, the arranged vocal quartet, singing in more or less "barbershop" style and harmony, appeared in the early decades of this century. Early quartets were often fostered by the same educational institutions, such as Fisk University and the Tuskegee Institute, that had played such an im-portant part in popularizing the spiritual in the nineteenth century. The quartet is still important in gospel music. Instrumental accompaniment of banjo, guitar, and later piano, with the addition on occasion of tambourine and even brass instruments, began to be used. This brought with it the same demands for simpler harmony and melody that we saw operating in the case of the Anglo-American ballad tunes. Some traditional spirituals were adapted to this accompaniment,[16] but for the most part the simpler tunes that were being turned out literally by the hundreds by professional religious songwriters replaced them. These tunes were invariably in the major mode, and got along for the most part, as did the white country tunes, with only the three well-worn pedestrian harmonies of tonic, sub-dominant, and dominant.[17] But also the blues, especially as regards form and harmony, began to be reflected in black religious song, as the singing of Bozie Sturdivant and others illustrates.[18] Jazz influences were evident as early as the 1920s, as some commercial recordings indicate.[19] (Perhaps, as has been said, the influence was really the other way around.) Finally, the heavier, boogie-related beat of rhythm-and-blues has been adopted by gospel music.[20] But always in the background of black religious music, sup-planted but neither eliminated nor forgotten, is the "mother lode" of the spiritual, fecund and inexhaustible.

SECULAR FOLK MUSIC

Early documentation and collection of secular music is scanty, for reasons already gone into in discussing the spiritual, though we are apt to forget that the very first collection, *Slave Songs of the United States*, did include a good many secular songs. In the preface of this collection an unidentified "gentleman from Delaware" is quoted on the subject of the importance of the secular music to any comprehensive view of Negro folk music:

> We must look among their non-religious songs for the purest specimens of negro minstrelsy. . . . Some of the best *pure negro* songs I have ever heard were those that used to be sung by the black stevedores, or perhaps the crew themselves, of the West India vessels, loading and unloading at the wharves in Philadelphia and Baltimore. I have stood for more than an hour, often, listening to them, as they hoisted and lowered the hogsheads and boxes of their cargoes; one man taking the burden of the song (and the slack of the rope) and the others striking in with the chorus. They would sing in this way more than a dozen different songs in an hour. . . .

These were the work songs, which we shall return to at the end of the chapter. But there were other kinds as well. Let us take a brief look at some of them.

Cries, Calls, and Hollers

A kind of musical expression among the blacks at once primitive and evocative is found in the cries, calls, and hollers. Early observers here described these occasionally, and they can still be heard in Africa. Frederick Olmsted, reporting on a journey through the South in 1853, tells of being awakened in his railroad car in the middle of the night by a gang of black workmen enjoying a brief break around a fire.

> Suddenly one raised such a sound as I had never heard before, a long, loud, musical shout, rising, and falling, and breaking into falsetto, his voice ringing through the woods in the clear, frosty night air, like a bugle call. As he finished, the melody was caught up by another, then by several in chorus.[21]

These cries and calls—of the field, the levee, the track—were highly individualized expressions, for communication, for relieving loneliness, for giving vent to feelings, or for simply expressing the fact of ones existence. Their city counterparts, the street cries, were more utilitarian; they advertised goods and services. Both types have all but disappeared from their original setting. A few have been recorded.[22] Musically, they are florid, melismatic vocalizations, usually based on a single interval or a single chord, with embellishing tones and often certain "blue" notes of variable pitch not capable of precise notation.

In fact, the embryonic blues scale is so apparent in some of these calls that it will be well to introduce its main features here. This will serve as a reminder of the close relation between some of these solitary, highly individualized calls and hollers and the primitive rural blues. For this purpose, it will be useful to examine two calls in some detail.[23] They are both cornfield hollers, or *arwhoolies*; these examples are specifically songs sung at quitting time. The first may be notated (though only approximately!) as follows:

Oh, __ the sun go-in' down and I won't be here long.

Oh, the sun go-in' down and I won't be here long.

Oh, __ then I __ be go - in' home.

Oh, I can't let this dark cloud catch me here.

Oh, __ I can't stay here long.

Oh, __ I be __ at home.

(*Transcription by the author*)

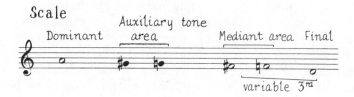

Scale

Dominant   Auxiliary tone area   Mediant area   Final

variable 3rd

It will be noted that there are only three essential pitch areas; a high one (which may be called the *dominant*) on which nearly all the phrases begin; a low one (which may be called the *final*) on which they all end; and an important area a third above the final, a *mediant*. The first two are relatively stable in pitch, but the mediant is variable. It sometimes gives a definite impression of major (marked with a sharp), and sometimes it sounds minor or neutral (indeterminately in between). The area between the mediant and the dominant is used as a relatively unessential auxiliary tone area. Careful listening will reveal that it is also subject to inflection, sometimes being so high as to sound like a flattened version of the dominant, a feature we will have occasion to note again.

The second example is more florid and more complex.

(*Transcription by the author*)

It will be seen that the range is greater; most of the phrases start an octave above the final. The dominant is also present, and an important tone. What is interesting to note is that the variable pitch area is now found a third above the *dominant*, or a seventh above the final, the third above the final being here fairly stable. Again the fourth degree of the scale, also inflected, is used as a passing tone. The falsetto ornaments (shown in small notes) are not uncommon, and may have been what caused Olmsted to refer to this music as "Negro jodling."

These two examples show the two areas of variable pitch in what has come to be known as the blues scale. If we make a composite of the pitch material of these two calls, adding additional tones to fill in the gaps, we have the complete blues scale in something resembling the form in which it is usually printed.

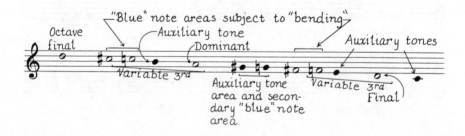

It should be noted that both the neutral (or indeterminate) third and the neutral seventh (which is actually a neutral third above the dominant, as we have seen) do not necessarily occur in every tune. There is, as we have said, also a tendency occasionally to inflect the dominant downwards as well, giving rise to yet a third area of variable pitch, and an alternative interpretation of the raised fourth-degree passing tone area.[24]

It should be noted that the performance of this music on an instrument of fixed and equal temperament such as the piano gives a highly conventionalized and falsified impression of its subtly inflected and extremely fluid nature as performed by the voice, whether in spirituals, hollers, or blues. Thus our conventional concept of this variable pitched scale is a somewhat mechanized and secondhand one.

Folk Blues

The Negro cries, calls, and hollers were intensely personal expressions, and this is also one of the most important characteristics of the blues. When we listen to *I Don't Mind the Weather* or *Joe the Grinder*,[25] we realize how this kind of elemental song gradually approaches the rural blues in proportions, and range and explicitness of expression. A further step would be represented by an extended holler such as the one beginning "Oh baby, what you want me to do?", captured in a field recording for the Library of Congress archive.[26] This is actually a primitive blues, albeit extremely rambling, improvisatory, and formless by "classic" blues standards. A less rambling song, in a rather tightly knit stanza form of four repeated lines, still unaccompanied, is the rather haunting and enigmatic *Another Man Done Gone*, as sung by Vera Hall.[27]

SOCIAL CHANGES AND THE BLUES

If these are a few steps away from the barely articulate field holler, it is readily apparent that they are very large steps. Furthermore, they are steps that could only have been possible after Emancipation, and the turbulent developments that followed in its wake. The spiritual began life in slavery; the blues could only have evolved afterwards. LeRoi Jones calls attention to at least five aspects of the profoundly changed life of the southern Negro after the Civil War that made the evolution of the blues possible.

There was a new dimension of leisure—circumscribed for most by hard economic necessity, but nonetheless real, as the absence of the overseer's lash was real.

There was, on the small individual farms, for either owner, tenant farmer, or sharecropper, a new degree of solitude that encouraged the cultivation of individuality—hallmark of the blues. This, in contrast to the older tribal nature of black culture, both in Africa and under the enforced tribal conditions the common bond of slavery imposed, gave a new and uniquely American dimension to Negro life and thought.

There was the confrontation with an entirely new set of social and economic problems, not the least being the need for money.

There was, as a consequence of broader contacts and experiences, a much greater fluency in the American language and a greater range of expression in its use.

Finally, and probably most important, there was a new mobility. This in itself gave access to a broader range of experience. The mobility was forced in most cases by the relentless (and new) necessity of finding employment—much harder, as Jones points out, for the men than for the women. But in the case of a few, the mobility was either not forced or was accepted willingly. There developed a small class of footloose wanderers, and it is among this class that many of the early blues musicians were found—genuine itinerant minstrels, in the original medieval sense of the term. To this class belonged also, perforce, the blind street musicians who had gravitated to the larger cities; making street music was the prime means of livelihood and independence available to those with even a modicum of talent. Thus it happened that the blues were propagated by a class of musicians who were to a degree outcasts, even among their own race—at least its more settled and established members, especially the most devoutly religious, to whom the blues were devil songs. Black author Richard Wright, going somewhat farther back and contrasting the origin of the spiritual with that of the blues, writes in his preface to Paul Oliver's *The Meaning of the Blues:*

> All American Negroes do not sing the blues. These songs are not the expression of the Negro people in America as a whole. I'd surmise that the spirituals, so dearly beloved of the Southern American Whites, came from those slaves who were closest to the Big Houses of the plantations where they caught vestiges of Christianity whiffed to them from the Southern Whites' cruder forms of Baptist or Methodist religions. If the plantations' house slaves were somewhat remote from Christianity, the field slaves were almost completely beyond the pale. And it was from them and their descendants that the devil songs called the blues came—that confounding triptych of the convict, the migrant, the rambler, the steel driver, the ditch digger, the roustabout, the pimp, the prostitute, the urban or rural illiterate outsider.[28]

It was perhaps inevitable, for a variety of reasons, that the prisons came to hold more than their share of bluesmen; many field recordings were made in the penitentiaries and prison farms of the South in the 1930s and 1940s, and some important blues singers discovered there.

BLUES TEXTS AND SUBJECTS

The subjects treated in the blues encompass a wide range. No area of commonly shared human experience is excluded. Some blues speak of a nameless depression.

> Early this morning the blues came walking in my room.

Some are about work—

> I worked all summer, yes, and all the fall
> Going to spend Christmas in my overalls.

or the lack of it—

> I'm goin' to Detroit, get myself a good job,
> Tried to stay around here with the starvation mob.

Some sing of gambling—

> Jack of Diamonds, you appear to be my friend
> But gamblin' gonna be our end.

of crime, of the law, of prisons—

> Judge gave me life this mornin' down on Parchman Farm;

of prostitution, of enslaving addiction, or of the necessity or the irresistible urge to move on—

> When a woman gets the blues, she hangs her head and cries.
> But when a man gets the blues, he flags a freight train and rides.

But the greatest number are in some way about the fundamental man-woman relationship. As blues singer Robert Pete Williams said: "Love makes the blues. That's where it comes from." [29] The man-woman relationship is displayed in the blues in a great variety of aspects—from a comment on the power of a woman's attraction

> Well, a long, tall woman will make a preacher lay his Bible down

or the exhilaration of being in love—

> Well, I feel all right and everything is okay.
> Yes, I feel all right, everything is okay.
> It's the love of my baby, oh, makes me feel this way.

to a scornful comment on infidelity—

> High yeller, she'll kick you, that ain't all,
> When you step out at night 'nother mule in your stall.

or the painful fact of separation—

> My man left this morning, jest about half past four,
> He left a note on his pillow, sayin' he couldn't use me no more.

or the most bitter rejection—

> If I was cold and hungry, I wouldn't even ask you for bread,
> I don't want you no more, if I'm on my dying bed.

Blues language is keen, apt, and colorful, if not grammatical, and is given to the use of irony, metaphor, and double entendre. No subject is off limits, and although broad social comment is foreign to such a personal medium, the blues poet finds a way to relate the most topical subject to an earthy metaphor with a telling phrase—

Uncle Sam ain't no woman, but he sure can take your man away.

BLUES FORM

The form of the blues is often described as though it were invariably conventionalized. It should be kept in mind that the rural blues is often quite free in form. The sung portions do not always arrange themselves into three-line stanzas, but may consist of a varying number of lines, often quite unequal in length. The standard form—a line, repeated, followed by a supplementing, concluding line—should be considered, in the country blues, as a tendency only.

My mama told me before I left home,
My mama told me before I left home,
You better let them Jacksonville women alone.

It was perhaps first crystallized in the published blues which began appearing as early as 1912, and which certainly influenced subsequent blues performers. The foregoing example also illustrates a feature common to much folk poetry—the casual inexactitude of both rhyme and meter. As in the case of the ballads, additional syllables in a line were simply crammed in.

The standard musical phrase is four bars long—hence the standard "twelve-bar blues" form. But in the case of the blues in its folk phase, single phrases could be four and a half, five, or seven bars long, with the singer beginning the next line whenever he or she felt like it (in the rural blues, it was almost invariably he). When there is instrumental accompaniment, which is nearly always, the sung line never takes up the whole musical "space," so to speak. The voice comes to its cadence about halfway through, and the phrase is always completed by an instrumental *break*. This paces the song, gives the singer time to think of the next line, and provides the opportunity for some more or less fancy and often highly individual instrumental playing. The blues is always introduced by an instrumental "warm-up," which may be the length of an entire stanza.

THE MUSIC OF THE BLUES

The melodic material of the blues has already been set forth in the discussion of field hollers, and the two or three pitch areas in the scale that are prone to inflection have been pointed out. But a sense of clearly defined pitch may be further obscured by a wide variety of highly personalized vocal techniques. Samuel Charters has made the point, in his notes to *The Rural Blues*, that the prime object of the blues is to express emotion, not to tell a story. Therefore the words themselves are not as important as, for example, in the ballad. The blues may thus be shouted (a manner of delivery related to the primitive field holler, which has been taken over successively by "rhythm and blues" and rock 'n' roll). They may be hummed; they may be sung in falsetto, or with falsetto breaks; they may be sung with the gravelly tone of the false bass voice; they may be chanted in the manner of a recitative; they may even be spoken.[30] In the folk blues, words and even lines may be left unfinished. As for melodic contour, there are many individual variations, but the general tendency is to start the phrases high and proceed downward, ending with a dropping inflection, as is true of the two field hollers previously transcribed. This is a trait of much primitive music.

Blues harmony may consist simply of a single chord with embellishments.[31] (This rudimentary harmony is likely to be associated with guitar tunings in which all the strings are tuned to the notes of a single chord.) The more usual practice involves the use of the three principal chords of the key in a pattern that *tends* toward the standard blues plan:

1st phrase	I	—	—	I⁷
2nd phrase	IV⁽⁷⁾	—	I	—
3rd phrase	V⁷	(IV)	I	—

Sometimes more sophisticated embellishing harmonies are used, especially at the end of the second phrase and the beginning of the last. This practice shows the influence of European harmony, probably by way of ragtime, and is typical of blues harmony as used in jazz.

The elemental blues, related to the field calls and hollers, was sung unaccompanied, of course. But at some undefined early date, the guitar was adopted as the natural instrument for accompanying the individual sung laments and comments that were the blues. The pungent nasal twang of the banjo was ideal for the fast breakdowns, but died too quickly to furnish sustained support for the slower blues. The fiddle was not widely used among blacks in the lowlands and delta regions, where the blues grew up; it also was thin-toned and incapable of providing harmonic support. But the guitar, with its deeper-toned strings and greater resonance, proved ideal. It could provide harmony, rhythm, and in the hands of an adept player, melody as well, for the warm-ups and the breaks. Skillful players developed their own individual sounds and techniques, elements of which could, by assiduous listening and imitation, be learned by others and so pass into general currency.

A sliding between tones was made possible by the use of the backs of knife blades on the strings, or the broken tops of bottles with the jagged edges annealed and worn on the little finger. This "bottle-neck" style, perhaps suggested by the Hawaiian guitar, overrode the tonal rigidity of the frets and provided a flexibility that made it possible for skillful performers to match the sliding and wailing of the voice. The playing of Robert Johnson, among many others, illustrates this.

Other instruments were used as auxiliaries to the ubiquitous guitar. The harmonica was fairly cheap and very portable, and this "blues harp" became, in the hands of virtuosos such as Sonny Terry, a very flexible and expressive instrument, capable of shadings and bendings that approached the subtlety of the voice. Improvised instruments were common. The jug served as a kind of substitute tuba; used as a resonator for the voice, it was also capable of the sliding tone. The washboard, fitted out with auxiliary metal pans and lids attached, was a whole rhythm section. The inverted washtub, with a piece of rope stretched between a hole through its center and a broom handle, was a substitute bass (and also a relative of the African earth bow!). Jug bands and washboard bands incorporating these instruments sometimes were recorded commercially, so that their sounds have come down to us—along with those of present-day revivals.

The piano occupies a unique position in relation to the blues. Basically an urban instrument, and far from portable, it did not figure in early rural blues at all. However, in the bars and bordellos of the cities and towns professional entertainers had early adapted blues guitar style and material to the piano. Thus boogie-woogie developed as a kind of parallel, and early urban, blues form. But that belongs to another part of the story.

The blues story is continued in chapter 8, as the story of a popular music evolving from folk roots. Admittedly it is difficult to draw a very precise line between the blues as folk music and the blues as essentially popular music, with professional entertainers catering to a "public" instead of casual music-makers performing within a closely knit community. But the distinction exists, nonetheless. LeRoi Jones has written:

> Socially, classic blues and the instrumental styles that went with it represented the Negro's entrance into the world of professional entertainment and the assumption of the psychological imperatives that must accompany such a phenomenon. . . . It was no longer strictly the group singing to ease their labors or the casual expression of personal deliberations on the world. It became a music that could be used to entertain others *formally*. The artisan, the professional blues singer, appeared; blues-singing no longer had to be merely a passionately felt avocation, it could now become a way of making a living. An external and sophisticated idea of performance had come to the blues, moving it past the casualness of the "folk" to the conditioned emotional gesture of the "public." [32]

It is at this real, if difficult to define, boundary that we take leave of the blues for the present.

Work Songs and Ballads

The blues, like the antecedent cries and hollers, were personal expressions that a lone singer might communicate to a few other sympathetic listeners, or simply sing to himself in his solitude. But there were other songs that, like the spirituals, were communal, social songs.

The use of singing to coordinate and lighten physical work, acting as both stimulus and lifter of spirits, is practically universal among men who must engage in hard communal labor, on land or sea. With blacks, work songs were prevalent during slavery; even the spirituals could be used in this way, and some of the earliest collected songs (such as *Michael, Row the Boat Ashore*) had this ambivalence about them. After the Civil War, work songs were needed wherever gang labor was used, in moving cotton bales, cutting sugar cane, chopping logs, and especially in the work of building railroads. There had to be a leader, of course; this called for a special skill involving not only a firsthand knowledge of the work and its pacing, and a gift for timing, but the ability to infuse into the work the balm of rhythm and song. A few of the recordings we possess of genuine work songs communicate this sense of rhythm and spirit.[33] With increased mechanization, of course, the work song almost disappeared. The only conditions under which it survived, at least until a generation or so ago, were those that closely duplicated conditions under slavery—that is, in the prisons and on the work farms, where, indeed, practically all the field recordings of work songs were made.

The ballad and the work song are both social forms of music making, though very dissimilar in function. However, the necessity on the part of the leader to prolong the work song to fit the task at hand often led to the adoption of the ballad, or storytelling, method, with its possibilities for improvisation and the proliferation of stanzas indefinitely. Thus it is that many of the Negro work songs and ballads are related; indeed, it may suggest the circumstances of composition for some of the ballads, or at least for some of the verses.

The ballad of John Henry, the steel driver, is probably the best known of all Negro ballads. So much attention has it attracted, as an important example of native folklore, that the ballad itself is the subject of two complete books. A hero-ballad, it also deals with the once-well-known occupation of hand-driving a steel drill to make a deep hole in solid rock for a blasting charge. The competition between mechanization and the "natural man" is an important feature in most versions of the ballad that have not been severely truncated. It is one of the few ballads that legend has attached to an actual event: the construction of the Big Bend Tunnel on the Chesapeake & Ohio Railroad near Hinton, West Virginia, in 1870–72. The ballad has been transmuted into both a work song and a blues.[34]

John Henry is an exception to the general truth that most of the Negro ballads are about murder and criminals. *Stagolee* (*Stackerlee*) is the archetypal "bad man" and a "bully from his birth." *John Hardy* (traceable perhaps to a man of that name hanged for murder in 1890) has killed for the most capricious of reasons. The crimes are not condoned, and in most versions the murderers eventually pay with their lives. Nevertheless, there is in the telling of these tales—black or white—an unmistakable strain of admiration for their almost superhuman embodiments of evil and meanness, or a strain of sympathy for the fugitive and the prisoner. *Frankie and Albert* (more popularly known as *Frankie and Johnny*) is on the other hand more of a domestic tragedy, and probably originated in a more urban milieu, even as a product of professional songmakers.

Students of the Negro ballad such as Malcolm Laws have pointed out the fecundity of invention that manifests itself in improvisation, and also (in contrast with white balladry) the greater emphasis on character and situation, rather than events per se.[35] This observation may well serve as a fitting conclusion to our brief survey of Negro folk music, for it serves to underscore a trait the perceptive reader and listener will have noted time and again—the ability to create, by means of an intensely personal and emotional kind of expression, a unique and characteristic degree of empathy with both subject and singer.

FURTHER READING

Collections with Some Expository Notes

* ALLEN, WILLIAM FRANCIS; WARE, CHARLES PICKARD; and GARRISON, LUCY McKIM (eds.). *Slave Songs of the United States.* New York, 1867. Reprinted since, most recently with piano accompaniments and guitar chords, Irving Schlein (ed.), New York: Oak Publications, 1965.

    A classic, of permanent importance as the first such collection published.

DETT, R. NATHANIEL. *Religious Folk-Songs of the Negro, as Sung at Hampton Institute.* Hampton, Va., 1927. Reprint, New York: AMS Press, 1972.

    This is the venerable Hampton Institute Collection, first published in 1874, as revised by one of Hampton's most famous choral directors and composers. As in the John Wesley Work collection listed below, most of the settings are for vocal quartet.

GRISSOM, MARY ALLEN. *The Negro Sings a New Heaven.* Chapel Hill, N.C., 1930. Paperback reprint, New York: Dover Publications, 1969.

    Good collection of 45 spirituals, with numerous stanzas of text included. The musical transcription is exceptionally carefully done, and

---

* Items thus marked are part of the suggested reference library to be available in connection with this book.

probably comes as close as is reasonably possible to representing in print the way the songs are actually sung in the folk tradition.

* JOHNSON, JAMES WELDON and J. ROSAMUND (eds.). *The Books of American Negro Spirituals.* 2 vols. in 1. New York: Viking Press, 1940.

Originally issued as two books, the first in 1925, this is a standard collection. James Weldon Johnson was a novelist and poet, author of *God's Trombones (Seven Negro Sermons in Verse).* His brother, J. Rosamund Johnson, made the piano arrangements.

* LOMAX, ALAN. *The Folk Songs of North America.* Garden City, N.Y.: Doubleday & Co., 1960. Paperback ed., 1975.

A fine general collection, as the name implies, with commentary.

* PARRISH, LYDIA. *Slave Songs of the Georgia Sea Islands.* New York, 1942. Reprint, Hatboro, Pa.: Folklore Associates, 1965.

An important work by an amateur folklorist working in an area that preserved much folklore, song, and speech into the mid-twentieth century. Includes some good photographs.

WORK, JOHN WESLEY. *American Negro Songs and Spirituals.* New York: Bonanza Books, 1940.

Some 40 pages of commentary, followed by a collection of songs of all types, with a preponderance of spirituals—mostly arranged for vocal quartet.

Primarily Studies, Which Include Some Complete Songs

CHARTERS, SAMUEL. *The Bluesmen.* New York: Oak Publications, 1967.

A study of rural blues singers by region, with some transcriptions of the music.

* COURLANDER, HAROLD. *Negro Folk Music, U.S.A.* New York: Columbia University Press, 1963.

An important and comprehensive recent study, with 43 complete songs.

* KATZ, BERNARD (ed.). *The Social Implications of Early Negro Music in the United States.* New York: Arno Press, 1969.

A collection of important articles and excerpts from books, dating from 1862 to 1939, most of which include a generous number of examples.

* KREHBIEL, HENRY EDWARD. *Afro-American Folksongs.* New York: Frederick Ungar, 1914.

An early musicological study, with examples to which piano accompaniments have been added, many by H. T. Burleigh. Includes African music, Creole music, and dances.

SCARBOROUGH, DOROTHY. *On the Trail of Negro Folk-Songs.* Cambridge, Mass., 1923. Reprint, Hatboro, Pa.: Folklore Associates, 1963.

A fine study, including a generous collection of ballads (including Negro versions of the Child ballads), reels, children's songs, lullabies, work songs, and railroad songs, many of which have become well known.

Studies and Background Reading

CHAPPELL, LOUIS W. *John Henry: A Folk-Lore Study.* Jena, Germany: Walter Biedermann, 1933.

* CHARTERS, SAMUEL B. *The Country Blues.* New York: Rinehart & Co., 1959. The first and still probably the most complete work on the subject, though the emphasis is biographical rather than on a study of the music itself. The first two chapters are relevant here; most of the book deals with the blues in its popular phase (commercial recordings, etc.).

————. Notes to *The Rural Blues: A Study of the Vocal and Instrumental Resources.* New York: Folkways record album RF 202.

————. Notes to *Roots of Black Music in America.* New York: Folkways record album 2694.

COOK, BRUCE. *Listen to the Blues.* New York: Charles Scribner's Sons, 1973. An informal but honest and perceptive study of the blues through selected bluesmen, involving eventually all phases, including the exploitation of some of the oldtime bluesmen.

DAVIES, REV. SAMUEL. Letters, quoted in Southern, *The Music of Black Americans* and *Readings in Black American Music*, both listed below. Davies was a Presbyterian minister who did missionary work in Virginia in the mid-eighteenth century. Consult Southern also for more specific bibliographical information on Davies and other missionary sources of his time.

EQUIANO, OLAUDAH. *The New Interesting Narrative of the Life of Olaudah Equiano, or Gustavus Vassa the African. Written by Himself.* London, 1789. Equiano, an early African writer in English, was an Ibo, a slave for ten years in Virginia and subsequently in England, where he purchased his freedom. A brief excerpt from his two-volume autobiography is included in Southern, *The Music of Black Americans*, p. 5.

FISHER, MILES MARK. *Negro Slave Songs in the United States.* Ithaca, N.Y.: Cornell University Press, 1953. A historical study of the spiritual, and the conditions that gave rise to it. In delving into the meanings of the spiritual, the author gives considerable emphasis to the colonization projects, whereby freed slaves were to be sent back to Africa. A detailed and perceptive study.

HERSKOVITS, MELVILLE. *The Myth of the Negro Past.* New York: Harper & Brothers, 1951. A landmark work, the result of a study begun in the 1930s. Traces Africanisms in New World black culture, daily life, and religion; one chapter deals specifically with language and the arts.

* JACKSON, GEORGE PULLEN. *White and Negro Spirituals: Their Life Span and Kinship.* New York: J. J. Augustin, 1944. Reprint, New York: Da Capo Press, 1975.

This is an important and often-cited work, by a scholar and an eminent authority in the field of the white spiritual. Especially interesting is the side-by-side comparison of the tunes of 114 spirituals from the black and white traditions. Jackson's main focus is the music. His contention that black spirituals are merely copies of white spirituals overstates his actual findings somewhat, and shows what seems to be an unfortunate bias. Lovell (listed below) is the leading author opposing the white-to-black theory.

JEFFERSON, THOMAS. *Notes on the State of Virginia.* 1803.

JOBSON, RICHARD. *The Golden Trade or a Discovery of the River Gambra and the Golden Trade of the Aethiopians.* London, 1623. Reprint, New York: Shoe String Press, 1968.
> Jobson was an English sea captain and explorer of West Africa. Relevant excerpts of his book are included in Southern, *Readings in Black American Music* (listed below).

JOHNSON, GUY B. *John Henry: Tracking Down a Negro Legend.* Chapel Hill: University of North Carolina Press, 1929.

JONES, A. M. *Studies in African Music.* London: Oxford University Press, 1959. 2 vols.
> This is perhaps the single most important study of African music to date, based as it is upon long and intimate acquaintance, and upon accurate transcription, using modern technological means. The musical transcriptions are beautifully reproduced as vol. 2. Both the virtues and the limitations of the study are candidly set forth in the introduction, which also includes a survey of other work done in the field.

———. "African Rhythm." *Africa,* vol. 24, no. 1 (January 1954). Reprint, London: International African Institute, as Memorandum no. 27, 1965.

* JONES, LeROI. *Blues People.* New York: William Morrow & Co., 1963.
> A perceptive social study of Negro music by a prominent black writer. The first six chapters are applicable to folk music.

LAWS, G. MALCOLM, JR. *Native American Balladry.* Philadelphia: American Folklore Society, 1964.
> This basic study, treating texts and subjects only, but with ample references to versions in print, has a section on Negro ballads.

* LOVELL, JOHN, JR. *Black Song: The Forge and the Flame.* New York: Macmillan Co., 1972.
> A major comprehensive survey, 686 pages long, of the spiritual. While no aspect is excluded, Lovell, a literary scholar, devotes his major attention to the texts and to the social background and implications. The book becomes at times somewhat argumentative in its denial of white influence on the spiritual. It is the leading work opposing George Pullen Jackson's contentions.

ODUM, HOWARD, and JOHNSON, GUY B. *The Negro and His Songs.* Chapel Hill, N.C., 1925. Reprint, Hatboro, Pa.: Folklore Associates, 1964.

A study of religious, social, and work songs. A rather exhaustive treatment of the texts, with many complete examples. No music.

OLIVER, PAUL. *The Story of the Blues.* Philadelphia: Chilton Book Co., 1969.

The first part of the book deals with the folk phase of the blues. There is an excellent collection of photographs.

———. *Savannah Syncopators.* Briarcliff Manor, N.Y.: Stein & Day, 1970.

Subtitled *African Retentions in the Blues,* it is a provocative if somewhat tentative study. Oliver has not claimed that his work is conclusive. Others, however, including A. M. Jones, have also pointed out that the presence or absence of Islamic influence is a basic distinction in African music.

* ———. *The Meaning of the Blues.* New York: Macmillan Co., 1960. Paperback ed., Collier Books, 1963.

An exhaustive and perceptive study of blues subjects and the milieu of its people, in the form of an extensive commentary on 350 blues texts arranged according to subject. Most of the blues lines used as examples in this chapter are quoted in Oliver's work.

OLMSTED, FREDERICK. *Journey in the Seaboard Slave States, with Remarks on Their Economy.* 1856. Reprint, New York: Negro University Press, 1969.

RAMSEY, FREDERIC, JR. *Been Here and Gone.* New Brunswick, N.J.: Rutgers University Press, 1960.

Among the numerous photographic studies with commentary this is surely one of the best.

* SOUTHERN, EILEEN. *The Music of Black Americans.* New York: W. W. Norton & Co., 1971.

A comprehensive, indispensable study of the entire field.

* ——— (ed.). *Readings in Black American Music.* New York: W. W. Norton & Co., 1971.

Excerpts from important source material ranging over the entire field.

* STEARNS, MARSHALL. *The Story of Jazz.* New York: Oxford University Press, 1956.

Early chapters deal with African influences, and their transplantation here, both directly and via the West Indies. Also discussed are the work song, the blues, and the spiritual.

TURNER, LORENZO. *Africanisms in the Gullah Dialect.* Chicago: University of Chicago Press, 1949.

WATERMAN, RICHARD ALAN. "African Influence on the Music of the Americas," in *Acculturation in the Americas,* edited by Sol Tax. New York: Cooper Square Publishers, 1967. Pp. 207–218.

WATTS, ISAAC. *Hymns and Spiritual Songs.* 1709. Words only.

Watts was an early eighteenth-century English theologian, whose hymn texts and paraphrases of psalms were well known. Phrases out of Watts's hymnody appear in both black and white spirituals right through the nineteenth century.

LISTENING

African Music

* *Negro Folk Music of Africa and America,* ed. Harold Courlander. Folkways: 4500.
  An excellent and far-ranging collection, edited by a noted authority.

Roots of Black Music in America: Some Correspondence Between the Music of the Slave Areas of West Africa, and the Music of the United States and the Caribbean, comp. and ed. Samuel Charters. Folkways: 2694.
  A highly interesting collection, juxtaposing, for example, African drumming with that of the early jazz drummer "Baby" Dodds. In listening to it, however, we must realize that the *very* selective excerpts, brilliantly chosen for their often superficial resemblances, may blind us momentarily to the very fundamental differences between African and American black music.

Music of the Jos Plateau and Other Regions of Nigeria. Folkways: 4321.

African Drums. Folkways: FE-4502.

Africa South of the Sahara, comp. Harold Courlander, notes by Alan Merriam. Folkways: 4503.

Religious Folk Music

FROM THE LIBRARY OF CONGRESS ARCHIVE OF AMERICAN FOLK SONG (AAFS)

* *Afro-American Spirituals, Work Songs, and Ballads,* ed. Alan Lomax. AAFS: L-3.
* *Negro Religious Songs and Services,* ed. B. A. Botkin. AAFS: L-10.
  Both these albums are valuable field recordings, with useful accompanying notes.

OTHER

Spirituals with Dock Reed and Vera Hall Ward. Folkways: FA-2038.

* *Anthology of American Folk Music,* vol. 2, *Social Music.* Folkways: 2952.
  This basic anthology consists of commercial recordings of folk music made in the 1920s and 1930s. The notes contain a great deal of information, including discography and bibliography. This volume includes sermons and early gospel songs.

An Introduction to Gospel Song, ed. Samuel Charters. Folkways: RF-5.

History of Jazz, vol. 1, *The South.* Folkways: 2801.

The Fisk Jubilee Singers. Folkways: 2372.

Negro Folk Music of Alabama, vol. 2, ed. Harold Courlander. Folkways: 4418.

* *Georgia Sea Island Songs,* from the *Recorded Anthology of American Music* (RAAM).

    A fine collection, with notes by Alan Lomax, who did the recording. Side 1 consists of spirituals.

Secular Folk Music

CRIES, CALLS, AND HOLLERS

* *Negro Work Songs and Calls,* ed. B. A. Botkin. AAFS: L-8.
* *Negro Blues and Hollers,* ed. Marshall Stearns. AAFS: L-59.
  Negro Folk Music of Alabama, vol. 1, ed. Harold Courlander. Folkways: 4417.

BLUES

* *Afro-American Blues and Game Songs,* ed. Alan Lomax. AAFS: L-4.
* *Negro Blues and Hollers,* ed. Marshall Stearns. AAFS: L-59.
* *History of Jazz,* vol. 2, *The Blues.* Folkways: 2802.
  The Country Blues, vols. 1 and 2, ed. Samuel Charters. Folkways: RF-1, 9.
  The Rural Blues: A Study of the Vocal and Instrumental Resources, comp. and annotated Samuel Charters. Folkways: RF-202.
* *Anthology of American Folk Music,* vol. 3. Folkways: 2953.
  The Jug Bands, ed. Samuel Charters. Folkways: RF-6.
* *Roots of the Blues,* notes by Alan Lomax. RAAM: NW-278.

WORK SONGS AND BALLADS

* *Negro Work Songs and Calls,* ed. B. A. Botkin. AAFS: L-8.
* *Afro-American Spirituals, Work Songs, and Ballads,* ed. Alan Lomax. AAFS: L-3.
  Negro Prison Songs from the Mississippi State Penitentiary, collected and annotated by Alan Lomax. Tradition: TLP-1020.
    Exceptionally fine recordings, and commentary, on prison work songs.
* *History of Jazz,* vol. 1, *The South.* Folkways: 2801.
* *Anthology of American Folk Music,* vol. 1, *Ballads.* Folkways: 2951.
* *Georgia Sea Island Songs.* RAAM: NW-278.
    See under religious folk music above. Side 2 consists of secular songs.

PROJECTS

1. Write a short paper on the South Carolina and Georgia Sea Islands as repositories of Negro folklore, speech, and song. Include whatever you can find out about conditions there today.

2. Review some of the significant studies that have been made of African survivals in American black music. Some of these are by Melville Herskovits, Alan Merriam, Harold Courlander, Richard Waterman, and Paul Oliver (*Savannah Syncopators*).

3. Make a brief study of the instruments used in Negro folk music.

4. Collect at least five quotations (other than those found in this chapter) from pre–Civil War writers bearing on the music, the musical aptitudes, and the musical practices of the Negroes.

5. Prepare a two-part sketch map of West Africa and the Caribbean and the southeastern United States, showing the original locations of various African tribes and the areas in the New World where slaves from these tribes were settled. (Stearns, *The Story of Jazz*, may furnish a point of departure.)

6. Compare the Latin, Catholic–dominated colonial areas (Louisiana, Florida, Hispaniola, Cuba) and the British, Protestant–dominated areas (Barbados, Jamaica, and the rest of the mainland South) for the survival of African traits among the blacks. (Refer to Stearns and at least one other source.)

7. Write a short paper on the influence of Isaac Watts (who never visited the United States) on American hymnody and spirituals, black and white.

8. Write a short paper on the work and significance of the Fisk Jubilee singers. (Locate if possible nineteenth-century works by Marsh and Pike in the bibliography of Katz, *Social Implications of Early Negro Music in the United States*.)

9. Write a short paper on textual themes in the Negro spirituals, including the double meanings they contain. (John Lovell's article in Katz, and Sterling Brown, *Negro Poetry and Drama*, could serve as points of departure.)

10. Compare a traditional version of a spiritual (as found in an early collection such as Allen et al., *Slave Songs of the United States*) with a concert version as sung by a recitalist or a trained concert choir. Discuss the advantages and disadvantages of such concert arrangements.

11. If you are somewhat experienced in music, make a brief study of the similarities between the music of the spirituals and that of the blues.

12. If you sing folk songs, learn two songs from the famous *Slave Songs of the United States*, using guitar or piano accompaniment if desired, and sing them for friends or the class. (See the reading list for this chapter for a modern edition with guitar chords and accompaniment added.)

13. Collect recorded examples of at least three different blues guitarist/

singers. Describe and compare their individual guitar techniques and styles, especially their treatment of the "breaks."

14. Collect recorded examples of blues illustrating at least four of the textual themes identified and treated in Paul Oliver *The Meaning of the Blues.*

Chapter Three

American Indian Music, and Spanish and French Folk Strains

IT IS AN IRONY INHERENT in our American experience that our oldest indigenous music—a music which has been heard here since prehistoric times—should be generally the most foreign to us. Except perhaps for Oriental music, no music has had less of an influence upon, or has proved more difficult to absorb into, our culture than the music of the American Indians.

The reasons for this are two. First, native American music is so different from European-derived music, both in sound and in function, that it may defy even understanding, much less assimilation, by non-Indians.

Second, this music belongs to a people that for too long were regarded by too many as being inferior, with little or nothing of value in their culture for the immigrant races. Even those Europeans who earliest took a sympathetic interest in American Indians, the Christian missionaries, most often viewed their music as "heathen," and strove to replace it (successfully in some cases) with the singing of psalms or Christian hymns. This prejudice has now largely disappeared, and we have entered an age in which other Americans are beginning to recognize and esteem the cultural achievements of America's first people, particularly their remarkable harmony with nature. The first difficulty, however, remains formidable. Much of the music is strange to non-Indian ears, unless the owners of those ears have had long and practiced acquaintance with it.

At the time of the first European exploration and colonization, at least 3 million native people lived in North America, split into several hundred separate independent cultural communities, each with its own language—and its own music. American Indian music is not folk music, then, in the strict sense of the term, but rather the tribal music of a great number of distinct peoples, displaying diverse cultural patterns and a wide variety of musical forms and styles. Scholars have made various attempts to divide the continent up into distinct geographical-tribal areas, on the basis of differentiated musical styles. These attempts, while yielding some significant results, have not thus far been completely successful. It is beyond the scope of this book to go into the characteristics of the various cultural areas; nevertheless, it is true that even a modest amount of careful listening will make one aware of important regional differences.

One other fact must be noted as we approach Indian music. We are discussing the music of native societies that once were aboriginal cultures but are so no longer. In the 300-odd years during which the whites completed their western advance across the continent, aboriginal Indian life was totally disrupted—native societies were dispossessed and decimated by disease and warfare; some tribal groups were totally destroyed; most others were relocated or confined on reservations, where they were first treated as a conquered, subject population. As a consequence, large elements of aboriginal cultural ways, including some musical elements, disappeared—destroyed, discarded, lost, or altered beyond modern recognition. Under these conditions, one of the most remarkable things about American Indian musical culture is that a significant remnant of it has indeed survived.

Not only has it survived, but it has entered a new phase of cultivation, as we shall note in due course. It will therefore be necessary to treat native American music in two distinct, though related, aspects: first, what can be learned of it as an integral part of the culture of an aboriginal people; and second, Indian music as it exists today.

MUSIC IN ABORIGINAL INDIAN LIFE

There are two ways to view an artifact, tangible or intangible, that is the result of artistic endeavor. The first is as a thing of interest and beauty wholly in and of itself. The second is as something to be viewed in the complete context of the society that brought it forth, having essential meaning only in this context. There is never an absolute separation of the two; we experience every art object with some mixture of both. But the closer we get to art in the folk or primitive state, the more necessary it becomes to take into account the second view. While never abandoning the study and apprehension of a work of art intrinsically, we must give a much greater proportion of our effort to understanding what the lives of those who made the art were like, and what its place and meaning was for them. This is in no case more imperative than with the music of the Indian people.

To non-Indian ears on first acquaintance, some Indian tribal music has instant appeal, but often much of it seems forbidding and unpromising esthetically—strange, monotonous, even ugly. Whatever one's immediate reaction, however, it must be realized that it was never created to be experienced in the essentially passive context in which we listen to music in the concert hall, or disembodied on phonograph recordings. Even more than in the case of folk music, its ambience is its very essence. As Willard Rhodes has said: "Primitive music is so inextricably bound up in a larger complex, ceremonial or social, that it is practically non-existent out of its functional context."

Here is a condensation of a description of a Hopi ceremony that included music, as in fact do most Indian ceremonies:

With a Hopi acquaintance I drove one July morning to Bakabi, to see the final ritual of the *Niman*. When I arrived in the village, I found that most of the Hopis had ascended to the line of roof tops, from which they could watch the ceremony in the plaza below. . . . The sky was cloudless and intensely blue. Sunshine flooded everything, illuminating the white walls of the houses along the plaza's farther side. . . . Soon a file of fifteen or twenty men came slowly into the plaza. . . . Each man's body, bare above the waist, was painted brown and marked with white symbols. Behind his right knee was fastened a rattle, made of a turtle shell. With each step that he took, the rattle gave out a hollow, muffled sound. In his right hand he carried a gourd rattle. . . . But the striking feature was the mask that each man wore. This covered his head completely and came down to his shoulders. The front was white and was inscribed with block-like figures, which suggested eyes, nose, and mouth. . . . Immediately the ceremony began. With measured, rhythmic step the long single file moved slowly forward, in time with a subdued chant. . . . With every step the turtle-shell rattle fastened behind the right knee contributed its hollow accent, sometimes suddenly magnified when all the dancers in unison struck the right foot sharply against the ground. Now and then the gourd rattles were shaken for two or three seconds, giving a curious accompaniment of elevated sound in contrast to the low, chanting voices. . . . When it was all over, I came away with the feeling that I had witnessed an ancient rite that was rich in symbolism and impressive in its significance.[1]

Even if a recording of this music had been made, how much could it convey to us, abstracted from its context?

Music had not only an importance in Indian life greater than is general among musically sophisticated societies, but also a *concreteness* unknown to such societies. The abstraction "music" would have been an unfamiliar and useless concept; it was only "this song" that had meaning. The important thing about a song is not its *beauty* but its *effectiveness*. Frances Densmore, one of the pioneering authorities on Indian music, has written: "The radical difference between the musical custom of the Indian and our own race is that, primarily, the Indians used song as a means of accomplishing definite results." [2] A recent incident illustrates the fact that this view of music is not totally dead even now. In a recent recording of gambling songs by the Yurok and Tolowa tribes of northern California, translations of the words could not be made, because, it was explained, "to do so would put the songs' luck in jeopardy." [3]

The degree of concreteness with which Indian songs are viewed is further illustrated by the fact that in many cases they are treated as strictly personal possessions, which may be transmitted to others only by being sold or given away. One old man, after being persuaded to record a noted war song, said that he would not live long, since he had given away his most valuable possession. There is, in fact, a sense of tangible reality, of magical power, of "presence," in *all* manifestations of what we would term art among primitive peoples. In the nineteenth century, after an eastern artist had been among the Plains Indians sketching the buffalo, an old Indian complained to a white friend that there were no longer so many buffalo on their range—a white man had put a great number of them in a book and taken them away with him. Is this not indeed an expression of the same magic-imbued world view that inscribed on rocks and in caves those often remarkably impressionistic likenesses of beasts the hunters needed to kill? It is this world we must be prepared to enter if we would understand what music originally meant to our first people.

Let us return to Frances Densmore's perceptive introduction to her chapter entitled "Why Do Indians Sing?"

Singing was not a trivial matter. . . . It was used in treating the sick, in securing success in war and the hunt, and in every undertaking which the Indian felt was beyond his power as an individual. An Indian said, "If a man is to do something more than human he must have more than human power." Song was essential to the putting forth of this "more than human power," and was used in connection with some prescribed action. . . . Thus it is seen that Indian music (both vocal and rhythmic instrumental) originally lay in the field of what we call religion.[4]

Music was thus a means of communication with what we would regard as the supernatural world—a world in which sun, moon, stars, lakes, rivers, mountains, and all animals each had an indwelling spirit (or to use the Iroquois word, *orenda*) that the Indian could call upon in need, provided he possessed and used the right "medicine."

Songs of great power, sung chiefly by medicine men or women, would be used in communal ceremonies for the general good, and would be very carefully passed on in oral tradition. The need for accuracy was all-important to their effectiveness. There could also be new songs, belonging to men who had acquired them in the course of "vision quests"—self-imposed ordeals of courage and self-denial that were known among virtually all tribes in their aboriginal state. Lonely fasts, often carried out in locations and conditions of extreme discomfort and danger, and lasting as long as four days, would, when successful, result in what appeared as tangible communication with the spirit dwelling in some animal or some natural phenomenon. With the impartation of the vision (which identified the seeker forever afterward with the particular animal, if that were the apparent source) would often come what was received as a new song. These, then, were the "real" songs—the property either of individuals or of the tribe. A clear distinction was made in most tribes between these songs, which had inherent power, and other songs, which were either borrowed from other tribes or were made up—consciously composed—and used to enhance various forms of recreation. In recent years, under the pressures of acculturation, the old songs have decreased in importance in the repertory of most tribes. Many that are known to have existed have been lost altogether.

The older ceremonial songs are heard in their purer form on the early recordings, sung often by old men whose memories stretch back to a time on the Plains and farther west when little acculturation had yet taken place. The following example is from the Menominee, an Algonquian tribe which, at the time this song was collected in the late 1920s, was still living along the Menominee River in Wisconsin, in the same locality they had inhabited for at least three centuries, going back to the time when they were first encountered by the whites. This dream song, which was said to have power in healing the sick and was so used, was sung by Louis

Pigeon, who secured it as a boy. After fasting for two days, he saw two birds, a crow and a raven, who gave him the song.[5]

Game songs are also present in the earliest collections. A favorite among many tribes was the moccasin game. The players were divided into two opposing sides; one side hid four small objects such as bullets or prune pits under four overturned moccasins. One of the objects was specially marked, and the point of the game was for the other side to guess under which moccasin the marked object lay. Wagers were often heavy, and assistants could be used to sing songs or otherwise bring luck. The songs could be sung by the side hiding the objects, to confuse the other side. The following is a Menominee moccasin game song.[6]

(Transcription by the author)

As for other functions of music in Indian life there were love songs, in the sense of songs sung or played to secure success in love. Social dancing, with its own music, was originally relatively unimportant, but it has now become much more prevalent—a manifestation of the changes that have come over Indian life. Work songs exist, as for example the corn-grinding songs of the Southwest. So do narrative songs, especially among the northwestern coastal tribes. Neither work nor storytelling songs figure prominently in Indian repertory generally, however. Songs for other social functions exist: to welcome and bid farewell to guests (very elaborate along the northwestern coast); to honor warriors and chieftains; and to use in contests and other purely social ceremonies.

CHARACTERISTICS OF INDIAN MUSIC

Indian music is predominantly vocal; there is very little purely instrumental music. The singing is usually accompanied, however, by a drum, or some sort of rattle, or both. The basic unit of the music is the song, which may last anywhere from less than a minute to several minutes. When the song accompanies dancing, which is very commonly the case, there is a good deal of repetition; it is common to sing a song four times.

The scales used in Indian music are found generally to correspond to our familiar diatonic scale—that is, the basic scale structure available on the white keys of the piano. When less than the full seven tones to the octave are used, as is often the case, some form of the pentatonic scale (that obtainable on the black keys) is very common, as it is in much folk and primitive music the world over. The piano has been mentioned merely as a means of reference; it must be understood that Indian music, in intonation, only *approximates* the tuning implied in our notational system. There are subtle deviations in the qualities of certain intervals that are consistent in repeated renditions of the same song. Even microtones are occasionally found. *Portamento,* or the sliding from one pitch to another, is common, particularly a descending slide at the end of a phrase. Singing in other than the unison (or octave, if the women sing also) is extremely rare, though not unknown—there are some interesting examples of an evolving polyphony.

Indian instruments include drums, whistles, flutes, hand-shaken rattles, and ornaments worn by the dancers (usually made of some type of shells), which produce a rhythmic kind of rattling during the dance. The drums range in size from small hand-held ones to quite large ones resting on the ground, or suspended between posts in the ground, and played by several people at once. They are made in a variety of ways, and even improvised from inverted baskets, washtubs or kettles covered with skin, or wooden boxes. Flutes are usually fashioned from some straight-grained wood, or cane, but in the Southwest they can be made of clay. Rattles are nearly universal, are of many types, and usually have (or had) ritual significance.

The flute is almost uniquely associated with love songs, and these songs constitute almost the only use of purely instrumental music. Here is a portion of a Sioux love song, as played on a flute.[7]

Repeated with slight modifications
(Transcription by the author)

As is the case in this example, words can be put to the melodies, so that they can also be sung.

The use of drums alone, without singing, is virtually unknown; this is in distinct contrast to African, and hence West Indian, tradition. The rhythms of drum and rattle are simple, the impulses usually grouped in pairs in a relation that ranges from perfectly even pulses

to those based on the triplet.

Very often it is somewhere in between. Longer songs may be divided into clearly defined sections, with definite tempo changes. The tempo of the drum, curiously, is sometimes independent of that of the voice.

Since the music is nearly all vocal, the question of the words arises. Interestingly enough, the songs are very often not in the language of speech. *Vocables*—simply vocal sounds—are often either interpolated between actual words or replace them altogether. (The same tendency, in the case of refrains, was noted in Anglo-American folk music.) To call these meaningless syllables is not quite correct; they may have either private or ritual significance, or they may be sounds whose original meaning has been lost, either through changes in the language or because they were borrowed from other tribes. Whatever their origin, the vocables are not improvised, but belong to the given song and are reproduced with complete consistency.

Indian music has not proved incapable of assimilating certain aspects of non-Indian music. On occasion, the tunes of Christian hymns and white secular songs have been adopted.[8] English words have been used, with either Indian tunes or disguised white tunes. A "forty-nine" song is a particular kind of humorous, often derisive, song with English words. A recent rendition of the Rabbit Dance, a social dance of the northern Plains Indians, contains the following lines, in a parody of a white cowboy song.

Hey, sweetheart, I always think of you.
I wonder if you are alone tonight.
I wonder if you are thinking of me.[9]

INDIAN MUSIC AND ACCULTURATION

As we have noted, acculturation has been going on continuously since the first contact with the white man—the French Huguenots were teaching the Florida Indians to sing psalm tunes in the sixteenth century. The length of time that the Indians have been exposed to the white man's culture varies widely from area to area, of course. We know the least about aboriginal Indian music in the eastern United States—where the cultural pressures (and the dispossessions and dispersions) have been longest-lasting and most severe—and in Mexico.

The Ghost Dance and the Peyote Cult

Two singular developments in the West since the encroachment of white civilization deserve mention, since they grew out of that cataclysm, directly or indirectly. The first of these was the spread of the Ghost Dance, with its accompanying music. Originating in the Great Basin area, the Ghost Dance cult represented a kind of messianic religious belief in the appearance of a savior and the expulsion of the white man, accompanied by the resurrection of dead Indian leaders and a return of the buffalo and of the old ways. In the 1880s the Ghost Dance spread rapidly, especially among Plains tribes. It was outlawed by the Bureau of Indian Affairs, and its repression by the United States Army culminated in the tragic massacre of Sioux Ghost Dance devotees at Wounded Knee in 1890. An active cult and ritual, vehicle of a fanatical hope, it died out as rapidly as it had spread. The songs of the Ghost Dance persisted, however, and were recorded among Plains tribes as late as the 1940s. It was a pan-Indian cultural phenomenon; Ghost Dance songs of various tribes show similar characteristics, of Great Basin origin, that are often markedly different from those of their own indigenous tribal music.[10]

A second development, not unrelated to the rapid spread and decay of the Ghost Dance cult, has been the spread of the peyote cult (the Native American Church), based on the use of the hallucinogenic buttons of the peyote cactus. Originating apparently in pre-Columbian Mexico, it had spread northward into the Rio Grande and Gila River basins by the eighteenth century, where it was known among the Apache. The cult reached the plains about 1870. Taking on there a somewhat different form, it became a group or community rite, with a well-defined ceremonial that incorporated some elements of Christian theology and symbolism. Its spread since then has been rather carefully documented, and is still going on; it reached some groups of the Navajo, and the Indians of Canada and

Florida, in the mid-twentieth century. Singing is an integral part of the meetings at which the peyote buttons are consumed, and while any songs, including Christian hymns, may be used, special peyote songs have evolved.[11] The relation of the peyote cult to the vanished Ghost Dance, and to the severe upheaval to which the American Indians and their aboriginal culture generally have been subjected in the modern world, is summed up by David McAllester:

> The wide spread of the Ghost Dance must have contributed to the receptivity of the Indians to peyote. After the brief currency of the former the Indians were left with little sense of spiritual direction, although the conditions of radical change and insecurity that fostered the Ghost Dance were intensified after its collapse. . . . In place of resistance a philosophy of peaceful conciliation and escape arose. . . . The vision, all-important on the Plains, was made easily available by the use of the cactus.[12]

Indian Music Today

The American Indian population, which had declined to half a million or less by the end of the nineteenth century, has begun again to grow at a rapid rate, and now numbers well over one million. Automobiles, radio, and television have ended the isolation of reservation life, and a large-scale movement of Indian people toward urban centers since the end of World War II has intensified cultural contact not only between Indians and whites but—most important for Indian music—between Indian peoples of different tribal traditions. It is important to recognize, then, that the indigenous and inherited culture of over one million native Americans is not dead. It is true that there has been an irreversible loss of much of the older music. Alan Merriam quotes a young Flathead musician, on being asked about the fact that the younger performers do not know the old songs: "Well, the old-timers are kickin' off fast, and that kind of song is gettin' to be old stuff nowadays." [13] And the exploitation of Indian music—at fairs, rodeos, and other tourist attractions, and for Hollywood films—has given currency to a certain standardized and stereotyped product, so that what has been described as a kind of pan-Indian "cultural front" has been created. But music has been part of a strong general movement of cultural revival since the 1950s. The pan-tribal *powwows* held annually on the large Plains reservations are primarily great social events today, but they include the performance of songs and dances that maintain distinct tribal identity and characteristics, and thus represent a return to tribal particularism and a movement away from pan-Indianism in matters of culture. The Crow Indians furnish an example of a tribe that has been particularly successful in maintaining its cultural identity. The fact that some groups, such as the Ponca Singers of Oklahoma, have become professionalized to the extent of traveling and performing regularly for pay at various pow-wows does not necessarily mean that they have corrupted or compromised Indian song itself, or even that they have blurred tribal and regional distinctions.

The movement of American Indians off the reservations and into the cities was given extra impetus in the 1950s by a Bureau of Indian Affairs program aimed at terminating eventually both the special status of the American Indians and the reservations themselves. This program has since been abandoned, but not all the Indians who were relocated returned to the reservations, and there exist very sizable communities of American Indians not only in virtually every small city in the West, but in and around large urban areas, particularly Chicago, Denver, Los Angeles, and Oakland and the San Francisco Bay area. These urban Indian communities also regularly enjoy large social gatherings, at which Indian songs and dances are performed—in Los Angeles, for example, by such groups as the Los Angeles Northern Singers, comprised of members of the Sioux, Arikara, Hidatsa, and Northern Arapaho tribes. At these gatherings, not only are the tribal songs and dances found to be flourishing, but along with the new emphasis on the social function of the music there are preserved unmistakeable traces of the older functionalism and attitude towards music as well. These can be seen, for example, in the custom of "sponsoring" an entertainment in honor of a person or event (which had its aboriginal counterpart in customs such as the *potlatch*), and in surviving manifestations of the concepts that certain songs are private possessions and certain songs bring luck. This blending of the old and the new is, according to the *functionalist* view of folk art and folklore, both a ceaseless process and a perennial condition.

HISPANIC FOLK MUSIC

The first European presence in America was that of the Spaniards. In the generation following Columbus's voyages, Spain, the foremost European power of the time, entered upon a period of phenomenal exploration and conquest. By the mid-sixteenth century the Spanish had begun extensive exploration by land and by sea from Florida to the northern California coast, and by the beginning of the seventeenth century the first attempts at colonization in what is the present area of the United States (many of which proved to be disastrous) had begun. Although Florida was the first point of contact, Spanish influence along the eastern coast of the Gulf of Mexico was not destined to be significant. In the Southwest, on the other hand, it was decisive. Beginning with the earliest missions and small colonial settlements in the upper Rio Grande valley of New Mexico in the 1600s, and culminating with the high watermark of Spanish penetration in the California mission period of the late eighteenth and nineteenth centuries, the foundation was laid for Hispanic influence, which is still of the greatest importance culturally in that part of the country, and which has been reinforced in all periods by almost continuous migrations from Mexico.

Sacred Music

The first musical influences were religious. Spanish sacred music reached the highest point of its development in the prosperous sixteenth century, rivaling in excellence and in the intensity of its cultivation that of Rome itself. It therefore accompanied the *conquistadores*, and music was found to be one of the priests' most powerful tools for converting and teaching the Indians. Before the end of the sixteenth century both vocal and instrumental music were intensively cultivated in Mexico, accompanied by musical-instrument manufacture and the printing of music.

Of course conditions were far more primitive in the small missions and settlements far to the northwest. Something of a distant and attenuated echo of the greatness of Spanish church music did belatedly reach this frontier, however. For example, it is now known that during the brief flourishing of the Franciscan missions in California from 1769 to their secularization beginning in 1834, there was a rather considerable musical culture. It embraced strictly liturgical music (at least some of which was probably composed there), as well as more informal and folk-like hymns and *alabados*, and even secular songs and dances, performed for festive occasions. Both vocal and instrumental music were taught to the Indians, who made up the choirs and small orchestras. After the secularization of the missions and the departure of the Franciscan priests, such manuscripts as existed (all of liturgical music) were destroyed or forgotten, and what little was preserved of a musical culture went over into oral tradition. Under the circumstances, it is remarkable that any survived; it is therefore rather surprising to come upon a remarkable photograph of the last Indian choir of Mission San Buenaventura, taken in 1860, with each of the Indians holding what appears to be a homemade instrument—a flute, for example, fashioned from an old gun barrel. That the singing of the Indian choirs survived even longer in some cases, without losing its intensity or meaning, is attested to by Robert Louis Stevenson's account of a festival at Mission San Carlos Borromeo (Carmel) in 1879: "I have never seen faces more vividly lit up with joy than the faces of these Indian singers. It was to them not only the worship of God, nor an act by which they recalled and commemorated better days, but was besides an exercise of culture, where all they knew of art and letters was united and expressed." [14]

Some of the sacred music of the missions has now been recovered and re-created; many of the simple liturgical pieces have a naive charm that is quite distinctive.[15]

A more living folk tradition is that of the religious folk plays, which are still performed, notably in New Mexico.[16]

Secular Music

The legacy of Spanish and Mexican secular folk music has been far more significant for American culture than has that of the religious music—although, as in many folk traditions, the two cannot always be entirely separated.

Of all the folk forms now popular, none is more distinctive or more interesting than the *corrido*. The Hispanic love of poetry, and especially the commemoration of people and events in poetry, here finds expression in what is still a vital tradition. The *corrido* is the modern equivalent of the folk ballad—a narrative strophic song. As distinguished from the older *romance*, of Spanish origin, it deals with actual people and events, often of immediate and topical concern, and in an earthy, frank, and unembellished way. It had its origins in Mexico in the turbulent mid-nineteenth century, where it was often political and satirical. *Corridos* were cheaply printed as broadsides (words only), just as they had been earlier in England and the United States.

The *corrido* of the southwestern United States is nearly as old as its Mexican forebear. An area rich in the production of *corridos* and other folklore has been the valley of the lower Rio Grande, from the two Laredos to the Gulf. A fertile valley in the midst of an arid plain, overlooked in early exploration and colonialization, largely ignored by Spain and Mexico, and spurned by the United States, it was inhabited by people of a fiercely independent spirit. When in 1836 Texas declared its independence of Mexico, it suddenly became a border area, and this ushered in a period of unrest, oppression, and bloodshed that was to last intermittently for nearly a century. Like many strife-torn border areas—those of England and Scotland, for example—it bred its heroes and its villains, and its ballads to commemorate them. An early *corrido* was *El Corrido de Kiansis*, known in the border area by 1870. It describes the experiences and hardships of the Mexican *vaqueros* in the cattle drives of the late 1860s and early 1870s from Texas to the western terminus of the railroad in Kansas.

One of the most famous *corridos*, still sung today, is *El Corrido de Gregorio Cortez*, based on an incident that took place in Karnes County, Texas, in 1902. The hero was a young Mexican who, having been falsely accused of horse stealing, shot and killed in self-defense the sheriff who had fatally wounded his brother. The *corrido*, in some twenty to thirty stanzas, goes on to trace Cortez's flight and capture, ending with the customary *despedida*, "Now with this I say farewell."

En el con-da-do del Car-men mir-
en lo que ha su-ce-di-do, Murió
el she-ri-fe ma-yor que dan-do Ro-mán he-
ri-do.

(Transcription by the author)

(In the county of El Carmen
Look what has happened;
The Major Sheriff died,
Leaving Román badly wounded.) [17]

This *corrido* shows the typical form of four-line rhymed stanzas, or *coplas*, each line customarily having eight syllables. The musical rhythm is simple, but rather characteristically irregular in its metrical structure. This combination of regular poetic form with irregular musical form is typical of Mexican-American music. Whether consciously contrived or not, it is a feature that enables the music to retain its interest through the repeated hearings inherent in the strophic form. The habitual singing in parallel thirds so typical of nearly all of this music is of uncertain origin, but it has been compared by John Donald Robb, authority on the folk music of New Mexico, with a medieval practice known as *gymel*.

In the *corrido* we encounter a ballad tradition still very much alive. *Corridos* are being composed and sung on topical events by amateurs and professionals alike. Many are recorded, and issued in the common currency of popular music, the 45-rpm "single." Subjects of recent *corridos* have included a Russian *Sputnik* ("la luna Rusa"); Cesar Chavez and the farmworkers' struggle; the infamous murder of eight nurses in Chicago; and "black September," the tragic killings at the 1972 Olympic games in

Munich. The following is a typical modern *corrido* by Rafael Ramírez entitled *La Muerte de Martin Luther King* ("The Death of Martin Luther King").[18]

Voy a can - tar para U -ste-des, Señ-or-es, La
dis- ta del a- ño vio-len-to. Fue un

glo-ria de un hom-bre va - lien-te. _____
hom-bre de es-fuer-zas ca- ba- les. _____

Que por sal - var un - a pa-tria, Señ-or- es. Ha -
Lu- chó por los hom-bres, lu- chó con cle-men- cia. Que

lló en su ca - mi - no la muer-te.
to - dos son crea-dos i - gua-les.
Fue un es-ta-

O - ye, pa-lo- ma que vue-las. _____ He -

ri -da en un cua-tro de a- bril. _____ Lle-va en tu

pi- co la es-que-ta, La muer-te de Mar-tin Lu-ther King.
(Transcription by the author)

(Gentlemen, I am going to sing for you
About the glory of a valiant man,
Who, while trying to save his country,
Found death in his pathway.

A statesman in a time of violence,
A just man of valor,
He struggled for mankind, he taught, with mercy,
That all are created equal.

Oh dove of peace, you who fly
Wounded on an April Fourth,
Take with you in your beak the sad notice
Of the death of Martin Luther King.)

(Translation by Joaquin Fernández)

Caribbean Music in New York City

Most of the world's super-cities are rich in ethnic mixtures, with a variety of racial and cultural enclaves—cities in themselves within cities. Thus the variety of ethnic musics represented in New York City alone could be the subject of a formidable and fascinating volume. Our survey of the Hispanic strain of American music would not be complete without mention of a twentieth-century development: the growth of a large Spanish-speaking population in New York City whose ethnic and cultural roots are in the Caribbean—mostly Puerto Rico, and to a lesser extent Cuba. Immigration from Puerto Rico (ceded to the United States after the Spanish-American War and given commonwealth status in 1952) has been significant since United States citizenship was granted to Puerto Ricans in 1917, but it reached a peak in the 1940s and early 1950s. Thus for two generations there has been heard in New York the strongly flavored music of the Caribbean: the Spanish-derived forms of the *danza*, the *seis*, and the *aguinaldo*, and the African-influenced *bomba*, *rumba*, and music of the *lucumi* ritual (*santería*). A unique feature of Caribbean culture has always been its mixture of the African with the Hispanic. African influence is especially strong on the islands of Cuba and Hispaniola (the latter is divided between Haiti and the Dominican Republic), where the importation of slaves by the Spanish colonizers was particularly heavy, forming the basis for a sizable black population. The chief musical influence has been that of rhythm; the variety of drums and other percussion instruments, and the pervasiveness and complexity of the rhythmic underpinning, set Afro-Caribbean music apart from all other North American Hispanic music. The most African-sounding music in the United States can be heard in the playing of the Afro-Cuban groups in New York.

The influence of Afro-Caribbean music on both jazz and rock has been crucial, as we shall see, and too often ignored or underestimated. It is also true that jazz instrumentation and style have been grafted onto the urban

Caribbean music, further validating the concept of folk music as a flowing and continually altering stream.[19]

THE FRENCH STRAIN: LOUISIANA

French influence in American folk music has been practically confined to southern Louisiana. There, within a relatively small geographical area—from the right bank of the Mississippi below its confluence with the Red River to the lowland Gulf coast between the mouths of the Mississippi and the Sabine, in a fertile and sultry land laced with estuaries, lakes, and bayous—the residue of France's brief period of colonialism in the New World is still palpable in a colorful, multifaceted musical culture. Actual French sovereignty over the area was remarkably brief, compared to that of Spain farther west and south—only the first two-thirds of the eighteenth century. Culturally, however, Louisiana clearly bore the stamp of France— and of the Caribbean—right through the brief period of Spanish rule and well after its purchase by the United States. This stamp is still visible.

The rich racial mixture of Louisiana, and the complex caste system it engendered, resulted in a "layering" of French-language folk music. Irene Whitfield has identified three such distinct layers: that of the Louisiana-French, the settlers and their descendants who came either directly from France or indirectly with a stopover of a few generations in the Caribbean; that of the Acadians, or *Cajuns*, refugees from Acadia (now Nova Scotia), who were welcomed into Louisiana and given land by the Spanish rulers after their expulsion from Canada in the mid-eighteenth century; and that of inhabitants at the bottom of the social order, those of African descent, comprising a complex caste system themselves—slave and free; black, mulatto, and quadroon.

Louisiana-French Music

The Louisiana-French folk music naturally bears the closest resemblance to that of France itself, and there are many songs and ballads that have Old World cognates. The famous *Malbrough s'en va-t-en guerre* is cited because of its interesting history (it was a satirical song aimed at the victorious duke of Marlborough by the French in 1709) and its ubiquitous tune, which may be even older than its association with its oldest known text.[20]

(Malbrough is going to war,
   mironton, ton, ton, mirontaine.
Malbrough is going to war,
God knows when he will return.
God knows when he will return.
God knows when he will return.)

Among old French ballads (possibly medieval) to have been recovered are *Le plus jeune des trois* and *Sept ans sur mer*.[21] These show the well-defined rhythmic sense that makes French folk music, even that of the narrative ballads, never far removed from the dance. *Sept ans sur mer* is worth citing here for its attractive tune.

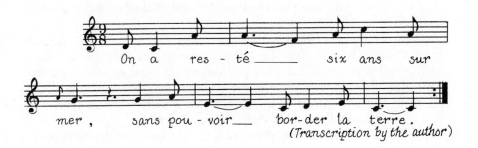

(*Transcription by the author*)

(Six years they were at sea,
   Without being able to touch land.)

Cajun Music

Though the Cajuns can trace the presence of their forebears in Louisiana to the forced migrations of French colonists from the old French-Canadian maritime settlements of Acadia in the eighteenth century, it is difficult to say how far back, or to what sources, their music can be traced. We do not encounter this rather narrowly regional music either written down or on recordings before the 1920s and 1930s. Going to the early sources, we find a music lighthearted in mood and theme, with a marked predilection for love songs, and a repertory consisting mostly of waltzes, pieces in duple meter related to fiddle hoedown music, and pieces clearly related to the blues. There was apparently little or no religious folk music.

The rhythmic vitality of some of this traditional music can be illustrated by the delightful folk song *Les clefs de la prison*, with its lively syncopations. (This song was used by the American composer Virgil Thomson in his suite *Acadian Songs and Dances*, adapted from his film score for *Louisiana Story*.) A similar tendency towards a syncopation in the vocal line can be heard in some of the early recordings, such as *La femme qui jovait les cartes*.[22]

One feature characteristic of traditional Cajun music is the use of the accordion, acquired probably from German settlers, as was the case farther west with the *musica norteña* of the Texas-Mexican border. To the accordion (originally the button variety) was added the violin and the guitar to form the small ensemble to accompany singing or dancing.

Cajun music began to be commercially recorded in the late 1920s, at the same time that so much other regional music was being marketed within the folk communities. Traditional folk songs do appear, of which *J'ai passé devant la porte* seems to be an example, apparently very well known; but since it did not appear in a folk music collection until after the first commercial recording, it is difficult to tell what relationship this had to its existence in oral tradition.[23]

Cajun musicians, though managing to retain a distinct regional identity in their music, have in true folk fashion appropriated for their use whatever appealed to them and their patrons outside of their own tradition. This early absorption of other music is shown in a rather amusing "Cajunizing" of *Home, Sweet Home* (it becomes a waltz), and an appropriation of the tune of the popular ballad *Casey Jones*.[24]

In the late 1930s and the 1940s, with the expansion of the oil industry and the influx of workers from the rural Southeast, Cajun music lost many of its earlier distinctive characteristics, and was nearly swamped in the flood of country-and-western music. It was about this time, for example, that the Hawaiian steel guitar, which had recently become so popular in country music, joined the Cajun band. And one hears in *Le côte farouche de la vic* a Cajun adaptation of *I'm Dreaming Tonight of My Blue Eyes.* Most of the recordings of the period can be rather succinctly described as hillbilly music sung in patois! Since the 1950s there has been a resurgence of the older styles; the accordion is back, and so are some of the older songs.

During the revival period of Cajun music there developed a style of black Cajun music known as *zydeco.*[25] Characterized by a resurgence of the accordion, this music is a kind of virtuosic reinterpretation of the older Cajun music, in much the same way that *bluegrass* is a reinterpretation by virtuoso performers of the traditional white mountain music of the southern highlands. Clifton Chenier, versatile black singer, accordionist, and harmonica player, became one of the chief exponents of *zydeco,* as well as performing the more broadly popular rhythm-and-blues.

Black Folk Music of Louisiana

That the folk music heard among the black people of Louisiana, and especially around New Orleans, should have been labeled "Creole" is an indication of the multiple and often confusing uses of this word. Strictly speaking, it applies to people of French, Spanish, and Portuguese descent born in the New World, and specifically in the United States to French-speaking descendants of the early French and Spanish settlers in Louisiana.[26] But the patois that the blacks evolved in struggling to speak a language they were not able (or permitted to learn) to read and write also acquired the *adjective* Creole. Thus the designation "Creole slave songs" was applied to an early study of Negro music using this dialect; and it was perpetuated in Irene Whitfield's classification of "Creole folk songs"—meaning again the folk songs of black Louisianians in this language. As a further confusion of usage, the word is sometimes applied to the black people themselves—as in "black Creoles"—and one of their own songs is even called *Criole Candjo* (a *candjo,* or *candio,* was a black chief).

George Washington Cable gives a descriptive account of this "Creole" music as it existed in and around New Orleans after the Civil War in two classic and often-quoted articles published in 1886: "The Dance in Place Congo" and "Creole Slave Songs." [27] These include musical examples.

What is immediately apparent in this early music of the Louisiana blacks is the nearly inseparable association of music and dance. If this was a tendency in French music, it was even more true of the music of Africa, as we have already noted in the previous chapter. The *bamboula,* the *counjaille,* the *calinda,* the *habañera*—these were types of songs, but they were also dances. The *bamboula,* for example, was named for a small drum made from a section of the huge bamboo that grows in the West Indies; the drum accompanied both song and dance. The dance itself was vividly described by Cable:

> A sudden frenzy seizes the musicians. The measure quickens, the swaying, attitudinizing crowd starts into extra activity, the female voices grow sharp and staccato, and suddenly the dance is the furious Bamboula.
>
> Now for the frantic leaps! Now for frenzy! Another pair are in the ring! The man wears a belt of little bells, or, as a substitute, little tin vials of shot, "bram-bram sonnette!" And still another couple enter the circle. What wild—what terrible delight! The ecstasy rises to madness; one—two—three of the dancers fall—bloucoutoum! boum!—with foam on their lips and are dragged out by arms and legs from under the tumultuous feet of crowding new-comers. The musicians know no fatigue; still the dance rages on:
>
> "Quand patate la cuite na va mangé li!"
>
> And all to that one nonsense line meaning only,
>
> "When that 'tater's cooked don't you eat it up!" [28]

The song was heard as early as the 1830s by the great Louisiana-born composer and pianist Louis Moreau Gottschalk (whom we shall meet later); he used it as the basis of one of his most popular piano pieces, *La Bamboula.*

Quand pa-tate la cuite, na va man-gé li, na va man-gé, Na va man-gé. Quand pa-tate la cuite, na va man-gé, Na va man-gé li.

The first measure of *La Bamboula* has a rhythm basic to much Latin American music—and, via New Orleans presumably, to much American black music as well—that of the *habañera*, or *danza*, which could be either song or dance.

The *calinda* was a satirical song/dance, and as such the heir of a considerable tradition in the West Indies and in Africa. Cable describes it as "a grossly personal satirical ballad . . . a dance of multitude, a sort of vehement cotillion." An example is given below of one *calinda* that he describes as "still familiar to all Creole ears; it has long been a vehicle for the white Creole's satire; for generations the man of municipal politics was fortunate who escaped entirely a lampooning set to its air." [29]

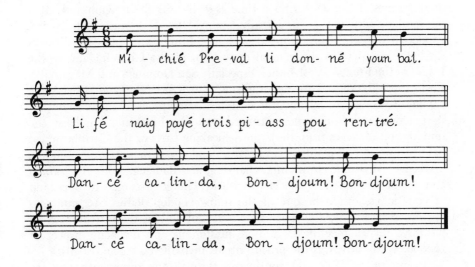

Mi - chié Pre - val li don- né youn bal.

Li fé naig payé trois pi - ass pou ren-tré.

Dan - cé ca - lin - da, Bon - djoum! Bon- djoum!

Dan - cé ca - lin - da, Bon - djoum! Bon-djoum!

(Monsieur Preval gave a big ball,
He made the blacks pay to dance.
Dance the Calinda, bondjoum, bondjoum
Dance the Calinda, bondjoum, bondjoum.)

There were numberless stanzas, of course, and new ones were fashioned to fit new occasions. Krehbiel gives the story of the original, insofar as it could be pieced together.[30]

There is a marked and interesting resemblance between the first part of the tune of this satirical song and that of the well-known Cajun *Saute crapaud*, which is, according to Whitfield, "one of the best known of the French folk songs of our state." [31]

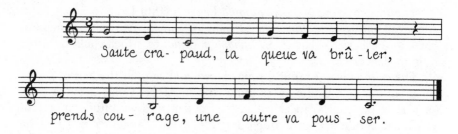

Saute cra- paud, ta queue va brû - ler,

prends cou - rage, une autre va pous - ser.

The enigmatic words—"Jump, toad, your tail will burn;/Take courage, another will grow"—suggest that this, too, may once have been a satire of some kind. Nothing seems to be known of the origin of either song.

A pervading influence among the blacks of French Louisiana—and among some of the whites for a time as well—was the religion and ritual of voodoo. Originating principally among the Dahomeans in Africa, voodoo had gotten intermingled with the liturgy and ritual of Roman Catholicism (despite the general opposition of the Church) among the blacks of the French West Indies, especially San Domingo and Martinique. From there it traveled to New Orleans, which became (and still is) the capital of voodooism in the United States. Attempts were made to outlaw its practice, and from time to time, before the Louisiana Purchase, the importation of slaves from the French-speaking parts of the Caribbean was banned in order to combat its growth. Voodoo ceremonies were, and are, marked by rhythmic drumming, chanting, and dancing. Both the *calinda* and the *bamboula* were associated with it. The goal seemed to be a kind of ecstatic possession by one of the ruling voodoo deities. According to eyewitness accounts, this possession was not unlike that to be seen at primitive revival meetings. (A more mysterious and menacing aspect of voodoo, apparently, was the private rituals invoking curses and spells.)

Beginning in 1817 and continuing through the nineteenth century, Sunday dances of the blacks in Congo Square, New Orleans, were legalized, subject to strict curfew laws. At that time the Place Congo was a large open field outside the city itself. This is the locale of the dancing Cable and others have described. The Sunday dances were supposed to act, as Marshall Stearns has said, as a kind of "safety valve" in allowing an outlet for some of the more public ritual of voodooism, and they eventually must have become something of a tourist attraction.

In describing and illustrating so briefly various aspects of the black folk music of Louisiana in the nineteenth century—the pronounced rhythmic character of the music, the drumming, the satirical element in the songs, the love of ritual that found expression in the activities of the fraternal organizations, secret and otherwise, climaxing in the elaborate funeral ceremonies—we are getting very close to at least some of the origins of jazz.[32]

OTHER FOLK STRAINS

The American melting pot has been flavored by many other folk strains, which unfortunately cannot be treated in detail here. Political unrest in Germany and central Europe in the mid-nineteenth century brought to a new peak the waves of immigrants from that part of the world, most of whom settled across the northern tier of the country. German influence, as we shall later see, has had the most important impact on American musical culture in the field of symphonic music and in music pedagogy— that is, at the professional level. But the prevalence of choral societies— *Sängerbunde*—wherever there is a sizable concentration of people of German descent is evidence of the preservation of a strong tradition of amateur music-making, and with it, of folk song. The same is true of the Scandinavians, who have perpetuated a great singing tradition in their settlements and in their schools and colleges in the northern states west of the Great Lakes. Slavic peoples from eastern Europe, especially Poland, have emigrated in successive waves since the mid-nineteenth century, and constitute a large and important cultural entity.[33] One is often surprised to come upon small pockets of folk culture that have resisted complete assimilation, such as those of the Armenians and the Russians in the Great Valley of California.

Oriental music (principally that of China, Japan, and the Philippines) as it has been preserved and cultivated, particularly on the West Coast of the United States, has until very recently been too little studied.[34] The highly cultivated traditional music of the Orient is not, strictly speaking, folk music at all, but it is appropriate to mention it here, since it is so clearly in the possession of communities that are, to an extent, culturally isolated. Like the tribal music of the American Indian, the music of the Orient was too radically different in nearly every way from our European-derived music to allow for any significant amount of assimilation or influence. However, with today's increased opportunities for hearing and studying Oriental music, plus a heightened receptiveness to the values of other cultures and our greater capacity for at least a superficial assimilation, this is all changing. Though the *koto* and the *sitar* may never actually sit down in full fellowship with the fiddle and the banjo, they can now at least make a contribution to a culture to which formerly they were all but total strangers.

It is not to be inferred from this that cultural homogenization will, can, or should occur. This would be impoverishment, rather than enrichment. A varied topography in a cultural terrain is as stimulating as in a physical one. We would indeed be poorer should our differentiated regional musics—even the small islands—disappear, to be replaced everywhere by that sterile uniformity with which mass production, and mass media in the service of mass culture, threaten our civilization. A look-alike dispenser of Kentucky Fried Chicken at every crossroads in the land (all the more ironic because of its phony appeal to a regional culture) might just possibly make good commercial sense; its cultural equivalent would be a dead and paved-over landscape—barren, monotonous, and utterly devoid of a vital sense of *place*.

FURTHER READING

American Indian Music

BURTON, FREDERICK R. *American Primitive Music, with Special Attention to the Songs of the Ojibways.* Port Washington, N.Y.: Kennikat Press, 1909. Reprint, 1969.

> A work written from the standpoint of an older approach to the music, including the consideration of its "art value." It includes some songs arranged with piano accompaniment.

* CURTIS, NATALIE. *The Indians' Book.* New York and London, 1907. Paperback reprint, New York: Dover Publications, 1968.

DENSMORE, FRANCES. *The American Indians and Their Music.* New York: Women's Press, 1926.

> An early comprehensive work on the subject by one of the foremost researchers in the field. It is supplemented by the following tribal studies.

> The following studies by Frances Densmore were, except as noted, published originally by the Bureau of American Ethnology of the Smithsonian Institution, and issued by the Government Printing Office, Washington, D.C. They are now available in reprint editions by Da Capo Press, 227 West 17th St., New York, N.Y. 10011. Far more than mere transcriptions and analyses of melodies, they treat in considerable detail the customs, ceremonies, and legends of the tribes, thus forecasting the type of study Alan P. Merriam (see below) was to do nearly a half-century later. The transcriptions themselves are not as accurate in either rhythm or pitch as modern standards would require (insofar as can be determined by comparing them with the recordings from which they were presumably derived); perhaps understandably overinfluenced by European music, they are too rigid in notation, especially as regards rhythm.

> > *Cheyenne and Arapaho Music.* Los Angeles: Southwest Museum, 1936.

---

* Items thus marked are part of the suggested reference library to be available in connection with this book.

Chippewa Music. 2 vols. 1910–1913.

Choctaw Music. 1943.

Music of the Maidu Indians. Los Angeles: Southwest Museum, 1958.

Mandan and Hidatsa Music. 1923.

Menominee Music. 1932.

Nootka and Quileute Music. 1939.

Northern Ute Music. 1922.

Papago Music. 1929.

Pawnee Music. 1929.

Teton Sioux Music. 1918.

Yuman and Yaqui Music. 1932.

FLETCHER, ALICE C. *Indian Story and Song from North America.* Boston: S. Maynard, 1900.

——. *A Study of Omaha Indian Music, with a Report on the Structural Peculiarities of the Music by John Comfort Fillmore.* Cambridge, Mass.: Peabody Museum of American Archeology and Ethnology, 1893.
   Another important study historically, by an early and eminent authority.

LA BARRE, WESTON. *The Peyote Cult.* Yale University Publications in Anthropology, no. 19. New Haven, Conn.: Yale University Press, 1938.

MCALLESTER, DAVID P. *Peyote Music.* Viking Fund Publications in Anthropology, no. 13. New York: 1949.
   This study includes music.

MERRIAM, ALAN P. *The Anthropology of Music.* Evanston, Ill.: Northwestern University Press, 1964.
   An introduction to the broad subject of ethnomusicology.

* ——. *Ethnomusicology of the Flathead Indians.* Chicago: Aldine Publishing Co., 1967.
   The jacket description is accurate: "The first complete survey of the entire musical output of a people in its cultural context, exemplifying a new technique of musical analysis." This important work has helped to set new standards for research and writing in the field. Though containing much detailed information, it can be profitably and enjoyably read by the layman.

MOONEY, JAMES. *The Ghost Dance Religion.* Bureau of American Ethnology, Smithsonian Institution, 14th annual report, part 2, 1892–1893.

* NETTL, BRUNO. *North American Indian Musical Styles.* Philadelphia: American Folklore Society, 1954.
   An important brief study, somewhat technical, of regional characteristics. Includes some musical examples.

PAIGE, HARRY W. *Songs of the Teton Sioux.* Los Angeles: Westernlore Press, 1970.
   A contemporary study, dealing with music in the lives of the Indians. No musical examples.

RHODES, WILLARD. "Acculturation in North American Indian Music," in

Acculturation in the Americas. Chicago: University of Chicago Press, 1952.

Hispanic Folk Music

STUDIES THAT INCLUDE MUSIC

DA SILVA, OWEN, O. F. M. *Mission Music of California.* Los Angeles: Warren Lewis, 1941.

A book of fine artistic quality, this presents a selection of liturgical music, and some useful expository information on the priest-musicians and on mission life as viewed by the Franciscans.

HAGUE, ELEANOR. *Spanish-American Folk-Songs.* Lancaster, Pa., and New York: American Folk-lore Society, 1917.

An old collection but available in many libraries; 100-odd songs, some from Mexico and Central and South America.

ROBB, JOHN DONALD. *Hispanic Folk Songs of New Mexico.* Albuquerque: University of New Mexico Press, 1954.

A valuable regional study by an eminent authority, with a representative sampling of music both sacred and secular.

STUDIES

LUCERO-WHITE, AURORA. *The Folklore of New Mexico.* Vol. 1. Santa Fe: Seton Village Press, 1941.

A collection (words only) of *romances* and *corridos,* as well as tales, proverbs, and riddles.

PAREDES, AMERICO. *"With his pistol in his hand."* Austin: University of Texas Press, 1958.

An extensive documentation of a ballad (*El Corrido de Gregorio Cortez*) and its hero, which supplies valuable background information on the Texas-Mexico border country.

RAY, SISTER MARY DOMINIC, O. P.; and ENGBECK, JOSEPH H., JR. *Gloria Dei: The Story of California Mission Music.* State of California Dept. of Parks and Recreation, n.d.

An informative illustrated booklet (24 pp.), with quotations from contemporary accounts.

TINKER, EDWARD LAROCQUE. *Corridos and Calaveras.* Austin: University of Texas Press, 1961.

Although this deals specifically with the *corrido* and related forms as found in Old Mexico, it is excellent background reading for the *corrido* as a genre. Especially fascinating are the reproductions of the old broadsides themselves, with their drawings by the famous artist José Guadalupe Posada, a forerunner of Rivera and Orozco. A delightful book, in a very artistic format.

The French Strain: Louisiana

* ALLEN, WILLIAM FRANCIS; WARE, CHARLES; and GARRISON, LUCY McKIM (eds.). *Slave Songs of the United States.* New York, 1867. Paperback reprint, New York: Oak Publications, 1969.

Seven Louisiana songs in patois are included in this famous early collection.

* CABLE, GEORGE WASHINGTON. "The Dance in Place Congo"; "Creole Slave Songs." Reprinted in Bernard Katz (ed.), *The Social Implications of Early Negro Music in the United States.* New York: Arno Press, 1969.

The importance of these articles, and the music they include, has been indicated in this chapter.

* KREHBIEL, HENRY EDWARD. *Afro-American Folksongs.* New York: Frederick Ungar, 1914. Reprint, 1962.

Krehbiel collaborated with Cable and with Lafcadio Hearn in collecting and studying black folk music in Louisiana in the nineteenth century. Chapters 9, 10, and 11, on "Creole" music, are the results of this collaboration.

LOMAX, JOHN A. and ALAN. *Our Singing Country.* New York: Macmillan Co., 1949.

The section "French Songs and Ballads from Southwestern Louisiana" contains seven complete songs collected there in 1934, including three of the songs mentioned in this chapter.

POST, LAUREN C. *Cajun Sketches.* Baton Rouge: Louisiana State University Press, 1962.

Deals with the geography, economics, traditions, and music of the region.

* WHITFIELD, IRÈNE THÉRÈSE. *Louisiana French Folk Songs.* Baton Rouge, 1939. Enlarged paperback edition, New York: Dover Publications, 1969.

The largest and most important collection in this area. Because of its uniqueness, its few weaknesses are all the more unfortunate: The musical transcriptions are, it must be suspected, not always trustworthy, and there is a lack of uniform documentation as to where, and especially when, the songs were collected. There are translations of the texts into standard French, but not into English.

LISTENING

American Indian Music

* *Songs of Earth, Water, Fire, and Sky: Music of the American Indian,* from the *Recorded Anthology of American Music* (RAAM). RAAM: NW-246.

An overall selection of modern performances, with excellent notes, bibliography, and discography.

* *Songs of Love, Luck, Animals, and Magic: Music of the Yurok and Tolowa Indians.* RAAM: NW-297.

  A second Indian album from the same series, this is a more detailed sampling of the music of two northern California tribes.

FROM THE LIBRARY OF CONGRESS, ARCHIVE OF AMERICAN FOLK SONG (AAFS)

Edited by William Fenton, recorded 1941–45:
  Songs from the Iroquois Longhouse. AAFS: L-6.
  Seneca Songs from Coldspring Longhouse. L-17.

Edited by Frances Densmore, recorded 1910–1930:
  Songs of the Chippewa. AAFS: L-22.
  Songs of the Sioux. L-23.
  Songs of the Yuma, Cocopa, and Yaqui. L-24.
  Songs of the Pawnee and Northern Ute. L-25.
  Songs of the Papago. L-31.
  Songs of the Nootka and Quileute. L-32.
  Songs of the Menominee, Mandan, and Hidatsa. L-33.

Edited by Willard Rhodes, *Music of the American Indian* series, recorded 1940–1952:
  Northwest (Puget Sound). AAFS: L-34.
  Kiowa. L-35.
  Indian Songs of Today. L-36.
  Delaware, Cherokee, Choctaw, Creek. L-37.
  Great Basin: Paiute, Washo, Ute, Bannock, Shoshone. L-38.
  Plains: Comanche, Cheyenne, Kiowa, Caddo, Wichita, Pawnee. L-39.
  Sioux. L-40.
  Navajo. L-41.
  Apache. L-42.
  Pueblo: Taos, San Ildefonso, Zuni, Hopi. L-43.

FOLKWAYS RECORDS, EXAMPLES FROM EXTENSIVE AMERICAN INDIAN CATALOG:

* *Anthology of North American Indian and Eskimo Music.* FS-4541.
  Music of the Sioux and the Navajo, recorded by Willard Rhodes. FE-4401.
  Music of the American Indians of the Southwest, recorded by Willard Rhodes. FE-4420.
  Hopi Katchina Songs, recorded by Jesse Fewkes, an early worker in the field. FE-4394.
* *Songs and Dances of the Flathead Indians,* recorded by Alan Merriam. FE-4445.
  Songs of the Seminole Indians of Florida, recorded by Frances Densmore. FE-4383.
  Washo-Peyote Songs (notes include reprint of paper in *American Anthropologist*). FE-4384.

Two other labels that have fairly extensive recordings of Indian music are Indian House and Canyon.

Hispanic Folk Music

California Mission Music, performed by the John Biggs Consort. Issued by the Regents of the University of California.
> While too eclectic and polished to convey much of an idea of the actual sound of the music of the mission period, it surveys the field in its broadest sense with some very elegant performances.

Catholic Mission Music in California. *Music in America* series of the Society for the Preservation of the American Musical Heritage, MIA-96.
> This older recording of mission music conveys in some ways a more authentic atmosphere, especially in the two *alabados* and the *Santo Dios*.

* *Bahaman Songs, French Ballads and Dance Tunes, Spanish Religious Songs and Game Songs*. AAFS: L-5.
> Side B is especially interesting for its inclusion of six brief excerpts from the religious folk plays, and a Mexican *corrido* as performed by a blind itinerant singer of Brownsville, Texas.

Spanish and Mexican Folk Music of New Mexico. Folkways: FE-4426.
> This sampling from the recorded collection of scholar and authority J. D. Robb includes his notes. It is a valuable companion to his book, referred to in the bibliography for this chapter.

Texas-Mexican Border Music, vols. 1–4. Folklyric: 9003–6. Available from Arhoolie Records, 10341 San Pablo Ave., El Cerrito, Calif. 94530.
> An excellent anthology of early recordings, with extensive notes, especially on the *corrido*.

Spanish Folk Songs of New Mexico. Folkways: FA-2204.
> Peter Hurd re-creates *ranchera* songs; the texts are included in the notes.

* *Caliente = Hot: Puerto Rican and Cuban Musical Expression in New York*. RAAM: NW-244.

POSSIBLY HARD TO GET OUTSIDE SOUTH TEXAS

Corridos Famosos. Falcon: FLP-2035.
Corridos y Tragedias del Siglo 20, 2 vols. Norteño: 803, 805.
El Corrido de Martin Luther King. Falcon: FLP-2091.

The French Strain: Louisiana

* *Bahaman Songs, French Ballads and Dance Tunes, Spanish Religious Songs and Game Songs*. AAFS: L-5.
> It is unfortunate that this catch-all album does not contain more of the French music, but the examples that are included are all valuable.

* *Folksongs of the Louisiana Acadians.* Arhoolie: LP-5009.

Louisiana Cajun Music. Old Timey. Available from Arhoolie Records, address above. Reissues of commercial recordings:

Vol. 1, *The 1920s: First Recordings.* OT-108.

Vol. 2, *The Early 1930s.* OT-109.

Vol. 3, *The String Bands of the 1930s.* OT-110.

Vol. 4, *From the 30s into the 50s.* OT-111.

Vol. 5, *The Early Years: 1928–1938.* OT-114.

Cajun Music: The Early 50s. Arhoolie: 5008.

Clifton Chenier: Louisiana Blues and Zydeco. Arhoolie: F-1024.

Street Cries and Creole Songs of New Orleans. Folkways: 2202.

PROJECTS

1. Select one American Indian tribe and listen to as much of its music as is available. (Try to work from a sample of at least 20 songs.) Note the musical characteristics, and see to what extent they conform to, or differ from, the description of the area characteristics as given by Nettl in *North American Indian Musical Styles.*

2. Make a study of the love songs of a particular tribe: their function, their origin, whether they were used by both men and women, whether they were sung or played on an instrument, and the beliefs regarding their efficacy. If you make a report orally or on tape, include musical examples.

3. Make a study of the relations of songs to visions or dreams in at least two tribes.

4. Make a study of the beliefs and practices concerning songs as personal possessions among American Indians. Consider at least two tribes.

5. Make a study of Indian games, and the functions of the songs that accompany them. If you make a report orally or on tape, include musical examples.

6. If it is possible to attend a live performance of Indian music and dancing, do so. By talking to the performers, and by doing some reading on the music of the particular tribe or tribes, try to determine to what extent acculturation has affected the music or the dance.

7. Consulting recent folk music periodicals such as *Sing Out!* (see the reading list for chapter 4), report on recent developments in Spanish-language folk music in the United States, including songs relevant to the Chicano movement.

8. If you are fluent in Spanish, transcribe and translate one or more *corridos* that are in current circulation on LP or 45-rpm recordings. Among other places, they are available from Nortena Records, 2606 Ruiz St., San Antonio, Tex.; and Arhoolie Records, P.O. Box 9195, Berkeley, Calif. 94709.

9. If you like to sing folk songs, learn *Pov' piti Momzel Zizi* from Cable's "Creole Slave Songs" (also known as *Lolotte* in Allen et al., *Slave Songs of the United States*, and *Pov' piti Lollete* in Krehbiel, *Afro-American Folksongs*). Familiarize yourself with Cable's interpretation, so that you can comment on its social implications in terms of the Louisiana caste system of the nineteenth century.

10. Consulting collections of French and Canadian folksongs, find a French (and if possible also a Canadian) variant of one of the songs in Whitfield's *Louisiana French Folk Songs*. Compare the versions.

11. If there are any ethnic groups in your vicinity that have preserved their folkways, especially their folk music, investigate, making some taped interviews if possible, and recording some of the music.

Chapter Four
Folk Music in Modern America

THE 1920s SAW THE DETERMINED ONSET of irreversible change for American folk music. Through the media of radio and recordings, urban popular music was brought to the "folk" (which at that time still rather clearly meant the rural people). It was then, too, that America's rural music, both black and white, was "discovered" by urban entrepreneurs. Not only was it being broadcast, but it was found commercially profitable to make recordings of it and sell them back to the folk. As we shall see in chapters 7 and 8, both rural Negro blues and white "hillbilly" music were first recorded in the 1920s, a development that had profound effects on both of these folk musics. It is interesting to note that one of the most important published collections of recordings documenting our folk music, the Folkways *Anthology of American Folk Music*, consists entirely of commercial recordings made in the 1920s and 1930s.

It was also true that increased industrialization and migration to the cities, spurred on subsequently by the depressed economic conditions of the thirties and the war effort of the forties, brought increased mobility to rural peoples, virtually did away with the isolation of any section of the country, and worked irrevocable changes in folkways. These environmental changes were paralleled by changes in the way people thought about folk music. The distinctly "non-folk" intellectual consciousness of folk music—as the expression of a vaguely defined spirit of a people, as a "cry for justice," as "art," or as artifact, to be collected and studied or else to be pressed into service for some specific purpose—began to replace the folk "unconsciousness" of it as something wholly integrated into daily life itself, and no more to be abstracted from it than the making of clothes or the building of fences (which have also become the objects of study as *folklore*). In other words, the singing of folk music has become, in our time, a much more self-conscious activity.

Americans' involvement with folk music has been going on in what might be thought of as three more or less distinct levels during the past fifty years. (1) Folk music, urbanized and adapted, has been used for propaganda. (2) It has been popularized, for entertainment and profit, beyond the confines of any definable "folk community." (3) It has been collected and studied extensively by scholars, both amateur and professional, who have been hard at work to preserve the artifacts of traditions that they saw as disappearing with increasing rapidity. We shall here consider briefly each of these involvements in turn.

FOLK MUSIC FOR PROPAGANDA

The use of folk music in the service of a cause is nothing new. John Powell, American composer and student of folk music, has called attention to an anecdote about the ingenuity and zeal of St. Aldhelm, seventh-century abbot of Malmsbury.

> According to this story, the Saint would station himself on a bridge in the guise of a gleeman and would collect an audience by singing popular songs. He would then gradually insert into his entertainment the words of the holy scriptures and so lead his hearers to salvation.[1]

From St. Aldhelm in the seventh century to the CIO labor organizer in the twentieth, the method is the same—adapting an already known and accepted song (or song *style*, in the case of newly composed songs) so as to transform it into an instrument of persuasion. The use of folk music as an adjunct to religion has continued right down to our own time, as we shall later note. Our present concern, however, is the association of folk music with social and political causes.

As John Greenway[2] and others have documented, protest songs have been composed and sung here since colonial times, mostly in the "broadside" tradition of printing the words only, to be sung to some preexisting and well-known tune. An example of this, a piece called the *Junto Song* that satirized what was seen as British avarice in taxing the colonists, was published in *Holt's Journal* in 1775. It runs in part:

'Tis money makes the member vote,
And sanctifies our ways;
It makes the patriot turn his coat,
And money we must raise.

(Chorus)
And a-taxing we will go,
A-taxing we will go,
A-taxing we will go.[3]

A lively tradition of propaganda songs continued right through the nineteenth and into the twentieth century, and Greenway cites many interesting examples. What was new about the period that began in the 1930s was not only the more conscious adoption of real folk tunes, and a folk style, but the attempt to appropriate virtually an entire folk tradition in the service of social and political causes. As D. K. Wilgus has said, in describing this period:

> The recognition that "singing has a direct and reciprocal relation to social, economic, and political issues" has led to an equation of the "cry for justice" and folksong. . . . The use of folksong for political purposes is an old device; what is new is the use of the folk concept, the magic term *folk*.[4]

Thus the *folk* became easily equated with the *proletariat*, or more specifically, with union members among the industrial workers. In terms of what the activists in the thirties and forties hoped to accomplish by means of folk music, it meant the imposition of an essentially rural song tradition upon urban workers.

There were two main motivations for it. In the first place, as Denisoff[5] has documented extensively, it was in the 1930s that the Russian Bolshevik example of using indigenous folk music for propaganda purposes during and after the 1917 revolution began to be urged upon American Communists, who had hitherto mostly used Soviet propaganda songs without much success. (A historian of the Southern Tenant Farmers Union, for example, reported that the *Internationale* "just didn't go over with the sharecroppers.")

A second and far more important motivation for the adoption of rural folk music and folk style was the fact that—as the northern labor organizers found when they went into the South to organize the mine and textile-mill workers—the tradition of folk singing, which was still vital in the rural South, was already at work providing songs to rally the workers in the bitter struggle. At the scene of the textile strike in Gastonia, North Carolina, in 1929 Ella May Wiggins, a ballad singer of some reputation, was singing songs like the following adaptation of a hymn:

Toiling on life's pilgrim pathway
Wheresoever you may be,
It will help you, fellow workers,
If you will join the I. L. D.[6]

And in Harlan County, Kentucky, scene of violent labor disputes in the coal mines in 1931, Aunt Molly Jackson (born Mary Magdalene Garland), a larger-than-life heroine who was midwife, doctor, union organizer, and ballad singer for the coal miners, and who had lost brother, husband, and son in the mines, was singing:

I am a union woman,
Just as brave as I can be.
I do not like the bosses
And the bosses don't like me.

(Refrain)
Join the CIO. Come join the CIO.

I was raised in old Kentucky
In Kentucky borned and bred,
And when I joined the union,
They called me a Rooshian Red.

(Refrain) [7]

As Archie Green has said:

In a sense, Piedmont mill villages and Cumberland mine camps became meeting grounds for the ideologies of Andrew Jackson and Karl Marx, Abraham Lincoln and Mikhail Bakunin. Few of the mill hands or coal miners were able to synthesize traditional and modern values into lasting literature, but some managed to compose folk-like songs which fused time-worn melodies with strange, revolutionary lyrics.[8]

Genesis of the "Urban Folk Song Movement"

When the union organizers and their supporters and chroniclers, such as John Dos Passos and Theodore Dreiser, returned to the North, not only did they take many of the songs with them, but some of the singers as well, including Aunt Molly Jackson herself, who had been banished, in effect, from Kentucky. In New York's Coliseum in 1931 she sang for twenty-one thousand people:

> I was born and raised in old Kentucky;
> Molly Jackson is my name.
> I came up here to New York City,
> And I'm truly glad I came.

> I am soliciting for the poor Kentucky miners,
> For their children and their wives,
> Because the miners are all blacklisted
> I am compelled to save their lives.[9]

This importation of the southern rural folk song tradition, and some of its singers, was the genesis of what has become known as the urban folk song movement. Its beginning was, in a sense, a transplantation of the rural South to Greenwich Village. In addition to singers from the Kentucky coal mining region, there were black singers associated with the blues tradition, such as Leadbelly, Josh White, Brownie McGhee, and Sonny Terry. Leadbelly (Huddie Ledbetter) was an interesting figure in the movement, though not typical. After a violent youth, he was discovered in a Louisiana prison by John and Alan Lomax, who secured his parole and brought him to New York. There he sang all sorts of songs from his vast repertoire, and added new ones based on his new experiences and appropriate to his new audiences, such as the *Bourgeois Blues:*

> Me and my wife run all over town,
> Everywhere we'd go people would turn us down.

> Lawd, in the bourgeois town, hoo!
> The bourgeois town.
> I got the bourgeois blues,
> Gonna spread the news all around.[10]

Other musicians and writers who entered or passed through the somewhat amorphous orbit of New York left-wing circles in the 1930s and 1940s included men and women who became well known in the folk song movement but who could hardly be classified as "folk" in background, as the term was still understood then: writer Millard Lampell, a graduate of the University of West Virginia; Earl Robinson, classically trained musician and composer from the University of Washington; Bess Lomax, daughter and sister of two eminent folklorists; and Pete Seeger, son of a distinguished ethnomusicologist, who left Harvard in his sophomore year, committed to the social and political causes he worked to further through singing (his own songs as well as those of others) and playing his banjo.

Woody Guthrie

Woody Guthrie was an exceptional and somewhat enigmatic figure in this circle. His Oklahoma background (he began early to sing and play at gatherings in Oklahoma and Texas) was certainly folk in any sense of the term. His complete absorption of his own heritage is evident in the many early recordings he made of traditional ballads and songs, both for commercial release and for the Library of Congress Archive—recordings that include *Buffalo Skinners, John Henry, Sourwood Mountain, Cumberland Gap,* and even the Child ballad *Gypsy Davy. Pretty Boy Floyd,* in the outlaw ballad tradition, was one of his own compositions. He early began to compose ballads and songs, something he did easily, naturally, compulsively, and with amazing fecundity. His preserved output, according to those who knew him, represents only a fraction of the songs he actually made up and sang.

As he began to move about the country, hoboing, working, barding, supporting in his own highly individualistic way various workers' causes as he found them, it can perhaps be said that he transcended the roots of the local tradition in which he had been brought up; but it is also true in a sense that he cut himself off from them, in his efforts to identify with a larger, more heterogeneous, and to an extent mythical, folk community. *So Long, It's Been Good to Know You* (originally a far more topical song about Dust Bowl life than its later popular form would indicate) and *Hard Travelin'* certainly have their roots in his personal experience. But they begin to show the effects of their separation from a definable folk community. The famous Dust Bowl Ballads were neither sung nor known by the migrant workers themselves who left the area for the West in the thirties. Songs like *I Ain't Got No Home in This World Anymore* and *Pastures of Plenty* show an increasing trend away from the specific and the individual—being applicable to many, they are about no *one,* and sung for no one group. Thus they lose some of the strength and validity of true folk song. This tendency reaches its ultimate conclusion in a song like *This Land Is Your Land.* It is so broadly inclusive—"from California to the New York island,/ from the redwood forest to the gulfstream waters"— that it sacrifices altogether the concreteness of folk music; though as popular song it is so far above the run-of-the-mill patriotic ditty as to beggar comparison. We have the feeling that Guthrie, at least, had *seen* the redwood forest and the gulfstream waters and the ribbon of highway and the golden valley—as indeed he had.

Guthrie's enormous talent, when brought to bear on a specific event, could produce a truly great song, through his faculty of making us sense at once the human dimension. The *Sinking of the Reuben James* was probably the best ballad to come out of World War II. Note his most arresting phrase: "Tell me, what were their names?" * (Guthrie's intention, from which he could barely be restrained, of incorporating into the ballad *all* the names of the men lost, should, ideally, have been realized, to make the ballad a true folk epic.) He could even bring to life an event twenty years or so in the past. His unusual commission to produce a set of ballads and songs on the famous Sacco and Vanzetti case produced work that was uneven in quality and to an extent forced, but the best real ballad in the collection, *Suassos Lane*, shows the true touch of the folk balladeer.

Guthrie was at his best as a balladeer. In later years, anything was grist for his mill. Being so prolific, he naturally produced a great deal that was nearly worthless. He felt acutely his limitations, as well as the pressures of the mantle he found himself wearing. A man of shrewd intelligence and diverse talents (he read voluminously, was a very prolific writer apart from his songs, a painter, the confidant of a president of the United States), he was no simple "man of the soil"; yet he often found himself having to deny his own acute perceptions and conceal his intellect behind a mask of simplistic doggerel in trying to fulfill his most difficult job of all—which was largely thrust upon him—that of being a kind of universal "folk poet" of the common man. By nature more perceptive than much of his more mediocre writing would indicate, Guthrie was not immune to brooding over the effects on him of such labels as "the best folk ballad composer whose identity has ever been known" or a "rusty-voiced Homer." In a typically self-revealing outburst he said:

> I kick myself in the britches pretty hard some times. You dont hate me any worse than I do. You dont bawl me out any more than I do. Oh well, dam it all anyhow, I never really set my head on a being a public figure. Its all what you mean when you say success. Most of the time success ain't much fun. Lots of times it takes a lot of posing and pretending.[11]

Charles Seeger writes sensitively of the changes wrought in the singers by the pressures of the situations in which they found themselves.

> Put, for example, any good "authentic," traditional singer before a microphone or on a platform before an audience not of its own kind and soon the peculiar requirements of the situation produce the typical traits of exhibitionism. To my personal observation, it took Molly Jackson only a

few months to convert herself, when expedient, from a traditional singer, who seemed never to have given a thought to whether anyone liked or disliked her singing, into a shrewd observer of audience reaction, fixing individual listeners one after another with her gaze, smiling ingratiatingly, gesturing, dramatizing her performance. Leadbelly was already an astute handler of the non-folk by the time I met him. Woody Guthrie was another case, almost swamping his native talent in Greenwich Villagese.[12]

The Almanac Singers and Their Successors

A trio of folk song enthusiasts, including Pete Seeger, who were at that time circulating in New York's left-wing orbit, formed in the late 1930s the nucleus of a talented, historic, and somewhat loosely organized group known as the Almanac Singers.[13] They were joined later by others—including, off and on for a time, Woody Guthrie. Their story is an interesting one of a well-intentioned, somewhat idealistic enterprise that was doomed to failure. The intellectuals and the Communists, who constituted almost the only audience for folk music in the cities in the 1930s, did identify fervently with their concepts of the "folk" and of the uses of folk art, but the goal of singers such as the Almanacs, to transform industrial workers into singing militants by giving them a ready-made body of protest songs in folk style, was never to any significant degree realized. Pete Seeger later reflected: "Most union leaders could not see any connection between music and porkchops. . . . 'Which Side Are You On' was known in Greenwich Village, but not in a single miners' union local." [14] Far more popular with the workers were productions in the popular Broadway style such as the famous *Pins and Needles*, a phenomenally successful satirical revue staged by the New York garment workers' union in 1937.

Another factor that severely hampered the Almanacs was their apparently dogmatic attachment to a political "party line." The weakness of being thus tied to an institutionalized ideology (a legacy of the early thirties) became painfully apparent as the tragically inhumane machinations of World War II unfolded. The songs were at first anti-Fascist, and urged intervention; the Spanish Civil War was the most important rallying cause, and *Los Quatros Generales* one of its best-known songs.

> The four insurgent generals, mamita mia,
> They tried to betray us.
>
> Next Christmas holy evening, mamita mia,
> They'll all be hanging.

Then, in August 1939, with the signing of the Nazi-Soviet pact, the line became pacifist and noninterventionist.

Franklin, Oh Franklin, we don't want to go to war.
Franklin, Oh Franklin, we don't want to go to war. .
We want to stay home.[15]

The sudden Nazi invasion of Russia in the summer of 1941 caused an immediate switch in the party line, which, according to Denisoff, "cut the Almanacs' repertoire in half. Anti-war songs were no longer appropriate now that German tanks thundered on Russian soil." After Pearl Harbor Pete Seeger, in a talking blues number, said:

So what I want is for you to give me a gun,
And we can hurry up and get the job done.[16]

The Almanac Singers, which in their heyday had become a somewhat large and amorphous group, with a stable of singers able to fill two or three simultaneous engagements, had ceased to exist as a group before the war's end. Their failure was an illustration of the pitfalls of trying to cloak a particular party line in the mantle of the folk.

After the war, two organizations founded and run by essentially the same people who had constituted the Almanac Singers continued the business of writing, publishing, and performing propaganda music. People's Songs, Inc., was formed as "an organization to make and send songs of labor and the American people throughout the land." During its three-year existence, which ended in 1949, it assembled a vast library of protest songs, encouraged and acted as a clearinghouse for the publication of new ones, taught classes in the "use of songs as a weapon," and published the *People's Song Bulletin.*[17]

A parallel organization of performers, formed to promote and manage live performances of folk music, was People's Artists, Inc. A special vehicle for this was the "hootenanny," a gathering featuring well-known folk performers, introducing new ones, and emphasizing audience participation in the singing.

The demise of People's Artists, Inc., in 1956 for lack of funds marked the end of the structured, institutionalized approach to propaganda songs.

Protest and the Folk Movement in the 1960s and 1970s

In the two decades since, the association of folk music with propaganda has not ceased, of course. But it has become more a matter of individual singers and songs addressed to specific issues, rather than an organizational effort. There is also a difference in the attitudes of the singers, and in the songs themselves. In the older movement the songs tended to be what Denisoff has termed *magnetic*—that is, suggesting concrete solutions or actions to be taken (such as joining a union). The newer songs are more likely to be *rhetorical*—simply dramatizing an issue. Seldom is a solution set forth, and the action to be taken, if any, is more likely to be on an individual, personal level, expressing a wide range of response—from the bitter and destructive:

> Burn, baby, burn

to the resigned:

> I can't do much more than to sing you a song

to the transcendent:

> Let us wrap you in our warm and freedom love.

Furthermore, rock music, as a protest in terms of musical *style*, has largely preempted the more explicit protest in terms of *content* that was the domain of the older folk-like music, in which the words themselves were all-important.

Bob Dylan

The career and work of Bob Dylan illustrate dramatically the differences of the sixties and seventies from the earlier thirties and forties. Dylan emerged into prominence from the same Greenwich Village milieu that had launched his idol Woody Guthrie before him into the role of protester and "folk poet." But the men, their backgrounds, and most of all their times, were vastly different, in ways that are worth considering if we are to understand their work in relation to the whole problem of folk music in our time.

First, the changed times that separated them are significantly indicated by the differences in their backgrounds. The hardships of Guthrie's early life were not self-imposed, whereas Dylan was a child of relatively less stringent times and circumstances who deliberately chose the vagabond life he really did lead in the beginning. Also, Guthrie never felt it necessary to change his style and approach on the basis of what he came into contact with and heard, or from any inner compulsion; in fact, as a folk musician, there is little evidence to show that he was ever much *aware* of such a thing as style. Dylan, however, coming along at a later and more self-conscious period, is very much a stylist and often *primarily* a stylist, albeit a very astute and talented one, capable of juggling several styles at once.

Dylan's talents as a songwriter, as well as a stylist, are great (as exemplified in songs such as *Mr. Tambourine Man*)—probably at least as great as Guthrie's. Certainly he is a far more distinctive and original *musician;* Guthrie apparently found his tunes and accompaniments by a largely offhand and unconscious process, as he himself has hinted. As a folk musician, he was an appropriator and an adaptor. Dylan, on the other hand, never really was a folk musician, but a composer in (among others) a folk-like style.

To put the work of both men in proper perspective, it must be realized that the majority of their songs can hardly be said to be in the realm of "social significance" at all; they deal with themes that are both more universal and more personal. Guthrie, essentially a balladeer rather than a writer of lyrical songs, was capable of using any event as the basis for a song. Dylan, more of a lyricist, tends to write songs that deal, like the majority of blues, with variants of the man-woman theme.

Dylan did create some memorable songs and ballads of protest, however, especially in the beginning. Some are explicit as to the issues and belong more or less to the older tradition: *The Lonesome Death of Hattie Carroll* and *Seven Curses* (the corruption of justice); *Only a Pawn in Their Game* and *Oxford Town* (the machinations of racial prejudice); *Masters of War* and *With God On Our Side* (war); *Let Me Die in My Footsteps* (bomb shelters). He also produced some very realistic ballads which are not overt protest songs, in that the target, as a defiantly general human condition, is less readily assailable: *The Ballad of Hollis Brown* and *North Country Blues* (poverty). Others are more highly distilled and convey more generalized feelings about the future: *Blowin' in the Wind; The Times They Are A-Changin'.*

But some, even among the early songs, begin to display that surrealistic kind of private imagery that marks much of the poetry and pseudo-poetry of the sixties and seventies, and is a sign of a distinct departure from the old tradition, in the direction of the esoteric. (*A Hard Rain's A-Gonna Fall; Subterranean Homesick Blues*). It was this trend that brought on the severe criticism of the old-line folk protesters.

Dylan has absorbed, most probably unconsciously, many influences. Even at his most esoteric, these are apparent, and link at least his early works to the dominant roots of American folk music and folklore. Perhaps this partly explains his appeal, and his enthusiastic adoption, in the beginning, by those who felt a special attachment to folk music. His debt to the Negro blues is readily apparent. Somewhat less obvious is his relationship to the Anglo-American ballad tradition and to the cultural milieu (including the religious) that nourished it. A few examples will suffice to draw attention to this. His *Girl of the North Country* is an offshoot of a perennial ballad. The tune of *Masters of War* is basically that of the haunting *Nottamun Town,* a song from the Appalachians. The question-and-answer incipits to the stanzas of *A Hard Rain's A-Gonna Fall* are an adaptation of the *Lord Randall* form; and *Who Killed Davy Moore?* is a modern version of *Cock Robin*, which, like many children's songs, has far older and more meaningful antecedents. *When the Ship Comes In* draws on the imagery of the revival spiritual, and *I Pity the Poor Immigrant* has the parallel construction of the Old Testament canticles.

Dylan's adoption, in 1965, of the instrumentation, style, and approach of rock was at the time a subject of much controversy. The resulting hybridization did apparently mark the beginning of a new subspecies of rock: so-called folk-rock. But it also coincided with the decline of folk-like music as a significant vehicle of propaganda. As indicated, rock itself was a form of protest, but more in terms of style than of overt content. Except in folk-rock, it often did not seem to matter much whether the words were intelligible or not (a condition that could never be allowed to prevail in actual folk music). And with the exception of a few performers such as Country Joe McDonald and Frank Zappa, there was a general turning away from material of obvious social and political satire and protest. The Beatles' *Revolution* was symptomatic:

> . . . if you go carrying pictures of Chairman Mao
> You ain't going to make it with anyone anyhow. . . .

Two Recent Movements

Protest songs in the older tradition, based on its assumptions about the power of song and the identity of the folk, and inspired by events, will always continue to be written and sung. Josh Dunson has identified two more or less distinct movements in the 1960s: "the *Broadside*-type songs in the North, and the songs of the freedom movement in the South." [18] Of these the latter has produced by far the most memorable songs, probably because of the immediacy and drama of events in the southern civil rights movement, but also because of the native singing tradition in the South, which was always stronger than in the North, and furnished a rich storehouse of traditional songs for adaptation. *We Shall Overcome* was the best-known example of this. But it was the northern movement that acted as the publishing and disseminating "wing," one might say, of the folk song movement as a whole, as represented chiefly by the output of Oak Publications, closely allied with Folkways Records. Here the older tradition of the protest song is kept alive, and such writers and performers as Tom Paxton, Peter La Farge, Mark Spoelstra, and, until his death, Phil Ochs, occasionally joined by the redoubtable Pete Seeger himself, are representative. But for *whom* the old tradition is being kept alive—that is, who its public actually is—is no longer as clear as it once was.

Who Are the Folk?

Attacking the problem of just who the folk are today, one folk singer's quasi-humorous remarks manage to point up the difficulties rather well: "I must regretfully class myself as an outsider in relation to any folk song, since my own community . . . [which] . . . we might call the Urban Literate Southern California Sub-Group of the Early Atomic Period has not yet produced a distinct body of folk music of its own." [19]

There were attempts in the 1930s and 1940s to identify a *new* folk tradition—a new "folk community." It was spelled out variously as "composed of progressives, anti-fascists, and union members" (Alan Lomax) and, as late as 1953, in more general terms, as "the industrial community" (John Greenway). These attempts at redefining the "folk," stemming as they did from a somewhat biased and unrealistic perspective, are not of much help in clarifying the state of folk music in modern America. Both the folk song and the song of persuasion have long histories. What was new in the twentieth century was the view implicit in many aspects of the so-called folk song movement that the two are identical—that, on the one hand, the protest song is *ipso facto* a folk song, and on the other, the folk are exclusively a militant proletariat whose every song is a protest. The following statement by the folk music scholar D. K. Wilgus helps to put the matter in clearer perspective:

> The inconsistencies and sophistries of the "democratic" interpretation, the substitution of politics for scholarship and well-meant sympathies for facts, should not lead one to conclude that folk-song is *undemocratic*; but one must recognize that it is *non-political* (in the sense that political considerations cannot rightly influence its definition or interpretation), even though it may in some cases arise from politics or be used for political purposes. American folksong is not exclusively Republican, Socialist, Prohibitionist, Vegetarian, AFL, or CIO; it resists all exclusive labels. [20]

THE POPULARIZATION OF FOLK MUSIC

The milieu which fostered the more earnest aspects of protest and propaganda in urban folk song was the same milieu from which sprang another, somewhat unexpected phenomenon: the "popular" phase of folk music so notable in the 1950s and 1960s. From the coffeehouses of Greenwich Village came not only the Almanac Singers and *Talking Union,* but Harry Belafonte, Burl Ives, the Weavers, and *On Top of Old Smoky.*

The Weavers

Pete Seeger and Lee Hays, who had been two of the founders of the Almanacs, joined with Ronnie Gilbert and Fred Hellerman in 1948 to form the new group. The Weavers still appeared at hootenannies, and sang some political material that was recorded without the use of the new name, but as the Weavers they eschewed politics and sang traditional material, and new folk (or folk-like) songs such as Leadbelly's *Goodnight, Irene* and Woody Guthrie's *So Long, It's Been Good to Know You.* They were among the first to bring folk music into a new setting, the concert hall. After concertizing widely and performing on radio and television, they achieved a considerable measure of commercial success. Their recordings made the Hit Parade, and in 1952 were said to have sold more than 4 million copies. This pattern of commercial success, on a scale that was impressive before the advent of rock 'n' roll, broke the ice for other "folk entrepreneurs." The group itself was widely imitated; though it disbanded in 1952, it was re-formed and was active in the period 1955–1963.

Other Purveyors of Folk Music

Of the individual folk entrepreneurs, Burl Ives and Harry Belafonte may be taken as typical. Ives was part of the Greenwich Village scene in the late thirties and the forties, singing for leftist audiences and drawing praise from the Communist press of the period. Though invited, he did not join the Almanac Singers; he later disavowed left-wing associations and went on to a professional career both as a singer of folk songs and an actor. Harry Belafonte's career represents a somewhat different pattern. He interrupted a promising pop music career to study folk music, delving into the Library of Congress Archive, among other sources. He began a second career in Greenwich Village, from which milieu he went on to Hollywood, television, and films. Born in New York of West Indian parentage, he spent some formative years in Jamaica. Identified primarily with Calypso music (he did more than any other single performer to popularize it), he has successfully purveyed the music of other traditions as well, including the spirituals.

A landmark in the popularization of folk music was the appearance in 1958 of a recording of a nineteenth-century North Carolina murder ballad, *Tom Dooley,* by a young group called (because of the then-current

Calypso craze) the Kingston Trio.[21] The trio had come to Greenwich Village from San Francisco, where it originated, performing in places like the hungry i and the Purple Onion. The recording was hugely successful, and led to an extensive career.

Another group to emerge from the New York folk scene was Peter, Paul, and Mary (Peter Yarrow, Noel Paul Stookey, and Mary Ellin Travers), who first recorded in 1962. Their career may be cited as evidence that the relationship between even some of the professionally successful folk singers and social and political causes was not over. In 1963 they recorded *Blowin' in the Wind,* by fellow Greenwich Village alumnus Bob Dylan. That same year they sang for the August march on Washington in behalf of civil rights. In 1968 they campaigned for Eugene McCarthy, the Democratic nominee for president; this was just twenty years after the Almanacs had stumped for Henry Wallace.

Festivals and "Stars"

In 1963 the high-water mark of the folk music "revival," as it has been called, was reached. That was the year of the memorable civil rights confrontations in the South, and of a somewhat revitalized and united folk singers' activist effort on behalf of the cause of the southern blacks. It was also the year of the reconstitution, after a two-year hiatus, of the Newport (Rhode Island) Folk Festival. The festival drew tremendous crowds, and the performers represented a broad spectrum. The southern traditional music was represented by Clarence Ashley, Doc Watson, Maybelle Carter, and Jean Ritchie; the older protest music of the thirties by Jim Garland; the southern civil rights movement by the Freedom Singers; the new topical song movement by Sam Hinton, Phil Ochs, and Tom Paxton; and finally, the "big drawers"—those singers who had achieved by then a significant popularity, but who kept in their repertory a number of songs reflecting social concern—by Pete Seeger, Joan Baez, Bob Dylan, and Peter, Paul, and Mary.

If the mid-sixties marked the height of the folk music revival, then the folk festivals were surely the "camp meetings" of this revival. The social concerns of the period (mainly civil rights) seemed to create, at least temporarily, a folk-singing "community," and particularly at the early festivals a feeling of fervent, almost religious enthusiasm was generated. The cohesion of this "community" proved to be short-lived and illusory, however. For one thing, the ideological commitments, for those who saw *these* in folk music, were far more diffused, individualistic, and transitory than they had been in the thirties and forties. Then, too, with the new popularity of folk music had come the inevitable commercialism. Performers, if they thought in terms of a career (and the blandishments were more attractive than ever) had to be very conscious of popularity charts, based on the sale of records and concert tickets. The "star system" rapidly evolved, which was completely foreign both to the very essence of folk music itself and to the ideals of the proletarian "folk movement" of the earlier period.

As for the mass audience represented by the popularity charts, its preoccupation with folk music was fleeting, and its exposure limited largely to the highly processed and commercially packaged article. Thus whatever mass audience folk music had in the fifties and sixties, it never viewed folk music as other than a branch of popular music—nor could it have been expected to. Having been introduced to "folk music" by groups such as the Kingston Trio, it drifted away with the coming of the Beatles.

MODERN COLLECTING, STUDY, AND THOUGHT IN FOLK MUSIC

Any assessment of folk music in relation to American life and culture worth making must be based on understanding. Understanding is based on disciplined study, and disciplined study requires not only trained and experienced minds but a body of material faithfully and carefully collected and preserved. This is the third level at which Americans have been involved with folk music in our time.

It is beyond our scope to include a survey of folk song scholarship in America. Yet the reader should be aware that by now a vast amount of American folk music has been collected, and is available for study and re-creation. This is due to the labors of a broad range of workers in the field. Harvard professors Francis James Child and George Lyman Kittredge began the work and laid down the guidelines around the turn of the century (incidentally making Harvard a leading center for folk song study). But the work of collecting subsequently was pursued with enthusiasm by both amateurs and professionals in all corners of the country. Jack Thorp, an easterner turned cowboy, published in Estancia, New Mexico, the first edition of his *Songs of the Cowboys* in 1908, to be followed soon by John Lomax's *Cowboy Songs and Other Frontier Ballads* in 1910. Collecting was meanwhile going on in Missouri, in Michigan, in Nebraska, in Kentucky, in West Virginia. The English collector Cecil Sharp, building on the work of American enthusiasts, collected folk songs in the southern Appalachians in the summers of 1916–1918. Roland Gray was collecting ballads among the Maine lumberjacks in the early twenties, while George Korson concentrated on the anthracite-coal miners in Pennsylvania at about the same time. In the thirties John Lomax and his son Alan first took their electric recording machine into the back country and prisons of the Deep South, and made historic recordings of Negro work songs, field cries, ballads, and blues. John Greenway delved into the material collected by the New York–based People's Songs, Inc., interviewed many of the singers connected with their endeavor, and came up with *American Folksongs of Protest* in 1953. Mike Seeger has found and recorded many old-time musicians such as Dock Boggs, as well as perpetuating traditional styles in his own playing and with the New Lost City Ramblers. And, central to all these endeavors and functioning as a great national repository of folk music is the monumental Archive of American Folk Song of the Library of Congress. This Archive, established half a century ago in 1928, has represented the collective efforts of many workers, but those most associated with it in the public mind, and with good reason, have been the Lomaxes. Its collection consists mostly of recordings made in the field, but such diverse figures as Woody Guthrie and Jelly Roll Morton have been brought to the recording laboratory in Washington by Alan Lomax to record songs, instrumental pieces, and reminiscences for posterity. The Archive now has preserved more than 60,000 performances, representing a resource that is bound to become increasingly valuable as students in the future look ever more penetratingly at the varied phenomena of folk music in America—tracing its paths and finding out what it can tell us about ourselves and our ways.

FURTHER READING

Studies and Background Reading

* DENISOFF, R. SERGE. *Great Day Coming: Folk Music and the American Left.* Urbana: University of Illinois Press, 1971.

    This short study is the most nearly comprehensive and objective study to date of this controversial topic.

———. *Sing a Song of Social Significance.* Bowling Green, Ohio: Bowling Green University Popular Press, 1972.

    Although this covers much of the same ground as *Great Day Coming*, it includes more statistical analysis and goes into more detail on more recent developments. There are chapters, for example, on folk-rock, on teen-age death songs, and a final one titled "Kent State, Muskogee, and the Ghetto."

DUNSON, JOHN. *Freedom in the Air: Song Movements of the Sixties.* New York: International Publishers, 1965.

    A brief account, with examples of song words, of the second flourishing

---

* Items thus marked are part of the suggested reference library to be available in connection with this book.

period of folk song as propaganda. Treats mainly the civil rights movement.

* GREENWAY, JOHN. *American Folksongs of Protest*. Philadelphia: University of Pennsylvania Press, 1953. New York: A. S. Barnes & Co. (paper), 1960.
  A rather detailed account of protest songs, especially those used in the labor movement. Many examples, including music.

* GUTHRIE, WOODY. *Bound for Glory*. New York: E. P. Dutton & Co., 1943.
  Autobiographical reminiscences, often of considerable poetic intensity, by one of the best-known authors and singers of the urban folk movement.

* JACKSON, BRUCE (ed.). *Folklore and Society*. Hatboro, Pa.: Folklore Associates, 1966.
  This collection of essays in honor of folklorist B. A. Botkin includes excellent articles by Charles Seeger, Willard Rhodes, Richard Dorson, and Ellen Stekert.

* MALONE, BILL C. *Country Music, U.S.A.* Austin and London: University of Texas Press, 1968. Chapters 4, 10.

NOEBEL, DAVID A. *The Marxist Minstrels: A Handbook on Communist Subversion of Music*. Tulsa, Okla.: American Christian College Press, 1974.
  A rather shrill and alarmist expression of dissenting opinion on the urban folk movement, based on the obvious and continuing bias of some leading segments of it towards the extreme Left, including communism.

REUSS, RICHARD A. *A Woody Guthrie Bibliography, 1912–1967*. New York: Guthrie Children's Trust Fund, 1968.

* WILGUS, D. K. *Anglo-American Folksong Scholarship Since 1898*. New Brunswick, N.J.: Rutgers University Press, 1959.
  A comprehensive survey and evaluation of the work of this century. As the work of an authoritative scholar treating subjects still often controversial, it is of great value. Includes a discography, useful even though out of date, and a very comprehensive bibliography.

See also the reading list for chapters 1 and 2.

Song Collections

Some general collections, such as Alan Lomax's *The Folk Songs of North America* and Carl Sandburg's *The American Songbag* (see chapter 1), have songs relevant to this chapter. Of the more specialized collections, the following should be mentioned:

American Folksong. Compiled by Woody Guthrie, edited by Moses Asch. New York: Oak Publications, 1961.

* *American Folksongs of Protest* (cited above).
  Contains many complete songs, with music for a few.

* *Bob Dylan*. New York: Warner Bros., 1974.

* *Hard-Hitting Songs for Hard-Hit People*. Compiled by Alan Lomax, with

notes by Woody Guthrie, music transcribed and edited by Pete Seeger. New York: Oak Publications, 1967.

> Probably the best collection concentrating on the period of the 1930s. Illustrated with fine photographs made under the auspices of the Farm Security Administration by Walker Evans and others.

We Shall Overcome. Compiled by Guy and Candy Carawan. New York: Oak Publications, 1963.

> Songs of the southern civil rights movement, with commentary.

* The Woody Guthrie Song Book. New York: Grosset & Dunlap, 1976.

Periodicals

Broadside. 215 West 98th St., New York, N.Y. 10025.

> This is a more topical publication, specializing in the more virulent and overtly propagandistic songs.

Crawdaddy. 72 Fifth Ave., New York, N.Y. 10011.

Sing Out! 270 Lafayette St., New York, N.Y. 10012.

> This more or less "official" organ of the urban folk movement prints articles of documentary value, as well as music.

LISTENING

General

* Anthology of American Folk Music, 3 vols. Folkways: 2951–53.
American Industrial Folksongs, ed. John Greenway. Riverside: RLP-12-607.
American Industrial Ballads, Pete Seeger. Folkways: FH-5251.

Colonial

* The Birth of Liberty, from the Recorded Anthology of American Music. RAAM: NW-276.

Pre-1930

The Songs of Joe Hill, Joe Glazer. Folkways: 2039.

1930s and 1940s

* Brother, Can You Spare a Dime?: Amerian Song During the Great Depression. RAAM: NW-270.

> A broad cross-section of songs from both the popular and folk domains.

Songs of the Great Depression, New Lost City Ramblers. Folkways: FH-5264.

Talking Union, Almanac Singers. Folkways: FH-5285.

The Songs and Stories of Aunt Molly Jackson. Folkways: 5457.

Aunt Molly Jackson, Library of Congress Recordings. Rounder-1002.

* *Dust Bowl Ballads*, Woody Guthrie. Folkways: FH-5212.

* *Hootenanny Tonight*, Pete Seeger and others. Folkways: FH-2511.

Hootenanny at Carnegie Hall, Almanac Singers. Folkways: FH-2512.

Songs of Struggle and Protest, Pete Seeger. Folkways: FH-5233.

Songs of the Lincoln Brigade, the Almanac Singers and Ernst Busch. Stinson: SLP-52.

Songs of the Spanish Civil War.

1950s and 1960s

Broadside Ballads, no. 1. Folkways: FH-5301.

A representative selection of protest songs of the sixties, with texts and notes.

We Shall Overcome, Pete Seeger. Columbia: CL-2101.

All the News That's Fit To Sing, Phil Ochs. Elektra: EKL-269.

Ain't That News, Tom Paxton. Elektra: EKL-298.

Newport Folk Festival 1963. Vanguard: 79148.

Newport Folk Festival 1964. Vanguard: 79184.

Woody Guthrie

Woody Guthrie: The Early Years. Everest. 2088.

The Legendary Woody Guthrie. Everest: 2058.

Woody Guthrie, Library of Congress Recordings. Elektra: EKL-271–272.

Original Recordings Made by Woody Guthrie: 1940–1946. Warner Bros.: BS-2999.

Ballads of Sacco and Vanzetti, Woody Guthrie. Folkways: FH-5485.

See also the list for the 1930s and 1940s.

Bob Dylan

* *The Times They Are A-Changin'*, Bob Dylan. Columbia: KCS-8905.

Freewheelin' Bob Dylan. Columbia: KCS-8786.

The Popularization of Folk Music

The Weavers' Greatest Hits, 2 vols. Vanguard: VSD-15-16.

* *The Weavers at Carnegie Hall*. Vanguard: 6533E.

Time to Think, Kingston Trio. Capitol: ST-2011.

Harry Belafonte: Pure Gold. RCA: ANL-1-0979-E.
Burl Ives' Greatest Hits. MCA: 114.
Peter, Paul, and Mary. Warner Bros.: 1449.
* *The Best of Peter, Paul, and Mary.* Warner Bros.: 2552.
The World of Pete Seeger, 2 vols. Columbia: CG-31949.

PROJECTS

1. Read Charles Seeger's thought-provoking article "The Folkness of the Non-Folk vs. the Non-Folkness of the Folk," in Jackson, *Folklore and Society*. Write a brief essay setting forth *your* interpretation of "folkness" and "non-folkness," drawing examples from the life and culture you see around you.
2. Make a study of the IWW (the "Wobblies") and their use of music. Consult, if possible, a copy of the *Red Song Book*, documenting where feasible the source of the songs. Are they fundamentally European or American?
3. Write a brief paper on the U.S. Communist party's views and attitudes towards music, and the uses of it advocated in various periods. (For a start, consult the bibliography in Denisoff, *Great Day Coming.*
4. Write a brief paper on the Lincoln Battalion and its role in the Spanish Civil War, with special attention to the songs that came out of the conflict.
5. Do a brief essay on the "hootenanny"—the term itself and the social gathering to which it was applied. (You may wish to consult, among other sources, Peter Tamony's article in *Western Folklore*, July 1963.)
6. For many of his songs, Woody Guthrie used tunes that were already traditional. (Consult his own description of his methods in *Born to Win.*) Trace the tune sources of at least three such songs, comparing them with Guthrie's versions.
7. Try to document a local example of a topical song or a protest song being used at a meeting, rally, or other gathering. Analyze the song itself (trying to determine its source) and as much of the context of its usage as you can. Consider, for example: How well did the people seem to know it? Was it sung primarily to sway the uncommitted or to promote solidarity and raise morale among the cause's adherents?
8. Interview some people prominent in local labor unions, to find out the current state of labor songs and singing in the labor movement,

and their views on what the role of singing either could or should be.

9. Analyze the body of songs in a year's issue of some topical song publication such as *Sing Out!* or *Broadside*. Consider (1) the number of topical issues involved and the proportion of songs devoted to each; (2) the proportion of *magnetic* songs to *rhetorical*, as defined by Denisoff and alluded to in this chapter.

10. Compare a popularized version of a folk song with a traditional one, giving attention to tune, words, style of singing, and accompaniment. Include some conclusions and comments. (An example would be Simon and Garfunkel's *Scarborough Fair/Canticle* as compared with a traditional rendition of Child 2—known by such titles as *The Elfin Knight* and *The Lover's Tasks*—from the Library of Congress Archive releases.)

11. Make a report on any recent "folk music festival," including such topics as the range of traditions represented; the proportion of what could be regarded as traditional folk singers to professional or popular singers of folk songs; any "stars" that were involved. What does the festival tell you about the state of folk music today?

Part Two

Sacred Music in the Possession of the Folk

America is too young to have been able to nurture such highly cultivated worship music as is represented, for example, by the rich efflorescences of Gregorian chant or the Lutheran cantata. Nor, the mere question of time aside, have the conditions been present that could produce such flowerings. With our broad spectrum of religious sects and our inherent distrust of ecclesiastical organization and wealth (indispensable for building a tradition of conscious religious art), to say nothing of our increased secularization, the intensity of focus has been lacking—that which in Europe, from the Middle Ages up to the time of the social and industrial revolutions, could put large resources of talent at the service of the Church, and produce, ultimately and at the apex, a Notre Dame Mass or a St. Matthew Passion. Thus our output of what might be called cultivated religious music has been meager, and up to now, mostly derivative.

At the relatively unconscious and unlearned level of folk art, on the other hand, we have produced religious music that, in accord with its homely character, has become embedded deeply into the culture of a broad segment of our people. Thus, as is true of so much of our music, the most significant of our religious music is that which has remained closest to folk sources. It has significance in our cultural life not only (and not even primarily) for what it is, but for the response it evokes. Indeed, the immediacy and depth of response, without the distancing of any art-consciousness, is part and parcel of the phenomenon of folk art. Charles Ives, one of our greatest composers, but also one of our greatest musical thinkers, has pointed up, in the epilogue to his Essays Before a Sonata, the importance of this near-folk music, in terms of its meaning in the lives of those whose music it is. He is speaking to the American composer, but his words have substance for anyone who would understand American music.

> The man "born down to Babbitt's Corners" may find a deep appeal in the simple but acute Gospel hymns of the New England "camp meetin'" of a generation or so ago. He finds in them—some of them—a vigor, a depth of feeling, a natural-soil rhythm, a sincerity—emphatic but inartistic—which, in spite of a vociferous sentimentality, carries him nearer the "Christ of the people" than does the Te Deum of the greatest cathedral. . . . [If] the Yankee can reflect the fervency with which "his gospels" were sung—the fervency of "Aunt Sarah," who scrubbed her life away for her brother's ten orphans, the fervency with which this woman, after a fourteen-hour work day on the farm, would hitch up and drive five miles through the mud and rain to "prayer meetin'," her one articulate outlet for the fulness of her unselfish soul—if he can reflect the fervency of such a spirit, he may find there a local color that will do all the world good. If his music can but catch that spirit by being a part with itself, it will come somewhere near his ideal—and it will be American, too.

Chapter Five

Religious Music of Early America

THE TWO RICHEST NATIVE TRADITIONS of religious music in America have been that of the Negro spiritual, on the one hand, and on the other a white quasi-folk tradition whose lineage can be traced from seventeenth-century psalm singing through the singing school of the eighteenth century to the shape-note hymnody of the nineteenth, with its offshoots and revivals in the twentieth. The Negro spiritual, as a predominantly folk form, has been treated in an earlier chapter. This chapter will deal with the earlier part of the psalm-tune-to-folk-hymn tradition, while also turning aside for a brief look at some worthy and fascinating music from the religious communities that functioned as more or less self-sufficient "islands" in our midst—such as are represented by the Moravians and the Shakers.

121

PSALMODY IN AMERICA

Very probably the first musical sounds from the Old World which the aborigines heard in that part of the New that is now the United States were the sturdy psalm tunes sung by Protestant settlers and sailors. Lest this image be confined to the Pilgrims and Puritans of New England, it should be noted that French Huguenots were singing psalms from their psalter in Florida half a century before the landing of the English Separatists at Plymouth—and, before their massacre by the Spaniards, were teaching them to the friendly and receptive natives. At the other edge of the continent, the California Indians were fascinated by the psalm singing of Sir Francis Drake's men in 1579. When the first permanent settlements were established in Massachusetts, the psalters were an important part of the few precious possessions brought over. Subsequently the psalms were sung both by the Indians and by many of the blacks along the eastern seaboard, as taught by missionaries. The psalm tunes were the most important body of religious music in constant use throughout those colonies founded by the English and Dutch, almost until the time of the Revolution. They were subsequently largely replaced by the music of hymns, anthems, and fuging tunes, but many of the old psalm tunes have survived, and tune names such as *Toulon, Windsor, York, Bristol, Old 104th, Old 112th, Old 120th,* and the famous *Old 100th* bespeak their presence in every major modern hymnal.

Calvinism and the Psalms

A glance at a map of Europe, together with some understanding of the situation there at the time of the Reformation, will make clear why it was the psalm tune, rather than the Lutheran chorale or the venerable and cultivated music of the Roman Catholic Church, that dominated our early religious music and left its mark on its development for three hundred years. It is beyond the scope of this book to fill in the background in any detail; suffice it to say that many of our earliest permanent settlers brought with them not only their psalters and their psalm tunes, but their pronounced aversion to state religion and temporal ecclesiastical hierarchy and power—all of which, to them, was summed up in one word: "popery." This was to have a profound effect on the development of American consciousness and culture.

Music in the Calvinist churches was rather severely limited to the unaccompanied singing in unison of metrical versions of the psalms. This limitation can best be understood in the light of the ancient and ever-present dichotomy that exists, when it comes to the uses of music in worship, between the musician and the theologian. The musician wishes to use all his skill and craft, and give the music free rein; the theologian wishes to keep music simple and ensure its subordination to the worship itself. The controversy is nearly as old as the Christian Church itself, and the history of Church music is the history of the swinging of the pendulum back and forth between the two positions. The Church recognized, as the Greeks had long before, the power of music over the human emotions. As two recent writers have aptly summarized the situation: "The Christian church has carried on a long, often fruitful relationship with music, governed, however, by the kind of uneasy truce man has struck with fire." [1] It so happened that in the sixteenth century the pendulum swung decisively to the side of strict control of music, both in the Roman Catholic Church and the new Reformed Church, but much more drastically and completely in the latter. In the Reformed Church, the new broom had no weight of musical tradition to encumber it. Psalm singing, then, was the product of an enforced musical simplicity on theological grounds.

Psalm Tunes and Psalters

With John Calvin's exhortation to psalm singing came the need for metered and rhymed versions of the psalms, and tunes to which they could be sung. This need began to be met immediately, and Calvin's first psalter was published in Strasbourg in 1539, followed by the Geneva Psalter in 1551, whose musical editor was Louis Bourgeois. Bourgeois is credited with composing many of the tunes himself, including both *Old 100th* and *Old 124th*, the ancestor of the modern *Toulon*. The sixteenth century saw the establishment of two great bodies of sacred tunes, the Lutheran chorales and the psalmody of the Reformed Church. They share similar characteristics: They are easily singable tunes of fairly simple construction, with vestiges of the old modal scales already encountered in our study of folk music.

The psalm tunes, especially those of French origin, display a rhythmic variety in the arrangement of long and short notes which was typical of Renaissance music, especially that for dancing. This rhythmic variety was lost sight of as succeeding generations tended to flatten out the rhythm into the rather pedestrian versions of the tunes as we have come to know them, plodding along in notes of equal value. Compare, for instance, the original version of *Old 100th*

with the version now commonly used.

Many of the tunes, especially when sung at a fairly lively pace, exhibit a kind of syncopation in relation to an implied steady pulse, as for example this version of Psalm 21 from the Ainsworth Psalter: [2]

That the psalms were not always performed slowly (at least outside of church) may be inferred from Shakespeare's oft-quoted allusion in *The Winter's Tale* to the Puritan who "sings psalms to hornepipes."

Of importance to America was the publication in 1612 in Amsterdam of a psalter in English for the use of the English Separatists who had taken refuge in Holland. Henry Ainsworth incorporated into his work, *The Book of Psalmes: Englished both in Prose and Metre*, thirty-nine fine and varied melodies, mostly from French sources. It was the Ainsworth Psalter that the Separatists (or Pilgrims, as they came to be known) brought with them when they founded the Plymouth Colony in 1620, and they used it in a number of editions until this colony merged with the larger Massachusetts Bay Colony in 1692.

The importance of psalm singing in the early Puritan colonies is attested to by the fact that the first book printed in what is now the United States was a newly translated, metered, and rhymed version of the psalms. *The Whole Booke of Psalmes Faithfully Translated into English Metre* was published in Boston in 1640, and has acquired the nickname of the Bay Psalm Book. It contained no music (nor did any subsequent edition until the ninth, of 1698); singers were referred to the two common English psalters of the day, those of Ravenscroft or Sternhold and Hopkins, for the tunes to be sung. The preface is scholarly, and the metered translations literal, if somewhat rough as poetry. It was no mean achievement for a community of less than twenty thousand people that had established itself on the edge of the American wilderness scarcely more than a decade before. The motive of these scholars is revealed in characteristic words at the close of the preface:

> If therefore the verses are not always so smooth and elegant as some may desire or expect; let them consider that Gods Altar needs not our pollishings: Ex. 20. for wee have respected rather a plaine translàtion, then to smooth our verses with the sweetness of any paraphrase, and soe have attended Conscience rather than Elegance, fidelity rather than poetry, in translating the hebrew words into english language, and Davids poetry into english meetre; that soe wee may sing in Sion the Lords songs or prayse according to his owne will; untill hee take us from hence, and wipe away all our tears, & bid us enter into our masters joye to sing eternall Halleluiahs.

Two Divergent "Ways"

By the 1720s a hundred years of psalm singing in America had produced not one but two discernible traditions, simultaneous but widely divergent. They amounted to a written and an oral practice of singing. It is plain from accounts of the period that the oral practice, or "Usual Way," as it was called, had gained the upper hand. In the written practice, the tunes would be sung according to the way they were notated in the psalm books of the time. But few in the congregations, especially in the rural areas, could read music, and so had to rely on a combination of their own memory and the singing of a deacon or precentor who led them with a powerful voice. Since there was little to ensure the accuracy (to say nothing of the vocal ability) even of the precentor, it is plain that the stage was set for the evolution of a distinctly oral, or *folk*, practice; and this is exactly what the Usual Way was.

It meant, first, that the number of tunes in common usage shrank to a very few (five or six, by most accounts), and that even these few were imperfectly remembered, so that local variations would develop, and fragments of one tune would find their way into another. It also meant that the pace of the music became slower and more erratic. There are probably two reasons for this. In the first place, in any communal singing that is not strongly led there is a tendency for each singer to sing in his or her own tempo, and this inevitably leads to a slowing of the general tempo in accommodation to the slowest singers.

But the pace of the tunes (originally, as has been indicated, probably quite lively) was slowed by another development—the practice of "lining out" the psalms, which called for the reading, by a deacon or the pastor himself, of each line before it was sung by the congregation. It is a hoary practice. It had its beginnings in England and Scotland, where it was prescribed by authorities as an antidote to the forgetting of the words on the part of the congregations, many of whose members could not read. In time it became an established practice, and then a cherished one, clung to tenaciously even when no longer needed as a prop to memory. Lining out was apparently introduced to American psalm and hymn singing at the end of the seventeenth century. Lining out naturally interrupted the flow and momentum of the tunes, which had to be started up anew with each phrase. This was a decisive factor in slowing the tempo. Just how slow it became in extreme cases is difficult to determine. Critics are apt to exaggerate, but one observer noted, "I myself have twice in one Note paused to take Breath."

The slowing down led to another development—the embellishment of the tunes in folk fashion with passing notes, slides, turns, and other devices—what one scholar has termed a "compensatory florid filling in"— perhaps by the more talented, inventive (and impatient), singers. The practice has been colorfully described (by those opposed to it) as consisting of "many Turnings of, or Flourishes with the Voice" or a "Tittering up and down." One observer counted as many as a hundred and fifty notes in a tune that, in its written version, consisted of thirty.

There was, at that time, no concept of "folk," "folklore," or "folk practice"; but there is no doubt that this is exactly what it was: a way of singing, understood and cherished in common by a community, unwritten, and passed from one generation to another as an oral tradition. It was more pronounced, of course, in the "country," where it persisted longest. If we were to search for a modern equivalent, it would be precisely in the "backwoods" that something at least analogous to it could be found today, in the singing in rural churches, chiefly in the South now—among the blacks or the mountain whites.[3]

Opposition to the Usual Way on the part of a more musically literate portion of the populace grew more outspoken as time went on, and came to a head in the 1720s. Those who favored reform were, as always, much more articulate than the "folk," who were perfectly content to enjoy what they had always known, and even highly suspicious of anything new. It has been pointed out that almost the only descriptions we have of the Usual Way come from those who were highly critical of it. They objected to the practice of lining out ("praising God by Peace-meal," as one critic put it), and they castigated the incompetence of the deacons who performed it.[4] They opposed the slow tempo, and the florid embellishments that resulted. They also wanted to enlarge the repertoire of tunes in common use. To replace the Usual Way they promoted what was called "Regular Singing."

Reform and Instruction

What the reformers, or proponents of Regular Singing, wanted to happen could only be accomplished by teaching people to read music. This is exactly what they set out to do. Instruction books such as *An Introduction to the Singing of Psalm Tunes in a Plain and Easy Method* (Rev. John Tufts) and *The Grounds and Rules of Musick Explained, or An Introduction to the Art of Singing by Note* (Rev. Thomas Walter) appeared in the 1720s, and went through many editions. As intimated in their titles, these books represented only the first of a long series of assaults by American ingenuity on the perennial problem of how to make music easier for the uninitiated. From *An Introduction in a Plain and Easy Method* through *Ragtime in Ten Easy Lessons* this elusive goal has been pursued—often, as we shall see, with some success. Tufts's device for removing some of the difficulties of reading ordinary notation was to place on the five-line staff, not the customary note symbols, but letters standing for the four solmization syllables (fa, sol, la, mi), which had long been in common use by then. As rendered by Tufts, the tune of *Old 100th* looked like this:

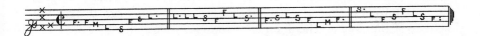

Tufts's system was never widely adopted, but a related and still more ingenious device of using notes of various *shapes* to stand for the syllables became very widespread in rural America in the next century, as we shall see.

But no one has ever learned to perform music just by reading a book. The need for instruction by a "master," and for practicing together under his tutelage, produced one of the most important and pervasive musical (and social) institutions in our history—the singing school.

THE SINGING SCHOOL TRADITION

That uniquely American institution, the singing school, may have had its beginnings in New England, but ultimately it spread far and wide. In the cities its descendants are represented by the numerous choral societies, great and small. In the rural areas it retained its original characteristics longest; here, as a social as well as musical gathering, it brightened the routine of lives that were otherwise all too often harsh and dreary. The firm place and meaning of the singing school in rural American life before this century can hardly be better attested to than by the following excerpt from the reminiscences, in folk verse form, of a pioneer woman writing of her life in Sangomon County, Illinois, in the mid-1800s.

We had so few things to give us pleasure
The memories of such times I love to treasure.
Our singing school, where we looked forward to meet
Our beloved teacher, and his pupils to greet.
Our singing books, few here now, ever saw
The old patent notes, fa, sol, la, sol, fa, me, la.
There were some good voices to lead the rest,
All long since gone to the home of the blest.
I seem to hear their voices now singing, loud and clear
And almost feel their presence hovering near.

How the Singing Schools Worked

Organized instruction in singing by note was being offered in the colonies as early as 1719 (in Virginia). From the 1720s on, the movement gradually picked up momentum, and the period 1760 to 1800, encompassing the Revolution and the founding of the new nation, saw the greatest activity of the singing school, especially in New England.

Just how did the singing school function? There were many variations in the details, but basically it was a private venture, taught by an itinerant master. The school would be advertised in advance in the community, and subscriptions taken. There was usually a close relationship with the local church; sometimes the church would pay part of the cost of the school in return for the improvement of its choir. But the singing school itself was not a denominational institution, and in fact the instruction did not always take place in the church; a room in a schoolhouse or local tavern was sometimes used. If the singing master had published a tune-book the pupils would be expected to buy and use it, thus somewhat augmenting his income, which was seldom large.[5] The length of the term and the frequency of the meetings varied, of course, but two or three meetings a week for three months seems to have been common, at least in and around Boston.

As for the actual instruction, the solmization syllables (fa, sol, la, mi) were invariably taught as a basis for learning to sing the correct pitches, and the words of the pieces were not allowed to be sung until the syllables had been mastered. As an ingenious device for getting the tempi exact, homemade pendulums (of a length carefully specified) were recommended, and Billings gives the following directions for making them in the preface to his *Continental Harmony:*

> Make a pendulum of common thread well waxed, and instead of a bullet take a piece of heavy wood turned perfectly round, about the bigness of a pullet's egg, and rub them over, either with chalk, paint or white-wash, so that they may be seen plainly by candle-light.

(It was usually stipulated that the students bring their own candles.) At the close of the term, there was almost always a public concert, or "exhibition" (sometimes called a "singing lecture" if the minister or some other dignitary graced the occasion with an address on music). The pupils thus got a chance to show off what they had learned; the singing master then moved on to another community.

Contemporary accounts show the pupils to have been mostly young people. The importance of the singing school as a social gathering has already been remarked; it seems, from the directions for the conduct of a singing school which have survived, that the ability to keep order was at least as important as the ability to teach music—an observation that has a familiar ring in all periods. Yet, generally, there is little question but that the singing schools accomplished their objectives very well. After the term was over, one or more of the ablest pupils might start teaching themselves, or even try their hand at composing psalm settings, anthems, or fuging tunes.

The singing schools had a great impact in raising the general level of musical literacy, in greatly expanding the repertory of music available, and, probably most importantly, in encouraging the development of native composers.

Billings of Boston and His Contemporaries

Not every singing master became a composer, of course, but the number that did is substantial, and in fact the singing school movement gave us our first school of indigenous American composers—who worked under the most fruitful conditions a composer can experience: writing music for which there is a clear demand and appreciation on the part of a well-defined public. This fruitful period for our first native composers did not last long—near-ideal conditions for art never do—but the productivity was intense (one scholar has termed it a "golden age"), for by 1800 one authority has estimated that there were over a thousand different compositions in print in American tune-books, most of them by native composers.[6]

It should not be assumed, however, that teaching singing schools and composing anthems was an occupation one could rely on as a sole source of livelihood. The singing masters and composers were for the most part humble craftsmen, artisans, or small businessmen, who composed and taught in addition to plying their trades. They were among the first in the tradition of the American "amateur" composer—a tradition that, from William Billings to Charles Ives, has been such an important feature of American musical life, but has nearly disappeared in the past half-century. The names and trades of these "native pioneers," as Gilbert Chase has called them, read like a litany of eighteenth-century New England names and occupations, and perhaps helps to give the flavor of the singing school movement in a way nothing else can: Supply Belcher, tavernkeeper; David Belknap, farmer and mechanic; William Billings, tanner; Amos Bull, storekeeper; Oliver Holden, carpenter; Jeremiah Ingalls, cooper; Jacob Kimball, lawyer; Abraham Maxim, farmer and schoolteacher; Justin Morgan, horse breeder; Daniel Read, storekeeper and maker of combs; Timothy Swan, hatter.[7]

William Billings (1746–1800), the best known among these, was also the most prolific, inventive, and enthusiastically dedicated. He was early apprenticed in the tanning trade, an occupation he pursued, except for brief intervals, throughout his life. But vocal music was his passion, which he indulged with indefatigable energy. At twenty-four, he had published the first tune-book in America consisting entirely of music by a single composer. The famous New-England Psalm-Singer, appearing in 1770, contained more than 120 compositions—all by Billings himself. In the next quarter-century he brought out five more books, the names of which give something of their flavor and usage: The Singing Master's Assistant (1778), Music in Miniature (1779), The Psalm-Singer's Amusement (1781), The Suffolk Harmony (1786), and The Continental Harmony (1794). All but one (Music in Miniature) consisted entirely of Billings's own compositions. They show an increasing mastery; he publicly deprecated some of the early compositions of The New-England Psalm-Singer, and consistently revised many of his own works in later publications. They also show an increasing tendency towards compositions of greater length, so that the later books contain fewer pieces.

He became quite well known in his time, and was certainly ranked as Boston's leading psalmodist. His fame spread outside New England; his works were performed in public concerts in Philadelphia, for example. Yet he was never able to give up his tanning trade permanently, and in fact records show him to have held down several civil posts in order to help make ends meet for himself and his family—posts such as Sealer of Leather for the city of Boston, and even jobs that had to do with keeping hogs off the streets, and keeping the streets clean in Boston's Eleventh Ward. He died in severe poverty.

Billings, a friend of Samuel Adams and Paul Revere, was an ardent patriot, and his patriotic song *Chester* was one of the most popular songs of the Revolution. As a stirring tune it is worthy of being quoted—and sung.

With its first stanza, it appeared in 1770 in *The New-England Psalm-Singer*; later, during the war, additional stanzas were added, with the names of five British generals, and the boast that "Their Vet'rans flee before our Youth,/And Gen'rals yield to beardless Boys"—and it was in this form that it appeared in *The Singing Master's Assistant* of 1778.

Billings was a colorful and energetic writer of prose as well, as his salty, conversational, and sometimes lengthy prefaces to his tune-books attest. His philosophical approach to music, as well as politics, was one of independence and self-reliance. Oft-quoted statements of his—such as "Nature is the best Dictator"; "I don't think myself confin'd to any Rules for Composition laid down by any that went before me"; and "I think it best for every Composer to be his own Carver"—may, taken out of their own context and the context of his work, suggest a degree of rebellion and iconoclasm far beyond Billings's actual intent, or what his works show. Nevertheless, he was among the first to sound here a note of independence that was more fully orchestrated half a century later by Emerson, and again a full century later by Charles Ives.

Perhaps the best summation of Billings as man and composer is contained in an entry in the diary of Rev. William Bentley of Salem, made a few days after Billings's death. Bentley, one of America's best-educated men of his time, and a man of broad interests and accomplishments (Jefferson had thought of him for the presidency of the University of Virginia), moved in circles unfamiliar and even inaccessible to Billings. Nevertheless, his insight into Billings's work and importance moved him to write: "Many who have imitated have excelled him, but none of them had better original power. . . . He was a singular man, of moderate size, short of one leg, with one eye, without any address, & with an uncommon negligence of person. Still he spake & sung & thought as a man above the common abilities."

Yankee Tune-Books by the Hundreds

Billings was but one among many. An examination of the singing school period during its golden age gives an impression of tremendous activity and vitality. By 1810 about three hundred of the distinctive tune-books, homely in appearance and typography, had been published. Their oblong shape gave rise to the terms "long boys" and "end-openers." The looks of their pages varied a great deal. The engraving could be clean and elegant, as in James Lyon's *Urania* (the first large-scale compilation, published in Philadelphia in 1761), or rather crude, as in Billings's *Psalm-Singer's Amusement.* Early typesetting for music, which was just beginning to come into use toward the end of the period, produced the rather stiff appearance of Billings's later *Continental Harmony*, in which the staff lines come out as a series of dashes.

The names of these old books tell us much. Some show the classical education or aspirations of their compilers: *Urania; Harmonia Americana.* Some of the names show clearly their use and purpose: *The Musical Primer; The Easy Instructor; The Psalmodist's Assistant* (reminiscent of Billings's *Singing Master's Assistant*); *The Psalmodist's Companion; The Chorister's Companion.* Many bespeak their own locale: *The Massachusetts Compiler; The Vermont Harmony; The Harmony of Maine; The Worcester Collection of Sacred Harmony; The Essex Harmony.* The word "harmony" in the title was widely used: *The American Harmony; The Northern Harmony; The Union Harmony; The Federal Harmony; The New England Harmony; The Christian Harmony;* and, as a final distillation, *The Harmony of Harmony.* To close the list, there appeared (with singular appropriateness to their environment) *The Rural Harmony* and *The Village Harmony.*

In view of their didactic purpose, most of the books begin with some sort of instruction in such rudiments of music as the scale, or "gamut," the names of the pitches and their syllables, and an explanation of rhythmic values, followed sometimes by rudimentary vocal exercises, or "Lessons for tuning ye Voice." On occasion the introduction would be expanded by the inclusion of a kind of Socratic dialogue between "Master" and "Scholar"; Billings's voluble nature makes this section one of the longest (for example, in his *Continental Harmony*), and incidentally one of the most revealing and interesting, as he roams freely from technical musical questions to matters of performance practice and even to philosophical questions.[8]

The Music of the Tune-Books

What kinds of pieces do we find in these tune-books? The terms "psalmodist" and "psalm-singer" that appear in the titles must be understood as being applicable in the strict sense to only a limited proportion of the music. The venerable psalm-tunes are well represented in some of the earlier collections (*Urania*, for example), but along with these appear the tunes for the short non-Scriptural *hymns* to composed texts, and the larger and more ambitious *anthems*—more elaborate settings of Scriptural texts, adapted Scriptural texts, or composed texts. It is evident that by this time hymnody had fairly well succeeded in replacing psalmody.

The *canon* (or *round*), as a composed piece, does not appear frequently, although Billings has given us a beautiful example in his first publication, the justly famous *When Jesus Wept the Falling Tear*.[9]

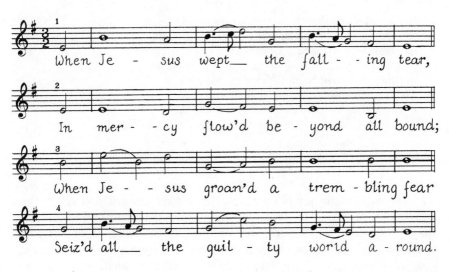

(original a major second higher)

Of particular interest are the famous *fuging tunes* (very possibly pronounced "fudging" in contemporary usage). The best simple description of the fuging tune is probably that of Alan Buechner, who writes of it as a piece that "begins like a hymn and ends like a round." It was the second section, or *fuge*, that was distinctive, and involved homespun imitative entrances of the voices, rather informally constructed. The fuging tune was very popular in its days; the rather thrilling effect of hearing the successive entrances coming from different parts of the U-shaped meeting-house gallery must have pleased both singers and congregation alike. Billings describes these pieces as being "twenty times as powerful as the old slow tunes." Although he composed many himself, there were other composers of the time who favored them even more, and it has been found that over a thousand were published by 1810. The fuging tune later fell into disfavor among reformers of church music, who urged that it was both too crude and too lively as music for worship. But its appeal among the rural folk persisted, and fuging tunes in considerable numbers appear in the shape-note songbooks of the nineteenth century, as we shall see in the next chapter.

A number of the larger anthems and set-pieces were written for specific occasions or observances—for Thanksgiving, for a Fast Day, for Ordination, for Christmas (a festival at this time still proscribed officially), for Easter, for thanksgiving "after a victory," to celebrate the landing of the Pilgrims, and so on. Some were of a still more topical nature, as illustrated by Billings's famous *Lamentation Over Boston,* a spirited paraphrase of Psalm 137 commemorating the British occupation of the city during the war, which begins:

By the rivers of Watertown we sat down and wept.
We wept when we remembered Thee—O Boston.
As for our friends, Lord, God of Heaven preserve them,
Defend them, deliver and restore them to us again.
For they that held them in bondage required of
Them to take up arms against their brethren.
Forbid it Lord, God forbid that those who have
Sucked Bostonian breasts should thirst for American blood.

The musical settings were practically all in the usual four parts: soprano (called treble), alto (called counter), tenor, and bass. In accordance with an already old practice, the melody was assigned not to the soprano but to the tenor. In actual performance, the distribution of parts among the voices was a matter of considerable flexibility; the tenor part could be sung (an octave higher, of course) by women as well as men, and the treble (an octave lower) by men as well as women. In the assignment of voices, it is evident that Billings himself preferred a somewhat "bottom-heavy" emphasis on the bass part, specifying "three or four deep voices suitable for the Bass to one for the upper parts." The bass part was also, as we shall see, often doubled on an instrument: a bass viol, cello, or bassoon.

The prejudice against instrumental music in the churches was strong, but instruments were gradually introduced before 1800 to support the voices. After the pitch pipe (to help the singers find the pitches) came the bass viol, though not without much controversy. (Churches using the "devil's fiddle" were branded as "cat-gut churches" at first.) Finally, the flute, clarinet, bassoon, and even the notorious violin (so much the secular instrument because of its use as an accompaniment to dancing) were admitted, and the small "gallery orchestra" evolved, being especially useful in churches that could not afford organs. Some pieces in the later nineteenth century tune-books even included very occasionally short sections for instruments alone, called "symphonies."

The End of an Era

By 1810, as McKay and Crawford have pointed out, a "reform" movement had successfully established a trend away from the native, unschooled, "innocent" art of the pioneer tradition, and towards the closer imitation of European models. Thus the first flourishing of indigenous musical art that America had experienced was pretty much over by then—at least in the cities.[10]

Much of the joy of the fuging tune and the anthem is in the singing of them oneself, and it cannot be too strongly emphasized that actually re-creating this music is by far the best way to understand and appreciate it. Fortunately, the availability of much of this music in modern editions, and its increasing popularity with church and amateur choirs, make it more accessible than at any time in the last century and a half. Hearing it sung is next best, and even through the thirdhand medium of recordings it is now possible to gain some experience of it; this, at least, is indispensable.[11]

MUSIC AMONG OUR SMALLER INDEPENDENT SECTS

Conditions in America have been such as to nurture from the beginning, despite glaring episodes of intolerance and persecution, a lively tradition of religious independence and nonconformity. Many sects have either been transplanted to this country or have sprung up here, where, especially in the eighteenth and nineteenth centuries, they found the space necessary to provide the measure of isolation and self-sufficiency they so deeply desired. Of these numerous sects, many did not place a particularly high value on music; some, like the Quakers, even abjured it. But there were a few to whom music was vitally important, and these sects cultivated music that often proved to be quite unique. The relatively small number of their adherents, as well as their relative isolation, has kept this music from significantly affecting the main development of American music. But they have contributed some vivid and irreplaceable patches to the quilt of a national music whose most salient characteristics are variety and nonconformity.

The Moravians

The most important of these sects musically was the Moravian Church, or *Unitas Fratrum*, to use the original name. It has had a venerable history, both in the Old and the New World. It was a pre-Reformation church, founded in what is now Czechoslovakia in the mid-fifteenth century by followers of the religious leader John Hus, who was burned as a heretic in 1415. Nearly exterminated during the bloody and disastrous Thirty Years' War of the seventeenth century, it emerged with new life in 1722, in exile from its native Bohemia and Moravia but under the protection of Count Nikolaus Ludwig von Zinzendorf of neighboring Saxony (in what is now East Germany). It was shortly after this that its history in the New World began, for the renewed *Unitas Fratrum* had a strong commitment to missionary work throughout the world. The first mission on the mainland of the New World was established in Georgia in 1735. This was abandoned after five years, but meanwhile work was going on elsewhere, and an important settlement was founded at Bethlehem, Pennsylvania, in 1742, with others in North Carolina (Bethabara, Bethania, and Salem) beginning in 1753. Bethlehem and Salem (later incorporated into Winston-Salem) became—and remain—the two important centers of the Moravian Church in the United States.

Considering the Czech origin and early German influence on the Moravian Church, it is not surprising that music was a vital part of life for its adherents from the start. Hus himself encouraged congregational singing in the vernacular, and wrote and translated hymns. The *Unitas Fratrum* produced the first Protestant hymnal in 1501, a generation before Calvin's first psalter came into being, and the Moravians brought their rich musical tradition with them to America. The singing of hymns was an integral part of their daily life—gathered as families in the morning and evening, at work, or at the love feasts, which were times of worship, fellowship, and song, where bread and drink were shared to the continuous accompaniment of music. Musical skills were taught and prized, even to the making of musical instruments. Not only did the Moravians perform the works of the European composers of the day—Karl Friedrich Abel, Johann Stamitz, Joseph Haydn, as well as many obscure ones—but they produced a large share of their own music. Over thirty Moravian composers working in America have been identified. As in the case of the New England singing school composers, these men were not professional musicians; most were ministers. The principal forms of music cultivated were the choral anthem, the solo song, and the hymn, or *chorale*, the latter resembling very closely the Lutheran chorale. This music differed from that of the singing school tradition in two important ways. First, it was more sophisticated musically, coming from a people who were much closer to the most advanced and dominant strain of European music of the time, the Germanic tradition. (John Antes, for example, Moravian composer and violinist, is said to have known Haydn and played in ensembles with him.)

Secondly, Moravian music was instrumental as well as vocal. The anthems and solo songs were all done with an orchestral accompaniment of strings, and a few winds were occasionally added. Almost all the music was religious, but a few examples of pure instrumental music have survived: string trios, string quintets, and a number of pieces for six wind instruments, ideal for informal outdoor music-making. The Collegium Musicum of Bethlehem may well have constituted the first symphony orchestra in the United States. Also famous were the trombone choirs, which played at funerals and on festive occasions. Their repertoire was mostly four-part chorales, often played, in the tradition of "tower music," from the church belfry. (One such performance is said to have been responsible for repelling an attack by hostile Indians.)

By the mid-nineteenth century Moravian communities had become more secularized, tastes had changed, and the period of musical cultivation and creativity was largely over. The legacy of their music was not rediscovered until the late 1930s in Bethlehem, and the 1950s in Winston-Salem.[12]

The Moravians furnish the most important example of a familiar phenomenon in the history of American music up until modern times: the more or less isolated, self-sufficient "pocket" of culture, relatively rich but destined to remain apart. In summarizing the Moravians' contribution, one eminent scholar has said: "Unfortunately for the history of American music, very little of this enormous quantity of music ever entered the stream of musical life in America."[13]

The Shakers

The most unusual of the sects to give much importance to music was the United Society of Believers in Christ's Second Appearing, commonly called the Shakers. The Society originated in the mid-eighteenth century as a kind of offshoot of Quakerism in the English Midlands, then in the throes of becoming industrialized. Its adherents were predominantly poor people who were attracted to its millennial teachings. Ann Lee, or "Mother Ann," as she came to be called, joined the Society in 1758 and soon became a dominant force in the movement. She and eight other members of the order came to America in 1774. In spite of persecution and imprisonment, by the time she died in 1784 eight Shaker communities had been established in New England and upstate New York. Their somewhat mystical teachings and practices were subsequently formulated—principally dedication to simplicity, humility, and service; communalism as regards property; equality of the sexes; celibacy; a reliance upon visions; and the importance of both song and dance in worship.

The order spread to the frontier during the first part of the nineteenth century (communities were founded in Kentucky, Ohio, and Indiana), where the spontaneity and abandoned fervor of its religious exercises accorded with the revivalism so prevalent there at the time. It reached its peak before the Civil War and declined afterwards; at this writing there are only two small communities of Shakers left.

The music of the Shakers represents, in all its aspects, a nearly pure folk art. Cut off by strict taboos in the beginning from almost all other music, the Believers had to evolve their own, out of improvisations and half-remembered scraps. For decades everything was in oral tradition; written music, which entailed the necessity of developing music reading, was not introduced until after 1800. In the early days, wordless songs were common. Some of these obviously accompanied the movements and dancing of the fervent religious exercises.

Many songs were received in "visions"—a phenomenon also prevalent among the American Indians, as we have seen.[14] These vision songs often had texts comprised of meaningless syllables, or "unknown tongues," as they were considered. Some of the vision songs were said to be received from the spirits of people of other races—American Indians especially, but also Persians, Abyssinians, Hottentots, Laplanders, Eskimos, Chinese, and others. When the Shaker sisters and brothers became "instruments" of these spirits (who were seeking salvation) during a "manifestation," they would pantomime appropriate actions, such as, Eskimos driving dog-sleds. The "words" of one vision song, in an "unknown tongue," begin:

O san-nisk-a-na nisk-a-na, haw, haw, haw,
    fan-nick-a-na, haw, haw, haw.
O san-nisk-a-na nisk-a-na yea se-ne-aw,
    fan-a-na, nisk-a-na, haw, haw, haw.

Most Shaker singing was unharmonized and unaccompanied. Many of the songs used the primitive pentatonic scale, or the archaic modes, as described in chapter 1. All these features identify the music closely with the folk tradition. As the repertory increased, it was inevitable that it be written down and then published. The first Shaker hymnal, *Millennial Praises*, was published in 1813. By this time, of course, borrowings and adaptations from other sources were quite evident; in particular the revivalism of the frontier had a considerable influence on the Shaker song repertory.

In bringing to a close our consideration of the music of the Shakers, we cannot do better than to present two examples of this unique body of song, with the hope that, as with the other examples, they will be *sung* as well as looked at. The first, called *The Humble Heart*, appeared in a hymnal from the New Lebanon, New York, community in 1822. It is a fine example of an old modal tune. The text (three of six verses are given) sets forth with rather felicitous imagery the Shaker philosophy.

Tall cedars fall before the wind,
The tempest breaks the oak,
While slender vines will bow and bend
And rise beneath the stroke.

I've chosen me one pleasant grove
And set my lovely vine,
Here in my vineyard I will rove,
The humble heart is mine.

Of all the fowls that beat the air
I've chose one little dove,
I've made her spotless white & fair,
The object of my love.
Her feathers are like purest gold,
With glory she does shine,
She is a beauty to behold,
Her humble heart is mine.[15]

One of the best known of all Shaker songs, both within the movement and without, is *Simple Gifts*:

'Tis the gift to be simple,'tis the gift to be free,'Tis the gift to come down where we ought to be, And when we find our-selves in the place just right, 'Twill be in the val-ley of love and de-light. When true sim-pli-ci-ty is gained, To bow and to bend we shan't be a-sham'd, To turn, turn will be our de-light,'till by turn-ing, turn-ing we come round right.

This song gives expression to the basic Shaker themes of simplicity and humility. In both words and music it stands as a consummate achievement of innocent religious art. Edward Deming Andrews, the uniquely qualified authority on Shaker music, dance, and ritual, has written: "Shaker ritualism was a true folk art." Elaborating further on its peculiar intensity, freedom, and imagery, he states:

> In no other way, in fact, could the restrained Shaker spirit find such freedom of expression. The Believer was disciplined to a precise and simplified functionalism in the crafts; in industry he followed strict routines and traditions; he was inhibited by the doctrinal taboos on recreation, reading, and intercourse with the world and the opposite sex; the normal sex impulses were suppressed by the great basic principle of the faith. But in songs and operations of worship the urge to play, to love, to create, found release in ways which revealed the very soul of the individual and the essential ethos of the sect.[16]

FURTHER READING

Psalmody and the Singing Schools

FACSIMILE EDITIONS

The following modern facsimile reprints of important old books are interesting and give us ready access to the only kinds of sources we have for an indispensable firsthand acquaintance with this music. Arranged in chronological order these are:

The Bay Psalm Book. Boston, 1640. Reprint, Chicago: University of Chicago Press, 1956.
> The first book published in the United States—words of a new translation only. Editions for the first 58 years contained no music.

TUFTS, JOHN. *An Introduction to the Singing of Psalm Tunes.* 5th ed. Boston, 1726. Reprint, Philadelphia: Musical Americana, 1954.
> One of the earliest instruction books, using the four syllables (fa-so-la-mi) on the staff in place of conventional notes. The tunes are harmonized in three parts.

LYON, JAMES. *Urania.* Philadelphia, 1761. Reprint, New York: Da Capo Press, 1974.

BILLINGS, WILLIAM. *The Psalm-Singer's Amusement.* Boston, 1781. Reprint, New York: Da Capo Press, 1974.

* ———. *The Continental Harmony.* Boston, 1794. Reprint, Cambridge: Harvard University Press, 1961. Includes an introduction by Hans Nathan.

---

* Items thus marked are part of the suggested reference library to be available in connection with this book.

BELCHER, SUPPLY. *The Harmony of Maine*. Boston, 1794. Reprint, New York: Da Capo Press, 1972.

MODERN EDITIONS OF MUSIC

Many publishers with substantial sacred-choral-music catalogs now include editions of music from the New England singing school tradition. An example would be Concordia, of St. Louis, which has a rather extensive series, *Sacred Choral Music from Colonial America by William Billings*, with useful notes.

ANTHOLOGIES, OR STUDIES WITH A SUBSTANTIAL AMOUNT OF MUSIC

* MARROCCO, W. THOMAS, and GLEASON, HAROLD (eds.). *Music in America*. New York: W. W. Norton & Co., 1964.
> A basic anthology for American music up to the Civil War, with an excellent selection of psalm tunes and singing school music. The notes are also valuable.

PRATT, WALDO SELDEN. *The Music of the Pilgrims*. Boston: Oliver Ditson, 1921.
> This valuable little book contains a transcription of the complete music of the Ainsworth Psalter, with excellent notes and a representative selection of texts.

STUDIES, SOME WITH INCIDENTAL MUSICAL EXAMPLES

BARBOUR, J. MURRAY. *The Church Music of William Billings*. East Lansing: Michigan State University Press, 1960.
> A thorough musicological study that has become a basic work for scholars, and is unlikely to be supplanted for some time.

BUECHNER, ALAN C. Notes to the record album *The New England Harmony* (FA-2377). New York: Folkways Records, 1964.
> This excellent 32-page booklet has much valuable information on the singing school tradition, on which the author wrote a doctoral dissertation at Harvard in 1960. The booklet is available separately from Folkways, although the record album is nearly indispensable as well.

* CHASE, GILBERT. *America's Music*. 2nd ed. New York: McGraw-Hill Book Co., 1966. Chapters 1, 2, 7.

DANIEL, RALPH T. *The Anthem in New England Before 1800*. Evanston, Ill.: Northwestern University Perss, 1965.

FOOTE, HENRY WILDER. *Three Centuries of American Hymnody*. Hamden, Conn.: Shoe String Press, 1940. Reprint, 1961. Chapters 1–5.

* LOWENS, IRVING. *Music and Musicians in Early America*. New York: W. W. Norton & Co., Chapters 2, 3, 8, 14, 18.
> A collection of valuable articles by one of the most eminent scholars in American music.

MacDougall, Hamilton C. *Early New England Psalmody.* New York: Da Capo Press, (reprint of original 1940 ed.)

* McKay, David P., and Crawford, Richard. *William Billings of Boston.* Princeton, N.J.: Princeton University Press, 1975.

> A fine recent, and very readable, addition to work in the field of the Yankee singing school. It includes much valuable background information, including a complete survey of sacred music in New England to the time of Billings. It is now a basic work on Billings himself and his time.

Scholes, Percy A. *The Puritans and Music in England and New England.* New York: Russell & Russell, 1962 (reissue of original 1934 ed.).

> A valuable and copiously documented treatise correcting the stereotype of the Puritans as being universally and implacably opposed to music, the fine arts in general, and the appreciation of beauty.

* Stevenson, Robert. *Protestant Church Music in America.* New York: W. W. Norton & Co., 1966. Paperback, 1970. Chapters 1, 2, 3, 7.

> A brief but invaluable survey, written with a broad perspective of the subject by a noted scholar. Begins with the all-but-forgotten Huguenot settlements in Florida more than half a century before the landing of the Pilgrims. Excellent bibliography.

Our Smaller Independent Sects

The Moravians

The best source of information on Moravian music is The Moravian Music Foundation, Drawer Z, Salem Station, Winston-Salem, 27108. It issues lists of the published music, of which there is by now a considerable amount, from various publishers. The foundation has also to date issued seven short monographs, of which *The Moravian Contribution to American Music* (no. 1) and *A Moravian Music Sampler* (no. 7) are probably of the greatest general interest.

Two pamphlets useful for background information on the Moravians are:

Davis, Chester S. *Hidden Seed and Harvest: A History of the Moravians.* Winston-Salem: Wachovia Historical Society, 1973.

Marrocco and Gleason. *Music in America.*

> Chapter 3 includes six examples of Moravian music.

Weinlick, John R. *The Moravian Church Through the Ages.* Bethlehem and Winston-Salem: Comenius Press, 1966.

The Shakers

* Andrews, Edward Deming. *The Gift to Be Simple: Songs, Dances and Rituals of the American Shakers.* Locust Valley, N.Y., 1940. Reprint, New York: Dover Publications, 1962.

> This short but excellent study is the basic one, and indispensable to any investigation of Shaker music. It includes over 70 complete songs.

In addition, the following general works have chapters relevant to this sect:
CHASE, *America's Music*, chapters 3 and 11.

STEVENSON, ROBERT. *Protestant Church Music in America*. Chapter 4.

LISTENING

Psalmody

* *Early American Psalmody*. The Margaret Dodd Singers. *Music in America* series, MIA-102.

Issued by the Society for the Preservation of the American Musical Heritage. Eight psalm tunes. Each tune is sung first in unison, with a precentor "setting the tune" for each line (i.e., singing it, in contrast with the more common practice of "lining out," which was a mere reading of each line). This is followed by harmonized versions, from European sources. The performance is polished, with impeccable rhythm and ensemble—far too much so, in fact, to convey an idea of what congregational singing must have really been like in seventeenth-century New England.

Music of the Pilgrims, Haydn Society. HSL-2068.

Side 1 presents nine psalms from the Ainsworth Psalter, interspersed with narration in the form of excerpts from Governor William Bradford's *Of Plimoth Plantation*. The performance, although too well drilled to be realistic historically, is spirited, and conveys well the lively rhythms of the old French tunes.

The Singing School Tradition

Choral Music in Colonial America, University of Utah Chorale and Chorus. Music in America Series, MIA-114.

Anthems by William Billings and Daniel Read. Credit is due to this early and worthy venture in re-creating this music. The performance is polished, anachronistic (for example, in its use of organ), and, unfortunately, dull.

* *The New England Harmony: A Collection of Early American Choral Music*. Folkways: FA-2377.

This excellent album of music recorded in the meeting house at Old Sturbridge Village, Massachusetts, in 1964, includes 26 pieces by Billings and his contemporaries. A medium-sized chorus of nonprofessional singers recruited from local church and school choirs is used, and this is surely indicative of the right way to perform this music. For instrumental accompaniment on a few of the pieces, a small re-creation of a "gallery orchestra" is used—five performers at most. The notes by Alan Buechner are excellent.

The Moravians

* *Music of the American Moravians*, the Moravian Festival Chorus and Orchestra; Thor Johnson, conductor. Columbia Odyssey: 32-16-0340.
   An excellent "sampler" of solo, choral, and instrumental music.
   American Colonial Instrumental Music. Folkways: FH-5109.
   Includes two string quintets by Johann Friedrich Peter, a Moravian.

The Shakers

Music of the Shakers. Folkways: FH-5378.
* *Brave Boys: New England Traditions in Folk Music.* RAAM: NW-239.
   Includes two Shaker Songs.

PROJECTS

1. Compare very succinctly the early musical traditions of the three major branches of the Reformation: the Reformed (Calvinist), the Lutheran, and the Anglican. Explain which had the most effect on early American music, and why.
2. If you like to sing folk songs, learn a psalm tune (from those reprinted in Marrocco and Gleason, *Music in America,* or from the Ainsworth Psalter as reproduced in Pratt, *The Music of the Pilgrims,* or any other authentic source); fit a psalm text of the same poetic meter to it from the Bay Psalm Book (or any other early translation); and add it to your repertoire. You may sacrifice historical authenticity to the extent of contriving a tasteful accompaniment to it on the guitar if you wish.
3. John Hus, John Calvin, Isaac Watts—none of these men were musicians, and none ever saw the New World. Yet each had a definite influence on American music. Write a brief paper on any one of them, identifying him and tracing his influence.
4. Find three psalm tunes (besides *Old 100th!*) that are still in use and appear in modern hymn collections in this country. Find out as much as you can about the origins of the tunes, and in which early psalters they appeared. Find and consult early versions of the tunes if possible. (Most hymnals have a good index of com-

posers and sources, which can help, as can the index of tune titles. The *Hymnal of the Protestant Episcopal Church in the U.S.A.*, for example, is rather rich in tunes from the old psalters of the sixteenth and seventeenth centuries.)

5. If you read and write music, transcribe two psalm tunes from John Tufts, *An Introduction to the Singing of Psalm Tunes*, 5th ed., into regular musical notation. Sing or play the tunes (or have them sung or played) for the class, and explain Tufts's syllable system for learning music. (You can reproduce just the melody—"cantus"—or the entire three-part setting as Tufts arranged it.)

6. Read William Billings's prefaces to his *Continental Harmony*— both "To the several Teachers of MUSIC, in this and the adjacent States" and "A Commentary on the preceding Rules: by way of Dialogue, between Master and Scholar." Comment on what these treatises seem to say about Billings himself: his sense of humor, his ability and ingenuity as a teacher, and his views on music, especially vocal music.

7. Compile a biographical listing of at least five of the New England singing school composers of the colonial and federal periods (besides Billings), listing their nonmusical occupations, some other biographical data, and some of their compositions.

8. Do an informal survey in your immediate area on the extent to which music of the New England singing school composers is included in the repertoire of church choirs. (Much of it is now available in modern performing editions.) If it is being sung, arrange to hear some of it. If not, perhaps you know a choir director who would be sympathetic to introducing some.

9. Make a study of Hussite hymns (those of the pre-Reformation precursors of the Moravians), noting their relationship to those of the later Lutherans.

10. Investigate and trace the relationship between John Wesley, founder of Methodism, and the Moravians, especially with regard to church music.

11. Make a study of music in the Moravian church today, and to what extent the Moravians incorporate into present-day services the music of their heritage.

12. Investigate music among a small independent sect other than those treated in this chapter. Examples would be the Seventh-Day Baptists of the Ephrata Cloister, the Mennonites, or the followers of Johannes Kelpius (the "Hermit of the Wissahickon").

13. Make a brief study of German Pietism and its effect on the music of its time.

14. Make a study of Shaker handicraft. Compare its characteristics with those of Shaker music.

15. Assemble some accounts of Shaker community life and ritual as recorded by outsiders who visited them. Try to include references or accounts by some of their famous visitors, such as Lafayette, Horace Greeley, Walt Whitman, or William Dean Howells. Consult the bibliography in Andrews, *The Gift to Be Simple.*

Chapter Six

Native Religious Music During and After the Time of Expansion

AMERICA'S EXPANSION, which can be said to have begun in earnest with the opening of the nineteenth century, manifested itself in two vitally significant directions at once: in the growth in size, complexity, and sophistication of our cities; and in the continuous rolling westward of our frontier. Both had profound effects on American thought, life, and art—including our indigenous religious music. We shall try to trace as well as we can some of these developments in this chapter, and explore in the process the unique legacy of music—ballads, hymns, and spiritual songs—that we have inherited from this tumultuous time of expansion and change.

NATIVE TRADITION SUPPRESSED IN
THE URBAN EAST

With the growth of the cities, there developed an increasing sophistication on the part of many urban churchgoers. They were being made more acutely aware of European music by outspoken musicians, both native-born and immigrant, who were either trained in its conventions or were at least aware of its more highly cultivated style, which they conceived as being more appropriate for worship. There developed, beginning about the turn of the century, what has been described as an "anti-American" sentiment regarding music. Though this may have been the first widespread expression of the conviction of American cultural inferiority to Europe, it was far from the last. (Emerson railed against it in the mid-nineteenth century, and Ives in the early twentieth; it plagues us still in some quarters.)

Andrew Law, a university-educated Congregational minister who was a composer, singing school teacher, and noted compiler of tune-books, virtually led off the campaign when he wrote, as early as 1794, that "American music is extremely faulty," and expressed regret that the products of native composers such as Billings "are actually preferred, and have taken a general run, to the great prejudice of much better music, produced even in this country, and almost to the utter exclusion of genuine European compositions."

The charge of being "unscientific" was leveled at American compositions, and tune-books for urban consumption compiled after 1810 show a marked decrease in the number of American works included, with a corresponding increase in European hymns and anthems, often by second-rate composers. The fuging tune especially was castigated. As an example, the Methodist Episcopal Church voiced mild disapproval even before 1800, stating in one publication: "We do not think that fuge-tunes are sinful, or improper to be used in private companies: but do not approve of their being used in our public congregations." In 1807 the preface of a new compilation characterized the fuging tunes as "those wild fugues, and rapid and confused movements, which have so long been the disgrace of congregational psalmody." [1]

Of European influences, the English was of course predominant, as represented not only by Handel but such lesser lights as Samuel Arnold, William Croft, William Boyce, Martin Madan, and Robert Wainwright. The German-Austrian influence also began to loom with prophetic strength. There were those who defended the virtues of the homespun Yankee tunes and their composers; some of this music was even reprinted in special collections in Boston throughout the nineteenth century. But for the most part, at least in the cities, it was true that, as one observer wrote in 1848, "the good old days of New England music have passed away, and the singing-masters who compose and teach it, are known only in history as an extinct race." [2]

THE FRONTIER

That the music of the New Englanders was in fact far from extinct is now clear to us. As is always the case, in the rural areas the "old ways"— and the old music—were clung to tenaciously long after they had been replaced in the cities. And the frontier, southwestward into the long valleys of the Appalachians and beyond into the broad river valleys of the Ohio and the Tennessee, was an extension of rural America. We can follow the movement of the singing school tradition along these paths just by tracing the continued appearance of its odd oblong books of tunes. Moving out of Boston and Philadelphia, we find compilations being made in Harrisburg, Pennsylvania; in the Shenandoah Valley of Virginia; in Hamilton, Georgia; in Spartanburg, South Carolina; in Lexington, Kentucky; in Nashville, in Cincinnati, in St. Louis. The names tell a story of both continuity and movement. As lineal descendants of *The New England Harmony* and *The Harmony of Maine*, we find *The Virginia Harmony*; *The Kentucky Harmony*; *The Knoxville Harmony*; *The Missouri Harmony*; *The Western Lyre*; *The Southern Harmony*; and finally, the famous *Sacred Harp*. These books clearly revealed their ancestry—in their shape and appearance; in their prefatory introductions to the "Rudiments of Music"; in their continued use of the four solmization syllables (fa, sol, la, mi); in their hymns in three and four parts, with the melody buried in the middle of the texture in the tenor voice; and in their sprinkling of more ambitious anthems and fuging tunes. Pieces by Billings himself were almost invariably included; far from being "extinct," as the Boston editor lamented in the middle of the nineteenth century, William Billings and some of his contemporaries have turned out to be the most continuously performed composers in American history. Indeed, their music has already entered its third century.

The singing schools continued to flourish in the nineteenth century, fulfilling their dual musical and social function much as they had done in New England in colonial times. Later came the institution of annual gatherings, or "singings," some lasting two or three days, with "dinner on the grounds" a fixed feature.

Thus we see that the "old ways" did not die. Two important additions were made, however, as the native tradition moved out of the East into the South and West. One was the development of the famous shape notes, and the other was the infusion of the folk element into the music.

The Shape Notes

We have already noted the perennial attempts to simplify and speed up the process of teaching people to read music through various modifications of musical notation, beginning with John Tufts's system in Boston in the early eighteenth century (see chapter 5). It has been pointed out that in this country these attempts have almost always been associated with religious music, for the encouragement and improvement of the democratic institution of congregational singing. There appeared in 1801 a book called, appropriately, *The Easy Instructor,* which introduced a simple but ingenious device that proved to be eminently practical. This consisted of the use of differently shaped notes for each of the four syllables then in use to indicate degrees of the scale. In the key of F major, for example, the scale with its syllables would look like this:

Fa   Sol   La   Fa   Sol   La   Mi   Fa

This system proved to be a successful blend of conventionality and novelty. The staff, with all its advantages of visual orientation, was preserved; key signatures and accidentals were provided for; and the troublesome problems inherent in inventing a new rhythmic notation were avoided, because the rhythmic values of the notes could still be rendered in the conventional way—only the shapes of the note heads were affected.

The device appears to have caught on rather quickly and well. *The Easy Instructor* (though its ownership changed hands) was reissued in various editions for thirty years; by the time it ceased publication there were at least eighteen other songbooks in print using the same device (many times this, if one takes into account the numerous editions most of these books went through). In 1816, in an attempt to secure the protection that the short duration of copyrights in those days (fourteen years) failed to provide, the shape-note device was actually patented—hence the term "patent notes."

The Easy Instructor was first published in the urban East (Philadelphia). It was so readily adopted by the compilers of the traditional rural songbooks, however, that the shape-note notation soon became associated with this tradition altogether, and for reasons probably having largely to do with this association, was in disfavor in urban circles of more "advanced" or "scientific" religious music. Thomas Hastings (of *Rock of Ages* fame) dubbed the shape notation "dunce notes." So it was that this quaint but practical device for learning to sing the pitches quickly and accurately became so indelibly associated with the rural tradition, and particularly with the South, that its vast literature—for so long all but unknown to outsiders—has taken on the name "southern shape-note hymnody." [3]

Infusion of the Folk Element

Another important development as this rural hymnody moved into the Southwest at the beginning of the nineteenth century was a fresh infusion of the folk element into the tune collections. Folk or folkish tunes of Anglo-Celtic cast, given sacred words and spare, austere harmonic settings, were found in the new books, alongside the established hymn tunes, anthems, and fuging tunes. This had actually already begun in New England. Jeremiah Ingalls, for example, in his *Christian Harmony* (Vermont, 1805), put sacred words to what was plainly a rollicking dance tune from the fiddlers' repertory.

George Pullen Jackson, who has done more than anyone else to bring this music to light, has said of Ingalls's contribution: "The conviction is unavoidable, after singing these romping tunes, that Ingalls was a musical daredevil. It is evident that he was the first in this land to dare put between the covers of a book those capering songs which others had had the courage merely to sing." [4]

The "borrowing" of folk tunes to supply the needs of sacred music—"plundering the carnal lover"—is a venerable practice, of course. The great body of Lutheran chorale tunes, for example, contains its share of melodies that began life as folk or popular tunes, in some cases love songs. [5]

An influential publication in which many folk hymns, as these came to be called, made their first appearance was John Wyeth's *Repository of Sacred Music, Part II*, published in Harrisburg, Pennsylvania, in 1813. It was evidently produced to satisfy the demand and taste of the people, mostly Methodists and Baptists, who sang these folk hymns and who took part in the revivalism that was so memorable a feature of rural, and frontier, life in America at this time. Issuing from a town that lay in the path of southwestward migration, it was remarkably successful, since it was said to have sold 25,000 copies.

One tune that was designated as "new" in this collection was *Rockingham*, which was reprinted in several later books. The following version, from *The Southern Harmony*, is interesting because of the compiler's attempt to approximate in notation, through the use of eighth notes and grace notes, the manner in which this tune was probably actually sung in oral tradition.

The procession of these books that followed in the next decades has already been alluded to. Nearly forty tune-books, some in several editions, were published before the Civil War, using the four-shape notation and including folk hymns. Of these, the two most influential were *The Southern Harmony* (1835), compiled by William ("Singin' Billy") Walker, of Spartanburg, South Carolina, and *The Sacred Harp* (1844), by Benjamin Franklin White and E. J. King, of Hamilton, Georgia. *The Sacred Harp*, which has gone through many editions and revisions, has outlasted all the others and been in continuous use for a century and a quarter.

A folk-like melody of unknown origin variously known as *Harmony Grove, New Britain, Redemption, Symphony,* or *Solon* appeared in shape-note hymnody at least as early as 1831 in *The Virginia Harmony*, with a text beginning:

There is a land of pure delight
Where saints immortal reign.

It became far better known with the text that was later associated with it, which has given it the name by which we know it—*Amazing Grace.*[6]

A - maz-ing grace! (how sweet the sound) That saved a_ wretch like me!   I_ once was lost, but now am found, Was blind, but now I see. *(Original a 4th higher)*

In certain cases the secular counterpart of a folk hymn can be identified. This modal tune still carried the name *Captain Kidd* when it was first printed in William Walker's *Southern Harmony* in 1835:

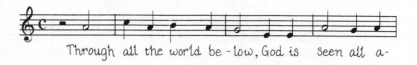

Through all the world be-low, God is   seen all a-

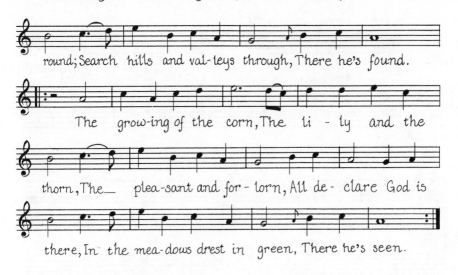

round; Search hills and val-leys through, There he's found.

The grow-ing of the corn, The li - ly and the

thorn, The— plea-sant and for - lorn, All de - clare God is

there, In the mea-dows drest in green, There he's seen.

The tune was originally associated with a broadside ballad composed on the occasion of the hanging of Captain Kidd for piracy in London in 1701. The first of at least nine verses runs as follows:

My name was Robert Kidd,
As I sailed, as I sailed,
My name was Robert Kidd,
As I sailed,
My name was Robert Kidd
And God's laws I did forbid,
And much wickedness I did,
As I sailed, as I sailed,
And much wickedness I did,
As I sailed.

Another aspect of the folkishness of these hymns as they appeared in the old tune-books was the harmonic setting, which abounds in the austere open consonances (octaves, fifths, fourths). The voice leading often yokes two or more voices together in parallel movement at these intervals—a practice scrupulously avoided in academically "correct" harmony. The spare openness of the harmonic texture, as much as the modality of the tunes, contributes to the distinctiveness of this music, which must be actually *heard* to establish any basis for its understanding. This style is nowhere better illustrated than in the three-voice setting of the famous folk hymn *Wondrous Love*, as found in *The Southern Harmony*.[7]

The fact is that this music is in some ways unlike any other music in existence in the nineteenth century. Isolated to a considerable degree from the main stream of cultivated music, it was almost as though the "primitive" musical craftsmen who harmonized the folk hymns were called upon to solve anew the problems of polyphonic music. The unique style that resulted from their solution resembles in some rather striking ways the church music of medieval Europe, with its primal reliance on the open consonances, the parallelism of its organum (a kind of pre-counterpoint), and its basically polyphonic conception of musical texture as the simultaneous sounding of individual sung lines, rather than a succession of chords. It is also interesting to note that some American composers in the 1930s and 1940s, such as Aaron Copland and Virgil Thomson, writing at a time when America had begun to find its own voice, were tending to adopt similarly lean textures and sounds.

Revivalism and the Camp Meeting

The successive waves of revivalism that have swept America since 1800 have had a decided impact on our native religious music. In the period of the expanding frontier before the Civil War this was most pronounced, for it was on the frontier that revivalism nurtured its most striking manifestation: the camp meeting. The camp meeting in turn nurtured, for its needs, one of our most distinctive forms of religious music: the revival spiritual. In order to understand the origin, nature, and function of the revival spiritual, it will be useful for a moment to turn our attention to the camp meeting itself, and see how it evolved and functioned, and something of what it meant in the lives of the sincere believers who attended.

The colonial South was far from being a religious society. The fundamentalist faith that later became so ingrained there was established as a result of two factors. One was the hardship of what amounted to a frontier existence throughout the antebellum South for the "plain-folk" who comprised the bulk of the population—white subsistence farmers, mostly, who were continually forced to move and take up less arable land as the large slave-run plantations spread into the fertile lowlands. This kind of existence bred a need for the reassuring and consoling ministrations that could be supplied by an evangelical religion—a religion which held out the promise in the hereafter of all the good that was so elusive and pitifully transient in the here-and-now. The other factor was the unremitting effort of the three most popular denominations after the Revolution: the Presbyterians, the Baptists, and the Methodists (the latter most especially, with their organized hierarchy and their corps of indefatigable circuit-riding preachers). These two factors set the stage for the Great Revival of the early nineteenth century.

At its beginning it was called the Kentucky Revival, for that state was its fertile seedbed. Of all the newly opened territories west of the Appalachians, Kentucky was the first to attract settlers, and to act as a kind of staging area for those who were eventually to move on. By 1800 it was a "boom" state, having a greater population (over 200,000) than all the other states and territories outside the original thirteen colonies combined. It was about this time that revivalism in its most sensational form came to this raw frontier state.

The early camp meetings of the Kentucky revival were huge, chaotic, turbulent affairs. Many traveled for days to get there. The famous camp meeting of August 1801 at Cane Ridge, in the gently rolling country of Bourbon County, northeast of Lexington, lasted six days, and estimates of the number in attendance ran between ten and twenty-five thousand. The preaching, praying, shouting, and singing went on day and night.

According to one of the many eyewitness accounts:

> The noise was like the roar of Niagara. The vast sea of human beings seemed to be agitated as if by a storm. I counted seven ministers, all preaching at one time, some on stumps, others in wagons, and one . . . was standing on a tree which had, in falling, lodged against . . . another. Some of the people were singing, others praying, some crying for mercy in the most piteous accents, while others were shouting most vociferously. . . . A strange supernatural power seemed to pervade the entire mass of mind there collected. . . . Soon after I left and went into the woods, and there I strove to rally and man up my courage.
>
> After some time I returned to the scene of excitement, the waves of which, if possible, had risen still higher. The same awfulness of feeling came over me. I stepped up on to a log, where I could have a better view of the surging sea of humanity. The scene that presented itself to my mind was indescribable. At one time I saw at least five hundred swept down in a moment as if a battery of a thousand guns had been opened upon them, and then immediately followed shrieks and shouts that rent the heavens.[8]

There was many a strange and disquieting sight to be viewed on the American frontier, and none more so at times than the camp meeting. But Cane Ridge represented the extreme. Subsequently the camp meetings, particularly under the Methodists, whose specialty they became, were much more carefully planned and organized—the more so precisely on account of the excesses and debaucheries that stigmatized the earlier and more spontaneous ones. In spite of their undenied excesses, their emphasis on emotionalism, and the dubious significance of many of the "conversions," most careful observers now conclude that the positive influence of the camp meetings outweighed the negative. As Charles Johnson has summed it up: "Among all of the weapons forged by the West in its struggle against lawlessness and immorality, few were more successful than the frontier camp meeting. This socioreligious institution helped tame backwoods America." [9]

What began as the Kentucky Revival became the Great Revival, spreading through Tennessee, the Carolinas, and Georgia like wildfire. The first conflagration had pretty well subsided by 1805. But the camp meeting had become by this time a regular institution of religion in the South. After the Great Revival of 1800–1805 a subsequent wave appeared, beginning in the 1830s, which has been called the Millennial Excitement. This millennialism was accompanied by all the same phenomena that characterized the Great Revival: large camp meetings, conversions in great numbers, and all the manifestations of religious hysteria. The old spirituals needed very little adapting to express in very explicit terms that time was running out in which to seek salvation. After the 1840s, the excitement subsided. Revivalism has nevertheless, in urbanized form, been periodically active right down to our own time. By the time of the Civil War, however, the heyday of the outdoor camp meeting, for a variety of reasons, was over.

The Revival Spiritual

Singing was a vital part of revivalism from the beginning—an effective opener to set the mood for an exhortation, an outlet for the emotionalism of the occasion, and a communal act into which one could pour all one's energies in fellowship with other believers. These have always been the functions of popular religious song. Another account of Cane Ridge tells of the powerful impulse of song: "The volume of song burst all bounds of guidance and control, and broke again and again from the throats of the people." Still another eyewitness reported that at the camp meetings the "falling down of multitudes, and their crying out . . . happened under the singing of Watts's Psalms and Hymns, more frequently than under the preaching of the word." [10] All agree that the singing was loud. "The immediate din was tremendous; at a hundred yards it was beautiful; at a distance of a half a mile it was magnificent." [11]

What was sung at the camp meetings? Since it was for so long a matter of purely oral tradition, evidence must be pieced together. The reference above to "Watts's Psalms and Hymns" refers to the words; certain hymns, and bits and pieces of hymns, of eighteenth-century English divines were much used. Tunes themselves were not written down and published before the 1840s, though pocket-sized "songsters" with just the words began to appear about 1805. There were several reasons why camp-meeting singing continued as an essentially oral tradition: Anything in print was scarce on the frontier; few could have read the music and many would not have been able even to read the words; in any case, many must have known at least portions of the tunes and words; probably the crowds often sang only the refrains or the choruses, which would have been easy to learn on the spot; and finally, the degree of participation, physical as well as emotional, would have made it not only inconvenient but actually impossible to try to read songs out of a book at a spirited revival meeting.

From later collections that recorded what must have been current in oral tradition for some time, we can get a pretty good idea of the camp-meeting repertory. Given the requirements of revival song, we know what the hallmarks of the true revival spiritual were. The tunes had to be lively and easily learned. There was an almost unvarying reliance on the verse-chorus form; everyone could at least join in on the choruses, even if the verses were not known, or if the leader introduced unfamiliar ones or even made them up on the spot. A further development along the line of what has been called "text simplification," for the sake of mass participation, was the single-line refrain, interpolated after a couplet of original text or even after every line. With the crowds joining in on the refrains, this turned the singing into the familiar call-and-response pattern. Indoor church hymns could thus be transformed into revival spirituals by this process.

It is interesting to observe this at work in the case of one of the most popular hymn texts of the time. The original hymn by the English clergyman Samuel Stennett (1727–1795) describes in Blakean imagery and language the beauties of heaven: "Canaan." The first of many verses runs:

On Jordan's stormy banks I stand,
And cast a wishful eye,
To Canaan's fair and happy land,
Where my possessions lie.
O, the transporting rapturous scene,
That rises to my sight!
Sweet fields array'd in living green,
And rivers of delight.

In the following version, as a revival song, only one couplet at a time is used, with a typical chorus added, spelling out in more homely language of action and urgency the conviction that the believer is actually *going* to the promised land so poetically described. The result is a spirited and popular revival spiritual that was first printed in William Walker's *Southern Harmony* in 1835.

On Jor-dan's storm-y banks I stand And cast a wish-ful eye, To _ Ca-naan's fair and hap-py land Where my pos-ses-sions lie. I am bound for the prom-is'd land,_____ I'm bound for the prom-is'd land; Oh, ___ who will come and go with me, I am bound for the promis'd land.

(Original a major 3rd higher.)

A further stage in the "revivalizing" of this hymn is illustrated in the following version, in which a one-line refrain is interpolated after every line of the text. Both the words and music of the refrain then become the basis for an added chorus. The whole appears in *The Revivalist* of 1868, set to a folkish tune that has acquired a decidedly Irish lilt.

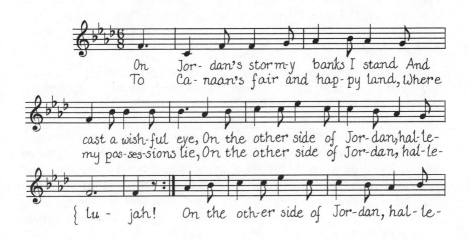

On Jor-dan's storm-y banks I stand And
To Ca-naan's fair and hap-py land, Where
cast a wish-ful eye, On the other side of Jor-dan, hal-le-
my pos-ses-sions lie, On the other side of Jor-dan, hal-le-
{ lu - jah! On the oth-er side of Jor-dan, hal-le-

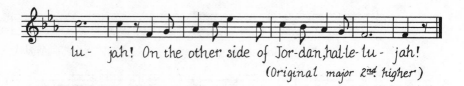

lu- jah! On the other side of Jor-dan, hal-le-lu- jah!

(Original major 2nd higher)

George Pullen Jackson says of songs in this familiar pattern: "It is safe to guess that the basic text was sung by one person or a few, while everybody came in on the refrain and chorus." Speaking further of the basic text, usually composed of rhymed couplets, he points out how these couplets became detached and took to "wandering"—turning up in various songs when and as needed. The same was true of entire "wandering choruses." [12]

Repetition was carried even further through the use of a form in which the mere substitution of a single word would suffice to make a new stanza.

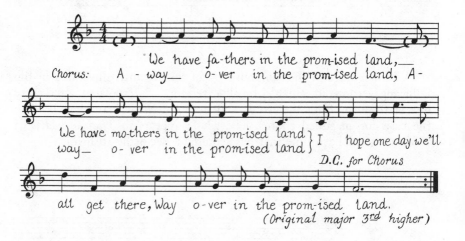

We have fa-thers in the prom-ised land,___

Chorus: A - way___ o-ver in the prom-ised land, A-

We have mo-thers in the prom-ised land ⎤ I hope one day we'll
way___ o-ver in the prom-ised land ⎦
                                      D.C. for Chorus

all get there, Way o-ver in the prom-ised land.

(Original major 3rd higher)

This spiritual was probably (according to Jackson) sung with "fathers" only in the first verse, then "mothers" in a second. Further multiplication of verses was easy, using "brothers," "sisters," "friends," "neighbors," and so on. The pattern has survived in many children's songs.

The revival spirituals (the complete name was "revival spiritual songs," a name that traces its lineage all the way back to Isaac Watts's *Hymns and Spiritual Songs* of 1709) were also distinguished by the style and content of their texts. These emphasized the basic themes of the prevailing theology—especially salvation, its attendant joys, and the glories of a heaven that was far removed from the present life. The examples already cited have been replete with the expressions that pervade the spirituals:

"promised land," "Canaan," "the other side of Jordan." Along with the descriptions of heaven and its joys is a dissatisfaction with this present life that is so pronounced as to amount at times to rejection of the world, and if not actually a wish for death, at least a poignant anticipation of the joys and release from pain it would bring to the righteous saints who had been converted:

Our bondage it shall end, by and by, by and by.

I am a stranger here below.

This world is not my home.

How blest the righteous when he dies!
How gently heaves the expiring breast
How mildly beams the closing eyes
When sinks a weary soul to rest.

Sweet home! Oh, when shall I get there.

Parallel Traditions: White and Black Spirituals

The black spiritual has been treated extensively in a previous chapter on Negro folk music. That parallel traditions of these "spiritual songs" existed among blacks and whites is incontrovertible, as has been documented, for example, by George Pullen Jackson, who included in his *White and Negro Spirituals* a comparative list of 116 tunes from both. There is also considerable evidence that white rural hymnody—the folk hymns and especially the revival spirituals—furnished a great deal of raw material, at least, for the black spirituals. John Lovell, Jr., black author of an exhaustive work on the Negro spiritual, has written: "There is hardly any doubt that the Afro-American songmaker borrowed from the hymns he heard, and from the Biblical stories he picked up."

The instructive point to consider here is that the main opportunities for this transmission occurred not in the large slave-holding areas of the South, and not through the master-slave relationship, but precisely in those regions and under those conditions that nurtured the folk hymn and the revival spiritual among the whites—in the uplands and on the frontier, among the plain-folk and at the camp meeting. They would later on have reached the "black belt" of the lowland and tidewater South. The frontier, not hospitable to barriers of race or caste, represented perhaps the most democratic region in America in the nineteenth century.

The camp meeting, a frontier institution, was the site of as uninhibited a meeting of blacks and whites as could probably be encountered in that time. Many of the early camp-meeting preachers, such as Lorenzo Dow and Peter Cartwright, preached against slavery, and were in fact among our earliest abolitionists.

An example of the parallelism of the black and white traditions was cited on pages 40–41: the famous *Go Down, Moses* paired with its white counterpart. Another striking parallel is that of the well-known Negro spiritual *Roll, Jordan, Roll* and a white revival spiritual whose basic text is a famous hymn by Charles Wesley. They are shown below (the white spiritual first).[13]

THE CITY

The opening decades of the nineteenth century, as we have noted, witnessed the beginnings of a growing cultural cleavage between the city and the country. In cities such as Boston the products of our native school of church composers were progressively cast aside by those dedicated to the improvement, as they saw it, of church music, who naturally turned to Europe for "rules" as to what was correct, and for tunes. The Boston Handel and Haydn Society was in the forefront of this movement, and its collection of church music, published first in 1822, was something of a landmark. It still had the shape and something of the look of the "long boys" that continued to flourish in the country; the tunes were still buried in the tenor voice; and there was the time-honored pedagogical preface, even incorporating the fa-sol-la-mi syllables. But the content was new. Gone were the fuging tunes, and there was not a single piece by Billings, Ingalls, Swan, and their ilk.| Instead, there were European hymn tunes, as well as adapted tunes by Handel, Mozart, Haydn, and Beethoven, complete with European *figured bass* (a shorthand device for indicating the harmony, of convenience to the organists who now nearly invariably accompanied choral and congregational singing in those churches wealthy enough to afford organs). Gone were all vestiges of the old modal scales of folk music, and the minor mode itself, a favorite of the folk, was nearly banished; most tunes were in major, and harmonized with European correctness. To use the terms found in the preface to this collection, the "gentlemen of taste and science in this country" went "to the fountains of Music in Europe" for refreshment, and material with which to further their "purpose of improving the style of Church Music" and insuring "increasing refinement in the public taste." Thus began the growth in this country of a progressively greater cultural schism, not only between city and country, but between "highbrow" and "lowbrow." It was an inevitable development. Our age of artistic innocence was over.

The compiler of *The Boston Handel and Haydn Society Collection of Church Music*, whose "taste and science . . . well fitted him for the employment," was none other than Lowell Mason, whom we shall discuss more fully later on. He was at the time just under thirty. Throughout the next fifty years he was to dominate American urban church music with his phenomenal industry—as composer, adapter, and arranger of hymn tunes; as publisher of numerous collections of sacred music; as choral director; and as educator.

Nineteenth-century America's capacity to consume published collections of sacred music seems phenomenal for the time. Mason himself published more than twenty; his *Carmina Sacra* sold half a million copies. And he was far from working alone. We have already mentioned Thomas Hastings, who was so scornful of the shape notes—he composed six hundred hymns and more than a thousand hymn tunes, and published fifty volumes of music. William Bradbury published more than fifty collections, one of which sold over a quarter of a million copies. Of course sales of this volume netted sizeable profits. Mason, who earned between $10,000 and $30,000 on his first compilation alone, is said to have made as much as $100,000 on a single volume later—a rather stark contrast to Billings, who, even with the help of his tanner's trade and several municipal posts, could not avert a virtual pauper's death.

The Urbanization of Popular Hymnody: Gospel Music

Religious music was no exception to the inexorable divergence between "highbrow" and "lowbrow" in American tastes after 1800. There was also, by midcentury, a pronounced "layering" of denominations in social and economic terms. For the worship services of the urban churches that had a pronounced liturgical bent, coupled with a substantial tradition and an intellectual, even esthetic, dimension to their appeal (Episcopal, Lutheran, Presbyterian to some degree, as well as Roman Catholic) there continued to develop a hymnody along the lines Lowell Mason had established— cultivated and eclectic, selecting and adapting from a wide range of traditions. The examination of any recent hymn-book of these denominations (such as *The Hymnal of the Protestant Episcopal Church in the United States, 1940*) will illustrate this. Here medieval plainsong, Lutheran chorales, Calvinist psalm tunes, and tunes from the classical and twentieth-century composers rub shoulders with American folk hymns such as *Kedron*, from the tradition discussed earlier in this chapter.

On the other hand, after 1800 the broadly popular evangelical denominations and sects continued to demand a popular type of song, particularly for special occasions such as revival meetings, which incorporated many features of the old camp-meeting spiritual.

WHITE GOSPEL SONG

Hymn tunes have been called by Stevenson "pre-eminently the food of the common man." We have just seen that there was, in the nineteenth century, a seemingly insatiable hunger for this food. In the period following the American Revolution, the demand for popular hymnody was met by drawing upon the wealth of folk music in the possession of the rural people, and creating thereby the folk hymn. After the Civil War, folk music, no longer a very vital part of the lives of a now much larger and increasingly citified mass of people, could not be drawn upon to satisfy this demand, which had become enormous. Instead, it was met by large numbers of hymn writers and composers, for the most part innocent of formal training, who maintained a prodigious output of what have come to be known as gospel hymns and songs. The outpouring of these became especially large after the revivalism of Dwight Moody and Ira Sankey swept the country beginning in 1875. In this year Sankey published, with P. P. Bliss, a volume called *Gospel Hymns*. This was followed by five sequels, culminating in *Gospel Hymns Nos. 1 to 6 Complete* in 1895, a compendium of more than seven hundred hymns and songs that typify the genre. As comprehensive as such a collection might seem, it represents only a fraction of the ephemera produced.[14]

Under these conditions of demand and production, mediocrity and a high degree of conventionality were inevitable. With extremely rare exceptions, all the tunes are now in the major mode, and are harmonized with the three most basic chords, embellished occasionally with some chromaticism in the style that has since become known as "barbershop harmony." The form is nearly always that of verse and chorus. The chorus is a feature that shows not only a direct lineage from the earlier revival spiritual, but also relates the music to the commercial secular songs of Tin Pan Alley. This chorus often embodies a sort of polyphony even more rudimental than that of the old fuging tunes; it imparts a similar "kick" to the second part of the hymn, and illustrates the perennial delight that the most naive manifestations of counterpoint have for the musically innocent. The following chorus from a hymn with music by the renowned Ira Sankey himself illustrates this feature.[15]

there_____ { And with Je-sus I long to be there .

to be there

As the example shows, the music was usually written on two staves in four-part harmony. The tune was now on top, in the soprano. This made it more prominent for congregational singing. The four-part harmonizations were also eminently convenient for the mixed solo quartet of soprano, alto, tenor, and bass (often paid professionals) that was such a popular feature in the churches from the Civil War on.

The words, as might be expected, show the same preoccupation with the central theme of salvation as did those of the revival spiritual, though there is less of the gloomy dwelling upon death, and, with the increased cheerfulness, a great deal more sentimentality. The relation of many of these gospel songs to country music is an intimate one, and is explored further in chapter 7.

Despite the ephemeral nature of most of this gospel music, a few survivals, of enormous popularity and some distinction, have found their way into modern hymn collections. What is more important, they have become woven into America's musical consciousness, as Charles Ives shows us when he quotes them so liberally in his works, and as other more recent composers like Virgil Thomson have demonstrated in their treatment and transformation of them. Perhaps a brief litany of nearly forgotten composers, with an even dozen of their hymn-tunes, will serve to recall for us this heritage that an English writer has characterized as "at best . . . honestly flamboyant and redolent of the buoyancy of the civilization that created New York and Pittsburgh and Chicago." [16] These composers and tunes are: P. P. Bliss, *Hold the Fort* ("for I am coming") and *Let the Lower Lights Be Burning;* William B. Bradbury, *Sweet Hour of Prayer* and *He Leadeth Me* and *Just As I Am;* Robert Lowry, *Beautiful River* ("Shall we gather at the river?") and *Where Is My Boy To-night?* and *I Need Thee Every Hour;* Charles C. Converse, *What a Friend We Have in Jesus;* George A. Minor, *Bringing in the Sheaves;* Simeon P. Marsh, *Jesus, Lover of My Soul;* J. R. Sweney, *Beulah Land.*

BLACK GOSPEL SONG

The term "gospel" today is largely associated with the popular sacred music of the blacks. Just as the white gospel hymns replaced the earlier folk hymns, so among black Americans a parallel tradition of gospel song gradually replaced the antebellum spirituals. Eileen Southern has written:

> The spiritual was born in the rural setting of the camp meeting, where thousands assembled under the stars amid the blaze of campfires and torch lights to listen to itinerant preachers. The gospel song evolved in urban settings, in huge temporary tents erected for revival meetings by touring evangelists, in football stadiums, and in mammoth tabernacles. The gospel song-makers borrowed the melodies and musical forms of popular songs— i.e., Tin Pan Alley materials—as their antecedents had borrowed folksongs and popular songs a half-century earlier. . . . Negro gospel music became essentially the sacred counterpart of the city blues, sung in the same improvisatory tradition with piano, guitar, or instrumental-ensemble accompaniment.[17]

This urbanization of black popular hymnody had begun as early as the turn of the century, notably with the work of C. A. Tindley, of Philadelphia. (A chorus of one of his songs, with the words "I'll overcome, I'll overcome, I'll overcome some day," was transformed a generation later into the well-known *We Shall Overcome*.) But it was not until the 1920s that gospel songs (previously known as "evangelistic songs") began to take hold as a popular form, and to be recorded. This was just the time when the blues also were undergoing a similar urbanization, and were becoming commercially successful.

Significantly, the one man responsible more than any other for the propagation of gospel music, Thomas A. Dorsey, was a blues pianist. As "Georgia Tom" he had played and recorded blues with such early singers as Ma Rainey and Tampa Red. He was first drawn to gospel music in 1921, while continuing to play and record the blues, but from 1932 on he devoted himself wholly to the latter's "sacred counterpart." It was in this year that he wrote his most famous song, *Precious Lord*.[18] Dorsey proved to be an indefatigable promoter, organizer, and manager, as well as composer, of gospel music. He published his own compositions, and went from church to church in Chicago, and later from city to city, with singers such as Sallie Martin and later Mahalia Jackson, performing and plugging gospel music. Dorsey published his songs, not in book collections, as had been the case with popular sacred music up to this time, but rather, in the manner of Tin Pan Alley, as sheet music. He and Sallie Martin founded the Gospel Singers Convention. Eventually, due largely to Dorsey's activity and influence, the solo gospel singer came into the limelight, alongside the earlier vocal ensemble. Just as most of the urban blues singers of the time were women, so were the gospel singers. Among the most prominent were Sallie Martin, Roberta Martin, Sister Rosetta Tharpe, Willie Mae Ford Smith, and Mahalia Jackson.

Negro gospel music had in the beginning the same folk hymn–revival spiritual heritage to draw upon as had the urbanized gospel songs of the whites. This is still apparent in some corresponding survivals: *Amazing*

Grace, for example, is as popular a traditional old hymn with blacks as with whites. But whereas the distinction in the nineteenth century between the white and black spiritual was largely one of differing modes of performance, with twentieth-century gospel music the divergence is more profound. Black gospel music was from the start much more influenced by its instrumental accompaniment, which gave it a "rhythm section" and a beat equivalent to that of the jazz or the rhythm-and-blues combo.

Nearly everywhere that we may look for the roots of blues we find the roots of gospel music as well. Street-singing evangelists, with a guitar and sometimes a tambourine, were there when the blues singers were on the streets.[19] Many black churches were hospitable to a mixture of the elements of jazz, blues, and gospel. This was especially true of the Sanctified (or Holiness) Church, a rather widespread Pentacostal sect among both blacks and whites, sometimes known as the Church of God in Christ, or by the blunter and somewhat disparaging nickname Holy Rollers. (*When the Saints Go Marching In* was originally a Sanctified shout.) The use of instruments such as the trumpet and the trombone in these churches had in effect introduced a counterpart of jazz into black worship services, probably early in the twentieth century.[20] Thus the introduction, later, of what might be thought of as a "secular" style was nothing new—any more than the rather contrived introduction of jazz into worship services in the sixties was new. Indeed, as we have already noted, the black people have never, by and large, felt the necessity of making a sharp distinction in musical style between sacred and secular.

Yet while black gospel music, especially in its vocal style and delivery, is indeed a counterpart of the secular blues, it must be noted that its singers, and the faithful among their followers, have insisted upon a firm line being drawn between the two on moral grounds. Committed gospel singers do not sing blues. Exceptions are rare, and the crossing of the line amounts to a serious transgression, if not to a betrayal.

In Conclusion: Popular Religious Music Today

Gospel music, both black and white, has become in our time an extremely successful popular music in itself. *Billboard* magazine, the leading trade journal of the popular music industry, began including extensive coverage of "The World of Religious Music" in 1965. As with any other commercially popular genre, the label "gospel" has come to be applied to an increasingly wide variety of performers and products, and to a kind of music that changes styles rapidly, in order to respond to popular taste and parallel the latest developments in other fields of commercial pop music.

The liturgically and esthetically oriented middle- and upper-class churches will continue to attract the services of enough talented and highly competent composers to keep things alive there artistically; the market is not large enough in any case to invite a degradation of standards through commercialism. But in the case of popular religious music, it would appear that its life as we have known it for three hundred years—a period of exuberance, of vitality, and of spontaneous self-renewal—may be over. It has become too big a business now. As in all other areas of popular art, the growth of a mammoth industry, with mass production and promotional methods, has wrought profound changes. Except for very isolated rural areas and deliberate enterprises aimed at conservation and revival (as in present-day performances of shape-note hymnody, for example), it is hard not to conclude that a tradition of indigenous religious music genuinely "of the people" is dormant, if not dead. Where its new breath of life is to come from, if there is to be one, is not now apparent.

FURTHER READING

Facsimile Editions of the Music

WYETH, JOHN. *Wyeth's Repository of Sacred Music, Part Second.* 2nd ed. Harrisburg, Pa., 1820. Reprint, New York: Da Capo Press, 1964.
> The first shape-note publication to include folk hymns. This reprint edition has an excellent introduction by Irving Lowens.

MASON, LOWELL. *The Boston Handel and Haydn Society Collection of Church Music.* Boston, 1822. Reprint, New York: Da Capo Press, 1973.
> A landmark of the "better music" movement, this interesting book retains the form and appearance of the older books, but contains very little American music, and was the harbinger of a flood of later popular urban collections.

* WALKER, WILLIAM. *The Southern Harmony.* Philadelphia, 1854. Reprint, Los Angeles: Promusicamericana, 1966.
> The revised edition of this important shape-note publication, which appeared first in 1835.

WHITE, B. F., and KING, E. J. *The Sacred Harp.* 3rd ed. Philadelphia, 1860. Reprint, Nashville: Broadman Press, 1968.
> This reprint of another very important shape-note publication includes George Pullen Jackson's essay "The Story of the Sacred Harp 1844–1944."

SANKEY, IRA, et al. *Gospel Hymns Nos. 1 to 6 Complete.* New York, 1895. Reprint, New York: Da Capo Press, 1972.

* Items thus marked are part of the suggested reference library to be available in connection with this book.

A large and very representative collection of late nineteenth century gospel hymns.

Anthologies

* MARROCCO, W. THOMAS, and GLEASON, HAROLD. *Music in America.* New York: W. W. Norton & Co., 1964.

This basic anthology contains a small but fairly representative selection of shape-note music transcribed, with good notes. It has nothing past the Civil War.

The George Pullen Jackson Legacy

Important enough to be in a category by themselves are these five volumes by the most eminent authority in the field of shape-note hymnody and American popular hymnody in general. Together they contain over 900 tunes. They are listed in chronological order.

* JACKSON, GEORGE PULLEN. *White Spirituals in the Southern Uplands.* Chapel Hill, N.C., 1933. Paperback reprint, New York: Dover Publications, 1965.

The basic history of the shape-note movement, and its background. It includes the seven-shape branch. It also includes a listing, with initial-phrase quotations, of the 80 most popular tunes in the tradition.

* ———. *Spiritual Folk-Songs of Early America.* New York, 1937. Paperback reprint, New York: Dover Publications, 1964.

This important collection has 250 complete tunes and texts, with sources and notes, and an extensive introduction. It is the basic annotated compendium of tunes and texts in the shape-note tradition.

——— . *Down-East Spirituals and Others.* New York: J. J. Augustin, 1939. 2nd ed. 1953.

A supplement to *Spiritual Folk-Songs,* presenting additional material which could not be included in the earlier publication, with some new material from the Northeast (hence the title). There are 300 complete tunes and texts.

——— . *White and Negro Spirituals: Their Life Span and Kinship.* New York, 1944. Reprint, New York: Da Capo Press, 1975.

This study further explores popular religious hymnody, including that of revivalist and millennial sects, and the relation of the black to the white spirituals. The core of it is a comparative tune list of 116 white and black spirituals, printed side by side. Some of the conclusions have aroused controversy, but the scholarship is sound and perceptive, and in itself virtually beyond dispute.

——— . *Another Sheaf of White Spirituals.* Jacksonville: University of Florida, 1952.

Another supplement to *Spiritual Folk-Songs* and *Down-East Spirituals;*

contains another 363 tunes. A foreword by Charles Seeger, and the introduction by the author (including a unique map), are valuable.

Studies

* CHASE, GILBERT. *America's Music.* 2nd rev. ed. New York: McGraw-Hill Book Co., 1966. Chapters 8, 10, 11.

FOOTE, HENRY WILDER. *Three Centuries of American Hymnody.* Hamden, Conn.: Shoe String Press, 1940. Reprint, 1961. Chapters 6, 7, 8.

HEILBUT, TONY. *The Gospel Sound.* New York: Simon & Schuster, 1971.
The area of black gospel music is ripe for competent study. In that regard, this book is disappointing in the extreme. The field awaits a genuine study, in the manner of what George Pullen Jackson did for nineteenth-century rural hymnody, or what Bill Malone did for country music.

* LOWENS, IRVING. *Music and Musicians in Early America.* New York: W. W. Norton & Co., 1964.
This collection of essays contains a detailed study of *Wyeth's Repository of Sacred Music, Part II*.

* STEVENSON, ROBERT. *Protestant Church Music in America.* New York: W. W. Norton & Co., 1966. Paperback reprint, 1970.
In this brief but well-documented study, chapters 8 and 10 are relevant.

The following works treat music only incidentally, but give valuable background on the camp meeting, and revivalism in general.

BOLES, JOHN B. *The Great Revival, 1787–1805.* Lexington, Ky.: University Press of Kentucky, 1972.

BRUCE, DICKSON D., JR. *And They All Sang Hallelujah.* Knoxville, Tenn.: University of Tennessee Press, 1974.

GOODSPEED, REV. E. J. *A Full History of the Wonderful Career of Moody and Sankey in Great Britain and America.* New York, 1876. Reprint, New York: AMS Press, 1973.

JOHNSON, CHARLES A. *The Frontier Camp Meeting.* Dallas: Southern Methodist University Press, 1955.

WEISBERGER, BERNARD A. *They Gathered at the River: The Story of the Great Revivalists and Their Impact upon Religion in America.* Boston: Little, Brown & Co., 1958.

LISTENING

Shape-Note Hymnody

* *White Spirituals from "The Sacred Harp,"* from the *Recorded Anthology of American Music* (RAAM). RAAM: NW-205.
24 folk hymns, anthems, and fuging tunes as sung by the Alabama

Sacred Harp Convention in 1959. It is to date the best recording by traditional singers available; the fidelity is excellent, the singing is spirited, and the remarks and prayers included help to convey the feeling these singers have for the music, and for these annual "sings."

* *Sacred Harp Singing*, from the *Library of Congress Archive of American Folk Song* (AAFS). AAFS: L-11.

This 1942 recording of the same Convention includes 19 pieces, only some of which are the same. Though technically inferior to the later recording, it is also a fine documentary.

Old Harp Singing. Folkways: 2356.

Made by the Old Harp Singers of eastern Tennessee, who evidently belong to the seven-syllable tradition. The singing is less spirited than that on the record above.

Gospel Music

Except for modern commercially recorded and issued gospel music, which is legion, the evolution of gospel hymns and songs through the last hundred years, if traced through recorded sound, has to be pieced together from various sources, a band or two from here and there. Ten basic source collections, either field recordings or reissues of old commercial recordings, are:

1. *An Introduction to Gospel Song*, ed. Samuel Charters (black tradition only). Folkways: RF-5.
2. *Country Gospel Song*, ed. Samuel Charters (both black and white tradition). Folkways: RBF-19.
* 3. *Anthology of American Folk Music*, vol. 2, *Social Music*. Folkways: 2952.
* 4. *Negro Religious Songs and Services*. AAFS: L-10.
5. *Negro Blues and Hollers*. AAFS: L-59.
6. *The Asch Recordings*, vol. 1, ed. Samuel Charters. Folkways: AA-1/2.
* 7. *Folk Song Types*. RAAM: NW-245.
* 8. *The Gospel Ship*. RAAM: NW-294.
9. *Where Home Is*. RAAM: NW-251.
10. *Brighten the Corner Where You Are: Black and White Urban Hymnody*. RAAM: NW-224.

WHITE GOSPEL MUSIC

In its early recorded state, this may be sampled by the following. Numbers in parentheses refer to the collections above.

ERNEST PHIPPS and his HOLINESS SINGERS (ca. 1930): *I Know That Jesus Set Me Free; Went Up in the Clouds of Heaven* (2); *Shine on Me* (3, band no. 54); *If the Light Has Gone Out in Your Soul* (7).

ALFRED G. KARNES: *To the Work*, (found in Sankey Gospel Hymns as no. 576) (2).

CARTER FAMILY: *Little Moses* (3, band no. 53); *Lonesome Valley, The Little Black Train* (2).

Since nearly all country singers, from Uncle Dave Macon down to the present, include some religious songs in their repertory, the tradition has merged almost inseparably with that of country music. See chapter 7 for an extensive treatment of this music.

BLACK GOSPEL MUSIC (EVOLUTIONARY OR FOLK PHASE)

Traditional Spirituals with Instrumental Accompaniment
Do, Lord, Remember Me, vocal duet with banjo, 1936 (4).
> This spiritual is found in Work, *American Negro Songs and Spirituals*, p. 82. See reading list, chapter 2.

I'm Gonna Lift Up a Standard for my King, congregation in Sanctified Church, 1941 (5).
> This spiritual is found in Grissom, *The Negro Sings a New Heaven*, p. 30. See reading list, chapter 2.

The Vocal Quartet
Roll, Jordan, Roll, Fisk University Jubilee Quartet, ca. 1913 (1).
I've Been 'buked and I've Been Scorned; Most Done Travelling, Tuskegee Institute Singers, ca. 1917 (1).
Moses Smote the Water, the Thrasher Wonders, n.d. (6).

Street Evangelists
Precious Lord (by Thomas A. Dorsey); You've Got to Move, the Gospel Keys, vocal duet with guitar and tambourine, n.d. (6).

Pronounced Male Blues Singer Correspondence
BLIND WILLIE JOHNSON, solo singer with guitar (2, 3); also *Blind Willie Johnson 1927–1930*, Folkways: RBF-10.
Ain't No Grave Can Hold My Body Down, Bozie Sturdevant, 1942 (4).
When Mother's Gone (traditional song), the Spirit of Memphis, ca. 1954 (1). "Soul" singing, with wordless chorus, trombone, and bass drum.

Pronounced Female Blues Singer Correspondence
SISTER ERNESTINE WASHINGTON: Does Jesus Care? and Where Could I Go but to the Lord (6), Did I Wonder (1), ca. 1946. Solo singer with jazz band.
MAHALIA JACKSON: When I Wake Up in Glory; I Will Move On Up a Little Higher, solo singer with piano and organ. Columbia: 644.

Music in the Sanctified Churches/Jazz Correspondence
I'm a Soldier in the Army of the Lord; I'm Gonna Lift Up a Standard for My King (5); I'm in the Battlefield for My Lord (3, band no. 56); I Looked Down the Line and I Wondered; Jesus the Lord is a Saviour (1).

Rhythm-and-Blues Correspondence
I Got Two Wings, Rev. Utah Smith and congregation, with electric guitar, 1951 (1).
He's a Friend of Mine, the Spirit of Memphis, solo singer with chorus, piano, organ, bass, drums, ca. 1954 (1).

A FEW CURRENT COMMERCIAL BLACK GOSPEL RECORDINGS

Mahalia Jackson: Greatest Hits. Columbia: CS-8804.
Sallie Martin. Savoy: S-14242.
The Best of Dorothy Love Coates. Specialty: S-2134E.
James Cleveland Presents the Sounds of Gospel. Savoy: 14336.
The Angelic Gospel Singers. Nashboro: 7047-E.
The Ward Singers. Buena Vista: S-3318.
The Mighty, Mighty Clouds of Joy. Peacock: 136.

PROJECTS

1. If you like to sing folk songs, learn two folk hymns from one of the nineteenth-century shape-note collections, and add them to your repertory. (The tenor, or next to the bottom line, has the tune.) Look up the tunes in Jackson, *Spiritual Folk-Songs of Early America*, and put together a brief commentary on the songs.
2. Try to find three folk hymns from the shape-note tradition that are included in present-day hymnals. As in project (1) above, find out what you can about the tunes and put together a brief commentary.
3. Try to find three revival spirituals in present-day hymnals. As in (1) and (2) above, find out what you can about the tunes and put together a brief commentary.
4. Find out what you can about the present state of shape-note singing (sometimes called Sacred Harp singing, or Old Harp singing) in this country, especially in your area. If there are regular meetings, or "sings," attend one and write a descriptive commentary. (More and more groups are being formed, in different parts of the country. They can often be located through the evangelical churches.) If there is no activity in your area, find out about sings and singing societies elsewhere, especially in the South. (The Knoxville Old Harp Singers is a typical group.)
5. Make a brief biographical study of at least four of the nineteenth-century shape-note singing book compilers, giving what data you can find and a listing of their books.
6. Write a commentary on the theology implicit in the texts of either the revival spirituals or the later gospel hymns.

7. Write a brief paper comparing the camp meetings of the Kentucky Revival with the large outdoor rock festivals of the 1960s.
8. Investigate the relationship between the revival spirituals and some types of children's songs sung at summer camps and elsewhere. Look for relationships of form and of tune, and even for parodies of the words.
9. See if you can discover counterparts in black gospel music of some of the white gospel hymns of the nineteenth-century. Note any differences or transformations they may have undergone.
10. Make a study of the Holiness Church (Church of God in Christ, Sanctified Church) and its musical practices.
11. Make a study of the works of the "pre-gospel" gospel writer Dr. C. A. (or C. H.) Tindley.
12. In the suggestions for listening are given two examples of traditional black spirituals performed with instrumental accompaniment, as a palpable link with gospel music. See if you can find other such links, and write a commentary on the relationship between the spirituals and gospel music, and on the survivals of the one to be found in the other.
13. Make a study of the hymn *Amazing Grace:* its sources, its history, and an annotated discography of performances in both the white and the black tradition.

Part Three

Three Prodigious Offspring of the Rural South

The rural American South, in its isolation and its conservatism, fathered, like a patriarchal Abraham, two musical offspring, reared in private within its confines and long unknown outside. Like Isaac and the outcast Ishmael, son of the bondwoman, white country music and the blues of the Negro are these two offspring—half-brothers, unlike in significant ways, yet sharing a patrimony and a native soil. As the prophecy runs, both have become in our time mighty musical nations with half a century of commercial success behind them. And their seed, so long segregated, have joined to form the basis for a third prodigious, electrified, urbanized offspring: rock.

How did the South come to produce its Isaac and its Ishmael? What were the antecedents, musically and culturally? Are there certain enduring characteristics of both? These questions we will attempt to explore, and we will trace the two musics as they emerged from the privacy of folklore into the bright public arena of popular tradition. For both assuredly come straight out of folk origins—so directly, in fact, that they are still considered folk music by some. Hardly better examples exist of forms of popular music whose characteristics so clearly derive from their cultural ambience than those furnished by country music and the blues.

And what of this ambience? The South, spelled with a capital S, seems to call up in the mind of most Americans more than simply a geographical area (that roughly coextensive with the states of the old Confederacy). If it is the land, it is also the people, the culture, the climate; further than this, it is a history, a lore, a habit of thinking, an aura, almost a mythology. It is not surprising that the South has constituted the largest and richest single reservoir of folklore we have.

Why should this be? Two key words have already been mentioned: isolation and conservatism. The isolation has been not only geographic (of the lowlands as well as the highlands) but also demographic—an isolation of the southern people, largely, from the greater mass of the American people. For once the frontier had passed through and moved on west, there was emigration from the South but little significant immigration to the South. And the conservatism, of course, owed a good deal to this isolation, but also to the almost exclusively agrarian economy; to the hierarchical (if not actually aristocratic) social and political structure; to the defensive attitude assumed almost monolithically by the southern whites towards the institution of slavery and its equally problematic sequel, white supremacy; and last but by no means least, to the prevailing orthodox religious modes of thought. Out of this soil, then, sprang the two most pervasive forms of rural music America has ever produced (or is ever likely to produce, so profoundly have cultural patterns altered), and as a second generation, a citified but visceral amalgamation that has revolutionized popular music throughout the English-speaking world. In the next chapters we shall take a closer look at each of them in turn.

Chapter Seven
Country Music

THE LATENT POPULARITY OF COUNTRY, or "hillbilly," music,[1] fully revealed only after it had spread beyond its original geographical limits in the 1930s and 1940s, was one of the surprises of the century, at least to those who were generally supposed to be wise in such matters—that is, city-bred entrepreneurs and savants of popular culture. Its base of popularity was found not only in the rural South, and as might be expected, among its people who had emigrated to the cities and to other parts of the country, but also among rural white people elsewhere who had no cultural ties with the South at all. We are dealing, then, with the closest thing to a universal "people's music" that rural white Americans have had.[2]

ENDURING CHARACTERISTICS OF THE MUSIC

Despite evolution and change, which have been as forcefully at work in country music as in any other, certain enduring characteristics have been consistently identified with it. The choice of instruments, the style of singing, the melody, and the harmony are all distinctive.

181

The Instruments

Country music, in the main, is music played on stringed instruments which, for good reason, are easily portable. (Rarely homemade, they were readily obtainable in the early days from mail-order firms.) The dominant instrument in country music is unquestionably the *fiddle*. As the only string instrument capable of producing a sustained tone, as played with the bow, it takes the lead, not only in the fiddle tunes intended for dancing (and it was long associated with dance music, both in America and in Europe) but in the long preludes and interludes in the songs and ballads. The straight, penetrating, vibrato-less tone and the sliding up into the longer held notes are characteristic, and are akin to the way in which the human voice, too, is handled.

All the rest of the stringed instruments are plucked or strummed. The *mountain dulcimer* and the *autoharp* belong more to the folk origins of this music, and did not survive long into country music itself. The *banjo*, however (possibly acquired in the lowlands, through contact with the blacks and minstrelsy), became an early mainstay of country music, where it established itself as being useful for solos, for accompanying songs, and for furnishing both harmony and rhythm in the small bands. In the second quarter of this century it was almost supplanted by the *guitar*, a somewhat more resonant instrument with a greater range, which took over the same functions. In the present era's revival of the older styles the banjo has come into its own again, and its pungent tone in the hands of virtuosos has remade it into a lead instrument, even rivaling the fiddle in importance. The *mandolin* entered country music in the 1930s, being at first associated with Bill Monroe and subsequently with the whole style known as "bluegrass." With its thin but penetrating tone, the mandolin for a time also competed with the banjo for the lead parts.

Country music has not been immune to outside influences, and new instruments have tended to bring with them their own peculiar styles of playing. Thus the mandolin, long associated with the popular music of Italy, has brought to country music the rapid *tremolando* sustaining of long notes characteristic of the Italian manner of playing.[3] Another exotic addition to the hillbilly band came from the other direction—in fact as far west as Hawaii, probably by way of the Hawaiian bands that were so popular in this country in the early decades of this century. The Hawaiian *steel guitar*, with its sliding, wailing sound, was appropriated by country musicians as far back as the 1920s and 1930s. (Similar sliding effects were obtained by many of the early Negro blues guitarists, stopping the strings with broken bottles, or knife blades.) A mechanically amplified version of it became known in country circles as the *Dobro*.[4]

The *string bass*, a much less portable instrument, came relatively late to country music, probably from the jazz band. Still later (and still less portable) additions have come with "rural electrification"; the steel guitar was the first to be electrically amplified, followed by the standard guitar and the string bass.

The Style of Singing

A characteristic manner of singing the songs and ballads has remained fairly constant throughout the years, and is in fact one of the features that has stamped country music indelibly. A direct carryover from the folk singing of the rural South, it is typified, in its more traditional phase, by a high, nasal, and somewhat strained tone.[5] The "lonesome," impassive manner of delivery (which gives an impression of the singer's detachment from the hearers, though not from the song) is suited to the impersonality of the ballad tradition. The clear, vibrato-less tone so akin to that of the country fiddle also lends itself to the kind of vocal ornamentation familiar in this music: the short slides and anticipatory flourishes heard in advance of the principal notes, especially in the slow tunes.[6] This is distinctly folk practice.

The high, tense, rigid vocal quality was later modified somewhat, particularly under southwestern influence. The tendency for the voice to "break," as if under the stress of the song's emotions, was introduced as a more subjective style crept into the music, and as the audience, seen or unseen, began to be more of a factor in the delivery of the song.

A familiar vocal feature, particularly in lowland and western styles, was the yodel. It became associated with cowboy music, but it was first recorded by a singer from Georgia,[7] and probably comes from a combination of influences: Negro field hollers and blues; Mexican song; and possibly (representing still another exotic influence on country music!) the yodeling of Swiss singers who toured the Midwest in the nineteenth century.[8] Jimmie Rodgers popularized the yodel, through his series of "blue yodels," around 1930; it is seldom heard today, except in specialty numbers deliberately evocative of some of the older railroad or cowboy songs.[9]

Essential to any consideration of vocal style is that utter sincerity of delivery without which country music is not genuine. This has been commented upon numerous times, by observers both within and outside the tradition. It is also a direct inheritance from folk origins. The impassive face, the often-closed eyes, the unashamed tear on the singer's cheek— these can be parodied and laughed at by sophisticates, but the sincerity and total immersion in the song and its subject of which they are only the visible manifestations is absolutely central to the meaning of country singing. Hank Williams expressed it vividly when asked about the success of country music:

> It can be explained in just one word: sincerity. When a hillbilly sings a crazy song, he feels crazy. When he sings, "I Laid My Mother Away," he sees her a-laying right there in the coffin. He sings more sincere than most entertainers because the hillbilly was raised rougher than most entertainers. You got to know a lot about hard work. You got to have smelt a lot of mule manure before you can sing like a hillbilly.[10]

Melody and Harmony

Richness of melodic and harmonic beauty is not to be found, by and large, in country music. There are reasons for this. We have seen in chapter 1 how much of the folk music of the ballad tradition that showed English and Scottish influence tended to preserve the old modal scales, with their attendant archaic-sounding melodic patterns. As country music sought to expand its public, and thus both to compete with and be influenced by urban popular music, the old quaint and often hauntingly beautiful modal tunes began to lose favor. They were still sung privately by singers brought up in the older tradition, but they were reluctant to record them, or sing them for "outsiders."[11] We have already investigated in chapter 1 the process by which the old tunes fell victims to the new practice of accompanying folk songs, chiefly on the guitar. Thus either the old tunes were greatly modified or else, most frequently, altogether new tunes were substituted—melodies that became inseparable from their accompaniment and therefore were tied to a harmonic framework of the utmost banality.

In the more traditional styles, such as old-time and bluegrass, there can still be heard, interestingly enough, occasional vestiges of the old modes. The most frequently encountered survivor is the Mixolydian mode, with its flatted seventh degree of the scale (as can be illustrated by playing in G major without benefit of an F sharp). This was one of the favorite modes of English folk music. Listen to *The Old Man and the Mill,* as sung by Clarence Ashley.[12] Here the ancient flatted seventh is harmonized in a way that paradoxically sounds quite modern. That it can sound that way to our ears is due to the fact that popular music has, in a way, come full circle; new expanded and more eclectic harmonic practices have found ways to embrace the old modal scales, so that they have now enjoyed a considerable revival in folk-oriented rock, and even in jazz. The same Mixolydian survival can be heard in a ballad made famous by the Carter Family, *John Hardy.*[13]

We cannot leave a consideration of the musical characteristics of country music without taking account of the influence of hillbilly music's half-brother, the Negro blues. There can be no doubt of the continuing musical exchange that went on between rural blacks and whites, especially in the lowlands. Many white country musicians, such as Dock Boggs and Jimmie Rodgers, learned much from Negro musicians in their formative years. Thus it was that musical characteristics of the blues went into the vocabulary of country music. The most evident influences were blues harmonies, and blues intonation; the variable, sliding pitch of the third degree of the scale, for example, was a vocal effect that could very well be imitated on the fiddle. These influences were of course most evident in the actual blues numbers, designated as such. From very early times, these blues were a part of country music.

ENDURING CHARACTERISTICS OF THE WORDS

The words of the songs and ballads, and their meaning for both performer and listener, are of paramount importance in country music, just as they are in folk music. They exhibit, furthermore, certain pervasive traits that have consistently characterized this genre through its half-century of change, and that may therefore be thought of as typical. Most significant are those having to do with fundamental attitudes and recurrent themes; less so, but nevertheless interesting, are characteristics such as the use of dialect and other regionalisms.

Fundamental Attitudes

Country music is steeped in a unique and somewhat paradoxical blend of realism and sentimentality. The realism reveals itself in a readiness to treat almost any human situation in song, and to deal unflinchingly with any aspect of life that genuinely touches the emotions. It shows up in extreme cases, for example, in the depicting of such grim scenes as the following:

> He went upstairs to make her hope
> And found her hanging on a rope.[14]

A later song, *Wreck on the Highway* updates this penchant for furnishing grisly details.[15] This unsparing realism (a characteristic of the ballad tradition) contrasts strikingly with the conventionalized subject matter and treatment of most urban commercial song before 1950, and identifies country music as a progenitor of the subsequent "revolution" in American popular music.

Paradoxically, the obverse of this realism is a nearly universal tendency towards sentimentality—a sentimentality that may often strike one outside the tradition as excessive, and even on occasion tinged with self-pity.[16]

Walking down this lonesome road,
I'll travel while I cry
If there's no letter in the mail,
I'll bid this world goodbye.[17]

The traditional song *I'm a Man of Constant Sorrow* is almost a prototype of this attitude, pushed to the verge of exaggeration:

I am a man of constant sorrow,
I've seen trouble all my days.
I bid farewell to old Kentucky,
The place where I was borned and raised.
. . . . . .
You can bury me in some deep valley
For many years where I may lay
Then you may learn to love another
While I am sleeping in my grave.[18]

The sentimentalizing of objects is common, especially in the "weepers" of the later, more commercial phase of country music, such as *Send Me the Pillow You Dream On*. The pathetic fallacy is frequently encountered: Objects in nature, or even inanimate artifacts, may be endowed with the capacity for human feelings and even the ability to manifest them visibly. The lyrics of Hank Williams's *I'm So Lonesome I Could Cry* are typical in this regard.

Perennial Themes

The subjects of country songs and ballads, while diverse, group themselves easily around certain perennial themes. One is love:

Tell me that you love me, Katy Cline.
Tell me that your love's as true as mine.[19]

Another is death:

There's a little black train a-coming
Fix all your business right;

> There's a little black train a-coming
> And it may be here tonight.[20]

Still another is religion:

> I am bound for that beautiful city
> My Lord has prepared for his own,
> Where all the redeemed of all ages
> Sing, "Glory!" around the white throne.[21]

And a fourth is nostalgia:

> There's a peaceful cottage there,
> A happy home so dear.
> My heart is longing for them day by day.[22]

Trains figure prominently in country music, as they do in blues.

> I'm riding on that New River train
> I'm riding on that New River train
> The same old train that brought me here
> Is going to carry me away.[23]

They were links with big cities and faraway places; they could put the overwhelming separation of distance between lovers, and they could overcome that separation. The railroad train, and the life of the rambler, were romanticized in rural thought. In recent times the truck and even the jet airplane have figured in country songs, but they have not seized the imagination with anything like the vivid intensity that the train has been able to evoke.

Songs about events were once an important part of country music, and any country singer worthy of the name could make up his own songs on important happenings of the day, local or national.

> Come all you fathers and mothers,
> And brothers, sisters too,
> I'll relate to you the history
> Of the Rowan County Crew.[24]

This trait shows clearly country music's relation to the earlier ballad tradition. And in fact a fine assortment of native ballads and near-ballads found their way into country music. Many songs and ballads collected by Cecil Sharp in the southern highlands in 1916–1918 appear in country music recordings of the 1920s and 1930s, often with the typical instrumental accompaniment of fiddle, banjo, and guitar.[25] *John Hardy*, already cited, was a ballad based presumably on an actual episode culminating in the execution of one John Hardy for murder in West Virginia in 1894. It was collected by Sharp in 1916, and subsequently recorded commercially by the influential Carter Family in 1930.[26]

The ballad tradition was kept alive in the event songs that continued to be written. With the coming of commercialism, it became vital to hit the market as soon after the event as possible. A song based on General Douglas MacArthur's speech before Congress, after President Harry Truman removed him from command in Korea, was written and recorded within hours of the event; while a song on the assassination of Senator Huey Long of Louisiana was written two years before his death—and even sung to him by its author.[27] The urbanization and sophistication of our time has virtually stopped the production of event songs, but songs such as *Whitehouse Blues* (on the assassination of President William McKinley) or *The Louisiana Earthquake* are still sung by those interested in the traditional country music.

Dialect and Other Regionalisms

The early country singers naturally retained not only their regional accent in their songs but their dialect as well, of which such usages as "a-going," "a-coming," "rise you up," and "yonders" may be given as samples. With the first wave of commercial success and the broadening of country music's public, there was a tendency (on the part of singers like Jimmie Rodgers, for example) to drop the dialect and substitute standard English. In more recent country music there are a few vernacular survivals, such as the well-nigh universal "ain't," and the dropping of the final g's of the *ing* suffix ("ramblin'," "cheatin'"), which have become virtual clichés. The loss of an authentic vernacular, together with the introduction of such devices as sophisticated rhymes ("infatuation," "sensation," "imagination"), has introduced an artificial conventionality to latter-day country music, which has already lost many of its distinctive regional characteristics in the general process of commercial homogenization.

A SURVEY OF THE MUSIC'S TIMES AND STYLES

We first encounter country music proper as it emerged from the folk tradition into the professional and commercial realm of the popular tradition in the 1920s. Within the folk culture, some professionalism had begun to develop even before the "discovery" of this music by the outside world. The fiddler and the itinerant entertainer were familiar figures. Just as traveling minstrel bands furnished an apprenticeship for many black musicians who later became jazz performers, so more than a few white country musicians got their professional starts as itinerant players and singers with the medicine shows that toured the rural South.[28] Thus there was no lack of performers, both singly and in groups, and ranging in ability from the mediocre to the highly proficient, who were on hand for the exposure that came in the twenties.

Commercial Beginnings: The Early Recordings and Radio

Although commercial phonograph recording was established before the turn of the century, its application to the genres of jazz, blues, and hillbilly music did not come for another two decades, principally because recording executives were either only dimly aware of their existence or were unsure as to whether a market for recordings existed. In view of later developments, this is somewhat ironic. When recording companies did move into the area of hillbilly music (camouflaging it at first under such names as "old-time music" or "old familiar tunes"),[29] they did so at least partly in response to growing competition from that other powerful new medium of the day, radio. Thus the roles of radio and phonograph recording in the dissemination and popularization of country music are elaborately intertwined, as we shall see.

The account of two old-time fiddlers—one from Texas, dressed in cowboy clothes, and the other from Virginia, dressed in a Confederate uniform—showing up in 1922 at the offices of the Victor Company in New York, fresh from a reunion of Civil War veterans in Virginia, to record their music, is one to give a pleasant stir to the imagination.[30] It was one beginning, and a rather inauspicious one. Another, more significant one was made the following year in Atlanta, when the Georgia moonshiner, circus barker, and political campaign performer Fiddlin' John Carson (who had recently become a locally popular radio performer) recorded *The Little Old Log Cabin in the Lane* and *The Old Hen Cackled and the Rooster's Going to Crow*. This recording proved to be phenomenally, and prophetically, successful—and the move to record hillbilly music was on. Recording companies made excursions into the South, set up temporary studios, and began recording country musicians by the score, either singly or in groups. In other cases the newfound artists were brought to New York to record. A few who were recorded in the twenties became famous—the stars of the ensuing period, such as Uncle Dave Macon, Jimmie Rodgers, and the Carter Family.

Radio broadcasting, until then an amateur's plaything, suddenly came of age in the 1920s. As receiving sets came within the economic reach of more and more Americans, broadcasting stations appeared and multiplied, and with them the demand for performers to cater to the new invisible audience. Some stations in the South began almost immediately to broadcast country music by local musicians, most notably WSB, Atlanta, in 1922. In 1925 WSM in Nashville began a show, with two unpaid performers and without a commercial sponsor, that was to evolve into the Grand Ole Opry. The early radio programs, like the early recordings, presented a highly traditional country music, still close to its folk origins.[31] But its very popularity generated winds of change.

Commercial Beginnings: The Age of the "Star" Singer

It is certainly not true that the radio and the phonograph record "created" country music. However, when a medium brings a particular genre into contact with a broader public, and transforms its performers into professionals whose success depends upon pleasing that larger public, changes are bound to be wrought. This was the situation in which country music found itself after its first wave of popularity and dissemination.

The work of country music's first real "star" embodied many of the changes that were to come. Jimmie Rodgers, the "Singing Brakeman" of Meridian, Mississippi, had an extremely short career as a performing and recording artist. But in a mere six years (from his first trial recording in 1927 to his death in 1933) he recorded 111 songs, sold 20 million records, became internationally famous, and led country music into greener pastures than it had ever dreamed existed.

Rodgers recorded many types of songs: sentimental love songs, melancholy nostalgic songs, cowboy and railroad songs, white blues. Many he wrote himself, many were written for him; he was able to put across a great variety of material, by the force of his sincerity and personality. His eclecticism was bound to lead him away somewhat from traditional country songs and traditional country style. He introduced the famous "blue yodel" into country music, and was really one of the first popular "crooners." With the advent of Jimmie Rodgers, the attention and emphasis in country music shifted to the solo singer.[32]

The appearance of its first real "star" marked the passage of country music into full-fledged commercialism. Yet it did not thereby cease to be a genuine "people's music," and some interesting interaction between the commercial country music of the thirties and what was held to be the "folk tradition" furnishes a valuable lesson in the difficulties of trying to define folk music at all after the advent of radio and recordings. For example, Polk Brockman, talent scout and entrepreneur who promoted the first recording by Fiddlin' John Carson, on hearing by radio of a tragic cave death in Kentucky in 1925, immediately commissioned a ballad on the subject by Rev. Andrew Jenkins, paying him $25 for it. The result, *The Death of Floyd Collins*, was recorded and put out by Columbia Records—and later discovered in oral tradition among the southern people and collected as authentic folk music. And folklorists, traveling through the South in the first wave of collecting on behalf of the Library of Congress and others, "discovered," collected, and catalogued songs that had been learned from the commercial recordings of Jimmie Rodgers!

The Western Image

America has long pursued a love affair with its own romantic conception of the West and the cowboy. The "western branch" of country music has played its part in the propagation of this romanticism. For just as the Southwest is in large degree a cultural extension of the South, so is "western" music an extension and adaptation of hillbilly music.

The link, of course, is Texas. Here the southern influence, especially in east Texas, is notably strong. The country was settled primarily by southern planters, and slavery and the raising of cotton flourished, along with southern religion, culture, and folklore. But Texas is also, as the song goes, "where the West begins." The dry and spacious topography, the open range and the raising and transporting of cattle to the new railroads, and ultimately the industrialization following the oil boom produced marked distinctions economically; while the influence of Mexican, Louisiana Cajun, and midwestern American culture distinguished Texas culturally from the old South.

Authentic cowboy and frontier songs existed, and it is some indication of the romantic interest in the West that they were among the first folk songs, after the Negro spirituals, to be collected and published in the United States, antedating even the attention given to southern mountain songs.[33] Early singers like Carl T. Sprague and Jules Verne Allen (who really *had* been cowboys) made important recordings of cowboy songs in the 1920s. And singers like Goebel Reeves and Harry McClintock (who really *had* experienced the life of the hobo) wrote and recorded hobo songs. But the "western" stamp was not fully impressed on country music until the advent and success of a singing star like Jimmie Rodgers. Rodgers, the "Singing Brakeman" from Mississippi, came ultimately to adopt the ten-gallon hat, Texas as his home state, and the image of the "singing cowboy." Others such as Gene Autry, Ernest Tubb, and Woodward Maurice "Tex" Ritter soon adopted and capitalized further on this image. Autry, Tubb, and Ritter were all authentic Texans, if not cowboys. Their background was the farm, rather than the range, but farm life has never been successfully romanticized in America.

Thus the western image and motif was established in country music. But paradoxically, few actual cowboy songs went into its repertoire. The country music entertainer adopted cowboy dress (often in fancy and exaggerated form) and continued to sing country songs. It was the production of cowboy films in Hollywood that spurred the writing of popular songs based on western themes, as opposed to authentic cowboy songs. Thus it was that songs like *Tumbling Tumble Weeds* and *Cool Water*, by Bob Nolan (a Canadian by birth), and *The Last Roundup*, by Billy Hill (who was born and grew up in Boston), became prototypes of the "western" song—and enormously popular.

A sub-genre of country music far more authentically representative of the real West of the twentieth century was "honky-tonk," whose milieu was the small-town, wide-open taverns and saloons. The open range, with its freely roaming cows and cowboys, was largely fenced and gone by 1900, but the oil boom-towns, and the lives and ways of oil workers and truck drivers, were real indeed. A special kind of country music evolved to fit this environment—frank and realistic in the country music tradition, but less concerned with religion and nostalgia, and more with loneliness and infidelity, and the new realities, equally harsh and bleak, of "western" life as it actually was for many. Honky-tonk used the piano (a basically urban instrument); it was bluesy, and it *had* to be loud to be heard at all. The use of amplified instruments really started, as a matter of necessity, with honky-tonk music. And much of the music reached its public second-hand, via that ubiquitous symbol of the music and its milieu, the jukebox.[34]

Movement and Change

By the time the western image had marked country music indelibly, the great upheavals and migrations that wrought such changes in American life in the second quarter of this century were underway. Their effect on country music was to spread it far beyond the provincial soil that had given it birth, and change it irrevocably in the process. The first migrations were poverty-driven, and were brought about by depression, mechanization, and drought. In the Deep South workers left farms for the cities, seeking, all too often in vain, to improve their lot by working in the textile mills. In the Southwest the labor-saving tractor and a few disastrously dry years in bleak and marginal farm country combined with the economic depression to set in motion the vast, epic movement of peoples from Texas, Oklahoma, Arkansas, and Kansas to the "promised land"—to green, fabled California, the last frontier that was no frontier, the last hope that was often hope tragically disappointed. However little these people were able to take with them in those forced and desperate migrations of the 1930s, they found solace in what they did *not* have to leave behind: their religion and their music. Thus country music and its people spread into the cities of the South, and into California. Los Angeles and the San Joaquin valley became second homes for hillbilly music. Scorned and despised by most Californians, it nevertheless, thus transplanted, began to take root and grow. The Beverly Hillbillies were there to stay.

The migrations of the next decade were the byproduct of war. Young men brought up on country music were inducted into the fighting forces and moved to other parts of the country, and to the theaters of war; others, who had never heard it, were moved into training camps in the South where they heard little else. Older men, women, families, moved to take advantage of work in defense plants. These migrations, marked by the fevered affluence of war, spread country music still further, setting the stage for the full-scale commercialization that was to follow. Country music was about to gain a whole world of commercial success, and all but lose its authentic soul in the process.

Full-Scale Commercialization: Nashville

On the eve of its coming of age as big business, country music had already undergone significant changes that had widened the gulf separating it from its folk origins. Most of its traditional repertoire had been abandoned in favor of newly composed songs; new instruments such as the Hawaiian guitar had changed the fundamental sound of the music; electric amplification had further and more drastically altered it; and a hybridization with swing-band jazz had introduced such essentially alien instruments as the piano, saxophones, brasses, and the jazz rhythm section, to produce a product known as "western swing."

A potent force in country music's adaptation to the popular taste of the young in the 1950s and 1960s was rock 'n' roll, which evolved out of a combination of country music and Negro rhythm-and-blues, largely for the newly affluent teen-age market. A fuller treatment of rock may be found in chapter 9; here it can simply be noted that the enormous popularity and commercial potential of this new form was not lost on the country music business. The hybrid "rockabilly" emerged; rock 'n' roll rhythms began to be used as background to country songs; many young rock-oriented country music "stars" appeared; and in general the boundaries between country music and the new "pop" music began to be less clear.

Since mid-century Nashville, Tennessee, has come to symbolize the full-scale commercialization of country music, and has become its business and recording capital; in the early sixties an estimated one-half of all records released in the United States were recorded in Nashville studios. This growth has coincided with a significant degree of crossing over of country music into the area of pop music in order to broaden its appeal. Sophisticated market research has come up with a description of country music's typical listener—and this listener is no longer "country," but urban or suburban, of the lower middle class. To provide music suitable for this new market, tremendous economic pressure has been brought to bear on recording artists to modify their music and make it more widely salable. "Country-pop" is the resultant product. The fiddles are gone, the electric guitar dominates the ensemble, with piano and drums added, and—a final touch of professional pop—a background chorus appears. This has become the "Nashville sound."

The Persistence and Revival of Traditional Styles

In the wake of full-scale commercialization has come a revival of interest in the older styles. Chiefly this has manifested itself in the upsurge of what has become known as "bluegrass" music. Bluegrass,[35] emerging in the late 1940s, is somewhat analogous to the "Dixieland" revival of early jazz styles that began in the same decade. It is music based on traditional styles and played on traditional instruments, but worked up to a high level of proficiency by very skilled performers. The basic instruments are the fiddle, the guitar, the mandolin, the string bass, and most importantly, the five-string banjo, as revived and played in a virtuoso manner based on traditional banjo styles. Earl Scruggs is the banjoist chiefly associated with this. Electrically amplified instruments are not used. Many old-time hillbilly songs and dances appear in bluegrass music, and although elements of commercialization and adaptation have not been lacking (as in so-called progressive bluegrass, for example), essentially it has maintained the authenticity and freshness of a traditional style as interpreted and improvised on by experts.

There have also been efforts to preserve and cultivate old-time music virtually intact—through the reissuance of old recordings; the recording anew of older surviving country musicians; and in the case of performers such as Mike Seeger and the New Lost City Ramblers, the deliberate re-creation, with studied accuracy, of old-time music by younger performers. (A parallel can be cited in the revival of traditional jazz styles by younger musicians.) This has taken place largely within the scope of the urban folk revival, and these recording projects, by Folkways, for instance, have been responsible for the availability of many of the examples of early country music cited in this chapter.

It has been said that real country music, like real folk music, is no more, because the outward conditions in which it evolved are no more. However this may be, the attitudes, inheritances, and social patterns of a rural life, of which country music is the expression, change or are discarded much more slowly. It seems likely, then, that the legacy of country music will furnish some ingredients for whatever people's music we have for some time to come. And it seems likely, too, that the appeal of, and the yearning for—if not the positive need for—a traditional music will keep the older styles green with cultivation.

FURTHER READING

CASH, WILBUR J. *The Mind of the South*. New York: Alfred A. Knopf, 1941.

GENTRY, LINNELL (ed.). *A History and Encyclopedia of Country, Western and Gospel Music*. 2nd ed. Nashville: Clairmont Corp., 1969.
> A useful work in two parts: an anthology of periodical articles from 1908 to 1968, and a large collection of short biographical entries of country musicians.

* MALONE, BILL C. *Country Music, U.S.A.* Austin, Tex., and London: University of Texas Press, for the American Folklore Society, 1968.
> This excellent study is the best comprehensive work available on the subject, and is highly recommended as a basis for any further investigation of country music.

* SEEGER, MIKE, and COHEN, JOHN (eds.). *The New Lost City Ramblers Song Book*. New York: Oak Publications, 1964.
> Primarily a songbook devoted to the older country songs as they were heard in the early recordings. The notes are highly informative, and the pictures add an interpretive depth to the subject. The book, published by a firm known primarily for its publications in the area of urban folk music, is valuable documentation of the early, folk-related phase of country music.

SHELTON, ROBERT. *The Country Music Story: A Picture History of Country and Western Music*. Indianapolis: Bobbs-Merrill Co., 1966.
> A book in popular style, profusely illustrated with photographs.
>
> Some of the books in the reading list for chapter 1 will prove useful, especially:

* LAWS, G. MALCOLM, JR. *Native American Balladry*.

* LOMAX, ALAN. *The Folk Songs of North America*.

* SHARP, CECIL. *English Folk-Songs from the Southern Appalachians*.

* Items thus marked are part of the suggested reference library to be available in connection with this book.

LISTENING

From the *Recorded Anthology of American Music* (RAAM)

* *Going Down the Valley: Vocal and Instrumental Styles in Folk Music from the South.* RAAM: NW-236.
* *Hills and Home: Thirty Years of Bluegrass.* RAAM: NW-225.
* *Country Music South and West.* RAAM: NW-287.
* *Country Music in the Modern Era: 1940s–1970s.* RAAM: NW-207.

Early Phases of Country Music

* *Anthology of American Folk Music.* Folkways: FA-2951, 2952, 2953.
    This three-volume, six-record set documents the earliest commercial stages of both country music and blues, through recordings made in the 1920s and 1930s. The album booklets accompanying this and other Folkways records noted here have, in most cases, the words and other important information.
* *Mountain Music of Kentucky.* Folkways: FA-2317.
    Uncle Dave Macon. Folkways: RF-51.
    Re-recordings from original masters by an important early "star" of country music.
    Tom [Clarence] *Ashley and Tex Isley.* Folkways: FA-2350.
* *Old-Time Music at Clarence Ashley's,* vols. 1 and 2, Folkways: FA-2355, 2359.
    Dock Boggs, vols. 1 and 2. Folkways: FA-2351, 2392.
* *Oldtime Country Music.* Folkways: FA-2325.
    Re-creations by Mike Seeger.
* *Mountain Music Bluegrass Style.* Folkways: FA-2318.
    Re-creations by younger musicians of important early bluegrass numbers.

Reissues by Commercial Record Companies

The Best of the Legendary Jimmie Rodgers. RCA Victor: LSP-3315 (e).
'Mid the Green Field of Virginia: The Carter Family. RCA: ANL-1-1107 (e).
Roy Acuff's Greatest Hits. Columbia: CS-1034.
24 of Hank Williams' Greatest Hits. MGM: SE-4755-2.
I Saw the Light, Hank Williams. MGM: SE-3331.
The Ernest Tubb Story. MCA: 2-4040.

The Best of Bob Wills. MCA: 2-4092.
Bill Monroe's Country Music Hall of Fame. MCA-140.
Flatt and Scruggs. Columbia: GP-30.

Useful Anthologies

Stars of the Grand Ole Opry, 1926–1974. RCA: CPL-2-0466.
Country Hits of the 40s. Capitol: ST-884.
Country Hits of the 50s. Capitol: ST-885.
Country Hits of the 60s. Capitol: ST-886.
The Very Best of Country Gold, vols. 1 and 2, United Artists: LA-412-E
and LA-413-E.

PROJECTS

1. Interview a number of people with varied backgrounds on the subject of country music, with a view to ascertaining the degree of correlation (if any) between a like or dislike of country music and a basically rural or urban background and orientation. It may be well to play some recorded examples as part of the interview. Include yourself as one respondent if you like.
2. Make a brief study of the blues in country music. See especially if you can find any actual Negro blues songs that have been taken over into white country music.
3. If you like to sing folk songs, learn two traditional country songs, either from records or from collections such as *The New Lost City Ramblers Song Book* or the *Anthology of American Folk Music* (both published by Oak Publications, New York) and add these songs to your repertoire. Find out as much as you can about the songs.
4. Investigate the state of country music in your own area to determine whether there are live performances of it by local groups, professional or amateur, and what styles are favored. If there is a sizable public for this music, try to determine something about its makeup. If possible, interview some local performers.
5. Find additional examples of country songs on subjects illustrating at least four of the "perennial themes" treated in this chapter. Transcribe the texts, with your own commentary.

Chapter Eight
Blues, from Country to City

IF COUNTRY MUSIC HAS BECOME A MIGHTY (and a wealthy) nation, the blues has prospered and increased mightily also, and the range of its influence on our music has been even broader. How was it that the South's Ishmael, offspring of the bondwoman, came to occupy such a prominent place in our musical vernacular? This is the object of our concern in this chapter.

The cultural ambience of the rural South that spawned both country music and the blues has already been alluded to in the previous chapter. And as we noted in chapter 2, in tracing the blues through its folk phase, it was a kind of music which, though belonging to a race that came to this continent in bondage, could not emerge until slavery itself was abolished. For the blues was neither a tribal nor a communal expression. It was (and is) the lament, the comment, often mocking or ironic, of the solitary individual, bereft of the support of tribe or close-knit society, facing *alone*, on personal terms, a hostile or indifferent world.

Yet long before our time the lament had become an entertainment, the solitary singer's comment had crystallized into a form that could be printed and sold, and the lone cry had become a commodity. It had become, in a word, popular music—even before the first recordings of it appeared.

But the legacy of its folk beginnings remained to characterize the blues indelibly: the way the voice is handled, the blues intonation, the range and treatment of its subjects, and above all, the basic blues feeling that has its roots in a solitary experience and life-view. Those who were to become its professionals and its stars had, like their white "hillbilly" counterparts, served their apprenticeship in the traveling tent shows and the minstrel and medicine shows, or in playing and singing for all-night parties and dances, or even (as many blind singers did) performing for passersby in front of country stores or on the streets of the cities.

EARLY PUBLISHED BLUES

It was inevitable that a type of music being sung and played in cities and small towns in the lowland South from the Piedmont to Texas should eventually find its way into print. This happened first in 1912, when by coincidence within a period of two months blues were published in St. Louis (*Baby Seals Blues*), Oklahoma City (*Dallas Blues*), and Memphis (*Memphis Blues*). The *Memphis Blues* had been widely played in that city for three years before its publication, by the enterprising composer-bandleader who was, more than any other early professional, to promote the blues as popular music and bring it to a wide public—William C. Handy. Handy's early experiences with the performance and publication of these compositions is interestingly set forth in his autobiography, *Father of the Blues*. In the beginning *Memphis Blues* netted him $50, the profits for years going to others. But Handy was to learn quickly. If the title "father of the blues" is something of an exaggeration (Bruce Cook has said that a more accurate one would be "rich uncle"), his place in blues history is still important, and his ties with its roots are perfectly genuine.

What was the blues like by the time it was being composed and arranged for broad popular consumption? For one thing, of course, the musical form had to be extended. It came to include at least two strains (in verse and chorus relationship), and sometimes three. The three-phrase, twelve-bar pattern with its usual harmonic plan (as outlined in chapter 2) was standard for at least one of the strains and was sometimes used for all of them, but there were also strains cast in the more European sixteen-bar form. These early published blues, as a matter of fact, showed a mixture of influences. The blues elements were often quite attenuated, and the music was sometimes pure ragtime, with its more elaborate European harmonies, as in the second strain of Handy's *Memphis Blues*. At times still other influences were evident; the best-known strain of the most famous blues of all, the *St. Louis Blues*, is actually, as Handy wrote it, a sixteen-bar tango! As he notes in his autobiography, the effect of this tango rhythm—the "Spanish tinge" of which Jelly Roll Morton spoke— on black dancers for whom he played was not lost on the observant Mr. Handy, and he used it again in his *Beale Street Blues* and *Aunt Hagar's Children*.

The relationship between the published blues and the blues as sung by a steadily growing number of professional blues singers is an interesting one, and difficult to unravel. While each had its own public and its own standards of what was admissible in terms of subject matter and language, there was undoubtedly some mutual exchange of musical and textual ideas. As a case in point, W. C. Handy wrote both the words and music of a song he copyrighted and published in 1915, *The Hesitating Blues*. The words are about a woman who stalls one suitor in the hope of marrying her absent, and hesitating, lover. The first verse sets forth the motif that runs through the song:

> Hello Central, what's the matter with this line?
> I want to talk to that High Brown of mine,
> Tell me how long will I have to wait?
> Please give me 298, why do you hesitate? [1]

In 1926 Gertrude "Ma" Rainey recorded *Sissy Blues*, which deals frankly with a homosexual theme, and runs in part:

> I dreamed last night I was far from harm,
> Woke up and found my man in a sissy's arms.
> Hello Central, it's bound to drive me wild,
> Can I get through, or will I have to wait a while? [2]

The music is essentially that of the first part of Handy's blues. Although the Rainey recording was made eleven years after Handy published his blues, it is not possible to say for certain who borrowed from whom, since Ma Rainey (and others) had been singing the blues professionally for years before they were recorded. Handy made a practice of noting down folk phrases he heard here and there ("Goin' where the Southern cross' the Dog"; "Ma man's got a heart like a rock cast in de sea") and incorporating them into his songs. The "Hello Central" motive, in common enough currency, could have been used in a folk blues that Handy heard—or it could well have been the other way around.

More important than the question of mutual borrowing is a comparison of the two pieces themselves, for they illustrate the divergence that had already occurred between the earthy blues of the tent shows (which were later to become so popular on recordings) and the blues as cultivated and polished specifically for general public consumption. The published blues of Handy and others are more developed in form and use more sophisticated harmonies. The rhymes are more exact and the lyrics facile, employing clever plays on words. But compared with the folk (and near-folk) blues, both words and music are apt to sound stilted and artificial. Though quoted perhaps somewhat unfairly out of context, an excerpt from the topical *Wall Street Blues* (published in 1929) illustrates the gulf that had already opened between the folk-derived blues and its commercial counterpart:

Never had the blues like the blues I'm blue with now,
Never had the blues like the blues I'm blue with now,
Oh, what I recall of the street called Wall and how!
Wailing Wall, Oh Jerusalem! There's one in New York too,
Where I got a whalin', now I'm ailin', Wailin' 'cause I'm blue.[3]

"CLASSIC" CITY BLUES

The blues as a more or less standardized form of popular music for a large public (mostly black, but with a growing constituency of whites) enjoyed what has been called its "classic" period from 1920, when the first recordings were made and sold, until the onset of the Depression in the early 1930s. It was a period of intense activity and popularity for the blues. Personal-appearance tours (mostly on vaudeville circuits) and nightclub appearances were a mainstay for the more popular blues singers, and there were some radio performances and even some films. But the principal medium for the propagation of the blues was the phonograph recording. Thousands of blues performances by dozens of singers were recorded, and millions of copies sold. There was a parallel development, of course, in instrumental jazz, in white hillbilly music (as we have seen), and in the rural blues (as we shall presently note).

The period of the classic city blues was dominated by the female blues singer. Various reasons have been advanced for this, but the most likely ones have to do with the nature of the show business of the time and the success of the women singers in the tent and vaudeville shows. Unlike the folk blues—which, as we have seen in chapter 2, encompassed a wide range of subjects—the classic blues were almost exclusively concerned with man-woman relations and written from the woman's point of view. The treatment of sexual themes ranged from the frank earthiness of much of Ma Rainey's material to the kind of slick and smirking double entendre heard in the sleazier vaudeville shows—a type of lyric exploited in both city and country blues by record companies eager to bolster sales in the early years of the Depression, when the amazingly prosperous era of the classic blues was waning.[4]

In view of the enormous popularity of blues recordings in the 1920s, it may seem strange that record companies were so skeptical at first about recording this music, but it was indeed regarded at the outset as a risky venture. The first singers recorded were not strictly blues singers at all, but professional entertainers with experience in cabaret and vaudeville singing in styles much like those of popular white singers. Mamie Smith made the famous first recording (*That Thing Called Love* and *You Can't Keep a Good Man Down*) in 1920. After its promising success she recorded the famous *Crazy Blues*, and the potential became unmistakable. Other professional black club and theater singers such as Lucille Hegamin and Edith Wilson recorded blues. The real blues singers in the southern tradition began to be recorded a few years later. Of these by far the best known and most influential were Ma Rainey and Bessie Smith, both of whom began recording blues in 1923.

Ma Rainey's early career, though only sketchily known, deserves some attention because of the light it sheds on the milieu in which the classic blues evolved. She was born Gertrude Pridgett in Columbus, Georgia, in 1886. Both her parents were in the minstrel-show business, and she herself was singing on the stage by the time she was fourteen. She acquired her familiar nickname "Ma" when, at age eighteen, she married William "Pa" Rainey, a minstrel performer, and they began touring with their song-and-dance routine. (She herself preferred to be called "Madame" Rainey.) Thus she had had more than twenty years of professional experience in the touring circus, variety, and minstrel shows by the time she made her first blues recording. Of all the classic blues singers she remained closest to the vernacular blues tradition. She never sang professionally outside the South, except to make recordings in New York and Chicago during a four-year period that ended in 1928. By then, a recording executive is said to have expressed the opinion that Ma's "down-home" material had gone out of fashion. During this brief period she recorded with some of the leading jazz musicians, including Louis Armstrong and Fletcher Henderson, but also made blues recordings with a jug, kazoo, washboard, and banjo band such as were traditional in the South. Significantly, her last recording, with just a banjo accompaniment, was a duet with Papa Charlie Jackson, who had been the first country blues singer to record.

By this time, blues form had become well standardized, and the conventional twelve-bar harmonic and structural mold was almost invariable.

As for the texts, Ma Rainey's material reflected to a certain extent the country-blues range of subject matter, and went beyond the perennial types of man-woman themes to touch on poverty, alcoholism, prostitution, topical references (*Titanic Man Blues*), and even, as already indicated, homosexuality. Contemporary accounts and pictures indicate that she was a stocky, somewhat ugly woman, imbued with what must have been an imposing stage presence indeed, and an uncanny degree of what can best be described by that much-abused term "charisma." In her surviving recordings what we hear, dimly transmitted through primitive recording techniques, is a voice and a kind of singing devoid of the slightest trace of artificiality.[5]

Bessie Smith, born in Chattanooga, Tennessee, and fourteen years younger than Ma Rainey, began her career as the latter's protégée, though she declined to acknowledge this in later years. She and Ma Rainey began recording about the same time, but Bessie Smith eventually became far better known, and was undoubtedly a more gifted and versatile singer. She became identified wholly with the sophisticated city-blues tradition, and her material was tailored largely for this market. She worked with the leading jazz musicians, and recorded with piano (with Fletcher Henderson, for example), with piano and one instrument (quite often with Joe Smith or Louis Armstrong playing muted blues cornet), with small jazz combo, and even with choral background, in some early "production" numbers. Her mastery of the idiom, and the forcefulness and directness of her delivery, are undisputed. But Bessie Smith, too, was out of fashion by the time she made her last recordings in 1933, and the dissipation and sad deterioration of her life toward the end were all too indicative of what could happen to the brightest popular stars propelled into fame and fortune by the phenomenal activity of the recording industry during the prosperous twenties.[6]

Other singers in the classic blues tradition included Ida Cox, Bertha "Chippie" Hill, Clara Smith, Sippie Wallace, and Victoria Spivey, all of whom performed with major jazz musicians of the 1920s and 1930s. It was the day of the woman blues singer, and while there have been eminent black female popular singers since (Ella Fitzgerald, Billie Holiday, Sarah Vaughn, Aretha Franklin), none after the classic period has been so exclusively identified with the blues. The role of dominance in blues singing has since passed largely to men.

BLUES AND JAZZ

Most of the great female blues singers performed with jazz musicians, as we have seen. The blues had evolved structurally in such a way as to demand the complementing role of an answering voice (or instrument) at the end of each sung line. This manifestation of call-and-response is, in fact, a distinguishing feature of genuine blues. The solitary blues singer filled in his own breaks on his guitar; in the city blues the piano, and later the collaborating instrumentalist, took up this function. Joe Smith and Louis Armstrong participated in many recordings with the classic blues singers in the 1920s. An interesting example of distinctive jazz breaks provided by a small combo can be heard in Ma Rainey's *Countin' the Blues*, in which each break in the three-line blues form is taken in turn by cornet, clarinet, and trombone.[7] These collaborations provide some of the finest moments in early jazz.

So closely identified was jazz with the city blues at this time that "blues" and "jazz" were taken by some to be one and the same. They are, of course, separate and distinct traditions; their parallel development is a rather complex history of periodically strong influence and identification. While the rural blues was slowly taking shape, something like its urban counterpart was having a hand in the early formation of jazz. There were bands in New Orleans (and possibly in Memphis and other cities as well) playing music by 1900 that was called "blues." None of it was published, so far as we know, and if any of it was written down it has not survived. Since this was nearly two decades before phonograph recordings of this kind of music were to be made, it is clear that we will never know what the blues played by these early bands sounded like. But the identification of blues with jazz remained exceptionally close through the classic blues period we have been examining. Then, in the 1930s, began a gradual divergence; the blues declined somewhat, and jazz itself evolved in other directions. While the blues as a harmonic and formal design can be heard in all ages of jazz, the blues references, as we advance through the so-called modern period, become increasingly attenuated. Recently, under the impact of the reenergized urban blues and the synthesis called "soul" music, jazz has been forcibly pulled back to a closer relation with its blues roots.

Three Examples

The form and feel of the blues has never been totally absent from jazz, and may be said to be in fact one of its vital ingredients. By the time the recorded history of jazz began, the blues had come to signify a well-recognized form, a harmonic matrix, and a melodic genre that gave special emphasis to the "blue" degrees of the scale. Within this well-recognized set of boundaries, jazz produced in the ensuing decades thousands of blues, all of them variations in some respect on the "given" premises. The following survey of just three contrasting examples will give a rudimentary idea, at least, of the way in which purely instrumental jazz continued to be involved at various periods with the blues:

1. *Dippermouth Blues* (1923).[8] In this early example you can hear the basic blues form and harmonic pattern used as a basis for variations. After the short introduction (four bars) there follow nine choruses of the basic twelve-bar blues pattern, following the usual harmonic path. There are some choruses in which the entire ensemble plays together, interspersed with choruses featuring solo instruments (clarinet, trombone, cornet). A two-bar "tag," or coda, ends the piece. This is a very clear and typical instrumental blues, in early traditional jazz style. Notice that the tempo, or speed of the beat, is not a reliable factor in defining the blues, which is not invariably slow.

2. *Ko-ko* (1940).[9] Here is instrumental blues on a very sophisticated level musically. The form is clear enough; after an eight-bar introduction there are seven choruses of regular twelve-bar blues, followed by a coda of the same length as one chorus. But the mode (minor instead of the more usual major) makes it somewhat more unusual, and the harmonies are much richer, subtler, and more complex than the ordinary blues chords.

3. *Parker's Mood* (1948).[10] This example, from a period of "modern" jazz characterized as having gotten away from the blues to a large extent, is an interesting and beautiful reinterpretation of it. It shows how the perennial forms that can be said to have become classic can be seen anew in each era through the temperaments of changing styles, and so become renewed. The small combo (alto saxophone, piano, bass, and drums) makes for the intimacy of expression of chamber music. There are just four choruses, with an introduction and short coda.

BOOGIE-WOOGIE

Boogie-woogie is a solo piano form, as is ragtime, but quite distinct from it in origin and style. Its progenitor and closest relative is the blues. Its sound is unforgettable—the driving left hand, with its hypnotically repeated pattern (the musical term for this, *ostinato*, is related to our word "obstinate"); the right often insisting equally obstinately on its own repeated figures; and, underlying all, the blues form and harmony. It was spawned as piano entertainment in bars, nightclubs, and houses of prostitution. Generically, boogie-woogie was probably an adaptation of what the blues singer-guitarists had been doing, with their intricate, ostinato-like accompaniments that had come to be known as "nigger pickin'." It is significant as further evidence of the close relationship with the blues that the early boogie-woogie soloists would often sing along, or talk to their audience, while they were playing.

Boogie-woogie, transferred out of the environment of its origins, went through a period of short but intense popularity in the late 1930s. This is apt to obscure the fact that it is a much older phenomenon. Jelly Roll Morton has said that many piano performers in his early days (shortly after the turn of the century) played in what must have been something like this style of piano blues with heavy ostinato-like left hand. W. C. Handy mentions adopting and orchestrating for his group a type of piano music played in the bordellos of the Mississippi delta region around the turn of the century. It was called "boogie-house music." In more recent times (from the 1950s on) the same concept can be heard in the heavier, or "hard" rock, beats that once again frequently underlie and underline the blues.

Boogie-woogie's resources are limited. Nevertheless, within those limitations a considerable amount of variety is found—variety of tempos (not all boogie is fast), of left-hand patterns, and of general feeling. The famous *Honky-Tonk Train* (1937) [11] can be considered a prototype. The right hand here is quite complex rhythmically, and shows some striking independence of the steady left. Many boogie-woogie numbers make similar allusions in their titles to railroad trains, and it is probable that some boogie has its origin in a programmatic imitation of the sounds of trains. The same thing had been done on the guitar, and the sounds would certainly have been familiar to both itinerant piano players and blues singers. Listen to *No. 29* (1929) as an interesting example of this. The work of Jimmy Yancey is especially noteworthy, in terms both of technical mastery and range of expression. Two final illustrations show contrasting aspects of boogie-woogie as played by Yancey: first, his hard-driving *Yancey Stomp*, and second, his *How Long Blues*, a marvel of rare and almost classical restraint.[12]

Before leaving boogie-woogie, it can be noted that it had a considerable influence on the big bands of the 1930s, especially in Kansas City, where the "jump" style was in many ways a translation of boogie idioms to the jazz band, just as the idioms of ragtime had been transferred to traditional jazz a generation earlier.

COUNTRY BLUES

The rural blues as a folk form has been examined in some detail in chapter 2, and its characteristics noted. It remains here to chronicle its emergence as "country blues"—largely through the medium of recordings—into the realm of a popular music, and the changes wrought in the process. Recordings of the city blues, which first appeared in 1920, were very successful, and as the business of selling records by mail grew it was realized that a large market existed among the black people of the rural South for recordings of their own country blues singers. (The market for white hillbilly music was discovered and began to be exploited about the same time; it was in 1923 that the first commercially successful recording of so-called old-time music, by Fiddlin' John Carson, was made in Atlanta.) It was 1924 before the first man who might be called a country blues singer made a recording. Papa Charlie Jackson was actually a minstrel and medicine show performer from New Orleans, and therefore more of a professional entertainer than a traditional country blues man—the parallel with Fiddlin' John Carson is interesting. Jackson recorded his *Lawdy Lawdy Blues* in Chicago, accompanying himself on his banjo-guitar, and in the promotional material accompanying its release more emphasis was placed on the fact that it was a man singing the blues (in competition with the women blues singers) than on its being rural blues. After an encouraging amount of commercial success, however, the search for country blues performers was on, and there soon followed recordings by singers from across the entire South, from Florida (Blind Blake) to Texas (Blind Lemon Jefferson). Although country blues singing was an almost exclusively male domain, the boundaries are never clear-cut, and there is a sense in which Ma Rainey, from Georgia, belongs here as well, since her background and singing owe almost as much to country as to city blues tradition.

For the earliest recordings, singers were brought to Chicago, where they worked in "studios" often primitive even by contemporary standards. But expeditions through the South with recording equipment were also undertaken, and new singers discovered. The collection and documentation of country blues recordings from this period, as with the rest of the "race" recordings (an informal trade name in the twenties and thirties for recordings by black musicians intended for black audiences), has been fraught with difficulties. The engineering and production of the records were for the most part as cheap as the promotional material was crass, and usually little attempt was made to preserve the masters. With notable exceptions the blues singers themselves were exploited while being treated with disdain.

Charles Keil has identified three fairly distinct country blues areas, with corresponding styles. While admittedly an oversimplification, his outline will serve well as a preliminary guide.[13]

The Mississippi delta region is the most famous blues area, and the most extensively documented in recordings, writings, and more recently, photographic essays as well. It is represented, in the early phase, by such singers as Charlie Patton, Willie Brown, Son House, and Robert Johnson, and later by Bukka White, Muddy Waters (McKinley Morganfield), and John Lee Hooker. The style is characterized by a chordal guitar technique that Keil describes as having a "heavy" texture, and that is very reminiscent of boogie-woogie styles on the piano. It is with the delta blues also that the bottleneck technique, with its sliding effects, is most often associated. The vocal delivery is apt to be impassioned, with phrases and utterances short, at times moaning, at times sliding in and out of falsetto, at times chanted without definite pitch, at times almost shouted, at times nearly inarticulate. This style, especially as cultivated by later delta blues singers, heavily influenced rock 'n' roll.

Texas has produced a significant number of country blues singers, including Blind Lemon Jefferson, Texas Alexander, Mance Lipscomb, and Lightnin' Hopkins. The blues of this region, as typified by the very influential Jefferson, who recorded between 1924 and 1930, are characterized by longer vocal lines, delivered in a more relaxed vocal style. The guitar style is more open and less chordal, with emphasis on melody playing on a single string during the breaks.

The eastern seaboard South and the southern highlands have produced some individually significant performers—Blind Blake, Blind Boy Fuller, Sonny Terry (Saunders Terrell)—but this part of the South is not rich in blues tradition nor does it have a particularly distinctive blues style. Fuller and Terry, both from North Carolina, worked as a team, and are probably the most important traditional blues men from this region. After Fuller's death, Terry and his new partner, Brownie McGhee, moved to New York for good, and have pursued successful professional careers.

Mention of McGhee and Terry brings us to what might be regarded as the final phase of the country blues: its absorption into the urban stream of popular music. This urbanization process was given some impetus, paradoxically enough, by a project designed to document and preserve important specimens of American folk music before they passed into oblivion—the archival recordings made for the Library of Congress in the 1930s and early 1940s. The project did indeed result in the recording of a large treasury of valuable folk material, as the references to it in this book have amply illustrated. But the interesting effect it had in addition was to help bring folk music, and the country blues in particular, to the attention of urban intellectuals at a crucial time—a time when the so-called urban folk movement, as we have seen in chapter 4, was just getting underway. Leadbelly of Louisiana, Muddy Waters of Mississippi, and Sonny Terry of North Carolina were among those recorded, all three of whom later became successful professionals. Leadbelly's story, including his release from the Angola prison farm in Louisiana,[14] at the behest of folklorist John Lomax, and his subsequent professional career, has been alluded to in chapter 4.

By the 1950s, the country blues had achieved significant popularity,

not only in the urban North but in Europe as well, where personal appearance tours were enormously successful. In addition to making recordings and touring, by 1960 country blues men had appeared in productions
on Broadway (*Cat on a Hot Tin Roof, Finian's Rainbow*). Folk festivals
such as the one at Newport, Rhode Island, have featured some of the
traditional country blues singers who have survived into the 1960s and
1970s, most of whose styles and accompaniments have, with greater or
lesser degrees of subtlety, adapted to the tastes and expectations of their
wider, and younger, audiences.

URBAN BLUES AND "SOUL" MUSIC

We have characterized the blues as an offspring of the rural South.
Paradoxically, there is nothing that epitomizes the harsher aspects of
urban life, especially for blacks, better than the urban blues. Unlike
white country music, the blues, except for the more or less self-conscious
revival or cultivation of older styles, has actually become urban music.
The heartwood of the blues is rural, but at the layer where it is adding
living tissue it is wholly of the city. Thus the blues, like the great mass
of the black populace whose music it is, has made the move from country
to city.

LeRoi Jones, in his *Blues People*, describes this phase in a perceptive
chapter titled "The Blues Continuum." This continuum bespeaks an ir-
reducible core of identity for the blues. The blues continuum (unlike
that of jazz, whose evolution has been at times very discontinuous) is less
easy to separate into movements. The thread of identity in this continuum
is, of course, the singer. Thus the singing of B. B. King, for example, has
far more in common with that of Blind Lemon Jefferson than does the
playing of Miles Davis, say, with that of King Oliver.

Blues *accompaniment* (here one could almost say "packaging") has,
of course, changed markedly with the times, and it is in this that the
blues has reflected the pressures for change which attend any form of
popular art. The guitar has remained in many cases as a kind of symbol
of continuity with its rural forebear, but the progression toward urban
blues and "soul" music has been one of increasing emphasis on instruments; there are more of them, and like the now-electrified guitar, they
are louder. This in turn has affected vocal style. The modern blues singer
has a microphone, of course, but the shouting style that southern Midwest
blues singers like Joe Turner and Jimmy Rushing had to adopt to be heard,
unamplified, over the big-band sounds of, say, Kansas City has remained
as a characteristic of much blues singing today. As LeRoi Jones has put it:

These Southwestern "shouters" and big blues bands had a large influence on Negro music everywhere. The shouter gave impetus to a kind of blues that developed around the cities in the late thirties called "rhythm and blues," which was largely huge rhythm units smashing away behind screaming blues singers.[15]

The symbolic distortion forced upon that most sensitive of all musical instruments, the human voice, by the stridency and abrasiveness of a stark urban milieu is summed up by Jones:

> Blues had always been a vocal music . . . but now the human voice itself had to struggle, to scream, to be heard.[16]

Although small instrumental ensembles (and occasionally large ones, in the theaters) accompanied the classic female blues singers, the real move toward modern urban blues was associated with blues men, and actually began, very probably, with the introduction of that quintessentially urban instrument, the piano, into the country blues ensemble. The combination of piano and guitar was used by the influential team of Leroy Carr and Scrapper Blackwell in the 1930s, and the piano almost invariably figured in Chicago blues recordings of the period. The style of piano playing, except for traces of ragtime, was, not surprisingly, essentially that of the blues-related boogie-woogie, with its heavy and incessant left-hand ostinatos so clearly presaging the main features of rock 'n' roll. Also significant was the addition of drums to many of the Chicago groups, showing the close relation to jazz. But this was a curiously transitional period in the citification of the blues; some of the recordings still included such down-home instruments as the harmonica and even the washboard. The blues, just before World War II, had one foot in the city and one still in the country.[17]

After the war the blues band began to take on some of its modern characteristics. The most significant development was its electrification. Aaron "T-bone" Walker, a Texas singer-guitarist who had moved to the West Coast, led the way with the electric guitar he had long used with his blues singing. Younger players quickly adopted it. Then came the electric bass, so well adapted to projecting with booming intensity the boogie-like bass patterns that could be produced on it with great facility. The electric organ was occasionally used, as was, ultimately, the electric piano. The dominant wind instrument was the saxophone. The wailing, honking, screaming saxophone, blown at full volume, had been the blues singer's alter ego since the days of the big Midwest blues bands, often taking a complete chorus after the singer had sufficiently established the mood. The saxophone was the instrumental counterpart in tone, inflection, and style to the blues singer's message, which itself had come to depend less upon words than upon conveyed emotion.

The electric guitar and bass as mainstay, a hard-driving drummer, a piano, and at least one saxophone—these were the main ingredients of the band backing the blues singer. If we add to this, in some cases, a small vocal ensemble of either men or women for the blues singer to "play" to, which gave the responses to his calls and echoed his key phrases, we have virtually complete the medium of the urban blues which, by the early 1950s, had been given the commercial designation "rhythm-and-blues."[18]

This rhythm-and-blues, especially as conventionalized by such entertainers as Chuck Berry and Bo Diddley, was still performed by black musicians for an almost exclusively black audience, reached either in person or via recordings—a market which rivaled that for the race recordings of city and country blues thirty years earlier. But it also unquestionably formed the basis for the subsequent rock 'n' roll music of the vast young white audience from the mid-fifties on. So closely, in fact, did early performers imitate Negro models that the early recordings of white performer Elvis Presley (who spent his adolescent years in the blues ambience of Memphis) sold primarily to black audiences. Rock 'n' roll itself, and subsequently the more eclectic popular music designated simply as rock, is dealt with in the next chapter.

The Potency of Negro Musical Styles in American Popular Music

The derivation, within the past generation, of rock music from a species of Negro urban blues is but the most recent confirmation of a salient and perennial fact of American musical life: Every vital new movement in our popular music has had its impetus from black musicians and black musical styles. The music of the minstrel show, ragtime, jazz, the blues in its many manifestations, including boogie-woogie, and finally rock—these are the really distinctive and important native developments in American popular music. Each began as an uninhibited and more or less coarse form of Negro music-making, cultivated in a milieu characterized as "lowbrow." Each in turn was resisted by the musical "establishment," and opposed by that segment of the populace with more cultivated tastes (both white and black), while being cultivated by "radicals" within that segment (largely of the middle and upper classes). Each, after commercially successful imitation by white musicians, eventually permeated and permanently changed our vernacular music.

This perennial revitalization of our popular music by Negro musical styles is not, at present, a source of unmixed satisfaction to black musicians. Though it confirms the dominant role of negroid musical traits and styles in American popular culture, the pattern of white imitation and appropriation of these successive musics is seen by some both as an exploitation of Negro music and an adoption, by the music industry and the populace generally, of its *manner* without its *substance*. Musical movements have appeared that have been, at least in part, both protests against the commercial appropriation of Negro styles and affirmations of black culture. Bop of the late forties was a kind of protest in the direction of increased complexity, virtuosity, and aloofness, while the raw, unrestrained emotionalism of the new black jazz of the sixties, and the earthy regressiveness of the so-called funky jazz of the same period (which had marked blues characteristics), were both attempts, in a sense, to redefine a black musical character and to differentiate it strongly from the increasingly homogenized "mainstream" of popular music.

The "Soul" Synthesis

A broader synthesis of Negro musical styles, and one embodying many elements of the blues, is embraced in the concept of "soul" music, which also has distinctly racial connotations that are broader than questions of musical style. It is for this reason difficult to define satisfactorily. Charles Keil writes: " 'Soul' may be partly defined as a mixture of ethnic essence, purity, sincerity, conviction, credibility, and just plain effort." He then proceeds to extensive documentation of the way in which those most caught up in the phenomenon express its essence.[19] The ethnic orientation of "soul" is clear; it began to evolve, as Keil points out, after the Supreme Court decision of 1954, one of the landmarks in a decade that saw the blacks' struggle take a definite turn towards strengthening racial and cultural *identity*, rather than achieving integration per se.

As a concept, soul embraces a wide spectrum of life's aspects, from religion to sexuality to food; indeed, it emphasizes a kind of synthesis of everything, and the communication and sharing of experience and strong emotion.

Musically, soul is a synthesis as well—of blues, jazz, and gospel. It is represented by the work of such performers as Otis Redding, James Brown, Ray Charles, Aretha Franklin, and Ike and Tina Turner. Its chief musical characteristics are a relentless ostinato, often with a prominent "back beat" (off-beat emphasis), and the use of a blues saxophone and a small vocal group to echo key phrases and sounds. Soul music is sometimes prone to use "camp" introductions.[20] Formally many of the pieces display a simple but effective buildup from a soft, underplayed beginning to a shouting, repetitive, near-hysterical catharsis, after which the intensity subsides.

As a commercial category the term "soul" has become so widespread that it bids fair to replace the older, narrower categories of "race" and "rhythm-and-blues" as applying generally to the work of any black singer who is accepted, and who sings with conviction and commitment for a primarily black audience.

Modern Blues Singers, and the State of the Blues

The category of soul musicians largely overlaps with, and includes, those singers of the 1960s and 1970s who might be most accurately described as present-day blues singers—those who have continued to cultivate the modern urban blues, largely for black audiences. B. B. King and Aretha Franklin are prototypes—singers of strong individuality who, although they use much non-blues material, still invest the blues, when they return to it, with conviction and a sense of authenticity.

Just what is the blues like today? The modern singers, especially the men, have large followings, both for their records and for their personal appearances, which (in common with the appearances of rock singers) take on the aspects of elaborately staged rituals in which the audience plays an important part.[21] The singing involves an exaggeratedly stylized vocal delivery, with melismatic shouting and moaning. The guitar, when used, is played with a technique heavily dependent upon electronic amplification and manipulation, and the whole is usually accompanied by a fairly large band with characteristics of both rock and jazz. It includes a prominent rhythm section of drums, electric bass, piano, and often electric piano and organ. There are usually a number of supporting "horns" (saxophones, trumpets, trombones). A fairly consistent feature is the vocal ensemble already referred to, for responses and echos. The more elaborate production numbers include strings as well.

Is the blues itself in a state of decline? This depends on one's point of view, of course. It is worth noting that in the case of any popular art still not too far removed from its folk roots, two contrasting attitudes develop eventually. On one hand there is the attitude of those who wish to see preserved the purity and integrity of a particular form of expression, as it evolved in a particular time, place, and set of circumstances. This attitude draws a circle around a specific corpus of music and performers, designating it as "authentic," and worthy of cultivation and study. Charles Seeger (writing of folk music proper) has characterized such an attitude as that of the *structuralists*.[22] He opposes to this the attitude of the *functionalists*, who regard the structuralists slightly as "purists" and characterize their outlook (in blues and jazz) with the term "moldy fig." The functionalists accept fully whatever happens to the music, which will in all circumstances, they feel, take whatever direction it *must*, and as a popular art form, whose first laws are those of adaptation and survival, appropriate to itself whatever seems to meet its needs at the moment.

Whichever view one takes, it must be recognized that there is a feeling among many blacks that the blues has outlived its time as a current form of communicative art; that its message is no longer relevant or appropriate; and that, indeed, it is too reminiscent of slavery and its residual consequences. And it is true that objective observation provides a good many indications to support the idea that the blues is in a state of decline. Except for revivalism, and the conscious cultivation of traditional styles, the music, both vocal and instrumental, has entered a stage of exaggerated mannerism typical of any popular music that feels itself in intense competition for a large market. The highly conventionalized lyrics seem to have lost the breadth, immediacy, and inventiveness of the traditional blues. Even the time-honored phrases and images, when they appear, seem, except in a very few hands, to have become clichés, delivered with showy stylization but without much conviction. Whether or not Paul Oliver, long-time blues writer and observer, may be of the "moldy fig" school is an open question. But his summation of the situation in 1969 raises issues that may well be pondered in relation to any popular music but must unavoidably be dealt with in assessing what has happened to the blues:

> In the past, blues has shown a remarkable capacity for survival; its demise has been predicted often enough and it may still survive the successive competition of Rock 'n' Roll, Soul and whatever comes next. But it shows every sign of cultural decline; the ascendancy of formal mannerism over content, the roccoco [sic] flourishes and extravagant posturings both physically and instrumentally are signs of an art form in its final stages. From direct and forthright origins as a functional art created of necessity, it has passed through the successive phases of development and maturity, the means evolving to meet the demands of meaning. As so often happens in an art form which has continued beyond its period of greatest value as expression and communication, it has reached a late stage of flamboyant embellishment. Not for a decade have lyrically significant blues appeared in any numbers, and its most meaningful expressions have been the tortured, impatient, openly aggressive abstractions of the playing of the music.[23]

Whatever the present and future state of the blues, there can be no doubt of its importance up to this point. Oliver's summation concludes by calling it "one of the richest and most rewarding of popular arts and perhaps the last great folk music that the western world may produce." [24]

FURTHER READING

CHARTERS, SAMUEL. *The Bluesmen*. New York: Oak Publications, 1967.
    A study by region of the country blues singers, with some musical examples.
* ———. *The Country Blues*. New York: Rinehart & Co., 1959.
    One of the first studies of the subject, and indispensable, especially as regards biographical information and the history of recordings.

* Items thus marked are part of the suggested reference library to be available in connection with this book.

Cook, Bruce. *Listen to the Blues.* New York: Charles Scribner's Sons, 1973. An informal but honest and perceptive study of the blues (primarily rural) through selected bluesmen, involving eventually all aspects including the exploitation of some of the old-timers.

Garland, Phyl. *The Sound of Soul.* Chicago: Henry Regnery Co., 1969.

Gillett, Charlie. *The Sound of the City.* New York: Dell Publishing Co., 1970. A history of rock 'n' roll, with a useful section on rhythm-and-blues.

* Handy, W. C. *Father of the Blues.* New York: Macmillan Co., 1941. In spite of the obvious kind of exaggeration implicit in its title, Handy's autobiography contains a wealth of background information, written from the standpoint of firsthand professional experience, on America's popular music business during the first four decades of this century.

* ——— (ed.). *Blues: An Anthology.* New York, 1926. Reprint, Macmillan Co., 1972. A famous collection of early published blues by Handy and others. A 1949 edition includes a rather extensive and valuable essay, "The Story of the Blues" by Abbe Niles. This is included in the most recent edition, which also incorporates additional blues, and guitar-chord symbols.

* Jones, LeRoi. *Blues People.* New York: William Morrow & Co., 1963. A survey by an eminent black writer, who uses music to illustrate and illuminate the history of his people in America.

* Keil, Charles. *Urban Blues.* Chicago: University of Chicago Press, 1966. An indispensable study, and one of the few to deal adequately and from a variety of angles with the modern urban component of the blues. His annotated outline of blues styles (Appendix C) is valuable.

* Oliver, Paul. *The Meaning of the Blues.* New York: Macmillan Co., 1960. Paperback ed., Collier, Books, 1963. Possibly more relevant to chapter 2, this deserves inclusion here as an exhaustive and perceptive study of blues subjects and the milieu of its people, in the form of an extensive commentary on 350 blues texts, arranged according to subject.

* ———. *The Story of the Blues.* New York: Chilton Book Co., 1969. A comprehensive study, profusely illustrated with photographs, this is a basic source, though concentrating mainly on the rural and "classic" blues. There is a fine bibliography and discography.

Redd, Lawrence H. *Rock is Rhythm and Blues.* East Lansing: Michigan State University Press, 1974. The first part of the book defends the thesis implicit in the title; the second is devoted to transcriptions of six interviews with Riley "B.B." King, Brownie McGhee, Arthur "Big Boy" Crudup, Jerry Butler, Dave Clark, and Jessie Whitaker.

See also various works in the reading lists for chapter 2 (additional background on the folk phase) and chapter 12 (jazz, especially the early jazz so closely related to blues).

LISTENING

General

* The Story of the Blues, notes by Paul Oliver. Columbia: G-30008.
    An excellent condensed anthology (which does not, however, cover adequately the more recent urban blues).

"Classic" City Blues

Ma Rainey, vols. 1 and 2. Biograph: 12001 and 12011.
The Bessie Smith Story, 4 vols. Columbia: 855–858.
    The above is an early LP reissue. Columbia, in a newer project, has recently reissued all 160 of its Bessie Smith recordings (nearly her entire output), with vast technological improvements to eliminate extraneous noises, on 20 sides. These are available in five volumes, under various individual titles, as CG-33, 30126, 30450, 30818, and 31093.
Rare Recordings of the Twenties, 4 vols. Columbia: CBS-64218, 65379, 65380, 65421.
    Part of the import series Aimez-vous le jazz?, these recordings feature Louis Armstrong playing with various blues singers such as Clara Smith, Sippie Wallace, Chippie Hill, and Victoria Spivey.
The Victoria Spivey Recorded Legacy of the Blues. Spivey: 2001.
Stars of the Apollo Theatre. Columbia: K-CG-30788.
    Sheds additional light on the vaudeville phase of the classic blues.

Blues and Jazz

Many entries in the previous category are also relevant here; in addition, the jazz anthologies listed below have much blues material. For full information on these, see the discography for chapter 12.
* The Smithsonian Collection of Classic Jazz.
* The Riverside History of Classic Jazz.
* The Folkways History of Jazz Series, especially vols. 2 and 10.
* The Encyclopedia of Jazz.

Country Blues

See also the suggestions for listening, chapter 2.
Blues Roots/Mississippi. Folkways: RBF-14.

The Jug Bands. Folkways: RF-6.
Brownie McGhee Blues. Folkways: 2030.
Blind Blake. Biograph: 12003.
Mississippi John Hurt. Vanguard: 79220.
John Lee Hooker. Everest: FS-222.
Big Bill Broonzy. Everest: FS-213.
Leadbelly. Everest: FS-202.
Lightin' Hopkins. Everest: FS-241.
Brownie and Sonny. Everest: FS-242.

Urban Blues and "Soul" Music

So vast are the numbers of recordings in this current and constantly changing category, that it is impossible to give anything but the merest suggestion of how to locate representative examples. To begin with, a few collections and anthologies, some with useful annotations, are valuable.

* *Anthology of Rhythm and Blues,* vol. 1. Columbia: CS-9802.
Blues Roots/Chicago–The 1930s. Folkways: RBF-16.
Includes notes by Samuel Charters, and complete texts.
Roots: Rhythm and Blues. Folkways: RBF-20.
Roots—The Rock and Roll Sound of Louisiana and Mississippi. Folkways: 2865.
Great Hits of Rhythm and Blues. Columbia: 30503.
* *History of Rhythm and Blues.* Atlantic: 9161, 8162–8164.
* *Straighten Up and Fly Right: Rhythm and Blues from the Close of the Swing Era to the Dawn of Rock 'n' Roll.* RAAM: NW-261.
Also useful are some fairly representative collections by individual artists, which go by such titles as "Greatest Hits" or "The Best of . . . ,", of which the following should be regarded as merely samples.
The Best of the Biggest. United Superior: 7718.
Early recordings by Ray Charles, B. B. King, etc.
The Best of B. B. King. ABCX-767.
Aretha Franklin's Greatest Hits, vols. 1 and 2. Columbia: CS-9473, 9601.
Diana Ross and the Supremes, Greatest Hits. Motown: 2-663.

PROJECTS

1. Based on W. C. Handy's autobiography (and any other sources you can find) describe in a brief essay what life was like for a

black musician in the Deep South in the first quarter of the twentieth century.

2. Make a further study, along the lines suggested in the chapter, of the relationship of the early published blues to those that appear in the recordings of the 1920s.

3. Assemble a list of at least ten male and ten female blues singers who recorded between 1920 and 1930, with a brief biographical sketch of each. Cite at least one recording for each, and listen to as many others as you can.

4. Besides those listed in the chapter, find three examples of blues' form and harmony in instrumental jazz. Try to select examples from different periods of jazz.

5. Make an annotated discography of at least ten entries by at least five different boogie-woogie pianists. Describe and classify as best you can the different styles that you hear. Select one or two examples, and analyze as best you can their relationship, in form and harmony, to the sung blues.

6. Compare three recordings of Mississippi delta blues performers with three recordings of Texas blues performers. Describe them, and determine to what extent they either support or contradict the stylistic generalities made in the chapter.

7. Make a collection of urban blues lyrics since 1950 (including rhythm-and-blues and soul). Compare them, in scope and treatment, with those in Paul Oliver's study *The Meaning of the Blues*, which are predominantly rural and date from before 1950.

8. Assemble a list of at least five singers from the rhythm-and-blues and soul categories whose work you feel still belongs to the authentic blues tradition, however you may interpret that. Cite examples, and explain what there is about their work that influences your choice.

9. Compile a short discography of two important blues saxophonists prominent since 1950. Describe their work, and include a brief biographical sketch.

10. Make a study of urban gospel music, and its relation to the urban blues.

11. Make a study of a commercial style such as the "Detroit sound" or "Motown" (as represented, say, by the Supremes). How much does it owe to the blues? Analyze the similarities and differences between such a stylization and the more mainstream blues tradition—the "blues continuum."

Chapter Nine

Rock

ROCK IS THE MOST DISTANT OFFSPRING OF THE RURAL SOUTH, and its patrimony is more varied than that of any of the others. The rock phenomenon is now a quarter of a century old. If it has been difficult up to now to fit it in proper perspective into the context of a survey of American music (and heretofore the generalists have all but ignored it, while the specialists have tended to give it exaggerated importance), this is at least partly due to the fact that its purely musical elements account for proportionately less of its impact as a cultural phenomenon than is the case with any other kind of music, excepting possibly primitive tribal music, with which it shares some cultural characteristics. It is more than the sum of its musical parts, in that it is an ambience, a set of attitudes, a total environment. Its musical factors have, in the main, been reduced to their most elemental functioning level, so that they have become easily conventionalized and synthesized; its obsessive repetitiveness is the most obvious manifestation of this. The music is, in general, less important in itself than for its function in providing an atmosphere for the projection of a message (however nonverbal), an image, a stance. Rock is burdened with a multitude of overtones—overtones of culture, politics, morals, and taste. These are part and parcel of the phenomenon, and a rock song, as perceived, includes them all.

To return to the analogy with tribal music, rock can be conceived of as a kind of folk art, in terms of the response it elicits. Carl Belz, who has faced this question more squarely than most other writers, has said of this folk response that it "is spontaneous, and it is directed to the thing-as-reality." [1] Thus the rock song, in the same sense as the folk ballad or the ritual tribal chant, has an immediacy in the lives of its participants that is not distanced by any sense of art-consciousness. When there is no consciousness of art (on the part of either performer or listener), there is no separation between art and life—no "frame" for the art, so to speak. The fade-out technique so much used at the end of recordings symbolizes this lack of frame; the illusion created is that of a performance with an existence independent of the limitations of the record—a tangible experience, of which only a portion happens to be made available on the recording. Thus the "thing-as-reality" has its impact in the domain of experience far more than in the domain of art. Even the ingenuously gushing commercialism of the record liner-notes (which, as Belz points out, can themselves be viewed as a kind of naive folk art) convey the sense that what is being bought is not just music, or even primarily music, but a shared experience. As the notes to a recent recording of a live performance put it: "If you weren't there, you are now."

This brings us to a second and equally significant consideration in connection with rock. It is a unique phenomenon that could only have come into being in our time. If it is a folk art in the sense described, it is one that was born and is living out its entire existence in the very maw of commercialism. This is what has imparted to rock its essentially equivocal nature. In a subject rife with paradoxes, the most basic one is that what began (and in essence still remains) as "underground" music—a vernacular, anti-commercial, "protest" kind of art—has become an almost unimaginably big business, turning upside down, and dictating to, an entire industry. As Charlie Gillett has written: "If rock 'n' roll as art and entertainment was the expression of a new generation, as commercial product it was the dynamite that blew apart the structure of the industry." [2]

This was not accomplished without considerable resistance, of course, in the early stages. But now that the "victory" has been won, the battles seem in retrospect to be viewed in the light of the struggle for popularity rather than in any artistic terms. It is significant that so much of the history of rock is written purely in terms of economics—of "covers" outselling originals, of the rise of the "independents" versus the "majors," and of course the ever-present "charts," finely tuned devices for measuring success in terms of records sold and other largely commercial indicators. Indeed, from this standpoint, what more reliable and irrefutable yardstick *is* there for measuring popular art than its popularity?

BEGINNINGS

The American South, as we have noted, has been a fertile source of much of our culture. Blues, jazz, and country music had their musical roots there. Rock also can trace its primal origins to this region. But its immediate background is urban. Like jazz before it, it has been described as "the sound of the city." And it is preeminently a part of the culture of the young. Let us now examine in more detail its origins and its growth.

Roots in Black Music

We have already noted that the most significant innovations in our vernacular music originated in the music of the blacks, from minstrelsy to jazz. The same is no less true of rock. There is no question but that so-called rhythm-and-blues, discussed in chapter 8, was the taproot of rock. The name itself was a trade designation, now as dated as "rock 'n' roll," but it was more accurately descriptive than most, and indicated a somewhat commercialized form of urban blues, in which either a single blues singer or a highly polished vocal ensemble was accompanied by a fairly small blues band, including a strongly marked rhythm section and usually at least one blues saxophonist.[3]

Rhythm-and-blues recordings had, in the early fifties, a somewhat narrow market, largely racially defined; it was music by black performers for black listeners. As such, it was a direct descendant of the previously described race records. The black folk elements were unmistakably present: the content, delivery, and hoarse tone-quality of the blues; the saxophone "responses"; the "back beat" (off-beats strongly marked in the drums, a direct legacy of the off-beat hand clapping so associated with black music-making); and the frank and unselfconscious treatment of sexual themes and lyrics.

On the other hand, there was already evident the influence of popularization, even of Tin Pan Alley—as indicated for instance in the adaptation of the old "standards" of popular music, such as *Blueberry Hill* or *Blue Moon*, without regard for the somewhat incongruous effect produced by the juxtaposition of cliché "pop" lyrics and the earthier musical style of the blues. The stylized, polished vocal ensembles point to the same influence, as does the unmistakable tendency towards the trivialization of themes and lyrics.

Had this music remained, as it began, nearly the exclusive province of a young black audience, the whole history of American popular music would have been vastly different. As it happened, black rhythm-and-blues, played on black radio stations in the large cities and recorded and sold through outlets primarily intended for the black public, began to be listened to and become popular with an increasingly large group of white youth. This coincided with a period of low inventiveness and pallid offerings from the established white popular music industry, and of increased independence and dissatisfaction with conventionality on the part of many young whites.

It was a disc jockey on a Cleveland radio station, Alan Freed, who first realized the potential inherent in the popularity of black rhythm-and-blues among white adolescents. In 1951 he began programming the music extensively. (It is probably true that he invented the name; his early radio program was called "Moondog's Rock and Roll Party.") He also arranged live stage shows of black rhythm-and-blues performers for predominantly white audiences. In 1954 he moved to New York as disc jockey for WINS, which quickly became the leading popular music station of the city. His activities, not only as disc jockey but as concert promoter, writer, and dedicated partisan, did much to publicize and advance rock 'n' roll in its early stages.

By 1954 white groups were "covering" (recording their own versions of) popular black rhythm-and-blues recordings; Bill Haley's *Shake, Rattle, and Roll* of that year, a version of an earlier recording by blues singer Joe Turner, was among the first of the very popular "covers." Freed himself played, and championed, the original black versions. But rock 'n' roll, as a new form of white popular music based on black rhythm-and-blues, began to evolve as a distinct music, and the black artists who were among the most popular with the growing constituency of whites were those whose styles were closest to the new idiom—Chuck Berry, Bo Diddley, Little Richard, and Fats Domino. Conversely, rock 'n' roll as a primarily white phenomenon began with those white performers who most closely patterned their work on black models—men such as Bill Haley, whose *Rock Around the Clock* (1955) has been recognized as the first white rock 'n' roll hit, and Elvis Presley, who was strongly imprinted with the blues ambience of Memphis. It was Presley (whose coming was presaged, as we have noted, by his early manager's search for a "white boy who could sing colored") who most forcefully exemplified the combination of black and white influences that constituted early rock. His famous *Heartbreak Hotel* (1956) accomplished the symbolic feat of achieving popularity in both black (rhythm-and-blues) and white (country-and-western) markets.

White Country Music and Early Rock

If black rhythm-and-blues was the taproot of rock, it was not its *only* root; white country music played an important role. As noted in chapter

7, white country music (or country-and-western, to use the trade term) had evolved out of folk roots as a traditional and conservative regional music. By the 1950s, however, its public was no longer as narrowly limited, thanks to the broad cultural mixing produced by the war years, and the popularity of western movies and movie stars.

When we recall that there was already a strong strain of the blues in country music, its part in the formation of rock can more easily be accounted for. The electric guitar had long been used in country music, and the singing guitarist, as basic to white country music as to black country blues, became the mainstay of the early rock ensemble, as typified by performers like Bill Haley, Elvis Presley, Carl Perkins, and Buddy Holly.

The country music style with the closest affinity to the urban blues style was honky-tonk, which, as noted earlier, used a piano and was strongly influenced by boogie-woogie. This early style, with its distinctly adult themes and lyrics, was cultivated by such performers as Jerry Lee Lewis, and some of the music was scarcely distinguishable from that of the black musicians on which it was based. But at the same time, country-influenced rock was moving in another direction—towards pop and the growing teen-age audience. The themes reflected the concerns and conflicts of adolescents (*Peggy Sue; Wake Up, Little Susie*) and also a tendency towards exaggeration, cliché, and trivia in the lyrics (*Blue Suede Shoes*).

THE IMPACT OF ROCK ON THE RECORDING INDUSTRY

It was in the mid-fifties that rock began to overturn the popular music recording industry. Prior to this time, the pop music field, representing the declining stages of Tin Pan Alley, had been dominated by a few major recording companies and was fairly stable, with its "hits" remaining at the top of the popularity charts for an average of five or six months. But given the new technology that allowed recordings to be produced nearly anywhere in the country, this situation was ripe for change, and the new idiom of rock, rejected and opposed at first by the major companies, was what brought this change about. Small independent record companies (the "indies"), which had been mainly responsible for supplying the heretofore limited black rhythm-and-blues market, now expanded and multiplied to meet the new demand for rhythm-and-blues and rock 'n' roll. Early rock thus belonged to the independents. The major companies, representing the conservative Tin Pan Alley tradition, found themselves left out of an increasingly large and volatile part of the market. Hits would zoom into prominence overnight, and disappear almost as fast. As in the early publishing days of Tin Pan Alley, a single hit would be enough to establish a company. In an effort to gain a position in the new pop arena, the major companies issued covers of their own of popular rock hits—cleaning and polishing them up but depriving them of their immediacy, and so misunderstanding that it was the rough edges engendered by its spontaneity and sheer energy which gave rock its appeal.

At the same time, rock itself, as it evolved, owed a great deal to commercial pop music in the matter of lyrics and themes, especially as it diverged from the more adult rhythm-and-blues and began to adapt itself to the increasingly large teen-age market.

Early Effects of Commercialization: The Teen Market

The shift away from the adult orientation of rhythm-and-blues in one area of "country rock" in the late fifties had become typical of rock generally by the early sixties, as the vast teen-age market began to be catered to. The preoccupation with cars, for example, was reflected in any number of "hot rod" songs, such as *Little Deuce Coupe*, which, in a manner curiously typical of folk art, combines vernacular expressions with oddly technical descriptions of the car's mechanical features. From California came the surfing songs (best represented, probably, by the highly successful and polished recordings of the Beach Boys). These, along with the entire surfing cult, spread rapidly throughout the country, having little to do, ultimately, with the actual practice of the sport, for, as Belz remarks, "the surf itself had been obviated as an essential ingredient." [4]

In a class of songs given over largely to a rather literal treatment of external things and concerns, there arose at this time a peculiar phenomenon—songs about death. (*Teen Angel* is perhaps the best-known representative.) Set in familiar adolescent surroundings and circumstances, they perhaps represented an attempt (however seldom it transcended the mawkish) to confront at least one of the most obvious themes associated with real poetry.[5]

VARIETIES AND DEVELOPMENTS

The British Influence

The state of rock music as the mid-sixties approached has been at least hinted at; its essential flavor and folk-like spontaneity had been dissipated in imitation, and in adaptation to the demands of a nearly all-devouring commercialism. At this point developments in England become a part of the scene, since it was from this source that revitalization of rock came.

This development was not as strange as it might at first appear, when one considers the long interdependence of British and American popular music. In one direction, English ballad opera was a staple here in colonial times; the English music hall provided songs and a song style for our musical comedy in the nineteenth century; and Gilbert and Sullivan has been almost as popular and perennially successful here as in England. Most important, British folk music, a subtly pervasive presence in nearly all English music, was a source of one of America's most important strains of folk music. In the other direction, our blackface comedy, ragtime, blues, and jazz were each, in their heyday, exports that were much in demand. A broad segment of the younger British public has always followed avidly developments in American popular music—especially the fruits of our black popular culture.[6] There have been times when the devotion to some particular phase was stronger in England than in America generally. The sixties was such a time. It was then that, in a kind of illustration of the folklorists' theory of "marginal survival" (according to which items of folklore will survive on the distant margins of a culture after they have ceased to become important at its core), the earthier manifestations of the blues, which no longer enjoyed very wide popularity here, were being assiduously cultivated by a segment of British youth. Big Bill Broonzy, Howlin' Wolf, Sonny Terry, and Brownie McGhee were known in England not only from their recordings but from personal tours. As adherents of a later style, such men as Chuck Berry and Bo Diddley were well known and influential in England after they had been largely supplanted here.

Young British groups developed their own kind of expression of the essential rhythm-and-blues ingredients, and though never more than an imitation, it showed in many cases a surprising mastery of the externals, at least. Thus it was that what the English groups gave back to America, when they were "discovered" and began to export their records and themselves, was America's own black rhythm-and-blues, filtered through the temperament and experience of British youth, and giving off echoes, when the beat was a little less relentless, of the music hall, and further in the background, of English folk music.

Some of these groups never went much beyond the somewhat limited range staked out by the shouting, "bragging" blues. The Rolling Stones, enormously influential, has typified this, in producing efficiently aggressive statements (and becoming efficiently aggressive symbols) of revolt, nihilism, and sexual bravado.

One group, however, succeeded amazingly well in transcending these limitations. The Beatles, born into the British equivalent of rhythm-and-blues, as were all the other groups, began their meteoric journey across the midcentury skies of popular culture by a reintroduction of innocence—an infectious pleasure in music making akin to what was felt in the folk-like singing and playing of such early black rock 'n' roll artists as Chuck Berry. This innocence proved to be the quality that opened the way to a much broader range of expression for the Beatles, which their collective talent enabled them to explore. In the process came inevitably sophistication, but also genuine musical and poetic development. Their work, from folk beginnings, gradually came to acquire that esthetic distancing from its subject that gave it a genuine *art*-stance. The *Sgt. Pepper's Lonely Hearts Club Band* album (1967), in its entirety, probably best signaled that arrival, of which even segments of the world of fine-art music had to take notice. Writing from the vantage point of this world, musicologists such as Wilfred Mellers and composers such as Ned Rorem could regard the Beatles' work as almost pointing the way towards a kind of salvation for fine-art music, or at least one avenue of escape from its paralyzing dilemma of noncommunication.

The inevitable eclecticism that the Beatles' work came to embody (running the gamut from synthesized sound to Renaissance music and Indian ragas) was widely imitated, of course, and has become symptomatic of much rock music from that point on. Having traversed, presumably, all the ground they could as a group, the Beatles broke up; whatever the immediate causes, this was inevitable. Their influence, especially here in America, was enormous.

In fact, from the mid-sixties on, so interwoven are the stories of British and American rock that it is impossible to trace native rock music without nearly constant references to what British groups were doing. They have continued to be a creative and innovative force, especially in the integration of rock with certain aspects of European art-music, a development that will be discussed in due course.

Uptown Rhythm-and-Blues: Rock on the Production Line

Rock, in its position of unimaginable affluence and influence, by now had attracted to its production an almost unlimited supply of inventiveness and trained skill, and had at its disposal all that recording technology could offer. The work of Phil Spector, who in a very literal sense "produced" such groups as the Crystals, the Ronettes, and the Righteous Brothers, using a studio orchestra and the full capacity of the studio to manipulate sound in recording, was representative. This trend was even more fully realized in the work of the so-called Motown groups: the Miracles, the Temptations, the Four Tops, and best known, the Supremes. In other words, the 1960s ushered in an era of studio-produced sound, wherein the sound studio itself, with the engineer at the control panel, became almost the most important musical instrument. Effects were developed that were impossible to duplicate in "live" performance; as

Carl Belz so perceptively pointed out, the recording itself became the "original." [7]

Folk-Rock

That phenomenon known as the urban folk movement—which transplanted the home-grown music, the anxious concerns, and even some of the folk musicians themselves from the Mississippi delta, the Oklahoma Dust Bowl, and the Kentucky coal mines to the coffeehouses of Greenwich Village, and ultimately to the tour circuit and the LP record—has been chronicled in chapter 4.

Folk music as popular entertainment flourished briefly in the late fifties and early sixties, as purveyed by groups like the Kingston Trio and Peter, Paul, and Mary, and by Joan Baez. Yet neither the urban folk movement nor popular folk music had any impact on rock itself until the mid-sixties, and this impact was initially produced largely by one man, Bob Dylan. Emerging with acoustic guitar, harmonica, and social-significance songs from the Greenwich Village scene in 1962, Dylan, who was never comfortably classifiable as either a pure folklorist or a protest singer, made his controversial switch to a rock style and approach (with electric guitars and hard-driving rhythm section) in 1965. This cross-fertilization of folk-oriented subject matter and approach with rock musical style had an influence at the time second only to that of the Beatles. It infused rock with a new element of conscious social comment: satirical, often bitter and angry. Dylan's subsequent musical styles have vacillated considerably—from rock back to ballad-type folk (*John Wesley Harding*, 1968), to a lighter, more easygoing country (*Nashville Skyline*, 1968–69), and ultimately back to a hard rock ballad–style (*Desire*, 1975). Dylan's work, especially in relation to the urban folk-song movement, has been discussed somewhat more fully in chapter 4.

Other alumni of the Greenwich Village coffeehouses, such as Paul Simon and John Sebastian, have moved at least onto the fringes of rock, helping to define what is known as folk-rock, and contributing also some memorable songs. Solo singers in the folk genre who have also written their own songs, such as Judy Collins and Joni Mitchell, have occasionally employed rock idioms; their work has added another dimension to the enormous breadth of popular music, and pointed up the difficulties inherent in trying to fashion and use labels.

Rock and Satire

An indication of rock's aging and sophistication by the sixties was an increased propensity for the wildest satire—satire of pop culture and pop music, even including rock itself. Rock became, in the hands of such clever and inventive talents as Frank Zappa and the Mothers of Invention, a kind of expressive game. The poses, the theatrics, the put-ons, made it purposefully difficult to determine whether the game was being played seriously at all. The elaborately staged contempt for the audience and for the conventional assumptions on which the live concert is based became mannerisms. They had their parallels in the actions of the bebop musicians of two decades previously, but there was also a remarkable resemblance, in attitude and even in action and event, to some of the staged "happenings" of the avant-garde fine-art scene. But while the fringes of the fine-art avant-garde *seemed* at least to always be in deadly earnest, performers like Frank Zappa, in spite of some occasionally very lucid statements made in interviews,[8] were able successfully to keep their public sufficiently in doubt about their intentions to create a considerable degree of tension and interest. The Mothers of Invention was illustrative of the fact that so many young and extremely talented, intelligent musicians gravitated to rock in the 1960s, and of the breadth of styles and resources they brought to it.

The Hybridization of Rock

One of the most important developments concerning rock in the 1960s was that it began noticeably to permeate other musical areas, such as the popular musical theater (as we shall see in the following chapter), and to hybridize with other musical styles—chiefly with jazz, and in a more superficial way with fine-art music.

The hybridization with jazz has been the most successful and productive. The relationship of both jazz and rock to the blues is what seems, more than anything else, to make this work. It has taken place chiefly at the hands of a new breed of young musicians whose talent and exposure to music are extensive enough for them to play with facility in a number of different styles. In terms of its instrumentation, "jazz-rock" usually means a rock band to which brass and saxophones have been added. In terms of musical style, more is implied. Over a rock beat and ostinato (expressed chiefly by the electric bass with elaborations and accents on the drums) jazz solos are spun out. The "square" rock beat, with its duple subdivisions and incessant repetitions, acts as a ground for the freer rhythm and melodic flights of the solos. Occasionally, as in Chicago's *Does Anybody Know What Time It Is?*, there is a dabbling in the asymmetric meters that preoccupied so-called progressive jazz for a time. By virtue of the jazz-derived improvisations, jazz-rock pieces are apt to be quite extended in length. Combining the elements of two very popular modes of expression, jazz-rock very often verges on pop, and is extraordinarily vulnerable to commercialization.

There have been repeated attempts at a synthesis of rock with symphonic music, and there are interesting parallels between this phenomenon and the kind of synthesis of jazz with symphonic music that was essayed earlier in the century. In both cases the attempt was made from both sides, so to speak. In the 1920s some serious composers took notice of jazz—in Europe, Stravinsky and the French; in America, John Alden Carpenter and Aaron Copland, among others. In the same way, in the 1960s and 1970s some serious composers have taken note of rock and its ambience, as illustrated by Leonard Bernstein's *Mass* written for the opening of the Kennedy Center for the Performing Arts in Washington, D.C., in 1971—described as "A Theater Piece for Singers, Players and Dancers." From the entertainment world, on the other hand, we find musicians (jazz-oriented in the 1920s and 1930s and rock-oriented in the 1960s and 1970s) similarly interested in such a synthesis—seeking to transcend somewhat the limitations of their genre, or seeking a degree of permanence, significance, or intellectual respectability. Young British musicians were attempting this in the sixties and seventies; for example, Keith Emerson, with the Nice, performed his *Five Bridges Suite* with symphony orchestra in Croydon in 1969.[9] It represents a serious attempt to integrate media and styles: Edwardian English symphonic music, mid-century jazz piano style, neo-baroque fugal piano style (somewhat in the manner of Dave Brubeck), virtuosic rock organ playing, rock song fragments with run-of-the-mill lyrics, and a jazz-rock finale that, as usual in these essays, manages somehow to leave the symphony orchestra far behind. The "bridges" of the title have reference, among other things, to the building of "bridges to those musical shores which seem determined to remain apart."[10] The attempt, while not especially distinguished, is typical.

Such attempts at a synthesis of "mass" and "elite" art will appear periodically, when such a union seems propitious—when for reasons economic, psychological, or artistic they "need" each other.[11] They will produce interesting phenomena, but the universal rule that only exceptional talent can produce anything of real significance and value is not waived for these enterprises, any more than in any other department of art. Of the experiments of the twenties and thirties which generated a similar interest, and from which much was hoped for, the works of Gershwin are virtually the only ones still in the repertory.

INGREDIENTS OF THE ROCK PHENOMENON IN THE SEVENTIES: A RECAPITULATION

The trends represented by individual albums, and even by individual performers and groups, date rapidly in a medium as volatile as rock, and a journalistic approach of trying to keep up with individual events in this shifting panorama is inappropriate to this present study. Instead, let us recapitulate some of the basic ingredients of the rock phenomenon in the seventies, since these are likely to be present for some time to come, and to be a part of whatever successive manifestations appear.

THE SEARCH FOR A MORE EXTENDED FORMAT

The exploration of a more extended format has been characteristic of latter-day rock since it transcended the limitations of the 45-rpm single. The most significant manifestation of this is the integrated LP album, as it became potentially more than a collection of singles, and acquired, at the hands of some musicians and producers, a unity of theme or treatment that made it akin to a forty-minute song cycle or suite. This level of development and sophistication has not been reached often, but some notable examples are the "underground oratorios" of Frank Zappa's *Absolutely Free* (1965) and the entire *Sgt. Pepper* album of the Beatles (1967). The latter is a stylistically wide-ranging *review*, with an opening song that is given a reprise at the end, after which, as a kind of coda, comes the serious *A Day in the Life*.

TECHNOLOGY AND THE ROCK RECORDING

It has already been noted that recording-studio technology has made possible the production of recordings that could not practically be duplicated in live performance. The sound studio itself has become a musical instrument, with the recording engineer nearly as important as the composer in the execution of the final product. Rock was one of the first genres, for example, to employ stereo capabilities (long taken for granted in the playing of its recordings) as an actual compositional device—as illustrated, for example, by the famous fox chase sequence in the *Sgt. Pepper* album. It is the recording, to recall Carl Belz's cogent point, which has become the "original" of a rock piece.

LIVE ROCK AS THEATER

Certain developments in rock may perhaps be viewed as attempts to achieve visual complements of the auditory sounds made possible by recording technology. In San Francisco, for example, during the late sixties there was the reinstatement of the live performance as a vital vehicle for rock, and its elaboration into what aspired to be a kind of "total environment" through the superimposition of visual projections and light shows. These light shows often aimed at simulating psychedelic experiences—as indeed did some of the music itself, such as *White Rabbit* by the Jefferson Airplane, a prominent San Francisco group.[12] Since then, the live indoor rock concert has become an elaborately staged spectacle, with three-dimensional stage sets, machines to create smoke and fog, and projections and laser displays, all contributing to the creation of the overwhelmingly kaleidoscopic total environment of sight and sound. The rock establishment, with its tremendous following and affluence, has been able to far outstrip technologically in this regard the efforts of one wing of the serious musical avant-garde, with whose staged happenings there was a curious parallel in the 1960s. Rock attracted much innovative talent of that period to the creation of its spectacles. It is something of a paradox that live rock concerts (and indeed much of rock *in toto*), representing a high and expensive level of technical sophistication, continue to be supported largely by a mass audience of relatively unsophisticated fans, for whom the phenomenon still functions at its most elemental, visceral level.

ECLECTICISM AND SYNTHESIS

Perhaps the most decisive ingredient in the rock phenomenon of the 1970s is its eclecticism—its tendency to appropriate other styles and sounds, including those from a broad band of European-American art music (ranging from the Renaissance to twentieth-century expressionism), from jazz, from folk music, and from Oriental traditional music, especially that of India. The hybridization with jazz and the attempted syntheses with fine-art music have been noted. These developments are certainly indications of the breadth of exposure to a wide variety of musical influences enjoyed by the young musicians of today, and their ability to absorb and reflect these influences. They may also be the symptoms of a popular art which has already passed the period of its most inherent vitality.

Beginning as a more or less spontaneous hybrid style, an unselfconscious folk-like expression of the first generation of youth with the means and motivation to create its own subculture, rock, in its twenty-five years of existence, has become, like commercial folk music, highly self-conscious and mannered. Its electrified, amplified thoroughfare has been the Tin Pan Alley of our time. The older Alley it so largely replaced, and the entire entertainment industry it so profoundly affected, will be our next subject.

FURTHER READING

Within the last decade, "rockwrite" has produced numberless books, articles, and essays. From the vast shelf of publications (many of them confined to a single figure or group) the following are suggested as among the most permanently valuable.

* Items thus marked are part of the suggested reference library to be available in connection with this book.

Books

* BELZ, CARL. *The Story of Rock.* 2nd ed. New York: Oxford University Press, 1972. Paperback ed. New York: Harper Colophon Books, 1973.

    This study, covering the period from rock's inception to 1971, is possibly the best one to date. It demonstrates not only a broad knowledge, but a thoughtful insight into its subject. A valuable bibliography (annotated) and discography are included.

* DENISOFF, R. SERGE. *Sing a Song of Social Significance.* Bowling Green, Ohio: Bowling Green University Popular Press, 1972.

  EISEN, JONATHAN, ed. *The Age of Rock.* New York: Vintage Books, 1969.

    A collection of essays from the late sixties emphasizing (to quote Belz) "popular sociology." A sequel (*The Age of Rock/2,* 1970) is far less significant.

* GILLETT, CHARLIE. *The Sound of the City.* New York: Dell Publishing Co., 1970.

    An excellent, informative study by a British writer, with a bibliography, exceptionally broad in scope, providing material for background reading.

  REDD, LAWRENCE N. *Rock Is Rhythm and Blues (The Impact of Mass Media).* East Lansing: Michigan State University Press, 1974.

    This informative study expounds a particular point of view—that rock 'n' roll and rhythm-and-blues are virtually the same, that it was the mass media which tended to create a separation between the two, and that therefore the black origins of rock have not been sufficiently recognized. That this study should have been written by an educator and radio and television producer/director is evidence of the broad impact of the rock phenomenon, not only musically but culturally and economically.

  STAMBLER, IRWIN, ed. *Encyclopedia of Pop, Rock and Soul.* New York: St. Martin's Press, 1974.

    A fairly extensive and informative reference work, this volume covers the period from rock's inception through 1973.

* WHITCOMB, IAN. *After the Ball.* London: Penguin Press, 1972.

    This very readable account of American popular music concludes with some views of rock from the inside, by one of its briefly shining British stars.

LISTENING

The numbers of recordings of rock music, and the volume of their sales, have been huge on an unprecedented scale. To distill from this deluge anything like a concise discography is a well-nigh overwhelming undertaking. Unfortunately, to date there have been very few significant anthologies (such as have appeared in jazz), and of those few that have appeared, most have gone out of

*print. In the beginning, the 45-rpm "single" was the sole medium for rock.
It is still a much-used vehicle, and accounts for a monumental volume of releases weekly, most of them very ephemeral. The LP album did not become
important as a rock medium until the mid-sixties. It is a somewhat more permanent vehicle, consisting mostly of re-releases of old 45-rpm singles in collections. In the case of single artists or groups, the nearest available approxima-
tions to anthologies are albums with such titles as "The Best of . . ." or ". . .'s
Golden Hits" or "Greatest Hits of . . . ."*

This very limited discography begins with the only anthologies of early rock
in print at this writing, and continues with a selective list, somewhat representative, the choices for which have been necessarily arbitrary.

Shake, Rattle, and Roll: Rock 'n' Roll in the 1950s. RAAM: NW-249.
Oldies but Goodies, 10 vols. Original Sound: 8850, 8852-60.
Roots: Rhythm and Blues. Folkways: RBF-20.
Roots: The Rock and Roll Sound of Louisiana and Mississippi. Folkways:
    FJ-2865.
Chuck Berry's Golden Decade, 2 vols. 2-Chess: S-1514.
Beach Boys Best. Capitol: DT-2545.
Meet the Beatles. Capitol: ST-2047.
Sgt. Pepper's Lonely Hearts Club Band. Capitol: SMAS-2653.
White Album, the Beatles, 2 vols. Capitol: SWBO-101.
Abbey Road, the Beatles. Apple: 50383.
The Rolling Stones. London: 375.
The Times They Are A-Changin', Bob Dylan. Columbia: KCS-8905.
Blonde on Blonde, Bob Dylan, 2 vols. Columbia: C2S-841.
John Wesley Harding, Bob Dylan. Columbia: KCS-9604.
Nashville Skyline, Bob Dylan. Columbia: KCS-9825.
Diana Ross and the Supremes Greatest Hits. Motown: 2-663.
Otis Redding. Atco: S-33-261-E.
Surrealistic Pillow, the Jefferson Airplane. RCA: LSP-3766.
Blood, Sweat and Tears, Greatest Hits. Columbia: PC-31170.
Chicago Transit Authority. Columbia: GP-8.
Absolutely Free, the Mothers of Invention. Verve: 65013.
Tapestry, Carole King. Ode: 77009.
Manassas, Stephen Stills. Atlantic: 2-903.
200 Motels, Frank Zappa. United Artists: UAS-9956.

PROJECTS

1. Find and listen to two early "covers" (recordings by white musicians
   derived from earlier recordings by black musicians) from the
   1950s, and their original versions. Write a descriptive comparison,
   trying to account for the differences.
2. If you have access (through friends, libraries, or a local radio
   station) to fairly representative record collections of both early

rock and country music of the 1950s, document the relationship of the two in that period. As background, read chapter 8 of *Country Music, U.S.A.*, by Bill Malone.

3. Do a taped essay on the role of the disc jockey in modern popular music, beginning with Alan Freed. Include taped excerpts of several current disc jockeys, with a brief commentary on their delivery, content, and style.

4. Describe the work of five British rock groups besides the Beatles that have been influential in the United States, detailing this influence.

5. Make a study of the complex array of popularity charts in *Billboard* magazine (the trade journal of American popular music).

6. Stephen Still's *Fallen Eagle* (from the album *Manassas*) is a "message" song from the early 1970s, done in a style that might be characterized as "bluegrass rock." Find other rock pieces that show definite relationships to other kinds of American music, such as Latin music, avant-garde fine-art music, Anglo-American folk music, or country music. Make your own brief anthology of about five such pieces, analyzing and characterizing their styles and influences as intelligently as possible.

7. Do a brief study contrasting rock drumming with jazz drumming.

8. If you have some background in English literature, assemble a small collection of rock lyrics from the 1970s and try to confront the question of rock "poetry"—the quality and consistency of the imagery, to what extent it can stand on its own as poetry, and so forth. You might wish to use the same approach for more recent material that Richard Goldstein did extensively for earlier rock lyrics in his *The Poetry of Rock* (New York: Bantam paperback, 1968).

9. Find an LP album that forms an integrated, unified whole in some way similar to that of Zappa's *Absolutely Free*, or the Beatles' *Sgt. Pepper's Lonely Hearts Club Band*. Analyze and describe the ways in which this integration is achieved.

10. Describe and analyze the theatrical aspects of a live rock concert you have attended.

11. Describe in as much detail as possible a recent synthesis of rock and symphonic music—on records or preferably in a live performance. Comment on its effectiveness.

12. Make a study of the modern sound recording studio and its equipment, and illustrate some of its effects on modern pop and rock music.

Part Four
The Broadway Galaxy

A byproduct of the specialization of human endeavor and the growth of the cities has been the evolution of a popular culture (made for the people by specialists) distinct from a folk culture (made for the people by the people themselves). By analogy with the strikingly similar production of goods, it is indicative of the state reached by a people when the store-bought replaces the homemade; the store-bought may not work any better or last any longer (if as long), but it is much less trouble to come by, it is without the individualistic and perhaps awkward quirks of the nonprofessional maker, and it tends to look more like everybody else's everywhere. Popular culture will emerge wherever and whenever the great mass of the people want, and can afford, art that has the look or sound of the familiar (it almost always has some points of resemblance with either the folk art or the well-accepted fine art that is known), that adds something desirable and even necessary to their lives without being too difficult to understand, and that can be mass-produced and widely disseminated. Because of the vast market, those who can create successfully this kind of art are naturally very well paid for doing it, but there are never very many around at any given time who can do it extremely well—who can meet, in other words, the exacting and often mysterious qualifications for being extremely popular.

Popular culture was formerly disdained or simply ignored by those who could have accurately described and assessed it for us in relation to its times, and seen to the preservation of some of its relics—the scholars. Hence we know as little of the popular art of former times as we know of the folk art, which is always less than we know of the fine art.

However, we do know that as far as popular music in America is concerned, we have nearly always had it. Popular music was a going concern in Europe (as we know, for example, from the broadside ballads and the ballad operas of England) before America was developing its own music of any kind. We imported it along with all of our other music, at first. It was not until shortly after the beginning of the Jacksonian period of political equalitarianism that we began to make our own distinctive kind (unless one considers as popular music the products of the Yankee singing-school composers). And we did not begin to develop a real popular music industry until the end of the nineteenth century. During the last fifty years—since the development of mass media other than print—Americans have manufactured music catering to popular taste as efficiently as we have fabricated 5,000 movies, 500 million automobiles, and 50 billion hamburgers.

Popular art is no longer ignored by scholars and observers of culture. Popular music (as a component of popular culture generally) is an extremely sensitive—even mercurial—indicator of the temperament and preoccupations of a people, and hence to be taken into account.

Nor is popular art ignored any longer by artists. It has become "subject *matter" itself.* We *have seen this come about only fairly recently in the pictorial arts, but Charles Ives was composing music "about" popular music in the first two decades of this century.*

Finally, it needs to be recognized that in the more than a hundred years of its existence, American popular music has grown up into its own sophistications, and arranged itself into its own layers of excellence, as does any kind of art. That popular music is a lively subject for study is undeniable; it is also true that the good popular song—the one in ten thousand that transcends the ephemeral nature of the genre and for reasons known, unknown, or only guessed at endures to stick in the minds even of succeeding generations—adds its own kind of luster to American music.

Chapter Ten
Broadway, Hollywood, and Tin Pan Alley

GEOGRAPHY FURNISHES LABELS that manage to convey *multum in parvo*. When considering that vast complex of the American entertainment business which, evolving gradually after the Civil War, came to function with such efficiency, such glamorous opulence, and such apparent omnipotence until the mid-twentieth century, one is tempted to think in terms of a "Broadway galaxy," whose nether regions embraced Tin Pan Alley and whose western extension was Hollywood. None of these geographical designations is precisely accurate (Tin Pan Alley, as a street, is wholly mythical, but its legendary ambience moved gradually uptown from 14th to 47th Street). Each, however, signifies a genre, and taken together they denote a historic musical and business empire that supplied America's popular music needs for nearly a century.

At the undisputed center of gravity of the galaxy, of course, was New

York. Long before the Civil War, New York City had firmly established its leadership as the entertainment capital of the United States. Even before 1800 a generous fare of pantomimes, masques, farces, and ballad operas was presented in the theaters of New York, which, outstripping Philadelphia, was soon to become our largest city. It was here, in one of the many popular variety theaters, that the minstrel show first came into being (in 1843); it was here that P. T. Barnum, appealing to a more sophisticated clientele, first introduced Jenny Lind in 1850; it was here, in the immediate wake of the Civil War, that the blend of ingredients which were to prove so successful as old-fashioned musical comedy was put together, virtually by accident, at fashionable Niblo's Garden; and it was in New York in the 1880s that Tony Pastor, from heterogeneous elements taken from the minstrel show and the circus, put together fashionable and respectable vaudeville.

Yet despite all this activity, what could be called a genuinely native American idiom of popular song was slow in evolving. Our popular music had first an Anglo-Celtic and later a Viennese accent, and in fact the latter influence has persisted well into the twentieth century. Some of the songs of Stephen Foster, especially those done for the minstrel stage, constituted a kind of first flowering of a native idiom—what James Maher has called a "brief false spring of American popular song." But this was not followed up in the decades after the Civil War; in fact, the last songs of Foster himself show a kind of retreat into an undistinguished banality, as, ill and discouraged, he was forced into hack work. Both the white and black versions of the minstrel show, crude but vital, were gradually relegated to the sticks, in favor of the more urbane and European-like popular music prevalent in the cities. Popular song has become one of America's most famous exports, but it was not really thoroughly Americanized until the twentieth century.[1]

The Three Genres of American Popular Song

A consistent theme among thoughtful observers is the stratification of American popular song as regards craftsmanship and sophistication— a stratification that would seem to be valid for most of the twentieth century and is still not altogether invalid as we enter its last quarter. At the top is the music written for the theater: the Broadway show songs. As Nat Shapiro has written: "The Broadway musical is traditionally the primary source of superior popular music in this country." [2] The theater songs constitute the great canon of American popular song, which includes most of the "evergreens" (such as *Smoke Gets in Your Eyes*). Almost everyone, with a little prodding, can probably whistle a few measures of the main strain of at least a dozen of these tunes.

Slightly below the theater songs, in terms of sophistication, is that class of songs which began to appear in the 1930s—the movie songs, meaning those written originally for films, and excluding, of course, those belonging to the numerous film versions of Broadway musicals. Notwithstanding a *general* level of craftsmanship slightly lower than that of the theater songs, this category includes many fine "standards" (many by theater composers), such as *Laura, The Way You Look Tonight*, and *You'd Be So Nice to Come Home To*.

Beyond the theater songs and the movie songs is that vast category of songs purveyed by what Maher calls "the marketplace-oriented music publishing companies known collectively as Tin Pan Alley." With notable exceptions (to be acknowledged by a sampling in due course), these songs are short-lived, manufactured to conform to the passing fashions of the year, the season, the month. They issue forth in prodigious quantities, and are mostly soon forgotten. The more instantly responsive the media have become, and the more intensively the songs are disseminated, the shorter their life expectancy. Among the Tin Pan Alley songs may be found novelties ranging from *Ta-Ra-Ra-Boom-De-Ay!* of the Gay Nineties (a song that has shown an amazing vitality) through such later insipidities as *Ja-Da* (the teens of the twentieth century), *Yes, We Have No Bananas* (the twenties), *Let's All Sing Like the Birdies Sing* (the thirties), *Mairzy Doats* (the forties), *I Saw Mommy Kissing Santa Claus* (the fifties), and *Itsy-Bitsy, Teenie-Weenie Yellow Polka-Dot Bikini* (the sixties). They range in sentimentality from the melodramatic (*She May Have Seen Better Days*) to the mawkish (*The Little White Cloud That Cried*). Among them may be found the occasional topical song, a genre basically foreign to Tin Pan Alley, but appearing in times of extraordinary stress and unity of concern and action—for example, *Comin' in on a Wing and a Prayer*, of World War II. Here also is the manufactured imitation, the pseudo-song (*The Last Round-Up*, pseudo-cowboy; *Scarlet Ribbons*, pseudo-folk). Yet there also appear among the Tin Pan Alley songs some few which have the enduring qualities that have made them standards: *Blue Skies, Stormy Weather, You Go to My Head*, and that amazing perennial *Star Dust*, which began life as a solo piano ragtime composition.

There have been exceptional composers (such as Irving Berlin) who have written extensively and successfully not just in two of these genres (which is not too uncommon) but in all three. But this is rare; for the most part the composer finds that his inclinations and talents place him in one particular niche. It is time now to consider each of these niches separately.

BROADWAY AND THE POPULAR MUSICAL STAGE

The American popular musical stage—what we usually mean when we use the term "Broadway"—has an interesting and varied ancestry. Such diverse popular entertainments as the early ballad opera (with its English background), the "speaking pantomime," the "burlesque" (in its original sense of caricature), the "extravaganza" (owing something to French influence), and certain aspects of the minstrel show (our first indigenous popular musical stage entertainment) are just as surely its lineal forebears as *The Black Crook* and the imported Savoy and Viennese operettas of a later period. Let us take a brief glance at some of its native roots.

Infancy: The Colonial Period to the Civil War

Colonial America was by no means devoid of a popular musical stage, although its development in the North was limited by religious and moral strictures that were actually written into law in some cities (Boston, for example). These strictures were not against music itself, but against the presentation of plays of any kind. But the public's appetite for popular musical entertainment was strong. Various subterfuges and circumlocutions were resorted to: An opera, for example, might be known as "a Lecture . . . properly diversified with music, scenery, and other decorations" or "a Monody . . . accompanied with vocal incantations." The strictures, for somewhat different reasons, were especially severe during the Revolution and immediately following it.[3] They were largely a thing of the past, however, by the end of Washington's first term, even in Boston.

What the public heard almost exclusively was ballad opera, the earliest form of musical theater known here. It was English in origin, and like latter-day musical comedy, used spoken dialogue. Also like musical comedy, it made a point of including popular tunes; these tunes, however, instead of being composed for the particular opera, were in most cases "borrowed" —from folk songs, from popular airs and ballads, or from Italian or English operas popular at the time. The ballad operas heard here went by such titles as *The Devil to Pay*, *Damon and Phillida*, *The Honest Yorkshireman*, *The Maid of the Mill*, and *The Padlock*, the latter famous for its Negro character, Mungo, played by a white actor in blackface. These were English operas. The relationship with the London stage was a close one; actors, managers, and whole companies came and went, and a popular opera such as *The Padlock* could be presented here the very next season after its initial success in London.

A perennial piece for many decades was John Gay's famous *Beggar's Opera*, as popular here as it was in England. With its colorful underworld characters and earthy atmosphere, it is still revived and played as a stylized period piece; and a twentieth-century adaptation of it by Kurt Weill and Bertolt Brecht (1928) has become well known, especially in its American translation by Mark Blitzstein (*The Three-Penny Opera*, 1954).

After 1800 other forms of popular musical theater began to supersede the ballad opera. Noteworthy was the burlesque. Not to be confused with the exploitative sex shows of more recent times, the burlesque, using the term in its original sense, was a humorous and satirical parody—of famous plays, of stories, or of well-known performers. A burlesque on *Hamlet* appeared in 1828; the first on an American subject was *Pocahontas* in 1855, followed the next year by a sequel, *Hiawatha*. The burlesque, with many of its devices, persisted into the latter part of the nineteenth century, as we shall note presently.

The pantomime was another form popular before the Civil War, with stories and characters adapted from fairy tales or the *commedia dell' arte*, and elaborate stage effects. Close upon the heels of the pantomime came the extravaganza, also with lavish stage spectacles, acrobats, and aerialists, and frequently with a topical theme. (*Novelty, with the Laying of the Atlantic Cable* played New York, by now the undisputed capital of entertainment, in 1857.)

The minstrel show, beginning in the 1840s, was an enormously popular form of entertainment, quite unsophisticated. (It will be treated in chapter 11.) In its original form, its heyday in the cities was over by the Civil War, to be replaced by other forms, as we shall see, but certain aspects of it (such as broad elements of burlesque) survived in vaudeville, in the more ambitious revue, and even in the early movies, through such performers as Al Jolson. Its links to musical comedy itself are somewhat tenuous.

Adolescence: The Civil War Through World War I

The adolescence of the American popular musical theater was a period of exuberance and experimentation that produced a profusion of overlapping genres. By the end of this period the quality and distinctiveness of the music had improved noticeably, and the shows and their music had come a long way towards being truly native in character.

An initial impetus towards this exuberance and experimentation came with a single production that reached the New York stage, in its final form, virtually by accident. This was the famous production *The Black Crook*, of 1866. The curious story of its genesis has been often told; the burning down of the Academy of Music, one of New York's large theaters, led to the incorporation of a stranded troupe of French ballet dancers into the production of a German-style melodrama. To the bodily allurements of the girls—two hundred of them, some in flesh-colored tights ("imitating nature so well that the illusion is complete," according to a disapproving clergyman)—was added stage spectacle on a scale hitherto unknown. William Wheatley, the producer, had completely rebuilt the stage of Niblo's Garden to allow for elaborate machinery and effects, which reached their climax in a final "transformation scene." Costuming (except for the seductive economy of the pink tights) was on an equally elaborate scale. *The Black Crook*, running for sixteen months and grossing more than a million dollars, became an American institution; it toured extensively and was revived eight times in New York. In the twentieth century it was revived as late as 1929, and subsequently the circumstances of its origin became the basis for Sigmund Romberg's last musical (unfortunately not successful), *The Girl in Pink Tights* (1954).

The Black Crook has been called the starting point of American musical comedy. But this is inaccurate, for as Cecil Smith has pointed out, real musical comedy was not to appear for another generation, and *The Black Crook*, with its thin, dated, and derivative melodramatic plot and its emphasis on stage spectacle, looked more to the past than to the future.[4] None of its ingredients were new, nor did any *one* of them—the ballet, the glorification of the female figure, the spectacular staging—prove to be an indispensable ingredient of the later musical, though all of them reappear consistently as elements. What was new was not only their combination but the prodigally lavish scale of the production (said to have cost more than $35,000, a record, and an astounding outlay for the time), and the fact that its long run (474 performances) established a new pattern that subsequent producers aimed to duplicate. It was the first real Broadway "hit."

After the impetus of *The Black Crook*, the New York stage became the arena for continued experiment on a new scale. Imports were periodically popular. Old concepts—such as the pantomime, the burlesque (with its "trousers" roles as a convenient institution for getting the female figure onstage in tights), and the extravaganza—were refurbished and combined in new ways. Occasionally a new idea emerged, such as vaudeville, which evolved as a show of individual unrelated acts.

Many of the types of musical shows actually made negligible contributions as far as music is concerned. The American popular stage languished musically, in fact, until the importation of comic opera of exceptionally high quality from London, Paris, and Vienna beginning in the last quarter of the century. This may be regarded as a mixed blessing, of course, depending upon one's viewpoint. It possibly delayed the development of a truly indigenous popular musical theater; certainly it imprinted on the American musical a European stamp that was still visible (in some quarters) well into the twentieth century. But at the same time it introduced new standards of quality to the popular stage—quality both of ideas and craftsmanship, without which the American musical could never have reached its own level of competence and sophistication so soon.

William Gilbert and Arthur Sullivan in London, Jacques Offenbach in Paris, Johann Strauss, Jr., in Vienna—each of these represented a peak of achievement in English, French, and German comic opera, all coming at about the same time. It was an unprecedented era of concentrated brilliance, which was bound to cast a few beams on this side of the Atlantic as well.

As far as the general public was concerned, the London "invasion" came first; *H.M.S. Pinafore* was heard (in a stolen version) in Boston in 1878, and became prodigiously popular at once. (The dismal story of the way Gilbert and Sullivan's comic operas were pirated here reflects little credit on the status of international copyright agreements or the ethics of American theatrical producers.) After *Pinafore*, there followed in short order *The Pirates of Penzance* (premiered in New York by the author's own company, to protect their rights), and then *Iolanthe, The Sorcerer,* and *Princess Ida,* climaxed by the phenomenal success of *The Mikado* in 1885. Well-knit comic plots, songs that grow naturally out of comic or romantic situations on the stage, well-crafted lyrics that make their points deftly, and memorable tunes that still never get in the way of the lyrics—these are some of the qualities that have made Gilbert and Sullivan continuously popular on both sides of the Atlantic for nearly a century. Furthermore, as both consumers and producers here recognized at once, these were precisely the qualities that musical comedy needed and had been lacking. It is not that musical comedy was henceforth to evolve precisely along the rather stylized lines of Gilbert and Sullivan; literal imitation, particularly of a foreign genre, is a peculiarly futile artistic exercise. But a new example of superior craftsmanship had been shown, and it was to help usher in a new era of competence on the musical stage.

Both French *opéra bouffe* and Viennese operetta had been known in the United States in the 1860s and 1870s, but for the most part in their original languages and therefore not accessible to wide audiences. (Both Johann Strauss, Jr., and Offenbach had visited America in the seventies, primarily as orchestral conductors.) The new popularity of English comic opera created a popular audience for other European light opera as well, and many were presented in English translations.[5]

After a lull in the nineties, Viennese operetta again enjoyed a great period of popularity here with the advent of *The Merry Widow* by Franz Lehar in 1907, and *The Chocolate Soldier* by Oskar Straus in 1909. A host of operettas more or less on the Viennese model were subsequently produced by our adopted composers, as we shall see. Vienna itself, and the atmosphere of the Viennese operetta, still haunts the American musical stage from time to time; in 1934, for example, there appeared a show ostensibly about the Johann Strausses, senior and junior, with a musical score from their waltzes and the appropriate title *The Great Waltz*.

While these foreign importations were enjoying their popularity, there was also in the process of development a more native kind of musical show. The Harrigan and Hart comedies of the period represented an important early step toward the Americanization of the musical. These plays with interpolated songs were the first to discover New York itself as a promising setting for a musical, and thus tap a vein that from *The Belle of New York* to *Wonderful Town* has yielded attractive pay-dirt. Portraying with accuracy and humor the Irish, the Negroes, and the Germans in believable comic situations growing out of the everyday lives of everyday people, they were an immediate success. The first was *The Mulligan Guard Ball* (1879), and this was followed by many Mulligan Guard sequels with the same characters, much in the manner of a television situation-comedy series. The songs, all by David Braham, a London-born musician who came here at the age of fifteen, became popular at the time in their own right and were sometimes borrowed for other shows. Some songs, such as *The Widow Nolan's Goat* from *Squatters' Sovereignty*, brought a true Irish folk flavor to the musical stage.[6]

The movement toward the Americanization of the musical comedy of this period culminated in the shows and songs of George M. Cohan, the energetic and ambitious showman who came up from vaudeville to become an author, composer, stage director, and performer who well-nigh dominated the musical stage in the first two decades of this century. In describing Cohan, the one word inevitably used by writers is "brash." The directness of his style, his informality, and above all his fast pace (Heywood Broun described him as "a disciple of perpetual motion") brought new vitality to the theater. Cohan was right for his time, and fittingly marked the last step in the adolescence of our popular musical theater, sounding a decisive note of independence from Europe. His three most important and characteristic shows came early in the century: *Little Johnny Jones* in 1904, and *Forty-five Minutes from Broadway* and *George Washington, Jr.*, in 1906. (*The Little Millionaire*, the last of this genre, came in 1911.) Of the first three, each has its American hero (a jockey, a reformed gambler, a young super-patriot), and the three shows together contain the best of Cohan's show tunes.

Cohan could write a good moderate-tempo tune (e.g., *Mary's a Good Old Name*, with its echoes of ragtime and barbershop harmony) and an American-sounding waltz (*Forty-five Minutes from Broadway*), but his most characteristic songs were his snappy up-tempo show tunes, in which he invariably made the most of the kind of rudimentary syncopation found in the chorus of *Dixie* (e.g., *Give My Regards to Broadway*; *Yankee Doodle Boy*; *You're a Grand Old Flag*; and one of his few non-show songs, *Over There*, the most popular song to emerge from World War I).

His lyrics could be good, or at times appallingly inept, yet he could come up with an unfailing catch-phrase, and much of the effectiveness of his songs is due to his ability to find just the right musical setting for those phrases, which were often the titles as well: "Give my regards to Broadway"; "You're a grand old flag"; "Over there"; "So long, Mary"; "I was born in Virginia" (this last was the closest in rhythm to ragtime that Cohan got).[7] Cohan's quotations from the other songs (*Yankee Doodle; Dixie; The Girl I Left Behind Me; The Star-Spangled Banner; Marching Through Georgia; Auld Lang Syne*) were an odd but characteristic quirk in his patriotic numbers.

George M. Cohan was a phenomenal success in his day, but given his limitations it was inevitable that his material, his approach, and even his songs should become dated, and the American musical theater passed him by in the 1920s. He continued his career as an actor, and was a success in *Ah! Wilderness*, and cast as President Franklin D. Roosevelt in the musical *I'd Rather Be Right*. Before his death, his career was dramatized on the screen in *Yankee Doodle Dandy*, with James Cagney, and his music was recently back on Broadway in the nostalgic reconstruction *George M!* (1968).

Our brief survey of the adolescence of the popular musical stage in America is nearly at an end, but there were three important developments which, because of their uniqueness and the fact that they overlap into the next period, demand separate treatment.

BROADWAY AND THE NEGRO

Late in the nineteenth century it began to be apparent that the contribution of the Negro to America's popular musical stage need not—in fact *could* not—be forever limited to the caricatured renditions of the minstrel stage. (The minstrel show was by this time more the province of the blacks than the whites as performers, but the stage stereotypes remained the same.) Change, however, was painfully slow, as we shall see.

It should be clear that there were two aspects to the Negro's contribution. The first was the talent that black professional writers and composers placed at the service of prevalent theatrical styles; the second was the infusion of styles that were essentially of black origin into the music of the popular stage—at first ragtime, and later blues, jazz, and ultimately rhythm-and-blues. The first kind of black participation has gone on more or less continuously since the turn of the century. For example, Robert Cole and the two brothers J. Rosamund and James Weldon Johnson were professional songwriters for the Broadway stage around 1900; their song *The Maid with the Dreamy Eyes*, for instance, was written especially for Anna Held in *The Little Duchess* of 1901. Later, Noble Sissle and Eubie Blake wrote *You Were Meant for Me* for Gertrude Lawrence and Noel Coward.

As for the infusion of musical elements of Negro origin, ragtime had reached Broadway in the 1890s; or actually it is more accurate to say that attenuated whiffs of ragtime reached Broadway, in the form of ragtime songs.* Songs of this type were *Mister Johnson, Turn Me Loose,* by ragtime composer and sometime minstrel performer Ben Harney, and *All Coons Look Alike to Me,* by black songwriter Ernest Hogan. Both songs were incorporated into *Courted into Court* in 1896 by May Irwin, popular singing comedienne who was famous for her renditions of "coon songs." The ragtime song soon became disreputable (Hogan suffered acutely for his contribution, mostly on account of its title, during his lifetime), but it was the form in which at least the flavor of ragtime was first brought to the predominantly white audiences of the time, even before the appearance of shows such as *Clorindy.* Outside the theater, songs by both black and white composers showing similar ragtime influence were making their way on Tin Pan Alley, as we shall see.

What of the appearance of black artists on the Broadway stage itself? The great difficulty these performers faced, as we have noted, was the image of the minstrel show, which cast a long shadow. Harrigan and Hart pioneered as early as 1883 in using a group of black dancers in one of the last of their white comedies, *Cordelia's Aspirations,* but the title of their number, *Sam Johnson's Cakewalk,* suggests strong minstrel influence still. An important step was the appearance in the 1890s of shows featuring beautiful Negro women (*The Creole Show,* 1890; *The Octoroons,* 1895). *Oriental America* (1896) was the first Broadway show with an all-Negro cast, and it broke significantly with minstrel tradition.

Two important landmarks came in 1898. Robert Cole produced the first full-length all-Negro musical show, *A Trip to Coontown.* But more successful and memorable was an all-Negro musical comedy sketch, *Clorindy, the Origin of the Cakewalk,* with music by the talented and well-trained black musician Will Marion Cook. This show, with its characteristic music, dancing, and choral singing, created a sensation and opened the doors for black music and musicians on the Broadway stage, performing for predominantly white audiences. The first wave of black musicals followed. Will Marion Cook himself wrote a succession of shows; the next three were unsuccessful, but *In Dahomey* (1902), a satirization of the scheme of colonizing American Negroes in Africa; *In Abyssinia* (1906), an extravaganza laid in Africa; and *In Bandana Land* (1907), laid in the American South, were hits.[8] The previously mentioned team of Cole and the Johnson brothers wrote two musicals, *The Shoo-Fly Regiment* (1906) and *The Red Moon* (1908), and J. Rosamund Johnson wrote the music for *Mr. Lode of Koal* (or Kole), of 1909. Thus the first period of activity of the black musical lasted for a decade.

* See chapter 11 for a discussion of ragtime.

After a lull during the second decade of this century, a second era of black musical shows was inaugurated in 1921 by the famous *Shuffle Along*, with lyrics by Noble Sissle and music by Eubie Blake. It was essentially a revue. Some of its fast numbers (of which *I'm Just Wild About Harry* was the most famous) are imbued with the ebullient but easygoing momentum of ragtime and early jazz; some (such as *Bandana Days*) are almost pure George M. Cohan. Of its slow songs, some are in the style of the standard sentimental show tune (*Love Will Find a Way*), which the authors feared, needlessly, might not be accepted by a white audience from black singing actors; other slow tunes are close to the blues (*Daddy, Won't You Please Come Home*). A recent reconstruction of some of the show's numbers from contemporary recordings shows the instrumental playing to give a fairly authentic flavor of ragtime and early jazz, while the singing represents the kind of compromise with currently popular show singing that attenuates its essential qualities.[9] This hybridization of styles is especially noticeable in the blues numbers, and is also a mark of the first actual blues recordings made a few years later, which were sung by show singers and not blues singers.

Shuffle Along brought together some distinguished black talent. In addition to Sissle as singer and Blake as both pianist and orchestra leader, Josephine Baker, Florence Mills and Paul Robeson sang; and in the orchestra pit Hall Johnson played the viola, and William Grant Still the oboe. The show is credited with helping to initiate the Harlem Renaissance of the 1920s—a period of interest in black culture. From that time until the Depression many all-black shows played Broadway. Blake and Sissle wrote three more, and among others of note were *Keep Shuffling* (1928) and *Hot Chocolates* (1929), with music by Thomas "Fats" Waller.

Shows for all-Negro casts were written by white writers as well; *Blackbirds of 1928*, with music by Jimmy McHugh (which included *I Can't Give You Anything but Love, Baby*) introduced tap-dancer Bill "Bojangles" Robinson to the Broadway stage. Later Oscar Hammerstein II brought out a very successful adaptation from the realm of opera in the all-black *Carmen Jones* (1943). In this connection, it is perhaps worth mentioning here that two important American operas appearing in the 1930s had all-Negro casts: Virgil Thomson's *Four Saints in Three Acts* (1934) and George Gershwin's *Porgy and Bess* (1935).

A more recent black musical idiom, rhythm-and-blues, has been brought to Broadway in a lavishly staged Negro adaptation of a classic (*The Wizard of Oz*) called *The Wiz* (1975).

OUR ADOPTED COMPOSERS

Building on the basic style, form, and approach of operetta, three adopted composers brought a consistent level of competence to the popular musical stage. During the forty years from Victor Herbert's first success, *The Wizard of the Nile* (1895), to Sigmund Romberg's last Viennese piece *May Wine* (1935), there was hardly a time when there was not an American operetta on the Broadway stage. What were the distinguishing features of the operetta? After tracing briefly this adopted form through its generation of popularity, we shall perhaps arrive at a rough-and-ready description that will differentiate it from the other types of shows competing for the public's attention.

Its three great American exponents were Victor Herbert, Rudolf Friml, and Sigmund Romberg. All three were European-born, and all received there a thorough musical training (though Romberg's was more practical than formal, gained by hanging around the very epicenter of German-language operetta, the Theater-an-der-Wien in Vienna). All came to America, thus fully trained and equipped, in their twenties. Although there is no question that they fully adopted and were adopted by America, and that their work belongs in any account of American music, it nevertheless remained basically European in style and approach, in contrast with the work of Cohan, Berlin, Gershwin, and Rodgers.[10]

Victor Herbert (1859–1924) had the broadest musical experience and competence of the three, with a versatility seldom encountered. He was a virtuoso cellist (premiering two cello concertos of his own composition here), a symphony conductor (of the Pittsburgh Symphony for five seasons), a bandmaster, and a composer of symphonic music and opera. He entered the field of the popular musical show at the age of thirty-five, but once in, he knew that the theater was his métier. He was extraordinarily facile; the shows that he wrote or contributed music to number in the dozens. With his thorough knowledge of the orchestra, he was one of the first popular composers to write his own orchestrations, thus improving enormously the quality of the sounds that emanated from the orchestra pit and bringing new high standards to this craft.

Herbert continued to write musicals right up until his death, but his major contributions were made in the two decades between *The Wizard of the Nile* (1895) and *Eileen* (1917), and included *The Fortune Teller* (1898), *Babes in Toyland* (1903), *Mlle. Modiste* (1905), *The Red Mill* (1906), *Naughty Marietta* (1910), and *Sweethearts* (1913). In addition to his gift for producing a memorable melody (surely a sine qua non in the business, in any period but the most moribund), Herbert's virtuosity as a composer enabled him to handle ensemble and choral scenes (e.g., the opening scene of *Naughty Marietta*, with its street cries) with a skill and inventiveness heretofore associated only with opera. He could produce telling variations (as in the theme piece in *The Serenade*) and stylistic parodies (his extended number *If I Were on the Stage* from *Mlle. Modiste* contains an evocation of *Die Fledermaus*, a polonaise, and one of his most famous waltzes, *Kiss Me Again*).[11] He could produce a rousing march

(*Tramp, Tramp, Tramp,* in *Naughty Marietta*) or an authentic-sounding Hungarian czardas (*Romany Life,* in *The Fortune Teller*). In short, the musical stage had in Victor Herbert a gifted, competent, and prolific composer.

Rudolf Friml (1879–1972), born in Prague, was another thoroughly schooled musician, who was in his early years a concert pianist. His range was somewhat narrower, but between 1912 (*The Firefly*) and 1928 (*The Three Musketeers*) he produced some enduring operettas, including *Rose Marie* (1924) and *The Vagabond King* (1925).

Sigmund Romberg (1887–1951) was more versatile than Friml. He identified himself completely with the popular musical theater, writing music for numerous revues for the Shuberts and others, including *The Passing Show* between 1914 and 1924. But his forte was operetta, with a pronounced Viennese flavor, and his main contributions were *Maytime* (1917), *The Student Prince* (1924), *The Desert Song* (1926), *The New Moon* (1928), and *May Wine* (1935).

From the major works of these three composers, we can arrive at a working definition of that form so popular in America from the Gay Nineties to the Depression—the operetta, or "light opera." Its setting was exotic, belonging to another place and time: perhaps Vienna itself (Romberg's *The Blue Paradise, Blossom Time,* or *May Wine*) or Heidelberg (Romberg's *The Student Prince*) or Hungary (Herbert's *The Fortune Teller*), but Paris would do (Herbert's *Mlle. Modiste,* or, in a late medieval setting, Friml's *The Vagabond King*). A New World setting could be made to work, if remote enough from the urban or rural humdrum in place and time. Eighteenth-century New Orleans was ideal (Herbert's *Naughty Marietta* and Romberg's *The New Moon*). The Canadian Rockies was a daring departure, but with Friml's *Rose Marie* it succeeded. (A near-duplicate setting, the Colorado Rockies, was chosen for a witty but slight satire of the genre in Rick Besoyan's *Little Mary Sunshine,* 1959). Romberg's late treatment of a New York setting (*Up in Central Park*) dealt, characteristically, with a time remote enough to be romanticized (the 1870s era of Boss Tweed) and given an appropriate Currier and Ives atmosphere.

The characters often included royalty or nobility, frequently incognito (*Mlle. Modiste, The New Moon, Sweethearts*), but gypsies, brigands, and opera singers were favorites. The plot usually involved either concealed identity or concealed fortune (*The Red Mill, Naughty Marietta, The Student Prince, The Desert Song*), and the hoary theatrical resort of look-alikes was employed (*The Fortune Teller, It Happened in Nordland*). In short, the stock theatrical devices were applied to characters remote enough to be romanticized.

The music was tuneful, often memorably so, and showed far better than average craftmanship. Like its Viennese counterpart, it placed its greatest faith in its waltzes, which really epitomized the genre, and we could do worse than to close our brief survey of a form once so popular with a litany of a few of its greatest waltzes, of which nearly every show had at least one: *The Absinthe Frappé* (Herbert's *It Happened in Nordland*); *Kiss Me Again* (Herbert's *Mlle. Modiste*); *The Streets of New York* (Herbert's *The Red Mill*); *I'm Falling in Love with Someone* (Herbert's *Naughty Marietta*); *Sympathy* (Friml's *The Firefly*); *Will You Remember?*, known also as *Sweetheart Waltz* (Romberg's *Maytime*).

THE REVUE FROM THE GAY NINETIES TO THE ADVENT OF TELEVISION

Thriving during the same period as the operetta was an even lighter form of entertainment, usually associated with the late spring or summer portion of the season, which could name among its humbler ancestors, if it chose, the olio of the minstrel show, and vaudeville, and among its more sophisticated and risqué the type of Parisian show from which it took its generic name—the *revue*. The "trade" names were many: "passing show," "follies," "scandals," "vanities." Dispensing usually even with a pretense of dramatic thread or interest, it was a succession of acts. Into it went the ancient elements of song-and-dance, burlesque, spectacle, and of course the display of feminine beauty. Of such elements (except spectacle) vaudeville and the older burlesque had been constituted. But brought "uptown" from the vaudeville theaters, the revue was produced with a lavishness and sophistication that made it appeal to the Broadway theater public. In short, it had "class." It concerns us in passing, only for the few good scores and songs to come out of this type of show, when gifted composers were called upon to write for it.

The revue as we know it began with *The Passing Show of 1894*, which was musically undistinguished but established the potential popularity of the genre. The pattern of shows with yearly editions was begun in 1907 with the famous *Ziegfeld Follies*, which with few exceptions were produced each year until his death in 1932 by the great show business entrepreneur Florenz Ziegfeld. (Three more *Ziegfeld Follies* were produced after his death, the last in 1943.) These productions set new standards for opulence, for the beauty of the girls, and for the quality of talent presented, a roster of which would read like a list of the greats of the entertainment world during the generation the shows encompassed: Anna Held (Ziegfeld's first wife), Fanny Brice, Sophie Tucker, W. C. Fields, Will Rogers, Eddie Cantor, Ed Wynn. Both Victor Herbert and Irving Berlin provided music on occasion; songs to come out of the *Ziegfeld Follies* included *Shine On, Harvest Moon* (1908) and Irving Berlin's *A Pretty Girl Is Like a Melody* (1919), which, like many of the hit songs in these shows, was made into a lavish production number.

Ziegfeld's competition was *The Passing Show* (reviving the title of the prototype of the form), whose editions ran from 1912 through 1924—for the last ten years with music by Sigmund Romberg. Its 1918 version introduced Fred and Adele Astaire, and two songs, *Smiles* and *I'm Forever Blowing Bubbles*, that were not by Romberg. *George White's Scandals* ran from 1919 to 1939; these are worthy of note mostly because George Gershwin wrote all the music for the five shows of 1920–1924, including *Somebody Loves Me*. Irving Berlin's *Music Box Revues*, 1921–1924, brought out his *Say It with Music*.

The revue furnished a welcome pattern for the musicals that were in demand as soon as sound was added to motion pictures, as we shall see. The form continues to exist, and many "book" shows, with ostensible plots, continue to be only one small step away from the revue (*Hair*, for example, in 1968), as indeed many always have been, with a continual freshening of topical material. But the heyday of the extravaganza type of revue ended with World War II. Changing tastes, and television spectaculars reaching millions instead of the stage show's thousands, are two factors in its decline.[12]

The Musical in Its Maturity: *Show Boat* to *West Side Story*

The musical show had its period of greatest achievement in the thirty years that began with *Show Boat* (1927) and ended with *West Side Story* (1957). (By the time *Pal Joey* came along, somewhere midway, the term "musical comedy" was no longer appropriate.) Naturally allowance must be made for the risks of trying to define an era precisely, but the point is that during this time the musical had set itself new musical-dramatic problems, and had solved them, without ceasing to captivate and entertain its audience. *Carousel*; *Kiss Me, Kate*; *Guys and Dolls*; and *My Fair Lady* came very close to perfection in the form. It was a period of sustained creation by major writers devoting their talents principally to the live musical stage, and it was, moreover, a period when the popular stage still had its audience. Broadway was in a clear position of leadership, and supplied America (and much of the world) with its best popular music.

Show Boat, long an acknowledged landmark, marks a fairly clear beginning of the era. Operetta had had its last spurt of great productions in the year or two previous. Jerome Kern, a veteran at forty-two, had been writing for Broadway for nearly a quarter-century, but this was clearly a new departure, and set its sights on new territory for the musical to explore. The end of the era is more difficult to establish precisely, but by the time of *West Side Story* the new ground that the musical had staked out had been rather thoroughly cultivated, and the work of the major writers and teams that had given their stamp to the period was done, or nearly so; the two subsequent and last collaborations of Richard Rodgers and Oscar Hammerstein II (*Flower Drum Song*, 1958, and *The Sound of Music*, 1959), and the last collaboration of Frederick Loewe and Alan Jay Lerner (*Camelot*, 1960), while successful, were by no means their best. New creators, new types of shows, and new patterns of entertainment were on the way.

A glance at the thirty years under consideration reveals the domination of five superbly equipped and successful composers: Jerome Kern, Irving Berlin, George Gershwin, Richard Rodgers, and Cole Porter, each of whom wrote the music for at least a dozen shows (with some falling outside the limits of our period). Four others also made important contributions: Kurt Weill, and near the end of the period, Leonard Bernstein, Frederick Loewe, and Frank Loesser. During these thirty years only one year passed without the appearance of a new show by at least one of these nine composers; in most years there were two or three. Their shows and the best-known of their hundreds of songs are so familiar that a mere listing would be pointless. What will be most profitable here will be to consider certain aspects of the musical itself—areas in which innovation and evolution occurred during its period of greatest achievement.

THE EVOLUTION OF DRAMATIC VALUES

During this period there was a great widening and deepening of the dramatic dimensions of the musical—a gain in both range and verisimilitude, without compromising the musical's essential nature as entertainment. Subject matter, plot, characterization, and range of emotion were all broadened. A brief look at eleven shows of the era should substantiate this.

Show Boat (1927, music by Jerome Kern, book and lyrics by Oscar Hammerstein II), our point of departure, clearly stood out as being of more substantial stuff, dramatically. Adapted from Edna Ferber's novel, it put real characters in valid situations—Magnolia, the sheltered daughter of the Mississippi show boat's owner, who survives a broken marriage with a riverboat gambler to make her way to the top as a musical comedy star; the half-caste Julie, singing two love songs that shattered the conventional sentimental mold, *Can't Help Lovin' Dat Man* and *Bill* ("an ordinary boy"). Also worthy of note was the realistic and sympathetic portrayal of blacks on the stage—in this case, as stevedores on the levee. *Old Man River* is not, and should not be confused with, real Negro song, but it is a superb theatrical song, right in its context.

Gershwin's *Porgy and Bess* (1935) had impressive dramatic dimensions, but since it was a venture into the realm of opera itself, it will be considered there (see chapter 14). Apart from this, satire and social comment absorbed a good deal of the musical theater's energies in the 1930s. After this preoccupation (which will be dealt with below), the musical made new dramatic strides in the 1940s.

Pal Joey (1940, music by Richard Rodgers, lyrics by Lorenz Hart, book by John O'Hara) was again substantial dramatically, based on O'Hara's stories, which the author himself had suggested as a framework for a musical. It is strongest in characterization: The hero is a crass, selfish opportunist, finally abandoned by the two women who have, each in her own way, been used by him. The shoddy night club milieu of Chicago marked a new venture into the seamier aspects of realism. Vera's unsentimental love song to a heel, *Bewitched, Bothered, and Bewildered,* which gained musical force through a characteristic Rodgers device of the almost obsessive development of a small melodic motive, carried its dramatic theme a step further than had Julie's two songs in *Show Boat*. So novel for 1940 were the elements thus introduced into a Broadway musical that *Pal Joey* did not succeed with the public until its revival twelve years later.

Lady in the Dark (1941, music by Kurt Weill, lyrics by Ira Gershwin, book by Moss Hart) plunges us into the realm of psychosis and the dream fantasy. As foreign as this theme may seem to musical comedy, it was not new; Rodgers and Hart had explored it in 1926 in *Peggy-Ann,* and Romberg's *May Wine* (1935), with book by Frank Mandel based on a novel, dealt with a psychiatrist who was himself the victim of a delusion. But *Lady in the Dark* presents an almost clinical treatment of the subject, as the heroine, Liza, undergoes psychoanalysis. The dream sequences, more than mere surrealistic burlesque, have a genuine bearing on the lady's problems, and the three men from whom she must choose are real, three-dimensional characters. The dramatic resolution is neatly paralleled by a musical one; the mysterious tune Liza remembers from childhood, which has haunted the play as a fragmentary motive, appears at the end, completed and harmonized, as *My Ship*.

From the psychiatrist's couch to an Oklahoma cornfield on a summer morning—the musical show was ranging far. *Oklahoma!* (1943, music by Richard Rodgers, lyrics and book by Oscar Hammerstein II, based on a play by Lynn Riggs, *Green Grow the Lilacs*) broadened this range, and posed the problem of a sophisticated medium dealing with a folk subject and setting. The treatment was sympathetic, and did not stoop to burlesque or caricature, nor did the music descend in sophistication to the imitation of folk music. *Oh, What a Beautiful Mornin',* for all the ingenuousness of its sentiments (sentiments basically foreign to folk music itself) is, melodically and harmonically, a quite sophisticated song. The plot has a classic design—two love triangles. The songs grow naturally out of the situations, which permit the introduction of a wide range of unconventional songs, from the refreshingly homely description of *The Surrey with the*

Fringe to the bizarre fantasy of *Pore Jud.* Even the love song, *People Will Say We're in Love,* has a fresh approach.

Carousel (1945, music by Richard Rodgers, lyrics and book by Oscar Hammerstein II, based on the play *Liliom* by the Hungarian playwright Ferenc Molnar) has elements of tragedy and symbolic fantasy, with a finale built on the age-old theme of redemption—heavy fare for a musical show. The hero is an outcast who must conceal his tenderness beneath a bullying, swaggering exterior. Thus he cannot, in life, communicate his love to Julie, nor can she to him—"*If* I loved you" is as much as they can ever say to one another. His suicide brings an opportunity for redemption; stealing a star that he gives to the daughter he has never seen in life, he conquers, for them both, the alienation that was threatening to warp her existence as it had his. Music has an ample role; the entire prelude is pantomimed to a carousel waltz, and there is a ballet-pantomime sequence in the second act.

In a period of such vitality and productivity, it was inevitable that some shows would attempt unsuccessfully to extend the boundaries of the musical. *Allegro* (1947, music by Richard Rodgers, lyrics and book by Oscar Hammerstein II) was such a show. But even the relative failures of the period are interesting when they are inventive. The chorus, used effectively in the dream sequences of *Lady in the Dark,* has here a much more expanded role; it is used, in the words of the authors, "to interpret the mental and emotional reactions of the principal characters, after the manner of a Greek chorus." It has somewhat the role of the Stage Manager in *Our Town,* with which the first part of *Allegro* has some points in common. The life of the son of a small-town doctor, who also becomes a doctor, is traced from birth to the time when, fed up with the compromises, intrigues, and general vacuity of his lucrative city practice, he returns home to work with his father. But thirty-five years of biography is difficult to stage with dramatic intensity, even with characters more interesting and vividly drawn than Joseph Taylor, Jr., and Jenny Brinker.

Street Scene (1947, subtitled in the score "An American Opera," music by Kurt Weill, lyrics by Langston Hughes, book by Elmer Rice, based on his play of the same name) is a slice of New York City tenement life. The starkness of its story, compressed within less than twenty-four hours and seen from a single vantage point, gives it some of the aspects of Greek tragedy, fundamentally unrelieved. As its subtitle indicates, it is very close to opera. The music has a dominant role and is present most of the time, often underscoring dialogue and action, while the "songs" (some of which are subtitled "aria") emerge from a more or less continuous musical texture, instead of being set apart. Especially noteworthy are the ensembles. Duets and trios (fairly rare in the conventional musical) emerge naturally out of the dramatic contexts. The trio with Rose and her father and mother (*There'll Be Trouble*) climaxes a scene that is operatic in conception and execution. Ensembles such as the Ice Cream Sextet (one of the few lighter moments) brought to the musical stage the unusual sound of a complex contrapuntal texture of interweaving voices.

Two more Rodgers and Hammerstein collaborations brought innovations in theme and setting. *South Pacific* (1949), one of the best-crafted musicals of the period, was able to deal in song with one of the play's basic themes, interracial marriage, in *You've Got to Be Taught* ("to hate and fear"). These virtuosos of the form were able next to execute the remarkable feat of bringing an exotic Oriental setting to the stage (*The King and I*, 1951) and treating it tastefully, without resorting either to crude spectacle or to caricature, and without subjecting the audience to imitations of Oriental music. They also showed the extent to which sentimental convention could be discarded by authors with sufficient talent and daring, in depicting a relationship between two principals devoid of love interest. (Five years later the authors of *My Fair Lady*, an otherwise nearly perfect piece, felt obliged to make a concession to conventional sentimentality—even more persistent than "middle-class morality," it seems—in bringing Eliza back to Henry Higgins, in a dénouement that is weak and unconvincing dramatically, and that George Bernard Shaw specifically precluded in a preface to a play written after *Pygmalion*, on which *My Fair Lady* was based.)

The Most Happy Fella (1956, music, lyrics, and book by Frank Loesser, based on the play *They Knew What They Wanted* by Sidney Howard) explores new dramatic depths for the Broadway stage while retaining its idiom and approach. This is manifested in the growth we see in an older man—Tony, the wine grower—up to the point where he has the capacity to forgive the young Rosabella (whom he has wooed by mail and brought to be his bride) her infidelity. A pervading theme is that of loneliness seeking companionship. A full and rich score, with the music present most of the time, emphasizes the characterization or furthers the action in a variety of forms, from recitative and song to large ensemble and choral numbers or instrumental interludes.

SATIRE AND "SOCIAL SIGNIFICANCE"

In the troubled political and economic climate of the 1930s, the theater did what it has always done in such times—it assumed the role of commentator, satirist, and gadfly. What was new was the fact that the musical show, hitherto the realm of entertainment, fantasy, and escape, began to get itself involved to an extent previously unknown. It is not that political satire had ever been completely absent from musical comedy, here or abroad, as a closer look at Gilbert and Sullivan would reveal. But it now became more pointed and overt. A trend was established, and the orbit of politics furnished a setting for shows from *Strike Up the Band* (1930) to *Louisiana Purchase* (1940).

The treatment given this theme represented a rather wide spectrum of approaches. Three shows by the team of George Gershwin (music), Ira Gershwin (lyrics), and George S. Kaufman and Morrie Ryskind (book) were brilliantly acidic and made use of outrageous fantasy. The first was *Strike Up the Band* (1930), followed by *Of Thee I Sing* (1931). The latter—with its right combination of the fantastic (a beauty contest to determine who is to be the new First Lady, "Miss White House"), of good show songs, and of genuinely humorous satire (the vice-president is such an anonymous figure that he cannot join the public library because he cannot produce two references)—was the most successful of the three, and the first musical to win the Pulitzer Prize. The third, *Let 'em Eat Cake* (1933), not only suffered the disadvantages of being a sequel, but carried its fantasy to the extremes of revolution and dictatorship, and failed.

Two shows of this period had an even more conscious emphasis on "social significance." *Pins and Needles* (1937) was a very successful revue produced by the garment workers' union; an amateur show, with emphasis on overt propaganda, it was nevertheless very successful, and ran (with updating) for three years. It marked composer Harold Rome's entrance into the field of popular music. *The Cradle Will Rock* (1938, music, lyrics, and book by Marc Blitzstein) was another timely propaganda piece, concerning the struggle to establish a steelworkers' union in a company-dominated town. It suffered the weaknesses of most propaganda drama, which must paint its characters either black or white, and can afford no real depth of characterization to reveal them as three-dimensional. Done without scenery or costumes, and with accompaniment and commentary by the composer, it revealed the brilliant and versatile talents of Blitzstein.

At the other end of the spectrum were shows that treated their themes with a lighter touch—musicals making use of satire, rather than satire taking the form of musicals. Veteran Irving Berlin wrote the music and lyrics for *Face the Music* (1932) and *As Thousands Cheer* (1933), both with books by Moss Hart, and *Louisiana Purchase* (1940), with book by Morrie Ryskind. All were in the nature of conventional musical comedy, with elements of the revue to allow for the incorporation of the satirical sketches. Rodgers and Hart's one venture into this field was *I'd Rather Be Right* (1937). Cole Porter successfully satirized not only American politics but the Soviet Union in *Leave It to Me* (1938). The hit of the show was the very nonpolitical *My Heart Belongs to Daddy*, which brilliantly etched one of Cole Porter's favorite hard-bitten female types. Porter returned to political satire, again of the Soviet Union, in *Silk Stockings*

(1955), of which the hit song was the politically neutral (if sexually partisan) *All of You*.

INCREASED SOPHISTICATION OF MUSICAL RESOURCES

During the period under consideration the Broadway show utilized more fully and freely the musical means that had long been at the disposal of opera—that is, all the resources European art music had so painstakingly evolved since the Middle Ages. Melody and harmony had already been absorbed; Herbert, Friml, and Romberg were of course thoroughly and classically schooled musicians. And the works of Jerome Kern and George Gershwin, even in the early songs, show them to have mastered thoroughly the craft of handling fairly complex chromatic harmonies. Kern showed that with skill it was possible to introduce into the limited dimensions of the popular song (which he, like Irving Berlin, completely accepted) rather startling juxtapositions of fairly remote tonalities, as he so deftly illustrated in *Smoke Gets in Your Eyes* (1933) and *Long Ago and Far Away* (1944, from a film score). This example was not lost on subsequent composers; Leonard Bernstein used it effectively in *Tonight* (1957).

Counterpoint (the sounding together of two or more melodies) is by nature an undramatic device, in a form where words are important, and the attention, for greatest dramatic effect, should be focused on only one thing at a time. But carefully introduced, it can be effective, if only as a foil for the otherwise constant monody. This is the basis for the ensemble number, which may involve, for example, two characters (*Marry the Man Today* from *Guys and Dolls* is a superb and witty illustration, incorporating a canonic sort of echoing effect between the voices); or the kind of integration of many parts that takes place in the *Street Scene* Ice Cream Sextet; or the superbly crafted ensemble near the end of the first act of *West Side Story*, when five characters present three different interpretations of what "tonight" means to them. Occasionally even imitative counterpoint has its place: Kern included a fugue in *The Cat and the Fiddle* as early as 1931, and the *Fugue for Tin Horns* (actually a three-part canon) in *Guys and Dolls* is one of the most effective opening numbers in any musical. As background for the dance sequence *Cool*, Bernstein used a fugue effectively in *West Side Story*.

The dimensions of the song itself—that still basic unit of popular music—were enlarged. The usual 32-bar format was discarded as early as 1932 in Cole Porter's *Night and Day* (from *The Gay Divorce*), which is built along ampler lines with a 48-bar chorus, and a verse so important in setting the mood that it can hardly be omitted.

Recitative (intoned speech, with the overwhelming emphasis on the words) had long been integral to opera, where everything is sung, but found its way into the musical as well, as in the introduction to the duet which is the title song in *Guys and Dolls*. A still more striking use of the recitative concept is shown in the opening scene of *The Music Man* (1957), when the rhythmically spoken chatter of the salesmen imitates the chugging of a train as it picks up speed.

Above and beyond the increased broadening and sophistication of technique, the musical during this period came gradually to assign a far greater role to music itself; there was more of it, and it was given more work to do. Instead of being called upon only when it was time for a song or dance, it underscored dialogue, accomplished transitions, or arranged itself in a sequence of movements that became the equivalent of the operatic scene. Furthermore, in the best musicals the entire score had a unity to it. Jerome Kern took a large step in this direction in the score of *Show Boat* when he employed a few key motives, associated with certain characters, at appropriate moments in the background. It was a technique long known to opera, but new to the musical.

INCREASED IMPORTANCE OF THE DANCE

Another evolutionary development that helped bring the musical to its high point in this period was the increased attention lavished on the dance. Song and dance had always gone together on the entertainment stage, and ballet was actually introduced (by accident) into the musical with the coming of *The Black Crook* in 1866. But a new era was begun when George Balanchine, noted choreographer and ballet-master of the Diaghilev Ballet and the Ballet Russe de Monte Carlo, was called upon to create a special jazz ballet for the Rodgers and Hart show *On Your Toes* (1936). The result was the famous *Slaughter on Tenth Avenue*, an extended "story" ballet sequence within the musical. After its considerable success two more collaborations of Balanchine with Rodgers and Hart ensued, *I Married an Angel* and *The Boys from Syracuse*, both of 1938. From this time forward, choreography and dance, in whatever style is appropriate, have become basic integrated ingredients in the best musicals, especially telling in drama and fantasy sequences, as in *Carousel* and *Allegro*. For *Oklahoma!* (1943) a new orientation for the dance was required, and Agnes De Mille created what were essentially folk-ballet sequences. The musical *On the Town* (1944), with score by Leonard Bernstein, had actually originated as a ballet, *Fancy Free*, by the same composer, with choreography by Jerome Robbins. Robbins also contrived the dance and movement for *West Side Story*, in which it played an important role in the unfolding of the action—indeed, it has been one of the few musicals conceived and directed by a choreographer. The score itself is nearly a succession of dances, with dance rhythms underlying even the love song. The two contrasting types (jazz-rock and Latin) in juxtaposition express the essential conflict that is the basis of the modern Romeo-and-Juliet-derived plot.

Thus we end with *West Side Story*, as we began with *Show Boat*, this brief examination of what went into the American musical show during the three decades that may well be regarded as its period of greatest effulgence.

The Musical in the Sixties and Seventies

The 1950s were the beginning of the end of the Broadway musical's dominance in American popular music. In the first place, the period of its extraordinary growth and flowering was drawing to a close, though there have continued to be talented artists creating for the Broadway stage, and some noteworthy individual achievements. In the second place, Broadway began to lose the ear of its heretofore large national public. The big bands no longer functioned as a medium for the dissemination of its tunes. The receptiveness to show tunes was narrowing, especially among the youth, as the new and affluent young market turned to rock 'n' roll, eschewing the musical sophistication of Broadway. Radio first, and eventually the record industry, followed the market; a gulf began to develop.

The element of continuity, which is never absent even in periods of change, was provided by the sustained activity of composers whose best works belonged to the thirty-year period we have considered. Thus Frank Loesser produced *Greenwillow* (1960) and *How to Succeed in Business Without Really Trying* (1961); Frederick Loewe, with Alan Jay Lerner, *Camelot* (1960); and Richard Rodgers, that perennial figure who has pioneered so many new departures in the musical theater, wrote *No Strings* (1962), providing for the first time his own lyrics, for a show that was venturesome in many respects. But in no case do these shows represent the best work of their composers.

There are later composers who have continued to cultivate the form pretty much as they inherited it. Jule Styne, after a number of shows going back to the 1940s (*High Button Shoes, Gentlemen Prefer Blondes, Two on the Aisle, The Bells Are Ringing*) produced his two best shows in the new period—*Gypsy* (1959) and *Funny Girl* (1964), both based on show business personalities, a part of a trend to be noted in due course. Two later-generation composers whose works belong almost entirely to this period are Jerry Bock (*Mr. Wonderful*, 1956; *Fiorello*, 1959; *She Loves Me*, 1963; *Fiddler on the Roof*, 1964) and Stephen Sondheim (*A Funny Thing Happened on the Way to the Forum*, 1962; *Anyone Can Whistle*, 1964; *Company*, 1970; *Follies*, 1971; *A Little Night Music*, 1973). Sondheim had provided brilliant lyrics for *West Side Story*. The work of these men has provided a continuity with the traditions growing out of the previous era.

The musical stage has always reflected, with greater or lesser distinctness, the culture of its times. The repertory of the American musical since 1960 contains pieces that reflect in a variety of ways the impact of the dominant youth culture, including rock. A sampling will suggest this variety, as heterogeneous in approach as is popular music itself in this age. *Bye Bye, Birdie* (1960, music by Charles Strouse, lyrics by Lee Adams) is simply a more or less conventional musical comedy that uses the phenomenon of the early rock star (Elvis Presley is the prototype) as material for rather good-natured satire. *Hair* (1968, music by Galt MacDermot, lyrics and book by Gerome Ragni and James Rado) appears to look not *at* but *out from* the culture. Themes of youth's concerns are treated with a light touch. The music eschews the harder, more aggressive style of rock, and the show, reverting basically to the format of the revue, includes some well-crafted and expressive songs reflecting both the degree of sophistication that had been achieved with the material of the new popular music and its eclecticism: The subjects range from a comment on environmental deterioration (*Air*) to an adaptation from Shakespeare (*What a Piece of Work Is Man*). *Tommy* (1970, music and words by Peter Townshend of the Who), billed as a "rock" opera, is a serious and even brutal piece, with its roots in the more morbid and tortured realms of the rock phenomenon. *Jesus Christ Superstar* (1971, music by Andrew Lloyd Webber, lyrics by Tim Rice), first appeared in recorded form in 1969. In spite of the unconventionality of the subject for the popular musical stage, it is commercial popular entertainment in every sense, with songs in a slightly sophisticated version of contemporary popular idiom, plus witty, up-to-date dialogue and also spectacle. Such controversy as was aroused concerning it centered on the treatment of the subject matter rather than on the music itself, which, to the extent that it was rock at all, was sufficiently attenuated as to be nearly pure pop. *Godspell*, somewhat less pretentious and perhaps more consistent dramatically, followed in 1971. *Grease* (1972, music, lyrics and book by Jim Jacobs and Warren Casey), a piece about high school kids in the rock 'n' roll era of the 1950s, is clearly geared to its own audience of those who belonged then, or belong now, to this milieu.

In all periods there have appeared shows designed with a particular performer in mind, and the genesis of such a show does not necessarily affect its quality. But during the past two decades there has been a special reliance on the show built around a striking female personality (whether real or fictional), and often designed as a vehicle for one star. *Gypsy* (1959), a bit ahead of the trend, was a special case in that the star, Ethel Merman, did not play the title role, but subsequently there appeared *Funny Girl* (1964, with Barbra Streisand), *Helly Dolly!* (1964, starring

Carol Channing, and in a later Negro version, Pearl Bailey), *Mame* (1966, with Angela Lansbury), *Coco* (1969, especially for Katherine Hepburn), and *Applause* (1970, for Lauren Bacall).

During this period the craft of the composer has appeared to be in an eclipse; his work—at times adequate or even well done, and at times undistinguished—has seemed to matter less. As a factor in the final result, it has tended to lag behind up-to-the-minute dialogue, behind the visual aspects of the show (in an age when modern stagecraft has produced breathtaking effects of costumes and setting, as in *The Wiz*), behind the presence of a star performer, or behind a catchy subject (the search for which has ranged from the New Testament to comic strips) or even a catchy title (*Stop the World, I Want to Get Off; The Roar of the Grease-paint, The Smell of the Crowd*). This eclipse of the music itself in the musical reflects a familiar situation in the history of the art of music, and these lulls are, in the final analysis, occasioned less by external conditions and tastes than by the absence of significant creative talent. The music will again matter when it is good enough to matter; and in the case of the musical show, this will only happen with the appearance of composers with that very specialized genius for writing what is still the cornerstone of the musical—the song.

HOLLYWOOD AND THE MOVIE SONG

Sometime before 1920 a songwriting team of Joe Young, Sam Lewis, and Walter Donaldson, who also produced *How Ya Gonna Keep 'em Down on the Farm?* ("after they've seen Paree"), wrote a sentimental blackface tear-jerker called "My Mammy." It became the trademark of vaudeville singer and blackface comedian Al Jolson, who interpolated it into a loosely constructed Broadway extravaganza called *Sinbad*. It would long ago have been forgotten if Jolson had not included his famous emotionally mannered rendition of it, along with five other songs, in the first motion picture to have sound. *The Jazz Singer* was premiered October 23, 1927, and it marked the beginning of a new era in American popular music.

The silent picture was doomed,[13] and as the "talkies" took over, the demand for music increased. The musical show, especially the less formal revue, was soon seized upon as an ideal vehicle for the medium. The *Hollywood Revue* of 1929 was a display case for a host of artists who were later to become major figures in the movies, and the film made one of Holly-wood's first contributions to the popular song with *Singin' in the Rain* (music by Nacio Herb Brown). Broadway composers began their trek west-ward as early as 1929, when the team of Buddy De Sylva, Lew Brown, and

Ray Henderson wrote songs for *Sunny Side Up*, as did Irving Berlin for *Hallelujah*, a rather extraordinary Negro folk piece. In 1929 also, one of the first important Broadway shows was adapted for the movies—Jerome Kern's *Sally*, which had originally been produced by Ziegfeld in 1920.

Within the next few years virtually all the successful Broadway composers had begun writing for the films. In addition to Irving Berlin, these included Vincent Youmans, Cole Porter, George Gershwin (with his brother Ira as lyricist), Richard Rodgers (with Lorenz Hart as lyricist), and only slightly later, Harold Arlen, Arthur Schwartz, Jimmy McHugh, and Sigmund Romberg. Jerome Kern, many of whose shows had been adapted for film, did not begin to write original film scores until 1935, but after this time he wrote almost exclusively for Hollywood. For these Broadway composers (Kern himself included) an era of "commuting" began, and American popular music for the next two decades and a half turned on a Broadway-Hollywood axis.

Since the beginning of sound films, movie versions of virtually every successful Broadway musical have been produced, some more than once. During the period of Broadway's leadership and greatest achievement, these accounted for most of the movie musicals of quality; in fact, as we shall see, the heydays of the Broadway and the Hollywood musical very nearly coincided. The film versions, which were predictably automatic events, will not be considered here, since most of the time, except when new songs were added (as when Jerome Kern added *Lovely to Look At* and *I Won't Dance* to the movie of *Roberta*), there was no new contribution in terms of popular song.

A number of original movie musicals have been noteworthy, however, most of them with scores by Broadway composers. *The Wizard of Oz* (1939), with a score by Harold Arlen, contributed a standard, *Over the Rainbow*, and first brought to serious notice one of the great stars of the next decade and a half, Judy Garland. She also starred in *Meet Me in St. Louis* (1944), which was a mature classic of the genre. The music, by Hugh Martin, included *The Boy Next Door* and *The Trolley Song*; the title song was an authentic period piece from Tin Pan Alley written in 1904 by Kerry Mills. Three subsequent original Hollywood musicals by renowned Broadway creators did not represent their best efforts: *State Fair* (1945), by Rodgers and Hammerstein; *Hans Christian Andersen* (1951), by Frank Loesser; and *Gigi* (1958), by Loewe and Lerner. A truly memorable movie of this genre, however, was *A Star Is Born* (1954, a remake of an earlier non-musical), which was Judy Garland's greatest triumph as both actress and singer; songs were by Harold Arlen.

Song-and-dance and the revue came in for a good deal of attention. The former was epitomized at its best by the work of Fred Astaire, who between 1933 and 1938 acted, sang, and danced in a series of musicals with Ginger Rogers, for which the songs were contributed by no lesser talents than Vincent Youmans, Irving Berlin, Jerome Kern, and George Gershwin. Both Astaire and Gene Kelly continued to cultivate what has been called the "dancer's musical." The revue, which Hollywood adopted early, continued to appear through World War II, including the *Gold Diggers* series (1933–1938, intermittently), the *Goldwyn Follies* (1938, George Gershwin's last film, which included *Love Walked In*), and that opulent, star-filled reminder of the form's most sophisticated Broadway prototype, *Ziegfeld Follies* (1944).

A development unique to the movie medium was the animated cartoon, first introduced as a short, and ultimately, in Walt Disney's hands, to become a full-length feature. Even before the full-length stage, songs had been introduced into the cartoons (*Who's Afraid of the Big Bad Wolf?*), but with the advent of *Snow White and the Seven Dwarfs* (1937), which included *Some Day My Prince Will Come* and *Heigh-Ho, Heigh-Ho*, the full-length animated cartoon became, in effect, a musical. Of the subsequent features produced by Disney through the 1940s, *Pinocchio* (1940), including *When You Wish Upon a Star*, was among the best.

While the Broadway musical was the traditional source of the best popular tunes, a substantial contribution on a somewhat less sophisticated level was made by the movies. A sampling of some of the best movie songs (in addition to those already alluded to) will substantiate this. In chronological order here is a baker's dozen of these popular music standards originating in films: *Blue Moon* (1933, Richard Rodgers, in the *Hollywood Revue of 1933*); *Flying Down to Rio* (1933, Vincent Youmans, in the same film); *It's Only a Paper Moon* (1933, Harold Arlen, in *Take a Chance*); *Cheek to Cheek* (1935, Irving Berlin, in *Top Hat*); *I'm in the Mood for Love* (1935, Jimmy McHugh, in *Every Night at Eight*); *The Night is Young* (1935, Sigmund Romberg, in the same film); *The Way You Look Tonight* (1936, Jerome Kern, in *Swing Time*); *Blues in the Night* (1941, Harold Arlen, in the same film); *That Old Black Magic* (1942, Harold Arlen, in *Star-Spangled Rhythm*); *White Christmas* (1942, Irving Berlin, in *Holiday Inn*); *You'd Be So Nice to Come Home To* (1942, Cole Porter, in *Something to Shout About*); *Don't Fence Me In* (1944, Cole Porter, in *Hollywood Canteen*; originally intended as a satire on cowboy songs, this one was taken up in earnest by country-and-western singers); *Long Ago and Far Away* (1944, Jerome Kern, in *Cover Girl*).

The title songs or theme songs from pictures that were essentially not musicals have occasionally been significant enough to have an existence independent of the film and enter the repertory of popular music. *Laura*, which ranks in quality with the best of American popular songs, is a case in point, and being one of the earliest (1945), it established something of a precedent that producers would like to have seen followed with more regularity. It originated as wordless theme music for the picture of the same name by film composer David Raksin; its subsequent popularity led to the addition of words by the noted lyricist Johnny Mercer. The song transcended the original film. Subsequent theme music of some substance that has become popular includes: the *Third Man* theme (1949, Anton Karas; famous for its use of an unusual instrument, the zither, which set off a minor fad for theme music using unusual instruments); the *High Noon* theme (1952, Dimitri Tiomkin); *Around the World in Eighty Days* (1956, Victor Young, in the movie of the same title); *Moon River* (1961, Henry Mancini, in *Breakfast at Tiffany's*); *Lara's Theme* (1965, Maurice Jarre, in *Dr. Zhivago*); *Born Free* (1966, John Barry, in the film of the same title); the *Love Story* theme (1970, Francis Lai); *The Way We Were* (1973, Marvin Hamlisch, in the film of the same title). The success of such theme music led producers to attempt to incorporate a "hit" song into every film score, whether a musical or not.

This points up the changes that have affected movie music and its relation to popular music in the 1960s and 1970s. The whole vast subject of film background music in and of itself is beyond the scope of this chapter, but recent developments have involved it with popular music in two ways. First, as we have seen, producers sought to exploit it by including songs that would hopefully sell well in recordings, regardless of the appropriateness of their presence in the film. As Mark Evans has written: "The ideal composer, according to the new norm in Hollywood, was one who could produce a hit tune and sell not only the film but thousands of records as well." [14] Then, as the youth market expanded tremendously, producers began to orient entire film scores to the currently popular jazz-rock idiom—"something for the kids," as one of them put it.[15] The use of jazz-oriented music for an entire film score began in a sporadic way in the 1950s, largely in vehicles for which it was appropriate, such as *A Streetcar Named Desire* (1951, Alex North), *On the Waterfront* (1954, Leonard Bernstein), and *The Man with the Golden Arm* (1955, Elmer Bernstein). But after Henry Mancini produced in 1959 an extremely popular jazz-oriented score for a television detective series, a somewhat mindlessly faddish trend towards using a commercially popular music-style for an entire film score was set in motion, and had ramifications for which Mancini himself can hardly be held responsible. As he has said:

> We've become a nation of followers when it comes to fashionable trends. Scoring *The Graduate* with a string of songs by Simon and Garfunkel was an excellent device for that particular film, but it set off repercussions, just as I did myself with the use of jazz in *Peter Gunn*. For years after that, jazz was used in films for which it wasn't suited. Now, everything is geared to the swinging youth scene. Sometimes it works well, sometimes it doesn't. As for integrity—we have the music departments thinking about the record album even before the picture is scored! It's the kind of thing where the tail is wagging the dog. I don't think the craft of film scoring is being furthered by this particular development.[16]

In extreme cases, this trend has resulted in the studio's bringing in popular recording stars of the moment, for the value of their names on the credits, and having them do the film "scores," which must then actually be ghostwritten by those trained and experienced in this difficult craft.

These developments, coupled with the fact that the film musical itself was in a period of noticeable decline by 1960—the end of its greatest period coinciding with that of its sire and mentor, the Broadway stage—have meant that the motion picture has contributed significantly less of substance in the past two decades to American popular music.

TIN PAN ALLEY

Tin Pan Alley—the term is as American as the phenomenon it refers to, and the images it evokes are as vivid as its temporal and geographical boundaries are vague. It has been our best-known and best-publicized factory of ephemera, turning out according to demand the musical artifacts of popular culture, most of which were as short-lived as the rapid changes in fashion and the short attention span of the public dictated. The level of sophistication and quality was correspondingly low. These limitations have *rarely* been transcended, although it has happened, as we shall see.

In a more concrete sense, we mean by Tin Pan Alley what James Maher calls a collective name for "the marketplace-oriented music publishing companies." Geographically, of course, it means New York City, its general location moving by stages uptown to follow the theaters, from 14th Street to 28th Street (its most renowned location in its heyday) to 42nd Street and finally to 47th Street and the Brill Building, its last stronghold. Chronologically, it can be said to have existed in a kind of low-key and sporadic way long before the Civil War. Stephen Foster, our first great popular song composer, was living out his last days in New York in the early 1860s, peddling his songs (written for a while at the rate of almost one a week) to publishers for what they would give him. However, the real period of Tin Pan Alley's greatest flourishing is somewhat more circumscribed. It is generally thought of as beginning just before the Gay Nineties (which it mirrored and to which it gave its own color), and it was dispersed in two stages: in the 1930s to Hollywood and in the 1950s to Nashville.

The Growth of an Industry: 1885–1920

Tin Pan Alley in this period was an industry based largely on the sale of printed copies of popular songs with piano accompaniment. It was therefore based on the sale of pianos, which increased significantly between the Civil War and the end of the century. Other media were in the offing. The player piano, a first step toward the automation of music for the consumer, was introduced about the same time as the phonograph recording. But the player piano's importance in the realm of popular music preceded that of the phonograph. It flourished in the first two or three decades of this century. At one time there were more of these in existence in the United States than regular pianos, and every piano manufacturer was producing them. They were supplanted only as the massive shift to recordings as a medium for popular music began in the 1920s.

But to return to Tin Pan Alley, its basic vehicle for the dissemination of its products during this period was what is known as sheet music, a commodity which, except for the design of its covers, has changed not at all in size or appearance in almost a hundred years. In the first years of this century sheet music sold for as little as ten cents a copy; extraordinarily, it might be unloaded for as little as two cents, but the average was around fifty cents. Sales figures for the very successful songs could easily top the million mark. George M. Cohan's *Over There* (1917) sold 2 million copies; Jean Schwartz's *Bedelia* (1903, "Bedelia, I want to steal ye"—labeled an "Irish coon song serenade"!) sold 3 million; *The Rosary* (1898, not a religious song, by Ethelbert Nevin) sold 4 million; and, probably the champion, *After the Ball* (1892, by pioneer Tin Pan Alleyite Charles K. Harris) sold more than 10 million. *On a Sunday Afternoon,* by another prominent Tin Pan Alley composer and entrepreneur, Harry von Tilzer, sold 10,000 copies in a single day in one New York department store in 1902.

To reach anything even approaching this volume of sales (and most barely paid for their printing costs), the songs of course had to be publicized, and this became a profession in itself, in which ingenuity and brashness paid off. Song pluggers were of course at work in music stores and department stores, playing and singing songs for prospective customers. Irving Berlin, Jerome Kern, George Gershwin, and Vincent Youmans all got started in the profession this way. But this in itself was not enough; a larger public had to be reached. In the days before radio and the sound movie, vaudeville and the revue, with their loose formats that allowed for the interpolation of songs, were the best media for this. Singers were paid handsomely to perform a particular song that was being "plugged," and the adoption of a song by a really popular singer could be a decisive factor. (Later the big-band leaders and the disc jockeys, each in turn, had this role and were subject to the same inducements.) Often the singer's picture appeared prominently on the sheet-music cover; later it was common practice to list the singer who introduced the song as coauthor (he or she *might* have contributed some extra verses), thus assuring the performer a share of the profits, while confusing, for uninitiated future generations, the real authorship of the song.

But securing the services of popular singers was not necessarily where the plugger's activities ended. He was limited only by the extent of his ingenuity and daring, and with the example of P. T. Barnum's publicity exploits behind him, he was alert to all possibilities. Amateur singers would be paid to sing the publisher's merchandise on the popular amateur-night programs that were given in many of the vaudeville theaters; the tunes were ensconced in the street organs leased to the immigrant organ grinders by an Italian *padrone*, with whom the song pluggers made it their business to maintain "close communication." In the early free-wheeling days, still more ingenious schemes were carried out. An anonymous "boomer" (a plugger who also sang) left this account from the early 1900s:

> I'm a song promoter. I'm the man who makes popular songs popular. I earn big money and I've grown into a necessity to the music publishing house that employs me. . . . Maybe I go to the swellest theater in town Monday night and sit in a lower box, in my evening clothes, like an ordinary patron. During the daytime I will have fixed the orchestra and had the music run over. Between the first and second act, perhaps, I stand up in my box and start singing. The audience is startled. Ushers run through the aisles. A policeman comes in and walks toward the box. About the time the policeman is where he can be seen by all the audience I step out on to the stage in front of the curtain and begin the chorus, with the orchestra playing and the audience, that is now onto the game, clapping so hard it almost blisters its hands.[17]

The World's Fairs of Chicago (1893) and St. Louis (1904) offered large-scale opportunities for plugging; *After the Ball* was essentially "made" at the former. Novelist Theodore Dreiser (whose brother, as Paul Dresser, had a fairly successful career as a songwriter, best known for *My Gal Sal*) left a valuable account of how the whole process worked in a magazine article written in 1898.[18]

What of the songs themselves? They were, for the most part, made with a view to supplying a proven demand. The shingle that the enterprising Charles K. Harris hung out in Milwaukee in 1886, before coming to New York to remake the industry, was indicative: "Charles K. Harris/ Banjoist and Song Writer/Songs Written to Order."

The music was in the European mold, owing the most, possibly, to English music hall songs. It had groove-worn, predictable harmonies—the same harmonies, in fact, that characterized the hybrid ragtime. Except for the more native ragtime-type songs to be discussed presently, and some of the slower sentimental ballads, the waltz dominated the field rhythmically. To name a few of the more familiar ones, there was *After the Ball* (1892, Charles K. Harris), *Daisy Bell*, better known as *A Bicycle Built for Two* (1892, Harry Dacre), *The Bowery* (1892, Percy Gaunt; a song that was said to have slashed the value of real estate along this street), *The Sidewalks of New York* (1894, Charles B. Lawlor and James

W. Blake), *The Band Played On* (1895, Charles Ward), and *Meet Me in St. Louis, Louis* (1904, Kerry Mills). The more lighthearted songs have lyrics that have retained some of their period charm. The "serious" songs—such as *The Pardon Came Too Late; The Letter That Never Came; Break the News to Mother;* and *She May Have Seen Better Days*—were nearly all afflicted with a sentimentality that derived from their essentially synthetic and either melodramatic or moralizing nature.

A more native style of music was making its way meanwhile into Tin Pan Alley. Ben Harney's *You've Been a Good Old Wagon, but You've Done Broke Down,* with its distinct folk flavor and its touch of ragtime rhythm, was a significant departure for published songs of the era. Written in 1894, it was published first in 1895, not in New York but in Louisville, Kentucky. Bought by the Alley firm of Witmark, it was published the next year in New York, with great success. (The first actual piano rags were not published until 1897.) This success was partly due to the fact that May Irwin, a white singer of "coon songs" and evidently one of the first of the "red-hot mamas," had introduced the song and also Harney's *Mister Johnson, Turn Me Loose* on the stage; it was also partly due to the fact that Harney himself was performing in New York by this time, and achieving notoriety with (according to a reviewer) "his genuinely clever plantation Negro imitations and excellent piano playing"—which must have been ragtime, but ragtime played, as Eubie Blake has said, "like white people played it." (Harney himself, according to Blake, was actually black, passing for white.)

Ragtime songs (an attenuated and vulgarized version of pure ragtime, as we have noted) began to be incorporated into stage shows and to appear more frequently in print. White composer Kerry Mills produced a memorable little piece, far above average quality, called *At a Georgia Camp Meeting.* It was published in 1897 as a piano piece, and later, in 1899, with words. (This was to be the origin of several famous songs.) The tune, with its ragtime syncopations, became very popular, and was much associated with the craze for the dance called the cakewalk that swept America and even invaded Europe. The cakewalk, originally a Negro plantation dance, had appeared in exaggerated form as the minstrel show "walk-around" for years. Other notable ragtime songs to stand out from the run-of-the-mill in the next few years were *Bill Bailey, Won't You Please Come Home* (1902, Hughie Cannon) and *Waiting for the Robert E. Lee* (1911, Lewis Muir).

Some of ragtime's most elemental syncopations (of the type found in pre-rag minstrel tunes like *Dixie*) enlivened many Tin Pan Alley songs that were otherwise simply fairly peppy tunes in duple meter. One such tune (labeled a march-schottische) is *Hot Time in the Old Town* (1896, Theo. A. Metz), said to have been based on a song heard in a famous St. Louis bordello. Interestingly enough, a slightly earlier song of the same type and origin, *Ta-Ra-Ra Boom-De-Ay!* (1891, credited to Henry Sayers on the sheet music), shows none of the same ragtime influence. A later song by the famous Tin Pan Alley entrepreneur Harry von Tilzer shows the same faint imprint of ragtime syncopation—*Wait Till the Sun Shines, Nellie* (1905). One of Von Tilzer's song pluggers, and an ardent admirer of his, the young Irving Berlin, had his first great success with *Alexander's Ragtime Band* (1911), which was still basically a march. This style of peppy tune with rudimentary dashes of syncopation was noticeable in many of George M. Cohan's songs, as we have seen, and appeared sporadically in hit tunes right up through the twenties: *Ja-Da* (1918, Bob Carleton), *'Way Down Yonder in New Orleans* (1922, Henry Creamer and Turner Layton, black composers), *If You Knew Susie* (1925, Buddy De Sylva), and *Yes, Sir, That's My Baby* (1925, Walter Donaldson).

The blues came out of the lower Mississippi Valley; the first ones to be published (those composed by W. C. Handy and others) were printed there in 1912 with piano accompaniments. The blues soon reached New York (Handy himself moved there in 1918), and by 1920 blues (or blues-derived songs) were as important a part of Tin Pan Alley's repertory as ragtime songs had been two decades earlier.

There appeared a few songs near the end of this period that strike us as belonging to a more mature era of our popular song. Mostly slower tunes, of the type henceforth called (confusingly enough) ballads, they are not palpably ragtime- or blues-influenced, and yet somehow they already sound distinctly American, as though they could not have originated anywhere else (as indeed they could not). They were a hint of things to come, and they surprise us with the early dates of their appearance: *Some of These Days* (1910, Shelton Brooks), *My Melancholy Baby* (1911, Ernest Burnett), *I Ain't Got Nobody* (1915, Spencer Williams). None of these was written by an otherwise well-known composer.

Recordings, Radio, and the Big Bands: 1920–1950

In the decades after 1920 there was a gradual shift in the role of the public from active to passive, as the radio and the phonograph replaced the parlor piano as a source of music in the home. Phonograph recordings of popular music sold well in the 1920s, already outselling sheet music, which was rapidly fading as a primary medium of distribution (and profit); the player-piano roll was also edged out. Figures for the sales of four Irving Berlin songs appearing about 1920 show record sales already slightly ahead of sheet music, on the average (in terms of units sold), with piano rolls a poor third. As the Depression arrived in the 1930s radio and the new talking pictures became the dominant media, dealing a severe blow to the phonograph recording, which did not really recover its position until the end of the decade, with recordings of the popular swing bands. Radio thus became a prime means for the dissemination and plugging of songs, as it has remained to this day (in changed form, and with a more specialized audience and material). Many of the prominent bands performed on weekly broadcasts in the 1930s, either from a permanent base or by remote hookup while on tour. Singers with the bands became increasingly important as purveyors of new popular songs. Some bandleaders were themselves composers, and a few of the best songs in this period came from the bands. These tended to be basically instrumental in conception, range, and design, and the words were incidental. Exceptionally, Isham Jones produced two notable songs in 1924 that were really vocal in nature, and have become standards: *It Had to Be You* and *I'll See You in My Dreams*. Duke Ellington contributed many, most of which are decidedly instrumental in character: *Mood Indigo* (1931), *Sophisticated Lady* (1933), *Solitude* (1934), and *Do Nothing Till You Hear from Me* (1943) are a few. *Caravan* (1937) was written with Juan Tizol, and the very instrumental *Take the "A" Train* (1941) was by Ellington's arranger, Billy Strayhorn. The important subject of the whole relationship of jazz to Tin Pan Alley will be dealt with presently.

A panoramic glance at the popular songs of the decades 1920–1950 (exclusive of show and movie tunes) is instructive. In the early years we find the occasional anachronistic song that belongs to an earlier period; *Three o'Clock in the Morning* (1922, Julian Robeldo) is a waltz song that could have been written in the Gay Nineties. There are the fundamentally instrumental big-band songs, of which the Ellington examples represent the best. A few topical songs appear, such as *Brother, Can You Spare a Dime?* (1932, Jay Gorney) or *The White Cliffs of Dover* (1941, Walter Kent; one of the better of a spate of songs relating to the war). At the lowest level of sophistication were inanities such as *The Music Goes 'Round and 'Round* (1935), *A-Tisket, A-Tasket* (1938), *Open the Door, Richard* (1947), *Rudolph, the Red-Nosed Reindeer* (1949), and others cited at the beginning of this chapter. Equally ephemeral was the brief fad of adapting melodies of nineteenth-century composers (chiefly Tchaikovsky) and fitting them with lyrics (*Moon Love* and *Our Love*, 1939; *Tonight We Love*, 1941). Prophetic of developments to come was the general popularity achieved by a few country songs before midcentury. *The Last Round-up* (by New York composer Billy Hill) and *Tumbling Tumbleweeds* (by Canadian Bob Nolan) were synthetic western songs, riding on the popularity of western movies (Hollywood westerns used almost no authentic regional music). But the appearances of *San Antonio Rose* (1940, Bob Wills) and *The*

Tennessee Waltz (1948, Pee Wee King) as nationally rather than regionally popular songs were straws in the wind. By the time Hank Williams's *Cold, Cold Heart* (1951) and *Your Cheatin' Heart* (1952) had similarly taken hold nationally, the trend that shifted a large segment of the popular music industry to Nashville had been established. This story, and what led up to it, has been treated much more fully in chapter 7.

The Latin American influence (too often overlooked in the study of both jazz and popular music) was apparent from time to time, in rhythm, melody, and occasionally even language and subject. The popularity of Latin American dance rhythms and dances—such as the rhumba, the samba, and the bossa nova—all attest to the perennial presence of Latin influence (an influence also apparent in the rhythms of rock). Some early Spanish-language songs to become popular were José Padilla's *La Violetera* ("Who'll Buy My Violets?", 1923) and *Valencia* (1926); Maria Grever's *Cuando vuelva a tu lado* ("What a Diff'rence a Day Made," 1934) and *Ti-Pi-Tin* (1938); and Emilio Uranga's *Alla en el Rancho Grande* (1934). Portuguese influence (by way of Brazil) was represented by songs like Zequinha Abreu's *Tico-Tico* (1943) and Antonio Carlos Jobim's *Garota de Ipanema* ("The Girl from Ipanema," 1964).

But these song-types were really peripheral to the mainstay of Tin Pan Alley in this period—the ballad, which included most of the best songs. This basic type of love song provided most of the "standards," those few songs that transcended in quality and appeal the quantities of ephemera produced. As illustration of the best the Alley had to offer in these three decades (again excluding show and movie tunes), here is a select list of a dozen independent songs: *I Cried For You* (1923, Arthur Freed, Gus Arnheim, Abe Lyman); *Blue Skies* (1927, Irving Berlin); *I'll Get By* (1928, Fred Ahlert); *Star Dust* (1929, Hoagy Carmichael; this perennial, one of the most recorded of all popular songs, began as a quasi-ragtime piano piece, which was later slowed down and given lyrics by Mitchell Parish); *Mean to Me* (1929, Fred Ahlert); *Sweet and Lovely* (1931, Gus Arnheim, Harry Tobias, Jules Lemare); *I'm Gettin' Sentimental over You* (1932, George Bassman); *Stormy Weather* (1933, Harold Arlen; written by this veteran Broadway composer for Harlem's Cotton Club, where it was introduced by Ethel Waters); *Deep Purple* (1934, Peter de Rose; another song that originated as a piano solo, words being added in 1939); *You Go to My Head* (1938, J. Fred Coots); *The Last Time I Saw Paris* (1940, Jerome Kern; this topical piece was originally written as an independent song, one of Kern's few, for which lyricist Oscar Hammerstein dictated the words over the telephone; it was later incorporated into a movie, and won an Academy Award); *I'll Remember April* (1941, Gene de Paul).

JAZZ VIS-A-VIS POPULAR MUSIC

A list of standards to come out of this thirty-year period would include, in addition to the above-mentioned Tin Pan Alley songs, such show tunes as Vincent Youmans's *Tea for Two*; Gershwin's *Somebody Loves Me*; *The Man I Love*; *Embraceable You*; *I Got Rhythm*; and *Summertime*; John Green's *Body and Soul*; Arthur Schwartz's *Dancing in the Dark*; Jimmy McHugh's *Don't Blame Me*; Kern's *Smoke Gets in Your Eyes*; and Morgan Lewis's *How High the Moon*; as well as such movie songs as *I'm in the Mood for Love* (Jimmy McHugh); *That Old Black Magic* (Harold Arlen); *You'd Be So Nice to Come Home To* (Cole Porter); and *Laura* (David Raksin). Most of these are firmly established in the canon of jazz. Therefore this is as appropriate a place as any to consider the important question of the relation of jazz to our popular music. For in spite of the disdain for popular music expressed by some jazz musicians, and more jazz fans, the relation is actually a symbiotic one—each is dependent, in a sense, on the other. Jazz has been heavily indebted to Broadway and Tin Pan Alley (and to a much lesser extent, Hollywood) for its basic material, its songs, whose melodies and chord changes become the basis for its variations and improvisations. Jazz has certainly brought forth its own composers, but since the fundamental genius of jazz is elaboration rather than composition, the popular song and its characteristic harmonic and melodic progressions have never been completely replaced as a basis for jazz pieces. Consider jazz without the hundreds of renditions of *Star Dust*, without Coleman Hawkins's *Body and Soul*, without Charlie Parker's *Embraceable You*, and without the score of bebop versions of *How High the Moon*.

On the other hand, popular music has been indebted to jazz at various periods for rhythmic revitalization (especially in the matter of accompaniment), for renewed contact with the dance, and for the innovations and general creative impetus that can come from a relatively uncommercialized form such as jazz ideally is. In a business way they are complementary; jazz musicians find employment in movie, television, and pop recording studios, and in the past, at least, pop music has been indebted to jazz singers who have sung and popularized it. Thus while jazz and popular music should never be confused, there has been a mutual relationship between them that is often ignored.

The Dispersion of Tin Pan Alley

In what terms is one to account for the decline and demise of Tin Pan Alley? From the standpoint of the structure of an industry, it can be said that one kind of publication, printed music, was superseded by another, the recording (an *acoustical* type of publication, as a vice-president of BMI explained).

In terms of the music itself, the demise can be accounted for as the end of "the professional tradition in song writing," as James Maher has said, placing this about 1950. By this was meant the end of an era that could produce the kind of songs we have cited as standards; note that this did not mean the end of the songs themselves. Song production itself, however, was already thinning out in the forties; indeed, by the end of that decade the products of Tin Pan Alley were so substanceless as to invite change even if events elsewhere had not been on the move—as they were.

These events began in the provinces, outside the orbit of the somewhat creaking but still functioning Broadway-Hollywood axis. A resurgence of what were in the beginning regional musics started in the postwar forties. And although it is a form of intellectual abdication to settle for the too facile and somewhat press-agentish term "revolution," by the mid-fifties the changes wrought in popular music were clearly apparent. Regional and ethnic musics, under suitable new names, were accounting for significantly larger shares of the market. Spawned in teeming and troubled urban areas like Chicago, there was black rhythm-and-blues; from the South came white "hillbilly" music (renamed "country-and-western"). And as an offspring of both, came rock 'n' roll.

The advent of new recording technology enabled the recording industry, at a crucial time, to be decentralized. This meant a corresponding decentralization of the music. Here again, the roots were in the forties, with the full force of the change being felt in the fifties. Robert Burton, vice-president of Broadcast Music, Inc., said in testimony before a Senate committee in 1967:

> In the 1940s and particularly after World War Two, technological improvements in the making of phonograph records and the reproduction of sound brought about a sweeping revolution in the music publishing business and in the exploitation of music. This revolution is the *prima facie* reason for hits being able to spring up from anywhere, just depending where a particular record happens to catch the public fancy. There isn't a market in the United States today of any size that isn't a place where a song may start. It may start in Portland, Oregon. It may start in Georgia, it may start anywhere.[19]

This development accompanied and made possible the rise of the "independents," which specialized in, and cashed in on, the new music. Rock was, for a time, the province of the independents. For that story and the kaleidoscopic convolutions of American pop music since the 1950s, the reader is referred to chapter 9.

FURTHER READING

Reference Works

Reference works are both numerous and essential in this field that encompasses such a vast amount of material. The following are among the best, and at least some will be found in most libraries.

BURTON, JACK (ed.). *The Blue Book of Broadway Musicals.* Watkins Glen, N.Y.: Century House, 1952–1969.

———. *The Blue Book of Tin Pan Alley.* Watkins Glen, N.Y.: Century House, 1950. Expanded new ed., 2 vols., 1962.

EWEN, DAVID (ed.). *The New Complete Book of the American Musical Theater.* New York: Holt, Rinehart & Winston, 1970.

    A useful single volume in four parts: (1) musical shows, alphabetical with date, composer, lyricist, and principals of the original cast, plus commentary, including synopsis; (2) librettists, lyricists, and composers; (3) chronology of the musical theater, 1866–1970; (4) outstanding songs.

KINKLE, ROGER D. (ed.). *The Complete Encyclopedia of Popular Music and Jazz.* 4 vols. New Rochelle, N.Y.: Arlington House, 1974.

    A multivolume work, probably the most comprehensive in the field. Vol. 1, music year by year, 1900–1950; vols. 2 and 3, biographies, alphabetical; vol. 4, appendices, including several indexes.

* LEWINE, RICHARD, and SIMON, ALFRED (eds.). *Songs of the American Theater.* New York: Dodd, Mead & Co., 1973.

    Another useful single-volume work, in four parts: (1) alphabetical list of 12,000 songs, with composer, lyricist, show (or movie or TV show), and year; (2) alphabetical list of productions, with date of opening, number of performances, composer and lyricist, titles of songs, cast album if issued, vocal score if published; (3) chronology of productions, 1925–1971; (4) index of composers.

LIMBACHER, JAMES (ed.). *Film Music: From Violins to Video.* Metuchen, N.J.: Scarecrow Press, 1974.

    Part 1: selected essays. Part 2: (1) film titles and dates, alphabetical; (2) chronological list of films and composers, 1908–1972; (3) composers and their films, alphabetical; (4) recorded musical scores, alphabetical.

MATTFELD, JULIUS (ed.). *Variety Music Cavalcade, 1620–1969.* 3rd ed. Englewood Cliffs, N.J.: Prentice-Hall, 1971.

    A somewhat unique work; for each year there is a select list of songs published, with show or film if applicable, and a brief synopsis of the year's events, cultural and otherwise. The list of songs is rather broad in scope,

---

* Items thus marked are part of the suggested reference library to be available in connection with this book.

including some fine-art and religious songs that have had wide circulation.

SHAPIRO, NAT (ed.). *Popular Music: An Annotated Index of American Popular Songs.* 6 vols. New York: Adrian Press, 1964–1973.
> Chronological by volumes, each of which contains: (1) list of songs, alphabetical year by year, with composer, lyricist, publisher, and who introduced; (2) index of titles, with year; (3) alphabetical list of publishers.

STAMBLER, IRWIN (ed.). *Encyclopedia of Popular Music.* New York: St. Martin's Press, 1965.

For more up-to-date information on Broadway musicals, a publication such as *The New York Times Reviews*, available in most large libraries, is helpful.

Song Collections, by Period or Genre

* APPELBAUM, STANLEY (ed.). *Show Songs from "The Black Crook" to "The Red Mill."* New York: Dover Publications, 1974.
> A useful volume covering the years 1866–1906. There are 60 songs from 50 shows, introductory notes and notes on each show, some pictures.

* FREMONT, ROBERT A. (ed.). *Favorite Songs of the Nineties.* New York: Dover Publications, 1973.
> 89 songs, with an introduction by Max Morath. A useful collection from the era in which the popular song industry was making its first phenomenal growth; many of the songs are still around.

Great Songs of Broadway. New York: Quadrangle/The New York Times Book Co., 1973.
> 74 songs from 63 shows, from 1904 to 1971. Introductions by Alan Jay Lerner and Jule Styne. No introductions to individual songs or shows.

Great Songs of the Sixties. New York: Quadrangle/The New York Times Book Co., 1970.
> 82 songs from "rock, soul, protest, alienation, folk, jazz, Broadway, and the movies."

World's Greatest Hits of the 20's/30's/40's/50's. New York: Charles Hansen Educational Sheet Music and Books, 1860 Broadway, N.Y. 10023. 4 vols., 40 songs each.

The Twenties/The Thirties/The Forties/The Fifties/The Sixties. New York: Consolidated Music Publishers/Music Sales Corp., 33 W. 60th St., N.Y. 10023. 5 vols., about 30 songs each.

Song Collections, by Composer

Merely a sampling, this category is subject to constant additions and subtractions.

ELLINGTON, DUKE. *The Great Music of Duke Ellington.* Melville, N.Y.: Belwin Mills Publishing Corp., 1973. 42 songs.

GERSHWIN, GEORGE. *Gershwin Years in Song.* New York: Quadrangle/The New York Times Book Co., 1973.
> A rather representative collection of over 50 pieces, including more pianistic versions of some of the choruses by Gershwin himself.

HERBERT, VICTOR. *Victor Herbert Song Album.* 3 vols. New York: M. Witmark & Sons, 1927–1938.

Jerome Kern: The Man and His Music. Santa Monica, Calif.: T. B. Harms Co., n.d.
> 41 songs, with pictures and connecting text of slight value. The rearrangements and transpositions of the songs detract considerably from the value of this collection.

KERN, JEROME. *The Best of Jerome Kern.* New York: T. B. Harms Co., 1972.
> 43 songs, reprinted from the original sheet music.

PORTER, COLE. *Music and Lyrics by Cole Porter.* New York: Chappell, 1972.

RODGERS, RICHARD. *The Rodgers and Hart Song Book.* New York: Simon & Schuster, 1951.

Vocal scores of most musicals are published, but some are out of print and all are now very expensive. "Books" (libretti) are published separately in many cases.

Studies or Histories, Some Specialized

* CHASE, GILBERT. *America's Music.* 2nd rev. ed. New York: McGraw-Hill Book Co., 1966. Chapter 29, "Popular Currents."

ENGEL, LEHMAN. *The American Musical Theater.* Rev. ed. New York: Macmillan & Co., 1975.

EVANS, MARK. *Soundtrack: The Music of the Movies.* New York: Hopkinson & Blake, 1975.
> Not confined to musicals, this covers the entire field.

EWEN, DAVID. *The Life and Death of Tin Pan Alley.* New York: Funk & Wagnall's Co., 1964.
> Covers the period ca. 1880–1930; appendices include a list of 100 standards of this period, and a list of lyricists and composers with dates.

* GOLDBERG, ISAAC. *Tin Pan Alley: A Chronicle of American Popular Music.* New York: Frederick Ungar Publishing Co., 1961. Paperback reprint.
> George Gershwin's introduction is interesting for what it tells us about him and his methods. The new edition of this work (originally published in 1930) has a supplement by Edward Jablonski, bringing it somewhat more up-to-date.

HUGHES, LANGSTON, and MELTZER, MILTON. *Black Magic: A Pictorial History of the Negro in American Entertainment.* Englewood Cliffs, N.J.: Prentice-Hall, 1967.

MARCUSE, MAXWELL F. *Tin Pan Alley in Gaslight*. Watkins Glen, N.Y.: Century House, 1959.
> A detailed account of the period 1880–1910.

MARKS, E. B. *They All Had Glamour: From the Swedish Nightingale to the Naked Lady*. New York: Julian Messner, 1944.

McVAY, DOUGLAS. *The Musical Film*. New York: A. S. Barnes & Co., 1967.
> A selective commentary on movie musicals, arranged by year from 1927 to 1966.

MEYER, HAZEL. *The Gold in Tin Pan Alley*. Philadelphia: J. B. Lippincott Co., 1958.

SHAW, ARNOLD. "Popular Music from Minstrel Songs to Rock 'n' Roll," in Paul Henry Lang (ed.), *One Hundred Years of Music*. New York: Grosset & Dunlap, 1961.

* SMITH, CECIL. *Musical Comedy in America*. New York: Theater Arts Books, 1950. Paperback reprint, same publisher and date.
> The best general work to date on the American popular musical theater, written from the standpoint of extensive knowledge and sound critical sense. It is to be regretted that a work of similar breadth and quality covering the quarter-century after 1950 has not yet appeared.

SONNECK, O. G. *Early Opera in America*. 1915. Reprint, New York: Benjamin Blom, 1963.
> The most authoritative source for information on popular musical theater in America up to 1800.

SPAETH, SIGMUND. *A History of Popular Music in America*. New York: Random House, 1948.
> Even allowing for the coloring of the author's personal (but well-informed) views, this is a most useful work, containing a great deal of information and covering an exceptionally broad period, from colonial times to the close of World War II.

THOMAS, TONY. *Music for the Movies*. New York: A. S. Barnes & Co., 1973.
> Covers the entire field, with biographical information on leading film composers, a listing of their scores, and a discography of film music available on records.

* WHITCOMB, IAN. *After the Ball*. London: Penguin Press, 1972.
> A breezy, slangy, perceptive, and readable account of American popular music from the beginnings of Tin Pan Alley to rock, by an intelligent young British author, whose own experiences as a rock star in the sixties add a dimension to the final stages of the narrative.

* WILDER, ALEC. *American Popular Song: The Great Innovators, 1900–1950*. New York: Oxford University Press, 1972. Paperback reprint, 1975.
> Written by a composer and songwriter of broad experience, this is the most comprehensive analytical study of the subject to date, and yet is eminently readable. There are hundreds of excerpted examples. Extensive treatment is given to Kern, Gershwin, Porter, Berlin, Rodgers, and Arlen, but virtually every other figure, and song, worthy of note is in-

cluded. There is a most perceptive and well-written introduction by James Maher.

Biographical Emphasis (Mainly One Person)

EWEN, DAVID. *Great Men of American Popular Song.* Englewood Cliffs, N.J.: Prentice-Hall, 1970, 1972.
   32 biographical articles on figures from Billings and Henry Russell to Bob Dylan and Burt Bacharach.

——. *Richard Rodgers.* New York: Henry Holt & Co., 1957.

——. *The World of Jerome Kern: A Biography.* New York: Holt, Rinehart & Winston, 1960.

——. *The Story of Irving Berlin.* New York: Henry Holt & Co., 1950.

FREEDLAND, MICHAEL. *Jolson.* New York: Stein & Day, 1972.

GOLDBERG, ISAAC. *George Gershwin: A Study in American Music.* Supplemented by Edith Garson. New York: Frederick Ungar Publishing Co., 1958.

GREEN, STANLEY. *The World of Musical Comedy.* Foreword by Deems Taylor. New York, 1960. Revised and enlarged edition, New York: A. S. Barnes & Co., 1968.
   "The story of the American musical stage as told through the careers of its foremost composers and lyricists." Hence, a biographical approach.

HART, DOROTHY. *Thou Swell, Thou Witty.* New York: Harper & Row, 1976. A biography of Lorenz Hart.

JABLONSKI, EDWARD. *Harold Arlen: Happy with the Blues.* Garden City, N.Y.: Doubleday & Co., 1961.

KIMBALL, ROBERT, and BOLCOM, WILLIAM. *Reminiscing with Sissle and Blake.* New York: Viking Press, 1973.

KIMBALL, ROBERT (ed.). *Cole.* New York: Holt, Rinehart & Winston, 1971.

MOREHOUSE, WARD. *George M. Cohan, Prince of the American Theatre.* Philadelphia: J. B. Lippincott Co., 1943.

TAYLOR, DEEMS. *Some Enchanted Evenings.* New York: Harper & Brothers, 1953.
   On Richard Rodgers, Lorenz Hart, and Oscar Hammerstein II.

VALLEE, RUDY, and McKEAN, GIL. *My Time Is Your Time.* New York: Ivan Obelensky, 1962.

WATERS, EDWARD N. *Victor Herbert: A Life In Music.* New York: Macmillan Co., 1955.

WATERS, ETHEL, and SAMUELS, CHARLES. *His Eye Is on the Sparrow.* Garden City, N.Y.: Doubleday & Co., 1950.

WOOLLCOTT, ALEXANDER. *The Story of Irving Berlin.* New York: G. P. Putnam's Sons, 1925.

LISTENING

A *discography in the field of popular music can be of only limited usefulness, due to the vast quantity of the recordings and their rapid obsolescence. There are a few good documentary collections and anthologies, and they are listed below, but popular music has not been anthologized as yet to the extent that jazz has. Albums devoted to selections from individual Broadway shows, and films with music, are available, but those from the older shows are not uniformly in print. Independent songs, not in shows or films, are the most difficult to find.*

* The Recorded Anthology of American Music (RAAM) has the following relevant issues. All are contemporary archival recordings.

Inventions and Topics in Popular Song, 1910–1929. NW-233.

The Golden Years of Tin Pan Alley: 1920–1929. NW-279.

The Golden Years of Tin Pan Alley: 1930–1939. NW-248.

Forgotten Songs from Broadway, Hollywood and Tin Pan Alley. NW-240.

American Song During the Great Depression. NW-270.

Sissle and Blake's "Shuffle Along." NW-260.

The Mighty Wurlitzer: Music for Movie Palace Organs. NW-227.

The Vintage Irving Berlin. NW-238.

Follies, Scandals, and Other Diversions, from Ziegfeld to the Shuberts. NW-215.

Also relevant: *Song and Dance Man: Popular American Song Hits of 1913–1928.* Folkways: FS-3858.

PROJECTS

1. Make a study of a ballad opera, either from printed sources or from recordings. Familiarize yourself with its background. Can you detect in it elements of burlesque or satire?
2. Write a brief paper on some of the famous theaters or places of amusement in New York City in the nineteenth century, and some of the performances associated with them, such as those at Castle Gardens (Jenny Lind's first American concert), Niblo's Garden (*The Black Crook* and many others), the Olympic Theater, and the Madison Square Theater.
3. Taking some "classic" story such as Jules Verne's *Around the World in Eighty Days*, or Frank Baum's *The Wizard of Oz*, trace its history through various musical stage and screen productions.

4. Read, and write a brief review of, Jacques Offenbach's diary of his visit to America in the 1870s (published as *Orpheus in America* [Bloomington: Indiana University Press, 1957]).

5. Trace and identify quotations of other popular songs in George M. Cohan's *Yankee Doodle Boy*. Find at least four additional songs of the same general period that themselves contain snatches of other popular songs, and identify these.

6. Make a study of the player piano in relation to American popular music.

7. Make a study of the popular dances of any given period, relating them to the contemporary popular music. (Examples would be the relation of the two-step to the Sousa march, the cakewalk to ragtime, the Charleston to the music of the twenties.)

8. Compare the "book," or libretto, of any musical show based on a play, with the original play. Note technical changes and changes of plot, emphasis, and characterization. What do you think were the reasons for the changes? (Examples would be *Oklahoma!* vis-à-vis *Green Grow the Lilacs; Carousel* vis-à-vis *Liliom; The Most Happy Fella* vis-à-vis *They Knew What They Wanted;* and *My Fair Lady* vis-à-vis *Pygmalion.*)

9. Make a brief study of the use of the popular musical theater as an instrument of propaganda, in any given age.

10. If you are sufficiently knowledgeable musically, make a study of remote key relationships in the songs of Jerome Kern or the popular songs of Leonard Bernstein.

11. If you are knowledgeable in the field of dance, make a study of the contributions of George Balanchine, Agnes De Mille, or Jerome Robbins to the popular musical stage.

12. Attend a performance, and do a careful review, of a musical show written since 1970. Assess such things as dramatic verisimilitude, depth of characterization (do the characters seem "real," believable, three-dimensional?), appropriateness of the songs to the situations in which they are sung, and distinctiveness and quality of the songs. Include a brief account of the breadth of your own acquaintance with musical comedy.

13. Write a thoughtful review of the music of a movie that has a title song or theme song. Assess the use and relevance of the song in the film, and the use of music in general throughout the film.

14. Sigmund Spaeth restated a thought expressed many times when he wrote of our popular song that it "captures the civilization of each period far more accurately than do many of the supposedly more important arts." Taking any decade from the 1890s to the

1970s, make a survey of its popular songs, and assess the extent to which this statement applies, and specifically how it applies.

15. If you are a jazz fan, find at least three jazz versions apiece of two different Broadway or Tin Pan Alley standards; identify the composer and the year of composition, and compare the versions.

Part Five

Jazz: The Unique Tradition of the Performer's Art

Jazz is yet a young music. It is true that its roots go deep into American soil—a cultural soil prepared by momentous human migrations, so that there occurred such a meeting of the musics of two continents of the Old World on one continent of the New as must be unique in man's cultural history. But as a music in itself it has evolved essentially only in the twentieth century. Synthesized out of its varied elements as a contribution of the Negro in America, it cannot be fully understood without seeing its brief history against that long and troubled pageant of emancipation still being played out in American life. Yet it can only distort our view of jazz to see it any longer as the exclusive music of a race. This gift of America's black musicians was made in installments that began long ago, though there may well have been some debts contracted that are still to a degree outstanding. As with all art in our century of broad cultural sharing, jazz has become part of the legacy of all humanity. Yet it is American, root and branch, nurtured here, and it is America's musical life that jazz has most vividly colored since the beginning of this century. It constitutes a teeming panorama in itself.

As numerous writers have demonstrated, jazz has antecedents in the tribal music of black West Africa, in the rich cultural amalgamations of the West Indies, and on this continent in the camp-meeting songs, the spirituals, the work songs, and the blues. These have been explored earlier—specifically in chapters 2, 3, 6, and 8. It remains in the first of the two chapters of this part to look at the important antecedents of jazz in the realm of our broadly popular entertainment music. In the second chapter we will follow the vivid procession of the times and styles of jazz itself, in order to fix in the mind the stages of its growth and establish a frame of reference into which can be fitted the details of more intimate knowledge.

Chapter Eleven
Minstrelsy, Ragtime, and Pre-Jazz

JAZZ HAS OCCUPIED a position in American music that is always ambivalent and often misunderstood. Folk in many of its origins, it has been both entertainment and fine art—both broadly popular in some of its manifestations and cultivated or even esoteric in others. Virgil Thomson has called it a "persecuted chamber music." This ambivalence surfaces to trouble any attempt to impose a convenient order on the whole panorama.

Yet it is in the nature of American music to defy easy categorization. Its history is full of instances of the merging and transformation of its individual streams, and of art forms developing out of popular vernacular forms. Thus we find in the background of jazz, as art music, not only folk and religious music but also Dan Emmett and the minstrel show. It is to these, and other popular forebears, that this chapter addresses itself.

All the kinds of music treated in this chapter had their part in the formation of jazz. But it falsifies and limits our perception to hear them only in this context. Each was a lively popular art in its day, making

287

its own contribution to our musical life. Some, having flourished and made their imprint, have passed from the scene. Others are still being cultivated, or re-cultivated, by ardent devotees. We begin our brief survey with the earliest of these native musics.

MINSTRELSY

The first secular music with uniquely American characteristics that became widely popular with the masses was associated with the blackface minstrel show before the Civil War. (Being American, it contained a generous mixture of diverse elements from two other continents—in this case black Africanisms and Irish jigs.) Since the earliest days of their presence here, black people had displayed their native talents as musicians, dancers, and entertainers both among themselves and for the benefit of the whites who made use of them in this capacity. There were many Negroes, for example, who had considerable reputations as fiddlers, and were much in demand to furnish music for dancing for both blacks and whites. Their faculty for spontaneous song and dance, and for unbridled comedy, was also well known. Lewis Paine, spending some time in Georgia in the 1840s, comments as follows in describing the festivities after a corn shucking:

> The fiddler walks out, and strikes up a tune; and at it they go in a regular tear-down dance; for here they are at home. . . . I never saw a slave in my life but would stop as if he were shot at the sound of a fiddle; and if he has a load of two hundred pounds on his head, he will begin to dance. One would think they had steam engines inside of them, to jerk them about with so much power; for they go through more motions in a minute, than you could shake two sticks at in a month; and of all comic actions, ludicrous sights, and laughable jokes, and truly comic songs, there is no match for them. It is useless to talk about Fellows' Minstrels, or any other band of merely artificial "Ethiopians"; for they will bear no comparison with the plantation negroes.[1]

It is clear from this that there was abundant material here for imitation by white entertainers, once they saw its potential. The original black minstrelsy was an informal, spontaneous, and exuberant affair of the plantation. But its reputation spread. Thus it came about that the native songs, dances, and comedy of the southern Negroes first reached the general American public in the form of parodies by white entertainers. These parodies, in the beginning at least, were done exclusively by whites for the entertainment of whites; their immediate origins were far closer to the Bowery than to the plantation. It is a subject that most Americans would approach with at least some embarrassment in our time, for the humor, the language, and the characterizations of black people were based on caricature, exaggeration, and stereotype which (even granting that this is the basis for most low comedy) appear in particularly bad taste today. (It should be noted that other ethnic groups were also caricatured by the minstrels, including the Germans and the Irish.) It is perhaps significant that the name "Jim Crow" itself originated in a very early minstrel song—albeit one that became enormously popular in due course with blacks as well as whites. And of course the music that was presented as "plantation melodies," "coon songs," and so on was far from being the real music of the Negroes, though there is no doubt that it exhibited some of its significant features.

All in all, today's prevalent attitudes towards the minstrel show are the reflections of hindsight. If we would understand and appreciate the place of the minstrel show in American musical life, we can only do so by seeing it in the context of the cultural milieu and mores of its own time. It is the same approach we must use, for example, in considering Mark Twain's basically sympathetic character with the name (unacceptable as it is in *our* time) "Nigger Jim." [2] Perhaps the time is now at hand when this important form of the popular musical stage can be studied with a humane dispassion. For it cannot well be ignored; as a form of entertainment enormously popular with the masses, it was also an influential link to later ragtime and jazz, and part of the great panorama of American popular music.

The minstrel show held the public's attention in the large cities for some time before it was superseded by the early variety shows and musicals, but it was in the smaller cities and the rural towns that it found its real public. There it proved to have remarkable vitality and staying power, for minstrel troupes were touring in rural America well into this century. There the coming of the minstrel show was as eagerly anticipated as the coming of the circus, with which it shared a good deal in common. The troupe's arrival was signaled by the inevitable parade through the town, winding up at the theater where the evening performance was to be given. At this performance the public's expectations of an evening of vivid and diverting entertainment were seldom disappointed; they laughed hard at the comic songs, repartee, conundrums, and grotesque antics of the "end-men," and the skits and parodies that made up the second half of the show. But there also may have been some moist eyes in the crowd at the close of the sentimental songs, ranging from *Old Black Joe* and *My Old Kentucky Home* to such later (and less slave-oriented) songs as *She May Have Seen Better Days* or *Just Tell Them That You Saw Me*.[3]

Beginnings

Impersonations on the stage of the black man by the white were taking place as far back as the eighteenth century, both here and in England (the source of so much of our early stage tradition and material). Two aspects were played up in these impersonations: the sentimental, exploiting a genuine sympathy of the times for the plight of the slaves, and the comic, exploiting through caricature the Negro's speech and appearance, and through stereotype his actions and attitudes. These two aspects of Negro impersonation persisted right into minstrelsy itself. As might be surmised, the Americans' impersonations soon went in the direction of a realism that was impossible for the English, who had so little contact with the black people themselves.

Even before the minstrel show was put together as a complete evening's entertainment, single-act impersonations, with accompanying songs, were common. Thomas Dartmouth ("Daddy") Rice, one of the most famous of the pre-minstrel song-and-dance men, capitalized on his well-known "Jim Crow" song and routine. Negro impersonation had evolved into two stage types. One, typified by "Gumbo Chaff" or Jim Crow himself, portrayed the ragged plantation or riverboat hand, joyous, reckless, uncouth. The other, typified by "Zip Coon" or "Dandy Jim," was the citified northern dandy, with exaggeratedly elegant clothes and manners. Incidentally, the extent to which some of the songs of the minstrel period have entered into the great body of perennial American tunes is illustrated by the fact that the tune of *Zip Coon* has been perpetuated since the Civil War as *Turkey in the Straw*.

The minstrel show itself was put together in the early 1840s. It consisted of songs (both solo and "full chorus"), dances, jokes, conundrums, satirical speeches, and skits. The performers, only four in number at first, seated themselves in a rough semicircle on the stage. The word "seated" may be misleading, however—they were much of the time dancing and cavorting around the stage, and even when in contact with the chairs, would be constantly in motion, executing the most comical gyrations and contortions. In the middle were the banjo player and the fiddle player (the instrument was played like a country fiddle, held against the chest). The two end-men played the tambourine and the bones, and these, along with the inevitable foot tapping of the banjo player, provided a kind of primitive "rhythm section." It was the end-men who indulged in the most outrageous horseplay. The bones, which were in the beginning actually just that, were held one pair in each hand and rattled together. The fiddle played the tune more or less straight, while the banjo played an ornamented version of it, so that their roles must have been somewhat analogous to those of the cornet and clarinet in early jazz, with the resulting heterophony. It is interesting to note that the banjo did not strum chords, as it did later in the jazz band, but played an actual melodic line, on one string at a time. Since the banjo music was eventually written down and published, along with method books for the instrument, we know the kind of music that must have been played on it, and it presupposes a good deal of agility.

What did the early minstrel band actually sound like? Hans Nathan, in his *Dan Emmett and the Rise of Early Negro Minstrelsy* (an excellent study and source of information on virtually all aspects of the subject), has this to say:

> The volume of the minstrel band was quite lean, yet anything but delicate. The tones of the banjo died away quickly and therefore could not serve as a solid foundation in the ensemble. On top was the squeaky, carelessly tuned fiddle. Add the dry "ra, raka, taka, tak" of the bones and the tambourine's dull thumps and ceaseless jingling to the twang of the banjo and the flat tone of the fiddle, and the sound of the band is approximated: it was scratchy, tinkling, cackling, and humorously incongruous.[4]

Dan Emmett

Daniel Decatur Emmett (1815–1904) was a pioneer performer in minstrelsy, and one of the most important composers and authors of its early folkish and rough-hewn material. Born in a small Ohio town just emerging from the backwoods, Emmett grew up in a frontier society similar to that in which Lincoln was raised, with all its virtues and vices—its examples of courage and fierce independence, its violence and prejudices, and above all, its rough-and-ready humor. Dan Emmett learned the printing trade, and began making up verses to be sung to popular tunes, in accordance with a prevalent custom of the times. At eighteen he enlisted in the army, mastering there the drum and fife. In the late 1830s he began appearing in circuses, singing and playing the drums, and later the banjo and the fiddle.

Blackface singing and dancing with banjo accompaniment was by this time common in the circus; of the four performers who formed the original Virginia Minstrels in New York City in 1843 (Dan Emmett, Frank Brower, William Whitlock, and Richard Pelham), at least three had had experience in the touring circuses. The Virginia Minstrels, the first group to use the classic instrumentation discussed above (fiddle, banjo, tambourine, and bones), and the first to put together a whole evening of minstrel music, dancing, and skits, caught on with both public and press in New York and Boston. A tour of the British Isles later that same year (1843) was less successful, and it was there that the original company broke up. But the popularity of this entertainment in the United States was so great that many imitators and competitors soon appeared— E. P. Christy and his troupe among them. Emmett, upon his return to this country in 1844, soon reestablished himself as an "Ethiopian" performer, working in urban theaters in the winter and touring with circuses in the summer until the middle fifties, when he tried several theatrical ventures in the Midwest. He had meanwhile composed many songs, some of which had been published as early as 1843. Returning to New York in

1858, he worked with Bryant's Minstrels, by then the foremost minstrel troupe, until 1866—as performer and as composer-author of songs and skits, especially for the shows' finales, the "walk-arounds."

It was for Bryant's Minstrels that Dan Emmett wrote *Dixie* (full title, *I Wish I Was in Dixie's Land*) in 1859. Perhaps the most phenomenally popular song of the nineteenth century, it was minstrelsy's greatest single legacy to American music. It soon acquired a significance entirely unintended and even resented by its composer, when it was adopted by the Confederacy at the outbreak of hostilities.

After the Civil War minstrelsy, as we shall see, lost much of its original flavor and character, becoming, as Nathan has said, "an efficient large-scale variety show which favored less and less the dry, tough humor of Emmett's texts and tunes and the primitive style of his performances." [5] With this development, Emmett's career in minstrelsy was virtually over; he went to live in Chicago, barely averting extreme poverty by working at various jobs, musical and otherwise. In the 1880s the entertainment profession came to his aid, with various benefit performances, and two touring engagements with minstrel companies, during which he appeared on the stage, usually to sing or fiddle *Dixie*, to tumultuous applause. In 1888 he returned to the town of his birth—Mount Vernon, Ohio—where, except for a "farewell tour" in 1895, he lived simply until his death in 1904.

Stephen Foster

Minstrelsy's best-known composer was Stephen Collins Foster (1826–1864), though he was not, like Emmett, a minstrel performer himself, nor did he write exclusively for the minstrel stage. Had he performed his own songs professionally, he would have made far more money from them. He almost surely had the talent, but his family background and upbringing, and in all probability his own temperament, precluded the career of a performer. Born near Pittsburgh into a large family that had formerly been quite well-to-do, Foster early showed signs of musical talent, and was exposed to many kinds of music. He heard not only the popular sentimental songs and pieces of the day (there was a piano in the home) but "plantation melodies" and blackface songs. He was taken to Negro church services by his family's mulatto servant, and later, working in a Pittsburgh warehouse, he heard the singing of the blacks working on the riverboats.

He had written songs and piano pieces earlier (*Open Thy Lattice, Love* was written when he was seventeen), but in 1845 he began writing "Ethiopian songs," at first for the enjoyment of a group of friends. In Cincinnati he met a member of a professional minstrel troupe (the Sable Harmonists) who introduced his *Old Uncle Ned* in one of their programs. In 1848 he wrote *Oh! Susanna*, selling it outright to a Pittsburgh publisher for $100. It became enormously popular. The next year he signed a contract with the leading New York music publisher, Firth, Pond & Co., and committed himself to a career of songwriting. In 1852 he made a brief steamboat trip down the Ohio and Mississippi to New Orleans—his only visit to the South. The 1850s brought him fame, and his music popularity. In 1860 he moved to New York City. He had virtually ceased writing by this time for the minstrel stage; instead he wrote, and sold for what they would bring in the commercial music market of pre-Tin Pan Alley days, sentimental songs (*Beautiful Dreamer*; *Lizzie Dies Tonight*), trite comic songs (*If You've Only Got a Moustache*), and war songs (*Better Times Are Coming*; *We Are Coming, Father Abraam, 300,000 More*; *Willie Has Gone to the War*). Poor, sick, ravaged by alcoholism, and alone, he died in New York City early in 1864.

While Foster's minstrel songs represent only a portion of his output, they represent, with few exceptions, his best. His minstrel songs belong to the two types then common: the fast tunes, often comic (*The Glendy Burke*; *Camptown Races*; *Nelly Bly*; and of course *Oh! Susanna*), and the slow, sentimental songs (*Massa's in de Cold Ground*; *My Old Kentucky Home*; *Old Black Joe*; and *Old Folks at Home*). The dialect so typical of minstrel material was used by Foster in the early songs (*My Brudder Gum*; *Ring de Banjo*), but Foster dropped this in the later songs, rightly thinking that it would restrict the universality of their appeal.

Zenith and Decline

The minstrel show reached its zenith in the years just prior to the Civil War. After that it began to lose its original flavor; with larger bands and casts and more varied fare, it increasingly resembled the variety shows, which indeed did replace minstrel shows almost completely in New York in the 1860s. But the latter continued strong in the smaller centers of population, as we have noted. After the Civil War, the Negro musicians and entertainers themselves began to participate, and all-black minstrel companies toured for another half-century or so. Minstrelsy thus became both a training ground and a source of employment for many black musicians who later branched out in the direction of jazz. W. C. Handy has been mentioned, as has "Ma" Rainey, who toured widely in the South with various minstrel shows and circuses in the first two decades of this century. Other jazz figures who played for a time in minstrel bands include Bunk Johnson, Lester Young, and Jelly Roll Morton.[6]

After the Civil War, blackface comedy done mostly by white performers continued to entertain audiences outside of the format of the minstrel show itself. Blackface acts, modelel after minstrel songs, dances, and skits, were a staple of vaudeville after the decline of genuine minstrelsy; according to one authority, a majority of the acts in vaudeville in the 1880s were in fact blackface.[7] Negro impersonations, of course, persisted right down through the first three or four decades of this century, through the heyday of singers like Al Jolson and Eddie Cantor, who got their start in the last waning epoch of vaudeville.

As to the black performers, we have already noted that they continued to perform in small touring minstrel shows, playing mostly the rural areas, until well into this century. In the cities, performers such as the team of Bert Williams and George Walker (singers and comedians who also worked in blackface makeup) brought new standards of integrity to the stage presentation of the black man. As George Walker himself said:

> The one hope of the colored performer must be in making a radical departure from the old "darkie" style of singing and dancing. . . . There is an artistic side to the black race, and if it could be properly developed on the stage, I believe the theatergoing public would profit much by it. . . . My idea was always to impersonate my race just as they are. The colored man has never successfully taken off his own humorous characteristics, and the white impersonator often overdoes the matter.[8]

Playing eventually in shows such as *In Dahomey* (1902) and *In Bandana Land* (1907), Williams and Walker were part of the first wave of black shows with black performers at the turn of the century—a development treated more fully in chapter 10. The shadow of minstrelsy still lingers over some aspects of these shows, even as late as the 1921 *Shuffle Along* of Blake and Sissle.[9] But let us return to the important musical contributions that the early minstrel show, in its heyday, made to American music.

Links to Ragtime and Jazz

Minstrelsy was not only a thriving entertainment form in its day, but it also furnished our first really indigenous popular music. But what is there discernible in the music of minstrelsy that enables us to connect it somehow with the popular music of our own time, especially jazz? The Negro elements in minstrel music, however diluted, constituted the only widely popular expression of pre-jazz musical traits before ragtime and the blues.[10] In the minstrel show, we find that the "buck-or-wing dance" and the later "cakewalk," especially, exhibited inherently jazzy rhythms. More specifically, we should focus our attention on what the banjo player was doing. Against the steady thudding beat of the tambourine and of the performers' feet on the floor (the early minstrel band's only "left hand"), the banjo player gave out lively and often syncopated rhythms similar to those that would appear in the next important source of jazz we will consider—ragtime. A comparison of the rhythm of the opening measures of Scott Joplin's famous *Maple Leaf Rag* (1899) with that of a minstrel banjo tune by Dan Emmett, *Nigger on de Wood Pile* [11] (1845), shows this relationship, especially at the places where identical or nearly identical rhythmic figures are marked.

It is unfortunate that as of this writing virtually no known re-creations of the music of the early minstrel show as it must have actually sounded to its mid-nineteenth-century audiences have been attempted. The material and the resources are available, and perhaps the time is ripe for such a venture. Meanwhile our acquaintance with the music of this rough-and-ready popular entertainment will have to be based on verbal descriptions, and on the printed music of the songs and banjo tunes.[12] As for the songs themselves, we all know a great many: *Dixie; Turkey in the Straw; Oh! Susanna* (and many others by Foster); *Buffalo Gals* (and its descendant, *Dance with a Dolly*); *Jordan Is a Hard Road to Travel* (popular in early hillbilly music); *Oh, Dem Golden Slippers; In the Evening by the Moonlight; Carry Me Back to Old Virginny.*[13] These and others give us the flavor of the minstrel legacy that has become woven into the common heritage of American song.

RAGTIME

The rapid growth, flowering, and fading of ragtime is one of the most vivid and arresting phenomena in the whole panorama of American music. Budding during the Gay Nineties, which it came to symbolize, it was in full bloom by the turn of the century, and had spent itself by the end of World War I, but not before many of its features had gone into new genres, including Harlem piano, and jazz itself. The soil of ragtime was prepared, as we have seen, by the coon songs and banjo work of the minstrel show, quite possibly fertilized by some of the Latin rhythms that could be heard in New Orleans in the nineteenth century. In fact, there was "hot" playing to be heard in dance halls, saloons, and bordellos all along the inland rivers of commerce emptying into the great Mississippi delta. Transferred to the piano (just how, when, and where first we do not know), the hot style of playing has been called "jig" piano,[14] though the exact vintage of this term is in doubt. It was known in Chicago in the early 1890s. Its center of development seemed to be the Midwest, especially St. Louis, but once it became known its spread was extremely rapid. Although its rhythms were definitely those that had evolved in the music of the American blacks, its harmony and form were European. Ben Harney, a black pianist from Kentucky, who passed for white, was the first to bring ragtime to significant notice in New York, through a concert he played there in 1896. In the next year the first rags were published, and the boom was on. There were at least two thousand rags published between 1897 and 1920, and some estimates run as high as ten thousand. While rags continued to be published after that, the output was down sharply, and the ragtime vogue was pretty much over in favor of jazz. Nineteen-seventeen was the year of the first jazz recording, but phonograph recording came too late to catch ragtime in its heyday. Outside the fairly limited scope of live performance, ragtime was spread chiefly through sales of the sheet music, which aspiring devotees would buy to take home and learn on their parlor pianos. But real ragtime is not easy to play. To aid the learner and cash in on the boom, instruction books in ragtime began to appear—the earliest by Harney himself in 1897. One truly valuable document is an all-too-brief set of six exercises by Scott Joplin himself, published as *School of Ragtime* in 1908, with accompanying explanations and admonitions. (Joplin concentrates most on accurate rendering of the rhythm, and warns the performer, as he was to do over and over again in his published rags: "Never play ragtime fast at any time.") To provide personal instruction, studios were opened to accept pupils—and yes, the first advertisement for "Ragtime Taught in Ten Lessons" appeared in Chicago in 1903.

Composers and Recordings

Who were the leading composers of ragtime? There are many to choose from, but at least the works of the following few should be known by the serious student of American music. First and foremost would be Scott Joplin (1869–1917), active in Sedalia, Missouri, then St. Louis, then New York. Also important were Tom Turpin (ca. 1873–1922) of St. Louis; James Scott (1886–1938), active in Carthage, Missouri, St. Louis, and Kansas City; and Joseph Lamb (1887–1960) of New York.

Ragtime available today on recordings is from three main sources. First, the music from the old piano rolls, very popular in the pre-phonograph days of ragtime, has been reconstructed and made available on discs. Many piano rolls were hand-played by the classic artists, including Joplin, and so a fairly accurate idea of their rendering has come down to us. The second source is recordings of performers like Jelly Roll Morton, who performed and recorded rags in the twenties and later, after the advent of phonograph recording, but also after the ragtime era itself had passed and the style was already undergoing changes. An interesting example is Morton's transformation of Joplin's *Maple Leaf Rag*, which he recorded in 1938.[15] The third source is modern performances of ragtime, and since we are now in an age of a considerable revival, not only in the performance but also in the composition of rags, there is much well-performed music to choose from, and we can in addition enjoy the luxury of modern studio-quality recording.[16]

Some Important Features of the Music

What of the music itself? The sound is familiar to most of us, and stereotyped images are all too easily evoked—honky-tonk piano, barroom pianist in shirt sleeves and straw hat, silent-movie music, piano-roll music, and so on and on. But the music beneath the stereotype repays careful attention and listening. Ragtime was an important link to jazz, yes, but it is also an authentic music in itself, with its own standards and its own excellences.

Ragtime rhythm

Since the "ragging" is in the rhythm, let us look more closely at this element and see how ragtime composers used the device of musical *syncopation*. Syncopation is so basic to the rhythmic life of much American music that it will be worthwhile to devote some time to an examination of it as it occurs in ragtime, as a basis for understanding it as encountered elsewhere. Syncopation is the displacing of accents from their normal position in the musical measure, so that they contradict the underlying meter.[17] Syncopation assumes a steady beat, stated or implied, and cannot be said to exist without it. This is normally supplied in ragtime by the "oom-pah" of the left hand, while the right hand has the melody, with its characteristically displaced accents. How does the right hand accomplish this syncopation, or displacing of accents? In ragtime it is done by simply arranging the succession of long and short notes so that *some* of the longer notes begin at rhythmically weak spots in the metric continuum, so that the accent they create at the moment of their attack serves to contradict rather than reinforce the prevailing background meter.

To turn to some examples to illustrate how this works, here is the rhythm of the first two measures of the fiddler's tune *Turkey in the Straw*:

Here all the notes except the last are the same length, so that there can be no accents by virtue of note length, and hence no syncopation. The running notes constitute a continuous background made up of what might be called the "lowest common denominator" of durations, since they are the shortest notes used. They occur in groups of four to a beat. This is exactly the same metric background that is used in ragtime—hence the "squareness" of its rhythmic figures, as compared to later swing-jazz.

Let us observe the ways in which longer notes can be superimposed on this background. If we want a longer note to reinforce the meter, it will do this most strongly if its beginning coincides with the first note of a rhythmic subdivision:

This is the normal position of the lowest, and hence the "heaviest," of the left-hand bass notes. Somewhat weaker, and in fact creating a mild contradiction, or syncopation, would be a note beginning on the third of the sixteenth notes of our background:

The only syncopation in Dan Emmett's minstrel tune *Dixie* is of this type.

Most contradictory to the meter would be notes beginning on either the second or fourth of the background sixteenths:

These jauntier syncopations are the ones typical of ragtime; in fact, these very rhythmic figures, or variants of them, may be found on every page.

If we now observe the way these syncopations are placed in genuine ragtime, we get an idea of the fine balance the best composers achieved between contradiction and affirmation of the meter within the phrase. In the following example from Scott Joplin's *The Entertainer* (1902), first strain, the contradictions, or syncopations, are marked with an S.

This well-known rag shows a typical number and distribution of syncopations. The rags from what might be called the classic period usually have between two and four to a phrase, fairly evenly distributed.

It will be readily apparent that given the subdivision of the beat into four parts, the variety of syncopated figures available to the composer is rather limited, and that rhythmically ragtime can all too easily take on the character of a series of clichés. This was undoubtedly one of its most severe limitations, which only the most gifted composers could transcend. As ragtime strove to evolve, there was a tendency in some works of the middle and late periods to crowd more syncopations into the phrase. Some of Joseph Lamb's compositions reveal this, such as the following example from his *American Beauty Rag* (1913), first strain. Here is a phrase in which there are seven syncopations in the first phrase—six of them within the first two measures, including four in immediate succession:

When we listen to the actual music, it is apparent that Lamb uses these syncopations with ease and grace, but there is a certain air of ripeness about it which suggests a genre that has almost reached the limits of its refinement.

RAGTIME HARMONY AND FORM

We have shown the relation of ragtime rhythm to that of the banjo tunes, minstrel songs, and Irish reels—if not actual folk music, these are very close to it. In terms of *harmony*, however, ragtime is farther removed from folk roots than any other music here discussed, with the exception of the more sophisticated jazz. It is miles away from blues, country music, and even most rock in this respect. Its harmonic sophistications are comparable (and indeed related) to the "close" harmony of "barbershop quartet" singing—which is to say, chromatic European harmonies acquired by way of Tin Pan Alley. Though it can become formula-ridden, the best ragtime composers have used this harmonic language with taste and skill; the rags of Joseph Lamb are noteworthy examples.

In terms of *form*, rags are closely related to marches, with their regular sixteen-measure strains, repeated, and subsidiary "trio" strains in the related key of the subdominant. An introduction is optional; Joplin, except in his single most famous rag, almost invariably uses one. Careful listening will reveal a typical pattern of AABB, followed by the trio, CCDD (each letter represents a sixteen-bar strain). Often the A strain is brought back, unrepeated, just before the trio. Sometimes the final strain returns to the principal key; more often (as in the march) the piece ends in a different key from that in which it began. Joplin, in his later rags, tried a somewhat more expanded form.

Of all the ragtime composers, Joplin had probably the greatest hopes and ambitions for his music, and tried the hardest to transcend the limitations inherent in ragtime. His hopes and ambitions were, sadly, doomed to disappointment. He wrote two ragtime operas, neither of which was ever fully staged in his lifetime, and one of which has subsequently completely disappeared. His second opera, *Treemonisha* (which does not consist exclusively of ragtime music), is being revived here and there in our time, mostly in concert form. Today's attitude toward ragtime, when it is not merely nostalgic or sociological, tends to be an acceptance and enjoyment of it on its own terms, just as we enjoy other idealized miniature dance forms for piano, like the mazurkas of Chopin. Within its small frame there is a wealth of music.

PRE-JAZZ

Minstrelsy, ragtime, and blues—those highly public and popular forms—were only the most audible and obvious of jazz's precursors.* Behind them, mostly unheard and unheeded by white Americans, were all the varied musical manifestations of what has been called the "black experience": the music of West Africa itself, and on this continent the ecstatic responsory cries and shouts of worshippers in the meeting houses and at the outdoor revivals, the work songs, the lonely field hollers, the hypnotic drumming of the Caribbean cults and ceremonies.

Where and when, from all this background, did actual jazz begin to emerge? This is a complex question, the first part of which cannot be adequately answered with the single place name New Orleans, important as its role was. It will be necessary to take a broader look geographically, for there were musical developments in all the cities and towns of the South, and in the larger cities of the North (wherever, in other words, there was a sizable black population) that set the stage for the emergence of jazz. The rest of this chapter will be devoted to shedding some light on these developments, and taking a look at what is known about the primitive jazz that preceded the first recordings of the 1920s.

Two developments in particular demand attention first: the popular black stage shows and "syncopated dance orchestras" of New York and other cities, and the Negro brass bands of the period.

Broadway and Black Bohemia

A series of successful non-minstrel variety shows with all-Negro casts were produced, in New York and elsewhere, beginning in the last decade of the nineteenth century. An account of these productions is found in chapter 10. What their audiences heard was not actual jazz, of course, but from what we know of the music, and the enthusiasm it aroused, it must have given them a foretaste. Will Marion Cook's *Rain Song*,[18] from 1912, uses syncopations that were already very prevalent in ragtime.

Well before this century, as we have seen, it was the time-honored role of black musicians to furnish music for dancing. As Eileen Southern has said: "In many places the profession of dance musicians was reserved

---

* Blues, largely coextensive in time with jazz, and coloring and shaping it in all eras, is treated in chapters 2 and 8.

by custom for Negroes, just as was, for example, the occupation of barber. Consequently, black dance orchestras held widespread monopolies on jobs for a long period in the nation's history—even after World War I." [19]

In the early 1900s New York's Black Bohemia (an area in West Manhattan around 53rd Street) furnished "syncopated dance orchestras" for all occasions, and these were much in demand. Such an orchestra gave a public concert in 1905, and by 1910 James Reese Europe had founded the famous Clef Club, whose orchestra gave public concerts, including a famous and highly successful one at Carnegie Hall in 1912. James Weldon Johnson, the famous black poet, wrote of this concert: "New York had not yet become accustomed to jazz; so when the Clef Club opened its concert with a syncopated march, playing it with a biting attack and an infectious rhythm, and on the finale bursting into singing, the effect can be imagined. The applause became a tumult!" [20] The reference to the band's singing is noteworthy; since the bands were still made up largely of string instruments (violins, cellos, mandolins, banjos, pianos) these performers could well sing while playing, and their style of singing probably contributed significantly to the origins of barbershop harmony.[21]

With the entry of the United States into World War I in 1917, Negroes joined the armed forces in large numbers, and bands were formed of black musicians whose services were much in demand. The most famous of these bands was formed and led by James Reese Europe himself. When this band went to France it was enormously popular, not only with the American troops but with the French as well.[22] Was Europe's band playing jazz? Probably not in the strict sense, since he laid great stress on its reading the music accurately. But read his own description of the band's playing:

> We accent strongly . . . the notes which originally would be without accent. It is natural for us to do this; it is, indeed, a racial musical characteristic. I have to call a daily rehearsal of my band to prevent the musicians from adding to their music more than I wish them to. Whenever possible they all embroider their parts in order to produce new, peculiar sounds.[23]

There could hardly be a more revealing hint of the jazz manner of playing.

This first significant introduction of the embryonic American jazz style to Europeans was to be followed by European tours after the war by both James Reese Europe and Will Marion Cook, with groups recruited from the best black dance musicians to be found in America. Many of these musicians, such as Sidney Bechet, later became famous jazz musicians. What one would give to have a recording, for example, of Bechet playing *The Characteristic Blues* with Cook's ensemble, as he did for King George V in a command performance at Buckingham Palace in 1919!

Brass Bands

More famous as precursors of jazz were the Negro brass bands that flourished not only in New Orleans but throughout the South, and in many cities in the North and Midwest as well. The town brass band, playing for park concerts, holiday parades, and numerous other civic occasions, is an American institution that still thrives in many small, and not so small, towns today. New Orleans, possibly owing to the French influence, had an exceptional number of bands, as well as dance orchestras. The French interest in the military, or brass, band goes back to Napoleonic times. There were also trained musicians playing in the French Opera House who regularly taught the instruments.

The bands were not large by present standards, consisting of only ten or twelve pieces, including trumpets or cornets, alto and baritone horns, trombones, tuba, clarinets, and drums. They could furnish music for concerts as well as parades; in addition, there was often a smaller group affiliated with the band that played for dances, since many of the men doubled on string instruments. The repertoire of both groups had of necessity to be broad, and by no means consisted entirely of the new ragtime (which was frowned upon by many of their patrons). They played marches and two-steps, of course—this was the very matrix of ragtime, and much early jazz—but they also played quadrilles, polkas, waltzes, and mazurkas.

It was their parade music for which they ultimately became the most famous, and not the least important job of the bands was playing for funerals. The lodges, or secret societies, to which the deceased might belong (often to more than one) would furnish the bands. In the legendary and often-described scene, the band would march solemnly to the graveyard, playing hymns such as *Nearer My God to Thee* or *Come Ye Disconsolate*, or "any 4/4 played very slow." After the burial the band would re-form outside the cemetery and march away to the beat of the snare drum only. After it was a block or two away from the graveyard, it would burst into ragtime—*Didn't He Ramble*, or a "ragged" version of a hymn or spiritual. It was then that the "second line" of fans and enthusiastic dancing bystanders would fall in behind the band.[24] No better evidence exists of the close relationship between early jazz and the march. It is interesting to compare an early "jazzed" march such as *High Society*, with its famous clarinet obbligato in the trio section (an obbligato solo, incidentally, that established the reputation of its earliest "jazz" performer, Alphonse Picou), with a march accepted as "standard," such as a Sousa piece of about the same time.

The Excelsior and the Onward were the most famous bands. No recordings exist, of course, of these bands in the formative period of jazz around the turn of the century (though it is frustrating for the student of jazz to realize that there *might* have been some; Sousa's band was recording before 1890). But a recording of the surviving Eureka Brass Band (an organization dating from the 1920s), which was made in the 1950s, gives some idea of the sound.[25]

There was keen competition among the bands, and "cutting" or "bucking" contests were common. A few legendary names emerge from this period—none larger than that of Charles "Buddy" Bolden, the New Orleans trumpet player. He was a versatile musician, reading music when necessary but preferring to play by ear. (The "uptown" New Orleans musicians, playing for the high-paying bordellos, were notable exceptions to the general practice among bandsmen of the period; these players for the most part prided themselves on being *unable* to read, feeling that it would inhibit their style.) Bolden played "sweet" music for the general public and "hot" music for the "district" and its patrons. It was for the latter that he became the most famous, introducing his "hot blues" about 1894. Was Buddy playing jazz, that far back? Ear-witnesses like Bunk Johnson say that he was. It is certain that he was heavily imbued with the blues. The New Orleans bass player "Pops" Foster has written of him: "He played nothing but blues, and all that stink music, and he played it very loud." [26] Thus there was ample evidence at an early date of the perennial and symbiotic relationship between blues and jazz.

Romantic legend has given New Orleans the reputation of being almost solely responsible for the birth of jazz. It is possible that the claim may be found to be somewhat exaggerated, as we learn more of the prehistory of this important genre. But there is no doubt that this unique city, with its rich blend of traditions, played an important part. In any event, this part was largely over by the end of World War I, and certainly by the advent of the first recordings. In the next chapter we will deal with the development of jazz itself, as we can trace it from the time of its earliest actual surviving recorded sounds.

FURTHER READING

General

* SOUTHERN, EILEEN. *The Music of Black Americans: A History.* New York: W. W. Norton & Co., 1971.
    The first comprehensive survey of the entire field of black music and musicians in America, this valuable work is written in nontechnical lan-

* Items thus marked are part of the suggested reference library to be available in connection with this book.

guage but contains a wealth of information. Each of the four major parts is preceded by a chronology of important events in black history, and the bibliography is considerable.

* ———. (ed.). *Readings in Black American Music.* New York: W. W. Norton & Co., 1971.
Selected source readings complementing the above.

* STEARNS, MARSHALL. *The Story of Jazz.* New York: Oxford University Press, 1956.
This excellent work on jazz has valuable material on the antecedents, especially in parts 2 and 3.

Minstrelsy

* HANDY, W. C. *Father of the Blues.* New York: Macmillan Co., 1941.
Chapter 4 is especially pertinent to the last days of minstrelsy.

* HOWARD, JOHN TASKER. *Stephen Foster, America's Troubadour.* New York: Thomas Y. Crowell Co., 1934. Rev. ed., 1953.
The standard biography, including a complete list of published works and a rather full chronology.

JACKSON, RICHARD (ed.). *Stephen Foster Song Book,* New York: Dover Publications, 1974.
Forty of Foster's songs in their original published versions, with original sheet-music covers, and with an introduction and notes on the songs by the editor. All the important minstrel songs are included.

* NATHAN, HANS. *Dan Emmett and the Rise of Early Negro Minstrelsy.* Norman: University of Oklahoma Press, 1962.
The single most important study of the early minstrel show, as well as Emmett himself. Nearly half the work consists of a valuable anthology of all types of minstrel material by Emmett and others, including, for example, the complete text of a skit, or "extravaganza."

PASKMAN, DAILY, and SPAETH, SIGMUND. *"Gentlemen, Be Seated!" A Parade of the Old-Time Minstrels.* New York: Doubleday, Doran & Co., 1928.

ROURKE, CONSTANCE. *American Humor: A Study of the National Character.* New York, 1931. Reprint, Doubleday & Co., 1953.

SIMOND, IKE. *Old Slack's Reminiscence and Pocket History of the Colored Profession from 1865 to 1891.* Chicago, 1891. Reprint, with preface by Francis Lee Utley and introduction by Robert C. Toll, Bowling Green, Ohio: Bowling Green University Popular Press, 1974.
Interesting documentation of black minstrelsy.

TOLL, ROBERT C. *Blacking Up: The Minstrel Show in Nineteenth-Century America.* New York: Oxford University Press, 1974.

WITTKE, CARL. *Tambo and Bones: A History of the American Minstrel Stage.* Durham, N.C.: Duke University Press, 1930.

Ragtime

* BLESH, RUDI, and JANIS, HARRIET. *They All Played Ragtime.* New York, 1950. 4th rev. ed., New York: Oak Publications, 1971.
  The best known and most comprehensive single work on the subject.
BLESH, RUDI (ed.). *Classic Piano Rags.* New York: Dover Publications, 1973.
  A fine collection of 81 rags by 13 composers, with original sheet music-covers and an introduction by the editor.
JOPLIN, SCOTT. *The Collected Works of Scott Joplin.* 2 vols. New York: New York Public Library, 1971. Belwin-Mills Publishing Corp., Melville, N.Y., has published vol. 1, *Works for Piano,* with an introduction by Rudi Blesh, in paperback. Vol. 2 includes Joplin's opera *Treemonisha.*
SCHAFER, WILLIAM J., and BIEDEL, JOHANNES. *The Art of Ragtime.* Baton Rouge: Louisiana State University Press, 1973.

Pre-Jazz

JOHNSON, JAMES WELDON. *Black Manhattan.* New York, 1930. Reprint, New York: Atheneum Publishers, 1968.
  An invaluable firsthand account of black musical activity in New York, from Will Marion Cook's *Clorindy* to Noble and Sissle's *Shuffle Along.*
LOMAX, ALAN. *Mister Jelly Roll: The Fortunes of Jelly Roll Morton, New Orleans Creole and "Inventor of Jazz."* Berkeley: University of California Press, 1950. 2nd ed. 1973.
* SCHULLER, GUNTHER. *Early Jazz: Its Roots and Musical Development.* New York: Oxford University Press, 1968.
  A thorough study, embodying musical analysis, of jazz from its origins to 1930. The early chapters are pertinent here.
See also the reading list for chapter 8.

Minstrelsy

As of this writing there are no known reconstructions of the music of the minstrel show as it would have sounded in its heyday. The songs of Stephen Foster are readily available, but not currently in versions approaching the style and instrumentation in which they would have been heard on the minstrel stage. *The Recorded Anthology of American Music* (RAAM) includes a few relevant items:

* *Songs of the Civil War* (NW-202).
  Includes a performance of *Dixie* as Dan Emmett wrote it, though not as it would have sounded on the minstrel stage.
* *Life in Nineteenth-Century Cincinnati* (NW-251).
  Includes a minstrel song, *Wake Up, Jake.*

* *Folk Song Types* (NW-245).

    Includes a minstrel-derived comic song, *Dr. Ginger Blue*, from the early country music tradition, probably sung by traveling medicine show performers.

* *Shuffle Along* (NW-260).

    The 1921 show by Sissle and Blake; includes a comic dialogue, "The Fight," of the type that reached the popular stage from minstrelsy by way of vaudeville.

See also *Tom Ashley and Tex Isley* (Folkways: 2350).

    Includes an old minstrel-type comic song, *I'm the Man That Rode the Mule Around the World*.

Ragtime

Ragtime in its original medium (piano solo) is abundantly available now on recent recordings by today's pianists who specialize in this (William Balcomb, Max Morath, Joshua Rifkin, and others). Documentary albums of interest are found in two categories:

TYPICAL PIANO ROLL PERFORMANCES

Scott Joplin, 2 vols. Biograph: 1013–14.

James Scott. Biograph: 1016.

THE DIFFUSION OF RAGTIME

* *Maple Leaf Rag: Ragtime in Rural America*. RAAM: NW-235.

    Ragtime 1: The City—Banjos, Brass Bands, and Nickel Pianos. Folkways: RBF-17.

    Ragtime 2: The Country—Mandolins, Fiddles, and Guitars. Folkways: RBF-18.

* *Steppin' on the Gas: Rags to Jazz, 1913–1927*. RAAM: NW-269.

    Includes James Reese Europe's bands and orchestras.

Pre-Jazz

A History of Jazz: The New York Scene 1914–1945. Folkways: RBF-RF-3.

Steppin' on the Gas (see above).

    Some of the earliest excerpts on these two albums are relevant here, especially those of James Reese Europe's groups.

The Music of New Orleans, vol. 2, *Music of the Eureka Brass Band*. Folkways: FA-2462.

PROJECTS

1. Make a study of the old-time minstrel skit with music known as *The Arkansas Traveler*. For a start, consult the versions in *The New Lost City Ramblers Song Book* (see the reading list for chapter 7) and in Carl Sandburg's *Folk-Say*.
2. Compare *Jordan Is a Hard Road to Travel* (in Nathan, *Dan Emmett, p.* 335) with *The Other Side of Jordan* (as found in *The New Lost City Ramblers Song Book*, and based on performances by Uncle Dave Macon, recorded on *Uncle Dave Macon*, Folkways release RBF-51). Find out as much as you can about the survival of such minstrel songs in traditional country music.
3. If you like to sing folk songs, learn an old-time minstrel tune by Stephen Foster, Dan Emmett, James Bland, or another minstrel composer, and add it to your repertoire.
4. Investigate the activities and accomplishments of Foster Hall, the organization housed on the campus of the University of Pittsburgh and dedicated to the collection, preservation, and dissemination of material pertaining to Stephen Foster. For a start, consult John Tasker Howard's biography included in the reading list.
5. Study Scott Joplin's brief *School of Ragtime* (included in the collected works published under the auspices of the New York Public Library, and available in most large libraries), and find examples in actual rags of the rhythmic figures Joplin presents in his *School* as teaching examples. If you are a pianist, work up a demonstration of these on the piano.
6. Make a study of Scott Joplin's opera *Treemonisha* (the score is included in the collected works cited in question 5). How much of it is ragtime? Include information on recent performances if possible.
7. Investigate the life and works of one or two of the lesser-known composers of ragtime—composers besides those mentioned in this chapter. For a start, consult the Blesh and Janis work on the reading list.
8. Do an investigation of the mechanical piano roll—its history, how it worked, its recorded literature (including ragtime), and the transcription of its music onto discs.
9. "Has the importance of New Orleans in the early development of jazz been overestimated in most standard books?" Taking either the negative or the positive side of this question, prepare a well-substantiated summary of your case.
10. Make a brief study of jazz and pre-jazz on the New York scene prior to 1925.

Chapter Twelve
Jazz: Its Times
and Styles

BEFORE THE ACTUAL SOUNDS of jazz began to be captured and preserved, however unsatisfactorily at first, by the phonograph, we can only speculate as to what this music really sounded like. We do have some re-creations, years after the fact, by a few of its musicians. What little has survived in notation gives no very accurate idea of this music that existed largely without being written down. And verbal descriptions, together with some knowledge of what instruments were used and under what conditions they were played, furnish imprecise clues at best. In the previous chapter we considered jazz before the advent of recordings—"primitive" jazz, according to the chronology of one prominent writer, André Hodeir.[1] We now pick it up with the first preserved sounds.

THE JAZZ OF THE EARLY RECORDINGS

Although jazz was first recorded in 1917, the most readily available early recordings date from about 1923, in the middle of Hodeir's period of so-called "old-time" jazz. What do we hear in these early recordings, rather dimly transmitted, as through a veil? Listen to King Oliver's *Dippermouth Blues* (solos by Louis Armstrong), *Snake Rag, Aunt Hagar's Blues*, or *Froggie Moore*; Jelly Roll Morton's *Grandpa's Spells, Black Bottom Stomp*, or *Big Foot Ham*; Freddie Keppard's *Stock Yard Strut*; or Kid Ory's *Society Blues*.[2] What we hear is the sound of a small band dominated by wind instruments, playing either fast numbers (rags, stomps, even speeded-up blues) that convey an infectious exuberance or slow tunes (usually with a female singer) that are invariably blues in their more typical aspect. Whether slow or fast, we are conscious of the tendency in the music towards an enriched and complex texture of individually felt and projected lines woven into a mostly harmonious but teeming heterophony and blown with informal and happy abandon.

THE BEGINNINGS OF DISSEMINATION AND CHANGE: CHICAGO

It is important to realize that jazz, by the time we encounter it on recordings, was already in a state of change. Where was it coming from, and what was its environment? New Orleans had put its stamp and name on it. But the recordings of this period were not made in New Orleans; they were made in Chicago, in New York, in Richmond, Indiana. Jazz had spread to the upper Midwest and to the East Coast, and its first great wave of popularity was beginning. New Orleans jazzmen had emigrated to the south side of Chicago, to New York, and to other urban centers. Musicians, both black and white, who had never been within a thousand miles of New Orleans were playing jazz. Considering the impact of its increasing popularity, and the numbers of new players that were taking it up, changes were inevitable, and gradually the traditional freewheeling, relaxed, improvised style was lost. We can sense this in some of the recordings of the so-called Chicago style made by the younger musicians. It was transitional; the white musicians were all, to a greater or lesser extent, learning from the blacks—and because of the attitudes. and conditions of the time, reaping a disproportionate share of the economic gains. The Chicago style shows jazz in a kind of adolescence between the carefree youth of the traditional stage and the maturity of the big-band stage, with its more sophisticated craftsmanship. It can be heard in the famous *Royal Garden Blues*, with Bix Beiderbecke and the Wolverines, and in both *Jazz Me Blues* and *There'll Be Some Changes Made*, with the Chicago Rhythm Kings.[3] It is a sort of derivative New Orleans style, but lacking some of the spontaneity, and it actually sounds more dated than the earlier jazz.

What was the milieu of jazz in the 1920s? Musicians played a great deal for and among themselves, after hours, but for the paying public (a rapidly growing constituency) its home was the nightclub and its orbit of related establishments. This was to constitute its basic environment, physically and economically, for years to come. One effect of Prohibition was to relegate the public dispensing of liquor to the tough guy—the mobster who could either dictate to the law or take it into his own hands. Consequently, especially in places like Chicago, jazz came under the aegis of the gangster. For a fuller understanding of jazz, its environment must be kept in mind, in terms not only of its effects on the lives of its musicians, but of the whole set of prejudices that grew up around it. The nightclub and its milieu is still basic to the day-by-day support of a sizable segment of jazz and the vast core of players who earn wages by playing it.

Except for isolated occasions, especially for recordings, the bands of this period were racially segregated. This led to what might be thought of as two parallel traditions in jazz. Although the color line began to be broken in the 1930s (often at high personal cost to those courageous enough to pioneer in this direction) and mixed bands eventually became fairly common, the jazz scene even today is still not free of vestiges of this unfortunate dichotomy along racial lines, as we shall see.

THREE NEW YORK DEVELOPMENTS IN THE PRE-SWING ERA

New York became the scene of intense jazz activity in the 1920s. But the stage was set for this activity long before, and any notion that jazz was imported wholesale from New Orleans and sprung full-blown on a public totally unprepared for such novel music is false. As we have noted in the previous chapter, all-black musicals and extravaganzas had been produced in Brooklyn and on Broadway before the turn of the century, and while they did not incorporate what would be called jazz, we know enough of the impression made at the time to sense that some of the authentic elements of jazz must have been present. Ragtime was very well known in the first decade of this century there. Black Bohemia had flourished as early as 1900, furnishing dance orchestras and musicians whose services were much in demand. James Reese Europe had given a concert with his Clef Club orchestra in Carnegie Hall in 1912, in collaboration with Will Marion Cook; again, what the audience heard must have been at least a foretaste of jazz.[4] The all-white Original Dixieland Jazz Band had played in New York as early as 1917. So the ground was prepared.

Harlem Piano

Three important developments began to emerge in New York before 1930. The first was a solo piano style that was an outgrowth of ragtime. "Rent-party," "parlor-social," "Harlem," "stride"—these names all describe, in terms of economics, geography, and left-hand agility, a solo piano idiom best illustrated in the work of its recognized founder, James P. Johnson. To get the flavor of his rollicking piano style, listen to his *Harlem Strut* (1921), *Carolina Shout* (1921), *You Can't Do What My Last Man Did* (1923), *You've Got to Be Modernistic* (1929), or *What Is This Thing Called Love?* (1930).[5] The atmosphere and function of the Harlem house-rent party of the twenties and thirties is succinctly described by Marshall Stearns when he calls it "an unstable social phenomenon that was stimulated by Prohibition and made necessary by the Depression." He continues: "The object of such a party is to raise the rent, and anybody who can pay a quarter admission is cordially invited. The core of the party usually centers around a pianist whose style was shaped by many similar situations: he plays very loud and very rhythmically."[6]

It should be noted that the work of Johnson, Fats Waller, and others far transcended the limited and highly functional milieu of the rent-party, and became influential in the mainstream of jazz itself.

Jazz and the Wider Public

A second development on the New York scene in the twenties, though somewhat peripheral to jazz itself, is interesting because it shows both the tremendous impact that jazz had by this time and the way in which the American penchant for assimilation was being indulged. New York, as the capital of the American entertainment business, has historically been not only the Great Marketplace but the Great Assimilator. Jazz was becoming enormously popular—a new force to be reckoned with in American music. As is usual, those *outside* the tradition itself saw it as "raw material"—vital and interesting, to be sure, but needing to be "worked over." (Somewhat in the same vein European composers in the nineteenth century started the practice of working over folk music.) Of course, there was a broad spectrum of reaction to jazz as raw material, with mixed and complex motives. Some were merely interested in "selling" it. For some this motive was mingled with a sincere desire to educate the public to its unique qualities. Some saw it as providing the basis for a new kind of concert, or fine-art, music. But almost all actual treatments of jazz involved setting it in a context that, while extending its temporal dimensions, diluted its essential "hot" quality. Paul Whiteman, whose work can be thought of typically as embodying all these motives, assembled a large orchestra of extremely able concert musicians and then employed a few genuine jazz players to impart to the ensemble the rhythm and flavor of jazz. The resulting "sweet" jazz thus became more acceptable to a broader segment of the public, many of whom may have thought that indeed what they were hearing *was* jazz.

Carrying assimilation a step further, we find in this period the composition of extended works intended for the environment and the audience of the formal concert, and using ensembles often approaching symphonic makeup and proportions. Of all such works of this period, probably the most successful was the famous *Rhapsody in Blue*, for piano and large ensemble (though in its original conception the ensemble was smaller and more jazz-oriented than the full symphony orchestra now used to perform the piece). The *Rhapsody* was written by George Gershwin for the now-memorable concert given by Paul Whiteman in Aeolian Hall, New York, in 1924. This work, which has not lost its freshness even today, is one of the best to come out of that first period of groping towards a successful amalgamation of jazz and concert music. The period was marked by the production of concertos, symphonies, and ballets strongly influenced by the jazz idiom. It also coincided with a period of great jazz popularity in Europe, and jazz influence on prominent European composers of the time, such as Maurice Ravel, Igor Stravinsky, and Darius Milhaud. While jazz here was attaining a rather slow and very reserved acceptance on the part of many Americans (on racial grounds as well as on grounds of its origins and environment), it was welcomed with open arms in Europe, especially in France. Accounts of the receptions American jazz musicians received abroad from the 1920s to the 1970s make educational reading indeed, and sound a consistent theme of enthusiastic, even worshipful, acceptance.

Early Steps in the Evolution of the Big Band

The third development in the New York scene at this time was squarely in the mainstream of jazz: the evolution of the big band. This led directly into the period of jazz's greatest stability, popularity, and economic security—an era that lasted until the end of World War II, and that has been designated by some (including Hodeir) as the classical era of jazz. New York can claim no monopoly in the development of the big bands.[7] But it did serve as a magnet to draw talented musicians from New Orleans (often by way of Chicago), from Chicago itself, from Kansas City, and elsewhere—musicians who helped forge the new institution that was to carry jazz to every part of the land, and ultimately of the world.

The term "big band" may be misleading. Compared with the orchestras, the bands were still small—scarcely more than about fifteen musicians.[8] But this was twice the size of the New Orleans-type bands, and many players and jazz fans thought the "big" bands a betrayal of the very principles and essence of jazz. We can see the big bands today as the kind of solution arrived at then to the problem of balancing the demand for a fuller, larger, and more varied sound with the need to retain the sine qua non of jazz—improvisational freedom, and the elusive hot quality that goes with it.

King Oliver, Louis Armstrong's mentor, and about the first of the real New Orleans jazzmen to make important recordings, recorded in Chicago in 1923 a number of his called *Dippermouth Blues*. It was in the authentic New Orleans style, done with only seven musicians. Fletcher Henderson, pianist and leader-arranger from Georgia, recorded the same piece in 1925 in New York, with slight additions, and now called *Sugar Foot Stomp*.[9] The differences make an interesting documentation of the beginnings of the big band. There are now eleven musicians, the most significant addition being two saxophones. The individual hot solos are still there, the most memorable being the choruses played by Louis Armstrong himself, who also plays essentially the same solos in King Oliver's earlier version. But the new trend toward *arranged* jazz is apparent in the way the instruments play predetermined figures together at the "breaks" (the fill-in passages at the ends of the phrases), in the tightly disciplined and rehearsed (if not written down) clarinet ensemble playing, and especially in the almost "chorale"-like presentation of the blues progression twice near the end. Another Fletcher Henderson piece, *The Stampede*, arranged by Don Redman and recorded in 1926, shows the trend carried further by using a still greater portion of arranged ensemble effects, while still allowing for individual improvisation.[10]

Of all the jazz musicians to be associated and come into prominence with the big band, none had a longer or more influential career than Duke Ellington, whose creative activity spanned half a century. He was a pianist, but he never pushed himself to the forefront as a soloist; his medium of expression was the band itself, and as leader, arranger, and composer he made music with a group that held together with exceptional consistency and continuity throughout the years. A famous early piece coming out of the very beginnings of his work with the big-band medium is *East St. Louis Toodle-Oo*.[11] Though an extremely early work as first recorded, and not to be compared with his mature work of a dozen or so years later, it shows already the smooth and disciplined playing that were evident even in his fast numbers, and the use of instrumental effects and colors typical of Ellington's essentially orchestral approach to jazz.

MID-AMERICA IS HEARD FROM

The big-band style, as it evolved in the East, drew on the New Orleans archetypal style, either directly or by way of Chicago. There had to be adjustments, as we have seen. But before the big-band style emerged finally, there was another part of the country to be heard from. This was "the West" to easterners, but it was actually the heartland—specifically Kansas City. In the days before mass media threatened to blanket the whole country and induce a homogenized culture suffocating to regional artistic identity, it was possible for different areas to develop artistic dialects as distinctive as their speech. What we are calling attention to here may seem like a fine distinction to the beginning listener to jazz, but listen to the hard-driving beat—"jump," it was called, or "four heavy beats to a bar, and no cheating" (to quote Count Basie)—of Bennie Moten's *Toby* or *Moten Swing* (both 1932), or Count Basie's *Roseland Shuffle* (1937), *Every Tub* (1938), or in a more understated vein, *Dickie's Dream* (1939).[12] You will then get a notion of that "Kansas City" ingredient that went into big-band jazz after the arrival in the East of Bennie Moten, Count Basie, Lester Young, and a host of other players from "the West." It was very akin, actually, to the drive of the boogie-woogie which came from the same part of the country.

THE ERA OF THE BIG BANDS

The so-called swing era, virtually synonymous with the heyday of the big bands, is usually thought to have come to full flower about 1935, and to have bloomed gloriously for nearly a decade. This was the period of the broadest popularity for jazz. By this time, after the repeal of Prohibition and partial recovery from the Depression, the mob-controlled nightclubs no longer constituted the nearly exclusive support and environment for jazz. Dance halls, eventually growing into large, well-appointed, and well-attended ballrooms by the mid-thirties, gave jazz a new forum and a broader popular base. The big "name" bands toured these, as well as giving stage shows in theaters. Recordings, of course, sold extremely well by this time, and could be heard on phonographs at home, in the jukeboxes that soon provided a ubiquitous accompaniment to nearly all public eating and drinking in the land, or on the new popular mass medium of the day, radio. The disc jockey, with his enormous influence, came into being. There were also weekly broadcasts of live bands. Movies featured jazz bands. This was unquestionably the period when jazz had its widest public.

Big-Band Music and Musicians

What was the jazz of this period like? Anyone born before 1925 can call up a litany of the big bands, a very few of which survived into the 1970s. We have already mentioned the leaders of two of the most influential: Duke Ellington and Count Basie. The work of Ellington's band at this period might be represented by Ko-ko (1940).[13] The fine, polished ensemble playing, the antiphonal writing (one instrument or section answering another), and the skillful and effective use of instrumental color, in consciously orchestrated effects—these are things to listen for in this work. As the scope of the jazz number widened, it was first the arranger's role that became important, and then the role of the composer began to develop. Ellington's work was crucial in both of these fields.

Another critically important musician of the swing era was Benny Goodman, clarinetist and bandleader. His highly skilled band of fourteen to sixteen musicians played an essentially hot style closely derived from that of the black jazz artists of the time. Goodman acknowledged this heritage, using arrangements written for him by Fletcher Henderson, some of them based on traditional New Orleans originals by King Oliver or Jelly Roll Morton. In addition, Goodman was one of the first to incorporate black musicians into his ensembles, using them at first as featured performers in his trio, quartet, and sextet. The disciplined but driving swing of his band helped to bring jazz to a new plateau of popularity and acceptance as dance music. This was dramatized by a famous breakthrough at the Palomar Ballroom in Los Angeles in 1935, where Goodman established that a tremendous audience, especially among younger people, existed for the hotter swing, alongside the more staid "sweet" jazz.[14] A series of recordings and broadcasts of the later thirties ensued, characterized by the hot solos of Goodman, trumpeter Harry James, and drummer Gene Krupa. Typical of this Goodman swing style are the Fletcher Henderson arrangements of Handy's St. Louis Blues or Oliver's Sugar Foot Stomp.[15] The latter is especially interesting for two reasons: first, because of the comparison it affords with two earlier versions of the work already cited, and second, because it was one of the Henderson arrangements that helped to accomplish the historic breakthrough for swing in 1935.

In considering Goodman's contributions, it may be noted further that the small jazz combo that played in conjunction with the larger band, consisting of clarinet, piano, and drums, occasionally augmented by vibraphone or guitar, was ahead of its time in concept and style, and forecast the sounds and approach of the postwar "cool" jazz. Goodman was also one of the first jazz musicians to be thoroughly schooled in classical music as well, performing and recording music by Mozart, Brahms, Bartok, and Stravinsky, the latter two contemporary composers having written works especially for him. Goodman thus forecast a catholicity of approach to music that is typical of many talented younger musicians of the 1960s and 1970s.

To name some bands is to leave out many more. Our purpose here, however, is not to present a catalog of the bands, but to try to characterize the sounds of the period and the milieu in which they flourished, and to trace the processes of change constantly at work on both.

Latin Influence

Before we move out of the swing era, we should note three other important aspects of the scene. The first is the work of the Latin bands popular at the time. The rhumba craze was no less intense than that of the tango earlier, or the mambo, samba, or cha-cha subsequently. What the purely Latin bands played was not jazz, of course, but it illustrates and reminds us of the perennial Latin presence and influence in American music. Jazz was by no means unaffected by it, and Latin drummers were soon to be incorporated into jazz ensembles (as were those from Africa, which has quite a different tradition, albeit with similar instruments). An interesting example, from somewhat later, of this Latin assimilation is *Tin Tin Deo* (1948), with the celebrated Cuban drummer Chano Pozo.[16]

The Small Combo

The second aspect is the simultaneous cultivation of the small ensemble in the era of the big band. This was no longer the old-time jazz ensemble (which did indeed enjoy a revival) but the intimate group of three to seven players that was the vehicle for the development of some of the newest ideas in jazz. Its commercial aspect was represented by the "cocktail combo" playing in small bars, but there were important artistic dimensions to the small combo as well. The Benny Goodman Sextet's recording of *I Found a New Baby* (1941) furnishes a good example.[17] Actually the small combo has always been present at every phase in jazz evolution; it was not an invention of the post-World War II "cool" or "progressive" schools. Louis Armstrong had recorded with from two to six musicians in the twenties.[18] The solo pianist also flourished; Earl

Hines, Fats Waller, Art Tatum, Buddy Powell, and Erroll Garner were leaders.

The Traditional Revival

The third aspect to be considered before leaving this period is the persistent vitality of the traditional (often called New Orleans) style of jazz. It has never wholly died out. An early copy of the New Orleans style (mostly white and more or less New York-oriented), known generally as Dixieland, was translated into big-band terms in the work of such white bandleaders as Bob Crosby (*South Rampart Street Parade*, 1937) and Eddie Condon (*Somebody Loves Me*, 1944).[19] But a real revival of the older style was one of the landmarks of the 1940s as well. In an episode in American music replete with both nostalgia and human interest, players who had been active in the very early days (some of whom had never played for recordings) were located, sometimes after considerable difficulty, and reinstated with honors in the kingdom of jazz, for the purpose of re-creating the authentic traditions and music of the long-gone New Orleans beginnings. How authentic such re-creations can be in any art so basically improvisational, and so dependent upon the player's subjective impressions of a *total* environment, may be open to question. But the documents are there now, recorded a generation after the fact, for all time. For examples, listen to Bunk Johnson, legendary symbol of this revival, in *Down by the River* (1942) or *Make Me a Pallet on the Floor* (1945),[20] or Kid Ory, in any number of revival recordings. Younger musicians also became interested in the old style, and the work of Lu Watters and Turk Murphy may be referred to in this regard.

Wartime and the Seeds of Change

With the entry of the United States into World War II there came, on one level, a kind of freezing of the status quo. In times of prolonged major crisis, especially war, we find certain kinds of art supported and indulged, both as a necessary release, and for the sense of stability afforded. But these times are not hospitable to changes and evolutions in art, which are apt to be disturbing. The feeling of security that a repetition of the accustomed can give is what is needed—and sought. During the war people flocked to the ballrooms to hear the name bands and bought the latest records; and overseas soldiers, sailors, airmen, and marines heard the same bands and the same pieces. (This is not to say that wartime hardships, including shortages of gasoline for touring, did not take their toll among the bands, some of which disbanded even before the war was over.) Meanwhile, underneath the desperately needed continuity of the surface, changes were being wrought that would profoundly alter the jazz scene once the war was over.

THE EMERGENCE OF THE MODERN PERIOD: BOP AND COOL

In the three decades since the end of World War II the whole fabric of Occidental music has frayed into so many different strands that it is difficult to keep track of them, or form any kind of overall picture of what has happened. Jazz has been no exception to this, though it has had its own peculiar set of influences to react to.

A restlessness, a ripeness for change, revealed itself first in the surfacing of new developments in jazz that had been in the making all through the war years, though for various reasons almost unnoticed. The first appearance was bepop, rebop, or simply bop, and it turned out to mark one of the most important turning points in the history of jazz, comparable to the earlier emergence of swing, which took jazz out of its ragtime rhythmic mold, or to the later emergence of rock, which again altered the rhythmic basis of jazz.

That bop was spawned at least partly in a spirit of revolt seems clear. Ross Russell, writing less than a decade after its appearance, has said: "Bebop is music of revolt: revolt against big bands, arrangers, vertical harmonies, soggy rhythms, non-playing orchestra leaders, Tin Pan Alley— against commercialized music in general." [21] This strain of revolt, of protest, has persisted in jazz since that time, and was manifested, as we shall see, in music with somewhat racial overtones in the 1960s.

The advent of bop marked a change in the function of the music itself that was to have a profound effect. There was a significant shift from jazz as music for dancing to jazz as music for listening. This started jazz off on new paths altogether—and also lost it a considerable portion of its public, a familiar situation when any art enters a period of innovation. It is significant that this was the period during which jazz began to attract the most serious attention of scholars and intellectuals, at the same time that the great mass of followers began asking whether it had not indeed ceased to be the same art at all. The question "Is it really jazz?" has been asked of every new development since, and answers have become progressively more arbitrary and less useful, until in the 1970s it is doubtful whether it is possible to formulate any very valid definitions as to what jazz is. But let us now go back to bop itself.

In its first manifestations it embodied a return to the small combo as its basic medium. Bop, it is pretty well agreed, began in a Harlem nightclub called Minton's Playhouse in the early 1940s. Not often do we know with as much assurance where, when, and by whom a new artistic movement is started. There Thelonius Monk, Dizzy Gillespie, the guitarist Charlie Christian, until his death, and the drummer Kenny Clarke were joined later by an alto saxophonist from the Midwest, Charlie Parker. It was a case of a few extremely talented musicians, in a kind of protest against and frustration with the artistic and commercial status quo, collectively evolving a new style. Gillespie and Parker both had keenly inventive musical minds, as well as extremely facile techniques on their instruments. It is not surprising that the resulting music was innovative harmonically and extremely difficult technically. Few listeners could follow it, and few musicians imitate it. This was apparently to a certain extent what its originators had in mind. Bop became controversial, even among jazz musicians, and the bop followers, whether or not they grasped the music, quickly formed a cult based on appearances that *could* very easily be grasped—the dark glasses, the berets, the goatees, the cultish "hip" language, the disdain of the public as outsiders.

What of the music itself? Besides the properties mentioned (the harmonic complexity, the virtuoso execution), the listener is aware of a rhythm section that has been much lightened. The cymbal, with its bright, insinuating tone, and the string bass, now "walking" at a fast pace, have together taken over from the drums the job of keeping the beat, and the drums can now be used both less frequently and more effectively for accentuation. From then on the jazz rhythm section—its color and its density—will have been permanently changed, in an evolutionary development outlasting bop itself.

The famous ban on the making of recordings imposed by the musicians' union in 1942 prevented the earliest experiments in this style from being either preserved or made known to the public at large. When recording was resumed in 1944, bop was a fait accompli; its circle of performers had widened, and it was sprung full-blown on an unsuspecting public. Thus our recordings pick it up already well along, and after its influence among jazz players had spread to a considerable extent. Listen to *Shaw 'Nuff* (1945), with Gillespie and Parker performing with just piano, bass, and drums, or *KoKo* (1945), with just four performers (Gillespie himself doubles on piano), for the essence of the style.[22] Notice the unison passages. This was new to jazz, and a contradiction of the old spirit of heterophony and polyphony that underlay the traditional jazz of the twenties and thirties. The unison lines became in turn a tradition that stuck, reappearing in post-bop works.

In due course bop was translated into big-band terms, just as traditional jazz had been before it. In *Oop-Pap-a-Da* (1947) Gillespie records with a band of seventeen pieces (large even for the big-band era) a work that not only transfers to the large ensemble the drive and virtuosity of bop, but shows another characteristic, the vocalizing on nonsense syllables (which incidentally provided titles for many of these pieces).[23] The singing exhibits the same fluidity and virtuosity that we hear in the instrumental solos. As an earlier example, we can recall the "scat" singing that Louis Armstrong began in the 1920s.

What has become known as "cool" jazz followed so closely on the heels of bop that it can almost be regarded as the other side of the same coin—the same dispassionate objectivity (symbolized, one could say, by the typical avoidance of instrumental vibrato), the same underlying complexity, the same careful avoidance of the obvious that almost tends to obscurity. But now these features were exhibited in a music of understatement, of restraint, of leanness. What had been interpreted by some as an attitude of disdain in bop became in cool jazz one of detachment. Virtuosity was at times refined into preciosity.

The briefness in our time of identifiable artistic movements is illustrated by the fact that many of the same musicians played both bop and cool, and a definite lineage can be established. An early example, in a kind of transitional stage between the two styles, is *Boplicity* (1949), with Miles Davis, trumpeter, J. J. Johnson, trombonist, and Kenny Clarke, drummer—all of whom were influential in the development and spread of bop.[24] The tempo has been slowed somewhat, but otherwise many bop characteristics remain: the light style of drumming, with the emphasis on the cymbal; the important role of the bass in keeping the beat; and, an important trademark of bop, the unison playing at the beginning of the piece (in this case harmonized by arranger Gil Evans).

In *Criss-Cross* (1951), by Thelonius Monk, there are more characteristics of the cool trend.[25] The vibraphone appears, here played by Milt Jackson. The tone of the "vibes"—warmed somewhat by its mechanical vibrato, but still restrained and detached—made it almost a symbol of cool jazz. There are only two other melody instruments, piano and alto saxophone, and a rhythm section of just bass and drums. The unison lines in the opening are still there from bop, as is the penchant for quotation that is found in both styles. Here, for example, we hear fragments of "Every little breeze seems to whisper Louise" as the alto saxophone enters for its solo.

Mention of the vibraphone leads to a consideration of one of the most influential small combos of this style, the Modern Jazz Quartet, with piano (John Lewis, also a composer), vibes (Milt Jackson, heard in *Criss-Cross*, as noted above), bass (Percy Heath), and drums (Connie Kay). With no wind instruments (in fact this entire ensemble is really a rhythm section, so to speak), their small combo epitomized the restrained understatement towards which cool jazz tended. *Django* (1960) is an example of the extended form some jazz had achieved by this time.[26] The series of short choruses that had characterized jazz form even through the big-band era was now replaced at the hands of innovative musicians by longer lines, and sections of greater dimensions. This was one breakthrough in both the cool and "progressive" schools; indeed, as we shall see, there was a great deal of overlapping between them.

Another late manifestation of the cool trend is *So What* (1959).[27] Miles Davis, of the earlier *Boplicity*, here shows further evolution. A residue of the unison lines (this time between bass and piano), is heard in the opening, as a kind of hallmark of continuity. The temporal dimensions are extended. The vibrato-less tone is straightforward and unadorned—a characteristic of cool jazz that outlasted the genre itself.

JAZZ OF THE THIRD QUARTER-CENTURY

If such a thing as a "mainstream" of jazz can be identified in developments since midcentury, it must certainly derive its principal characteristics from the twin stages of bop and cool jazz. Principally these are (1) the renovated rhythm section, already described, with its steady pulse lightened and given to the cymbal and bass, consequently freeing the drums for highlighting and solos; (2) an emphasis on unison playing; (3) an emphasis on instrumental virtuosity, which is tempered by (4) a manner of delivery tending towards an objective detachment from the material, an avoidance of sentimentality, even a tendency towards the cryptic, the incoherent. (Tone color is in many ways an index of this, with the use of vibrato-less, blunt, or even harsh tone quality a frequent element of playing style.) Closely allied to this cryptic, almost "private" kind of communication, is another characteristic of most jazz since World War II—the tendency to obscure the thematic basis of the composition. "What happened to the tune?" is the question frequently heard about "modern" jazz. The "tunes" may only appear at the beginning, or not at all, and even their identifying sequences of harmonies, such an important basis of "classical" jazz, may be augmented, changed, obscured, or done away with entirely in favor of either an intensive development of short motives from the theme or simply improvisation on a much larger and freer scale than had been used before.

Given these new characteristics, how can we make sense out of the vast, confusing, overlapping panorama of jazz since midcentury? There is always a danger of oversimplifying, and nothing will substitute for extensive exploration of the music itself. It is possible, however, to identify five major influences. (1) The first is a kind of intellectual ferment, expressed in the desire to expand the range and resources of jazz, and this to a considerable extent means a renewed influence of the European cultivated-music tradition—which indeed has always had a hand in the evolution of jazz. (2) The second is in a sense a reaction to this, a back-to-the-roots tendency often manifested in a music consciously abjuring refinement and sophistication, and highly charged emotionally—often indeed consciously seeking raw emotional expressiveness as a goal. (3) The third is related to the second, but is of such great impact as to constitute a distinct and definable influence in itself, and this is the impact of rock music on jazz. (4) The fourth came with the advent of rock, but must be considered on its own, and this is the impact of electronic technology. (5) The fifth is an eclecticism that (aided by the explosive growth of media technology and industry) has affected all the arts. Purity of style has given way to the mixture, the absorption, the juxtaposition, of styles. The collage is the symptomatic art form in many ways.

There is overlapping, of course, but in terms of these five elements most of the developments in what may still be called jazz in the third quarter of our century can be viewed. Let us examine them one by one.

Jazz Seeking New Resources

With the advent of cool jazz (and that which has been termed "progressive" or "modern"—the words are ill-defined and overlapping in usage) we see evidence of a restless, searching kind of intellectual force within jazz itself, paralleling the experimentation that took place in European and American fine-art music after the war. It manifested itself in two ways. One was the conscious attempt to assimilate the instruments, devices, and techniques of Euro-American fine-art music into jazz itself. Instruments such as the flute, oboe, bass clarinet, French horn, and even the cello, previously thought foreign to jazz, were incorporated. For an early example of the use of the flute, listen to Eric Dixon's work in Count Basie's band in *Blues for Eileen*. (The flute has since become very common as a "doubling" instrument—one played as an alternate instrument—in the jazz ensemble.) An interesting example of the integration of the cello into the small jazz combo can be heard in *Dexterity* (1958), with Fred Katz.[28]

Rhythmic innovations were introduced that took jazz out of the duple or quadruple grouping of the pulses (expressed by the meters 2/4 and 4/4) that had characterized it since its earliest associations with the march and two-step. The first change in this direction was the introduction of triple meter, typified by the waltz.[29] Then followed so-called asymmetrical meters in which groupings of two, three, and four pulses were mixed in recurring sequence. A well-known piece involving asymmetrical meter is *Take Five*, by Paul Desmond,[30] in which the pulses are grouped as follows:

Dave Brubeck's *Unsquare Dance* and Don Ellis's *Tears of Joy* [31] both use the following asymmetrical grouping of seven pulses:

Such meters are not indigenous to western music, but are quite common in the folk music of certain areas in southeastern Europe. There are interesting exceptions, however; the rhumba, of Latin origin, is actually an asymmetrical grouping of eight pulses, though written with deceptive simplicity in 4/4:

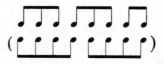

Brubeck's *Blue Rondo A La Turk* [32] groups nine pulses asymmetrically, against which, later in the piece, can be heard the more usual triplet grouping shown in parentheses:

In the matter of pitch material and tonality, there were borrowings from older music, such as the use of the modes known to folk music. John Coltrane's work illustrates this in some pieces; listen to his *Alabama* (1963).[33] Jazz also showed a continuing preoccupation with increasingly complex harmony, including new methods of building chords, and with a progressively greater obscuring of tonality (the relation of all tones to a single "home" tone). In all this, jazz tended to follow—at some distance—developments in Euro-American fine-art music.[34]

The second manifestation of contemporary expansion had not so much to do with changing the basic nature and language of jazz itself, but with preserving that identifiable language (more or less), and placing it in fruitful juxtaposition with the language, style, and instrumentation of fine-art music. The "third stream" concept is a manifestation of this. An early work in this vein, the Concerto for Jazz Band and Symphony Orchestra by Rolf Liebermann, dates from the mid-fifties.[35] Dave Brubeck has participated in similar collaborations. The Modern Jazz Quartet has recorded in conjunction with a string quartet. On a more integrated and avant-garde level, Gunther Schuller's *Abstraction, Variants on a Theme of John Lewis,* and *Variants on a Theme of Thelonius Monk* are interesting pieces in which a small group of jazz instruments is integrated with strings and flute. Each type of instrument preserves its normal mode of speech; the jazz instruments are heard in a kind of evocation of mainstream bop and cool, while the strings are written for in what might be termed a "mainstream avant-garde" style.[36]

Many jazz players would not, of course, consider this to be jazz. Fortunately we need not try to determine whether it is or is not—it is a kind of music that is being made, and it is significant enough in the panorama to take note of. Many see it as a pointless exercise, while others hold out great hope for this kind of musical integration. Whether or not these essays are actually jazz, they do point clearly towards a breaking down of mutually exclusive categories of music, with hard and fast lines between them. The training and practice of musicians themselves is the most convincing evidence of this. Many young musicians intensively schooled in fine-art music go into jazz, while for a long time now many of the more thoughtful jazz musicians, interested in growing and broadening musically, have sought out traditionally trained teachers and composers from whom to study.[37]

Jazz Seeking a Return to Its Roots

Appearing in a sense as a reaction to this sophistication and expansion of means in jazz—a sophistication that can be seen as a divergence from its roots—a trend towards a renewed contact with these roots is evident. It can be seen as a kind of literal and conscious "throwback" to earlier styles, without constituting an actual revival of these styles (for instance, a return to the pre-bop style of heavy drumming heard in so-called funky jazz); or else, in a less literal way, it can be seen as a reassertion of emotional expressiveness as a dominant element in jazz, such as is found in "soul," and more noticeably, in the "new-wave" jazz.

Very often this renewed contact with roots meant a return to the blues. As a good example of the funky style, listen to *Back at the Chicken Shack* (1960).[38] There is a driving beat, but the frenetic tempo of much of bop has been modified into a kind of rollicking swing beat, with off-beat accents on the drums that are a definite reference to pre-bop drumming. A new element is the electric organ, which featured prominently in jazz from this time on. With its blues basis, its electric sound, its driving beat, this is already (except for the drumming and the lack of electric bass to play the boogie-like ostinato) very close to rock.

The epitome of emotional expressionism is found in the so-called new wave. Given the times from which it emerged, it is not surprising that jazz of the new wave was made and marketed with the most overtly racial overtones since the "race" records of the twenties. (In surveying the music, however, one must be careful not to be unduly influenced by contemporaneous written commentary about it, nor to accept such writing as a literal "translation" of the music; indeed this is true of *all* writing on jazz.) The movement must be seen in the context of the deeply upsetting turmoil of the sixties, and the emergence and cultivation among certain musicians and writers of an understandably conscious black cultural identity. Jazz was one natural medium for this expression; theater has been another.

The new wave exploited the enlarged time dimensions that had been established in the cool trend, and made much use of free and open-ended improvisation. With new-wave jazz, this improvisation tended more and more to push the expressive possibilities of the instruments to their limits in a highly subjective kind of playing ranging from ironical understatement to frenzied outbursts that at times reached incoherence. This was particularly true of the group of tenor saxophone players associated with this trend, from John Coltrane—whose work was not confined to this school by any means—through Archie Shepp, Pharaoh Sanders, and Albert Ayler. Coltrane's *Nature Boy*, Archie Shepp's *Hambone*, and Albert Ayler's *Holy Ghost*, all recorded on one occasion in the course of a benefit concert for the Black Arts Repertory Theater/School in 1965, may be listened to as typical examples.[39]

Categorizing is always dangerous. There are many who regard the new-wave jazz as being avant-garde, and in its extension of formal boundaries through the use of long improvisational sections, it may be said to be a species of "free-form" jazz. But its basic thrust is probably best understood in terms of its avowed emotionalism, and its attempted negation of European influence. Albert Ayler has said: "It's not about notes anymore. It's about feelings!"

Jazz Under the Impact of Rock

In the 1950s rock 'n' roll was much closer to its own roots than was jazz. Certainly its emotional content and delivery was unmistakeable.

Albert Ayler's statement above might well have been applied to early rock, and in a sense rock, like new-wave jazz, also brought jazz into renewed relation with its own roots; rock utilized blues elements to do so. But so distinct and massive was the impact of rock on jazz that it will be best to consider it here separately.

Rock itself was treated in a previous chapter. Our concern here is to note its influence on jazz. The most striking influence is that of rhythm. The light rhythm section and walking bass that were characteristic after bop were replaced in rock-influenced jazz by a return to the drum-oriented beat, with complex patterns involving several drums and bass, and incessantly repeated as an almost hypnotic ostinato foundation for the entire piece. The beat patterns, though complex, are based on duple division, rather than the characteristic triple division of the more relaxed swing, and so have a kind of machine-like precision and drive. In this they are related closely to the Latin beats, though the effect of the beat in rock is much more pronounced. Here is an example of such a beat, as transcribed from the playing of the rhythm section in *Beginnings*, a jazz-rock number by the group called Chicago Transit Authority.

(The composite cymbal and drum and tom-tom part, played by a single drummer, changes somewhat from measure to measure; what is given is a sample.) The metronomically precise and insistent beat of rock-influenced jazz is one of its most salient features.

Another important influence has been the renewed emphasis on the voice. Rock, stemming as it does from both country music and the blues, has as its primary vehicle the song. Rock-influenced jazz is therefore once again oriented to the singer and the song in a way jazz has not been since the early blues recordings.

The serious amalgamation of jazz and rock began in the late 1960s. By this time rock itself, in the hands of the musically adventurous and talented, had already achieved a considerable degree of both sophistication and eclecticism, so that influential recordings of this period display a rather wide range of styles in juxtaposition. Important and illustrative are the albums *Blood, Sweat and Tears* and *Chicago Transit Authority*, by those groups respectively, which show the incorporation of jazz elements, especially solos, into the work of highly skilled young rock musicians conversant with a variety of traditions and techniques.[40] More recent examples, recorded by groups whose leaders are primarily jazz-oriented, can be heard in albums such as *Chase* and *Electric Bath*.[41] In *Chase*, for example, jazz instruments (especially trumpets) are prominent on the melodic lines, but the beat and rhythm section are rock, and there is precise, hard, on-the-beat drive.

Jazz in the 1970s has entered an era of amalgamation and eclecticism in which its boundaries become less and less clear. Except for conscious revivals and cultivations of older traditions, jazz and rock seem apparently to have very nearly fused in the mid-seventies.

Electronics and Jazz

A kind of urban electrification came gradually to jazz. The microphonically magnified intimacies of the swing-era crooners was one beginning; the paradoxical necessity to amplify the hushed delivery of private sentiments all the way up to the very public volume level of the big band made the microphone a permanent part of the jazz singer's equipment from then on.

The electrically amplified guitar made its way almost unobtrusively into jazz in the early 1940s, and made it possible for that instrument, now competitive in volume, to leave the rhythm section and join the "front line" of melody instruments.

The electric organ, long a mainstay of the cocktail combo, joined the jazz band later, becoming associated with both funky jazz and soul.

The electric camel—metaphorically speaking, of course—had his head in the tent of jazz. After rock, he came in with all four feet. Rock, having been suckled on electronics as mother's milk, with never a thought of weaning, grew up totally dependent on amplification. The impact of rock on jazz coincided both with new technical possibilities for electrifying every existing instrument in the band and with the introduction of such instruments as the electric bass and the electric piano, which, while using traditional instruments as their point of departure, are actually new instruments. The effect of these developments on the size and makeup of the jazz ensemble is graphically illustrated in the chart on pages 330–31.

To this picture we must add such radically new possibilities as totally synthesized electronic sound and the advent of the sound studio as a musical instrument itself, so to speak, where, in the studio-spawned recordings, the most elaborate effects become possible—reverberations, echoes, electronic transmutations of sounds, and so on.* It is clear that by this time not only is the electric camel all the way *in* the tent, but it has in some cases virtually *become* the tent.

Eclecticism and Jazz

In a way eclecticism is a kind of summing up of all but one of these influences we have already discussed, but it is a sufficiently important and widespread symptom of many of the arts of our time to invite consideration in and of itself.

In our era the world of human culture has shrunk in both time and space; in neither dimension are the distances as great as they once were. In music, for example, when one can easily buy recordings of everything from thirteenth-century Notre Dame organum to the classical music of India to the songs of the Australian aborigines, it is clear that scholarship and entrepreneurship have combined to bring a multitude of heretofore obscure or exotic cultural artifacts within easy reach of anyone with sufficient curiosity. Perhaps this major cultural sampling began in earnest in our age with the great international expositions (which brought the music of the Far East to Europe around the turn of the century, for example), but recording technology and marketing have finished the job of cultural spreading about as thoroughly as anyone needs to have it done.

That jazz, once considered an exotic product itself, should in turn seek in our time to reach out and incorporate elements from other musics is not surprising. Besides availing itself of the well-mapped explorations of avant-garde European music already discussed, and the ministrations of the electronic studio, jazz is delving into the medieval modes of folk music, into concepts and practices of Hindu classical music, and into European practices of the Renaissance and baroque periods, as well as borrowing from its own past.

In looking for examples, the amalgamation known as jazz-rock tends to be the most eclectic, although, as we have seen, the fusion of styles that has taken place in our time makes it difficult to isolate this particular style from most other types of jazz. But one approach is through the

---

* This was dealt with in more detail in chapter 9; for a treatment of electronic fine-art music, see chapter 17.

THE JAZZ BAND:

RHYTHM

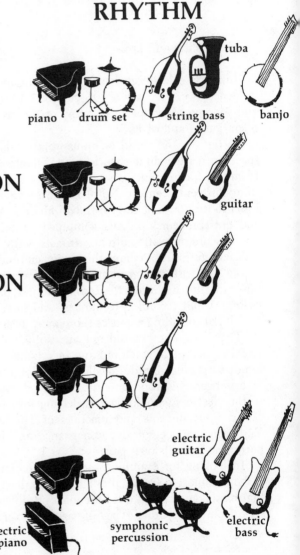

KING OLIVER
1923

piano · drum set · string bass · banjo · tuba

DUKE ELLINGTON
1926

guitar

DUKE ELLINGTON
1941

STAN KENTON
1958

GILL EVANS
1973

electric piano · symphonic percussion · electric guitar · electric bass

0 YEARS OF GROWTH

MELODY

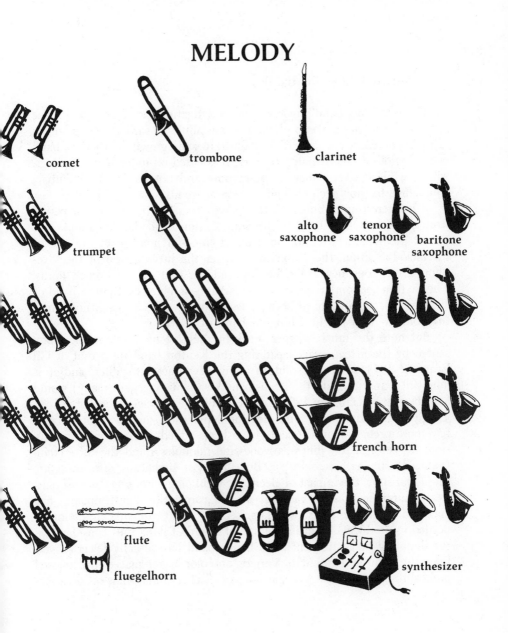

cornet

trombone

clarinet

trumpet

alto
saxophone

tenor
saxophone

baritone
saxophone

french horn

flute

fluegelhorn

synthesizer

identity of the performers and arrangers themselves. As a sample of eclecticism in the work of one arranger whose credentials in the field of jazz are impressive and of long standing, listen to a 1973 work by Gil Evans, titled, appropriately, *Blues in Orbit*.[42] With a rhythm section of rock timbre that at times plays swing figures, the piece presents in montage fashion synthesized electronic sounds, a quotation from a Sousa march, a short section of vintage bop, an expressionistic saxophone solo in the manner of free-form or new-wave jazz, and a polyrhythmic bass duo—for one performer!

A Postscript: How Big the Band?

The term "big band" invites some investigation, not only into its size alone but into the makeup of the jazz ensemble in various periods of its history. The chart on pages 330–31 illustrates the growth of the jazz band over a period of exactly half a century. It is based on individual samplings, which, while chosen somewhat at random and not absolutely definitive, will suffice to show well enough the major trends.

It is interesting to note that the growth over the thirty-five-year period from the King Oliver band to the Stan Kenton band shows a simple and almost predictable evolution in a direct line—an increase in the size of the melody section, the "front line." After the introduction of the saxophones, only one new color has been added, that of the French horns. The rhythm section has remained remarkably stable. The Kenton band of 1958 would certainly have been at least conceivable, by extension, from the point of view of the Ellington band of 1926.

But note the much sharper break in the line of development represented by the fifteen years separating the Kenton band from that of Gil Evans of 1973. Here is evolution along new lines altogether, and it is doubtful if anything like the Evans band (which is typical of many) would have been predictable in 1958. Let us look more closely at the differences. To give the more predictable developments their due, we note that a few more orchestral instruments have been added—"symphonic" percussion, for color; a few flutes as woodwind "doubles"; and the tuba (reintroduced after half a century!). But the most significant differences are those that show the impact of electronic technology. For one thing, sophisticated amplification has radically altered conventional instrumental balance and tonal intensity so that large sections of instruments are no longer needed to produce a requisite volume of sound. Taking into consideration the doubling on instruments, the Evans band has actually fewer players than the Kenton band did. Variety of color has replaced the massed monochromatic effects. A single flute or electric guitar can, on occasion, be made to sound with as much penetrating power as was formerly available from an entire trumpet section.

But even beyond this is the fact that there are actually new instruments present. The electric piano, bass, and guitar are quite different from their nonelectrified predecessors, and the synthesizers *have* no acoustical predecessors!

FURTHER READING

Jazz has stimulated the production of an enormous volume of written material, which runs the gamut from sound, well-informed studies by competent musicians and scholars (too few) to the kind of press-agent-inspired writing typical of many (but not all) record-jacket notes. There are biographical and autobiographical works (some of considerable value), there are pictorial studies, and there are works written with a pronounced racial, social, or musical bias. The discerning student will soon become discriminating and find what is most informative and individually helpful in this vast array of printed matter. An exhaustive reading list is beyond the scope of this book. The following list is quite selective, and should be viewed as merely a beginning.

General

BLESH, RUDI. *Shining Trumpets*. 2nd ed. New York: Alfred A. Knopf, 1958.

DE TOLEDANO, RALPH (ed.). *Frontiers of Jazz*. 2nd ed. New York: Frederick Ungar Publishing Co., 1962.

* HODEIR, ANDRÉ. *Jazz: Its Evolution and Essence*. Translated by David Noakes. New York: Grove Press, 1956.
   A respected historical-analytical work that deals with many of the fundamental problems of jazz.

* SARGEANT, WINTHROP. *Jazz: Hot and Hybrid*. 1938. 3rd ed., New York: Da Capo Press, 1975. 2nd ed., published as *Jazz: A History*, New York: McGraw-Hill Book Co., 1964.
   A valuable analytical work, dealing with jazz origins and characteristics from the standpoint of comparative musicology.

SHAPIRO, NAT, and HENTOFF, NAT. *Hear Me Talkin' to Ya*. New York, 1955. Reprint, Dover Publications, 1966.
   Quotations from more than 150 jazz musicians, arranged to shed light from firsthand sources on nearly every aspect of jazz.

* STEARNS, MARSHALL. *The Story of Jazz*. New York: Oxford University Press, 1956.

---

* Items thus marked are part of the suggested reference library to be available in connection with this book.

Highly recommended as probably the best single volume on the subject for the general reader, with much reference material for the musician as well. Embodies a broad approach to the subject, with a very extensive bibliography, and a syllabus of fifteen lectures, with discographical references.

TIRRO, FRANK. *Jazz: A History.* New York: W. W. Norton & Co., 1977.
A comprehensive, up-to-date, musically literate study. The breadth of the author's sources and references makes possible an exceptional integration of the subject into the picture of American music generally. The transcriptions are valuable, especially those of performances included in the *Smithsonian Collection of Classic Jazz,* to which the music examples in the book are mostly keyed.

WILLIAMS, MARTIN. *The Jazz Tradition.* Rev. ed. New York: Oxford University Press, 1970.
The 16 chapters in this latest edition each deal primarily with one figure in jazz, ranging from Jelly Roll Morton to Ornette Coleman. The more recent chapters thus supplement works such as those of Stearns and Hodeir.

—— (ed.). *The Art of Jazz.* New York: Grove Press, 1960.
A collection of essays.

Pre-Jazz and Early Jazz

ARMSTRONG, LOUIS. *Satchmo: My Life in New Orleans.* New York: Prentice-Hall, 1954.

LOMAX, ALAN. *Mister Jelly Roll: The Fortunes of Jelly Roll Morton, New Orleans Creole and "Inventor of Jazz."* 2nd ed. Berkeley: University of California Press, 1973.
Based on an extensive series of recorded interviews in the Music Division of the Library of Congress.

* SCHULLER, GUNTHER. *Early Jazz: Its Roots and Musical Developments.* See the reading list for chapter 11.

* SOUTHERN, EILEEN. *The Music of Black Americans: A History.* See the reading list for chapter 11.

* —— (ed.). *Readings in Black American Music.* See the reading list for chapter 11.

WILLIAMS, MARTIN (ed.). *Jazz Masters of New Orleans.* New York: Macmillan Co., 1967.

Pre-Swing and Swing

GOODMAN, BENNY, and KOLODIN, IRVING. *The Kingdom of Swing.* Harrisburg, Pa.: Stackpole Sons, 1939.

HADLOCK, RICHARD. *Jazz Masters of the Twenties.* New York: Macmillan Co., 1965.

LAMBERT, GEORGE. *Duke Ellington.* New York: A. S. Barnes & Co., 1961.

* MEZZROW, MEZZ, and WOLFE, BERNARD, *Really the Blues.* New York: Random House, 1946.

STEWART, REX. *Jazz Masters of the Thirties.* New York: Macmillan Co., 1972.

SUDHALTER, RICHARD M., and EVANS, PHILIP R. *Bix: Man and Legend.* New Rochelle, N.Y.: Arlington House, 1974.

Emergence of the Modern Period

GITLER, IRA. *Jazz Masters of the Forties.* New York: Macmillan Co., 1966.

RUSSELL, ROSS. *Bird Lives: The High Life and Times of Charlie (Yardbird) Parker.* New York: Charterhouse, 1973.

Jazz of the Third Quarter-Century

GOLDBERG, JOE. *Jazz Masters of the Fifties.* New York: Macmillan Co., 1965.

JONES, LEROI. *Black Music.* New York: William Morrow & Co., 1967.

THOMAS, J. C. *Chasin' the Trane: The Music and Mystique of John Coltrane.* Garden City, N.Y.: Doubleday & Co., 1975.

WILLIAMS, MARTIN. *Jazz Masters in Transition, 1957–1969,* New York: Macmillan Publishing Co., Inc., 1970.

Periodicals

Down Beat. 222 Adams St., Chicago, Ill. 60606.
   A weekly magazine, with articles and record reviews.

Journal of Jazz Studies. Transaction Periodicals Consortium, Rutgers University, New Brunswick, N.J.,08903.
   An excellent scholarly periodical, issued semiannually.

Consult also the often copious notes published with certain of the jazz anthologies referred to in the suggestions for listening.

LISTENING

Last year's jazz discography is often about as useful for obtaining current information as a year-old newspaper. There is hardly a commodity more ephemeral and more capricious in its availability than the jazz recording. However, two trends in the industry today tend to mitigate this capriciousness: the current reissuings of old recordings of individual artists or bands (often billed as

"The Best of . . ." or "Greatest Hits of . . ." or "The —— Story") and the recent compilation of genuine anthologies, some with very complete notes, and data on recording dates and personnel. For convenience, the recorded examples from this chapter have been drawn insofar as possible from five of these anthologies. While each anthology has somewhat different limits and emphasis, there is considerable overlapping. With this in mind, duplicate examples are cited in many instances, so that even if only one or two of the anthologies are available to the listener, a fairly broad range of listening examples will be at hand, correlated with the text. The five anthologies are:

* The Smithsonian Collection of Classic Jazz.
>   Distributed by W. W. Norton & Co., New York. Six records, with a long booklet of notes by Martin Williams. The recordings span 1916–1966.

* The Folkways History of Jazz Series.
>   Available from Folkways Records. Eleven separately jacketed records, 2801 through 2811, each with a booklet of notes. More emphasis on roots and earlier music; stops about 1940.

* The Riverside History of Classic Jazz.
>   Released by Bill Grauer Productions, 553 W. 51st St., New York, N.Y. 10019. Five records (RLP:12-112–116), available separately, or in one volume with an essay by Charles Edward Smith and very complete notes. Emphasis on roots, and jazz of the 1920s.

* The Encyclopedia of Jazz, ed. Leonard Feather.
>   Six records, MCA: 2-4061–4063. The first four records of this set are denoted Jazz of the 20's, 30's, 40's, and 50's respectively, and are also available as Decca DXS-7140E.

* Recorded Anthology of American Music (RAAM).
>   At least nine albums are relevant, ranging from ragtime and traditional jazz to avant-garde and third-stream. Since RAAM's editorial policy seems to be to avoid extensive treatment of groups and performers already well represented elsewhere, this anthology is most useful as a well-annotated supplement, valuable for the additional (and sometimes different) light it throws on certain areas.

Also Useful

The King of Swing: Benny Goodman's Complete 1937–38 Jazz Concert no. 2. Columbia: OSL-180.

* Three Decades of Jazz. Blue Note: BST-89902–89904.
>   Six records, in three sets subtitled 1939–1949, 1949–1959, and 1959–1969.

The Bebop Era. RCA Vintage: LPV-519.

Adventures in Time, Dave Brubeck. Columbia: G-30625.

Tears of Joy, Don Ellis. Columbia: KG-30927.

New Directions, David Mack. SRS 12009.

Concerto for Jazz Band and Symphony Orchestra, Rolf Liebermann. RCA: LM-1888.

* *Jazz Abstractions.* Atlantic: 1365.
* *The Definitive Jazz Scene,* 3 vols. Impulse: SA-99, 100, and 9101.
* *The New Wave in Jazz.* Impulse: AS-90.

Blood, Sweat and Tears. Columbia: CS-9720.

Chicago Transit Authority. Columbia: GP-8.

Chase. Epic: 30472. Also with *Ennea* as Epic: BG-33737.

Electric Bath. Columbia: CS-9585.

Gil Evans Svengali, Atlantic: SD-1643.

PROJECTS

1. The culture, and the music in particular, of black Americans has gone through periods of discovery or rediscovery by white Americans. Study any one of the following, or make a comparative study of them: (a) discovery and popularization of Negro music in the minstrel show; (b) popularization of the Negro spirituals after the Civil War; (c) the "Harlem Renaissance" of the 1920s. What similar phenomena have occurred since?
2. Assemble a brief documentary description of jazz in Chicago as it existed under the rule (and patronage) of the gangsters of the 1920s and early 1930s. Firsthand accounts such as found in Mezzrow's *Really the Blues* will be a logical starting place. See also Shapiro and Hentoff, *Hear Me Talkin' to Ya.*
3. Make a brief study of the narcotics problem as it has related particularly to jazz musicians. The two sources referred to in question 2 above make a good place to start.
4. Make an assessment of jazz in your local area. Is there music being played that can be distinguished as jazz, as distinct from rock or merely pop music? Where is it being played, and for whom? What styles can one hear—are there bands playing in a revival of the big-band style? of traditional (Dixieland) jazz? of cool?
5. If you feel qualified to accept the challenge, make a beginning study of the use of quotation in the jazz of the last thirty years. Some mention of it has been made in the text; it is a fertile field for exploration, especially in bop and much overtly black jazz since bop.
6. If you have access to a library with good periodical holdings, make a comparative study of two or three periodicals devoted more or less exclusively to jazz. For example, choose from *Down Beat;*

Jazz; Jazz Report; Journal of Jazz Studies; Jazz Journal (London); or back volumes of *Metronome* (no longer published).

7. Keep a diary of jazz listening for a month, noting pieces and artists heard, and making some general comments on the music and where it fits into the overall panorama of jazz outlined in this chapter. Make it a point to listen to at least 25 pieces during this time, and include as great a variety of styles and periods as you can.

8. If the calendar of musical events in your area allows, or your travel capabilities permit, attend three separate live jazz performances. Try for a variety of experiences. Write a commentary on the music of each, placing it in the general framework of contemporary jazz as outlined in this chapter.

9. Investigate and write on the jam session in jazz—from the legendary "cutting contests" in New Orleans to the staged jam sessions of today's jazz festivals.

10. Using as references newspapers such as the *New York Times* or the *Christian Science Monitor*, or general magazines such as *The New Republic* or *Saturday Review*, or music magazines such as *Etude*, trace the attitudes toward jazz and the treatment given it through any ten-year period.

Part Six

Fine-Art Music: The Comprehensive Tradition of the Composer's Art

The cultivated tradition of the art music of the composer, since it has the capacity to assimilate the materials and modes of expression of folk music, popular music, and jazz (and indeed, of any other music), is our most comprehensive and varied tradition. This we have called, for convenience, fine-art music, reserving for that uniquely American art of the performer its own name—jazz.

The pursuit of fine art in America, as far as music is concerned, had a prehistory marked by European domination (at first British, and then German), with a voice in the wilderness now and then protesting the state of affairs but with only a few hints of a genuine national music appearing. This prehistory came to an end after World War I. Since then, in a century of which a decade may witness as much evolutionary change as did a half-century previously, things have happened swiftly. Our fine-art music emerged from adolescence into strong-featured adulthood between the wars, finding its own mature voice. In the second half of the century, it has become divided, and no longer sings with one voice to the extent that it did before. The ground broken in the "definitive decade," as Virgil Thomson has called the 1930s, is still cultivated by some, who have shown it to be capable of yielding new and fresh crops, while at the hands of others, pursuing new technical and esthetic concepts, our fine-art music has, in self-effacement, merged its identity with that of a new international music (though there are those who maintain that American music inevitably possesses still, even under these circumstances, its own definite character).

Unfortunately, the barriers to understanding and acceptance that hedge in fine-art music have nowhere been more pronounced than in America, where, in particular, the gulf between fine art and popular art began to widen perceptibly in the period of expansion and industrialization after the Civil War. It was at this time that the aspirations to culture in the new middle and upper economic and social classes began to be manifested. Thus the real and inherent distinction between popular and fine art became obscured, and a false distinction began to appear, based on the social stratification that was becoming so pronounced in this period. To this was added the stratification of sex; it was largely the business of women to support fine-art music—they were the teachers, the arrangers of concerts, the fund raisers, the patronesses. To the common man, then, fine-art music became either "highbrow" or "sissy," or both. The devastating effect of this on a young man with musical talent and the drive to develop it is dramatically illustrated in the case of Charles Ives. This set of attitudes lingers on, though it is waning.

The very existence of this gulf, which has appeared troublesomely inconsistent with democratic concepts, has seemed to give rise to an almost idealistic yearning to bridge the gap by either bringing fine art to the masses or amalgamating "mass" art and "elite" art so as to nullify the distinction between them. The visionary Arthur Farwell tɔ the first approach, arranging concerts to bring music to the people of crowded urban areas in natural out-of-doors surroundings. Gershwin and Copland in the twenties took the second, each attempting to bridge the gap from his own side of it, with symphonic works employing the idioms of popular music and jazz. Similar attempts have subsequently appeared from time to time, showing that the urge towards some sort of reconciliation, whether idealistic or simply opportunistic, is still there— "third stream jazz" and "symphonic rock" are manifestations of this. It is perhaps significant that in most cases the labels and the intended results are remembered longer than the music.

Whatever may be the precise nature of future attempts to amalgamate our various musics, our cultivated tradition of fine-art music is, to recapitulate, our most comprehensive tradition. If it is in any sense elite art (and woeful are the misunderstandings that attend this question!), it is so only in the sense that the greater the artist, the closer he is working to the cutting edge of art, so to speak, with a long tradition of artistic cultivation behind him, and that at any given time not all of his contemporaries—or their successors, for that matter—are equipped by experience and exposure to grasp what he is doing. All truly new developments come from this sector of art, which maintains at most times a lively research department and experimental wing.

But the fact that what is new in fine art may be strange to many, and have a small following at first, does not mean that this art as a whole is by nature inaccessible. That which has stood the proverbial test of time, and become well assimilated, has a secure place in our culture—some of it may indeed be very popular, though it need not be to survive.

Since it is the domain more than any other of the solitary worker, its story is largely the story of individual achievers and achievements.

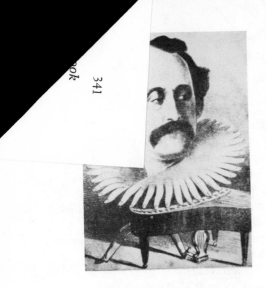

Chapter Thirteen
Eight Pioneers

AMERICAN FINE-ART MUSIC cannot truly be said to have found itself, and entered into its period of full and characteristic maturity, until after World War I. But its infancy and adolescence prior to this time was colorful, to say the least, and not devoid of solid accomplishments. It was a period of gradual preparation and growth, punctuated by episodes of unique fascination and peopled with some extraordinary individuals.

It is these individuals who arrest our attention. While this book does not place its main emphasis on biography, something of an exception is appropriate here, since the gradual maturation of the American fine-art tradition is most vividly portrayed in the lives and times of a succession of unique, hard-working, strong-willed individuals who can best be described, in the context of their careers, as pioneers. Sometimes singly, sometimes as representatives of whole groups of similarly oriented musicians, eight men out of many claim our attention here for one reason or another. In becoming acquainted with each of them, we will have illuminated for us some important aspects of our musical salad-days.

342

FRANCIS HOPKINSON AND THE 18TH
CENTURY GENTLEMAN AMATEUR

The career of a man like Benjamin Franklin astounds us with its tremendous range. The eighteenth century, the Age of Reason, was the last to give its geniuses such scope for their activities. Science, invention, politics, letters, the arts—in none of these had specialization yet closed the door to real accomplishment for the well-educated, well-rounded, and keenly intelligent individual. Genuine contributions could be made especially in the new and not-yet-exploded fields of science and invention (the latter we would now call technology), in which one man of exceptional ability could actually encompass all that was known of a given discipline.

In the fine arts, of course, the open door was in many respects an illusion. Since this area of human endeavor was already laden with the fruits of centuries of cultivation, supreme talent alone was the key to real accomplishment. But the spirit of optimism and enthusiasm that so properly belonged to eighteenth-century politics, science, and technology was infectious, and it was natural to assume that no doors could be shut to the industrious man of ability. And it is true that in certain more or less technological aspects of music, the doors were still open. Thus one of the signers of the Declaration of Independence (Benjamin Franklin) could make decisive improvements in the design of a musical instrument (the famous glass harmonica, now obsolete), make keenly perceptive contributions to musical criticism, and (if its unsubstantiated attribution should prove accurate) write a string quartet ingeniously devised to be played all on open strings (especially tuned). And another signer (Francis Hopkinson) could devise a new method of quilling the harpsichord (the introduction of quills made of leather, a material still much used, was his invention), invent a new musical instrument,[1] become an accomplished harpsichordist, assume an active—even decisive—role in the musical life of one of the most important cities in the colonies, and compose some music that can still be heard today with pleasure.

Into what kind of musical world was Hopkinson born? There were only four cities large enough to support any significant theatrical or concert life before 1800: Boston, New York, Philadelphia, and Charleston. But conditions there were not as primitive as might be supposed. The first public concert in the United States that we know of was given in Boston in 1731; Charleston began still more ambitiously the following year with what was evidently a series of concerts. These early concerts (much like those in contemporary Europe) consisted of music for a variety of combinations: solo pieces for harpsichord or piano; songs;

chamber duos, trios, and quartets; concertos for violin, violoncello, French horn, clarinet, or bassoon; and symphonies, sometimes billed as *overtures* and probably played by quite small ensembles at first. Novelties such as "Pot Pourris on the Harmonia" might be included, and even recitations and orations. After the concert itself, there could be further diversions: card tricks, "Manly Feats of Activity" (whatever they might be), and very often music for dancing. This reminds us that the early music masters, in demand in fashionable colonial America, also frequently taught dancing and fencing.

Colonists enjoyed another civilized delight, summer concerts in the out-of-doors—with or without refreshments or fireworks afterwards. New Yorkers could thus indulge themselves as early as 1765; similar concerts were begun in Charleston two years later.

O. G. Sonneck, the most eminent authority on our music of this period, has summarized the musical ambience into which Hopkinson and other gentleman amateurs were born with the statement: "Music in America was provincial but not primitive."

Francis Hopkinson (1737–1791), a near contemporary of George Washington, to whom he dedicated his most important surviving music, belonged, as had his father before him, to that natural intellectual aristocracy made up of men of ability, at least modest affluence, and a sense of public service. His name has a way of cropping up in many interesting connections in the colonial and early federal periods. Elected to the Continental Congress in 1776, he was an ardent advocate of independence, and became an active pamphleteer, satirist, and allegorist in the American cause. He was also in effect our first secretary of the navy. He had some artistic ability, too—in this field, his was the singular accomplishment of designing the American flag.

An active Anglican, he was secretary of the convention that organized the Protestant Episcopal Church after the advent of American independence. He was also a poet and an inventor (of a ship's log and a shaded candlestick, in addition to the previously mentioned harpsichord-quill design).

What of Hopkinson the composer? His output, not large, consisted mostly of songs, though he also composed anthems, odes (akin to cantatas) for various occasions, and an interesting occasional piece called *The Temple of Minerva*. This last was described in Hopkinson's own manuscript book as "An Oratorial Entertainment performed in Nov. 1781 by a Company of Gentlemen and Ladies in the Hotel of the Minister of France in the Presence of his Excellency General Washington and his Lady." (It was evidently a kind of miniature patriotic opera in two scenes, celebrating America's friendship with France.)

Whether Hopkinson was, in fact, our first composer cannot definitely be established. But we can certainly be satisfied with Sonneck's carefully researched conclusion that "Francis Hopkinson was the first native American composer of songs of whom we know, and his song 'My Days Have Been So Wondrous Free' is the earliest secular American composition extant, dating back to 1759." [2]

This song has survived.[3] Almost thirty years later, Hopkinson's most important surviving group of songs was published: his *Seven Songs for the Harpsichord*, dedicated to George Washington.[4] The songs, as printed, consist merely of a melody line (treble) and a bass line. According to earlier eighteenth-century practice, which was already being superseded in Europe, this was all the composer supplied; the harpsichordist filled out the harmonies at the keyboard in performing the piece. The poems set to the music deal with romantic love, with romanticized pastoral scenes, with a lover gone to sea, with a traveler lost in a storm. The music itself is in the rather *galante* style of eighteenth-century European classicism; the musical language, though not its degree of mastery, resembles that of Johann Christian Bach, the fashionable "London" Bach, son of the great Leipzig master—or, to make a comparison with a far greater and better known composer, that of Haydn.

No one claims greatness for this early American music of our gentlemen amateurs.* But there is no doubt that Hopkinson himself was modestly gifted, and what little has survived of his music can be listened to without undue embarrassment, and in fact with some pleasure and a measure of pride. Not only was it a first step, but more importantly, it demonstrated the important place that music and the arts generally occupied in the lives and thoughts of many of the eighteenth-century founders of the republic. This has not always been the case with the men of affairs who followed them.

The death of Hopkinson coincided with the end of the heyday of the gentleman amateur. The Revolution had of course put a stop to public concerts and theatrical entertainments. After the war, the concert and theatrical life of the new nation resumed slowly; the tenor of the times was one of sobriety, and those who opposed concerts and plays on moral grounds were more successful in suppressing them than they had been before the war. By the time the desire for such entertainments had overridden this opposition and the momentum had picked up again— and it was in full swing by the time of the Constitutional Convention in Philadelphia in 1787—the situation had changed somewhat. For one thing, the prosperous cities of the North (Philadelphia, New York, and Boston, but especially Philadelphia) were in the lead, and those of the South (Williamsburg, Charleston) did not regain their prewar cultural

---

* The descriptive and accurate phrase "gentlemen amateurs" has been used in our time by Gilbert Chase and other writers; in origin it is at least as old as the early nineteenth century, when the "amateurs" (who were most often "gentlemen" as well) were contrasted with the "professors"—a term equivalent to our "professionals."

eminence. For another, these rapidly growing cities of the North began to attract more and more professional musicians from Europe, principally England. The cultivated music of America's cities entered a new phase; with music, both sacred and secular, more in the hands of the professional —often the recently immigrated professional—the standards of performance and composition were bound to rise, the amateur was relegated to a secondary role, and we entered a period of conscious and prolonged dependence on European music, musicians, and music teaching that was to persist undiminished for at least another century.

LOWELL MASON AND "SINGING AMONG THE CHILDREN"

Lowell Mason's life work was nurtured in the same soil that produced the Yankee singing school, which we have explored in chapter 5. Indeed, it was a natural outgrowth of the singing school tradition, urbanized and rendered cosmopolitan. We have already encountered Mason, the "improver" of church music, in chapter 6; he was instrumental in driving a native, folk-oriented religious tradition out of the cities. Yet, in the large view, his work can be seen as a continuation of a New England cultural tradition; it is not so surprising that Bostonians, who took the lead in teaching people to read music in the eighteenth-century, were the first to make music a regular part of public school education in the nineteenth.

Lowell Mason (1792–1872), born in a village southwest of Boston, went to a singing school at the age of thirteen. His grandfather had been a singing master; Lowell himself taught singing schools, led the parish choir, organized and led instrumental groups, and composed at least one anthem before he was twenty. He was a voracious learner, and made himself proficient at all the instruments he could lay his hands on.

His period of preparation for what he then little suspected would be his life's work was passed in Savannah, Georgia, from the time he was twenty until he was thirty-five. While working there as a banker, he studied harmony and composition with a competent "scientific" (German) musician, held a post as organist and choirmaster, and was superintendent of one of the first Sunday Schools in the country—significant in view of his later concern with teaching music to children. A work that proved to be most important for his future was a compilation of psalm and hymn tunes, ultimately published by the young Boston Handel and Haydn Society. The contents and significance of this work have been dealt with in chapter 6; it set the trend of adapting and reharmonizing the melodies of European classical composers as hymn tunes, thus "improving" the domestic product. It was only the first of many such publications edited by Mason and others.

What concerns us here is Mason's all-important pedagogical work, and the impact on American musical life of what he was so instrumental in beginning. When he moved permanently to Boston in 1827, his life work gradually but surely unfolded. His first accomplishments were in the field of church music; his church choirs attracted notice far and wide for their excellence. But more importantly, his developing interest in teaching children to sing soon bore fruit. Mason was convinced that, if it was done in the right way, nearly *all* children could be taught to sing. He began extensive teaching under the auspices of his church (the Bowdoin Street Church, of Lyman Beecher), and his classes ultimately became very large. The public concerts he gave with his children's choirs proved his point, and attracted wide and favorable attention. Today we take pretty much for granted the fact that children are taught to sing; it is hard to realize that formerly the musical capacities of the *average* child (as with so many other capacities of children) were undernourished or ignored completely.

Mason, ever the practical man, saw the vital need for organization. The Boston Academy of Music was a means to this end. It was established in 1833 after the performances by his singing classes for children had aroused community interest. A private organization, it did not have to wait for official school board action, but set about at once to teach vocal music to children, both at the Academy itself and in the schools—a few private ones at first. Mason himself did this teaching single-handedly to begin with; soon George J. Webb, Boston organist and teacher, joined him, and other "professors" were added. The Academy itself offered both juvenile and adult classes, as well as private instruction. Children were accepted into singing classes Wednesday and Saturday afternoons free of charge, provided they would promise to attend for at least a year.

The activities of the Academy were in fact broad, and its goals embraced the improvement of church music and the training of music teachers, as well as what appears to have been the primary one: "to introduce vocal music into schools, by the aid of such teachers as the Academy may be able to employ." When, in 1837, in a familiar kind of situation, Boston's school committee adopted resolutions recommending that music be introduced experimentally in four public schools but failed to get funds from the city council, Mason offered to teach in one of the schools gratuitously. The offer was accepted, and this was the beginning. His impressive results led, the next year, to the adoption of resolutions authorizing the introduction of music as a branch of popular education into the public schools of Boston—a step the Boston Academy termed the "magna charta of musical education." This time funds were forthcoming, and Mason became the country's first "supervisor of public school music." The traditional goals of public school music were established—not to produce trained musicians, but to give all students "the power of understanding and appreciating Music."

Still another venture in which Mason pioneered was the editing and publication of music especially suited for use in the teaching of children. Beginning with the *Juvenile Psalmist* in 1829 (for church use) and the secular *Juvenile Lyre* in 1831 (for school use), Mason produced a number of songbooks for this purpose, culminating in a three-volume graded music series, the first representative of a type of publication now legion. He also led the way in the writing of teaching manuals, from the *Manual of the Boston Academy of Music* in 1834 to *The Pestalozzian Music Teacher* in 1871.

Music, in Mason's words, "should be cultivated and taught, not as a means of mere sensual gratification, but as a sure means of improving the affections, and ennobling, purifying, and elevating the whole man." [5] Mason's conviction about what he saw as the highest function of music, beyond the sensuous, the intellectual, and the artistic, was the mainspring of his life work.

There is no doubt that Lowell Mason was an astute businessman. He had a keen sense for a potential market, especially in sacred music. (For example, he published in 1846 *The Cherokee Singing Book*, a compilation of hymns in the Cherokee language, the result of a collaboration with Sequoia, the famous Indian linguist.) But the temptation to characterize him as a musical exploiter, whose career was motivated largely by the desire for profit, must surely be tempered by a closer acquaintance with the man and his work.

Mason's gifts as a composer were modest, but he seldom essayed what he knew to be beyond his powers; he knew what he could do, and for whom he was composing. Among his many hymn tunes, his *Missionary Hymn* ("From Greenland's icy mountains") and *Nearer, My God, to Thee* have become part of the common store of American religious music.

LOUIS MOREAU GOTTSCHALK AND THE VIRTUOSO IN NINETEENTH-CENTURY AMERICA

In 1853 there appeared on the New York scene, just arrived from Europe, one of the most brilliant pianists of the age. He had recently completed a triumphant concert tour of Spain, where the queen had made him a Cavalier of the Order of Isabella the Catholic; Chopin had predicted a great future for him; the great French composer Hector Berlioz was his friend and mentor. Louis Moreau Gottschalk would have been an outstanding figure whatever his origin, but his importance is all the greater because he was an American. He was, in fact, the first American musician to rank unquestionably with the greatest in Europe in his time—there is abundant documentation for this. As a pianist, he must have been superb, especially in the performance of his own works; as a composer, he has left some colorful piano pieces based on the folk music of Louisiana and the West Indies that will continue to hold their place in the world's piano music; as a diarist, he has left some brilliant, witty, and highly perceptive observations of the United States, the West Indies, and South America during eleven years of travel and concertizing. Proud of being an American, he was an ardent patriot, but also a keen and critical observer. The circumstances of his life were such that he spent more than half of it outside his native land.

Louis Moreau Gottschalk (1829–1869) was born in New Orleans, the oldest of seven children. His father (probably at least partly of Jewish extraction), a well-educated gentleman, had emigrated from London. His mother, Aimée de Bruslé, was a Creole, a cultured woman of French extraction whose parents were both refugees from bloody slave insurrections on the island of Santo Domingo in the West Indies. Gottschalk's father, Edward, became a successful businessman, and was able to provide for his family all the cultural advantages that New Orleans offered at the time.

New Orleans in the 1830s was a cultural melting pot in which relatively new American influence, a generation after the Purchase, vied with the established French. The St. Charles Theater gave performances in English (and in Italian, by visiting Italian opera companies); the Théâtre d'Orléans, with its orchestra and opera, was the focal point of French culture. Of considerable significance also was that colorful mixture of the African, the West Indian, and the Hispanic that constituted the folk ambience dealt with in chapter 3.

It was into this multicolored and multi-cultured world that Louis Moreau Gottschalk was born. He soon showed the unmistakable signs of musical precocity—picking out on the piano, at the age of three, tunes his mother (an accomplished singer) had sung; beginning lessons in piano and sight singing with the director of music at the St. Louis Cathedral soon afterward; substituting as organist at the cathedral at the age of seven; playing from memory melodies that he heard from operas given at the St. Charles Theater and the Théâtre d'Orléans; and playing the piano regularly in public beginning at the age of nine. By the time he was eleven, his teacher was saying that there was nothing more he could learn from any musician in New Orleans; when he was thirteen, his parents sent him to Paris to study.

The young American prodigy's reception by the director of piano classes at the Paris Conservatoire in 1842 is significant to our story of

American music—he rejected him without even hearing him play, because, in his opinion "l'Amérique n'était qu'un pays de machines à vapeur" ("America was nothing but a country of steam engines"). That Gottschalk, seven years later at the age of twenty, was invited to sit as a judge at examinations at this same conservatory is a fitting sequel, and indicative of how rapidly he took his place among the leading young pianists of the day. Not only musically, but socially, he was soon in the most exalted company. We have noted his acquaintance with Berlioz and Chopin; among the younger musicians, his contemporaries, he was the friend of Jacques Offenbach, Georges Bizet, and Camille Saint-Saëns. Among writers who knew and admired his playing were Victor Hugo, Alexandre Dumas *père*, and Alphonse de Lamartine. His remarkable appearance, stage presence, and charm were universally commented upon throughout his life; he was to become, in effect, one of the first "matinee idols."

The closing highlight of his eleven-year European sojourn, first as student and then as concert artist, was his triumphal tour of Spain. Made under the direct patronage of the queen herself, it was rich with characteristic incident, including Gottschalk's adoption of a homeless Andalucian waif, and a severe injury to his hand (from which he fortunately recovered completely) by a jealous court pianist.

By the time Gottschalk went to Spain he had already established himself as a composer. Especially popular were three piano pieces he had written when still in his teens in Paris, based on folk tunes of the Louisiana blacks that he remembered from his childhood—*Bamboula: Danse des Nègres* (which he dedicated with foresight to the queen of Spain on its publication), *Le Bananier: Chanson nègre*, and *La Savane: Ballade créole*. Responding to the demand for musical "acrobatics" (especially in Spain), he began writing pieces such as his brilliant paraphrase on *The Carnival of Venice*, his Spanish-flavored étude *Manchega*, and his caprice on three Spanish dance tunes, *Souvenirs d' Andalousie*. And in response to the popularity of programmatic pieces he produced a *Grande Symphonie* for ten pianos, *El Sitio de Zaragoza* ("The Siege of Zaragoza"). This "symphony," of which a popular fragment (*La Jota Aragonesa*) has survived, exhibits another phase of nineteenth-century concert-giving that was by no means an exclusively American phenomenon—the multiple-piano piece. (A concert of Gottschalk's in San Francisco thirteen years later included a piece for fourteen pianos and gave rise to a bizarrely humorous anecdote that he recorded in his *Notes of a Pianist*.)[6]

Gottschalk's initial concerts in New York appeared to have been carefully planned by his advance agent, who may have profited in a more dignified way from the example set by P. T. Barnum in his advance campaign for Jenny Lind's New York appearances three years before. It is interesting to look at the program for Gottschalk's opening concert—a relatively intimate one given at Niblo's Salon on February 11, 1853. It was the usual medley, consisting of songs, a flute and piano duet, duets for two pianos, and piano solos performed by Gottschalk that included two operatic transcriptions and three "poetic caprices" (one was *Le Bananier*), ending with his *Carnival of Venice.* We look in vain on concert programs of the day for Beethoven sonatas, Bach preludes and fugues and even the works of Chopin. These Gottschalk knew and loved, playing them for his friends, but to play them at public concerts would have been out of the question.

Gottschalk's large concert followed in Niblo's Garden six days later. There a full orchestra accompanied him in Carl Maria von Weber's *Concertstück*; he also played solos and shared the program with a second pianist and with two singers. The concerts, though they cost Gottschalk more than $2,000, were an unquestioned success with the public and paved the way for his subsequent career in America. Following the second concert, P. T. Barnum offered Gottschalk a contract for a two- or three-year tour; Gottschalk, on the advice of his father, turned it down, on the grounds that Barnum's price was too low and that he was a vulgar showman who would do more harm than good to his career.

Gottschalk went to Philadelphia, where he played to enthusiastic response a reworked version of *The Siege of Zaragoza* that included *Yankee Doodle*; *Hail Columbia*; *The Star-Spangled Banner*; *Oh, Susanna*; and *Old Folks at Home* in place of the Spanish tunes. Gottschalk played in Louisville, and then boarded a river steamer for the return to his native New Orleans. (On board the steamer, he is said to have asked permission to play daily for the slaves below decks, who were bound for the New Orleans slave market. The captain refused. The incident is thoroughly characteristic of Gottschalk.) After a tremendous reception and round of concerts in the city of his birth, he set out once more. His life continued to be one of almost constant travel and concert giving.

His years in the United States were twice interrupted by sojourns in the West Indies. The second of these, beginning in 1857, lasted five years—years in which Gottschalk virtually dropped out of sight. He himself describes them as

> years foolishly spent, thrown to the wind, as if life were infinite, and youth eternal; six years, during which I have roamed at random under the blue skies of the tropics, indolently permitting myself to be carried away by chance, giving a concert wherever I found a piano, sleeping wherever the night overtook me—on the grass of the savanna, or under the palm-leaf roof of a *veguero* (a tobacco-grower) with whom I partook of a tortilla, coffee, and banana, which I paid for on leaving in the morning, with *"Dios se lo pague"* (God repay you); to which he responded with a *"Vaya usted con Dios"* (God go with you)—these two formularies constituting in this

savage country, the operation so ingeniously perfected among civilized people, that is called "settling the hotel bill." [7]

Much as he loved the United States (to which he formally declared allegiance in Havana before returning to his war-torn country in 1862), there is no question that he felt more at home in Latin America, that he was better understood there, and that his receptions there were more spontaneous and enthusiastic.

The lines quoted above are from the important journal that Gottschalk began the year he embarked upon his long West Indian rambling. Published as *Notes of a Pianist,* they cover the nearly twelve years from that time until the year before his death. They are brilliantly written (in French), and reminiscent of the essays and memoirs of his older mentor Berlioz in their wit and insight. As valuable descriptions and commentaries on American life of the time, they rank with the journals and writings of Frances Kemble, Frederick Law Olmsted, and Alexis de Tocqueville. Who knew better, for example, or could better have expressed, the American state of mind with regard to the fine arts a century ago than Gottschalk, writing in 1862:

> There is no doubt that there are immense lacunæ in certain details of our civilization. Our appreciation of the *beaux-arts* is not always enlightened, and we treat them like parasites occupying a usurped place. The wheels of our government are, like our managers, too new not to grate upon the ear sometimes. We perhaps worship a little too much the golden calf, and do not kill the fatted calf often enough to feast the elect of thought. Each of us thinks himself as good as (if not better than) any other man— an excellent faith that engenders self-respect but often leads us to wish to reduce to our own level those to whose level we cannot attain. These little faults happily are not national traits; they appertain to all young societies. We are, in a word, like the beautiful children of whom Montaigne speaks, who bite the nurse's breast, and whom the exuberance of health sometimes renders turbulent.[8]

It is characteristic that Gottschalk, who had suffered much at the hands of the rude and boorish among his countrymen, should still have been able to write so understandingly of the young America's "turbulence," even as he wrote sympathetically of the plight of the slaves who had massacred so many of his maternal relatives in Santo Domingo.

When Gottschalk did return for the last time to the United States, it was to undertake a nearly killing schedule of concerts that took him, in three and a half years, to every large city in the wartime United States (he did not travel into the Confederacy) and to many of its smaller towns. He played many concerts in New York, Philadelphia, Boston, and the beleaguered nation's capitol, where Lincoln was once in the audience. He played in Portland, Maine, and Peoria, Illinois; in Harrisburg, Pennsylvania, his concert was canceled because the Confederate army was too close; Gottschalk recorded vividly the chaos that reigned there two weeks before the Battle of Gettysburg. He played for benefits for wounded soldiers and wrote feelingly of the tragedies of war. Of the rigors of the traveling concert artist he wrote:

> I have just finished (it is hardly two hours since I have arrived in New York) my last tour of concerts for this season. I have given eighty-five concerts in four months and a half. I have traveled fifteen thousand miles by train. At St. Louis I gave seven concerts in six days; at Chicago, five in four days. A few weeks more in this way and I would have become an idiot! Eighteen hours a day on the railroad! Arrive at seven o'clock in the evening, eat with all speed, appear at eight o'clock before the public. The last note finished, rush quickly for my luggage, and en route until next day, always to the same thing. . . . The sight of a piano sets my hair on end like the victim in the presence of the wheel on which he is about to be tortured.[9]

Finally, in April 1865, he left for California via the Isthmus of Panama. In San Francisco, and towns of northern California and Nevada, he played numerous concerts. Then, in September 1865, disaster struck; it was apparently Gottschalk's enemies who seized upon the late return of two young women students to the Oakland Female Seminary after a Sunday afternoon carriage drive with Gottschalk and an acquaintance, and succeeded in blowing it up into a scandal of such menacing proportions that Gottschalk had to be smuggled secretly onto a boat bound for Panama.

He spent the remaining four years of his life in South America, concertizing and arranging huge festivals that often involved the entire resources of a community, choral and instrumental. It was Berlioz, in Europe, who had first promoted and directed this kind of mammoth musical event; Gottschalk may even have helped him with some of the rehearsals. They were very popular in South America, where the entire city felt itself involved in the excitement. It meant a tremendous amount of work for the director, of course—writing or adapting special music, supervising the copying, and then undergoing countless hours of rehearsals. It was during one of these mammoth festivals in Rio de Janeiro that Gottschalk collapsed. He died less than a month later.

Gottschalk's compositions have already been discussed in part. The overwhelming majority, like those of Chopin, are for piano solo. In accord with Gottschalk's needs as a concert artist in the nineteenth century, these compositions fall into three main categories. First, there are the folk-tune-based ethnic pieces, such as *Bamboula*. These distillations of folk dances and songs, in the tradition of Chopin's mazurkas and Liszt's Hungarian Rhapsodies, were always popular—as much in Europe as in America. With the Creole pieces should be included some pieces based on Spanish dances, and some of West Indian origin. A second class of compositions is the virtuoso concert pieces, or "paraphrases," consisting of medleys of operatic airs, or popular tunes that were often patriotic. *The Union*, for example, so popular during the Civil War, includes the *Star-Spangled Banner*, *Hail Columbia*, and as a final tour de force, *Hail Columbia* and *Yankee Doodle* played at the same time. This seldom failed to bring down the house. A third class is the so-called salon pieces. These Gottschalk liked the least, but as a popular artist and "matinee idol," he had to write, play, and publish them. They are sentimental creations, with titles such as *The Dying Poet*. The most famous of these is *The Last Hope: Religious Meditation*. Published, it sold extremely well, and was found on many a parlor piano. Young ladies who played the piece, attending his concerts, would invariably ask Gottschalk to play it; it became almost a ritual for him to end his concerts with it, head bowed and eyes closed. (The main theme from *The Last Hope* lives on in a different guise. Almost two decades after Gottschalk's death, a Congregational minister put sacred words to it, and it has since led an independent existence as the hymn-tune *Mercy*.)

Gottschalk also wrote songs, a small number of works for multiple pianos, a small amount of chamber music, some works for piano and orchestra, two symphonies, and three operas. A great deal of the music he is known to have written cannot be found.

As a performer, Gottschalk made an indelible impression in the United States as undoubtedly our greatest nineteenth-century virtuoso. Yet he did not have an easy time of it. He had to play for an extremely varied audience, in a time of transition. Actually, he was caught between two publics, and neither was large enough for a professional concert artist to cater to exclusively. On the one hand were those so unsophisticated musically that even his most obvious crowd-pleasers were beyond them. On the other were those who thought Gottschalk's music too light—who wanted the "classics." In the realm of fine-art music, America was rapidly becoming increasingly dominated by German music. Gottschalk could play the "classics," but they were not what he did best, and he knew better than to try to build a career on performing them publicly. He saw his mission as entertaining, and on occasion consoling, his fellow human beings, individually or in assembled multitudes; this he did, by all accounts, superbly well.

THEODORE THOMAS AND THE SYMPHONY ORCHESTRA IN AMERICA

In 1862, when Gottschalk returned from the West Indies to begin anew his concertizing in the United States, he invited to appear with him one of New York's leading violinists, the twenty-seven-year-old Theodore Thomas. Three years later, Thomas, who was just beginning his innovative career as a conductor, returned the favor, and Gottschalk appeared as both performer and composer on the first of a new series of "symphony soirees" with Thomas's own orchestra. The next week Gottschalk again appeared as soloist and composer in a version of *The Union* for piano and orchestra. Thus the orbits of two of America's most celebrated musicians intersected briefly. The contrast between the two men is interesting. Gottschalk, the Creole, the mercurial virtuoso, French in temperament and musical taste, sought to entertain his public. Thomas, the German, the thoroughgoing farsighted planner—convinced, like Lowell Mason, of the moral value of music—sought to elevate and educate his. Following Thomas's lead and responding to his tireless and meticulous labors, American orchestral music was to develop, through the next fifty years, along the lines of the German tradition.*

Theodore Thomas (1835–1905) was born in a small town in north Germany, where his father was the town musician (*Stadtpfeifer*). The family emigrated to America when Theodore was ten, settling in New York. The boy, already an accomplished violinist, found employment where he could, playing in the theater orchestras of course, but also for dancing schools. At fifteen he set out alone on a tour of the South, giving solo recitals in hotel dining halls. He would put up his own posters (billing himself as "Master T. T."), collect the money at the door, and then unpack his violin and play the concert. This episode shows the youth's boldness and initiative; in a daguerreotype of him at that age he looks the picture of complete self-possession and confidence. When he returned to New York he got a job as a leading violinist in the new German theater there. With complete candor he wrote later of himself at that period: "I played everywhere, in opera and concerts, and was very popular."

In 1860 came a singular opportunity to conduct (though not Thomas's first conducting experience, as research has shown); as is often the case, it was suddenly thrust upon him by the illness of the regular opera conductor, and Thomas stepped in, conducting at sight an opera he had never played or seen. He must have done well, for he was then and there engaged as regular conductor for the opera. The experience convinced him that this was where his life's work lay.

In 1862 he assembled the first of his own orchestras; in 1864 it was formally organized as the Theodore Thomas Orchestra, and it was to

---

* Of course this was not solely due to Thomas's influence; the influx of German musicians to this country in the latter half of the nineteenth century was a significant factor. The identification of orchestral music as a largely German tradition in American life persisted until well into this century; when Leopold Stokowski took over the Philadelphia Orchestra in 1912, he found that the rehearsals were still being conducted in German.

remain in virtually continual existence for twenty-four years. Although during that quarter-century Thomas also conducted the Brooklyn Philharmonic, the New York Philharmonic, and the ill-fated America Opera Company, and founded the Cincinnati Festival, his own orchestra was the main vehicle for his accomplishments. After it finally disbanded in 1888, Thomas's attention shifted to the Midwest, which was coming of age culturally. In 1889 a Chicago businessman, Charles Norman Fay, undertook to secure enough guarantors among the business community to found a permanent orchestra in that city expressly for Theodore Thomas. He was successful, and in 1891 the Chicago Symphony gave its first concert under Thomas's direction. This orchestra became the second principal vehicle for Thomas's realization of his orchestral ambition; he conducted the Chicago Symphony until his death in 1905.

Thomas worked and planned tirelessly, in the face of disinterest, opposition, and calamity (the Chicago fire of 1871 nearly ruined one of his earlier ventures), to establish the symphony orchestra and its legitimate repertory firmly in American musical life. To a great extent he succeeded. His achievements were fourfold:

1. He raised the standard of orchestral playing in the United States with his uncompromising policy of hiring only the best players available, and his insistence upon thorough rehearsals and strict orchestral discipline. The Theodore Thomas Orchestra soon had an enviable reputation in Europe as well as in America; on a trip there in 1867, Thomas satisfied himself that his American orchestra was already rivaling the best orchestras in Europe.

2. He toured widely with his own orchestra. This was necessary in order for the orchestra to play enough concerts to survive, but it had benefits beyond those of offering fairly secure employment to his musicians—it gave to many communities their first sight and sound of a symphony orchestra. This was seed work, inspiring musical enthusiasts in cities without orchestras to form them. The past hundred years has seen a phenomenal growth of orchestras throughout the country. Opera (whose time may now be coming, as the signs show) could be rather accurately regarded until very recently as an immigrant. Not so the symphony orchestra; since the time of Theodore Thomas America has been a country of orchestras, their numbers unequaled and the quality of the best ones unsurpassed.

3. By 1867 a judicious combination of summer outdoor concerts (in which he pioneered), tours, and regular concerts enabled Thomas to take the bold step of offering a full season's engagement to his musicians. Thomas lived up to his contracts, even though it meant going into debt personally on occasion. Comparatively few orchestras now offer full-time employment; in Thomas's day, before the advent of recordings, which

now account for a large share of the income of our major orchestras, it was a monumental undertaking.

4. Thomas became famous for his carefully planned programming, which was designed to offer some of what the audience knew and liked while carefully introducing longer, more involved, and less familiar works; eventually he presented complete symphonies. His early programs show a carefully balanced mixture of arias, polkas, and waltzes with overtures and the movements of symphonies. The care he lavished upon the details of such programming extended even to selecting, for a given program, a piece of light dance music that had a tune similar to the theme of a symphony he was going to introduce. His programming shows a steady progression over the years, so that concerts of the later years in Chicago resemble those of today, except in their somewhat greater length. But this type of programming at the beginning of Thomas's career would have meant playing to virtually empty halls. With his uncanny skill, he *led* his audiences, which for symphony orchestra concerts, were consistently large. He was uncompromising in his dedication to quality in performance, but he never believed that symphonic music was for the elite.

The subsequent history of the symphony orchestra in America shows that the seed work began to yield results even in his lifetime. In Boston, where the Theodore Thomas Orchestra had often played, Major Henry Lee Higginson founded an orchestra in 1881, saying later that "Theodore Thomas made the Boston Symphony Orchestra possible." The St. Louis Symphony was founded the same year, followed by the Pittsburgh Symphony in 1895, the Cincinnati Symphony in 1896, the Los Angeles Symphony (later to become the Los Angeles Philharmonic) in 1897, and the Philadelphia Orchestra in 1900. Today there are more than a thousand orchestras in cities throughout the United States, including not only major professional orchestras but semiprofessional, community, and college orchestras. The place of the symphony orchestra in American musical life is secure.

JOHN PHILIP SOUSA AND THE AMERICAN BAND

What Theodore Thomas did for the American orchestra, John Philip Sousa was to do for the American band. In fact, Sousa had a lifelong admiration for Thomas and his work. There are certain interesting parallels in their careers; both began their musical education with a study of the violin, and both served brief terms of service in military bands while still in their teens. (The military bands of the day were an alternative to the theater orchestras as a source of employment for instrumentalists.) The most significant parallels, however, were the qualities of leadership both possessed and their uncompromising devotion to the highest standards of disciplined ensemble performance. The joint dedicatory concert at the Chicago World's Fair in 1892 by the newly formed Sousa Band and Thomas's Chicago Symphony brought together the two most important pace-setting musical organizations of the time.

John Philip Sousa (1854–1932) was born in Washington, D.C. His father, born in Spain of Portuguese parentage, was an accomplished linguist and an amateur musician. At the age of six Sousa began the study of the violin. An early impression, significantly, was that of the many bands of the Union army in Washington during the Civil War. At the age of thirteen his father (possibly, so the story goes, to keep him from running away with a circus band) enlisted him in the marine corps as an apprentice in the band. In two separate enlistments, he served in the marine corps until he was nearly twenty-one. This was not a full-time job, however, and Sousa continued to study music and play the violin professionally in Washington theaters and elsewhere; he even did some conducting and composing. After his discharge from the marines, he did some traveling as professional conductor and arranger with a theatrical group, ending up in Philadelphia for the Centennial celebration. There he heard Thomas's orchestra and also the band of Patrick Gilmore for the first time. He stayed in Philadelphia—playing, conducting, and composing—until 1880. His first comic opera, *The Smugglers*, was produced at this time.

At twenty-six his life took a decisive turn; he returned to Washington to take over the direction of the United States Marine Band. Like Theodore Thomas, Sousa was to have in his lifetime two performing organizations that served as vehicles for his talents and innovations. The first was the Marine Band, which he led from 1880 to 1892, and the second was his own Sousa Band, which he continued to lead until his death in 1932.

With the Marine Band, and to even a greater extent the Sousa Band, touring was a way of life. The latter made annual tours throughout the United States and Canada, took four trips to Europe (in 1900, 1901, 1903, and 1905), and from December 1910 to December 1911 toured around the world. Commercial recordings of the band (an enterprise Sousa himself long disapproved of and disassociated himself from) began to be made on wax cylinders as early as 1893; disk recordings began in 1897. (Some wax-cylinder recordings had been made with the Marine Band as early as 1890.)

In addition to leading a strenuous life as a director of bands, Sousa remained prolific as a composer. Best known, of course, are his marches.

The Stars and Stripes Forever, composed during a return voyage to America in 1896, is our unofficial national march, internationally known and popular. Sousa composed 136 marches; the best of these bear his unique imprint, and are unsurpassed in quality and spirit. Though only his marches are known (or even available) today, it is not generally realized that he composed in other forms as well. His operettas, fifteen in number, occupied him between 1879 and 1915, during the very heyday of his band activities. The most successful, *El Capitan* (which includes the famous march), was produced in New York in 1896 and in London the following year. He also wrote some seventy songs, eleven programmatic suites, and various other pieces. An author as well, he wrote seven books (including an autobiography and three novels) and more than a hundred articles for periodicals.

The Sousa Band was not a marching band; it continued to develop the tradition of the concert bands that had been well started by Patrick Gilmore's band. Sousa's programs were varied and featured vocalists, solo violinists, and harpists. Almost a trademark was the cornet solo; Herbert L. Clarke, who had been with Gilmore, was for years Sousa's featured cornet soloist, playing his own compositions. Clarke's virtuoso pieces are now dated, but they were very popular in their time, and attempted by every young aspiring cornetist.

Much of the music Sousa played was transcribed from the orchestral repertory—Italian opera overtures, for example, or the music of Wagner, which both Thomas and Sousa admired. Later Sousa himself wrote suites, overtures, and fantasies for band. His famous marches were, of course, an important part of every program, but they were usually played as encores to larger works.

No musical career better illustrates the hazards of trying to organize American music in categories than does that of John Philip Sousa. His work, and much of the repertory of his band, certainly established the concert band as a vehicle that contributed to the fine-art tradition. But a closer look at Sousa's output (of operettas and songs, for example), at his repertory (of rags as well as marches), and, above all, at his own statements of his philosophy shows him to have been, like Gottschalk before him, basically committed to entertaining his public, rather than —like Lowell Mason and Theodore Thomas—educating them. He himself made this distinction; he wrote in his autobiography:

> Thomas had a highly organized symphony orchestra with a traditional instrumentation; I a highly organized wind band with an instrumentation without precedent. Each of us was reaching an end, but through different methods. He gave Wagner, Liszt, and Tchaikowsky, in the belief that he was educating his public; I gave Wagner, Liszt and Tchaikowsky with the hope that I was entertaining my public.[10]

He railed against what he considered artistic snobbery.

Experience taught him to become an astute businessman. Some of his earliest (and most famous) marches he sold outright for as little as $35; later, by retaining a percentage of the proceeds, he earned as much as $35,000 on one march. *The Stars and Stripes Forever* is said to have earned him more than $300,000. The income from his compositions and from years of public appearances as a famous bandmaster made him eventually a wealthy man. His conviction that the composer should benefit financially from the performances of his music (rather than simply through the one-time sale of the music itself) led him to pioneer, with Victor Herbert, in the establishment of the American Society of Composers, Authors, and Publishers, a performance-licensing organization.

Sousa was a unique figure in American music. Anton Rubinstein said on hearing his band, "They have Thomas' orchestras in other countries, but America has the only Sousa." Yet he did not invent the concert band; he built on the work of Gilmore and others. Nor did the concert band cease with his death. A distinctly American institution, it was carried on by some of Sousa's own musicians. Cornetist Herbert L. Clarke, and trombonist Arthur Pryor both subsequently formed and led their own bands. Perhaps the most eminent bandmaster after Sousa was Edwin Franko Goldman, whose Goldman Band, founded after World War I, gave concerts in New York City and also toured.

The repertory of the modern symphonic band has increased significantly, and some able composers have contributed to it. Transcriptions of music for orchestra are no longer played, as they were in Sousa's day. Nevertheless, the professional band that concertizes, tours, and records, seems to have declined in recent years in the face of the phenomenal rise of the symphony orchestra, with its greater tonal range and its far greater repertory. But the band as a municipal or collegiate institution still occupies an important niche in American musical life; well loved and irreplaceable, the band and its best music are secure. It is a tribute to Sousa's contribution that, in a reversal of the usual direction of borrowing, his marches are virtually the only music for band that is regularly played by the symphony orchestra.

JOHN KNOWLES PAINE AND NEW ENGLAND'S CLASSICAL SCHOOL

Boston, the hub of New England life, has always been an important cultural center, but it occupied an especially commanding position of leadership from the mid-nineteenth century to World War I. Including in its orbit Cambridge and nearby Concord, its intellectual life had already, by the time of the Civil War, been marked by the great literary and philosophical tradition that included Emerson, Hawthorne, Longfellow, Whittier, and Thoreau. Musically the ground had been cultivated by the formation of the Handel and Haydn Society in 1815; the Boston Academy of Music, founded under the aegis of Lowell Mason in 1833, which gave musical instruction, much of it free, to schoolchildren; and the Harvard Musical Association, established in 1837. From 1840 on, orchestral and chamber music concerts were fairly regular occurrences. In 1862 lectures in music were instituted at Harvard; in 1867 the New England Conservatory (today one of our leading music schools) was founded; and in 1881 the Boston Symphony Orchestra was formed, partly due to the example of Theodore Thomas. It was a time of great patrons and patronesses. The two most notable were Henry Lee Higginson, who founded and supported (for long nearly single-handedly) the Boston Symphony and built Symphony Hall for it in 1900, and Mrs. Jack Gardner, the colorful and generous patroness who surrounded herself with a large circle of artists and musicians to whom she gave help. She provided composers with places to work and with performances, engaging musicians to give chamber music concerts, orchestral concerts, and even operas at her two successive palatial Boston establishments, 152 Beacon Street and the even more sumptuous Fenway Court.

It is not surprising, then, that Boston should have nurtured during this fifty-year period a tradition of musical composition and a group of composers who are often (conveniently but somewhat inaccurately) considered together as a "school." Actually, what these composers had in common was a dedication to excellence of musical craftsmanship and to the highest ideals of "serious" composition as they saw them. In both instances this meant looking to Germany, and to German teachers and composers. This was not only the great period of German postromanticism, but the period when German cultural influence was strongest in this country. Not surprisingly, many of the New England composers went to Germany to study almost as a matter of course.

Notwithstanding the stimulating cultural climate generally, it was not an easy time for American composers. To go into the music profession, especially for an educated person of some means who obviously had alternatives, was considered a dubious step. Some of the New England composers made the decision fairly late. George Chadwick, until he was twenty-one, was slated for a career in his father's business; Arthur Foote at the same age was a Harvard graduate and had not yet decided to devote himself to music. And even after they had become trained and productive composers, performances were not always easy to secure— conductors and the public generally balked at the idea of an American composer's name on the program. (The battle for the American composer, joined in the 1850s by William Henry Fry and George Frederick Bristow, did not really show significant results until the third decade of this century.)

Let us get better acquainted with some of the pioneers (there was one woman among them) who broke ground for the American composer, helped to establish the place of music in our colleges and universities, and left behind an impressive body of music. Because he was earliest on the scene, and gifted with tenacity and a sense of purpose, to John Knowles Paine (1839–1906), competent and dedicated, though not the most talented composer among the New Englanders, fell the role of the first pioneer. Born in Portland, Maine, he was the grandson of an organ builder and the son of a bandmaster. At nineteen, Paine, already an accomplished organist, was giving subscription organ concerts to raise money for study in Europe. He soon succeeded; went to Berlin, where he studied organ and concertized; and returned to the United States in 1861. In the next year he began the association with Harvard that was eventually to entail his most important life work. He was first engaged as chapel organist and choirmaster, but convinced that music should have a regular place in the college curriculum, he offered to give a course of lectures on musical form. Against opposition he was allowed to do so— without extra remuneration and with no credit given his students towards a degree. Courses in harmony and counterpoint were subsequently added; and recognition finally came in 1873, when he was given the rank of assistant professor, and in 1875, when he received the first full professorship of music at Harvard—and in the United States. Thus our oldest college became also the first one to establish courses in music as a regular part of its curriculum. Eventually other colleges followed suit; Harvard's curriculum became a model, and Paine was a leader in doing for music in the colleges what Lowell Mason in the earlier part of the century had done for it in the public elementary and high schools—also in New England.

Paine was in another way an important leader, in that he began to attract serious students; among them Arthur Foote, Daniel Gregory Mason, and John Alden Carpenter became important American composers of the next two generations.

Another New England pioneer, George Chadwick (1854–1931), was brought up in a typical Yankee musical atmosphere: His father, in his spare time from his varied pursuits, taught singing school and organized a community chorus and orchestra. George, who had learned the piano and organ, decided at twenty-one to go into music. After some study at the New England Conservatory and a year's teaching at a college in Michigan, he went to Germany at age twenty-three for three years of study. Soon after his return he joined the faculty of the New England Conservatory, to begin an affiliation that was to last nearly fifty years. In 1897 he became its director, a post he occupied until his death.

Among his students were many important American composers: Horatio Parker, Edward Burlingame Hill, Henry Hadley, Frederick Converse, Daniel Gregory Mason, and William Grant Still.

The range of Chadwick's compositions was broad. In addition to symphonies, choral works, and chamber music he wrote overtures with classical allusions (*Thalia, Melpomene, Adonais, Euterpe*), a symphonic ballad based on Robert Burns's *Tam o'Shanter*, serious operas (among them *Judith*, and *The Padrone*, the latter on the realistic native subject of the Italian immigrant and the political boss, the *padrone*), and comic operas, of which *Tabasco* was the best known. His works exhibit qualities of exuberance, vitality, and humor, reflecting his energy and the breadth of his interests and perceptions. Perhaps his best (and best known) work is a suite for orchestra entitled *Symphonic Sketches*: four separate pieces (*Jubilee, Noel, Hobgoblin, A Vagrom Ballad*) written between 1895 and 1904. With its humorous incongruities, flashes of satire, and pervading good spirits (except for an enigmatic episode of rather somber and even bitter reflection just before the end of the last one), it is perhaps the most "American"-sounding piece to come out of the New England group of composers.

Horatio Parker (1863–1919), suddenly taking an interest in music in his teens, made such rapid progress in learning piano and organ (his mother being his first teacher) that at sixteen he was a church organist —a calling common to our New England composers, as we have seen. He studied with Chadwick, and at the age of nineteen went to Germany for three years of further study. On his return he settled in New York as organist and teacher. In 1894 he became professor of music at Yale University, and from then on was active not only in New Haven (where in addition to teaching he formed the New Haven Symphony) but in New York and Philadelphia also.

He is noted chiefly today for his choral works and for two operas, the first of which, *Mona*, was produced at the Metropolitan Opera House in 1912. His best-known work is the cantata *Hora Novissima*, a setting of portions of a twelfth-century satirical poem in Latin. With this work he achieved great success, not only in this country (it was first performed in New York in 1893) but in England as well. For England, a country devoted to choral music and great choral festivals since the days of Handel, Parker wrote two more works, for the Hereford and Norwich festivals. *Hora Novissima* is still performed occasionally; it was given a Carnegie Hall performance forty-four years after its premiere, at which time *New York Times* critic Olin Downes described it as "irretrievably old-fashioned and genuine, glorious music."

Our first prominent woman composer was a New Englander. Mrs. H. H. A. Beach (1867–1944, born Amy Marcy Cheney) very early showed talent as a pianist, making her Boston debut at sixteen, and playing the next year a Chopin concerto with the Boston Symphony and a Mendelssohn concerto with the Theodore Thomas orchestra. She also began composing early. Two well-known songs of hers are *Ah, Love but a Day* and *The Year's at the Spring*. She wrote larger works, including a piano concerto and a *Gaelic* Symphony. There has been a recent revival of interest in her work, and some new recordings are now available, as reference to the discography will show. Except for some rather interesting late works such as her *Five Improvisations* for piano, her musical ideas are expressed in the full-bodied romantic language associated with, say, Brahms.

There is always a problem of whom to leave out in an introductory survey of this kind, which aims not so much at comprehensiveness as at giving the reader a sampling, and a feel for the meaning, of significant trends. Some composers who belong spiritually and stylistically to the "Boston school"—the third generation, one might say—were active until well into the twentieth century. Daniel Gregory Mason (last scion of the notable American musical dynasty founded by Lowell Mason) wrote his best-known work, *Chanticleer*, as late as 1929. But by the twenties American music had come under other influences (the German, already on the wane, had been dealt a severe blow by World War I), was moving in other directions, and had acquired a new sound.

The music of the nineteenth-century New Englanders represented an important cultural flourishing, and some of its artifacts, such as Arthur Foote's E major *Suite*, will be around for some time to come. But there is no question that it was based, artistically and esthetically, on the past— even in its day. The reasons why most of the music was not destined to be a part of our active repertoire for long are not to be found (as is sometimes implied) in the fact that it was written by educated New Englanders who belonged to a certain tradition, "genteel" or otherwise, or who either happened or did not happen. to teach in colleges and conservatories. Rather, it lacked that distinction which can only come from a strong talent working in a style that has not already been fully formulated.

EDWARD MacDOWELL, ROMANTIC IDEALIST AND ACCLAIMED COMPOSER

America had its first success story, in terms of a composer, in the brief career of Edward MacDowell (1860–1908). His native land not only accepted but encouraged and heaped praise upon him (often so extravagantly as to put his sensitive nature ill at ease). Practically everything that he desired to preserve was published during his lifetime, in most cases immediately after its composition; some works were published in Europe while he was still there as a young man. His orchestral works were performed by our leading symphonies. He was also recognized in Europe, especially in Germany, which for ten years in his youth was his adopted home. The changing European attitude toward American music is illustrated by the fact that a rather famous "American concert" was given at the Paris Exposition in 1889. At this concert MacDowell himself performed his own piano concerto, and the concert also included works by Paine, Foote, and Chadwick. The notion, voiced about half a century earlier, that America was nothing but a country of steam engines was beginning to fade.

MacDowell was endowed artistically with a broad range of sensitivities, abilities, and interests. With his gift for drawing, he might have become a successful artist. (He was offered what amounted to a handsome art scholarship as a young man in Paris.) He was widely read, with a particular penchant for medieval lore and poetry, and felt a lifelong affinity for the Celtic culture of his background. After his boyhood in New York City, his brief career of scarcely thirty years divides itself into three well-defined periods: a lengthy European sojourn, during which he completed his education and established a reputation as a pianist, composer, and teacher; his "Boston" period, when he concertized, wrote, and had his largest and most significant works performed; and finally, the period of his professorship at Columbia, when he concertized rarely, and despite constant work at composition produced only shorter works.

At fifteen, MacDowell went to Europe to study, first in France and then in Germany. While still in his twenties he became a successful pianist, teacher, and composer, and a protégé of the great Franz Liszt. MacDowell had virtually settled in Germany (he and his American wife, a former pupil, had bought a house in Wiesbaden) when he was persuaded to return to the United States and take an active part in our rapidly developing musical life. By the time he came back and settled in Boston in 1888 (at that time enjoying a great epoch of cultural activity, as we have noted) he had spent nearly half his life in Europe. During the next eight years he concertized, composed, and had his works widely performed. After his trip to Paris to play his Second Piano Concerto in 1889, his reputation became even more firmly established. From this period come many songs; many solo piano pieces, including the famous *Woodland Sketches*; and some of his most important orchestral compositions, including the *Indian Suite*, published in 1897.

MacDowell's use of genuine Indian themes in this suite represents one of the earliest, and perhaps most successful, attempts to use material of this kind in a symphonic composition. The songs (of Iroquois, Chippewa, and Kiowa origin) were taken from a collection made by a young German musicologist. MacDowell altered the material somewhat, and used it on his own terms. The themes retain some of their character when first presented, but are soon absorbed and transmuted in symphonic expansion and development. However relevant or irrelevant this may be, the *Indian Suite* is certainly one of MacDowell's best works, and one of the best American orchestral compositions of the nineteenth century.

It might seem natural that our leading composer of the time (and as such he was generally recognized) should write music using native melodies. Actually this was somewhat untypical of MacDowell, who otherwise (except for a few piano pieces) did not make use of folk material; who declared in a lecture, "Folk-Song in its Relation to Nationalism in Music," that "purely national music has no place in art"; and who disparaged as "childish" what he regarded as artificial "means of 'creating' a national music." Charles Ives later voiced, and amplified, the same convictions. Ives, as we shall see, quoted often from indigenous material (American hymn tunes, for example), yet there is no real inconsistency, either here or in the case of MacDowell's *Indian Suite*, since neither was setting about consciously to create a nationalistic American music. The whole issue was an important one in American music at this time.

In 1896 MacDowell took what was to be a decisive and even fateful step. He accepted a newly created professorship of music at Columbia University. This meant curtailing drastically his concertizing, and to a certain extent his composing, for MacDowell was far from regarding his new duties as perfunctory. He conceived ambitious plans for instruction at the university that reflected the breadth of his own artistic concerns and were to embrace both the technical and cultural aspects of music— in other words, the curriculum of both the conservatory and the liberal arts college. As MacDowell himself expressed his two aims, they were: "First, to teach music scientifically and technically, with a view to training musicians who shall be competent to teach and to compose. Second, to treat music historically and aesthetically as an element of liberal culture." In connection with the second aim, he laid great stress on the importance of the musician's understanding the other arts.

MacDowell took a sabbatical leave in 1902–1903, touring and playing concerts in Europe and America. Returning in the fall of 1903 to Columbia, he found the new administration unsympathetic to his ideas, and he resigned early in 1904. A year later began an increasingly debilitating mental collapse, possibly brought on or aggravated by overwork, and he died early in 1908.

MacDowell's legacy—five orchestral works, two piano concertos, some choral works, forty songs, four piano sonatas, and numerous short piano pieces, mostly arranged in groups—was not large or really varied. His range of expression we can now see to have been rather narrow. Perhaps his talent for art gives us a clue to his musical nature; he was fundamentally a pictorialist, and furthermore one who was most at home in miniature forms. An America still attuned to the muses of Europe called him her "greatest composer"; that he was indeed distinguished there is no doubt, but it was the last era in which a composer of his range, temperament, and inclination could have been so called.

An enduring legacy that the MacDowells left for American composers, writers, and artists is the MacDowell Colony at Peterborough, New Hampshire. In 1896 MacDowell purchased a farm there, as a summer retreat for composing. After her husband's death, Mrs. MacDowell worked to establish a colony where other artists could find the same peace and freedom from interruption that he had enjoyed. The original 50-acre farm has now grown to 600 acres, with 24 studios available throughout the year where individual artists, writers, and composers may work for periods of from one to six months. The MacDowell Colony, prototype of several others, is an institution well known and significant to the arts in America.

ARTHUR FARWELL, IDEALISTIC PROMOTER OF A NATIVE MUSIC

At the same time that MacDowell and the Boston classicists were at their honorable work of cultivating in America what were basically European musical forms and modes of expression, there were other musical winds stirring in the land. To understand these, it is necessary to recall a few things that had happened meanwhile on the broad musical scene. In the 1870s the Fisk Jubilee Singers (followed soon by other groups) had begun to open up a reservoir of black musical culture vastly different from the popular caricatures of the minstrel stage. In the 1880s American Indian music was beginning to be seriously collected and studied. On the popular musical stage at about the same time, Harrigan and Hart were presenting plays with music that dealt with a cross-section of the everyday life of the people of New York. Ragtime arrived from the Midwest in the 1890s. From 1892 to 1895 the great Czech composer Anton Dvořák was in America as director of the National Conservatory in New York. His black student Harry Thacker Burleigh, later to become a prominent composer, arranger, and concert singer, was a frequent visitor to his New York apartment, and repeatedly sang him spirituals. He heard the songs of Stephen Foster. He spent summers in Iowa, where he heard Indian music. Dvořák issued what was in effect a challenge to American composers, to look to their own native music as a foundation on which to establish in America what he termed "a great and noble school of music."[11] And there were composers of the time who were more than ready to accept this challenge. A spirit of ferment and optimism accompanied the advent of the new century, which seemed to portend a new era. One pioneer composer, writing in 1903, addressed himself to "all composers who feel the pulse of new life that marks the beginning of an era in American music," inviting them to join those workers who had been striving

> to draw out of the dawning, though widely distributed realities and possibilities of American musical life, the elements and forces necessary to form a definite movement which shall make for the untrammeled growth of a genuine Art of Music. Such an art will not be a mere echo of other lands and times, but shall have a vital meaning for us, in our circumstances, here and now. While it will take the worthier traditions of the past for its point of departure, it will derive its convincing qualities of color, form, and spirit from our nature-world and our humanity.[12]

So wrote Arthur Farwell (1872–1952), a man of his time, and one whose initiative, enterprise, and integrity of ideals made him a leader and a mover. Coming out of the Midwest (he was born in St. Paul, Minnesota), he was headed for a career in electrical engineering, and earned an S.B. degree from the Massachusetts Institute of Technology in 1893. However, his attention had meanwhile been turned to music. He studied in Boston, got some help and encouragement from MacDowell, and then went to Germany and France for further study. He returned in 1899, accepted a lectureship at Cornell, and at this time began the study of Indian music. In 1901, his family having resettled in Newton Center, Massachusetts, Farwell returned there, and entered upon one of the most important ventures of his life—and the most significant for American music. Having tried unsuccessfully to get his *American Indian Melodies* published, and having met other American composers who suffered similar rejections, he resolved to try to overcome the resistance to American music, and to create for himself and other American composers an outlet for their works. What he did was to found a composers' press; the Wa-Wan Press, of Newton Center, Massachusetts, came into being late in 1901, and two publications were issued that same year, the second being Farwell's *American Indian Melodies*. (The name "Wa-Wan" is that of an Omaha Indian ceremony of peace and brotherhood.) Issues were sold by subscription, but some pieces were published separately as sheet music. The emphasis was on quality—quality not only of the music chosen but of design and typography as well. In this Farwell was inspired by the examples of such predecessors as William Blake and William Morris. A glance at the complete output of the Wa-Wan Press (reprinted in five volumes by the Arno Press and the *New York Times* in 1970), shows it to have maintained exceptional standards of workmanship and appearance.

The press was in existence for ten years, during all of which time it remained Farwell's venture. His lecture tours helped to support it, since the subscriptions did not always cover the costs. After he moved to New

York in 1909 to take a job as staff writer for *Musical America,* issues dwindled; the last came out in 1911. A pioneering venture was over. But during the decade of its existence it published the work of thirty-six American composers, including nine women. Indian music (set by Farwell and others) formed an important but by no means exclusive part of it. Farwell himself did most of the editorial writing—stating, restating, and amplifying the cause for which the publication stood.

The aims of the Wa-Wan Press, as Farwell set them forth, were two-fold. The first was "to promote by publication and public hearings, the most progressive, characteristic, and serious works of American composers, known or unknown." This meant, by and large, the younger, more "radical" composers, who could not get publication or a hearing elsewhere. Farwell insisted on quality, however (to the best of his ability to determine it), and the adjective "serious," referring to seriousness of *intent,* was important. Like William Morris before him, who had partially inspired the enterprise, he completely eschewed commercialism, being likewise aware of the extent to which it could perpetuate and surround peoples' lives with shabbiness and mediocrity. For this reason, Farwell's work has special meaning for today.

The second aim of the Wa-Wan Press, and of Farwell himself, is less easily stated, but it had to do with developing an American music more in touch with American life. "It must have an American flavor," he wrote. "It must be recognizably American, as Russian music is Russian, and French music, French." He even suggested some of the ingredients: "ragtime, Negro songs, Indian songs, Cowboy songs, and, of the utmost importance, new and daring expressions of our own composers, sound-speech previously unheard." In this he showed his full awareness of, and appreciation for, the folk and popular currents that had surfaced, as we noted, in the last quarter of the nineteenth century. He spoke out boldly against German influence in particular, and recommended as an antidote more attention to the music of France and Russia, countries which, he said in 1903, "lead the world today in musical invention." Yet he never stooped to the narrow chauvinism and wholesale condemnation indulged in by the lesser minds. "The German masterpieces are unapproachable," he wrote, adding: "All that we do toward imitating them must necessarily be weak and apologetic." Of the role of European influence generally, he made one of the fairest and most perceptive assessments:

> It was natural that as the conditions for peaceful life were being wrung, step by step, from the land, there should follow the standards and the enjoyment of European culture. During this period it was the destiny of American musical activity to perpetuate the fundamental principles of the musical aspects of that culture in the New World. This accomplished simultaneously several important things. It gave crude America a general view of the spirit and form of European music. Through its own unavoidable crude-

ness it cleared that music of the ultra-refinement appropriate to an alien and venerable art evolution, but without meaning for pioneers about to face the task of expressing the broader feelings of a new and vast land, innocent of culture ideals. Moreover, it secured the distribution of trained musicians throughout the land, and thus provided a tolerably complete outfit of musical machinery, ready to be set into more purposeful operation when the right time and the right controlling minds should appear.

"But," he continued, "to-day this is past history."

The swiftly increasing group of American composers of the present generation has tasted of the regenerative sunlight flooding the wide stretches of our land, has caught glimpses of the wealth of poetic lore in the traditions of Negroes and Indians, and seen that justice must be done at last to the myriad sights and sounds of our own country. Europe will never respect America artistically, until she sees the results of this rebirth. And American composers are pressing to the mark.[13]

The Wa-Wan Press, then, was more than just a publishing venture; it was the embodiment of an ideal—an ideal held with tenacity and vision by one man above all in his time. Arthur Farwell sounded for American music the same note that Emerson, two generations earlier, had sounded for American literature: First, find your own voice, cultivate your own field; second, do not divorce art from life.

It should not disillusion us to realize that the actual music published in the Wa-Wan Press, including that of Farwell, is in general less impressive than are Farwell's optimistic and inspiring pronouncements. His ideals *were* in time fulfilled, but it took another generation. The age and the people who perceived the need were not capable, at the same time, of substantially filling that need. Like Moses, they could show the way prophetically to the promised land, but they were not destined (or equipped) to enter it.

But we are not yet done with the remarkable Arthur Farwell. Let us follow a little further his career and interests. In addition to his many other concerns, he was active as a composer throughout his adult life, as his catalog of 168 compositions, extending from 1893 to 1950, shows.[14] These include a far broader range than compositions on Indian themes. One of his most important orchestral works was a suite made from incidental music to Lord Dunsany's fantasy-play *The Gods of the Mountain* (1928).[15] Many of his works were done for special occasions, such as music for the *Pilgrimage Play* produced at the Hollywood Bowl in 1921, and *Grail Song*, a masque for community singing, dancing, and acting (1925).

Farwell's concern with making music an active part of the lives of the great mass of the people expressed itself in many novel ideas, which his abilities as a leader and organizer enabled him to bring to fruition. While working in New York, he organized with Harry Barnhart the New York

Community Chorus, which eventually grew to 800 singers. In 1916, using this chorus, he collaborated in the production of a Song and Light Festival on the shores of a lake in Central Park. The lighting effects, spectacular for their day, were described in a contemporary account:

> One-half million candle power of illumination shining through hundreds of artistic panels and huge globes gave the lake at the end of the Mall a fantastic aspect of colorful fairyland. No two of the colored panels were alike. The reflections of delicate red, blue, green and gold shades twinkled in the water, which was dotted with gay boats carrying passengers through the festival of song and light.[16]

An orchestra and the 800-voice chorus performed some standard works by Handel, Wagner, and others, but integrated with these were songs such as *Old Black Joe* and *Nearer, My God, to Thee* in which the entire assembled audience of 25,000, gathered on the opposite shores of the lake, participated. The total effect must have been truly moving. Farwell later incorporated audience participation into his *Symphonic Song on "Old Black Joe."* Interestingly enough, the Swiss-born immigrant composer Ernest Bloch (1880–1959) did the same thing in his "epic rhapsody in three parts for orchestra" entitled *America* (1927), at the final climax of which the audience is to rise and sing the anthem that the composer has included in the score. And it was Roy Harris, a pupil of Farwell's, who composed a *Folk Song Symphony* for chorus and orchestra, utilizing American folk tunes and written with the express purpose of bringing about "a cultural cooperation and understanding between the high school, college and community choruses of our cities with their symphonic orchestras."

In California, where Arthur Farwell lived and worked from 1918 to 1927, he was connected with many projects for involving people more directly with music than the conventional concert format would allow, often in an out-of-doors setting. While teaching at the University of California in Berkeley he wrote *California*, a masque of song, given in the Greek Theater with audience participation; later, in southern California, he was instrumental in the establishment of the Hollywood Bowl, and he wrote music for *La Primavera, a* "Community Music Drama" produced in Santa Barbara in 1920. In 1925 he organized a series of outdoor concerts in a natural amphitheater that he named The Theater of the Stars, near Big Bear Lake, in the mountains of southern California.

Arthur Farwell's music may not impress us today as being his most important contribution (though it has been unduly neglected), but many of his ideas, as he eloquently expressed them, and the example of his accomplishments, are relevant in today's world and amply repay an acquaintance. It is thus that he looms large, and he is a fitting figure to be considered as the last of our pioneers.

We have, with ruthless and perhaps arbitrary selectivity, chosen and introduced our eight pioneers (or groups of pioneers), who each in his or her own way made some significant contribution to the coming of age of a fine-art musical tradition in America. Many others have had to be left out. The student eager to explore further the fascinating period of our musical adolescence will want to listen, for example, to the individualistic tone painting of the gifted Charles Tomlinson Griffes (1884–1920), or the polished, urbane, and *à la mode music* of a gentleman amateur from Chicago, John Alden Carpenter (1876–1951), or the richly wrought sounds of A *Pagan Poem* by Charles Martin Loeffler (1861–1935), an Alsatian immigrant who became a recluse composer in Massachusetts. But an acquaintance with our eight pioneers should form at least an adequate background for a proper appreciation of the flowering of a mature American fine-art music, which came after World War I and is our next concern.

FURTHER READING

This list includes references to editions of music, where appropriate.

Francis Hopkinson; the Colonial and Federal Periods

* CHASE, GILBERT. *America's Music.* 2nd rev. ed. New York: McGraw-Hill Book Co., 1966. Chapter 5.

   HOWARD, JOHN TASKER. *Our American Music.* 4th ed. New York: Thomas Y. Crowell Co., 1965. Chapter 2.

* LOWENS, IRVING. *Music and Musicians in Early America.* New York: W. W. Norton & Co., 1974.
   Includes essays on Benjamin Carr's *Federal Overture* and James Hewitt.

* SONNECK, OSCAR G. *Early Concert-Life in America (1731–1800).* New York: Musurgia Publishers, 1949.

———. *Francis Hopkinson and James Lyon: Two Studies in Early American Music.* Washington, D.C., 1905. Reprint, New York: Da Capo Press, 1966.

MUSIC

   HOPKINSON, FRANCIS. *Seven Songs for the Harpsichord.* Philadelphia, 1788. Facsimile reprint, Philadelphia: Musical Americana, 5458 Montgomery Ave., 1954.

* Items thus marked are part of the suggested reference library to be available in connection with this book.

* MARROCCO, W. THOMAS, and GLEASON, HAROLD. *Music in America.* New York: W. W. Norton & Co., 1964.

This useful anthology, covering the period 1620–1865, contains two of Hopkinson's songs: *My Days Have Been so Wondrous Free* and *A Toast.*

Lowell Mason

* CHASE, *America's Music.* Chapter 8.

HOWARD, *Our American Music.* Chapter 5.

MASON, LOWELL. *Musical Letters from Abroad.* New York, 1854. Reprint, New York: Da Capo Press, 1967.

—— (comp.). *The Boston Handel and Haydn Society Collection of Church Music.* Boston, 1822. Reprint, New York: Da Capo Press, 1973.

RICH, ARTHUR L. *Lowell Mason, "The Father of Singing Among the Children."* Chapel Hill: University of North Carolina Press, 1946.

Louis Moreau Gottschalk

* CHASE, *America's Music.* Chapter 15.

* GOTTSCHALK, LOUIS MOREAU. *Notes of a Pianist.* New edition, with notes by Jeanne Behrend. New York: Alfred A. Knopf, 1964.

One of the most perceptive and brilliant documentations of nineteenth-century American life by a musician that we have.

HOWARD, *Our American Music.* Chapter 6.

LOGGINS, VERNON. *Where the Word Ends: The Life of Louis Moreau Gottschalk.* Baton Rouge: Louisiana State University Press, 1958.

OFFERGELD, ROBERT. *The Centennial Catalog of the Published and Unpublished Music of Louis Moreau Gottschalk.* New York: Stereo Review, 1970.

An invaluable assembling of all known information on the nearly 300 known works of Gottschalk.

MUSIC

Piano Music, edited by Richard Jackson. New York: Dover Publications, 1973.

Includes 26 pieces.

The Piano Works of Louis Moreau Gottschalk, edited by Vera Brodsky Lawrence. 5 vols. New York: Arno Press and The New York Times, 1969.

The most complete and authoritative edition.

Theodore Thomas and the Symphony Orchestra in America

RUSSELL, CHARLES EDWARD. *The American Orchestra and Theodore Thomas.* New York: Doubleday, Page & Co., 1927.

THOMAS, THEODORE. *Theodore Thomas: A Musical Autobiography*, edited by George P. Upton. 2 vols. Chicago, 1905. Vol. 1 reprinted, with introduction by Leo Stein, New York: Da Capo Press, 1964. 2 vols. reprinted, Grosse Point, Mich.: Scholarly Press, 1974.

John Philip Sousa and the American Band

BERGER, KENNETH. *The March King and His Band*. New York: Exposition Press, 1957.

BIERLEY, PAUL E. *John Philip Sousa: American Phenomenon*. New York: Appleton-Century-Crofts, 1973.

* CHASE, *America's Music*. Chapter 29.

GOLDMAN, RICHARD FRANKO. "Band Music in America," in Paul Henry Lang (ed.), *One Hundred Years of Music in America*. New York: Grosset & Dunlap and G. Schirmer, 1961.

———. *The Wind Band: Its Literature and Technique*. Boston, 1961. Reprint, Westport, Conn.: Greenwood Press, 1974.

SCHWARTZ, HARRY WAYNE. *Bands of America*. Garden City, N.Y., 1957. Reprint, New York: Da Capo Press, 1975.

SOUSA, JOHN PHILIP. *Marching Along*. Boston: Hale, Cushman & Flint, 1941.

MUSIC

Sousa's Great Marches in Piano Transcription: Original Sheet Music of 23 Works. New York: Dover Publications, 1975.

Show Songs from "The Black Crook" to "The Red Mill." New York: Dover Publications, 1974.

> Includes the title song from the operetta *El Capitan*, from which the march of the same title was derived.

John Knowles Paine and New England's Classical School

No one book has treated comprehensively this group of composers or this period. Aside from the works cited below, the main source of information remains articles on individual composers in periodicals such as *Musical Quarterly*.

* CHASE, *America's Music*. Chapter 16.

FOOTE, ARTHUR. *Arthur Foote, 1853–1937: An Autobiography*. Norwood, Mass.: Plympton Press, 1946.

HOWARD, *Our American Music*. Chapter 11.

MASON, DANIEL GREGORY. *Music in My Time, and Other Reminiscences*. New York: Macmillan Co., 1938.

Edward MacDowell

* CHASE, *America's Music*. Chapter 17.

GILMAN, LAWRENCE. *Edward MacDowell, A Study*. New York and London, 1908. Reprint, New York: Da Capo Press, 1969.

HOWARD, *Our American Music*. Chapter 11.

MACDOWELL, EDWARD. *Critical and Historical Essays*. Boston, 1912. Reprinted, with introduction by Irving Lowens, New York: Da Capo Press, 1969.

Arthur Farwell

* CHASE, *America's Music*. Chapter 19.

FARWELL, ARTHUR. "An Affirmation of American Music." Reprinted in Gilbert Chase (ed.), *The American Composer Speaks*. Baton Rouge: Louisiana State University Press, 1966.

—— (ed.). *The Wa-Wan Press*. Newton Center, Mass.: 1901–1911. Reprinted in 5 vols. prepared by Vera Brodsky Lawrence, with an essay by Gilbert Chase. New York: Arno Press and The New York Times, 1970. An invaluable republishing venture for American music, this incorporates Farwell's considerable editorial writing.

FARWELL, BRICE (ed.). *A Guide to the Music of Arthur Farwell*. Briarcliff Manor, N.Y.: privately printed, 1972. "A centennial commemoration prepared by his children," this guide includes a chronological list of Farwell's compositions, a list of his writings, reprints of some of his later music, various articles, and other miscellany. It is available from Brice Farwell, 5 Deer Trail, Briarcliff Manor, N.Y. 10510.

LISTENING

Francis Hopkinson, and the Colonial and Federal Periods

No music of Hopkinson himself is currently available on recordings, the Margaret Truman performance of My Days Have Been So Wondrous Free *being out of print. The* Music in America *series, made by the Society for the Preservation of the American Musical Heritage and distributed free of charge at one time to colleges and other qualified public institutions, is still currently the best source for recorded music of the colonial and federal periods. It includes music by Raynor Taylor, Alexander Reinagle, James Hewitt, Giovanni Gualdo, and Joseph Gehot. The string quartet attributed to Benjamin Franklin is available in a collection of American quartets on Vox: SVBX-5301 (three records).*

Two recent and useful additions to the Recorded Anthology of American Music *are* The Birth of Liberty: Music of the American Revolution *(RAAM: NW-276) and* Music of the Federal Era *(NW-299), both with notes by Richard Crawford. Also useful for this period is a three-record album titled* An Anthology of American Piano Music *(1780–1970) (Desto: DC-6445–47). The performances by Alan Mandel include Benjamin Carr's* Federal Overture *(a potpourri that included the first appearance in print in America of* Yankee Doodle*) and works by Alexander Reinagle, Raynor Taylor, and James Hewitt.*

The Colonial Williamsburg Foundation has issued several recordings of vocal and instrumental music of the time (available direct by writing to the Foundation at Box C, Williamsburg, Va., 23185), but this is mostly music by contemporary English, Italian, and French composers—sources which did, indeed, account for most of the music heard in colonial America.

Louis Moreau Gottschalk

Current Schwann catalogs indicate that a fairly broad selection of Gottschalk's music is now available on recordings. The American pianist Eugene List has pioneered in performing and recording much of it.

John Philip Sousa and the American Band

RAAM includes reissues of original recordings on *The Sousa and Pryor Bands: Original Recordings 1901–1926* (NW-282) and new recordings by the Goldman Band on *The Pride of America: The Golden Age of the American March* (NW-266), both with extensive notes. Of Sousa's music itself practically all that is available now are the marches, and in addition to the above releases, they are nearly always available in some version or other on commercial recordings. A good current recording is that by Donald Hunsberger and the Eastman Wind Ensemble (Philips: 9500151).

John Knowles Paine and New England's Classical School

The following recordings in the basic collections are supplemented in the case of most of the composers by currently available commercial recordings listed in the Schwann catalogs.

MRS. H. H. A. BEACH

Sonata in A Minor for Piano and Violin. RAAM: NW-268.

Song, *The Year's at the Spring,* from *When I Have Sung My Songs: The American Art Song 1900–1940.* RAAM: NW-247.

Symphony in E minor (Gaelic). *Music in America* series, MIA-139.

GEORGE CHADWICK

Sinfonietta in D major. MIA-104.
Symphony no. 3. MIA-140.

ARTHUR FOOTE

Four Character Pieces After the Rubaiyat. MIA-127.
Selected Piano Compositions. MIA-123.
Sonata in G minor for Piano and Violin. RAAM: NW-268.
Suite in D minor for Orchestra. MIA-122.
Symphonic Prologue "Francesca da Rimini." MIA-127.

EDWARD BURLINGAME HILL

Stevensonia. MIA-142.

JOHN KNOWLES PAINE

Fantasie über "Ein' feste Burg." RAAM: NW-280.
Mass in D. RAAM: NW-262–63.
Moorish Dance from Azara. MIA-132.
Overture "As You Like It." MIA-141.
Symphonic Poem, "The Tempest." MIA-130.
Symphony no. 1. MIA-103.
Symphony no. 2. MIA-120.
Dance; A Funeral March (in memory of President Lincoln); *Under the Lindens.* In *An Anthology of American Piano Music.* Desto: DC-6445–47.

HORATIO PARKER

Fugue in C minor. RAAM: NW-280.
A Northern Ballad. MIA-132.
Second Symphonic Poem "Vathek." MIA-138.

Edward MacDowell

The following recordings in the basic collections are supplemented by currently available commercial recordings listed in the Schwann catalogs.
First Suite for Orchestra and *Two Fragments after "The Song of Roland."* MIA-119.
Third Sonata. In *An Anthology of American Piano Music.* Desto: DC-6445–47.

Second Suite for Orchestra (Indian Suite). MIA-137.

Songs, *Long Ago, Sweetheart Mine; A Maid Sings Light,* from *When I Have Sung My Songs.* RAAM: NW-247.

Symphonic Poem, Hamlet and Ophelia. MIA-130.

Symphonic Poem, "Lamia," and *Sea Pieces.* MIA-133.

Symphonic Poem, "Lancelot and Elaine." MIA-131.

Arthur Farwell and Other Wa-Wan Press Contributors

CHARLES WAKEFIELD CADMAN

Four American Indian Songs. RAAM: NW-213.

ARTHUR FARWELL

The Gods of the Mountain. MIA-128.

Various Indian-inspired songs, choral pieces, and piano pieces are included in the excellent album RAAM: NW-213, with notes by Gilbert Chase on the "Indianist" movement.

HENRY B. F. GILBERT

Humoresque on Negro Minstrel Tunes. MIA-128.

Nocturne. MIA-141.

Other Important Composers

JOHN ALDEN CARPENTER

Sea-Drift for orchestra. MIA-142.

Songs, *When I Bring You Coloured Toys; Light, My Light,* from *When I Have Sung My Songs.* RAAM: NW-247.

See also current Schwann listings.

CHARLES TOMLINSON GRIFFES

RAAM: NW-273 is devoted to Griffes, with notes by Donna K. Anderson, and includes songs with both piano and orchestral accompaniment; *Three Tone-Pictures* for chamber ensemble; and *The Pleasure-Dome of Kubla Khan* for orchestra. See also current Schwann listings.

PROJECTS

1. Trace one of several organizations such as the Handel and Haydn Society (Boston), the St. Cecilia Society (Charleston), or the

Musical Fund Society (Philadelphia) from their beginnings to the present time, and indicate their importance to American music. Periodicals, local historical societies, works by O. G. Sonneck, and scholarly theses (which may be traced with the aid of reference librarians) may be of help.

2. Irving Lowens, in his introductory essay, "Music in the American Wilderness" (in *Music and Musicians in Early America*), has written: "Sometimes we almost forget that it was the land that was uncivilized rather than the men." He was writing primarily of seventeenth-century America in this context, but his remark applies equally well to popular misconceptions about the concert life of America in the eighteenth century. In order to partially clear these up, take any five-year period between 1730 and 1800 and summarize what was going on in the way of concerts in the four major cities (Boston, New York, Philadelphia, Charleston). Your major source will be Sonneck's informative and carefully researched study, *Early Concert-Life in America*.

3. Write a brief paper on Benjamin Franklin as composer, musical theoretician (he had some ideas on the improvement of musical notation), and originator of an invention to improve the glass harmonica.

4. Comment on the political aspects of music in eighteenth-century America, using as your point of departure such compositions as Hopkinson's *The Temple of Minerva* (see Sonneck, *Francis Hopkinson and James Lyon*) and Benjamin Carr's *Federal Overture* (see Lowens, *Music and Musicians in Early America*).

5. The tradition of medleys of patriotic and topical tunes perhaps began in America with Benjamin Carr's *Federal Overture* (which can be heard in *An Anthology of American Piano Music*, Desto DC 6445/47, as performed by Alan Mandel) and can be traced in a direct line through Gottschalk's *The Union* (which can be heard on a variety of recordings). Listen to both of these, if possible, and familiarize yourself with the circumstances surrounding their performance (see question 4 for background on the Carr piece). If such a piece were to have been written during the last fifty years, what tunes might it have included? What would be the effect of such a piece in our time? Is there as much potential power in a tune to evoke a response now? Why?

6. Investigate the teaching of vocal music to elementary-school children in your own immediate community today. Compare this with the opportunities for learning to sing that the children of Boston had (1) before Lowell Mason opened the Boston Academy of Music; (2) after the Academy was in full operation, around 1840.

7. Describe in a paper P. T. Barnum's enterprise of bringing the Swedish singer Jenny Lind over to America for a concert tour. (His promotional skill is said to have amassed a gross intake of nearly three-quarters of a million dollars for 95 concerts, and this around 1850!) It is a fascinating episode in American concert life. For a start, you can refer to *Barnum's Own Story* (New York: Dover Publications, Inc., 1961), an engrossing autobiography, even if not to be taken altogether too literally. Check this against the Maretzek book referred to in Question 10.

8. Do a paper entitled "Louis Antoine Jullien and the Fireman's Quadrille: A Bizarre Episode in American Concert Life." (See Howard and Bellows, *A Short History of Music in America* [New York: Thomas Y. Crowell Co., 1957], pp. 120–121, for a start.)

9. Read Louis Moreau Gottschalk's *Notes of a Pianist*, and write a paper on any of a number of subjects suggested by this brilliant musician and diarist—e.g., "The Life of a Concert Artist in Mid-Nineteenth-Century America" or "Music in the Mining Towns of the West."

10. Do a short paper on opera in nineteenth-century America. The vicissitudes of this exotic import can be traced through readings in Chase, *America's Music*, and Howard, *Our American Music* and *A Short History of Music in America*. For an interesting personal account, read Max Maretzek's *Revelations of an Opera Manager in Nineteenth-Century America* (New York: Dover Publications, Inc., 1968).

11. Try to locate, through the facilities of a large library, volume 2 of Theodore Thomas's autobiography (*Theodore Thomas: A Musical Autobiography* [Chicago: A. C. McClurg & Co., 1905, 2 vols.]). This interesting volume, consisting of "Concert Programmes, 1855–1905," was omitted from the 1964 reprint of the autobiography. Consult it to compare samplings of early, middle, and late programs during this fifty-year period, comment on the changes made, and on Thomas's own "system of programme-making" as he sets it forth.

12. Write a paper on the gigantic music festivals held in nineteenth-century America, using as a prototype those produced by Patrick Gilmore in Boston in 1869 and 1872. For a start, see Howard, *A Short History of American Music*, pp. 137–138, and Nicolas Slonimsky, "The Plush Era in American Concert Life," in Lang, *One Hundred Years of Music in America*.

13. Compare the concert band programs of the late nineteenth and early twentieth centuries (before 1920) with those of today. Note and comment on the differences. (Consult the reading list.)

14. Write a short paper on Sidney Lanier, American poet *and* musician.

15. Many composers of the so-called New England classical school, composing between 1875 and 1925, wrote programmatic pieces— pieces with extramusical associations. Examples are John Knowles Paine's overture *As You Like It* or Arthur Foote's symphonic prologue *Francesca da Rimini*. (Composers such as Victor Herbert and Charles Tomlinson Griffes, who were not New Englanders, also wrote such works.) Make a survey of the programmatic works written during this half-century, and summarize the kind and variety of literary influences on composers of this period. Would your results justify its designation as the "American Romantic Period"?

16. Referring to MacDowell's *Critical and Historical Essays* and other sources, summarize his views about the place of music in "liberal culture," and specifically, the directions in which he wished to ultimately develop the music department at Columbia. Include his thoughts on the relation of music to the "sister arts."

17. Peruse rather thoroughly the five-volume reprinted edition of the Wa-Wan Press output, edited by Arthur Farwell. Summarize the variety of influences—literary, social, and if possible, musical—that are evident in the works published.

18. As indicated in the text, in 1916 Arthur Farwell began a series of projects designed to bring music closer to the great mass of people and thereby enrich their lives. He organized community choruses open to all who were interested, community "sings" with orchestra, and community pageants and masques, the performances taking place nearly always in the out-of-doors. Summarize and comment upon Farwell's work in this vein between 1916 and 1927. Much information is to be found in Brice Farwell's *Guide to the Music of Arthur Farwell*. What do you think are the concrete results of such idealistic enterprises? Are they likely to be undertaken today, and why?

19. The Wa-Wan Press venture has been documented and evaluated, and its editions preserved. (See Chase's *America's Music*, chapter 19, and his long essay in the reprint of the Wa-Wan Press editions by the *New York Times*.) Summarize subsequent ventures in which American composers, singly (including Farwell himself) or in groups, have published their own music.

Chapter Fourteen

Music with Film, Dance, Drama, and Poetry

AMERICA FINDS ITS OWN VOICE

WORLD WAR I MARKED a kind of watershed in American music. In the peace that followed, temporary and illusory though it proved to be, exciting things happened here artistically. "It was an adventurous time," as Aaron Copland put it. For it was then that an indigenous fine-art music, the coming of which had been prophesied by so many of the pioneers we encountered in the last chapter, and made possible certainly in part by their labors, began to flourish. The two decades between the wars, especially, were years of ferment and change—"fervent years," as they have been called. They were years of optimism and productivity. A perhaps comparable "Americanization" had happened earlier in the more immediately responsive field of popular music, but these were the years when the American "serious" composer really began to find (or make) his place in American life, and to find an audience.

Partly this was the result of the existence of a group of young musicians of considerable talent, who, fairly early in their lives and at that time unknown to each other, made the irrevocable decision to become composers, and who dedicated themselves fully and knowledgeably to preparing themselves for productive careers. (Roger Sessions, born in 1896, had already decided by the time he was thirteen that he was going to be a composer; Aaron Copland, born in 1900, reached the same decision by the time he was fifteen. Virgil Thomson, born in 1896, and Roy Harris, in 1898, each came to this point at about the age of twenty-four.) That composing hardly existed at the time as a profession in America, and that the audience for American music was practically nonexistent, did not daunt them. They managed to acquire the preparation they needed, they found out (by ingenuity, persistence, and trial and error) how to establish themselves as professional composers, and they set about building an audience. As Roger Sessions put it:

> The striking fact is that those who aspired to genuine and serious achievement, no longer a handful of ambitious individuals who remained essentially isolated, were young Americans who had begun to learn what serious accomplishment involved. They were determined to find their way to it. Such seeking had not occurred before in the United States, but they did not find what they sought within the then existing framework of American music life.[1]

Americans in Paris

Not finding "what they sought within the then existing framework of American music life," most did turn, once more, to Europe. Postwar Europe, then, was by no means without its influence during this period, but it was a different Europe and a different sort of influence. It was not merely the war and its aftermath that curbed somewhat the German influence—it was that more venturesome things, visibly, at least, were taking place elsewhere. Arthur Farwell had already noted, two decades earlier, the greater musical inventiveness of France and Russia. By the third decade of this century the Russian Revolution had stifled musical innovation there; many of the most important Russian musicians were in western Europe by this time anyway. But in France, and specifically in Paris, there was an atmosphere of fervent concern for music (and for the arts generally), which was evidenced in a burst of new music being performed (some of it written during the war years) and in the new artistic movements (Dada, for example, as a rejection of artistic formalism and rationality). This ferment attracted younger composers. The young French group of Les Six—Darius Milhaud, Francis Poulenc, Arthur Honegger, Georges Auric, Louis Durey, and Germaine Tailleferre—in the artistic company of the older iconoclast Eric Satie, held together and motivated by the writer Jean Cocteau, was making itself heard. But there was also important music by non-French composers: Igor Stravinsky, Arnold Schoenberg, Paul Hindemith, Béla Bartók, Serge Prokofiev. Serge Koussevitzky, noted Russian conductor, began in 1921 in Paris the Concerts Koussevitzky, at which many new works were performed.

And along with the young émigré writers, the young American composers were there as well. In the same year that Koussevitzky began his celebrated concerts, there was established in the palace at Fontainebleau a music school for Americans. Although Paul Vidal of the Paris Conservatory was the composition teacher, it was an exceptional woman in her thirties, Nadia Boulanger—an organist and a teacher of harmony, counterpoint, and composition—who was destined to have the most influence on a host of American composers who came to her for instruction, guidance, and encouragement throughout the twenties and thirties. A list of these young "Americans in Paris" who studied at least for a time with Mlle. Boulanger, gaining not only perceptive criticism but the confidence to find and strike out on their own paths, would include many of the most important American composers of the past fifty years: Virgil Thomson, Aaron Copland, Walter Piston, Roy Harris, Douglas Moore, Marion Bauer, Bernard Rogers, Robert Russell Bennett, Elliott Carter, Ross Lee Finney, David Diamond, Arthur Berger, Irving Fine, Theodore Chanler, Richard Franko Goldman, and Easley Blackwood.

A European composer who became an enthusiastic adopted American, and who was also responsible for teaching and guiding many young American composers during this period was the Swiss-born Ernest Bloch, who taught in New York, Cleveland, and San Francisco between 1917 and 1930.

Americans Back Home

American composers returning from Europe in the 1920s found reasons for both pessimism and optimism. Certainly there was as yet no great audience, or demand, for the music of American composers, and many could justifiably join H. L. Mencken in condemning our tendency to shallow materialism and our lack of interest in, or understanding of, the arts. Some of the young émigrés had left for good. But this did not include many composers. As Copland, with characteristic optimism, has pointed out, positive forces (mostly generated by the composers themselves) were at work, and things were happening. The International Composers' Guild and its offshoot, the League of Composers, were active, and gave concerts of new music. In 1924 Serge Koussevitzky, whose celebrated concerts in Paris had introduced many new works, was appointed conductor of the Boston Symphony, thus beginning a long tenure during which he not only played many new American works but was often responsible, through commissions, for their creation. From 1928 to 1931 the Copland-Sessions Concerts, a collaborative venture on the part of two of our leading composers, was also a forum for the presentation of new works. The 1920s, before the crash, was a time of opulence in American life, and patrons of the arts were available. In the mid-twenties the Guggenheim Memorial Foundation was established, and Aaron Copland was given the first fellowship awarded to a composer. In 1929 the RCA Victor Company offered an unprecedented award of $25,000 for a symphonic work (the prize was finally split five ways). American "serious" music was finally underway, it seemed.

The Drive Toward an "American" Music

It was natural that composers of the time should be seeking to write music that was "recognizably American." In this they were responding to the same urges that had been expressed two and three decades earlier by Farwell, Henry F. Gilbert, and others. As Roger Sessions has stated:

> The principal concern of music in the twenties was the idea of a national or "typically American" school or style and, eventually, a tradition which would draw to a focus the musical energies of our country which, as Rosenfeld once said to Aaron Copland and the author, would "affirm America." [2]

For the new generation of composers who took the business of writing music with intense seriousness, it was no longer a matter of simply incorporating folk material into compositions or using it as a basis for symphonic elaborations, although both of these practices were and still are followed, and remain valid in themselves. But as Copland put it:

> Our concern was not with the quotable hymn or spiritual: we wanted to find a music that would speak of universal things in a vernacular of American speech rhythms. We wanted to write music on a level that left popular music far behind—music with a largeness of utterance wholly representative of the country that Whitman had envisaged. [3]

There was much experimentation in this search for "a music that would speak of universal things in a vernacular of American speech rhythms." It was natural, for example, that as earlier composers had looked to Indian music, Negro spirituals, and minstrel tunes, composers of the third decade of the twentieth century should look to jazz. Among the older generation of composers, Chicago-based John Alden Carpenter had written the score to a ballet entitled *Krazy Kat* (after a cartoon figure) that was performed there in 1921 and that employed jazz idioms, as did his more ambitious ballet score, *Skyscrapers* (commissioned by the Russian impressario Sergei Pavlovich Diaghilev), which was performed at the Metropolitan Opera House in New York in 1926. On Koussevitsky's suggestion, the League of Composers commissioned an orchestral work from Aaron Copland; he responded with his jazz-based *Music for the Theater* in 1925, and the next year utilized jazz motifs again in his Concerto for Piano and Orchestra. It should be noted that many European composers were also fascinated with jazz at about this time; Darius Milhaud's famous ballet *La Création du monde*, for example, was presented in Paris in 1923.

George Gershwin's *Rhapsody in Blue*, Concerto in F, and *An American in Paris* (the latter two commissioned by Walter Damrosch for the New York Symphony)—pieces intended for the concert hall by a composer already firmly established as a writer of popular songs and musical comedies—date from this period also. But after the 1920s, the tendency to turn to jazz as a stylistic source for American fine-art music waned; from this time on, as jazz entered its successive stages of expansion and development, the borrowing was much more in the other direction, with jazz incorporating harmonic, melodic, and formal ideas that had been evolved in the fine-art music of both Europe and America.

The American Composer Comes Into His Own

Virgil Thomson has labeled the thirties as "the definitive decade" in American music. The Depression had ended the period of general affluence, but paradoxically these were rather good times for the American composer. His work had begun to be known, he had a public, and there was, possibly for the first time, an actual need for his music. Copland has written:

> In all the arts the Depression had aroused a wave of sympathy for and identification with the plight of the common man. In music this was combined with the heady wine of suddenly feeling ourselves—the composers, that is —needed as never before. Previously our works had been largely self-engendered: no one asked for them; we simply wrote them out of our own need. Now, suddenly, functional music was in demand as never before in the experience of our serious composers. Motion-picture and ballet companies, radio stations and schools, film and theater producers discovered us. . . . No wonder we were pleased to find ourselves sought after and were ready to compose in a manner that would satisfy both our collaborators and ourselves.[4]

From the advent of the Depression to the end of World War II, then, were years of greatly expanded productivity for the American composer. Having found a public—a demand for his music—he began, in those works intended for that public, to speak a musical language that it could understand. Thus were born in this period many of those works that have become known, both in America and abroad, as most "typically American."

MUSIC WITH FILM

It is from this period, and from works written for the medium of the sound film, so largely developed in America, that we choose the first of the works to be considered in some detail. Sound had been added to the movies before 1930, and we have already encountered the rash of musicals that were rushed into production to fill the instant demand, as more and more theaters became equipped to show the "talkies." After 1930 Broadway composers went in increasing numbers to Hollywood to work in films, but their contributions generally consisted of writing individual songs. The 1930s also saw the rise of the so-called symphonic film score, with lush orchestral music mostly by European composers brought up in the European symphonic-operatic tradition. These were extremely talented and facile composers; they moved to Hollywood and became specialists in the new craft, adapting their talents to the requirements of the industry and turning out many scores a year. Among them were Max Steiner, a Viennese composer who arrived in Hollywood in 1929; Erich Wolfgang Korngold, another Austrian, who came to Hollywood in 1934; and Franz Waxman, born in Poland and trained in Berlin, who did his first film score in 1933.

Film scoring rapidly became a very specialized job. The relation to the film industry of those who have established themselves as composers in more or less autonomous media (symphonic and chamber music, opera) has in this country been from the beginning rather tenuous and spasmodic. Not until 1936 did one of our major composers write film music, and then it was in the field of the documentary, a genre that is independent of the pressures of the entertainment industry and thus freer to concern itself with the artistic excellence of the whole, including the integration of quality music.

A Realistic Film of the American West

In the middle thirties, the United States Resettlement Administration, a government agency, wanted a documentary film to propangandize on behalf of its program to aid farm families driven out of drought-stricken areas—mainly the Dust Bowl of the Southwest. Pare Lorentz, a film reviewer turned film maker, was engaged to make this, his first movie. The result was a powerful and even dramatic documentary called *The Plow That Broke the Plains.* Excerpts from Lorentz's own narration for the film give its outline and tenor:*

I: Prologue

This is . . . .
a story of the Great Plains:
the 400,000 acres of
wind-swept grass lands that
spread up from the Texas

Panhandle to Canada . . .
A high, treeless continent,
without rivers, without streams . . .
A country of high winds
and sun . . .
and of little rain . . .

III: Cattle

First came the cattle . . .
an unfenced range a thousand
    miles long . . .
an uncharted ocean of grass,
the southern range for winter grazing
and the mountain plateaus for
    summer
It was a cattleman's Paradise. . . .

The railroads brought markets to
    the edge of the plains . . .
land syndicates sprang up overnight
and the cattle rolled into the West.

IV: Homesteader

But the railroad brought the world into the plains . . .
new populations, new needs crowded the last frontier.
Once again the plowman followed the herds
and the pioneer came to the plains.
Make way for the plowman!
High winds and sun . . .
high winds and sun . . .
a country without rivers and with little rain.
Settler, plow at your peril!

VI: War and Tractor

Many were disappointed, but the great day was coming . . .
the day of new causes—new profits—new hopes.
"Wheat will win the war!" . . . .

* Four ellipses points within sections indicate deletions made for these excerpts; three ellipses points are from the original narration.

VII: Blues (Speculation)

Then we reaped the golden harvest . . .
then we really plowed the plains. . . .
By 1933 the old grass land had become the new
wheat lands . . . a hundred million acres . . .
two hundred million acres . . .
More wheat!

VIII: Drought

A country without rivers . . . without streams . . .
with little rain . . .
Once again the rains held off and the sun baked the earth.
This time no grass held moisture against the
winds and sun . . . this time millions of acres
of plowed land lay open to the sun.

IX: Devastation

Baked out—blown out—and broke!
Year in, year out, uncomplaining
   they fought
the worst drought in history . . .
their stock choked to death on the
   barren land . . .
their homes were nightmares of
   swirling dust night and day.
Many went ahead of it—but many
   stayed
until stock, machinery, homes, credit,
food, and even hope were gone.
On to the West! . . . .

No place to go . . . and no place to
   stop.
Nothing to eat . . . nothing to do . . .
their homes on four wheels . . . their
   work a desperate
gamble for a day's labor in the fields
   along the
highways, price of a sack of beans or
   a tank of gas. . . .
The sun and winds wrote the most
   tragic chapter
in American agriculture.[5]

The film still makes a stunning visual impact today, with its expressive
footage of prairie grasslands; devasted, dust-blown farms; and hard-hit,
long-suffering farm families; and its visual analogies, as for example between military tanks and mammoth harvesters, and between a collapsed
ticker tape machine and bleached bones on the plowed-over, denuded
land.

Virgil Thomson was engaged to write music for the film. The score,
completed in 1936, showed what could be done by an experienced composer thoroughly acquainted with our indigenous music and able to manipulate its varied materials in an original, effective manner to emphasize
the film's message. Both Thomson and Lorentz felt the rightness of "rendering landscape through the music of its people," as the composer has put

it. The music therefore integrates material representative of the vastness and variety of our vernacular music, including a Calvinist psalm tune, cowboy songs (with their strong suggestions of Irish origin), Negro blues, and war songs of the early twentieth century.

The film itself, twenty-seven minutes long, is still available.[6] Even more readily available is the music, in the form of a fifteen-minute suite for orchestra fashioned by the composer himself (it omits the music of the three middle sections). The music is quite effective apart from the film (in which it is actually covered at times by the narration), and in fact John Cage has written: "Unless Muzak-inclined, one would do better to hear *The Plow* accompanied by pictures of one's own invention, which, thanks to the composer's faithfulness to those of Lorentz, may well resemble them."[7]

The *Prelude* is an austere evocation of the virgin prairie (which now exists only in music like this, and in the imagination), and it incorporates the first two phrases of the psalm tune *Old 100th* in a setting in which it manages to sound perfectly natural.

Pastorale (Grass) is a short movement making much of canonic imitation (in the manner of the round). The theme, related to that of the first movement, is here vaguely reminiscent in its opening notes of the Lutheran chorale tune *How Beautifully Shines the Morning Star*.

The two middle movements, rather symetrically framed by the outer movements, as we shall see, are the ones in this documentary of the Plains most clearly related to the "music of its people." *Cattle* blends in an appropriate setting reminiscences of three authentic cowboy tunes. The first one recalled is *I Ride an Old Paint*, which appears in Carl Sandburg's *The American Songbag*.

I ride an old paint, I lead an old Dan, I'm goin' to Mon - tan' for to throw the hool-i - an. They feed in the cou-lees, they wa - ter in the draw, Their tails are all mat-ted, their backs are all raw.

(original a fourth lower)

Thomson's version of the tune is polyrhythmic—that is, it superimposes on the waltz (or Irish jig) rhythm of the tune itself a slower, broader waltz rhythm as accompaniment.

This treatment is extended to the second tune as well, *The Cowboy's Lament*, shown here as found in Vance Randolph and Floyd Shoemaker's *Ozark Folksongs*.

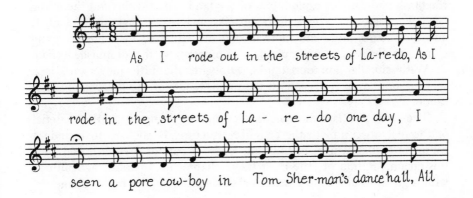

dressed in his buck-skins an' fit for his grave.

The third is a brief recollection of *Whoopee Ti Yi Yo, Git Along, Little Dogies,* shown below as it appears in John Lomax's *Cowboy Songs and Other Frontier Ballads,* in juxtaposition with Thomson's quotation.[8]

Thomson

Lomax

As I was a-walk-ing one morn-ing for pleas-ure, I

spied a cow-punch-er a - rid- ing a - long;
(Original a 3rd lower in Lomax)

It is interesting to compare Thomson's treatment of this tune with Copland's very different usage in *Billy the Kid* (see music example, p. 399).

The fourth movement of the suite is *Blues,* appropriately conventionalized and urbanized in the style of 1920s commercial jazz, to underscore the brash and ruinous exploitation of the land. Toward the end the music becomes progressively more dissonant (it is marked "Rough and violent"), and the themes more and more incoherent, climaxed by a final jangling chord that has as its underpinning, appropriately, the diminished triad.

With singular appropriateness, *Drought,* the fifth movement, is a shorter, more somber version, in the minor mode, of the *Pastorale (Grass)* canon.

The sixth and last movement, *Devastation,* brings back the material of the first, to complete the arch-like structure. It goes on to include a complete fugue (which, in the film, is also a part of *Prelude*), and ends this documentation of "the most tragic chapter in American agriculture" with a gigantic tango on a stretched-out version of the fugue theme.

In 1937, the year after *The Plow That Broke the Plains* was finished, Thomson collaborated with Pare Lorentz on another documentary, *The River*, also for the United States government. Thomson again used folk material—this time delving into the southern shape-note folk hymnody described in chapter 6. This film is also still in circulation [9] and from this music the composer also drew a suite.

Since then Thomson has written scores for at least five more films, three of them documentaries. Best known is his score for *Louisiana Story*, using some of the indigenous material we have encountered in chapter 3. Two suites have been made from this: *Suite from Louisiana Story* and *Acadian Songs and Dances*.

VIRGIL THOMSON (born 1896, Kansas City, Missouri) set about early preparing himself for what he knew would be a professional career, either as a musician or a writer (it turned out to be both). Precocious and a prodigious learner, he participated fully and confidently in the musical and intellectual life of his growing midwestern city, meanwhile observing, absorbing, and being responsive to every feature of its ambience. Thus he could say later: "During my second twenty years I wrote in Paris music that was always, in one way or another, about Kansas City. I wanted Paris to know Kansas City, to understand the ways we like to think and feel on the banks of the Kaw and the Missouri." [10] (Thomson's generation of American composers have been a decisive influence, as we shall see. Of this generation, only Thomson and Howard Hanson are from the Midwest—Thomson from the big-city Midwest and Hanson from the small-town prairie Midwest.)

After World War I Thomson decided on music as a career, and went to Harvard. Membership in the Harvard Glee Club entailed a concert tour to Europe, and this was his introduction to Paris. The recipient of a fellowship from Harvard, he stayed on for a year, studying organ and composition with Nadia Boulanger. He returned to America for three years, completing his degree, filling the post of organist at King's Chapel in Boston, studying counterpoint and conducting, and composing. In 1925 he returned to Paris, where he spent most of the next fifteen years, composing, writing pieces of musical journalism for American periodicals, and keeping up his friendship with virtually everyone of importance in the arts in the Paris of that time—and in the United States also, during his return visits. He returned in 1940, after the onset of the war in Europe, to take up the post of music critic for the *New York Herald Tribune*, a highly influential position he held for fourteen years, writing about all the important musical events of the period with wit and perception.[11] In the more than two decades since leaving the job, Virgil Thomson has been active as a composer, conductor, lecturer, and author.

He has written for virtually every medium. Besides his film music, some noteworthy works include three operas (two of which will be discussed presently, and a third, *Lord Byron*—a properly, though not conventionally, romantic opera with an arch-romantic hero, which premiered in 1972), his *Symphony on a Hymn Tune*, his orchestral "landscapes" *The Seine at Night, Wheat Field at Noon*, and *Sea Piece with Birds* (collectively known as *Three Pictures for Orchestra*), his *Five Songs to Poems of William Blake*, and his *Requiem (Missa pro Defunctis)*. A form of composition he engaged in frequently was the writing of musical portraits of his friends; these were mostly done for piano, but some were for violin, some for chamber ensembles, and some he has orchestrated.

Virgil Thomson writes deftly and expertly music that is functional and often appears deceptively simple. It avoids profundities, and is devoid of pretensions. In this it may be said to have the French touch—certainly he has often been compared to Erik Satie, who had similar ideas about music. Thomson is an intensely practical man of music, and in spite of the apparent traditionalism of his style he is a genuine innovator. His music can be very affecting; at its best it has the pure and simple beauty of the indigenous music (such as hymn tunes) that he has so thoroughly assimilated into his artistic vocabulary.

Two Films About the Small Town and the Big City

In the 1930s, when our major composers were occupied with film scores, it was for the most part for documentaries. In 1939 and 1940, however, Aaron Copland (who had done one documentary, *The City*, in 1939) did two film scores for the "industry"—both for stories of exceptional quality by eminent American writers. The first was John Steinbeck's *Of Mice and Men*, and the second Thornton Wilder's *Our Town*.

When our established fine-art composers did work on feature films in the thirties and forties (which was not frequently in this country, in contrast to European practice), certain standard industry concepts—such as the "symphonic score," with its consistent reliance on rich, thick orchestral sonorities and its debt to older European styles, and the "assembly line" methods whereby the composer's music is clothed in its final orchestral garb by someone else—were abandoned. Thus the collaboration of composers of independent stature on films generally had the effect of *simplifying* the music, in texture and orchestration, rather than making it more complex, and this slimming down, this letting in of light and air to the score, managed in itself to give the music a more American character.

This is nowhere more evident than in Copland's score for *Our Town*, Thornton Wilder's play about life and death, the commonplace and the universal, dramatized in episodes in the lives of two families in a small New England town.[12] As with the Thomson film scores, the music is more readily available in the form of an orchestral piece called simply *Our Town: Music from the Film Score*. Copland's music from the film score seems to lean on its program more than does the Thomson suite from *The Plow*. Without reference to the play, it would be difficult to see the reason for ten minutes of calm, slow, elegaic music; knowing the play, and its extraordinarily deliberate pace, one is able to restage it in one's own imagination. For if the magic of Thornton Wilder's drama comes off, the calm and quiet of the commonplace gradually and subtly become the calm and quiet of the whole star-inhabited universe; and Grover's Corners, New Hampshire, is a window on that austere, lovely, lonely universe.*

Quite different from the music for *Our Town* is the score Leonard Bernstein created for the Elia Kazan film *On the Waterfront* (1954).[13] This film is about a longshoreman who is possessed of a degree of sensitivity and moral integrity totally at odds with, and seemingly inappropriate to, the harsh brutal world of the waterfront in which he lives. The quiet opening melody, unaccompanied (one of the main themes of the score), has a spacious diatonic simplicity about it, until the introduction of the one "blue note" (a master stroke of inflection and timing) at once affects the whole feel of the music. For all the spareness of its opening, and its references to jazz (appropriate to the urban setting and the theme of alienation), it is soon apparent that this is a "symphonic film score," basically of the older vintage, with well-crafted orchestral effects and the piling of statement upon statement of its motives to build its climaxes. In its themes, and especially in their development, the score owes as much to Broadway (and to Richard Strauss and Gustav Mahler) as to jazz. Like much of Bernstein's music, it is inherently choreographic. The score has also been made into a symphonic suite.

LEONARD BERNSTEIN (born 1918, Lawrence, Massachusetts) studied composition at Harvard, spent two years in Philadelphia at the Curtis Institute, and studied conducting with Koussevitzky at Tanglewood. In the 1940s he burst upon the scene as the versatile *Wunderkind* of American music: pianist, composer, and conductor. A fortuitous last-minute opportunity to conduct the New York Philharmonic in 1943, which he did with legendary success, was the start of a conducting career that led to his eventual appointment as permanent conductor of that orchestra in 1958, a post he held until he left it (assuming the title and role of "laureate conductor") in 1969 to move on to other arenas. While leading the New York Philharmonic, his television appearances in highly informative and imaginative programs demonstrated his brilliance as a lecturer on a variety of musical subjects.

We have encountered in chapter 10 Leonard Bernstein's works for the popular musical stage, the most noteworthy being his masterpiece

---

* For additional discussion of Aaron Copland, see pp. 403–404.

West Side Story. He is one of the few composers who have functioned successfully in both the concert and the entertainment fields. To his concert works he often brings his predilection for jazz—as in his Symphony No. 2 (*The Age of Anxiety*) and his *Serenade* for violin, strings and percussion—and for more recent popular styles, as can be heard in his *Mass*. To his works for the popular musical stage he brings the musical sophistication that enables him to utilize with perfect naturalness crafts and techniques of the fine-art tradition, such as canons and fugues.

Bernstein is a restless, peripatetic talent—clearly, in all he does, a "star." His gifts are most evident in endeavors in which music is combined with other arts: in musical comedy, in his quasi-dramatic works such as the symphony *Kaddish* (for which he also wrote part of the text) and the semi-staged *Mass*, and in his phenomenal success in conducting opera since leaving the New York Philharmonic.

MUSIC WITH DANCE

The 1930s was a vital period of new beginnings for ballet, as well as for film. It was in 1936, you will recall, that George Balanchine was called upon to create the first jazz ballet sequence (*Slaughter on 10th Avenue*) by a "serious" choreographer to go into a musical show, setting new standards for the dance routines on the popular musical stage. But ballet itself began looking for new material and fresh approaches; its real "Americanization" began at this time (taking into account earlier venturesome essays, such as Diaghilev's production of *Skyscrapers*, with a score by John Alden Carpenter, in 1926). In 1937 Lincoln Kirstein commissioned for his Ballet Caravan the ballet *Filling Station*, with music by Virgil Thomson—a score consisting of twelve numbers, with copious references to popular dances (the waltz, the tango, the Big Apple) and other Americana, "all aimed," as Thomson has written, "to evoke roadside America as pop art."

Billy the Kid

The next year Kirstein again commissioned a ballet score from an American composer, and brought into being the first "western" ballet. This was Copland's *Billy the Kid*. A more unequivocally "American" theme could hardly be imagined. (Musical comedy did not take up the American West until five years later, with *Oklahoma!*) Kirstein himself devised the scenario, around the short career of the legendary William Bonney (1859–1881).

The scenario is given in the score as follows:

The action begins and closes on the open prairie. The central portion of the
ballet concerns itself with significant moments in the life of Billy the Kid.
The first scene is a street in a frontier town. Familiar figures amble by.
Cowboys saunter into town, some on horseback, others with their lassoes.
Some Mexican women do a Jarabe which is interrupted by a fight between
two drunks. Attracted by the gathering crowd, Billy is seen for the first
time as a boy of twelve with his mother. The brawl turns ugly, guns are
drawn, and in some unaccountable way, Billy's mother is killed. Without
an instant's hesitation, in cold fury, Billy draws a knife from a cowhand's
sheath and stabs his mother's slayers. His short but famous career had begun. In swift succession we see episodes in Billy's later life. At night, under
the stars, in a quiet card game with his outlaw friends. Hunted by a posse
led by his former friend Pat Garrett. Billy is pursued. A running gun battle
ensues. Billy is captured. A drunken celebration takes place. Billy in prison
is, of course, followed by one of Billy's legendary escapes. Tired and worn
in the desert, Billy rests with his girl. (Pas de deux.) Starting from a deep
sleep, he senses movement in the shadows. The posse has finally caught up
with him. It is the end.*

A suite was made from the ballet score, and it is more readily available
both in score and on records, but it omits music important to the action.
The following description refers to the music of the suite.

The introduction, subtitled *The Open Prairie* in the score, is an evocation of the loneliness of the vast arid plains; if the "rightness" of this
music is remarkable in a composer born in Brooklyn, and as Arthur
Berger points out, a "thorough-going New Yorker," he goes on to remind
us of the psychologically not-so-different solitude and aridness of the
teeming city streets. This same "openness" (achieved partly through the
use of the open consonances) can be heard in many other works of
Copland as well. The prologue of *Billy the Kid* also has a vast static
quality about it—if it can be called a dance, it is a lean, somewhat harsh,
but majestic sarabande, a huge dilation upon its rhythmic motive:

$$\downarrow \quad \downarrow$$

that dwarfs merely human figures. When human figures do appear, in the
first scene, their smallness is emphasized by the slightness and fragility
of the little tune given to the solo piccolo.

---

* Copyright 1941 by Aaron Copland. Renewed 1968. Reprinted by permission of Aaron
  Copland, Copyright Owner, and Boosey & Hawkes, Inc., Sole Licensees.

(sounds an octave higher)

The tune is based on the folk song *Great Granddad:*

A careful comparison reveals that Copland is not merely quoting, however; whereas the folk tune, after a promising start, goes flat in its second half, Copland's tune, using the folk tune as a point of departure, introduces changes (beginning with a simple one-note substitution to fix the weakness of the fourth bar) that keep the tune interesting to the end.

The street scene is in fact a collage of derivatives of actual cowboy tunes. There appears presently a distillation of *Git Along, Little Dogies,* which alternates with phrases of *Great Granddad.* The rough-edged, drunken effect is enhanced by the occasional disagreements among the instruments as to what the right notes of the tune are, and by the hiccoughing grace notes. (This is quite different from Thomson's version of the same tune. For the original cowboy song, see page 392.)

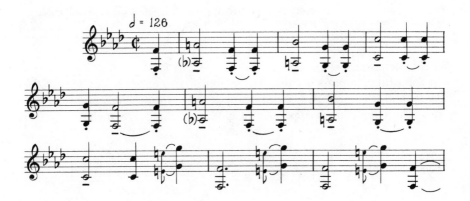

The effect of clumsy tipsiness is further engendered by the incongruous intrusion of a halting waltz rhythm, which so persistently contradicts the basically square duple meter of the simple cowboy tune as to nearly bring the whole musical proceedings to a halt. Duple meter reasserts itself strongly, however, and there appears next *The Old Chisholm Trail,* with the first two lines of the song

becoming

in the orchestra.

Soon there appears an adapted version of the verse of *Good-bye, Old Paint,* and the first two tunes reappear. A raucous version of *Come Wrangle Your Bronco* appears in a giddily lurching 5/8 meter.

This gives way to a long variation on the familiar *Good-bye, Old Paint,* beginning with the chorus portion.

The next section ("at night, under the stars") is a quiet movement based on *Oh, Bury Me Not on the Lone Prairie*. Except for an expressive lengthening of the stressed notes, it is very faithful to the original.[14]

There follows in the suite the music for the gun battle, and then the drunken celebration scene after Billy is captured. In the latter, the garish little tune is made to sound still more tipsy by having its bass sound a half-step too high:

After this extended sequence, the music of the suite omits the escape scene, the music of the love pas de deux in the desert, and the death of Billy at the hands of the posse, and goes directly to the recapitulation of the impressive "open prairie" music.

Billy the Kid is in a sense an American *Petrouchka*, done on an appropriately simpler scale, with the detached artistic stance and even some of the same techniques of the Russian master. Like Stravinsky's masterpiece, it uses indigenous material, often in collage fashion (for crowd scenes), with expressive "distortions," all in neoclassic style. Like *Petrouchka*, Copland's *Billy* (both as ballet and orchestral suite) has become firmly established in the repertory.

Copland followed this up four years later (1942) with another "western" ballet, *Rodeo*, a slighter but attractive work for Agnes De Mille and the Ballet Russe de Monte Carlo. Another masterpiece, the music of which is as well known as that of *Billy the Kid*, is Copland's ballet *Appalachian Spring*, written for Martha Graham in 1944. A pastoral ballet, the focus of which is a newly wedded farm couple in the Pennsylvania hill country, it is not so much a dance-drama as a dance-celebration, of spring, of love, and of life. The one folk tune used by Copland is that of the Shaker song *Simple Gifts*, already quoted in chapter 5 (see page 140); in the ballet score it becomes the subject of a rather elaborate set of variations.

The whole question of what the composer does *with* or *for* folk material is of some interest here. With characteristic but reasoned perverseness, Oscar Wilde once turned around the old saw "Art imitates nature" by declaring that "Nature imitates art," supporting this with the illustration that, for example, no one had ever really *seen* vivid sunsets until Turner began painting them. In other words, the observant, selective eye of the artist is capable of revealing beauties in nature that would escape the notice of the average eye. So it is often with the composer and folk music: His highly selective ear reveals and points up for us (sometimes by making seemingly slight but significant changes) beauty and character in folk music that may have lain fallow, or forever have gone unnoticed by the average ear. This has been the case with both Thomson and Copland, who after Ives were our first major composers to deal successfully with folk music, revealing the beauty inherent in at least a few of its rough gems. Who would have seen, for example, what a little masterpiece was "Simple Gifts" had Copland not made so much of it in his ballet score *Appalachian Spring*? Arthur Berger, another highly literate composer, has written: "It might even be said, with a certain irony, to be sure, that Copland has had more influence on American folk music than it has had on him." [15] This is *almost* the equivalent of the Oscar Wilde dictum. If future observers cannot say that "American folk music has imitated Ives,

Thomson, and Copland," at least their role in bringing it to our attention, and revealing its essence, must be taken into account.

AARON COPLAND (born 1900, Brooklyn) found his way to music from an unpromising background and milieu, knew by the time he was fifteen that he was going to be a composer, and set about plotting his course to this end, though he knew not in the beginning how it would lie. There were no well-worn paths, and for each of our early-day "commandos" (as Virgil Thomson has called those who have now become our elder statesmen) it was a lonely search at first. The comradeships-in-arms of the twenties and thirties were still a few years away.

Copland was led to discover modern music almost instinctively (the conservatism of his first harmony teacher served merely to whet his appetite), and in 1921 went to Paris, the postwar mecca for American artists. Having found out Nadia Boulanger on his own (independently of Virgil Thomson) he stayed three years to study. On his return, he began to establish himself as a composer and to lay plans for leading his colleagues in the battle to gain a hearing for the new American music they were in the process of writing. Copland's Symphony for Organ and Orchestra, which Mlle. Boulanger premiered with the New York Symphony under Walter Damrosch early in 1925, was a beginning. Serge Koussevitzky, newly arrived from Paris to take over the Boston Symphony, was responsible for Copland's writing his *Music for the Theater* for small orchestra (1925), and for the premier performance of his Concerto for Piano and Orchestra (1927). These works show Copland's preoccupation with jazz at that time, as one possible basis for the new American music. (As we have noted, Gershwin's works for orchestra date from the same period, as did John Alden Carpenter's ballet *Skyscrapers*.) After this, Copland (and most other American composers) turned their backs on jazz as a basis for fine-art music—Copland because of what he termed its "limited emotional scope."

The next years saw the production of some of his "difficult" works—difficult for performer and audience alike: the Piano Variations (1930), the *Short Symphony* (1933), and the *Statements for Orchestra* (1935). Although Copland has continued to produce works of this kind, such as the Piano Sonata (1941), the *Piano Fantasy* (1957), and the *Connotations for Orchestra* (1963, for the opening of Lincoln Center in New York City), he began in the mid-thirties to write more accessible works as well, for American music's "new public." To this continuing series of works belong (not surprisingly) those by which Copland is best known to the general public. Beginning with *El Salon Mexico*, first performed in Mexico City in 1937 (Copland has been a leading advocate and practitioner of our musical Good Neighbor Policy), these works include the film scores (already mentioned), the ballets and such works as the play-opera for high school performers *The Second Hurricane* (1937), *Outdoor Overture* (1938, written for the High School of Music and Art of New York City), *A Lincoln Portrait*, for speaker and orchestra (1942), and his opera *The Tender Land* (1954).

Although, like Thomson, Copland has never taken a permanent university appointment, he has been an influential teacher, especially at the summer music establishment at Tanglewood, in western Massachusetts. In the late 1940s he began a career as conductor, mostly of his own compositions. He has lectured widely, and he is a candid, lucid, and perceptive writer. (His books will be found in the reading list for this chapter.)

A Circus and a Ballad in Dance Form

For further exploration of American music for the dance from this period, two other ballet scores are suggested. The first, *The Incredible Flutist*, is by another major American composer, New Englander Walter Piston. Making its appearance in May 1938, after Thomson's *Filling Station* and before Copland's *Billy The Kid*, Piston's *Incredible Flutist* has, by contrast, an Old World village setting, strongly suggestive of Mediterranean Spain, and concerns the visit of a small traveling circus troop with its wonder-working flutist, who transforms the village. An orchestral suite has been drawn from the score, which includes as its hit tune a ravishing tango in quintuple meter.

The second ballet score from the same period is an unusual one based on a popular native ballad. *Frankie and Johnny* was composed by Brooklyn-born Jerome Moross. It is based on jazz, blues, and ragtime idioms, and makes considerable use of folk tunes. An unusual feature is the use of women singers, dressed as Salvation Army workers, who interject portions of the ballad as commentary.

MUSICAL DRAMA

Opera, as sung drama (as opposed to the musical show, which is a play, usually a comedy, with popular songs and dances interjected) has required a long time to take root here. It was for nearly a century virtually an exotic importation. The music, the singers, even the language, were largely foreign until well into our century. Add to this another difficulty—namely, that no other form of music making has carried with it in this country, until fairly recently, such connotations of appealing only to an affluent musical or social elite. It is indeed the most elaborate and expensive of all forms of either music or theater, involving as it does the work of the composer, the dramatist, the poet (who furnishes the sung text), the artists who create the staging and costuming, the orchestra, usually a chorus, and the soloists—who ideally are both acting singers and singing actors. (Another distinction between opera and musical comedy surfaces here: When a choice must be made, opera favors the acting singers, as it must, because of its technical demands on the voice, while musical comedy inclines to singing actors.) Yet with all its problems (which will always remain formidable), its challenges have continued to attract composers, producers, and performers—and now audiences, on a broader basis. For when opera works (and the harmonious dovetailing of all its diverse elements is nothing short of a minor miracle), it works a magic such as no other form of either music or drama can work.

Opera in America is now beginning to lose (except in a very few of its entrenched bastions) its snobbery. It is being tackled, with enthusiasm and a healthy respect for its challenges, in more places than ever before in this country. There are signs that opera, getting back to its basic nature as sung drama, is beginning to develop as an indigenous form. Let us take a brief look at how it got where it is.

Opera, primarily French, became established in New Orleans fairly early, as we can recall from our survey of the life of Louis Moreau Gottschalk. There was an opera house there as early as 1808, and opera became a more or less permanent feature of New Orleans life from that time. (As mentioned earlier, it was the musicians of the opera orchestra who taught many of the early jazz instrumentalists.)

Italian opera was introduced first to New York by Manuel Garcia, who came from London with a small troupe that included his daughter, the famous Mme. Malibran, in 1825. An interesting footnote to the history of American music is the fact that Garcia's most ardent supporter in his enterprise of bringing Italian opera to America, a teacher of Italian language and letters in New York at the time, was none other than Mozart's celebrated librettist, Lorenzo da Ponte. Hounded from one European country to another by scandals and debts, he had finally taken refuge in America in 1805. He was instrumental in arranging for the first American performance of his—and Mozart's—*Don Giovanni* in 1826.

Opera on a regular basis was not established in New York, however, until mid-century. German opera, a relative newcomer, first reached the city during the Civil War; characteristically, its strong points were its orchestra and its chorus. For the next three-quarters of a century, opera audiences there (and on a lesser scale in Philadelphia) had presented to them a European bill-of-fare, with mostly imported singers, in which there was a seesawing of success and popularity back and forth between the Italian and the German repertory. There was generally a separate stable of singers and conductors for each, whole companies being devoted to one or the other. The extent to which opera in these two languages dominated the American scene is illustrated rather interestingly by the fact that the first American performance of Gounod's *Faust* (written in French) was given in German (1863); twenty years later, to open the new Metropolitan Opera House, it was given in Italian! To have given foreign opera in our language would have been, in this time, unthinkable (as it still is in some quarters), although Theodore Thomas did some pioneering in this in the 1880s. That the history of American opera is so often told almost exclusively in terms of singers (who made his or her debut singing what role),[16] is indicative of where the emphasis so long lay. The nineteenth-century cult of the *prima donna* was only equaled later by its symphonic counterpart, the cult of the conductor.

As for American opera, there was *some*—William Henry Fry's *Leonore* was first performed in Philadelphia, in English, in 1845. (In its New York revival in 1858 it had to be given in Italian.) And George Frederick Bristow's *Rip Van Winkle* (the first opera by an American composer on an American subject) was given at Niblo's Garden in 1855. But these early operas contributed nothing to the building of an indigenous opera tradition. The same must be said, unfortunately, of even later attempts, of which there were many prior to 1930. A partial listing of operas by American composers during our years of musical adolescence (the typical story of which was a premier, a few additional performances, and abandonment) would include: *The Pipe of Desire* (Frederick Converse, performed in Boston, 1906, and in New York, 1910); *Mona* (Horatio Parker, 1912); two operas on American Indian subjects, *Natoma* (Victor Herbert, 1911) and *Shanewis* (Charles Wakefield Cadman, 1918); and two fairly late operas that enjoyed more than average success, *The King's Henchmen* (1927) and *Peter Ibbetson* (1931), both by Deems Taylor.

In the modern period of our maturity, opera, like the other musical forms, has begun to flourish. What has contributed to this is not only the appearance of talented and well-equipped composers, and not only the use of more indigenous settings and plots, but even more importantly, a new degree of attention to dramatic values, and to the musical setting of the American language in such a way as to be true to American speech patterns. For opera is, to revert to our opening definition, sung drama. As Virgil Thomson has put it, "Basic opera is nothing more or less than an intoned play." If the musical setting of the language is apt, the otherwise forbidding convention that everything is sung instead of spoken need bother us even less than the convention in Shakespeare that most of the characters speak in iambic pentameter.

Two Important Operatic Landmarks

It was in the mid-1930s that two major landmarks in American opera appeared. These works marked the beginnings of a genuine and indigenous opera, and brought to a close the period of historically noteworthy but derivative essays in American opera. The first of these was the Virgil Thomson–Gertrude Stein collaboration *Four Saints in Three Acts*, first performed in 1934. The other was George Gershwin and Du Bose Heyward's *Porgy and Bess*, which came the next year. Both, interestingly enough, introduced all-black casts, though for different reasons. Each was a work *sui generis*—neither could establish a genre that could be productively explored by others. Yet each represented in its way a breakthrough for American opera. As individual works, they are worlds apart.

Four Saints in Three Acts has been described as a "deeply fanciful work." It is laid in Spain, and its principal characters are Saint Teresa and Saint Ignatius. Yet before going any further, you should be warned against any very literal expectations. A hint of this is provided at the outset, in that there are actually fifteen saints, in four acts, and one of the saints is represented by two singers identically dressed. The text, simply and beautifully set by Thomson so that every word can be heard and understood, often defies understanding in the literal sense. This work resists any sort of "interpretation"—religious, mythical, psychological, or otherwise. Yet it is more than mere playing with words and sounds; it creates its own atmosphere, and given a chance, and a setting in which to work its magic (the memorable sets for the first production were of draped cellophane), it transports us into a saintly world of innocence and bliss.

Porgy and Bess

It is a quite different world that we enter in *Porgy and Bess*. In Charleston, South Carolina, in the early part of this century there was a crippled black beggar named Samuel Smalls who got himself around by means of a cart pulled by a goat, and thus acquired the name of Goat-Sammy. A Charleston writer, Du Bose Heyward, wrote a short novel—his first—based on this character, whom he renamed Porgy. He set the story in Cabbage Row, a large ancient mansion with a courtyard that had become a Negro tenement, rechristening it Catfish Row. By means of his knowledge of his city and its black people, he surrounded Porgy with thoroughly believable characters, and spun a tale of humor, foreboding, violence, brief joy, and desolation. The novel appeared in 1926. George Gershwin read it, liked it, and wrote to the author proposing that they collaborate in making an opera out of it. (Heyward was at the time working with his wife on a play adaptation, which was staged in 1927. The play, in turn, *nearly* became a musical produced by Al Jolson, with music by Jerome Kern.) Gershwin had many commitments at this time; after many delays, there was a period of intensive effort. Gershwin went to Charleston during the winter of 1934, and spent the summer of the same year on one of the Sea Islands off its coast—composing, observing, and absorbing all he could of the atmosphere and the Negro music, with which he felt a great affinity. By August 1935 the opera was completed, and its first performance was in Boston in September of that year, with the New York opening the following month.

For those acquainted only with some of the superb songs of the opera (and who does not know *I Got Plenty o' Nothin'*; *Bess, You Is My Woman Now*; *It Ain't Necessarily So*, and above all, *Summertime?*) the experience of the opera as a whole must come as something of a revelation. *Porgy and Bess* is a full-fledged, full-scale opera, in the realistic tradition. The story has been transformed into a tightly knit tragedy, though not without elements of joy, optimism, and especially (a thing Gershwin insisted upon) humor. The volatile central figure is Bess, around whom the action revolves.

ACT 1, SCENE 1 is laid in Catfish Row on a summer evening. Clara sings a lullaby (*Summertime*) to her baby. A crap game is soon underway. Clara's husband, Jake, leaves the game to sing another kind of song to his infant son ("A woman is a some-time thing"), in which all join. Porgy arrives, and joins the game. Bess arrives with her lover, Crown—a powerful, brutish stevedore. Drunk and doped, he soon breaks up the game he has joined by killing Robbins with his cotton hook. He flees alone, and all doors are shut against Bess except that of the cripple Porgy, with whom she takes refuge. ACT 1, SCENE 2 is a moving scene of mourning for Robbins, in which a collection must be taken up by his widow to bury him ("Gone, gone, gone"; "Overflow, overflow, fill up de saucer till it overflow"; "My man's gone now"; "Oh, we're leavin' for the Promise' Lan'"). ACT 2, SCENE 1 is a tranquil interlude. Porgy and Bess discover a love for each other (Porgy has secretly loved her for some time), Bess gives up her "high-life" habits (disdaining the wares and the propositions of the dope-peddler Sporting Life), and they are happy together. The scene includes Porgy's ebullient *I Got Plenty o' Nothin'*, his warning "Buzzard, keep on flyin' over," and the love duet "Bess, you is my woman now." ACT 2, SCENE 2 shows a lodge picnic on a nearby island, opening with an evocation of African-style drumming and dancing. Sporting Life entertains the crowd with his humorously mocking "It ain't necessarily so. . . . De t'ings dat yo' li'ble to read in de Bible/It ain't necessarily so"—the lyrics of which reveal Ira Gershwin's unmistakeable touch. Bess encounters Crown, ("What you want wid Bess?") who has been hiding there since the murder, and once more unable to resist him, stays on the island with him. In ACT 2, SCENE 3 Bess has returned to Porgy; she is ill and delirious. In an episode of remarkable authenticity (Gershwin, in the company of Heyward, had visited the black churches in and around Charleston, and heard the singing and praying) Robbins's widow, Serena, prays for Bess. When she recovers (Porgy, with his intuitive gifts, knew that she was with Crown) she tells him that she has promised Crown to go away with him soon, but she would really rather stay with Porgy ("I wants to stay here"). At the end of the scene, the hurricane bell sounds ominously. ACT 2, SCENE 4 takes place in Serena's room, where the whole community has gathered for safety and companionship during the violent storm that is raging outside. At the height of the storm, Crown dramatically reappears. He mocks the praying of the assembled blacks, drowning it out with an earthy blues song ("A redheaded woman make a choo-choo jump the track"). The boat of Jake, the fisherman, is sighted upside-down in the river; Clara, his wife, gives her baby to Bess and rushes out in the storm to look for him. Crown, taunting Porgy for his infirmity, goes out to try to save her. In ACT 3, SCENE 1, after the hurricane has subsided, the people of Catfish Row are mourning those who have been lost in the storm. Bess sings Clara's lullaby (*Summertime*) to her baby, for whom she is still caring. It is night. Crown comes back for Bess; Porgy kills him. In ACT 3, SCENE 2 an investigation ensues, and Porgy is taken off to identify Crown's body. Sporting Life deceives Bess into believing that Porgy will not be released for a long time, if ever, and in her distraught state she takes some of the "happy dust" he gives her. He proposes to take her to New York with him ("There's a boat dat's leavin' soon for New York"). She repulses him, but in the interim before the last scene she goes off with him. In ACT 3, SCENE 3, a few days later, Porgy comes home. He has been jailed for contempt for his refusal to look at Crown, on account of his superstitious fear of looking on his victim's face. He has brought presents to Bess, and to the others. He is finally told that she has gone to New York with Sporting Life. In a spirit of undaunted optimism, glad that she is still alive, he sets off to New York after her in his goat-cart ("Oh Lawd, I'm on my way").

Gershwin always insisted that *Porgy and Bess* was a "folk opera." We can by no means be sure what this term means. (Douglas Moore also used it for *The Devil and Daniel Webster*, although neither opera uses folk music.) But it is certain that there are touches of unmistakeable realism in the music. Among these are the complex six-voiced prayer set against a hummed drone with which the storm scene opens and closes (this was inspired by what Gershwin heard while standing outside a Negro church in Hendersonville, South Carolina); almost all of the mourning scene, with its solo and response section ("Gone, gone, gone"), its spiritual-like "Overflow," and Porgy's preacher-like exhortations, with their ejaculatory responses; Serena's prayer for Bess in act 2, scene 3; the fishermen's rowing song ("It takes a long pull to get there") from act 2, scene 1; the African-like drumming at the beginning of the picnic scene; and, an especially authentic touch, the street cries of act 2, scene 3 (those of the Strawberry Woman, the Honey Man, and the Crab Man).

Gershwin used no actual folk tunes in his music, but he did thoroughly immerse himself in the musical ambience of the South Carolina blacks, as we have noted—an ambience he found thoroughly compatible with his own, which is not surprising in view of the fact that the American popular music with which Gershwin grew up was based so largely on Negroid musical style. Du Bose Heyward has described how, on a visit to a meeting of the Gullah blacks, on a remote Sea Island, Gershwin joined wholeheartedly in the "shouting." Of his whole South Carolina experience, Heyward said, "To George it was more like a homecoming than an exploration." Perhaps this accounts for the extraordinary success of this unique opera.

GEORGE GERSHWIN (1898–1937) was, like Aaron Copland, born in Brooklyn. At sixteen he left high school and went to work as a song plugger in Tin Pan Alley, and he soon began writing songs of his own. By 1919 he had produced his first show, and from then until 1932 he wrote the music for at least one show a year that appeared on Broadway, most of the songs of which had words by his brother Ira. In the early thirties he moved to Hollywood and worked on films. Although Gershwin's milieu and language was basically that of popular music (an area in which he functioned instinctively and superbly), he never set limits for himself in this regard, as did Irving Berlin and Jerome Kern, for example. He was ambitious to compose serious music as well; what we have labeled fine-art music he saw as the only musical genre with permanence (in this he was somewhat mistaken, of course). He worked and learned unceasingly, studying counterpoint (as Beethoven and Brahms had continued to do in their mature years), modern harmony, and orchestration. The *Rhapsody in Blue* (1924) was his entry into the field of concert music, though it was hardly envisioned as such initially. He later contributed the Concerto in F for piano and orchestra, the descriptive orchestral piece *An American in Paris*, three *Preludes for Piano*, and a second *Rhapsody*. Much was looked for, in this time, from the cross-fertilization of our popular and fine-art music. Except for a few important pieces (most of them by Gershwin), this exceptation, like our preoccupation with Indian music a generation earlier, never came to much. But it is an indication of the strength of this hope at the time that Gershwin, as we have already noted, had two commissions from Walter Damrosch for the New York Symphony, and he premiered his *Second Rhapsody* under Koussevitzky, with the Boston Symphony. Whether he ever truly succeeded in solving the problems of producing an integrated, longish symphonic work is open to question, but his talent for the theater, his love for the subject, and his genius as a musician enabled him to produce a unique masterpiece in *Porgy and Bess*.

A Thriller, A Pageant, and a Biblical Tale "Southernized"

Three slightly more recent works will be mentioned to further your acquaintance with American opera. It is indicative of where most of the adventurous work in opera has been occurring since before midcentury that all three of these—although they subsequently went to opera houses throughout the country—were first produced at universities. In chronological order these works are *The Medium, The Mother of Us All,* and *Susannah*.

The Medium, with music and text by Gian-Carlo Menotti, was commissioned by the Alice M. Ditson Fund of Columbia University, and first performed there in 1946. That it is gripping and suspenseful theater is demonstrated by its successful run on Broadway the next year, in company with its companion curtain-raiser comedy *The Telephone. The Medium* is a compact thriller in two acts. Baba (also known as Madame Flora), an aging medium, holds faked séances, aided by her daughter Monica and by Toby, a mute boy whom Baba picked up as a destitute gypsy on the streets of Budapest. As the opera progresses, Baba herself falls victim to the very illusions she has peddled for so long to her clients. Demoralized, tortured by fear and uncertainty, she finally, inadvertently, kills Toby.

GIAN-CARLO MENOTTI (born 1911, Milan, Italy) represents a reversal of the characteristic pattern in that he came to America to study, at the age of seventeen, and has lived here mostly ever since. Previous to *The Medium* he wrote two operatic comedies that are still performed (*Amelia Goes to the Ball* and *The Old Maid and the Thief*). After *The Medium* he wrote another thriller, *The Consul,* the tragedy *The Saint of Bleecker Street,* and for television, perhaps his best-known work, the short Christmas opera *Amahl and the Night Visitors*.

The Mother of Us All, with text by Gertrude Stein and music by Virgil Thomson,[17] was also commissioned by the Alice M. Ditson Fund, and produced at Columbia University in 1947. It was the second Stein-Thomson operatic collaboration (after the significant *Four Saints in Three Acts* of the previous decade) and the last; Gertrude Stein, one of the most important women of American letters, died in 1946, before the music of the opera was completed. To quote from the printed score:

> *The Mother of Us All* is a pageant. Its theme is the winning in the United States of political rights for women. Its story is the life and career of Susan B. Anthony (1820–1906). Some of the characters are historical, others

imaginary. They include figures as widely separated in time as John Quincy Adams and Lillian Russell. Through poetical license they are all shown in the opera as personally acquainted or as associated in public life. . . .

Thomson's music is for the most part very consonant, and supports unobtrusively the play of the words and the pageantry of the characters. There are some effective orchestral interludes, and some beautiful hymn-like passages in the last scenes of each of the two acts. The text often plays wittily with the language in the manner so much associated with Gertrude Stein. It even seems a good deal of the time to carry out the notion expressed at one point by the "chorus of the V. I. P.": "It is not necessary to have any meaning." But this is deceptive; the opera's meaning, in terms of the work and character of Susan B. Anthony herself, becomes stronger and clearer as the opera progresses, culminating in the extremely effective Epilogue in which the heroine, appearing as a statue of herself, "ends the opera singing about her long life in semi-darkness to an empty stage."

Susannah, with text and music by Carlisle Floyd, was first performed at Florida State University in 1955. It is a transference of the Apocryphal story of Susannah and the Elders to rural Tennessee. The drama is thus played out in a setting of rural and primitive southern orthodoxy—stern, intolerant, and hypocritical. However exaggerated and (in many cases) unfair a regional picture it may present, there is no question of its matchless potential for dramatic tension. Furthermore, it was a setting in which Floyd (born in Latta, South Carolina) was a native, so that the musical dialect (with touches of fiddle tunes, play-party songs, and hymn tunes) and the speech patterns have the ring of authenticity.

Floyd has written other operas, including an adaptation of *Wuthering Heights*, but none has to date matched the success of *Susannah*.

As these and other contemporary works indicate, there is today the promise of an operatic tradition in America, though as yet this promise has not been fulfilled.[18] A nation of 200 million, which had (in 1961) twenty-six "major" symphony orchestras (each with an annual budget of more than a quarter of a million dollars and many operating on a year-round basis), we had, in the same year, only two full-time professional opera companies. There is no reason why sung drama, well conceived and well performed in the American language, should not eventually take its place as an artistic experience just as available to us as symphony orchestra concerts.

MUSIC WITH POETRY: FOR SOLO VOICE

The solo song, with accompaniment, has been an important form of musical expression since at least as long ago as the Middle Ages, and there is a vast and impressive repertory in many languages, though it has not been cultivated with equal fervor in all eras.

In America the art song, as it is called, has developed parallel to (though not in competition with) our vigorous tradition of popular song. The distinction is not necessarily as much one of *quality* (there are extremely well written popular songs and many mediocre art songs) as of *kind*, and of the level of sophistication on which it operates. The art song is not bound by the conventions that have long dictated to popular song its form, its degree of difficulty, its subject matter, and above all, its *approach* to that subject matter (though the distinctions in this regard have lessened considerably since the advent of the Beatles). Art songs have generally been written with the capabilities of the trained singer in mind; indeed, many if not most have been written for specific singers. The accompaniment is more independent of the vocal line than in the popular song (it does not usually incorporate, or *double*, the voice part); it is more developed musically; and most important, it is fully written out by the composer. In the case of the popular song, only the tune—and *sometimes* the harmony—is traceable to the composer; all the other aspects of a given performance as we hear it, including accompaniment, instrumentation, tempo, and even harmony, are determined by the singer and the arranger. In the art song, the composer is much more specific about every aspect of the song. Finally, the art-song composer usually works with a text that is more sophisticated and developed *as poetry*; often the works of authentic if not always major poets are set to music. Thus American composers have set works of Walt Whitman (one of the most frequently used poets), Sara Teasdale, Vachel Lindsay, Edwin Arlington Robinson, Archibald MacLeish, E. E. Cummings, Emily Dickinson, Tennessee Williams, Mark van Doren, Wallace Stevens, Paul Goodman, and James Agee, as well as such other English-language poets as William Blake (a great favorite), Robert Browning, Rudyard Kipling, and James Joyce. Occasionally a composer has been gifted enough to write successfully his or her own texts, but this is less common than it is in the field of popular music.

American art song may be said to have begun in the colonial period, when some of our earliest composers (chiefly Francis Hopkinson) wrote songs, or "airs," firmly in the English mold. The solo song somewhat languished after this. There was a large output of songs from the mid-nineteenth century on, in either a sentimental or a melodramatic vein, as typified by Henry Russell's *Woodman, Spare That Tree*, or *My Mother's Bible* by the singing Hutchinson family, and such songs of Stephen Foster's non-minstrel output as *Beautiful Dreamer*. The simpler of these songs were intended for home consumption (the parlor piano was, as we have noted, a prominent feature in middle-class homes until replaced by the radio and the phonograph); the more melodramatic productions, such as Russell's *The Ship on Fire,* or *The Maniac,* were the stock in trade of the professional singers and singing groups who toured quite successfully in the latter part of the nineteenth century. Some songs of Ethelbert Nevin (*The Rosary* and *Mighty Lak' a Rose*) and Carrie Jacobs Bond (*A Perfect Day* and *I Love You Truly*) have endured to remind us of this period of our development in song.

At the very end of the nineteenth century and during the first two decades of the twentieth, some songs were written that clearly began to transcend former limitations and to lay the foundations for a mature American art song, even though (like much American music of the time) they showed, in most cases, strong German or French influence. Among these were songs by Edward MacDowell, George Chadwick, Horatio Parker, John Alden Carpenter, Charles Wakefield Cadman, and Charles Griffes. The many songs of Charles Ives are surely very important in any consideration of American art song, but since his work as a whole belongs so clearly in chapter 16, as that of one of our great innovators, it will be taken up all together there.[19]

Three Contemporary Songs

From a wealth of contemporary songs, three are suggested as an introduction. The first is a setting by the composer John Duke of a poem by the American poet Edwin Arlington Robinson (1869–1935).[20] *Richard Cory,* one of Robinson's concise and sometimes cryptic verse portraits, is from his *Children of the Night,* written before the turn of the century. In Duke's setting, as Ruth Friedburg has pointed out,[21] the piano moves (until the climax) in an elegantly tripping rhythm (6/8), expressive of the hero's glitter and grace, while the singer (as narrator) sets forth the tale in a more pedestrian meter (2/4) appropriate to the townspeople.

Richard Cory

Whenever Richard Cory went downtown,
We people on the pavement looked at him:
He was a gentleman from sole to crown,
Clean favored and imperially slim.

And he was always quietly arrayed,
And he was always human when he talked;
But still he fluttered pulses when he said,
    "Good morning,"
And he glittered when he walked.

And he was rich, yes, richer than a king,
And admirably schooled in every grace:
In fine, we thought that he was everything
To make us wish that we were in his place.

So on we worked, and waited for the light,
and went without the meat, and cursed
   the bread;
And Richard Cory, one calm summer night,
Went home and put a bullet through his head.

(An interesting reinterpretation of the *theme* of *Richard Cory*, without using the actual text, is Paul Simon's song of the same title. Done in terms of contemporary pop-rock, its lyrics specify a somewhat conventionalized first-person narrator—"I work in his factory"—in a repeated chorus that blurs the sharp focus of Robinson's poem.) [22]

The second and third songs are settings by Paul Bowles of two *Blue Mountain Ballads* by Tennessee Williams: *Cabin* and *Heavenly Grass*.[23] The first, marked by the composer to be played "like a ballad," is indeed written in a meter and style related to the folk idiom in its simplicity, but showing in every measure the subtleties of harmony and nuance the skilled composer can bring to such material. In this it is a match for the poetry. The comparison of both words and music with a real ballad would be instructive.

Cabin

The cabin was cozy and hollyhocks grew
Bright by the door till his whisper crept through.
The sun on the sill was yellow and warm
Till she lifted the latch for a man or a storm.

Now the cabin falls to the winter wind
And the walls cave in where they kissed and sinned.
And the long white rain sweeps clean the room
Like a white-haired witch with a long straw broom!

The second, except for the telling refrain, is more ambiguous tonally.

Heavenly Grass

My feet took a walk in heavenly grass.
All day while the sky shone clear as glass.
My feet took a walk in heavenly grass,
All night while the lonesome stars rolled past.

Then my feet come down to walk on earth,
And my mother cried when she give me birth.
Now my feet walk far and my feet walk fast,
But they still got an itch for heavenly grass.
But they still got an itch for heavenly grass.

Knoxville: Summer of 1915

Written on a larger scale than songs for voice and piano are those more extended compositions for a single voice and orchestra. The larger canvas demands poems of correspondingly greater length and compass. Because of the greater resources involved and the corresponding rareness of performances, this form is much less frequently used by composers. One outstanding example will suffice here—an American masterpiece that represents a rare coincidence of gifted poet and first-rate composer, each working at his best. This is the hauntingly beautiful *Knoxville: Summer of 1915* by Samuel Barber, on a text by James Agee. The text is a fragment of the prologue to Agee's novel *A Death in the Family*; it consists of the wonder-filled observations, through the eyes of childhood, of an uneventful summer evening. Barber, a composer noted for his lyricism, manages, in one of his greatest scores, to evoke an innocence and nostalgia that perfectly complement the text.

It has become that time of evening when people sit on their porches, rocking gently and talking gently and watching the street and the standing up into their sphere of possession of the trees, of birds' hung havens, hangars. People go by; things go by. A horse, drawing a buggy, breaking his hollow iron music on the asphalt: a loud auto: a quiet auto: people in pairs, not in a hurry, scuffling, switching their weight of aestival body, talking casually, the taste hovering over them of vanilla, strawberry, pasteboard, and starched milk, the image upon them of lovers and horsemen, squared with clowns in hueless amber. A streetcar raising its iron moan; stopping; belling and starting, stertorous; rousing and raising again its iron increasing moan and swimming its gold windows and straw seats on past and past and past, the bleak spark crackling and cursing above it like a small malignant spirit set to dog its tracks; the iron whine rises on rising speed; still risen, faints; halts; the faint stinging bell; rises again; still fainter; fainting, lifting, lifts, faints foregone: forgotten. Now is the night one blue dew.

Now is the night one blue dew, my father has drained, he has coiled the hose.

Low on the length of lawns, a frailing of fire who breathes . . .
parents on porches: rock and rock. From damp strings morning glories hang their ancient faces.

The dry and exalted noise of the locusts from all the air at once enchants my eardrums.

On the rough wet grass of the back yard my father and mother have spread quilts. We all lie there, my mother, my father, my uncle, my aunt, and I too am lying there. . . . They are not talking much, and the talk is quiet, of nothing in particular, of nothing at all in particular, of nothing at all. The stars are wide and alive, they seem each like a smile of great sweetness, and they seem very near. All my people are larger bodies than mine, . . . with voices gentle and meaningless like the voices of sleeping birds. One is an artist, he is living at home. One is a musician, she is living at home. One is my mother who is good to me. One is my father who is good to me. By some chance, here they are, all on this earth; and who shall ever tell the sorrow of being on this earth, lying, on quilts, on the grass, in a summer evening, among the sounds of the night. May God bless my people, my uncle, my aunt, my mother, my good father, oh, remember them kindly in their time of trouble; and in the hour of their taking away.

After a little I am taken in and put to bed. Sleep, soft smiling, draws me unto her; and those receive me, who quietly treat me, as one familiar and well-beloved in that home; but will not, oh, will not, not now, not ever; but will not ever tell me who I am.[24]

After a brief orchestral opening, a gently rocking, singsong-like theme carries the first portion of the text.

The passing of the streetcar becomes a major musical event in this setting, and a descriptive orchestral passage makes much of it. When it is past, the singer calls it forgotten; the orchestra, however, cannot forget it so easily, but mulls over the streetcar theme, ever more faintly, even after the singer has returned to the night that is "one blue dew." Upward-tending figures bring us back to the "rocking" theme once more, as our attention is drawn again to "parents on porches." The "dry and exalted noise of the locusts" is suggested fleetingly, and then there is a change of scene, to the "rough wet grass of the back yard." The woodwinds anticipate a new theme at this point—one based on a simple three-note motive that has a quality of "nothing in particular" and is repeated over and over, becoming the main building block of this section.

This innocent motive, stretched and intensified, carries us to the emotional climax of the work—even as an intensified and purified observation of the simple things around us leads inevitably to a realization of the untellable "sorrow of being on this earth . . . among the sounds of the night."

The benediction "May God bless my people . . ." is accompanied by a return to the music of the opening bars. Finally the rocking theme returns for the third time as the boy is taken in to be put to bed. The boy's unsatisfied quest to find out "who I am" is voiced calmly, in a high, detached *pianissimo*, whereupon the orchestra finishes softly with a final statement of the rocking theme.

SAMUEL BARBER (born 1910, West Chester, Pennsylvania) wrote *Knoxville: Summer of 1915* on a commission from the noted soprano Eleanor Steber (the work's first, and greatest, interpreter) in 1947. Barber has been described, in a phrase of Ned Rorem's as succinct as it is generous, as "an American glory." Indeed, the singing quality of his music (related to an important component of his early background, since his aunt was a noted singer and he himself a good baritone), together with his tendency to use resonant and sensuously pleasing sonorities, which he never allows to become cloying or vulgar, have made him perhaps the most accessible and certainly one of the most-played of American composers. He was trained entirely in America, but went to Rome as a prizewinner (of the American Prix de Rome) at the age of twenty-five. His operas, songs, concertos, symphonies, and chamber music are standard repertory pieces; all give evidence of Barber's superior craftsmanship and elegance.

MUSIC WITH POETRY: FOR CHORUS

As a nation we have grown up with choral singing. The psalm tunes were sung by whites and blacks both; the singing schools early implanted among us a vigorous tradition of part-singing and fostered a native school of choral music that we are only now fully rediscovering and learning to value; the urban singing societies of the nineteenth century saw to it that the major works of the cultivated tradition were heard; the singing of the Fisk Jubilee Singers and similar groups from other black colleges started the choral singing of spirituals among blacks and whites alike, and introduced a new dimension to choral music; and by 1900 we had begun to compose our own large choral works, created mostly by New England organist-choirmaster-composers beginning with Dudley Buck (1839–1909) and including Horatio Parker (see chapter 13), whose *Hora Novissima* (1891–1892) for orchestra, chorus, and soloists has become a standard repertory work, and probably the first American work of its kind to succeed in England, a nation with a great choral tradition.

Two contrasting works are suggested as an introduction to American choral music of the last half-century. The first is *The Peaceable Kingdom* by Randall Thompson, a sequence of choruses for unaccompanied mixed voices on Biblical texts from Isaiah. The title is that of a famous piece of folk art by the American painter and Quaker preacher Edward Hicks (1780–1849), illustrating the millennial text of Isaiah 11: 6–9, which begins, "The wolf also shall dwell with the lamb, and the leopard shall lie down with the kid; and the calf and the young lion and the fatling together; and a little child shall lead them." Thompson's procession of eight choruses (the verses illustrated in the painting are not actually used in the composition it inspired) are settings of text that contrast the prophesies of woe and destruction to the wicked with the beautifully reassuring prophesies of joy to the righteous. The music shows a mastery of choral writing and exhibits a wide range of textures and devices, including the biting dissonance of "their faces shall be as flames," the quiet desolation of "the paper reeds by the brooks," the delicious word-painting of "the trees of the field shall clap their hands," and the exuberant polyphony of "as when one goeth with a pipe to come into the mountains of the Lord."

A more recent significant choral work of sharply contrasting character is a setting by Roger Sessions of Walt Whitman's poem *When Lilacs Last in the Dooryard Bloom'd*. Described as a cantata, for soprano, contralto, baritone, mixed chorus, and orchestra, it was commissioned by the University of California and completed in 1970.[25]

Whitman's poem is a dirge on the death of Lincoln. The cantata is thus partly a comment on the death of public figures (it is inscribed "To the memory of Martin Luther King, Jr., and Robert F. Kennedy"), and more broadly, a commentary on death itself. Sessions, shortening the long poem only by a dozen lines or so, has arranged its sixteen irregular-length stanzas into three parts.[26]

The first four stanzas form a kind of prologue, introducing Whitman's "trinity" of "Lilac blooming perennial and drooping star in the west,/And thought of him I love." It also introduces the symbol of the mourning bird—a symbol Whitman had earlier used so effectively in his *Out of the Cradle Endlessly Rocking*.

The second section describes the procession of the coffin, and the tribute of the poet: the sprig of lilac, the perfume ("sea-winds") for the grave, and the pictures—broad Whitmanesque scenes with people— to adorn the burial-house.

The third section is the bird's carol of death ("dark mother," "strong deliveress"), Whitman's retrospective view of a Civil War battlefield, and a final passing beyond and leave-taking.

As would be expected in a dirge, the colors are basically somber, and the underlying movement, despite occasional rapid coloratura figuration, is slow-paced. A certain repeated "lamenting" rhythmic figure (occurring at the opening and in all sections) is prominent:

Also noteworthy, as a kind of associational word-painting, is the call of the bird (the hermit-thrush):

(*sounding an octave higher*)

Roger Sessions, WHEN LILACS LAST IN THE DOORYARD BLOOMED. © 1974 Merion Music, Inc. Used by permission.

Sessions's musical language in this work, as elsewhere, tends to be complex and dissonant, but it is a complexity and dissonance arrived at with the most purposeful care.

ROGER SESSIONS (born 1896, Brooklyn) was of New England ancestry, graduated from Harvard, and then studied with Horatio Parker at Yale and with Ernest Bloch, with whom he was associated for some years and who was a considerable influence on him in his formative period.

He then spent some years abroad—not, like many of his contemporaries, in Paris, but in Florence, Rome, and Berlin. In this country he has worked hard and consistently on behalf of new music and the American composer. With Copland, Thomson, Harris, and Piston, he belonged to what Thomson has referred to as the "commando unit"—the first wave to storm the citadels of the musical establishment. The Copland-Sessions concerts of new music made history around 1930. Sessions has remained in the vanguard; in 1959 he became one of the directors of the new Electronic Music Center maintained jointly by Princeton and Columbia universities. From 1935 on he has taught in universities—Princeton chiefly, with a sojourn at the University of California at Berkeley. Sessions brings his seriousness of intent and his perfectionism to every activity relating to his art—as composer, as teacher (he has written a comprehensive harmony text, *Harmonic Practice*), and as occasional author (see the reading list for this chapter).

We have in this chapter explored American music written during the "definitive decade" of the 1930s, and some of it before, and a good deal of it after. All of it has had some extramusical association—a film, a story (danced or sung or both), or poetry. These associations have come from sources as old as the Old Testament, but most are American, from the realm of legend or balladry, or the works of American playwrights, authors, and poets. The music itself has often acknowledged in its own way an association with the indigenous—through the quotation of hymns and folk tunes or a reference to the idioms of jazz, ragtime, or country fiddling.

But our composers during the past half-century have also written much music that is just as "recognizably American" (to use Arthur Farwell's prophetic phrase) without tangible extramusical associations. It is to this music that we turn next.

FURTHER READING

General

* CHASE, GILBERT. *America's Music*. 2nd rev. ed. New York: McGraw-Hill Book Co., 1966. Chapters 24, 25, 26, 30.

HOWARD, JOHN TASKER. *Our American Music*. 4th ed. New York: Thomas Y. Crowell Co., 1965. Chapter 12.

LEICHTENTRITT, HUGO. *Serge Koussevitzky, the Boston Symphony Orchestra and the New American Music*. Cambridge: Harvard University Press, 1946.

* Items thus marked are part of the suggested reference library to be available in connection with this book.

REIS, CLAIRE R. *Composers, Conductors, and Critics.* New York, 1955. Reprinted, with new introduction by the author and preface by Aaron Copland, Detroit: Detroit Reprints in Music, 1974.

Important as a source of information about the influential League of Composers; written by the woman who was its director for 25 years.

ROSENFELD, PAUL. *Musical Impressions: Selections from Paul Rosenfeld's Criticism.* Edited and with introduction by Herbert Leibowitz. New York: Hill & Wang, 1969.

A reprinting of some important and flamboyantly written essays by this controversial critic and enthusiastic supporter of our new music.

——. *An Hour with American Music.* Philadelphia: J. B. Lippincott Co., 1929.

——. *Discoveries of a Music Critic.* New York: Harcourt, Brace & Co., 1936.

Works on the Period by Important Composers

All these books are important—written from the vantage point of composers who are also literate and lucid writers.

* COPLAND, AARON. *Our New Music.* New York: McGraw-Hill Book Co., 1941. Revised and enlarged, as *The New Music 1900–1960,* 1968. Paperback, New York: W. W. Norton & Co., 1969.

While this deals with twentieth-century European music as well, there is an important section on "Composers in America," with additions updating it as of 1967.

——. *Copland on Music.* Garden City, N.Y.: Doubleday & Co., 1960.

A collection of essays on various topics; of most interest are the writings of each decade from the twenties through the fifties, with sketches of the then-promising composers of each.

* ——. *Music and Imagination.* Cambridge: Harvard University Press, 1952.

The last two of these six Charles Eliot Norton lectures at Harvard relate to music and the composer in America, and are highly recommended reading.

* SESSIONS, ROGER. *Reflections on the Music Life in the United States.* New York: Merlin Press, 1956.

* THOMSON, VIRGIL. *American Music Since 1910.* New York: Holt, Rinehart & Winston, 1970. Paperback, 1972.

Informative essays on individual composers and on issues; includes, as a final section, sketches of 106 American composers and a list of the major works of each.

——. *Music Reviewed, 1940–1954.* New York: Vintage Books, 1967. Paperback.

A collection of many of Thomson's reviews and articles, on diverse musical subjects, for the *New York Herald Tribune.*

* ——. *The State of Music.* 2nd rev. ed. New York: Random House, 1962. Paperback, 1962.

Originally written in 1939, this penetrating, informative, down-to-earth analysis of the musical scene and its actors is a classic (now brought up to date), and makes good reading for musician and nonmusician alike.

Collections of Essays, Mostly by Composers

BORETZ, BENJAMIN, and CONE, EDWARD T. (eds.). *Perspectives on American Composers.* New York: W. W. Norton & Co., 1971.

* CHASE, GILBERT (ed.). *The American Composer Speaks.* Baton Rouge: Louisiana State University Press, 1966.
  An anthology of writings by composers from 1770 to 1965.

* COWELL, HENRY (ed.). *American Composers on American Music: A Symposium.* Palo Alto, Calif., 1933. Paperback reprint with new introduction, New York: Frederick Ungar Publishing Co., 1962.
  An interesting set of essays in which composers write about each other, and about musical issues, in the early 1930s.

Films

EVANS, MARK. *Soundtrack: The Music of the Movies.* New York: Hopkinson & Blake, 1975.
  Good all-around coverage of the subject by a musician.

LIMBACHER, JAMES L. (comp.). *Film Music: From Violins to Video.* Metuchen, N.J.: Scarecrow Press, 1974.
  A collection of articles on many aspects of film music, and a reference work on film composers and their music.

THOMAS, TONY. *Music for the Movies.* South Brunswick, N.J.: Barnes, 1973.
  Gives attention to individual film composers and their work, including Thomson and Copland.

Opera

DRUMMOND, ANDREW. *American Opera Librettos.* Metuchen, N.J.: Scarecrow Press, 1973.
  A study of the librettos of 40 American operas performed in the period 1948–1971, with copious bibliography.

HAMM, CHARLES. "Opera and the American Composer," in Chase, *The American Composer Speaks.*
  A thought-provoking article placing the blame on American composers themselves for the undeveloped state of American opera, with some suggestions for the future.

Art Song

CARMAN, JUDITH, et al. *Art-Song in the United States: An Annotated Bibliography*. National Association of the Teachers of Singing, 1976.

A monumental bibliography of 1,400 songs, listed by composer, with indexes by "subject," poet, and title. Though the annotations are chiefly of interest to singers (range, degree of difficulty, "mood," "uses," etc.), the mere compilation of such a list, with dates and publishers, makes it a most valuable reference work.

STEVENS, DENIS (ed.). *A History of Song*. New York: W. W. Norton & Co., 1961.

This general work includes a long and fairly comprehensive chapter on American song by Hans Nathan.

UPTON, WILLIAM TREAT. *Art-Song in America: A Study in the Development of American Music*. Boston: Ditson, 1930.

———. *A Supplement to "Art-Song in America," 1930–1938*. Philadelphia: Ditson, 1938.

Works By or About Individual Composers

These are arranged alphabetically by composer.

BRODER, NATHAN. *Samuel Barber*. New York: G. Schirmer, 1954.

BRIGGS, JOHN. *Leonard Bernstein: The Man, His Work and His World*. Cleveland: World Publishing Co., 1961.

GRUEN, JOHN (text), and HEYMAN, KEN (photographs). *The Private World of Leonard Bernstein*. New York: Viking Press, 1968.

EDWARDS, ALLEN. *Flawed Words and Stubborn Sounds: A Conversation with Elliott Carter*. New York: W. W. Norton & Co., 1971.

BERGER, ARTHUR. *Aaron Copland*. New York, 1953. Reprint, Westport, Conn.: Greenwood Press, 1971.

A short but good study, by another literate composer, of the first quarter-century of Copland's active life as a composer; we lack a study of similar quality of the next quarter-century.

ROREM, NED. *The Paris Diary of Ned Rorem*. New York: George Braziller, 1966.

———. *Music and People*. New York: George Braziller, 1968.

Of Rorem's seven books of observation and introspection (nearly one a year beginning in 1966), this sampling conveys the flavor and style.

SCHREIBER, FLORA RHETA, and PERSICHETTI, VINCENT. *William Schuman*. New York: G. Schirmer, 1954.

SESSIONS, ROGER. *The Musical Experience of Composer, Performer, and Listener*. Princeton, N.J.: Princeton University Press, 1950. Paperback, 1971.

A set of six lectures dealing with general questions, not particularly related to the American scene.

––––. *Questions About Music*. Cambridge: Harvard University Press, 1970.

THOMSON, VIRGIL. *Virgil Thomson*. New York: Alfred A. Knopf, 1966.
A stimulating and readable autobiography.

HOOVER, KATHLEEN, and CAGE, JOHN. *Virgil Thomson: His Life and Music*. New York, 1959. Reprint, Freeport, N.Y.: Books for Libraries Press, 1970.

LISTENING

We have finally arrived at an area of American music, in these and succeeding chapters, that is fairly well represented by commercial recordings, as listed in current issues of the Schwann catalogs. Nearly every work examined here in any detail is available (as of this date) in at least one in-print recorded version, some by many more. When this is not the case, or when reference to one certain recording has seemed advisable, this is footnoted in the text. It merely remains here to list some important anthologies, especially in the somewhat elusive field of art-song.

When I Have Sung My Songs: The American Art Song 1900–1940. RAAM: NW-247.

But Yesterday Is Not Today. RAAM: NW-243.

Songs of Samuel Barber and Ned Rorem. RAAM: NW-229.

Songs of Charles Ives, Theodore Chanler, Norman Dello Joio, Irving Fine, and Robert Ward. RAAM: NW-300.

Toward an American Opera. RAAM: NW-241.

The Art Song in America, 2 vols. John Kennedy Hanks, tenor; Ruth Friedburg, pianist. Duke University Press, Durham, N.C.

Songs by American Composers. Eleanor Steber, Mildred Miller, John McCollum, Donald Gramm. Stand Records, Inc., 105 West 55th St., New York, N.Y. 10019. Recording project initiated by the Alice M. Ditson Fund of Columbia University.

PROJECTS

1. Read Irving Lowens's perceptive essay, "American Democracy and American Music (1830–1914)," in his *Music and Musicians in Early America* (see Bibliography, chapter 13). He describes American democracy as having two important components, equalitarianism and libertarianism, and American music as also being comprised of two components, a popular music and a fine-art

music. He sees, furthermore, "a certain correlation between the dominance of the equalitarian urge and the vitality of popular music, and a similar correlation between the dominance of the libertarian urge and the vitality of fine-art music." He declines, however, to comment on whether this correlation exists past the time of World War I. After careful reading and thought, arrive at your own assessment of the situation in America, either between the World Wars or since World War II. Does such a correlation exist, and if so, how it could best be illustrated? If it does not, what factors make it no longer applicable?

2. Write a brief paper on the League of Composers and its periodical, *Modern Music*. Include the principal American composers associated with it, and its work for, and place in, American music. For a start, consult "Conversation with Aaron Copland," in Boretz and Cone, *Perspectives on American Composers*, and also Reis, *Composers, Conductors and Critics*.

3. Aaron Copland, in the above mentioned "Conversation" (and Roger Sessions in his *Reflections*), paid tribute to critic Paul Rosenfeld (1890–1946) as one of the most important and perceptive of the chroniclers and supporters of innovative American music in the 1920s and 1930s. Do a brief paper on Rosenfeld and his writings. (Copland's expressed wish for a reprint of some of Rosenfeld's essays has been fulfilled; see his *Musical Impressions* and *Discoveries of a Music Critic* if his original *An Hour with American Music* is not available. There is also a volume of tributes to Rosenfeld that may be available in some libraries: Mellquist, Jerome, and Lucie Wiese, *Paul Rosenfeld, Voyager in the Arts*. New York: Creative Age Press, 1948.)

4. Interview a composer in your community who has written music for a film or a ballet, concerning the problems peculiar to the medium, and the methods used to solve them.

5. Read a story or a play that has been made into an opera by an American composer, comparing the original with the opera. Note the changes that have been made, and try to account for them in terms of the requirements of opera. (Examples would be Du Bose Heyward's novel *Porgy*, or the play adapted by the author and his wife, vis-à-vis the opera *Porgy and Bess*; Emily Brontë's *Wuthering Heights* vis-à-vis Carlisle Floyd's opera of the same name; or Arthur Miller's play *The Crucible* vis-à-vis the opera of the same name by Robert Ward.)

6. Listen to Samuel Barber's short opera *A Hand of Bridge*. Compare the differing musical characterizations of the four players, whose unspoken thoughts are sung as the game goes on perfunctorily.

7. Douglas Moore's opera *The Ballad of Baby Doe* and Meredith

Willson's musical *The Unsinkable Molly Brown* both have the same setting (Colorado), and both deal with actual historical figures, women who faced the challenges of the mining-camp era of the West. Compare these two works, as a means of pointing out some of the differences—musical, dramatic, and in overall approach—between opera and the musical show.

8. Write a short paper on American poets (or an American poet) whose poems have been set to music by American composers. You could summarize a survey of the field or could concentrate on a single poet and compare settings by various composers. Carman's *Art-Song in the United States: An Annotated Bibliography* would be an invaluable—almost indispensable—help.

9. In past ages composers have not been notably literate, or prone to express themselves in writing, except in letters. This has changed in the twentieth century, and nowhere more noticeably than in the United States. Textbooks aside, Leonard Bernstein, Aaron Copland, Ned Rorem, Roger Sessions, and Virgil Thomson have several books each to their credit, not to mention numerous articles and essays by these and other composers. Read three books by three American composers, and write a brief paper with some such title as "The American Composer as Author."

10. Write a brief paper with the title "American Composers Write About Each Other's Music." In it, for example, you might review in juxtaposition Virgil Thomson's chapter on Aaron Copland in Thompson's *American Music Since 1910* and Copland's chapter on Thomson in Copland's *The New Music 1900–1960;* or John Cage's analysis and assessment of Thomson's music in Hoover and Cage, *Virgil Thomson, His Life and Music* and Thomson's chapter "Cage and the Collage of Noises" in *American Music Since 1910.*

Chapter Fifteen
Music by and
for Itself

MOST COMPOSERS, whatever kind of music they find themselves occupied with most of the time, inevitably feel an urge to write music to be heard alone—music by and for itself. This is true even of those composers who are known to us almost exclusively for the writing they do to a scenario, a libretto, or a poem. Thus we find Gian-Carlo Menotti writing a piano concerto, and Carlisle Floyd a piano sonata. Music independent of literary, pictorial, or dramatic association has its own appeal, both for composers and for listeners, and since America's coming of age musically her composers have indulged anew in the kind of "pure," non-programmatic music-making that was so highly developed in Europe in the eighteenth and early nineteenth centuries. Indeed, a return to the ideals and procedures of classicism was a prominent feature of our art music beginning in the 1920s. Forms such as the sonata, the string quartet, and the symphony have been extensively and assiduously cultivated, along with

428

ballet, opera, and song—often by the same composers. The uncompromising way in which "pure" music was kept "pure" showed itself in the avoidance of even the suggestive titles that romantic and post-romantic composers were wont to attach to their sonatas and symphonies. Around 1910 we could find MacDowell writing a "Keltic" sonata, and Mrs. Beach a "Gaelic" symphony. Not so for most composers after 1920. To them, a symphony or a sonata had, once again, to stand on its own feet, as it were; whatever "meaning" it might have was to be conveyed to the receptive listener by its sounds alone, unaided by even so much as a title. (There is evidence of a swing of the pendulum in the opposite direction now; in the last decade or so, the more avant-garde composers have been returning to programmaticism. This interesting, and perhaps inevitable, movement will be discussed in the last two chapters.)

In this chapter we shall examine some of this music "by and for itself"—the fruits of a mature fine-art tradition.

MUSIC FOR SOLO PIANO

It should perhaps be made clear at the outset that the absence of *extramusical* references has not prevented American composers on occasion from making purely *musical* references to their cultural inheritances and environment, and thus writing music as native in its way as that related to an American play or poem. Indeed, it was by drawing sustenance from indigenous musical idioms that many of our composers sought to develop a "recognizably American" music.

This is illustrated in an interesting way by three sets of short piano pieces by Gershwin, Copland, and Barber. All three sets relate to American popular idioms, and display what amounts to a characteristic (indeed, almost impulsive) American gesture of trying to achieve a reconciliation between our "mass art" and our "elite art." Here we see the gesture coming from both sides. Gershwin, in writing his three Preludes for Piano, is the composer of popular music writing in a short classical form (the independent prelude), which has been in use since Chopin's time, using in an unaffected way the musical language that is natural to him. Copland, on the other hand, in his *Four Piano Blues,* and Barber, in his *Excursions for the Piano,* exhibit the stance of the fine-art composer. Their works consciously *refer* to blues, boogie-woogie, and hoedown music, while maintaining a certain esthetic distance that makes their music rather a sophisticated commentary on these popular forms and idioms. We are conscious of an ingredient of *play* that is absent from folk and popular art.

Gershwin: *Preludes for Piano*

George Gershwin composed five piano Preludes in 1926, to be played by himself as part of a concert (later taken on tour) with the Peruvian singer Marguerite d'Alvarez, who sang Gershwin's songs with the composer himself at the piano. Of the five, three were published the next year [1]—two bright movements, both marked *Allegro ben ritmato e deciso*, flanking a central blues-like *Andante con moto e poco rubato*, the best-known of the three. The first Prelude uses the jazz-Latin rhythm of the Charleston (very close to a speeded-up tango) with variants:

The catchy asymmetry of its rhythms is matched by simultaneous cross-relations in the chords (e.g., A-natural against A-flat), which constitute renditions, in terms of the piano, of the blue notes of the scale.

The second Prelude is a blues with a piano texture akin to that of a Chopin nocturne. The accompaniment of the first and last sections uses a familiar Gershwinesque chromatic undulation, which seems to bespeak the combined influence of Negro and Jewish musical characteristics, expressed here as the continuous vacillation between major and minor.

The third Prelude, "well-rhythmed and decisive," is somewhat closer to Broadway, and might be characterized as up-tempo ragtime—including pianistic "breaks"—interpreted with Gershwin's unique harmonic and melodic sense.

Copland: *Four Piano Blues*

The first of Copland's *Four Piano Blues* [2] (written in 1947) is almost a meditation on the theme of Gershwin's second Prelude. Marked "freely poetic," it is spare music, its blues harmonies transmuted, and its "rubato" immutably fixed in measures of 5/8, 7/8, and 8/8. The second, "soft and languid," dates from 1934. It is sophisticated play, with piquant poly-harmonies (in the first section) against the stylized blues sonorities. The

second section (marked "graceful, flowing") introduces a theme somewhat more French than bluesy, which Copland wittily combines with
the opening material in the last section. The third (1948), marked "muted
and sensuous," is a play of sonorities and lines, its *rubato* and improvisatory nuances again fixed in carefully notated rhythm, as in the opening
bars and in the 7/8 measures. The last of the group is the earliest (1926).
Marked "with bounce," it has an infectious lilt in its syncopation, and its
impulsive stops and starts are carefully calculated.

Barber: *Excursions for the Piano*

On the flyleaf of Samuel Barber's *Excursions for the Piano*,[3] written
in 1945, appears the following note: "These are 'Excursions' in small classical forms into regional American idioms. Their rhythmic characteristics,
as well as their source in folk material and their scoring, reminiscent of
local instruments, are easily recognized."
    They each capture the features of their respective "regional American
idioms" with an unerring ear, yet maintain, in their elegance, an esthetic
distance from their "subjects" that is even greater than in the case of
the Copland pieces. The first is an excursion into the realm of boogie-
woogie in a small rondo form (ABACA, with the returns defined chiefly
in terms of tonality). The second is a slow, restrained blues, in four
variations of the classic twelve-bar form (with some extensions and con-
tractions). The third evokes a cowboy ballad sung to a "guitar" accompaniment, and is a set of twelve variations on a four-bar *ground*, with
interspersed "vamp" sections as prelude/interlude/postlude. (It is actually
quite reminiscent of the *diferencias* of Renaissance Spain, cradle of the
classical guitar and its literature.) The fourth is an excursion into the
realm of the hoedown—a lively evocation of fiddle and banjo figuration.
It is interesting to compare this with Louis Moreau Gottschalk's *The
Banjo*, a similarly polished "translation" of banjo idioms into a piece for
the concert hall a century earlier.

The Piano Sonata

In addition to writing small pieces for piano, American composers
have not been reluctant to essay the large gesture as well—the serious
work of extended proportions that, out of an intense awareness of tradition, is still most often given the name *sonata*. Thus we have piano
sonatas by, among others, Samuel Barber, Ernest Bloch, Elliott Carter,
Aaron Copland, Charles Tomlinson Griffes (although Griffes died in
1920, his piano sonata, one of his last works, belongs to our period of

maturity), Leon Kirchner, Peter Mennin, Roger Sessions, and Virgil Thomson. It is significant that with the exception of Sessions (who has written three) and Thomson (who has written four short ones) these composers have, to date, written only one piano sonata apiece; presumably, having once fought their way through to say what they had to say in this monochromatic and somewhat recalcitrant medium, they have been disinclined to return to it, whereas the composition of a string quartet or a symphony has usually proved to be habit-forming.

THE STRING QUARTET

The string quartet, since Joseph Haydn developed it (and he wrote over sixty of them), acquired in the mature classic period a prestige that it has never since lost. It was Beethoven especially who entrusted some of his most important musical thoughts to the medium, and after him composers almost traditionally lavished great care on their string quartets, if they essayed them at all. With the advent of musical romanticism, with its program music and its penchant for the more varied colors of the orchestra, the string quartet was cultivated only by such European classicists as Johannes Brahms, or by New Englanders such as George Chadwick, Arthur Foote, Charles Martin Loeffler, and Daniel Gregory Mason. The French impressionists Claude Debussy and Maurice Ravel each contributed one unique quartet to the repertory. The string quartet became a major vehicle for modern music when the Hungarian composer Béla Bartók composed his six major quartets between 1908 and 1939, and the Austrian Arnold Schoenberg his four between 1907 and 1936.

The "commando" generation of American composers began anew the cultivation of the string quartet as early as the 1920s, Howard Hanson writing his quartet in 1923, Roy Harris his first two before 1930, and Aaron Copland his *Two Pieces for String Quartet* in 1928. The 1930s saw the production of two quartets by Virgil Thomson, one by Samuel Barber, a third by Roy Harris, two by Walter Piston, one by Roger Sessions, and three by William Schuman. Since then the string quartet has been cultivated, not often, but with particular care, by nearly every important American composer. Of the eldest generation, Wallingford Riegger, Roger Sessions, and Walter Piston continued to write them; of the next-to-eldest, Ross Lee Finney, Elliott Carter, William Schuman, David Diamond, and Leon Kirchner; and of the composers born in the 1920s, Lukas Foss, Peter Mennin, Andrew Imbrie, and Gunther Schuller, among others.

The newcomer to the string quartet might wish to begin his or her acquaintance with its less intensely serious side—through the pleasantly soporific eleven-minute *Lullaby* of George Gershwin (written about 1920, but not performed in its original form until nearly half a century later) or the graceful four-minute waltz that is the second movement of Virgil Thomson's String Quartet No. 2, composed in 1932.[4] The entire four-movement Thomson work is a clear, melodious, and unproblematic neoclassical/romantic quartet, with long arches of singing lines.

Two vigorous and energetic string quartets representative of the period are the String Quartet No. 3 by William Schuman and the String Quartet No. 2 by Peter Mennin. Other string quartets suggested for further exploration are the highly chromatic Second String Quartet by Roger Sessions, the String Quartet No. 5 by Walter Piston, and the Three Variations on a Theme (String Quartet no. 2) by Roy Harris.[5]

CHAMBER MUSIC FOR WINDS

With the advent of the new era in music that began in the 1920s, the wind instruments assumed a more important role in chamber music. This may have been due partly to the influence of French music—the French had cultivated the woodwinds with special care for more than a century, and the new French composers, influenced some of the time by American jazz, were writing music that featured winds.

It is also true that the wind instruments, with their "cooler," more objective sound, their capacity for expressing both the sardonic and the whimsical, and their suitability to the "light touch," accorded well with the musical esthetics of the age and the sounds of the new neoclassicism. This movement rejected the emotional involvement, the dead seriousness, and the complex chromaticism and "expressiveness" of post-romanticism (as exemplified by composers like Gustav Mahler, Richard Strauss, and Arnold Schoenberg) in favor of a more detached stance, tending toward the ironical, and a return to classical and contrapuntal forms and the diatonic scale (without renouncing dissonance). This new stance, and this new sound, relying heavily on wind instruments, was epitomized by Igor Stravinsky's very influential *Octet* for flute, clarinet, two bassoons, two trumpets, and two trombones, written in 1923. Virgil Thomson produced an American neoclassical work (or "neo-baroque," as he has called it) in his *Sonata da Chiesa* of 1926, written and first performed in Paris. Instrumentally it involves a quintet (significantly including only one member of the string family) of seemingly disparate instruments: a viola, a small clarinet in E-flat, a small trumpet in D, a French horn, and a trombone. A "church sonata" that includes not only a chorale and a double fugue, but also a tango, it does indeed, as its composer has said, make "funny noises."

Barber: *Summer Music*

The standard woodwind quintet consists of flute, oboe, clarinet, bassoon, and one brass instrument, the French horn. This combination was first used in Europe at the end of the eighteenth century, but it has really come into its own, with significant repertory being written for it, in the twentieth. American composers in particular have been attracted to it.

Samuel Barber's *Summer Music*, for woodwind quintet,[6] (first performed in 1956) consists of a single uninterrupted movement. It evokes the feeling of summer with an opening marked "Slow and indolent."

The first half of the piece is in the form of an arch, which moves, in contrasting tempos and themes, from the initial "Slow and indolent" through "A little motion," with its languidly graceful theme (p. 4, ca. 40")*

to "Faster," with its rhythmic chords (p. 5, ca. 2')

* For this piece and the Harris *Third Symphony*, where the music is surveyed event by event, page numbers and approximate timings are given for the convenience of the score watcher and the listener.

to "Lively, still faster," with its light, rapid chattering (p. 6, ca. 2' 35")

and then, by reverse progression, back to "Slow and indolent" again. The second half concerns itself mainly with a theme of relaxed gaity, which jogs along pleasantly in a vaguely ragtimey way (p. 12, ca. 6'35")

and which reminds us of Barber's facility for subtle allusion demonstrated in the earlier *Excursions for the Piano*.

There are two more brief suggestions of the slowness and indolence of the opening, and an intense and sweeping interlude marked "Joyous and flowing"; and the work ends with the bassoon toying playfully once more with the little ragtime theme.

Riegger: Concerto for Piano and Woodwind Quintet

A return to the domain of neoclassicism is represented by the austere but impressive Concerto for Piano and Woodwind Quintet by Wallingford Riegger, composed in 1953.[7] The seeming austerity of the work can be attributed to its lean texture, its dissonance (avoiding altogether conso-nant triads and lush sonorities), its wide melodic intervals (the diminished octave is prominent), the rhythmic abruptness of some of the themes, and finally, the wide spacings that often occur between the instruments, emphasizing the disparity of their tone colors (the piccolo, for example, is answered by the bassoon in an imitative passage in the first movement).

It is a piece firm in its musical logic, and of great power. For all of its craggy and forbidding visage on first acquaintance, it is a highly expressive piece once one is familiar with its materials and accepts its premises. It is one of the most original chamber works for winds by any American composer.

The work is in three movements. In the first, the main theme is announced at once by the piano alone; its doubling by the left hand two octaves away gives it a hollow, arresting color.

This fourteen-note theme contains all the twelve tones of the octave, with two duplications. In this regard it resembles the musical materials used in the twelve-tone serial technique, a compositional technique in which the musical pitches must always appear in a prescribed serial order, according to various series that are derived from a prototypical original "row" of tones, which remains the same for an entire composition. This technique was developed by the great Viennese composer and teacher Arnold Schoenberg, who came to this country in 1933, and taught and composed here (mostly in Los Angeles) until his death in 1951. Schoenberg and his method were highly influential, and there developed an American school of twelve-tone composers, which has included among others Riegger, Ross Lee Finney, George Perle, and George Rochberg. Like most of the Americans who use serialism, these composers have adapted it liberally for their own needs. This is true of Riegger's use of his material in the first movement of the Concerto; he develops extensively certain intervals, and certain cell-like groups of notes, which may serve melodically, or become the basis for chords.

This is not the place for a detailed analysis of this movement; suffice it to say that if you can become familiar with the basic theme, you will gradually become aware that this series of notes forms the basis of virtually the entire first movement. It appears right side up, upside down, and in imitation, and fragments of it generate both melody and harmony.

The concerto has its ingratiating moments, such as the duet between the flute and the bassoon that opens the second movement; it reappears in its original form near the end, and with different scoring near the beginning. It shares this movement with a more dynamic and abrupt kind of material, which culminates in a passage in imitative counterpoint—almost a trademark of neoclassicism. The main theme of the first movement is heard near the end.

The last movement is one of great originality and daring, partly because, in accord with the typical American composers' non-doctrinaire approach to matters of this kind, it rejects serial chromaticism and expresses unequivocally a tonal center—in fact, hammers away at it with Beethovenian insistence. But it is also daring in its relentless unfolding of its initial march-like theme, which only gradually gathers strength and momentum from its fragmentary, drum-like opening. Presently winds and piano are answering each other. There follows next a passage that is distinctively American in conception, and written from a precise "metronome sense." The unit of rhythm suddenly becomes the twice-as-fast eighth note, and we have a series of asymmetric measures containing, successively, six, seven, six, four and five of these units. The steady-quarter-note march returns and this time an insistent, singing, diatonic tune appears as a countermelody—similar in feel to the kind one finds in the trio of a good march by Sousa (pp. 34–35, ca. 50").

With these materials the movement sweeps along to a stirring climax, after which the main theme of the first movement returns to conclude the Concerto in a soft, fading-away manner.

WALLINGFORD RIEGGER (1885–1961) was born in Georgia, but moved at an early age to New York City, where he graduated from the Institute of Musical Art. Riegger was a decade or so older than the "commandos" who came into prominence in the 1920s here; he finished his studies in New York and went to Germany in 1907, when Sessions and Thomson were only ten years old. He remained mostly in Berlin, studying and conducting, for the next ten years. When the United States entered World War I, he returned, teaching for a time at conservatories and colleges and finally settling in New York, where he earned his living doing music editing and arranging. His compositions, until 1927, were conservatively romantic, but his *Study in Sonority* of that year, for ten violins or any multiple thereof, was his first work in his new, dissonant, atonal style. He wrote music for dance groups in the 1930s. Recognition for his more serious works did not come until his Third Symphony was performed with great success in 1948. Like the Concerto described here, this symphony combines serial procedures with a sense of tonality. Riegger, like Copland, has his "difficult" works—beginning with the *Study in Sonority* and including *Dichotomy* (1931–1932) for orchestra and his Second String Quartet—and also his more accessible ones, including the popular *Dance Rhythms* (1955) for orchestra and the *Festival Overture* (1960).

THE SYMPHONY

Like the string quartet, the symphony evolved as an important musical form in the eighteenth century, and by the death of Beethoven (1827) had come to represent the ultimate vehicle for the expression of serious musical thought in terms of "absolute," or "pure," music. But Beethoven had already planted the seeds of programmaticism in the field of the symphony; his sixth (subtitled "pastoral") was frankly descriptive of the countryside, and of feelings evoked by the countryside, and the ninth used voices, in a setting of Schiller's "Ode to Joy." The succeeding century proceeded to view the symphony two ways: as a form of absolute music (used as such by Bruckner, Brahms, Dvořák, and Sibelius) and as program music (used as such by Berlioz, Liszt, and Mahler). Early American symphonists, writing between 1850 and 1925—such as George Frederick Bristow, John Knowles Paine, and George Chadwick—mostly adopted the more classical, non-programmatic view of the symphony, though this did not prevent them from sometimes attaching programmatic titles to their works (such as Bristow's *Arcadian* Symphony, and Mrs. Beach's *Gaelic* Symphony). Such freakish anomalies as William Henry Fry's *Santa Claus* Symphony (ca. 1853), complete with sleigh bells and cracking whips, might be embarrassing to acknowledge, were they not typical of our musical adolescence, and did they not add a certain spice to its story.

The new generations of American composers, writing from the 1920s on, regarded the symphony in its classical sense, and the typical American symphony since that time has been a non-programmatic work, generally in several independent movements, and plainly regarded as a vehicle for the composer's most serious musical thoughts. A composer is bound to feel the weight of tradition in calling something a symphony; it is not to be taken lightly. This has not prevented certain American composers from cultivating the form rather extensively. Since the advanced development of our symphony orchestras, and the breakthrough of the 1920s and 1930s as regarding performances of American works by American orchestras, there has developed a corresponding predilection to write music for them.

Not all composers have become writers of symphonies, however. It is generally true that our composers can be divided into symphonists and non-symphonists. Confirmed symphonists are Roy Harris (with fourteen to date), William Schuman (ten to date), David Diamond (nine to date), Walter Piston (eight) and Peter Mennin (eight to date). Those who have become involved only peripherally (two or three at the most, and mostly early works) are Virgil Thomson, Aaron Copland, Elliott Carter, and Samuel Barber.

Harris: Third Symphony

We shall begin our consideration of the American symphony with one of the most remarkable and successful of them, the seventeen-minute Third Symphony by Roy Harris,[8] first performed in 1939. The symphony, rather untypically, is in one continuous movement, though divided rather clearly into sections. These sections Harris has characterized for us in the following outline.

    I. Tragic—low string sonorities
   II. Lyric—strings, horns, woodwinds (p. 14, measure 139, ca. 5′)
  III. Pastoral—woodwinds with a polytonal string background (p. 23, measure 209, ca. 7′)
  IV. Fugue—dramatic
      A. Brass and percussion predominating (p. 57, measure 416, ca. 10′)
      B. Canonic development of materials from Section II constituting background for further development of Fugue (p. 72, measure 505, ca. 12′)
   V. Dramatic—tragic
      A. Restatement of violin theme of Section I: tutti strings in canon with tutti woodwinds against brass and percussion developing rhythmic motif from climax of Section IV (p. 82, measure 567, ca. 13½′)
      B. Coda—development of materials from Sections I and II over pedal tympani (p. 93, measure 634, ca. 14½′)

The symphony is not programmatic in a very literal sense, but it will be noted that Harris has attached to each section a word which has a significance beyond the purely musical. Like Arthur Farwell, who was one of Harris's early teachers, and in a sense his "discoverer," Roy Harris has consistently and consciously sought the expression of human states of mind and even cultural values, especially those belonging to what he calls "the American spirit," according to his credo that the "creative impulse is a desire to capture and communicate feeling."

To become receptive to the unique qualities of this symphony, and indeed of Harris's work as a whole, you would do well to purge your ears of complex sounds and sensitize yourself to the drama inherent in the simple but basic conflict between the major and the minor triad.*

Of this Harris makes much, changing through the movement of one voice (that entrusted with the harmonic "coloring agent," the chord *third*) the inflection of an entire chord

or else sounding successively two versions of an implied chord third in a melodic line.

Sometimes he will allow both coloring agents to sound together momentarily.

* Music examples pages 440, 441, and 442 Copyright 1939 by G. Schirmer, Inc. Used by permission.

Harris has, in fact, developed a theory of light and dark in musical sonority based on the "coloring" of chords and entire scales through these inflections.

Another Harris device, to be seen in the foregoing example, is the juxtaposition of distantly related simple chords, also illustrated in this more extended example near the climactic end of the symphony.

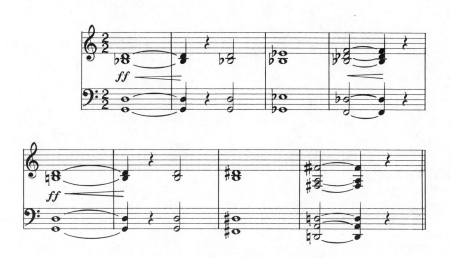

Harris in this work is primarily a harmonist; that is, harmony appears to be a prime motivating element of the music. For the most part the melodies themselves appear to grow out of basic chords, with a few embellishing tones, as can be seen in the opening tune that the cellos play

Con moto

or the melodic idea of the second ("Lyric") section, which assumes a number of forms, but appears first as

or the woodwind solos of the third ("Pastoral") section, sounding over the multi-layered chordal background that Harris labels "polytonal."

Even the energetic fugue subject

has as its skeleton a simple chord, with embellishing subordinate harmonies implying nothing beyond the basic three chords of D major known to every beginning folk guitarist.

The form of the work, according to Harris's own description, is sufficiently clear to allow the listener to follow the unfolding of its essential musical drama, even on first hearing. It has been, and continues to be, widely performed; Virgil Thomson has called it "to this day America's most convincing product in that form."

ROY HARRIS (born 1898, Lincoln County, Oklahoma) belongs to the same generation as Copland, Piston, Sessions, and Thomson—composers who matured in the 1920s and 1930s, and battled for a hearing for the American composer in the same decades. Unlike the others, however, Harris has tended to be a peripatetic "loner," imbued with a sense of his own destiny to express "the American spirit," and like the poet Robert Frost, caught up in his own legend: that of a man close to the soil (for Frost, New England; for Harris, the plains) and able to speak to and of the "common man." Harris, to whom Paul Rosenfeld referred in 1929 as "this awkward, serious young plainsman," was indeed born in a log cabin in Oklahoma on Lincoln's birthday. But he moved to California at the age of five, where his family continued farming in the San Gabriel Valley. In his teens Harris found himself increasingly interested in music, poetry, and philosophy; the conflict between these concerns and values and those implicit in his life as a farm boy was severe. Harris soldiered (during World War I), drifted, went to college for a while, drove a truck. At twenty-four, he decided with finality to become a composer. In Arthur Farwell, then living in Los Angeles, he found a teacher who gave him not only training but unstinted encouragement. Furthermore, Farwell's ideals with regard to the mission of the American composer, and the high seriousness of his art, were similar to those Harris was later to express.

It was Farwell who secured a performance at a Hollywood Bowl concert of Harris's *Andante* for orchestra. This was the beginning of his success; the piece was later played at a summer concert in New York City, and when Harris went east to hear a subsequent performance of it under Howard Hanson in Rochester, New York, it proved to be a decisive move. He spent some time at the MacDowell Colony, and then went to Paris to work with Nadia Boulanger, studying and composing there until 1929. A back injury forced his return, and during his convalescence he wrote his first string quartet, freeing himself of dependence on the keyboard for composing.

In the early thirties, Harris had his works performed by the League of Composers, and Koussevitsky began his long-term commitment to Harris's orchestral works by performing his first symphony (*Symphony 1933*) in Boston in 1934. There has followed a steady stream of symphonies, which by 1976 reached fourteen.

Harris, moving frequently, has held a succession of academic posts, typically occupying the position of composer-in-residence for a few years and then moving on. His output has been large, and while he has written occasionally for ballet and films, and more than occasionally for chorus (mostly folk-based or patriotic music), his most important music is instrumental. The chamber music is mostly early, including three string quartets, the Concerto for Piano, Clarinet, and String Quartet, the Quintet for Piano and Strings, and the Sonata for Violin and Piano. For orchestra, in addition to the symphonies, there are numerous other works as well, with titles such as *Farewell to Pioneers* (1935), *American Creed* (1940), *Ode to Truth* (1941), *Ode to Friendship* (1947), *Memories of a Child's Sunday* (1945), *Kentucky Spring* (1949), *Ode to Consonance* (1957), and *Horn of Plenty* (1967).

Roy Harris, as his writings and his works show, is concerned with the expression of a national spirit, as was his early mentor, Arthur Farwell, and has held that music is only valuable to society when "it is created as an authentic and characteristic culture of and from the people it expresses." He has, not surprisingly, used the poetry of Walt Whitman a great deal. Sometimes, in creating this "authentic and characteristic culture," he uses means that are even more overt, as in the *Folk Song Symphony* (No. 4, 1940); in his basing of the Sixth Symphony (1944) on Lincoln's Gettysburg Address; and in his use of the preamble of the United States Constitution in the Ninth Symphony (1963), "dedicated to the City of Philadelphia as the cradle of American Democracy." In his prose writing, Harris often essays a Whitmanesque sweep.[9]

Harris's work has already been described to a certain extent in discussing the Third Symphony. The essential elements are there that are present in nearly every work: the attention to sonorities, out of which grow melodies that tend to develop themselves in long lines; the often exuberant rhythms (which Harris identifies as being a peculiarly American trait); and the capacity for writing passages that sustain a mood of seriousness and even tragedy (Virgil Thomson has called this a "deeply meditative quality").

Other American Symphonies

For a further acquaintance with the twentieth-century American symphony, four additional works are suggested. The first is an early work, the Symphony no. 2 (*Romantic*) by Howard Hanson. As its subtitle implies, this ever-popular work is warmhearted, large of gesture in the romantic manner, and opulent in harmony and orchestration. Written in 1930, it was a virtual manifesto by its composer, intended in his words to be "lyrical and romantic in temperament," as opposed to what he saw as the tendency towards "cerebral" music.

The next work, chronologically, is another Second Symphony—that of Roger Sessions, dating from 1946. Since the death of Franklin Delano Roosevelt occurred while the work was being composed, it was dedicated to his memory. Two more different symphonies could hardly be found coming from a single country in a single era than the second symphonies of Hanson and Sessions, a fact that demonstrates the breadth of the American tradition—even that tradition which might be designated, with perilous inexactitude, as "mainstream." The Sessions work is dense, complex, and dissonant; it fits the classic notion of "modern music," and the adjectives called up to describe it might well have been applied more than thirty years earlier to Stravinsky's *The Rite of Spring*. Indeed, it bears an odd resemblance at times to that now-familiar but still bewitching dragon of modernity, not in structure or technique, but in the sheer sound-image it creates. It is "modern music" in the good old-fashioned scandal-creating sense—the kind that used to cause riots among audiences in the days when they were less inhibited. Yet this four-movement work has strength, expressiveness, moments of fascinating, beguiling sound, and a "difficult" kind of beauty that is more apt to make its greatest impression in retrospect—after the sounds themselves have died away.

The perennial dichotomy invoked by Hanson (which one can hear debated at almost any period in the history of music) between music of the intellect ("cerebral") and music of the emotions can easily lead us astray if we try to apply it concretely to specific works and composers, since any music worth consideration has both aspects, and the mix is not easy to determine. If Hanson and Harris are taken as representative of the view that music is a matter primarily of the feelings (an oversimplification that does violence to complex artistic truth, as oversimplifications about art invariably do), is it a fair assumption that Roger Sessions, our most respected "difficult" composer, may be taken as representative of the view that music is primarily a matter of the intellect? This is a highly questionable assumption. Listen to Sessions himself, in his comments on his Second Symphony: "My music is always expressive in intent, and often has very concrete associations for me." He goes on to qualify this: "In composing, however, I follow not the associations, but the impulsion of the musical ideas themselves in terms of melody, rhythm, and harmony. . . . The hearer must therefore get from the music whatever it may have for him." [10]

The third listening suggestion, chronologically, is Walter Piston's Symphony no. 6, written in 1955.[11] This work for large orchestra by a master craftsman is noteworthy for its moments of intriguing sound, and the sheer virtuosity required for its performance. The second movement, a scherzo marked *Leggerissimo vivace* ("lively, and as light as possible") is a tour de force.

The final suggestion is William Schuman's Symphony no. 8, commissioned by the New York Philharmonic for its opening season in the Lincoln Center for the Performing Arts, and first performed there in 1962. In the first two of its three movements it is, like the Harris symphony, a work of intense seriousness, with the same penchant for long, singing lines and rich, resonant sonorities (like Harris, Schuman bases much of his harmony on modal coloring, favoring the triad with both major and minor thirds present). The texture is often punctuated by staccato rhythms in the winds and percussion, a trait noted also in Harris. The final movement falls somewhat short of the others, and fails to cohere with anything like their expressive intensity; like all too many fast movements in contemporary American music, it becomes little more than a collage of capriciously shifting colors and nervous, jerky rhythms.

THE CONCERTO

The concerto, as a work for solo instrument (or instruments) and orchestra, takes on a different character from that of the symphony, a character dictated by the presence of the solo performer. It is a dialogue. It also can hardly avoid the function of being to some extent a display piece, very often composed for a specific performer. It was quite usual formerly for the composer to write a concerto for himself as performer. This was the origin of most of the piano concertos of Mozart and Beethoven; in this country MacDowell wrote his piano concertos for himself, and Copland appeared as soloist in his own early piano concerto. But the increasingly rigorous demands of the professions of both composer and concert performer have rendered this practice rare in our time. Many concertos in the twentieth century have their genesis in a commission from a concert artist himself, or on his behalf.

In the 1920s the concerto for piano and orchestra was a natural vehicle for the incorporation of jazz and popular-music idioms into symphonic works, the piano having established itself as a jazz instrument. Gershwin's popular Concerto in F, written in 1925, has become a standard repertory work, and probably the best in this vein. It can form an ideal introduction, for many, to the twentieth-century American concerto. Also employing jazz idioms is the one-movement Concerto for Piano and Orchestra by Aaron Copland, first performed in 1927. A more highly distilled and sophisticated work than the Gershwin, it has not found as firm a place in the repertory. Another concerto for a jazz instrument that employs jazz idioms is the difficult Concerto for Clarinet with Strings, Harp, and Piano that Aaron Copland wrote for Benny Goodman in 1948. Written more than twenty years after the piano concerto, this is

Copland's only other concerto, and something of an anomaly for its time, since the period of substantial concern with symphonic jazz had passed.

After the passage of the "jazz age," American composers turned in the 1930s to the writing of concertos largely in the neoclassic or neo-romantic vein; compact works such as the Concertino for Piano and Orchestra (1937) by Walter Piston and the sonorously romantic Concerto for Violin and Orchestra (1939) by Samuel Barber are typical. An exception to this, and to the generally conservative tendency of the times, was the composition of the large-scale, four-movement Concerto for Violin and Orchestra by Roger Sessions in 1935. This difficult piece of "modern music" was considered unplayable by some violinists at the time—as have been quite a few new concertos when they first appeared. It was not performed with orchestra until 1940. It is actually a very lyrical work, and the unusual instrumentation—no orchestral violins, but a large wind section that includes alto flute, two English horns, a bassett horn (a clarinet pitched between the normal-sized one and the bass clarinet), and a contrabassoon—yields some very interesting and attractive sounds.

Since the "definitive decade" of the 1930s the concerto has continued to be cultivated, and as twentieth-century American music has gained more of a foothold in the concert field, more works, and more extended works, have been written. The classic three-movement form consisting of a fairly expansive and varied movement, moderate to fast in tempo, followed by a slow, expressive movement, and ending with a brilliant, virtuosic, fast movement has been the rule. The concerto, by virtue of its position in the economic and artistic scheme of things (Where does it get played, and by whom?) tends to be the most conservative of musical forms. Professional concert soloists must of necessity confine themselves to a fairly small and highly traditional list of works geared both to the tastes of paying concert audiences and to the number of new works they can learn and add to their own active repertory. The piano concerto, like the piano sonata, has proved to be a one-time venture for most American composers. In chronological order George Gershwin (1925), Walter Piston (1937), William Schuman (1942), Howard Hanson (1948), David Diamond (1949), Roger Sessions (1956), Peter Mennin (1957), Samuel Barber (1961), and Elliott Carter (1966) have each, to date, produced one piano concerto.

The piano and the violin have continued to dominate the concerto field, as they have since the eighteenth century, with the cello a rather distant third but coming up fast. Notable American contributions to the literature for cello and orchestra are concertos by David Diamond (1938), Samuel Barber (1945), Virgil Thomson (1950), and Peter Mennin (1956), and the somewhat unique *A Song of Orpheus* (1961) by William Schuman, an expansion for solo cello and orchestra of a song to a text from Shakespeare's *Henry VIII*.

Concertos for other instruments, such as the viola, flute, clarinet, saxophone, and percussion instruments, are rarer but appear occasionally; Ross Lee Finney's Concerto for Alto Saxophone and Orchestra of Wind Instruments is a noteworthy example.[12] The concerto for multiple soloists harks back to an earlier concept of the concerto—one belonging to the late seventeenth and early eighteenth centuries, known as the baroque period. Such works, partly because they are usually conceived on a smaller scale, and partly to avoid needless complexity and confusion in the sound, usually use a smaller orchestra, often just strings. Samuel Barber's *Capricorn Concerto* (1944) for flute, oboe, trumpet and strings is of this type. The seventeenth-century Italian term *concerto grosso* is sometimes applied to these twentieth-century works.

Still another type is the "concerto for orchestra." A seemingly confusing title, this applies usually to a work that treats the various instruments of the orchestra itself in a soloistic fashion, as typified by the early and compact Concerto for Orchestra (1934) by Walter Piston, and the recent work with the same title by Elliott Carter (1970).

Carter: Double Concerto for Harpsichord and Piano with Two Chamber Orchestras

On September 6, 1961, at a meeting of the Eighth Congress of the International Society for Musicology, in the presence of nearly a thousand musicians and scholars from around the globe, there was performed for the first time Elliott Carter's impressive Double Concerto for Harpsichord and Piano with Two Chamber Orchestras.[13] It was an entirely fitting audience to witness the premiere of this work, which represented the most advanced level of complexity, sophistication, and virtuosity that music still derived and conceived in the evolving line of tradition had yet attained.

The piano and the harpsichord (which it replaced historically) have tone qualities and basic modes of tone production that are usually regarded as incompatible. Carter has enlarged upon this incompatibility, and made it a basic structural feature of the work. The total instrumental forces involved are divided into two small groups of equal size, one associated with each solo instrument, and placed as far away from each other as possible on the stage. A seating plan is given in the score. (The recording, like some sophisticated rock recordings, thus makes very functional and structural use of stereophonic playback capabilities.) As the composer explains in his notes to the recording:

> The harpsichord is associated with an ensemble of flute, horn, trumpet, trombone, viola, contrabass and percussion (largely metallophones and ligniphones) while the piano is joined by an ensemble of oboe, clarinet,

bassoon, horn, violin, cello, and percussion (largely membranophones). In addition to being isolated in space and timbre, the antiphonal groups are partially separated musically by the fact that each emphasizes its own repertory of melodic and harmonic intervals. . . . The motion of the work is from comparative unity with slight character differences to greater and greater diversity of material and character and a return to unity. The form is that of confrontations of diversified action-patterns and a presentation of their mutual interreactions, conflicts and resolutions, their growth and decay over various stretches of time.

The work is in one continuous movement lasting approximately twenty-three minutes, but as the composer has stated, "falls into seven large interconnected sections," which include written-out cadenzas for the soloists. The notated score is extremely detailed and complex, but like much contemporary music, its sound paradoxically resembles sounds achieved through improvisation. As Eric Salzman, who reviewed the premiere for the *New York Times*, wrote, "In a larger sense the entire work is a cadenza."

ELLIOTT CARTER (born New York City, 1908) brings to his art a remarkable breadth of intellectual background. He studied English at Harvard (from which he holds two degrees) and is a student of classical language and culture. (While on the faculty of St. John's College in Annapolis he taught Greek, mathematics, physics, and philosophy in addition to music.) It was not until his later years at Harvard that he turned seriously to music, studying then with Walter Piston, and later in Paris with Nadia Boulanger. He has taught not only at St. John's but at Peabody Conservatory, Columbia University, Queens College, Yale University, and the Juilliard School of Music. Assuming a professional composer's responsibilities to his craft and his colleagues, he has served on the boards of directors of important organizations such as the League of Composers, the International Society for Contemporary Music, and the American Composers' Alliance.

Early in his career (in the 1930s) he was music director of the Ballet Caravan, for which he wrote his first ballet, *Pocahontas*. His ballets, and choral works such as *The Defense of Corinth, The Bridge,* and *Emblems,* belong to the thirties and forties; since that time (shortly after the advent of the Piano Sonata, which was something of a landmark) he has concentrated almost exclusively on the production of chamber and orchestral works with no programmatic or extramusical associations. Important among these is the Double Concerto for Harpsichord and Piano, just discussed. Other works of importance are the Woodwind Quintet (1948), two string quartets (1951 and 1958–1959), *Variations for Orchestra* (1955), a Piano Concerto (1965), and *Concerto for Orchestra* (1970).

Carter's music tends to be complex, but endowed with a clarity that makes it much easier to follow than much modern music. As Virgil

Thomson has written: "His genius is to have combined intellectual elaboration and auditory delight with no loss of intensity to either." [14]

A tour de force such as the Carter Double Concerto brings us into the rarified atmosphere of exploration and innovation in American twentieth-century music. It is this restless, challenging, uncomfortable, sometimes harsh, sometimes quixotic, but nearly always stimulating area of our artistic endeavor that remains to be explored in the two concluding chapters.

FURTHER READING

The fairly extensive reading list for chapter 14 is relevant to this chapter as well.

LISTENING

Here, as in the previous chapter, the works examined in any detail are available in recorded versions listed in the current Schwann catalogs. In addition, the following deserve mention as being especially valuable.

Works Treated in This Chapter

* AARON COPLAND, *Four Piano Blues*. RAAM: NW-277.

* WALTER PISTON, *Symphony no. 6*. RAAM: NW-286.

Works Not Treated in Text but Relevant

* COPLAND, *Piano Sonata and Piano Variations*. RAAM: NW-277.

* DAVID DIAMOND, *Symphony no. 4*. RAAM: NW-258.

* ROSS LEE FINNEY, *Concerto for Alto Saxophone*. RAAM: NW-211.

* ROY HARRIS, *String Quartet no. 2*. RAAM: NW-218.

* LEON KIRCHNER, *Piano Concerto no. 1*. RAAM: NW-286.

* PETER MENNIN, *Symphony no. 7*. RAAM: NW-258.

* *American String Quartets*, vol. 2, 1900–1950. Vox: SVBX-5305.
   This useful three-record collection consists of the following quartets, all relevant to this chapter: Copland, *Two Pieces for String Quartet*; Gersh-

---

* Items thus marked are part of the suggested reference library to be available in connection with this book.

win, *Lullaby*; Hanson, *Quartet in One Movement*; Ives, *Scherzo*; Mennin, *Quartet no. 2*; Piston, *Quartet no. 5*; Schuman, *Quartet no. 3*; Sessions, *Quartet no. 2*; Thomson, *Quartet no. 2*.

PROJECTS

1. Assemble and write program notes for an imaginary ideal program of American concert piano music based on native folk or popular idioms. Music from all eras may be used, with Gottschalk as a likely starting point, but including twentieth-century composers.
2. Become familiar with, and write a brief essay on, an American piano sonata written within the last fifty years.
3. Interview a concert pianist on the subject of American piano sonatas and concertos in the active repertory. Prepare by becoming acquainted with at least three of each. (There are many touring artists, as well as artists-in-residence at colleges and universities. Advance planning, through consulting the offerings of local concert series and contacting the artist's management well ahead of time, will make this go more smoothly and be more productive.)
4. Interview a member of a professional string quartet on the subject of American string quartets in the active repertory. Prepare by becoming acquainted with at least four quartets by different composers. (There are several quartets that tour regularly, and quite a few attached as quartets-in-residence to some of the larger universities and music schools.)
5. Attend a concert that includes the performance of an American symphony. Write a brief essay on any aspect or aspects of it that you wish. Your own observations and impressions are important. As supporting material, you may find it possible (if it is a local orchestra) to interview the conductor with regard to why he or she chose the particular symphony, some of the problems involved in its preparation, and the place of the American symphony (in general) in the active repertory of our symphony orchestras.
6. If there is a symphony orchestra in your community (a college or university orchestra, or amateur community orchestra, or a professional or semiprofessional orchestra), survey the entire season's programs; report on the percentage of American works included, and their type and vintage. You may want to include an interview with the conductor on the subject of programming American music.
7. If you have some musical background, and access to scores as well as recordings, do a brief study of the *fugue* in American music

since 1925. To what extent can its use be regarded as an expression of neoclassicism?

8. If you have some musical background, do a study on the rhythmic characteristics of American fine-art music. You might use as your point of departure relevant portions of the article by Roy Harris quoted in this chapter—"Problems of American Composers," in Chase, *The American Composer Speaks*. Include many examples.

9. Make a brief survey and study of American concert pieces (both concertos and smaller works) for wind or percussion instruments and orchestra.

10. Consulting biographical and other material, and listening to recordings, do a brief essay on an American composer who, due to limitations of space, has had to be omitted from the preceding two chapters or mentioned only briefly. Such composers, in alphabetical order (a list still arbitrarily limited) might include: Ernst Bacon, Marion Bauer, William Bergsma, Paul Creston, Ingolf Dahl, Norman Dello Joio, David Diamond, Irving Fine, Ross Lee Finney, Lukas Foss, Howard Hanson, Alan Hovhaness, Andrew Imbrie, Leon Kirchner, Peter Mennin, Daniel Pinkham, Walter Piston, Quincy Porter, Bernard Rogers, William Schuman, Arthur Shepherd, Elie Siegmeister, Leo Sowerby, William Grant Still, Howard Swanson, Robert Ward.

Chapter Sixteen

Exploration and Experiment: New Ways with Old Tools

"To EXPERIMENT AND TO EXPLORE has never been revolutionary for an American; he is unaffectedly at home in the unregulated and the untried." So wrote Henry and Sidney Cowell in the first chapter of their valuable book on Charles Ives.[1]

We have already encountered this unorthodoxy, this confident "tinkering" spirit in the arts, infused with a strong sense of self-reliance and independence of conventionality, and combined with a pronounced bent for the practical, manifested in the work of William Billings, who said that "every composer should be his own Carver" (and described a practical metronome to help the singers keep time); in the writing of a string quartet, presumably by Benjamin Franklin, with tunings that allow it to be played on the open strings only; and in the invention of shape notes to facilitate learning to read music.

Yet for all their interest as signposts, these were limited ventures; they did not deal with the basic question of what music was, or should be, and they did not extend any musical horizons. Our genuine exploratory and experimental tradition begins with George and Charles Ives, whose work really did push back our horizons, and suggested areas of musical experience that have still not been fully explored.

In these two concluding chapters we shall try to trace this tradition of exploration and experiment from the Iveses, father and son, to the present—a span of nearly a century. The first of these chapters will deal with expanded concepts as they have been applied to the traditional means of writing and making music. Thus "new ways with old tools" refers to music written largely in traditional notation, re-created by musicians playing traditional instruments more or less in the way they were built to be played. The second chapter deals with the new means of synthesizing and manipulating sound that expanding technology has made available, and with more radically different esthetic concepts of the nature and function of music, and of art in general. The work of some practitioners belongs in both, of course: Edgard Varèse and John Cage both began their explorations (in quite different directions) before the advent of electronics, but remained on the scene long enough to utilize new technology in their music making. Harry Partch is well-nigh unclassifiable, but his chronology, his esthetic premises, and his return to monophony and pure intonation all seem to make him go better in this chapter, in spite of his brand-new and beautiful instruments. Otherwise, the main line of demarcation between the chapters should be clear.

CHARLES IVES (1874–1954)

In 1947, when the composer Henry Cowell and his wife, Sidney, were planning their book on Charles Ives, Mrs. Harmony Ives wrote to Sidney Cowell: "How he is going to get Charlie into a book I don't know." Indeed, the multifaceted Charles Ives does defy being put into any sort of book, as he defies being looked at from any single point of view. Every approach to him soon suggests others, and leads one off in many directions—as does listening to his music or reading his *Essays Before a Sonata*. (It is much the same experience one has in reading the essays of his spiritual mentor, Ralph Waldo Emerson.) Perhaps it is nearer the truth to say that every approach leads us around, or *through*, the career or the music to the ideas that animated and infused both. For it is the ideas, when all is said and done, that account for the man's increasing stature today. We go to Ives not so much for a crystallized corpus of well-ordered works as for a pandemonium of ideas, interrelated and prodigally fecund.

It is an interesting and perhaps significant commentary that in a comparatively young culture such as that of America, which has heretofore placed such value on tangible activity and its fruits (including technology), a man whose life was outwardly so uneventful (like that of Henry David Thoreau), and whose importance rests so largely on the ideas and ethical principles that both his career and his music embody, should be emerging as one of our major American heroes—of already legendary proportions. Henry Cowell, who knew him as well as any other musician did, anticipated the current assessment nearly fifty years ago when he wrote: "Ives is independent, and is truly great; both in invention and in spirit he is one of the leading men America has produced." [2]

As impossible as it is to "get Charlie into a book" (or to get anyone into a book, for that matter), we can perhaps give some help to the reader interested in making Ives's acquaintance by organizing our approaches to him along three main lines: first, the life; second, the music, together with the issues and ideas suggested by it; and third, some account of the reception accorded the music over the past half-century, the assessments made of it, and the impact of Ives's music and ideas on our intellectual and cultural life.

The Life and Career

A brief treatment of his life and career is essential, not only for its intrinsic interest, but because of the fact that for all of what appears to us as his modernity (a concept to which he could not have been more indifferent), and for all the freshness and relevance of many of his ideas and his music today, it is nonetheless true that his world was quite a different one from ours, and he cannot be fairly understood without reference to that world. Philosophically and musically, as well as chronologically, his world was that of nineteenth-century America, which can be thought of as lasting into the first two decades of the twentieth century and ending with World War I, a cataclysm that dealt Ives a crushing blow, and indirectly, at least, brought his composing career to a close.

Charles Edward Ives, the older of two boys in his family, was born October 20, 1874, in Danbury, Connecticut, a growing manufacturing town in the southwestern corner of the state. His boyhood in Danbury, where he spent his first nineteen years, was of exceptional significance to his work; he drew upon its impressions throughout the whole of his fairly short creative life.

Pervading nearly all these impressions was the extraordinary figure of his father. George Ives (1845–1894) had an exceptional breadth of interest in, and knowledge of, music for his time and place, a forever curious and inquiring mind, and the spirit of an explorer, especially in musical acoustics. He had been the youngest—and reputedly the best—bandmaster in the Union army during the Civil War.[3] Returning to Danbury, he became virtually the town musician, playing the piano, organ, violin, and cornet, directing the music at the Methodist church, leading the Danbury Band, leading the singing at camp-meetings, organizing and leading chamber music groups, and arranging music for his many and varied ensembles. Yet Danbury, a microcosm of growing industrial America, held these musical activities in very low esteem. Music, except for the most popular, earthy variety (such as country fiddling) was an effeminate pursuit and no fit profession for a man—this was the prevailing attitude in nineteenth-century middle class America. It was the burden of this attitude, with its subtle influences on George Ives's attitudes and behavior, that Charles had to bear all his life.[4] If his father was not exactly a black sheep, he was certainly not considered a very illustrious member of his prominent Danbury family of bankers, businessmen, and fairly substantial property owners.

If his regular musical pursuits were not recognized in the community, there was still less understanding and approval of his really venturesome experiments in music and musical sound, such as the experimentation with musical intervals smaller than the half-steps on the piano (quarter-tones, and smaller) through the tuning of glasses, and even through the invention of a special contraption, strung with twenty-four or more violin strings, built to play scales and tunes in these small intervals; or the tuning of a piano to the actual acoustical partials of a given fundamental; or the attempt to duplicate the complex sound of a church bell on the piano (one of Charles's earliest memories, and a crucial experiment that led to many of the others). There was exploration in the realm of conventional tuning as well—exercises imposed on Charles and other members of the family to "stretch the ears," which included playing or singing a tune in one key and playing the accompaniment in another.[5]

One instance of the simultaneity of musical sounds made a lasting impression on Charles. It has not been established whether this particular effect was deliberately planned or not, but on one occasion two bands, his father's and another, marched past each other in opposite directions around the park in Danbury, each playing a different tune, in a different key, and at a different tempo. The effect produced fascinated both father and son; Charles re-created it years later in an orchestral piece called *Putnam's Camp*. Another experiment carried out by his father dealt with the factors of space and distance as they affected the sounds of music. It is best described in Charles Ives's own recollection:

> The writer remembers hearing, when a boy, the music of a band in which the players were arranged in two or three groups around the town square. The main group in the bandstand at the center usually played the themes, while the others, from the neighboring roofs and verandas, played the

variations, refrains, etc. . . . . The bandmaster told of a man who, living near the variations, insisted that they were the real music and it was more beautiful to hear the hymn come sifting through them than the other way around. Others, walking around the square, were surprised at the different and interesting effects they got as they changed position. . . . The writer remembers, as a deep impression, the echo part from the roofs played by a chorus of violins and voices.[6]

The account would seem to invite us to revise somewhat our opinion of the musical receptiveness and curiosity of at least *some* of Danbury's inhabitants in the 1880s; it seems that there was even some kind of vote taken on the effectiveness of the experiment. Ives made use of the spatial dimension, including the effect of distant sounds (which he justly observes as being quite different in *quality* from sounds produced softly at close range), in his later works. This kind of distance perspective can be heard in his famous orchestral piece *The Unanswered Question*.

The experiments of George Ives are worth treating in some detail for at least two reasons. They show him to have been a man with a lively curiosity and rare ingenuity, and worthy of note in his own right; some of the ideas he tried out in rough form were devices that sophisticated avant-garde composers hit upon three-quarters of a century later. And they also show the kind of stimulation and example Charles was exposed to as a boy. Of all the influences on him, Charles Ives was proudest to acknowledge that of his father. George Ives composed little or no music himself, but, as Henry and Sidney Cowell have written, "it is not too much to say that the son has written his father's music for him."

It should be made clear, however, that there were two complementary sides to Charles Ives's early musical background, and his father showed rare wisdom in insisting on a balance between them. On one hand there was the curiosity, the openmindedness to tinkering and experimentation, of which his father set such a remarkable example. On the other was the solid grounding in musical rudiments that the boy received from his father and from others. He was taught the drums, the violin, the cornet, the piano, and the organ. His father also taught him sight-reading, harmony, and counterpoint. He began early to compose, and at thirteen wrote a piece, *Holiday Quickstep*, that his father's band played.[7] Ives's earliest extant song, found years later in the cellar by his mother, dates from his fourteenth year and is a dirge for the family dog.

The same year he began playing the organ occasionally in church, and at fourteen he got his first permanent job as church organist—a kind of work he did steadily for the next fourteen years in Danbury, New Haven, and New York City. He also gave organ recitals; one at the age of fifteen included the *William Tell Overture*, a Bach toccata, and a Mendelssohn sonata. All this is cited to dispel the notion that Ives was a musical amateur, a dilettante, or some sort of "primitive." Nothing could be more misleading. His innovative and experimental tendencies showed up early (as in his *Variations on "America"* for organ, which he wrote in 1891, with touches of polytonality and plenty of tongue-in-cheek humor), but his father insisted that this sort of thing be supported by an underpinning of solid knowledge and technique. As he told him on one occasion, "Charlie, it will be time enough to write an improper fugue and do it well when you can write a proper fugue and do *that* well."

At twenty Ives entered Yale. His record shows him not to have been a particularly good student, except in music. He studied with the renowned composer Horatio Parker. Parker, a strict taskmaster and academician, is conventionally disparaged as intent on stifling Ives's creative impulses through his insistence on formally "correct" music. Though Ives soon gave up showing Parker his more adventuresome essays, he admired and respected Parker and most of his music, of which Ives later said: "It was seldom trivial."

While at Yale, Ives had an important church job. A sociable and well-liked person, he joined several clubs and wrote music for fraternity shows. He substituted occasionally at the piano in the Hyperion Theater orchestra, and it was with this orchestra that he began to have some of his music tried out. We have already had occasion to note the importance of theater orchestras in American music. Ives liked these small orchestras and the musicians who played in them, and he wrote or rearranged many of his pieces for them.

When Ives graduated from Yale in 1898, he decided, for reasons that will be explored later, to go into business, thus initiating one of the most astounding aspects of his career. For the next twenty years he was to pursue under full steam two careers at once: that of business executive and that of composer. The business he chose was life insurance. It was for him a dynamic and idealistic field. In brief, he threw himself as fully into his chosen business profession as he had into his music; his creative and humane approach (he pioneered in the field of estate planning and the training of insurance agents) made him and his partnership (Ives and Myrick) enormously successful, and when he finally retired in 1930 because of ill health, he could have been many times a millionaire. Instead, in accord with his principles, he took out of the business only enough to provide comfortably but modestly for himself and his family, and to set up a fund for the promulgation of his (and others') music.

The period of two decades between 1898 (when Ives first went into business) and 1918 was one of furious and unrelenting productivity. Ives literally led a double life, giving full attention to the business on weekdays and composing at night, on weekends, and during summer vacation. His output during this time would have been impressive for a full-time composer; considering the conditions under which he worked, it was prodigious. There was a simultaneity in his composing methods that corresponded to the simultaneity in the music itself; he would usually be working on many pieces at once. During the very active five-year period 1911–1916, for instance, he was composing some of his most important songs, the third and fourth violin sonatas, the Second String Quartet, the *Concord* Sonata, the orchestral *Three Places in New England*, the *Second Orchestral Set*, the *Holidays Symphony*, the huge Fourth Symphony, and the gigantically conceived *Universe Symphony* that was never to be finished. Working often at a white heat, he would throw sheets of sketched notes over his shoulder as he finished them, to be gathered up and sorted later. Naturally many works remained in an unfinished or semifinished state. Some sketch sheets (his music manuscript was extremely difficult to decipher) remained still unsorted, piled in drawers in his West Redding barn at his death, some thirty or forty years after they had been written. Ives did make some attempts, between 1910 and 1915, to have some of his music played over; these attempts were mostly disastrous, and left the sensitive composer scarred and embittered—determined to continue writing but with virtually no thought of performance, an action of which only an extremely strong and determined will is capable. But it was not to be for long.

In 1917 came the onset of radical and tragic change. The entry of the United States into the war was a severe blow to Ives. He was unreservedly opposed to war, but once his country was in, he worked in very practical ways (as was characteristic of him) for the war effort—selling bonds (he advocated a new small-denomination bond of $50 so that more people could participate, in accord with his philosophy of involving the masses of common people, whether in art, politics, or business)—and making a gift to the government of two completely equipped ambulances. His increased activity meant the end of composing.

In 1918 his health broke severely. He recovered somewhat in 1919, but never resumed his former prodigious productivity. The short burst of new works that appeared in 1921 represented, with few exceptions, the finishing of works previously underway—mostly songs. Not yet fifty, his career as a composer was over. By 1927 his business career was practically over; he formally retired in 1930. That he was able to live on, vitally interested in new music and in larger human concerns generally, for another quarter of a century, leading a carefully secluded but by no means unhappy existence, is due in large measure to the care and devotion of his wife, Harmony Twichell Ives, whom he had married in 1908.

As early as 1919, sensing and accepting the change in his life, Ives began to make plans for the future of some of his most cherished compositions. He finished the important *Concord* Sonata (which had been composed mostly in 1909 and 1910) and had it published at his own expense. To accompany the sonata, he wrote a prologue, four essays (on Emerson, Hawthorne, the Alcotts, Thoreau), and a lengthy epilogue.

Since these proved too lengthy to be printed with the sonata, they were published separately in 1920, as *Essays Before a Sonata*. The *Essays* are a kind of artistic and philosophical manifesto, and constitute the single most valuable documentation of Ives's thought. The sonata itself was ready for distribution in 1921. Both were sent free of charge to friends and interested parties; there was a time when almost anyone requesting a copy of either from Ives himself would receive them. (John Kirkpatrick, the first and foremost interpreter of the sonata, received his first copy from Ives in this way, having chanced to see a copy of it in Paris.) Shortly afterward, he prepared an addition of *114 Songs*, again published at his own expense and distributed free of charge. The songs, a rich and varied collection, were again accompanied by some of Ives's voluble and brash prose, in a postface.

Ives was far from idle in his long retirement, nor did he withdraw completely from the world of music and musicians. He supported attempts to get his music, and that of other composers of "new music," before the public by subsidizing concerts and by financial support of ventures such as the periodical *New Music*, launched in 1927. He supervised the editing of his own music by other devoted musicians (a task his frail health did not allow him to do himself), and it is due to their intensive and exhausting labors that much of Ives's music has reached the public. These people include Elliott Carter, Henry and Sidney Cowell, Lou Harrison, John Becker, Nicolas Slonimsky, and John Kirkpatrick. Ives was all his life determined to receive no money from his compositions. When some of his works were printed by *New Music* in the 1920s and 1930s, he insisted on paying the costs. He disdained the copyrighting of his music, and exclaimed in connection with the publication of part of his Fourth Symphony, "If anyone wants to copy or reprint these pieces, that's FINE! This music is not to make money but to be known and heard. Why should I interfere with its life by hanging on to some sort of personal legal right in it?" [8] In later years, royalty checks were returned, or given away. When he received the Pulitzer Prize for his Third Symphony (written mostly in 1904, first performed in 1947), he is said to have told the committee, "Prizes are for boys. I'm grown up," and to have given the money away.

The Music

IVES'S RANGE AS REVEALED IN THE SONGS

Ives wrote nearly a hundred and fifty songs, his output spanning his entire creative career. The earliest songs were composed before he left Danbury for Yale, and the latest in 1923. The songs, in addition to comprising a rich repertory in themselves, are an excellent introduction to the music of Ives. Their range is large—musically, from the simple to the complex and dissonant, and textually, over nearly every aspect of human experience. Romantic love (staple fare of the popular song) is the only significant area of experience not represented; possibly Ives's New England reticence accounts for this. The songs resulting from what he did choose to set have the universality that can only come from vivid impressions and feelings. Nine songs, arranged in an approximate order of difficulty and dimension, are suggested as a beginning.

The easy songs show Ives using the simplest of means. *A Christmas Carol* (1897) has an unforgettable charm, and the unexpected rhythms at the ends of the phrases are entirely unconventional. *At the River* (1916), one of four songs based on hymn-tune themes published in the *114* collection, shows Ives's reworking of some of the musical material he likes best. The hymn by Robert Lowry is seen as it passes through the prism of Ives's unique musical imagination; it emerges fractured and colored with unusual harmonies. For a fuller Ivesian treatment, listen to the last movement of the Fourth Violin Sonata; this song was made out of the last portion of it. Ives had a habit of transferring his ideas from one medium to another (all composers do it to a certain extent); thus many of his songs have their counterparts in choral or instrumental works.

Some songs—growing out of, or depicting, some vivid human scene— have a little more of the Ivesian complexity about them. The text for *The Greatest Man* (1921) Ives found, as often happened, in a newspaper. It was a poem by Anne Timoney Collins, which told "in a half boasting and half wistful way" (to quote from the score) of a boy's pride in his father. Ives's setting captures both the spirit and the speech patterns. Like Modest Moussorgsky, he had a gift for musical realism in his songs. *Tom Sails Away* (1917) has a prose text by Ives himself:

> Scenes from my childhood are with me, I'm in the lot behind our house upon the hill, a spring day's sun is setting, Mother with Tom in her arms is coming towards the garden; the lettuce rows are showing green. Thinner grows the smoke o'er the town, stronger comes the breeze from the ridge, 'Tis after six, the whistles have blown. The milk train's gone down the valley. Daddy is coming up the hill from the mill. We run down the lane to meet him. But today! Today Tom sailed away for, for over there, over there, over there! Scenes from my childhood are floating before my eyes.*

The song is set in Ives's more expansive and dissonant "prose" style. One of three war songs in the *114*, it includes a quote from George M. Cohan's *Over There* in the vocal line, while the piano quotes a tune apparently always in the back of Ives's mind when it turned (as it so often did) to thoughts of his country—David Shaw's *The Red White and Blue* ("O Columbia, the Gem of the Ocean").

Some of the songs make a more philosophical comment on the human

* Copyright 1935 Merion Music, Inc. Used by permission.

condition. In *The Cage* (1906) the voice intones Ives's short prose text, again using mostly the noncommittal whole-tone scale, while the piano, in a rhythmically independent part, uses severe sonorities based on the interval of the perfect fourth, to depict the restless pacing of the leopard in the cage.

A leopard went around his cage from one
    side back to the other side; he
    stopped only when the keeper came
    around with meat;
A boy who had been there three hours began
    to wonder, "Is life anything like that?"

Several songs reflect Ives's social idealism. Of these, *West London* (1921), to a sonnet by Matthew Arnold, is one of the most successful, possibly since it has as its basis a concrete scene of vivid realism. Less concrete is the song Ives placed first in the *114*, a startling work, big in conception, which he titled *Majority* or *The Masses* (1914). The text, by Ives, expresses one aspect of his rather complex and sometimes contradictory idealism—a deep faith in democracy.

The Masses! The Masses! The Masses have toiled,
Behold the works of the World!
The Masses are thinking,
Whence comes the thought of the World!
The Masses are singing, are singing, singing,
Whence comes the Art of the World!
The Masses are yearning, are yearning, are yearning.
Whence comes the hope of the world.
The Masses are dreaming, dreaming,

The Masses are dreaming,
Whence come the visions of God!
God's in His Heaven,
All will be well with the World! *

Ives himself noted on the music, "Preferably for unison chorus; it is almost impossible for a single voice to hold the part against the score." *Majority* is a thesaurus of Ives's harmonic vocabulary; in addition to a few plain triads it uses extended chords built in thirds, fourths, and fifths, and also—possibly with programmatic connotations—appropriately massive, all-embracing tone "clusters" (chords built in seconds), two octaves in extent, combinations which strike not only the ear but the eye:

Two verses were omitted from the version in the *114*; to one of these verses, Ives wrote music in 1914 that anticipated the twelve-tone row technique later developed by the Viennese composer Arnold Schoenberg.[9]

It is possible that many of the recipients of the *114 Songs* were put off, or at least puzzled, by this opening song, with its strident dissonances. (The album was the butt of many contemporary jokes.) The fact is that Ives, for perhaps a variety of reasons, felt very strongly about the use of dissonance. It was, in a way, an indication for him of *manliness* in music. He complained vociferously about the "sissies, that couldn't stand up and take the full force of dissonance like a man." Ives was, by all accounts, a master of the art of cussing, but the most damning adjective in his vocabulary was "nice." Recalling his boyhood, and the traumatic conflict between his natural bent for music (a form of activity dominated by "nice ladies") and his love of sports and natural honest regard for his peers (among whom music was a "sissy" thing to be spending one's time on), we can begin to understand *one* of the possible sources of Ives's whole set of attitudes on the emasculation of art. (Ives was not the only American artist to suffer from this conflict and the consequent obsessive need to assert "manliness"; among others may be mentioned Roy Harris and Ernest Hemingway.)

But Ives was far from being a simple man, and dissonance had other shades of meaning for him as well. For one thing, he felt the need to use whatever suited the expressive purpose at hand, which might in one instance be a crashing chord with ten or twelve different pitches in it, and in another an uncomplicated C major triad. There is also a sense for Ives in which dissonance, if used in the service of an art that emphasizes "substance" rather than "manner" (a favorite Ivesian polarity), can be virtuous. In his *Essays Before a Sonata* he wrote, "Beauty in music is too often confused with something that lets the ears lie back in an easy chair." Ives was always contemptuous of any "easy way." He continued the essay:

> Many sounds that we are used to do not bother us, and for that reason we are inclined to call them beautiful. Frequently—possibly almost invariably —analytical and impersonal tests will show, we believe, that when a new or unfamiliar work is accepted as beautiful on its first hearing, its fundamental quality is one that tends to put the mind to sleep. A narcotic is not always unnecessary, but it is seldom a basis of progress—that is, wholesome evolution in any creative experience.[10]

Earlier in the *Essays* his lack of regard for what is merely superficially or conventionally appealing in music provoked him to an even more vehement and epigrammatic outburst: "My God! What has sound got to do with music!" Here we catch a glimpse of Ives the Transcendentalist.

A brief survey cannot hope to touch on all the kinds of songs we find in Ives. We shall suggest here only one more type: the longer narrative songs, which have their roots in the vernacular. There are two of these that are noteworthy, and they are among his best songs. *Charlie Rutlage* (1920 or 1921) is a cowboy ballad. The text appeared in John Lomax's *Cowboy Songs Without Music*, printed at first as anonymous folk poetry but later attributed to D. J. "Kid" O'Malley. Ives takes as his point of departure for the first and last verses a popular ballad style, which he transmutes with a few characteristic touches (such as the rhythmic displacements in the second line of each of the stanzas, and the word repetitions on "the golden gate," "in eternity," and "the shining throne"). In the middle three stanzas, the narrative itself, he reverts to melodrama; behind the recitation of the singer, the piano works up bits and pieces of *The Old Chisholm Trail*, and other cowboy tunes, to a frenzied climax on the words "fell with him." This is followed by a memorably apt setting of "beneath, poor Charlie died" as a retransition to the final stanza, with its pointing up of the colloquial accentuation: "His *ree*lations in Texas." The whole is one of the gems of American song.

Another good cow-puncher has gone to meet his fate,
I hope he'll find a resting place within the golden gate.
Another place is vacant on the ranch of the X I T,
'Twill be hard to find another that's liked as well as he.

The first that died was Kid White, a man both tough and brave,
While Charlie Rutlage makes the third to be sent to his grave,
Caused by a cow-horse falling while running after stock;
'Twas on the spring round-up—a place where death men mock.

He went forward one morning on a circle through the hills,
He was gay and full of glee, and free from earthly ills;
But when it came to finish up the work on which he went,
Nothing came back from him; for his time on earth was spent.

'Twas as he rode the round-up, an X I T turned back to the herd;
Poor Charlie shoved him in again, his cutting horse he spurred;
Another turned; at that moment his horse the creature spied
And turned and fell with him, and, beneath, poor Charlie died.

His relations in Texas his face nevermore will see,
But I hope he will meet his loved ones beyond in eternity.
I hope he will meet his parents, will meet them face to face,
And that they will grasp him by the right hand at the shining
      throne of grace.

General William Booth Enters Into Heaven (1914) is perhaps Ives's
best known song, and justly so. The text is a portion of Vachel Lindsay's
poem (minus six lines) that Ives saw in a review. The drama and imagery
of the imaginary scene put into play all of Ives's powers of musical
characterization. Lindsay evidently conceived the poem to be sung with
instruments—a bass drum in one spot, banjos in another, and in another
"sweet flute music." His opening alliteration, "Booth led boldly with his
big bass drum," furnishes Ives with a motive that begins the piece

and also frames it; the ending is a faint dying away of the drumbeats in the distance. (One cannot help remembering here that Ives as a boy had played the drum parts in his father's band on the piano during their practices.) Vachel Lindsay had suggested *The Blood of the Lamb* as a tune to which the poem could be sung, but Ives chose instead a tune called *Fountain* ("There is a fountain filled with blood"), by Lowell Mason (see chapter 13), whose hymn tunes he recalled so frequently in his music.

The tune is overtly present only at the very end, the verse being quoted fully over the resumed bass drumbeat beginning with the words "marched on spotless," as Lindsay's phrases are made to overlap those of Mason's tune. Prior to this, the hymn tune is a kind of shadowy presence—Ives's settings of "Are you washed in the blood of the Lamb?" are based on a derivative of the tune, which is also present, unobtrusively, in the piano left hand under the words "Jesus came from the courthouse door." Other touches of text painting are evident: the "banging banjo" tune, the trumpets, the memorable treatment of "round and round and round and round." The nearest that Ives comes to negating a tonal center is in the section beginning "Ev'ry slum had sent its half-a-score"; here he uses polychords in the piano,

and as often happens in this type of context, a whole-tone scale for the voice (cf. *The Cage*). *General William Booth* is a vivid musical drama in miniature on the theme of salvation as is Schubert's *The Erl King* on the theme of death.

> Booth led boldly with his big bass drum
> (Are you washed in the blood of the Lamb?
> Are you washed in the blood of the lamb? of the Lamb?)
> Hallelujah
> Saints smiled gravely and they said "He's come."
> (Washed in the blood of the Lamb? The blood of the Lamb?)

Walking lepers followed rank on rank,
Lurching bravoes from the ditches dank.
Drabs from the alleyways and drug fiends pale—
Minds still passion-ridden, soul powers frail:—
Vermin-eaten saints with mouldy breath,
Unwashed legions with the ways of Death
(Are you washed in the blood of the Lamb?
Are you washed in the blood of the Lamb?)

Ev'ry slum had sent its half-a-score
The round world over. (Booth had groaned for more).
Ev'ry banner that the wide world flies,
Bloomed with glory and transcendent dyes.
Big-voiced lassies made their banjos bang, bang, bang,
    made their banjos,—
Tranced, fanatical, they shrieked and sang—They
    shrieked and sang: "Are you?
Are you washed in the blood?
In the blood of the Lamb?—of the Lamb? Hallelujah!
Hallelujah, Hallelujah, Lord, Hallelujah, Lord, Hallelujah!"
It was queer to see
Bull-necked convicts, bull-necked convicts with that land make free.
Loons with trumpets blowed a blare,
On, on, upward thro' the golden air!
(Are you washed in the blood, in the blood of the Lamb,
in the blood of the Lamb, the Lamb, of the Lamb, the Lamb?) . . .

Jesus came from the courthouse door,
Stretched his hands above the passing poor.
Booth saw not, but led his queer ones,
Round and round, round and round and round and
    round and round and round and round and round—
Yet! in an instant all that blear review
Marched on, marched on marched on marched on marched
    on marched on marched on spotless, clad in raiment new.
The lame were straightened, withered limbs uncurled
And blind eyes opened on a new sweet world.
Are you washed in the blood of the Lamb?
Are you washed in the blood of the Lamb?

IVES AND PROGRAMMATICISM

That Ives was fundamentally a composer of program music can hardly
be questioned; even his "pure" music—his sonatas and his symphonies—
at least has (except for the very early music) programmatic titles, and in
many cases the references go further than that. Much of his music bristles

with quotations, tunes that are either familiar or are unfamiliar with a familiar ring to them, and in most cases one is aware of a deliberate reference intended. One can hear Ives concurring with Emerson: "Borrowing can come of magnanimity and stoutness.... You do not quote, but recognize your own."

Perhaps it is Ives's nearly constant reference to a larger framework that at least partly accounts for his increased appeal today. Ives is coming into his own at a time when we are witnessing a resurgence of program music—music which, even if only by virtue of a title (and it can hardly be denied that an engaging title is an important attribute of a composition in the 1960s and 1970s) invokes something outside itself. The quotation, in advanced jazz as well as in concert music, is a frequent mannerism; and the montage, with its implicit capacity for commentary, is as frequently used in music as it is in art. All this Ives was doing more than fifty years ago.

If Ives is a programmatic composer he is also an impressionist, and the impressions he works his pieces out from are always vivid and keenly felt. *The Housatonic at Stockbridge* is an excellent place to start with in examining Ives the impressionist. Written before 1911, it forms the last movement of his *First Orchestral Set*, called more familiarly *Three Places in New England*. Ives's own account of what suggested the piece gives us a point of departure; rarely is he so explicit about the genesis of a work.

> The last movement, *The Housatonic at Stockbridge*, was suggested by a Sunday morning walk that Mrs. Ives and I took near Stockbridge the summer after we were married. We walked in the meadows along the River and heard the distant singing from the Church across the River. The mist had not entirely left the river bed, and the colors, the running water, the banks and trees were something that one would always remember.[11]

Yet with Ives nothing is ever simple, and as sufficient as the above might seem to be in accounting for this short and lovely piece, there is another influence at work as well—a poem (from the title of which Ives took the title of the piece) by Robert Underwood Johnson, which begins "Contented river! in thy dreamy realm....", personifies the river as having "grown human laboring with men"; and ends with the poet's restless determination to accompany the river "by fall and shallow to the adventurous sea." It is this final call to movement and action in the poem rather than the passive impression of the Sunday morning walk that better explains the accelerating, eddying turbulence of the last section of the piece—turbulence that subsides with utter suddenness, leaving a soft string sound and one of Ives's inconclusive, questioning subdominant endings. At least ten years after the composition of the orchestra piece Ives made a song out of it, incorporating selections from

Johnson's text. The vocal line, with its fragment of Heinrich Zeuner's
Missionary Chant (presumably the distant singing from the church to
which Ives referred), can be traced note for note in the orchestral version,
mostly in the French and English horns, until it finally becomes lost in
the complex texture of the ending rush to the sea.

The first two movements of *Three Places in New England* show
Ives's impressionability to scenes from American history. *The "St.
Gaudens" in Boston Common* (ca. 1911), subtitled *Col. Shaw and His
Colored Regiment*, evokes the Civil War. Again there is a double refer-
ence; the Negro regiment of Col. Robert Gould Shaw that fought in the
Civil War was memorialized in the bronze relief by Augustus Saint-
Gaudens, unveiled in Boston Common in 1897. Ives's piece, a ghostly
sort of march, evokes the marching regiment as the sculptor caught it.
There are impressionistic echoes of the songs from the era, such as
Stephen Foster's *Old Black Joe* and Henry Work's *Marching Through
Georgia*. The piece furnishes an interesting example of the way Ives dis-
tills the essence of his tunes and allows their motives to suffuse his works.
The interval of a minor third is important throughout *The St. Gaudens*;
it is presented at once in the flute and piano.

This same minor third is common to the choruses of both songs—a kind of
hidden link. (*Old Black Joe* is shown below followed by *Marching
Through Georgia*.)

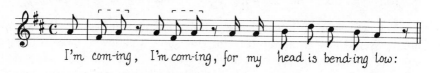

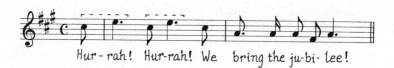

The associational process is so subtle as to appear almost subconscious.

Putnam's Camp, Redding, Connecticut (ca. 1912), the second of the
Three Places in New England, harks back to the Revolution, and the tunes

used are *The British Grenadiers,* a snatch of *Yankee Doodle,* and a march tune Ives had used in his rollicking *Country Band March* nearly ten years earlier. (The same tune appears in the *Hawthorne* movement of the *Concord* Sonata and the second movement of the Fourth Symphony.)

Ives's rather elaborate program depicts a child wandering away from a Fourth of July picnic at the site of the Revolutionary War encampment, falling asleep, and seeing the old soldiers marching out of camp with fife and drum, with Major General Israel Putnam himself coming over the hill. Ives's use of two different march tempos simultaneously will be discussed a little later.

A longer set of compositions, finished about the same time, further illustrates Ives's programmaticism. This is the symphony labeled *Four New England Holidays.* It consists of four movements, which may be played as separate pieces. In addition to treating specific holidays, there are references to the four seasons; each begins with an impressionistic evocation of its season and then proceeds to the celebration. Ives has described the pieces as "attempts to make pictures in music of common events in the lives of common people (that is, of fine people), mostly of the rural communities." Of the four movements—*Washington's Birthday* (winter), *Decoration Day* (spring), *The Fourth of July* (summer), and *Thanksgiving* (autumn)—we shall take a closer look at the third.

For *The Fourth of July* (summer), we have Ives's own description:

It's a boy's '4th. . . . His festivities start in the quiet of midnight before, and grow raucous with the sun. Everybody knows what it's like—if everybody doesn't—Cannon on the Green, Village Band on Main Street, fire crackers, shanks mixed on cornets, strings around big toes, torpedoes, Church bells, lost finger, fifes, clam-chowder, a prize-fight, drum-corps, burnt shins, parades (in and out of step), saloons all closed (more drunks than usual), baseball game (Danbury All-Stars vs Beaver Brook Boys), pistols, mobbed umpire, Red, White and Blue, runaway horse,—and the day ends with the sky-rocket over the Church-steeple, just after the an-

nual explosion sets the Town-Hall on fire. All this is not in the music,—
not now.[12]

The multitude of impressions, seemingly random, crowding each other,
superimposing themselves—all this is startlingly parallel to Ives's musical
composition. Everywhere he looks there is something to record; he cannot get it all down. "All this is not in the music,—not now."

But what *is* in the music is a good deal. There is the quiet opening
in which the violins and string basses begin *Columbia, the Gem of the
Ocean,* a great favorite of Ives's and the tune that is to be the mainstay
of the movement. There is a gradual gain of momentum, as bits and
pieces of a dozen other tunes are heard; there is an explosion of fireworks;
the band finally comes on with a great tumultuous rendition of the main
theme, wrong notes, missed beats and all; there is a final explosion—and
again quietness. The sound of the band in full swing in this movement
is one of the most vividly realized moments in all of Ives's music: The
tunes (*Columbia, the Gem of the Ocean, The Battle Hymn of the
Republic,* and *Yankee Doodle,* all at once), recklessly off key, are heard
through the buzz and roar of the crowd noises. Ives has built up a musical
equivalent of the scene he has seen and felt so vividly. A look at the
score conveys the same sense of exuberant detail (especially in the explosion) that one hears in the sounds. Originally thought possibly unplayable, even by Ives himself, these are some of his grandest and most
successful pages.

SIMULTANEITY AND PERSPECTIVE

You will encounter many manifestations of simultaneity in Ives's
music. His impressionistic bent—his fidelity to his model, which was life
itself as experienced—led him to try to render the sense of two or more
things going on at the same time. Though his works are full of this, one
famous example will suffice by way of illustration. In *Putnam's Camp*
(the second of *Three Places in New England*) we hear one march beat
established, and presently another—in a different tempo, marked "as a
distant drum beat"—is heard superimposed. The rhythms are:

There are many examples of even more complex simultaneous meters in Ives's music, but this one is particularly clear, and has a direct relationship to the boyhood experience described earlier of hearing the two bands marching around the park. Such a representation in music was not entirely without precedent; Mozart, the superb dramatist (whom Ives, partaking of the prevalent contemporary misunderstanding, grossly underestimated), had put three dance orchestras on the stage in *Don Giovanni*, each playing a different dance in a different tempo. Mozart's orchestras harmonize, however; Ives was after a more clashing effect.

The concept of *perspective* finds its way into Ives's work as well—a sense of relative nearness and distance. His father had studied the difference in *quality* between a sound and its echo, and between a distant sound and a sound played softly at close range. Ives himself wrote: "As the distant hills, in a landscape, row upon row, grow gradually into the horizon, so there may be something corresponding to this in the presentation of music." This spatial sense can be heard in two works, both of which have philosophical connotations.

Some time before June 1908 Ives composed a short work he called *The Unanswered Question, A Cosmic Landscape*. It has become one of his most famous pieces. As Cowell describes it:

> The orchestra is divided, the strings playing very softly throughout offstage, representing the silence of the seers who, even if they have an answer, cannot reply; the wind group, on stage, is dominated by the trumpet, which asks the Perennial Question of Existence over and over in the same way, while "the Fighting Answerers (flutes and other people)" run about trying in vain to discover the invisible, unattainable reply to the trumpet. When they finally surrender the search they mock the trumpet's reiteration and depart. The Question is then asked again, for the last time, and the "silence" sounds from a distance undisturbed.[13]

The piece, as usually performed, requires two conductors; the sense of perspective is enhanced if the strings play offstage, or behind a curtain.

Not all the explorations of Ives's inventive and far-ranging musical mind can be traced here—his work with the twelve tones of the chromatic scale used in series, for example, and his work with quarter-tones, represented by three pieces for two pianos (tuned a quarter-tone apart) that he has left us. In much of his work he anticipated the work of later major innovators, a fact that never seemed to interest him greatly. "That's not my fault," was his reply on one occasion, when this was pointed out to him. He *was* adamant, however, about clarifying the fact that he had not gotten his experimental ideas from any of the European composers of the time.

IVES'S HUMOR

There are few composers with as demonstrably keen a sense of humor as Ives. It is obvious from his writings (in which the heated intensity and occasional acidity are nearly always counterbalanced by some remark of humorous detachment), from the marginal notes penned in his scores (mostly to "Rollo," his name for the unimaginative musician or listener who has to have everything according to the rules, and to what he is familiar with), and from the accounts of all those who knew him in life. The important thing to consider here is that it shows up in his music as well. It may show itself in just a sudden gesture, as in his thumbing-the-nose ending of the Second Symphony with a loud dissonance. It may appear in the crafting of an entire fantasy-comedy piece, such as the *Hawthorne* movement in the *Concord* Sonata or the vastly complex second movement of the Fourth Symphony, which is related to it—a piece of Falstaffian proportions in which he uses once again part of the *Country Band March* he wrote years before. Many of the short pieces he called *Cartoons* or *Take-offs* show a keen sense of humor.

The songs show several aspects of Ives's humor. He can use epigrammatical and witty texts, as in *Ann Street*, or a song to words he wrote himself, called *1, 2, 3*:

Why doesn't one, two, three seem to appeal
to a Yankee as much as one, two! *

(This was from an early sketch from Ives's bachelor days with his companions in Poverty Flat, entitled *Rube trying to walk 2 to 3!*—"written as a joke, and sounds like one! Watty McCormick only one to see it! and Harry Farrar! at 2:45 A.M.") Some songs describe a comic situation, as in the first of the two *Memories* songs ("sitting in the opera house—waiting for the curtain to arise") or *The Circus Band*:

Where is the lady all in pink?
Last year she waved to me I think;
Can she have died? Can! that! rot!
She is passing but she sees me not! †

Ives makes humorous allusions in the music itself. In the otherwise serious *On the Antipodes*,

* Copyright 1935 Merion Music, Inc. Used by permission.
† Copyright 1953 by Peer International Corporation. Used by permission.

Sometimes Nature's nice and sweet, as a little pansy, and
Sometimes "it ain't." *

is set with the expected "nice" saccharine sounds on the first line, followed by crashing dissonances on the second. Finally, an instance of
rarified, sophisticated humor is to be found in a song called *The Side
Show*. The stumbling of an old lame horse that turns the merry-go-round
is imitated by an uneven rhythm of five beats that Ives says makes the
carousel tune sound "a bit like a Russian dance," at which point he
quotes two bars of Tchaikovsky's famous 5/4 waltz from the *Pathétique*
Symphony!

THE SOURCES OF IVES'S MUSICAL LANGUAGE

Although Ives's music has an unmistakable and distinctive sound,
which has begun to influence other American music to a certain extent,
it is difficult to define an Ives *style*, since he wrote in so many diverse
ways. The sources of his musical language are his own inventive imagination with tones—and the music he heard and played in Danbury and New
Haven before he was twenty-five. As the Cowells have written: "Ives'
music had its roots in the church, stage, parlor, and dance music of a
small American town—the popular music of his time, in short. . . . He was
the first composer in the United States to commit himself unreservedly
to the vernacular for the grammar of a new symphonic speech." [14]

Of course there are pages and pages in works such as the *Concord*
Sonata and the Second String Quartet, and passages even in the songs, in
which it would be far-fetched to try to detect any relationship to popular
music. But whenever Ives needs a musical *subject*, it is almost invariably
to the popular sources that he turns. In 1917 he wrote a song (both words
and music) called *The Things Our Fathers Loved*. With appropriately
evocative music, it is in effect a short ode to Ives's musical roots.

I think there must be a place in the soul all
    made of tunes, of tunes of long ago;
I hear the organ on the Main Street corner,
Aunt Sarah humming gospels;
Summer evenings,
The village cornet band, playing in the square.
The town's Red, White and Blue, all Red,
    White and Blue
Now! Hear the songs!
I know not what are the words

* Copyright 1935 Merion Music, Inc. Used by permission.

But they sing in my soul of the things
our Fathers loved.

IVES'S ATTITUDE TOWARDS THE PERFORMANCE OF HIS MUSIC

We can be sure that Charles Ives had, at least as a young man, the normal composer's desire to hear his works realized in performance. The piano and organ works he could, of course, play himself; he once wrote, "There is nothing that I have ever written for a piano that I haven't been able to play." [15] It is likely that a good many of the germinal ideas to be more fully realized in later works were first played on the organ, and that some were even tried out on unsuspecting congregations until Ives finally gave up his church job in 1902, feeling that it was unfair to inflict his explorations on "captive" listeners. But it was at least possible for him to hear ideas for this medium. With the instrumental and orchestral works, it was different. Until about 1915 he made efforts to secure performances, or at least to hear some of his works. He occasionally hired individual performers to play with him, and groups of musicians from the theater orchestras. The latter he had great respect for; and little could he have realized at the time that these informal readings were the nearest thing to performances of some of his works that he was to hear until after he had stopped composing. When the musicians really tried, he was respectful of their efforts; years later he declined to allow the premiere of a work to be billed as a "first performance," feeling it would not be fair to "those old fellers" who had done their best with his music in the early days.

So there is no doubt that in the beginning he wished, and even expected, to hear his works. As time went on, however, and after some bitter and humiliating experiences with performances and readings, his attitude towards performance seemed gradually to change. His music itself became less and less geared to actual realization in sound—less in touch with the practical problems.

As evidence of this we have the music's difficulties and enormous complexities—about which Ives manifested a curiously dualistic attitude. On one hand, he sometimes freely castigated the laziness, indifference, and lack of ability of performers who would not come to grips with the difficulties of new or hard music, including but not limited to his own. He described, for example, his own successful efforts to master complex simultaneous rhythms: "I have with much practice been able to keep five, and even six, rhythms going in my mind at once, so that I can hear each one naturally, by leaning toward it." On the other hand, at times he seemed quite ready to acknowledge that some of his music was possibly unplayable. Of the *Fourth of July* movement he wrote: "I did what I wanted to, quite sure that the thing would never be played, and probably *could* never be played." In the postface to the *114 Songs* he wrote:

"Some of the songs in this book, particularly among the later ones, cannot be sung, and if they could, might perhaps prefer, if they had a say, to remain as they are; that is, 'in the leaf'—and that they will remain in this peaceful state is more than presumable." It will be noted that the idea of the music's impossibility—an idea proved wrong by the more recent higher standards of musicianship—is linked with a certain half-bitter resignation traceable to the neglect, indifference, hostility, and ridicule he experienced.

Another evidence of his growing remoteness from the realistic arena of performance is seen in his apparent casualness with regard to the resources called for in a particular piece. He suddenly wants a flute in a piano sonata, or an organ pedal tone in a song (*On the Antipodes*). In another song, he writes at one point: "These four measures sound better sung with string quartet if one is available." It is true that many of these indications are marked *ad libitum*, that Ives was in later years notoriously and often exasperatingly permissive with regard to the details of performance of his works, and that these indications often seem to spring from an imaginative sense very akin to his sense of humor. Though these seeming caprices may be justified purely from the standpoint of the composer's imagination, and though they may sometimes be given a philosophical garb ("Why can't a musical thought be presented as it is born—perchance a 'bastard of the slums,' or a 'daughter of a bishop'—and if it happens to go better later on a bass-drum than upon a harp, get a good bass-drummer"), they nevertheless betray Ives's detachment from the professional world of music and the realities of performance. Bernard Herrmann, practical professional musician, for years a conductor with CBS radio, who devoted a great deal of time and care to bringing out performances of Ives's music, said: "Ives, after all, was a very impractical man when it came to performances of music. By not being a professional musician in the sense that he did not have to make a living of music, he entered into an abstraction of music. Because it was an abstraction, it didn't deal with any of the realistic problems." [16]

This detachment took on at times the aspect of dealing with a reality of music that transcended any actual realization in sound, a realization that he seemed actually to disdain at times. His famous "My God! What has sound got to do with music!" is his most succinct and often-quoted statement of this attitude. He continues cogently:

> The waiter brings the only fresh egg he has, but the man at breakfast sends it back because it doesn't fit his eggcup. Why can't music go out in the same way it comes in to a man, without having to crawl over a fence of sounds, thoraxes, catguts, wire, wood, and brass? [17]

Beethoven, it may be remembered, voiced a similar impatience with the mechanism of performance, and this even before total deafness removed him, too, from the more mundane realms of music.

This sense of the unimportance of actual performance showed itself in another symptom occasionally found in composers, even sometimes among those who are much more in touch with the world of performance—the disinclination to regard works as *finished,* or in final form. All his creative life Ives was rearranging his musical ideas—transforming them from one medium to another. The *Emerson* movement of the *Concord* Sonata he kept continually working at, changing bits here and there, cutting out or elaborating ("I may always have the pleasure of not finishing it"). This became also for him a philosophical question, and its most striking manifestation is in the *Universe Symphony.* A plan for this exists:

    I. (Past)   Formation of waters and mountains.
    II. (Present) Earth, evolution in nature and humanity.
    III. (Future) Heaven, the rise of all to the spiritual.

There are also some sketches and fairly explicit notes, which are fascinating, and have to do with the matters of perspective and simultaneity previously discussed. Ives did work on the *Universe Symphony* from time to time, even as late as 1951, but it is possible that it was conceived as a work never to be finished.

IDEALISM VERSUS PROFESSIONALISM IN MUSIC

Of the many aspects of Ives's idealism regarding art that might be explored, a central one, involving eventually all the others, is his attitude towards professionalism, and what it does to an artist's independence and self-reliance. Ives was one of the last of our "amateur" composers (in the sense of not depending upon music for a living), and certainly a uniquely rugged individualist in the matter of the principle involved in deriving any income for his music. Ives himself speaks to the point as follows:

> We hear that Mr. Smith or Mr. Morgan, etc., et al., design to establish a "course at Rome," to raise the standard of American music (or the standard of American composers—which is it?); but possibly the more our composer accepts from his patrons "*et al.,*" the less he will accept *from himself.* It may be possible that a day in a "Kansas wheat field" will do more for him than three years in Rome. . . . If for every thousand-dollar prize a potato field be substituted, so that these candidates of Clio can dig a little in real life, perhaps dig up a natural inspiration, art's air might be a little clearer.

And again, in a strong statement that summarizes his attitude:

> Perhaps the birth of art will take place at the moment in which the last man who is willing to make a living out of art is gone and gone forever.[18]

Whether these are rationalizations by Ives of his early insight that he could not expect any degree of success, monetary or otherwise, from the only kind of music he was interested in writing is beside the point. The fact is that he made an early decision to go into business, so that the family which was still in the future would not have to "starve on his dissonances." He apparently never regretted his decision, but saw a relationship between his daily work in the world and his art that tended to develop a "spiritual sturdiness" which showed itself in "a close union between spiritual life and the ordinary business of life." Emerson said: "There is virtue yet in the hoe and the spade, for learned as well as for unlearned hands." Ives said:

> I have experienced a great fulness of life in business. The fabric of existence weaves itself whole. You cannot set an art off in the corner and hope for it to have vitality, reality and substance. There can be nothing *exclusive* about a substantial art. It comes directly out of the heart of experience of life and thinking about life and living life. My work in music helped my business and work in business helped my music.[19]

Ives's Music and the World

We have surveyed rather painstakingly the career, the music, and the ideas of Charles Ives, out of the conviction that Ives is one of the central figures in our story. It now remains to trace very briefly the story of the acceptance of his music, and to survey contemporary assessments of it.

Charles Ives's music was not suddenly discovered after his death, nor did he emerge dramatically from obscurity, Minerva-like, a full-grown hero made to order for the adulation of a new generation in the decade of his centennial (though one would think so to peruse some latter-day writing). The truth is more complicated, and as usual more interesting, for the list of hard-working and courageous protagonists in "the Ives case" is rather long and distinguished. After the discouragements of the teens, some recognition came as early as the twenties. Henry Bellamann, poet and lifelong friend of Ives after their first meeting, wrote and spoke in his behalf, and arranged performances of the *Concord* Sonata (a movement at a time) as early as 1920. A Town Hall concert in New York by the venturesome Pro-Musica group presented two movements of the Fourth Symphony, with Eugene Goosens conducting, in 1927.

As the Cowells have pointed out, the thirties was a time when mostly composers, and a few critics, championed Ives's music. Henry Cowell had introduced Ives to Nicolas Slonimsky, a Russian-born composer, conductor, and writer who must have a significant place in any recounting of the story of American music beginning in the 1920s, when he came to America as an opera coach and, later, as Koussevitzky's assistant. Slonimsky conducted *Three Places in New England* in Boston in 1930, and *Decoration Day* in San Francisco in 1932. He also conducted Ives's music in Europe about the same time, with considerable success. It was, in fact, the acceptance of the music in Europe that had a lot to do with its being taken more seriously in America at this time—evidence of the still-strong influence of European taste and opinion. Around 1930 the critic Paul Rosenfeld wrote enthusiastically about Ives, as did Aaron Copland, with some reservations, in 1933. Copland arranged for some of the earliest public performances of the songs.

The 1940s, as the Cowells have noted, was a time when Ives's music began to be championed by important performers. A landmark event, touching off much of the success of the forties, was the first complete public performance of the *Concord* Sonata in 1939 by John Kirkpatrick. (Kirkpatrick, who had discovered the sonata in 1927, subsequently became a leading Ives interpreter, scholar, and authority, and curator of the Ives collection at Yale University.) This performance in Town Hall, which had to be repeated, marked the beginning of widespread favorable critical acclaim of Ives's music; Lawrence Gilman called the *Concord* Sonata "the greatest music composed by an American." Thus the stage was set for important performances of the next decade. Violin virtuoso Joseph Szigeti put the Fourth Violin Sonata in his repertory, and in 1944 the influential Los Angeles Evenings-on-the-Roof concerts, under Peter Yates, honored jointly Charles Ives and Arnold Schoenberg, both then seventy. In 1946 West Coast composer and conductor Lou Harrison premiered the Third Symphony; the next year it was awarded the Pulitzer Prize. The first performance of the Second Symphony took place under Leonard Bernstein in 1951.

By this time Ives's music was well on its way, and the 1950s saw its acceptance and acclaim by a far greater segment of the general musical public, who had now had a chance to hear a fair amount of it. (Ives himself, who died in 1954, heard very little; he had virtually stopped going to concerts after the 1920s and is said to have owned neither a radio nor a phonograph.) The principal barrier to the performance of Ives's music (except for the comparatively few published works) for the last thirty years has not been hostility or indifference to it, but the extreme difficulties of making performable editions out of the chaotic and jumbled manuscripts. Thus the Fourth Symphony had to wait until 1965 for its first complete performance. After Ives's death, much care was lavished on sorting out, cataloguing, and photostating the manuscripts. As has been noted, only the painstaking efforts through the years of such people as Henry and Sidney Cowell, John Kirkpatrick, Elliott Carter, Lou Harrison, and Bernard Herrmann have made much of Ives's music accessible at all.

For Ives the man there is no lack of admiration; his idealism, his grit, his humor, and his generosity have fired the imagination of succeeding generations. For the music there is admiration and love—tempered, for many who know it well, with certain reservations. Copland has pointed out the deleterious effect on Ives's music of his having worked in virtual isolation—"cut off from the vitalizing contact of an audience." We have already noted some of the musical evidence of this loss of contact. Elliott Carter points to the "large amounts of indifferentiated confusion," and is forced, reluctantly, to the conclusion that Ives's work often "falls short of his intentions." And, as Virgil Thomson has reminded us in connection with Ives, "Intentions are no guarantee of quality." He goes on to point out the necessity of distinguishing purely musical quality from the wealth of not-strictly-musical associations that have grown up around Ives's work: "When time shall have dissolved away his nostalgias and ethical aspirations, as they have largely done for Beethoven and for Bach and even for the descriptive leitmotifs of Wagner, what sheer musical reality will remain in Ives's larger works?" Then there are the reservations engendered by the unevenness of his large output, much of it left in rough state. It is certainly inevitable that, given the pace at which Ives worked during the period of his "double life," he could hardly have achieved a very complete realization of all his ideas, or a very conclusive form for all his works. In the early years, the free rein he gave his imagination channeled all his energies into a kind of furious sketching approach to composition. One has the impression that his ideas were too legion, and tumbled in upon him too fast, for many of them to be fully realized.

Yet there is enough. Ives's most cogent and nearly perfect realizations—many of the songs, *The Unanswered Question, The Housatonic at Stockbridge*, practically all the *Holidays*—have been indispensable to us. Virgil Thomson, speaking for all subsequent composers, hailed Charles Ives as "whether we knew it or not, the father of us all."

CARL RUGGLES (1876–1971)

The picture most of us have of Carl Ruggles is that of a craggy New England nonegenarian who worked in a made-over schoolhouse in Vermont, and whose entire output (those works he has allowed to survive) consists of less than a dozen pieces: music of consistently high integrity, density, and dissonance. And this is one artist about whom the first impression—and the legend—is essentially accurate. Further investigation, as we shall see, will reveal that nothing about the legend needs revising, only filling out.

Ruggles is often mentioned with Ives. Indeed, they had much in common; they were nearly exact contemporaries, and both New Englanders of a highly independent spirit and temperament. Although they did not meet until 1930, when both were over fifty (Ruggles was involved at the time with a particular New York wing of the avant-garde that held a disparaging view of Ives), they immediately became fast friends and great admirers of each other's music.

There are further points of similarity in career and attitude. Both had early practical acquaintance with music (Ruggles studied violin as a child; he once played for President Grover Cleveland!) Both received academic training from the best that the New England musical "establishment" had to offer (Ives from Horatio Parker of Yale, and Ruggles from John Knowles Paine at Harvard). Both were uncompromising idealists in music and indifferent to popularity, and when each struck out to find new paths, these paths (though quite dissimilar) both led into the domain of dissonant and "difficult" musical utterance.

Unlike Ives, however, Ruggles had an extremely small output, and the individual pieces themselves were compact. His orchestral "symphonic poem" *Sun Treader*, which was six years in the making, is, at seventeen and a half minutes, one of Ruggles's longest pieces. His complete surviving works could be performed in a single program of less than two hours. They are remarkably consistent, and each is honed to an amazing degree of perfection. There is no nostalgic or impressionistic display of Americana; in fact, Ruggles's music has no discernible relationship to American popular music, and very little to any other music. Ruggles was a most meticulous craftsman. But he was also not in a hurry. With the support of a patron and in good health, he was able to work in his forty-foot-square studio in Vermont, dividing his time between painting (his abstract canvases have been exhibited in several museums), composing (he often covered the walls like a mural with his music, written with different-colored crayons on huge staff paper, so that he could see an entire section at once), and entertaining a vast range of friends, treating them to samples of his skill as a raconteur. Ives expressed himself often in writing, and Ruggles seldom, but he was known for his voluble, opinionated, talk—laced with salty profanity. (The cliché is for once apt: Ruggles descended from a seafaring family, grew up on Cape Cod, and went to Boston originally to study ship design.)

Also unlike Ives, Ruggles did involve himself in the working world of music. At age thirty-six he went out to Winona, Minnesota, where he taught in a conservatory, and most importantly, founded an orchestra and conducted opera and symphony concerts. When he returned to New York (1917), he was over forty. It was about that time that he found his patron, but he continued to involve himself in the promotion of new music in New York, first with the International Composers' Guild with Edgard Varèse (1923–1927) and then with the Pan-American Association of Composers (1927–1933). Later in the thirties he taught seminars in modern composition at the University of Miami, Florida.

The Minnesota years seem to have been his last years of apprenticeship. When they were over, he began writing the music we know today. Nothing he wrote before 1919 has he allowed to survive. (He also destroyed an unfinished opera, *The Sunken Bell*, based on a German play.)

Ruggles has left only two works for voice: the early *Toys*, a song for voice and piano, and *Vox Clamans in Deserta* for voice and orchestra. *Angels* (rearranged in 1938 from an earlier work called *Men and Angels*) is for four muted trumpets and two muted trombones. For piano solo he has written a group of pieces called *Evocations*, and for three pianos a piece called *Polyphonic Composition*. The rest are for larger forces. *Men and Mountains* (1924) consists of three movements: *Men* (for strings), *Lilacs* (also for strings, and frequently played alone), and *Marching Mountains* (for orchestra). *Portals*, for string orchestra, dates originally from 1926, but has been revised several times. His two works for large orchestra are *Sun Treader* (1932, the title from a line in Browning) and *Organum* (1945).

Unlike Ives, a musical impressionist who sometimes did his tone painting in a remarkably photographic way, Ruggles only did his painting on canvas, and even there he dealt with abstractions. His music never reflects overtly outward scenes. His melodies are often long sweeping lines, gathering in intensity and covering a great range. He is usually very careful not to repeat a note too soon. The opening melody of *Portals* shows these features.

His texture is usually contrapuntal, but he doubles parts extensively, and unlike Ives, seldom has more than three real parts going at once. When he pauses on a chord, on the other hand, it is often complex. Of the following two sonorities in *Portals*, the first has seven tones and the second eleven; in each there is only one tone doubled.

Ruggles's music is never dance- or march-like; there are no strong recurring accents. Even the prominent drumbeats in *Sun Treader* are speeded up, so that they set up no pulse. The form, like the rhythm, is rhapsodic, and virtually seamless.

Ruggles is not apt to produce a detachable "tune" that one remembers, and he never quotes. Still, his music, in terms of its sound, and even more importantly, in terms of its *gesture*, leaves an unmistakable impression. It is dissonant and often dense, but it sings in a way much dissonant music does not, and it never seems to falter or lose its way.[20]

Though the sounds, to its first audiences, were new, the esthetic is old. Ruggles believed in a quality in art he called the "sublime." To him the greatest composers were Bach and Handel (and the greatest living composer Charles Ives). Charles Seeger, in a 1932 article that still gives us the most well-rounded picture of the man and his music, has referred to Carl Ruggles's work as a "distinct type of artistic effort—the attempt to convey the most approved ideal by the least approved means." [21]

HENRY COWELL (1897–1965)

Henry Cowell came into the world gifted with the kind of observant, eagerly absorbing mentality that was able to reap the full benefit of growing up in the richly polyglot atmosphere of the San Francisco Bay area just after the turn of the century. It was the same milieu in which had grown up, a generation earlier, Jack London and Gertrude Stein. Unburdened by even modest means, and free of any predetermined set of cultural values, Cowell was free to accept his musical stimulus where he found it—in Irish folk tunes (from his family), Gregorian chant (from a neighbor), Oriental music, and rural American hymnody (from early sojourns in Kansas and Oklahoma). In San Francisco, young Cowell heard Chinese opera more frequently than Italian. At five he started studying the violin, giving it up at eight. When he got hold of a battered up old upright piano, he soon found he had an instrument that would open up new possibilities, and he began experimenting. In 1912, at the age of fifteen, he played in public in San Francisco a piece called *The Tides of Manaunaun*; it was a prelude to an opera he was writing based on Irish mythology. Manaunaun was the maker of great tides that swept through the universe; to convey the sense of this vast motion, Cowell, interestingly enough, hit upon the same device that Ives, on the other side of the continent, and at about the same time, was using to convey the sense of the masses in *Majority*—huge groups of tones sounded together that could only be played with the entire forearm. These were soon to become known as tone "clusters." Cowell used them in many of his piano works—became known for them, in fact—but nowhere more effectively than in this very early piece.[22]

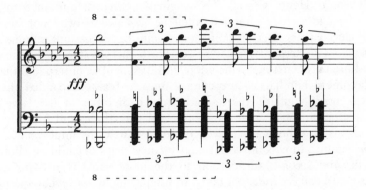

This would seem quite a start for a boy just turned fifteen, but Cowell had been composing since he was eleven, and there was far more to come. By the time he was twenty, he had composed 199 pieces, including an opera and a symphony. By this time he had become persuaded of the value of some systematic study, and found an ideal person to supervise it in Charles Seeger, then teaching at the University of California. His formal education had ended with the third grade, but he was a voracious learner—when he was twenty he was seeing Seeger for lessons in music every morning in Berkeley, studying English with Samuel Seward every afternoon at Stanford, working at night as a janitor—and writing a book! Cowell went east to New York for further study, and began appearing in concerts playing his own works on the piano. Between 1923 and 1933 he made five important tours of Europe (including a trip in 1928 to the Soviet Union, which he was the first American composer to visit); his new music stimulated interest, not only in and of itself, but interest in the new American music generally.

When in this country, Cowell divided his time for the next thirty years between teaching and lecturing (mostly at New York's New School for Social Research, where he was director of music, but also at Columbia and Stanford universities; Mills, Bennington, and Adelphi colleges; and the Peabody Conservatory), editing, writing, championing the new music of others, and of course continuing to compose a prodigious amount of music himself.

There are many sides to Cowell's work. There is Henry Cowell the teacher—one of our best, and an important influence on such composers as Lou Harrison, John Cage, and other free spirits of the musical left.

There is Henry Cowell the tireless worker for new music, and new ideas in music. In 1927 he founded the important periodical *New Music Quarterly*, which published a great many new scores (though not a note of his own). It was through this that he met Charles Ives, becoming his first important discoverer, his lifelong promoter, with his wife Sidney Cowell his first biographer, and after Ives's death his musical executor.

There is Henry Cowell the imaginative theorist and inventor. The book he had virtually finished when he was twenty-two (not published until eleven years later, in 1930) was a slim but important volume called *New Musical Resources*. In it he sets forth the possibilities for new relationships between tones (including the dissonant counterpoint that was to become a familiar feature of new music); for an expanded rhythmic system, using regularly the less accustomed divisions of five, seven, and so on simultaneously with the more usual two, three, and four (Ives was doing this also, but Cowell even invented a new rhythmic notation and nomenclature to encompass it); and for new ways of building chords (in fourths and seconds in addition to the more usual thirds—his clusters he came to call *secundal* chords). An interesting, if somewhat speculative, feature of his work is his scheme of associating the frequency ratios of pitch intervals with rhythmic ratios. According to Cowell, there could be established an analogy, for example, between the major triad, with its three pitches in a ratio of 3, 4, and 5,

and a rhythmic relation of three parts having the same ratios.

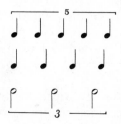

This integration of rhythm and pitch he sought to illustrate in two early quartets called the *Romantic* and the *Euphometric*.[23]

Cowell the inventor collaborated with Professor Leon Theremin to produce, about 1931, an instrument called the "Rythmicon," capable of rendering the rhythms of complex ratios. It was never widely used, but it made its point; what it did can now be easily done by electronic means.

There is also Henry Cowell the student of a variety of musical cultures, worldwide. In 1931–1932 he studied comparative musicology in Berlin with Professor Eric Moritz von Hornbostel. Oriental music he had already heard a great deal of in his youth. His works subsequently bore witness to the detailed study of musical cultures as widely separated as those of Japan, Persia, and Iceland.

And finally there is, as our major concern, Henry Cowell the prolific composer. We left him as the fifteen-year-old composer of a remarkable piano piece. What of his subsequent output?

It is, of course, as varied as the interests of the man himself. The experimental works—those which place him in this chapter as one of our innovators—were for the most part early works. Of these, the short works for piano are the most accessible and open up the most interesting possibilities.

Cowell used tone clusters for their descriptive appropriateness in other short works after *The Tides of Manaunaun*. About 1914 he wrote *Amiable Conversation*, which is a kind of dialogue between a low-pitched voice and a high-pitched one. It was suggested by an argument he overheard in a Chinese laundry; not understanding the words, he was free to listen to the voices simply as sounds that rose in pitch and intensity as the conversation proceeded. Another early work of about the same vintage is *Advertisement*, in which small clusters are struck with the fist. Cowell describes it as a "humorous impression of the repetitive advertising in the flashing lights of Times Square." He gives the performer the option of repeating one section, "to emphasize the absurdity," as many times as desired.

About 1923 Cowell began to produce works calling for the performer to play directly on the strings of the piano. (A grand piano is required for these.) In *Aeolian Harp* (named after a small harp with silk strings played upon by the wind) the performer silently depresses the keys of the successive chords, releasing their dampers; the strings are then swept with the other hand (somewhat in the manner of the autoharp), sometimes with the fingers and sometimes with the thumbnail. They are also plucked. Another small descriptive piece using this technique is *The Fairy Answer*: Chords played normally are "echoed" (slightly changed, to identify it as the work of the fairies) by the strings swept by hand. In *The Banshee* (ca. 1923) the dampers are all released, and the performer, standing in the crook of the piano, plays directly upon the strings—at times sweeping across them in various ways, at times sweeping lengthwise on one or more strings, at times plucking them. This remarkable piece consists of sounds the farthest removed (until John Cage began playing on the outside of the piano) from the normal ones a piano makes—sounds that gave a foretaste, significantly, of those that were to be produced electronically a quarter of a century later.

Still other possibilities were explored in a piece written about 1930, when Cowell was nearly finished with his experiments on the piano (he was completing his Piano Concerto) and was ready to turn to other matters. The piano piece in question is called *Sinister Resonance*. It involves further direct manipulation of the strings: the playing of several pitches on one string, through "stopping" the string; the "muting" of strings with the hand; and the playing of harmonics, by lightly touching the strings in the center while they are played from the keyboard.[24]

Cowell's restless inventiveness often suggested areas of exploration that he himself made only a few sallies into, before turning to something else. He never followed up consistently or to any great depth the means suggested in his *New Musical Resources*, nor was it ever his intention to do so. Of the early piano pieces, *The Banshee* and *Sinister Resonance* proved to be the most prophetic. Both suggested a practice that became a trademark of the mildly avant-garde in the fifties and sixties—producing sounds on traditional instruments in ways other than that for which they were designed: blowing air through mouthpiece-less brass instruments, clicking the keys on woodwind instruments, or thumping on the bodies of string instruments. Cowell himself directs players to "tap back of instrument with padded drum stick" in his *United Quartet* (after the early years he was singularly prosaic in his choice of titles), but adds the thoughtful if unnecessary precaution "not hard enough to injure." The muted, damped, and otherwise manipulated sounds of the piano strings in *Sinister Resonance* also led directly into the sounds of the "prepared piano" of John Cage, a device that, more than any other single idea, launched Cage's career. Indeed, Cowell had himself experimented with various mechanical objects used to damp or mute the strings.

After the 1930s Cowell's experimentation with new musical resources began to give place to his eclecticism. He sought to apply the compositional processes appropriate for the writing of longer, more complex works to the musical materials (ethnic, folk, and traditional) of cultures in which the aims and esthetics of fine art were unknown.

Around 1940 he discovered (as had Virgil Thomson before him) the tradition of native religious music, which began with the New England singing-school masters and continued into the rural South and Midwest in the shape-note music—the tradition described in Part 2 of this book. This interest resulted in a series of compositions known by the title *Hymn and Fuguing Tune*, written for various combinations. They are much enlarged elaborations of the basic binary plan of the old *fuging psalm tunes of* Billings and company; there is a first section, primarily chordal, emphasizing open consonances, and consonant triads, and a second "fuguing" section, contrapuntal but still fundamentally consonant. Cowell used this material as a point of departure in other works of the period as well, from his Fourth Symphony (1946) to his Tenth Symphony (1953), both of which have hymn and fuguing sections, as well as Irish jigs, a Celtic kind of music-making that greatly appealed to Cowell.

In 1956–1957 Cowell went on a world tour, sponsored in part by the Rockefeller Foundation and the United States government. He spent a considerable amount of time in Iran and in Japan, both studying their music and bringing a knowledge of our music to them. This marked the beginning of a series of works based on Persian music (*Persian Set*, 1957, and *Homage to Iran*, 1959) and Japanese music (*Ongaku* for orchestra, 1957). Later his interest expanded to include the music of Iceland; his Symphony no. 16 (1962) is subtitled *Icelandic*. In these works, as in the works inspired by American and Celtic music, Cowell only rarely uses traditional tunes, but writes his *own* Persian, Japanese, or Icelandic music. Always skillfully scored, even to suggesting the timbres of national instruments or the voicing of national choral singing, it nevertheless has the flavor of pleasant musical tourism, of the same type that issued forth in the nineteenth century when Russian and French composers were writing Spanish music.

Because of Henry Cowell's relentless efforts on behalf of all new music, American music and American composers are much in his debt. His mind was inventive, but quite literal, at times in an almost childlike way. He worked prodigiously at a complicated craft in an uncomplicated fashion. It was his role to suggest new sound resources, without troubling deeper musical waters.

LOU HARRISON AND JOHN CAGE

Henry Cowell was the first American composer to remind us that the West Coast of the United States is, culturally as well as geographically, farther from Europe than is New York, and closer to Asia. The orientation of our East Coast to Europe continues to survive our colonial period (which lasted much longer culturally than politically); our West Coast, with more tenuous European ties and a greater variety of influences, has been more open to choices. In music, this openness to a vocabulary of sounds larger than that inherited from the European fine-art tradition, which we first noted in Cowell, has been carried further, both in terms of exploration and refinement, by two composers, both of whom were at one time students of Cowell.

One of these composers, Lou Harrison (born 1917 in Portland, Oregon), went east in the 1940s to become an important part, for a time, of the New York musical scene. (It will be recalled that in 1947 he conducted the first performance of Ives's Third Symphony.) But he was, and is, a West Coast man in his independence of "establishment" music and thinking (including that of the avant-garde establishment), in his concern with the music of the entire vast Pacific basin, and in the liberal breadth of his outlook. Concerned with plants and animals, Harrison has been a florist. (It is interesting to note that Cowell at one time made his living collecting wild plants, and that John Cage, our third free-wheeling Pacific coast composer, is an avid collector of mushrooms.) Harrison has also been a dancer, and is a painter, playwright, conductor, and maker of musical instruments. He acknowledged and partook of the European twentieth-century tradition, as evidenced by his having studied with émigré Viennese composer and teacher Arnold Schoenberg, who settled in Los Angeles in the mid-thirties and became the center of a circle of students and devotees. This phase of Harrison's work is represented by a few twelve-tone works (not necessarily atonal) such as the largely proportioned Symphony on G. (Harrison also found an alternative way of organizing highly chromatic music, through controlling the number and kind of melodic intervals used, as he did in his Concerto for Violin and Percussion Orchestra, 1940–1959.) His interest in a return to the pure intonation of just intervals* is exemplified in his Four Strict Songs for Eight Baritones and Orchestra, on his own text, patterned after the "making-things-right-and-good-again songs of the Navaho." The orchestra consists of a specially tuned piano, harp, percussion, and such other conventional orchestral instruments as can adjust to the pure tunings—i.e., strings and trombones. Harrison's interest in pre-tonal music (both medieval and Renaissance) is evidenced in works such as his Mass (1954) and his Suite for Symphonic Strings (1961). His abiding preoccupation with percussion sounds is apparent in many works, including several Canticles, a Suite for Percussion, and concertos for flute and for violin with percussion orchestra. Finally, his knowledge of, and love for, the music of the Orient is evident in many works, including Solstice (1950) for gamelan (a Javanese orchestra of percussion instruments), Concerto in Slendro for Violin, and most notably, Pacifika Rondo, a piece in seven movements for an orchestra of both Western and Oriental instruments.[25]

Another of Cowell's students, John Cage (born 1912 in Los Angeles), is a West Coast composer who went east permanently when he was thirty. In his early years he combined the need to impose a systematic

---

* See the discussion of pure intonation on page 495.

organization on his materials (which would be natural in one who studied under Schoenberg) with a love of percussion sounds, particularly those of an Oriental character. His *Construction in Metal* (1937), one of his earliest works available on recordings, shows clearly these two concerns. The rhythmic structure is of a rigidly predetermined type that Cage used until he turned to indeterminacy and electronics in the early 1950s. It partakes of Schoenbergian determinism, but is also, in Cage's words, "analogous to Indian *tala* (rhythmic method)." As he explains it, "The whole has as many parts as each unit has small parts, and these, large and small, are in the same proportion." Thus the 16-measure units have an internal arrangement of 4–3–2–3–4, and there are sixteen of these 16-measure units, grouped similarly, with a 12-measure coda added as a concession to the "Western" need for an ending. The West Coast–Oriental aspect of the work is evident in the use of gamelan, and of Japanese temple gongs, while the eclectic noise preferences are seen in the use of brake drums and anvils.

Cage also formed an early attachment to the dance, which came about partly because some of his earliest jobs consisted of playing for dance classes and partly because he soon discovered that in the 1930s, when it was difficult otherwise to find an audience for percussion music, dancers were eager for new sounds to accompany their new choreographic creations. About 1936 Cage went to Seattle, where he was on the faculty of the Cornish School, as composer-accompanist for the dance group. It was there that he first hit upon the idea of the "prepared piano." A dancer had requested a score for a new ballet, *Bacchanale*, to emphasize percussion. Since the company could not afford a whole percussion orchestra, Cage (who was the son of an inventor) followed up on some of Cowell's experiments and modified the sound of a grand piano by muting or damping the strings with various objects, thereby in effect creating a percussion orchestra inside the piano, at the control of a single player. This was in 1938, and it was followed by many works for prepared piano, mostly for the dance. Cage then turned to other things, but in 1946–1948, after he had moved to New York, he returned to the prepared piano, writing the well-known Sonatas and Interludes for Prepared Piano. There are sixteen sonatas and four interludes; the sonatas are in the short binary form, with each of the two parts repeated—a common form in the eighteenth century. This short form is appropriate, since each of the sonatas and interludes reveals its musical essence rather quickly and there is little change or development. Cage was at this time becoming interested in Oriental teachings, and these represented an attempt to express, in terms of his gamelan-like instrument, the "permanent emotions" of the Indian tradition: the heroic, the erotic, the wondrous, the mirthful, the sorrowful, the fearful, the angry, and the odious.

Cage's tenuous Concerto for Prepared Piano and Orchestra (1951), based on a strictly ordered rhythmic structure that incorporates silences, is a kind of culmination of this aspect of his endeavors. From this point on, electronics, with its new sound sources, engaged him. (Here it must be noted that he had already delved into this realm, as far as the technology of the time would allow, in his *Imaginary Landscape no. 1* of 1939.) Also, the Oriental teachings, as he understood and interpreted them, were leading him in the direction of indeterminacy as to musical results, and an abdication of the role of composer. These developments belong to the next chapter.

HARRY PARTCH (1901–1974)

There was another westerner, born at the turn of the century, who also struck out on his own—the embodiment, as a musician, of Blake's dictum "I must create a system, or be enslaved by another man's." Harry Partch, working for years alone and virtually unknown, rejected three of the most basic elements of his immediate musical heritage: conventional instruments, a scale of twelve equidistant notes to an octave, and counterpoint. His musical influences, as he himself listed them, are, like Cowell's, varied and typical of the West: "Christian hymns, Chinese lullabyes, Yaqui Indian ritual, Congo puberty ritual, Cantonese music hall, and Okies in California vineyards." Yet Partch did not become a "collector," either of exotic instruments or exotic systems. Instead, he found what he needed as a base for his own music in two ancient ideas that had become eclipsed in Western music: purely tuned intervals and monophony (the harmonized singing or reciting of a single voice). And he soon saw that his return to pure intervals would draw him into another endeavor—that of building his own instruments.

Harry Partch, the son of apostate former missionaries to China, was born in Oakland, California, but soon moved with his family into the southwestern desert area of Arizona and New Mexico, where he grew up. His father, who understood Mandarin Chinese, worked for the immigration service, moving frequently from one small railroad-junction town near the Mexican border to another. Thus the boy grew up, lonely and largely self-educated, among the polyglot people of "the declining years of the Old West," as he puts it—including the Yaqui Indians, the Chinese, and the hobos and prostitutes his father and mother occasionally brought home. Young Harry Partch read a great deal, especially enjoying Greek mythology; and musical instruments, obtained by mail-order, were in the household. At fourteen Partch began to compose seriously. A few years later he began to have doubts about accepting both the intonational system and the concert system of European-derived music. At twenty-one he found Hermann von Helmholtz's famous book on musical acoustics, *On the Sensations of Tone,* and began writing works using pure, or just, intonation. At around twenty-six he wrote the first draft of his own treatise and manifesto, *Genesis of a Music.* At twenty-eight he burned, in a big iron stove, all the music he had written up to that time, and set out with determination and (as he describes it) "exhilaration" on new paths.

His first works of the early thirties were for Intoning Voice and Adapted Viola—a viola to which has been attached a longer cello finger-board, marked so as to facilitate playing the smaller just intervals. These early works had texts from Chinese poetry, the Psalms, and Shakespeare. After much experimentation, other instruments were added: an Adapted Guitar, a Chromelodeon (an adapted reed organ), and a Kithara (a lyre-shaped plucked stringed instrument with movable bridges, allowing for a sliding tone). Using these instruments, Partch wrote his first major work, *U.S. Highball.*[26] "A hobo's account of a trip from San Francisco to Chicago," with an adagio dishwashing interlude at Little America, Wyoming, it is to a great extent autobiographical, for Partch's life between 1935 and 1943 consisted in large measure of hoboing, dishwashing, WPA jobs, and wandering. This phase of his life came to an end only with the award of a Guggenheim Fellowship; his first work completed under this was *U.S. Highball,* which was premiered in New York in 1944.

U.S. Highball has a Subjective Voice (the protagonist) and several Objective Voices, whose words consist of "fragments of conversations, writings on the sides of boxcars, signs in havens for derelicts, hitchhikers' inscriptions"—all of which Partch had recorded in a notebook he always carried during his wanderings.

In succeeding years Partch built many new instruments, and rebuilt many earlier ones. The "string and voice" instruments eventually came to include, in addition to those mentioned above, Harmonic Canons (zither-like instruments with movable bridges for tuning, played with a pick), a retuned Koto, a bellows-operated Bloboy, consisting of auto horns and organ pipes, and a Crychord, with which sliding pitches are attained by changing the string tension with a lever. The percussion instruments feature various Marimbas. The Marimba Eroica is the largest; its lowest tone, below any of the notes on the piano, is produced by a Sitka spruce plank more than seven feet long suspended over a resonator eight feet long and four feet high. Many of the Marimbas are made of bamboo. The smallest and softest is the Mazda Marimba, made of twenty-four light globes "with their viscera removed," and yielding a sound, according to Partch, like the "bubbling of a coffee percolator." Other percussion include a Gourd Tree, Cone Gongs, and the bell-like Cloud-Chamber Bowls—the tops and bottoms of twelve-gallon glass carboys suspended.[27]

Appealing in sound, his instruments, especially as he redesigned them, came to have a great visual appeal as well; they are very much "part of the set" of a Partch performance, which, in accord with the composer's ideas of corporeal music, has always, and increasingly in the later works, a strong element of theater in it. The players themselves (who must be specially trained) are also aware at all times that they are "on stage."

Major compositions since *U.S. Highball* have been *Plectra and Percussion Dances* (1949–1952, a three-park work that includes *Castor and Pollox*); *Oedipus—A Music-Dance Drama* (1951); *The Bewitched—A Dance Satire* (1955); *Revelation in the Courthouse Park* (1960); *And on the Seventh Day Petals Fell in Petaluma* (1963–1964); and Partch's final large work, *Delusion of the Fury* (1963–1969).

In the 1940s, Partch thought of the realization of his works in terms of recordings (recordings he himself, for a time, issued under his own Gate 5 label). Since then, beginning approximately with *Oedipus*, they have been conceived more and more as theatrical works, with sets (including, of course, the instruments), costumes, dancers, singers, and actors; the players themselves, costumed, often serve as a chorus or take part in the action. Greek legend and drama and Japanese and African tales, figure as sources for the larger works.

Partch's *Genesis of a Music* (first published, after many drafts, in 1947, with a revised and enlarged second edition completed in 1972) is, as has been noted, both manifesto and treatise. Unlike Cowell's earlier and comparable smaller work, *New Musical Resources*, it is not a suggestion of what *might* be done but a painstakingly thorough description of what Partch spent a lifetime doing—together with his reasons for doing so. The theoretical portions include, in terms of the *ratios* which Partch used to express intervals, a complete description and derivation of his scale of forty-three tones to the octave.

It takes a bold, energetic, and singularly dedicated and single-minded composer to develop and commit himself to a system of intonation impossible to produce on existing instruments; to build new instruments to the new specifications; and then to create new works exploiting the resources of both the intonation and the instruments.

Partch's music does not, of course, exhaust or even begin to explore significantly the vast implications of his system. His is largely a music in which instrumental color, especially that of percussion, plays a dominant role. The consequently lesser role that melody and harmony play, together with his penchant for sliding tones, which blur the sense of finely tuned pitch, do not allow for much exploration, from the standpoint of what the listener can perceive, of the resources of his elaborate 43-tone pitch system. Then, too, without the visual impact of a stage presentation, the music alone, after one gets used to the sounds, does not always seem to sustain interest over long periods. (Several of the major works last more than an hour.) Yet the sounds themselves are often very arresting and very beautiful. There are inevitable limitations in what Partch did, but considering the task he set himself, he certainly did all any creator could in one lifetime.

The most poignant limitation in such a life work is that Partch's music can only be performed by specially trained performers, on only his own instruments—one of a kind, and difficult and expensive just to maintain, let alone duplicate. It is not certain, following his death in 1974, what the future of his music—*live*—will be. But it is likely that this was of little concern to Harry Partch. He had done his work. In 1972 he wrote:

> I am not trying to institute a movement in any crypto-religious sense. If I were, *idea* would soon turn into something called *form*, and the world is already plagued with its ephemera. . . . [The pathbreaker's] path cannot be retraced, because each of us is an original being.[28]

Pure Intonation: A postscript

It is interesting to note that three of the individualists treated in this chapter were concerned with pure, or just, intonation—that is, with the musical intervals resulting from simple and rational mathematical frequency ratios, in contrast with the irrational ratios and with the "clouding" of all intervals except the octave that results from the compromise of twelve equal-tempered semitones to the octave. Cowell dealt theoretically with the concept, in his *New Musical Resources*. Lou Harrison has written music to be played in pure intonation, and Partch committed himself to it wholly. There are others who have further explored it, including Ben Johnston, who studied with Partch. His String Quartet no. 2 (1964) combines just intonation (in a 53-tone scale) with, oddly enough, the very serialization of both pitch and duration that has been so characteristic of the dodecaphonic composers who have been utterly committed to equal temperament. Johnston's Sonata for Microtonal Piano (first performed in 1965) uses a piano especially tuned to a complex scale of eighty-one different pitches, only seven of which appear in octave duplications.[29] Still others have been at work (necessarily as instrument builders and modifiers) exploring the ramifications of a return to purely tuned intervals.

EDGARD VARÈSE (1883–1965)

In the matter of putting genuinely new sounds and sound sources at the disposal of an expressive purpose, Harry Partch and Edgar Varèse have been our two most original composers. They worked in very different ways, yet neither regarded sounds (as does John Cage) as ends in themselves. Both were dissatisfied with traditional instruments and with the tempered scale of twelve equal semitones to the octave (Partch rejected these outright, while Varèse, whose ties to European tradition were stronger, used both while awaiting the development of technology that would furnish him with new sound sources). Both men, interestingly enough, felt the need of sounds of flowing, sliding pitch; Partch achieved this through the use of movable bridges on his stringed instruments, while Varèse at first did so with sirens (*Amériques, Hyperprism,* and *Ionisation*) and later used electronic means. Both began composing afresh in their thirties, their earlier output having been destroyed—Partch's deliberately, and Varèse's probably at least partially so. There were fundamental differences, of course. Partch was committed to a very "corporeal" concept of music; the presence of a musician performing was a vital part of the artistic transaction, which always took place in terms of something staged. Varèse conceived of his music as structures in sound; the human performer was dispensable.

In terms of the man himself and his milieu, Edgar Varèse could hardly present a greater contrast to Harry Partch. Parisian-born, and educated there and in Italy, Varèse acknowledged his roots in the European tradition, which he knew thoroughly. He knew and associated with many of the great contemporary European musicians of his time, especially Claude Debussy and Ferruccio Busoni, whose advanced ideas, contained in his *Sketch for a New Aesthetic of Music,* had a considerable influence on Varèse. Whereas Partch was a lone worker, in the manner of the frontiersman, building his instruments, writing his music, and working out his theories almost totally on his own, Varèse was immersed in the current, urban world of his time (he loved cities, especially New York)—musical, literary, artistic, and political. During the European years he lived in Paris and later in Berlin. He was helped by Jules Massenet and Richard Strauss; he also knew Ravel, Picasso, Lenin, and writers Jean Cocteau, Hugo von Hofmannsthal, and Romain Rolland. Both in Europe and America he conducted concerts, and was a leader and cofounder of organizations devoted to furthering the cause of new music.

Varèse did not come to America until 1915, after the outbreak of World War I (he had served in the French army and been discharged because of ill health); he was then thirty-two. He is almost universally considered an American composer, however. He started composing anew here, taking his music in new directions; and his important—in fact, his sole surviving—output was composed after he arrived in his enthusiastically adopted land. His *Amériques* (1918–1922), the first important piece written here, is a vast work, the significance of which is not, as Varèse wrote, "purely geographic, but as symbolic of discoveries—new worlds on earth, in the sky, or in the minds of men." [30]

Once established in America, for the last half-century of his life Varèse directed his enormous energies in several directions at various times. In addition to composing (with which he was always, of course, preoccupied, although new completed works appeared comparatively infrequently and at irregular intervals), he was a conductor, an organizer for new music, a researcher into new controllable sound sources, and a teacher, lecturer, and writer.

Varèse's Conceptions of Music

In a preparation for examining his music, it will be useful to let Varèse himself, through his writings, describe some of his conceptions of music. When he was about twenty, Varèse discovered a definition of music that fired his imagination, to which he kept returning again and again throughout his life—the definition of music by the Polish philosopher Hoëne Wronsky as "the corporealization of the intelligence that is in sounds."

This concern for "the intelligence that is in sounds" was indicative of the importance Varèse always gave to the study of acoustics. The son of an engineer, and destined as a boy for the same career, he early acquired (even though he was severely and permanently estranged from his dictatorial father) a taste for science. He regarded music as an "art-science," and pointed out its association by medieval philosophers with mathematics, geometry, and astronomy. He strongly advocated composers' making use of the latest scientific developments.

> We all think it very sensible that tools that have become outmoded should be replaced by the very newest thing in "efficiency." . . . Composers like anyone else today are delighted to use the many gadgets continually put on the market for our daily comfort. But when they hear the sounds that no violins, wind instruments, or percussions of the orchestra can produce, it does not occur to them to demand those sounds of science. Yet science is even now equipped to give them everything they may require. . . . If you are curious to know what . . . a machine could do that the orchestra with its man-powered instruments cannot do, I shall try briefly to tell you: whatever I write, whatever my message, it will reach the listener unadulterated by "interpretation." It will work something like this: after a composer has set down his score on paper by means of a new graphic, similar in principle to a seismographic or oscillographic notation, he will then, with the collaboration of a sound engineer, transfer the score directly to this electric machine. After that anyone will be able to press a button to release the music exactly as the composer wrote it—exactly like opening a book.[31]

This remarkable forecast of electronic-tape music was written in 1939. Twenty years later, Varèse qualified and clarified somewhat his apparent rejection of the performer.

> Because for so many years I crusaded for new instruments with what may have seemed fanatical zeal, I have been accused of desiring nothing less than the destruction of all musical instruments and even of all performers.

This is, to say the least, an exaggeration. Our new liberating medium—the electronic—is not meant to replace the old musical instruments, which composers, including myself, will continue to use. Electronics is an additive, not a destructive, factor in the art and science of music.[32]

Varèse conceived of music as spatial, and of musical sounds as analogous to masses in space, with quasi-geometrical characteristics. He used sirens in some early scores to achieve what he called "parabolic and hyperbolic trajectories of sound."

In a lecture given as early as 1936 in Santa Fe he described his projected "corporealization" of music in a startling illustrative paragraph worth quoting in full.

> When new instruments will allow me to write music as I conceive it, the movement of sound-masses, of shifting planes, will be clearly perceived in my work, taking the place of linear counterpoint. When these sound-masses collide, the phenomena of penetration or repulsion will seem to occur. Certain transmutations taking place on certain planes will seem to be projected onto other planes, moving at different speeds and at different angles. There will no longer be the old conception of melody or interplay of melodies. The entire work will be a melodic totality. The entire work will flow as a river flows.[33]

Varèse had to wait another twenty years before he heard his music literally "projected into space." But his music had inspired a writer as early as 1925 to write of "great masses in astral space." Let us now examine some of the music of a composer who has been described as "the first astronaut."

The Music of Varèse

The music of Edgard Varèse falls clearly into three chronological groups. First are the early works, all written in Europe prior to World War I, and all lost or deliberately destroyed. (These included a symphony, *Bourgogne*; a symphonic poem, *Gargantua*; and an uncompleted opera, *"Ödipus und die Sphinx,* on which he was collaborating with Richard Strauss's librettist, Hugo von Hofmannsthal.) The second group includes the nine works written in America between 1918 and 1936. (Varèse, in the sparseness of his output, is surpassed only by Ruggles.) He was an extremely careful workman; often years would elapse between the initial conception of a work and its appearance in final form. Beginning in the mid-thirties there was a fifteen-year hiatus in his composition; whether this was due to his not wishing to write for conventional instruments and not having sophisticated electronic ones at his disposal, or to his own depressed feelings and the lack of acceptance of his music, is not certain. He lived in the West for a while, returned to New York for the war years, and did do some work on a vast project called *Espace* ("Space"). In theme it was the counterpart of Beethoven's Ninth Symphony, or Ives's *Majority* ("Theme: TODAY, the world awake! Humanity on the march.... Millions of feet endlessly tramping, treading, pounding, striding, leaping.") In scope it was to be a kind of counterpart to Ives's *Universe Symphony*; Varèse at one time imagined a performance of it broadcast simultaneously from all the capitals of the world, with a choir in each singing in its own language! Like the *Universe Symphony*, it was never finished.

The third group of Varèse's works are those few written between 1949 and 1960: *Déserts* for orchestra with electronic-tape interludes; organized sound (electronic) for a sequence, *Good Friday Procession in Verges*, in a film called *Around and About Joan Miró*; *La Poème électronique*; and two unfinished works, *Nocturnal* [34] and *Nuit*, both on texts from Anaïs Nin's *The House of Incest*.

It will be useful now to treat several significant works of Varèse briefly in the order in which they were composed.

HYPERPRISM (1922–1923)

Varèse's works tend not to be long, but *Hyperprism* is the shortest—only four minutes. "Little Hyperprism," as his wife called it, nevertheless caused a riot at its first performance, at an International Composers' Guild concert in 1923 with Varèse conducting. For this work he arrived at a type of instrumentation well suited to his ideas, and one he was to use, with various additions, in three more works (*Intégrales, Ecuatorial, Déserts*)—an orchestra of eight to a dozen wind instruments and a large percussion section of four to six players playing many different instruments. For *Hyperprism* these include a siren and a string drum, or "lion roar," which makes a unique and quite audible effect. As Varèse describes it, in another score, it is "a single-headed drum; a piece of heavy twine is attached to the center of the membrane. The sound, approximating a lion's roar, is produced by drawing a piece of leather or canvas along the string, causing the membrane to vibrate."

INTEGRALES (1924–1925)

In *Intégrales* Varèse further explored the ground he had broken in *Hyperprism*, enlarging his wind section and expanding the work to three times the length of the earlier one. Robert Craft, who has conducted and recorded most of Varèse's music, has called attention to the "repeated one-note rhythmic figure with interrupting appoggiaturas, that is a kind of germinal figure throughout Varèse's music." [35] This trait is nowhere more apparent than in *Intégrales*; at the beginning, for example, the note b flat'' persists, in various instruments, through seven pages.

It is possibly in *Intégrales*, as a matter of fact, that we find the majority of Varèse's characteristic musical traits most fully exemplified. When all is said and done, what kinds of sounds does a composer choose to make music with? This is a revealing common denominator in all of a composer's works. With Varèse one hears, first of all, and a good deal of the time, *sustained* sounds—extremely low, extremely high, getting louder, getting softer (this less often), and often articulated in repeated notes, as Craft has pointed out. One hears sliding sounds: a trombone *glissando*, a siren, a lion roar—later he will make more of these with electronics. And one hears certain favorite percussion sounds: a snare drummer executing rudimental flams and rolls (which somehow injects a disturbingly mundane element into the music), little scraping noises, various noises of rattles and ratchets, the sounds of small hollowish wooden objects being hit(castanets, wood blocks, Chinese temple blocks, coconut shells), and of course the cymbals and gongs. These are the most salient elements of Varèse's vocabulary.

Interestingly enough, they have their close counterparts in the later purely electronic music of *La Poème électronique* and the organized-sound interpolations of *Déserts*. Varèse makes music with tone color and rhythm. Harmony has been replaced by a sense of the mass and density of sounds. (He can make a "chord" out of several percussion instruments sounding together, as he shows us in *Hyperprism* and *Ionisation*.) His counterpoint is the juxtaposition of sound masses. By the time he wrote *Hyperprism*, he had succeeded more than any other composer (how well in the long run it is still probably too soon to tell) in dispensing with melody. Even small fragments of melody (such as the quasi-jazzy bits in the middle of *Intégrales* or the oboe cadenzas in the same piece or the curious, almost Ivesian, little high woodwind tune in *Arcana*) sound by this time out of place. Only when the human voice sings (as in the incantation-like *Ecuatorial*) does melody still seem to fit this kind of organized sound, as Varèse himself called his music.

IONISATION (1930–1931)

Varèse's output became more sparse after he completed *Arcana* in 1927. In 1928 he went to France for five years. During that time he completed only one work, the famous *Ionisation*. For this five-minute work he used nothing but percussion—an orchestra of thirteen percussionists playing thirty-seven instruments (though not all at once). It was premiered in New York in 1933 by Nicolas Slonimsky. As the creation of a composer working in what could be considered the mainstream of Occidental music, it was epoch-making; however, the time of the percussion instruments had surely come in any case, owing more than is generally realized to the Latin-African music of the Caribbean. The Cuban composer Amadeo Roldán, for example, had written six *Ritmicas* for percussion orchestra in 1930.

DESERTS (1949–1954)

After Varèse's long hiatus, he produced *Déserts*, for much the same kind of instrumental forces he had used before—twelve winds and a large assortment of percussion, but with the important addition of ten minutes' worth of electronic-tape sounds interpolated at three points into the thirteen and a half minutes of live instrumental music. This makes *Déserts*, at twenty-three and a half minutes, one of Varèse's larger works, although he has indicated that the electronic interpolations can be dispensed with; there is some evidence that the decision to include them came fairly late. The genesis of the work is interesting. Varèse had evidently first conceived of the music as associated with a film that was to be made *afterwards*—a film that would show "the deserts of earth (sand, snow); the deserts of the sea; the deserts of outer space (galaxies, nebulae, etc.); but particularly the deserts in the mind of man." [36] The film was never made, but the conception was realized musically in terms of this piece. All the characteristics of Varèse's vocabulary previously noted are present; *Déserts* is, if possible, an even more severely refined music of pure timbre and rhythm.

LA POÈME ÉLECTRONIQUE (1957–1958)

Varèse's eagerly awaited liberation, which he had long asked of science, from the limitations of the human performer and the traditional acoustical instruments came with the opportunity to create eight minutes of sound to be projected literally *in space* through the medium of 425 loudspeakers in the Philips Pavilion designed by Le Corbusier for the Brussels International Exposition in 1958. (*La Poème électronique* was actually the name of the entire concept, which included visual projections designed by Le Corbusier; the pavilion was simply the "vessel" to contain both.) Here the sound masses (a montage made up of a combination of manipulated "real" and synthesized sound carefully assembled by Varèse, who worked for six to eight months in the Philips laboratory in Eindhoven, Holland) could literally move in space, thanks to a three-track tape and an elaborate "routing" of the sound channel's through the maze of speakers installed in the roof of the pavilion.

Some of the components of this achievement Varèse had envisioned forty years before. (In 1916 he had said, "We ... need new instruments very badly," and in 1922, "The composer and the electrician will have to labor together.") He had participated in and encouraged actual research for thirty years before. The technology that finally made *La Poème électronique* possible had already, in the post–World War II years, added a lively new electronic wing to the edifice of music, from which much was hoped for by many. It is to these developments, together with some contemporaneous new esthetic concepts, that we now turn.

FURTHER READING

General

CHASE, GILBERT. *America's Music.* 2nd rev. ed. New York: McGraw-Hill Book Co., Chapters 20, 27.

HOWARD, JOHN TASKER. *Our American Music.* 4th ed. New York: Thomas Y. Crowell Co., 1965. Chapter 12.

MELLERS, WILFRED. *Music in a New Found Land: Themes and Developments in the History of American Music.* New York: Alfred A. Knopf, 1965.

> An English musicologist views American music; all the composers in this chapter are given interesting and rather extensive treatment—Ives "as American hero," Ruggles "as American mystic," etc.

REIS, CLAIRE R. *Composers, Conductors and Critics.* New York, 1955. Reprinted, with new introduction by the author and preface by Aaron Copland, Detroit: Detroit Reprints in Music, 1974.

> Important as a source of information about the influential League of Composers (begun as an offshoot of Varèse's International Composers' Guild), written by the woman who was its director for 25 years.

ROSENFELD, PAUL. *Musical Impressions: Selections from Paul Rosenfeld's Criticism.* Edited and with introduction by Herbert Leibowitz. New York: Hill & Wang, 1969.

> Includes early critical assessment of Ives (1936), Ruggles (1928), and Varèse (1929).

* YATES, PETER. *Twentieth-Century Music: Its Evolution from the End of the Harmonic Era into the Present Era of Sound.* New York: Random House, 1967.

> A readable and perceptive introduction to his subject by a Los Angeles author, lecturer, and critic who has produced concerts of new music and written regularly for *Arts and Architecture* and other periodicals. Relevant are chapters on Ives and Cage, and two on "The American Experimental Tradition."

---

* Items thus marked are part of the suggested reference library to be available in connection with this book.

Collections of Writings by American Composers

* CHASE, GILBERT (ed.). *The American Composer Speaks*. Baton Rouge: Louisiana State University Press, 1966.

> Excerpted writings of composers covering a 200-year span, from William Billings to Earle Brown. Included are pieces by Ives, Cowell, Cage, Partch, and Varèse.

* COWELL, HENRY (ed.). *American Composers on American Music: A Symposium*. Palo Alto, Calif, 1933. Paperback reprint with new introduction, New York: Frederick Ungar Publishing Co., 1962.

> The prototype of such collections, this excellent "symposium" of the early thirties, focusing on the contemporary scene, includes 31 articles on American composers and on general tendencies.

* SCHWARTZ, ELLIOTT, and CHILDS, BARNEY. *Contemporary Composers on Contemporary Music*. New York: Holt, Rinehart & Winston, 1967.

> This collection covers the European scene as well, but part 2 deals with "Experimental Music and Recent American Developments." There is some inevitable duplication of this collection with Chase, *The American Composer*.

Individual Composers

CHARLES IVES

From the vast amount of material, the following is suggested as a basic Ives library:

* COWELL, HENRY and SIDNEY. *Charles Ives and His Music*. New York: Oxford University Press, 1955. Rev. ed. (paperback), 1969.

> Always valuable as the firt biography (the section written by Sidney Cowell) and the first important study of the music (written by Henry Cowell), this is an excellent introduction to both, by an eminent composer and his wife who knew Ives personally and helped to bring his music before the public over a period of many years.

* Ives, Charles. *Essays Before a Sonata, and Other Writings*. New York: W. W. Norton & Co., 1961. Paperback, 1964.

* ———. *Charles E. Ives: Memos*. Edited by John Kirkpatrick. New York: W. W. Norton & Co., 1972.

> These two books may be considered well-nigh indispensable primary sources for Ives's life, work, and most importantly, thought. With some regrettable exceptions (such as the "Conductor's Note" to the Fourth Symphony) they contain nearly everything Ives wrote. The *Memos*, in addition, carefully and knowledgeably edited, contain some almost equally valuable appendices, including an annotated list of all Ives's compositions.

* PERLIS, VIVIAN (ed.). *Charles Ives Remembered: An Oral History*. New Haven: Yale University Press, 1974.

> Evidence of the new wave of interest in Ives, this consists of transcripts of recorded reminiscences of many who knew him: family members, business associates, friends, neighbors, and of course musicians, many of them well known. There are many photos, and reproductions of manuscript pages and programs. The actual voices of some of the contributors may be heard in excerpts from this oral history in the album *Charles Ives: The 100th Anniversary* (Columbia: M4-32504).

ROSSITER, FRANK R. *Charles Ives and His America*. New York: Liveright Publishing Corp., 1975.

> An up-to-date and well-researched biography—and more; it also examines the issues faced, and raised, by Ives as an artist in early-twentieth-century America. Rossiter writes: "I became more and more convinced that the Ives Legend which has grown up around him gives a very imperfect picture of the man. I think that the key to an understanding of his place in American culture lies in his extreme artistic isolation."

CARL RUGGLES

HARRISON, LOU. *About Carl Ruggles*. Yonkers, N.Y.: Oscar Baradinsky at the Alicat Bookshop, 1946.

> This slim volume is the only book known, to date, devoted exclusively to Ruggles. It is written by an eminent, widely knowledgeable composer, who much admires Ruggles's music, and sees in it a renewal of the tradition of serious, contrapuntal music represented by Bach and Handel.

HENRY COWELL

COWELL, HENRY. *New Musical Resources*. New York, 1930. New ed., with preface and notes by Joscelyn Godwin, New York: Something Else Press, 1969.

> The importance of this youthful treatise, at times penetrating and prophetic, and at times naive, has been discussed in the chapter.

LOU HARRISON

HARRISON, LOU. *Music Primer: Various Items about Music to 1970*. New York: C. F. Peters, 1971.

JOHN CAGE

* CAGE, JOHN. *Silence*. Middletown, Conn.: Wesleyan University Press, 1961. Paperback, Cambridge, Mass.: M.I.T. Press, 1966.

> The best single source of Cage's writing and lectures, including material from 1939 to 1961.

Harry Partch

* Partch, Harry. *Genesis of a Music*. 2nd ed. New York: Da Capo Press, 1974.

In this 500-page volume Partch sets forth the esthetic and acoustical basis of his work, and describes his instruments (which are illustrated by photographs) and his compositions. Aside from his music and his instruments, this book is Partch's major work. He worked on it for twenty years before the first edition was published in 1947. The second edition is enlarged by a new preface; by chapters on new instruments built after 1947 and on the background of six of his major works; by some important appendices listing all the music; and by a chronology of the instruments.

Edgard Varèse

Ouellette, Fernand. *Edgard Varèse*. Translated by Derek Coltman. New York: Orion Press, 1968.

A biography that takes up the works in the context of Varèse's life. With its list of works and very extensive bibliography, which includes a great number of periodical articles and interviews, this "first biography" is informative and well-nigh indispensable, despite its effusively worshipful tone.

Varèse, Louise. *Varèse: A Looking-Glass Diary*. Vol. 1, 1883–1928. New York: W. W. Norton & Co., 1972.

Rich in detail as in insight, this account by Varèse's wife is far more objective than the Ouellette biography.

LISTENING

Current Schwann catalogs indicate a rather wide selection of available recordings of works by composers treated in this chapter. The Ives list grows continuously, all of Varèse is available, and most of Ruggles and Partch; Cowell, Harrison, and Cage, with their relatively large output, are nevertheless fairly well represented. It only remains to suggest a few individual albums of some particular usefulness or significance.

Charles Ives

* *Charles Ives: The 100th Anniversary*. Columbia: M4-32504.

This four-record album consists of a sampling of the music, but also includes two sides of Ives playing of his own music, and a "bonus" record of excerpts from the interviews that make up the oral history

project *Charles Ives Remembered* (see the reading list). A lengthy illustrated booklet is included.

Old Songs Deranged: Charles Ives, Music for Theater Orchestra. Columbia:
M-32969.

This interesting recording by the Yale Theater Orchestra contains some
rarities, such as the *Holiday Quickstep* written for his father's Danbury
band; it also reminds us of Ives's fondness for the theater orchestras of
his own time, in which he occasionally played while at Yale, and with
which he tried out some of his music.

Nine Songs by Charles Ives. RAAM: NW-300.

The selection of Ives songs occupying the first side of this album (the
second is devoted to the songs of more recent American composers) is
noteworthy for its rarities, including four French songs.

Henry Cowell

* *The Piano Music of Henry Cowell.* Folkways: FM-3349.

This consists of 20 pieces played by the composer himself, including all
the ones treated in this chapter, with Cowell's own verbal annotations.

Quartet Euphometric. RAAM: NW-218.

Quartet Romantic. RAAM: NW-285.

This album also includes work relevant to this chapter by Wallingford
Riegger, John J. Becker, and Ruth Crawford Seeger.

John Cage

* *The 25-Year Retrospective Concert of the Music of John Cage.* Produced by
George Avakian, 10 West 33rd St., New York, N.Y. 10001

A recording of a live performance at Town Hall, New York, in May
1958, this three-record album, with extensive notes and sample pages
of the scores, is a good survey of Cage's work up to that time.

Also of Interest

Nicolas Slonimsky: Historic Premieres. Orion: 7150.

An interesting documentary recording of Slonimsky conducting four
pieces he had premiered: Ives, *Barn Dance* (from *Washington's Birthday*) and *In the Night*; Ruggles, *Lilacs*; and Varèse, *Ionisation*.

Sound Forms for Piano. RAAM: NW-203.

This recording of experimental music includes Cowell, *The Banshee,
Aeolian Harp,* and *Piano Piece (Paris 1924)*; excerpts from Cage,
Sonatas and Interludes for Prepared Piano; Ben Johnston, *Sonata for*

Microtonal Piano; and Conlon Nancarrow's *Three Studies for Player Piano.*

PROJECTS

1. Frank Rossiter, in *Charles Ives and His America,* quotes the American conductor Walter Damrosch as having written in 1923: "I do not think there has ever been a country whose musical development has been fostered so almost exclusively by women as America." Read Rossiter's book, with special attention to the first chapter, and comment in a brief talk or essay on the reflection of this observation in Charles Ives's attitudes and writings. Conclude with any observations you may have from your own experience, either past or present, and an assessment of the situation today.
2. If you play the guitar, banjo, or dulcimer, use one of these instruments to demonstrate quarter-tone tuning, devising some simple melodies using such a tuning.
3. Contrive a series of "ear-stretching" experiences similar to those of George Ives, in which a melody is sung or played in one key, and the accompaniment in another.
4. Devise and put on a simple musical performance demonstrating the spatial element in music—similar to, but less elaborate than, the experimental performance devised by Georges Ives in Danbury, described on pp. 456–457.
5. Write a brief paper on Charles Ives as business executive, including an account of his important contributions to the life insurance business. Refer to his innovative concepts and his writings (such as his pamphlet *The Amount to Carry—Measuring the Prospect*).
6. From the approximately 120 songs by Charles Ives, most of which are available in print and many of which are recorded, make up a list of twelve (exclusive of the ones treated in this chapter) and write program notes for a hypothetical performance of them, "cataloguing" them in some manner similar to that used in this chapter.
7. Write original program notes for two or three of the following Ives compositions: *Central Park in the Dark,* String Quartet no. 2, *Hallowe'en, Calcium Night Light, The Pond.* Comment upon the programmaticism involved.
8. After a careful study of the sources of Ives's musical language, and his use of quotation, write a brief essay assessing to what extent his work *is,* and to what extent it is *not,* "pop art."
9. Review thoughtfully Ives's statements about "idealism versus pro-

fessionalism in music" in the section so-labeled in this chapter, and read Ives more fully in this regard (starting with the complete Epilogue of the *Essays*). In what ways do you agree or disagree with his stance? Is this stance possible today? Make this the subject of a brief talk or paper.

10. The French-born Americanized composer Dane Rudhyar wrote in the early 1930s a very brief, nonspecific article titled "Oriental Influence in American Music." (It is printed in Cowell, *American Composers on American Music.*) His last paragraph reads: "The gateway to the Orient is through Occidental America. It is therefore natural to assume that it will be through America that the influence of Oriental music will first be felt in the Occident." To what extent has this happened in the nearly fifty years since this was written? Explore the topic from any aspect you choose, and write a brief but more specific essay with the same title as Rudhyar's.

11. Henry Cowell and Harry Partch both began fairly early to write treatises on their conceptions of the directions and resources required of the "new music"—Cowell in *New Musical Resources,* and Partch in *Genesis of a Music.* Make a brief comparative study of these.

12. John Cage's "Four Statements on the Dance" (four articles written between 1939 and 1957, and included in his *Silence*) allude to the correlation of new sounds (especially percussion) with modern dance. If you have the opportunity, attend a performance of "modern dance" (now frequently incorporated into ballet itself) that uses new sounds, percussive or electronic, and review the program and its impact, including references to the Cage articles.

13. In his *Gensis of a Music,* p. 9, Harry Partch clarifies his distinction between Corporeal and Abstract music, giving instances of each from a broad range of music. Read this and the material leading up to it, ponder this distinction, and think about your own listening habits and preferences. Of which type is the music that most (and least) appeals to you? Make an annotated diary of the music you listen to for a week or a month, describing the degree of Corporeality or Abstractness of each piece, giving your reasons for making the distinction, and describing your reaction to the music in terms of this distinction.

14. Harry Partch has called *U.S. Highball—A Musical Account of a Transcontinental Hobo Trip* "the most creative piece of work I have ever done." It is autobiographical, and Partch explains at some length its genesis and why in his view, it "suggests epic feelings." (See *Genesis of a Music,* pp. 322–323.) Listen carefully to the work (issued on Gate 5 Records—as of this writing unfor-

tunately out of print, but available in many library collections).
Compare it to other works based upon some aspect of American
experience that you might consider to similarly suggest "epic
feelings" (the *Dust Bowl Ballads* of Woody Guthrie?).

15. Edgard Varèse said: "Science is the poetry of today." Comment on
both the truths and fallacies implicit in this, and on the ways in
which whatever Varèse meant by this was reflected in his music.

16. John Cage wrote a two-page article on Varèse, which is printed in
his *Silence*. Using this as a point of departure (but acquainting
yourself further with the ideas and music of both men), contrast
the views of each on the use of sounds in music.

Chapter Seventeen
Exploration and Experiment: Technology and New Esthetic Concepts

FOR THE INDIVIDUAL who is serious about making the acquaintance of the radically new music written since midcentury, there are two approaches possible. One is through reading about it. This can be an absorbing and time-consuming pursuit in itself. The new music has occasioned a great deal of writing: books, articles, printed lectures, record-jacket notes. One can thus become familiar with its various rationales, and read descriptions of the methods used in its composition, the game rules given its performers, and the theatrical-environmental conditions of its performance.

The other approach is through simply listening to the sounds themselves. Although the genetic aspects of the works cannot be left out of account altogether for a sympathetic appreciation of this music (and we shall deal with them in due course), a first approach through the sounds themselves has much to recommend it. As Roger Sessions (a composer who has long championed the avant-garde) has said:

> One cannot insist too strongly or too frequently that, in the arts generally and in music in particular, it is only productions that really count, and that only in these—music, written or performed—are to be found the criteria by which ideas about music, as well as music itself, must finally stand or fall: not the converse.[1]

To the listener who approaches this music through the sounds themselves the whole picture of the new music is somewhat less complicated than it would seem from reading about it. It is, in fact, less revolutionary than evolutionary. (The hyperbolic image of the radical genius "destroying the past," as irresistible as it may be to the record-jacket annotator, has validity, after all, only in the realm of polemics.) For there can be observed a fairly consistent overall progression, independent of the genetic rationales and intellectual justifications, into the typical sound patterns of the new music of the 1960s and 1970s.

What are the points of departure? If we were to look for archetypal sounds, we would come closest to finding them in the music of Edgard Varèse (treated in the previous chapter) and of the Austrian Anton Webern, in the sounds of Far Eastern music (especially the gamelan orchestras of Indonesia), in the playing of such bop and post-bop jazz virtuosos as Charlie Parker and John Coltrane, and in the sounds of early electronic music. From these starting points (and others), present-day new music has developed a vocabulary of sound types and sound gestures that lend themselves fairly well to generalized description—description that is to a remarkable degree independent of whether the sounds are produced electronically or by live performers. Thus it is possible (with due regard for the dangers and limitations involved) to characterize in a general way both the sounds and the way in which these sounds are used. Much of the new music in fact invites this approach—this attention purely to the aural surface. Unlike Ives's ideal music, what it sounds like *is* what it is.

THE SURFACE OF THE NEW MUSIC

In this music, as John Cage has said, "nothing takes place but the sounds."[2] These sounds, however, tend to avoid the middle ground of the formerly usual. They are much of the time very high or very low; very soft (as in the case of many of Morton Feldman's compositions through-out) or very loud (George Crumb has specified that the dynamic level of his electrified stringed instruments in *Black Angels* be "on the threshold of pain"). Furthermore, they tend to manifest the preference for the unusual in quality. With stringed instruments, resources such as harmonics, *col legno* (playing with the wood of the bow), *sul ponticello* (bowing far up on the bridge, to produce an eerily rasping sound), playing without the usual vibrato, playing with excessive bow pressure, and bowing the strings on the opposite side of the bridge (to say nothing of such effects as thump-ing on the body of the instrument) are common. In the case of the woodwinds, new "multiphonic" effects (more than a single pitch sounding at once) are sought after and used,[3] as are simpler effects such as clicking the keys. Brass players may be called upon to blow through their horns without forming the usual embouchure with their lips, producing thereby a windy amplification of the sound of their breath. We have already encountered modifications of piano tone in the music of Cowell and Cage; recent works such as *Makrokosmos II* (1973) by George Crumb, and *Ni Bruit Ni Vitesse* by Lukas Foss, are successors to the early Cowell and Cage pieces, and show a continuing preoccupation with the tonal possibilities of the grand piano. Electronic music has available standardized synthesized tone qualities that go by such names as "square wave" and "saw-toothed wave." Percussion continues to yield new sounds, and some both new and old (like the sounds of gongs and rattles, and the scraping of the güiro, a serrated gourd) have furnished useful sound models for electronic music. "Gamelan-like" percussion sounds (the sounds of reso-nant metal or wood bodies being struck, which resemble the sounds of the percussion orchestras of Java or Bali) are favorites, both for live and for electronic music.[4]

Sliding sounds are used; Varèse's sirens perhaps furnished the prototype. The effect is a basic element of writing for strings in the new music (practically all avant-garde string quartets incorporate it), and of course it is easily managed electronically.

The use of "noise-like" sounds has been endemic to electronic music, but has continued to be part of the music for live performers as well, with a long lineage extending from John Alden Carpenter's typewriter and Varèse's sirens of the 1920s to the tray of dishes thrown into a trash barrel at the climax of a composition of the 1960s.

There are also characteristic ways in which sounds are used. For one thing, the durations of tones tend to be either very short (often so short that their tone quality hardly registers with the listener) or very long, avoiding the middle-ground durations upon which traditional music is based. There is also much use of what has been known (by analogy with the visual arts) as "pointillism"; the sounds come singly, disconnectedly, and often widely separated in range and in tone color. (Many contemporary works illustrate both pointillism and durational extremes, but Christian Wolff's *Duo for Violinist and Pianist* does so to a striking degree.)

Silence is an important element—a more pronounced structural feature than in traditional music. The silences are apt to be longer in a work by Cage, or one of the circle of composers he has most directly encouraged or influenced, such as Morton Feldman, Earle Brown, and especially Christian Wolff. As early as 1952 Cage himself preempted the ultimate position as far as the use of silence is concerned with his famous and often-cited piece *4′ 33″*, in which no intended sounds whatever are produced, and which may therefore be performed by "any instrument or combination of instruments."

Certain sound complexes are characteristic, and often seem to have prototypes in nature. A texture of dry, crackling sounds (such as may be heard in Earle Brown's String Quartet of 1965 or Mel Powell's *Filigree Setting for String Quartet* of 1959) finds its analogy in the sound of fire. Soft twittering, scraping sounds, whether produced electronically or by live performers (Leon Kirchner, in his Quartet no. 3 for Strings and Electronic Tape, uses both), give the impression of having been suggested by the activities of small birds, animals, or insects. (Amplified, as in George Crumb's *Night of the Electric Insects* from *Black Angels*, this effect can be terrifying.) Similarly, certain *gestures* are frequently encountered in both live and electronic music—rapid, frenetic flurries of notes, for example. (This could find its prototype, among other places, in the frenzied spurts of virtuosity of some jazz performers, from bop onwards.)

Rhythmic complexity (engendered by the consistent use of a complicated and nonrepeating series of durations) is a crucial characteristic. This complexity is of the type used by Ives, as shown in the notes from *In the Night* reproduced below—considered unplayable by most performers in his day.

With the advent of electronic music, it became possible to realize such complexities in the laboratory, so to speak. But there has arisen a new generation of virtuoso performers (challenged, like the John Henry of the ballad, to compete with the machine) who can execute these rhythms manually, and these performers are now given complex series of durations to realize, such as the following from Elliott Carter's Double Concerto:

Rhythmic complexity has obscured or eliminated entirely the sense of *pulse* in this music—a feature both broadly typical and of the most decisive importance to its basic nature.

In terms of larger formal dimensions (often determined, as we shall see, by extramusical considerations, mathematical or programmatic, or both) it is generally true that no one kind of sound, or one musical procedure or gesture, lasts very long. From the listener's point of view, it it a music comprised of a series of moments, put together mosaic-like, often with little *obvious* connectedness. As the composer Ralph Shapey has said: "The 'image' must create and sustain the unforgettable moment, and it is a series of such moments that result in a dynamic, unforgettable experience." [5]

Yet it is interesting to observe that certain mundane but nearly inescapable principles of form apply: for example, in the procession of textures and intensities, a complex, active section is apt to necessitate a following section that is more or less quiet, if the piece is to "work," regardless of how this procession of events is rationalized.

THE RATIONALES AND METHODS OF
THE NEW MUSIC

If the surface of the new music, as the ear alone perceives it, gives the impression of having simply assimilated (with greater or less success) more sounds into its vocabulary, and having found ways of putting them together that differ only in degree from the ways used before, the situation in the 1950s and 1960s was far less simple from the composer's point of view. He or she had, as never before, to *rationalize*. Innocence was no longer possible; the new "advanced" composer knew too much. Even the decision *not* to rationalize had to be rationalized. There lay in wait for the serious young aspiring composer a maze of ideas, ideologies, methods, dogmas, and intellectual abstractions and justifications. The European climate of academicism and intellectualism had made European composers more prone to rationalization, but American composers had also become involved, despite a certain ineradicable residue of independence and distrust of hierarchical system. Among composers dedicated to advanced music, fortunate were those such as Morton Feldman, who succeeded in extricating themselves and confronting autonomously once more the basic function of the composer—to make music. Feldman himself has said: "Unfortunately for most people who pursue art, ideas become their opium. The sickness that you feel about the situation today is a piling up of multitudinous suggestions and multitudinous misconceptions, each tumbling over the other. There is no security to be one's self." [6]

A sign of the times was the extent to which these "multitudinous suggestions" were verbalized in the abundant writing about contemporary music. A few samples will convey the sense of the terms in which composition was either conceived by composers themselves or was *presumed* by observers to have been conceived by them. The well-worn "time and space" theme, reverted to again and again, furnishes some typical examples.

> music as an object in Time and Space . . .
> In my music, the initial space-time image generates through expansions of *itself* all textures and a structural totality. Through permutations of this image I continue, rather than destroy, its state of being.[7]

> Sounds do not progress, but merely heap up and accumulate in the same place. . . . This blurs and obliterates the past, and obliterating it, removes the possibility of a future. . . . What is offered is not just music in time, but a new idea of time.[8]

In terms of rationale and method, the paths that composers took varied in detail with each individual, but two fairly clear general routes were followed—routes that diverged widely. Cage, in an address given in 1957, pointed up the difference rather clearly in terms of the amount of *rational* control exercised by the composer over the aural result: the production.

> Again there is a parting of the ways. One has a choice. If he does not wish to give up his attempts to control sound, he may complicate his musical technique towards an approximation of the new possibilities and awareness. (I use the word "approximation" because a measuring mind can never finally measure nature.) Or, as before, one may give up the desire to control sound, clear his mind of music, and set about discovering means to let the sounds be themselves rather than vehicles for man-made theories or expressions of human sentiments.[9]

The almost diametrically opposed positions represented by the ideal of maximum rational control on the one hand (Milton Babbitt: "I believe in cerebral music, and I never choose a note unless I know why I want it there" [10]) and a minimum of such control on the other (John Cage: "Discovering means to let sounds be themselves") polarized the new music in the 1950s and 1960s to the extent that the two approaches were given separate names: *avante-garde* for the first and *experimental* for the second. Let us now examine briefly some of the premises and the manifestations of each.

Toward Maximum Rational Control by the Composer

The trend towards ever-greater control over the end result of musical composition was manifested in two distinct but related areas. The first was the control over every aspect of performance, going beyond the historically basic specifications of pitch, rhythm, and tempo (which evolved in that order) to include the most detailed instructions regarding tone color and dynamic nuance. Increasing control is a process that has been going on progressively from the time that specific instrumentation and instrumental effects began to be called for by composers of the Renaissance. Its ultimate realization, naturally, is the composition directly on tape (electronic music), which eliminates the performer entirely.

The composer Richard Maxfield has furnished one of the most lucid and best-reasoned briefs for electronic music in his article "Music, Electronic and Performed." [11] And the carefully crafted compositions—some of them large-scale, and by no means inexpressive—of composers such as Vladimir Ussachevsky and Otto Luening, and after them Mel Powell, Kenneth Gaburo, and especially Morton Subotnik, are representative of what is possible in this medium. But by and large the elimination of the performer did not prove to be the altogether worthwhile victory it was once thought to be, and Maxfield's article also opens up lines of retreat from the ultimate position of control that tape music represents. It is precisely the degree of predetermination that this control involves, as well as tape music's "perilously limited array of options," as Mel Powell has said, which has so drastically limited the currency and success of pure electronic music. Maxfield's compromises with this absolute predetermination include live performers playing the machines in a concert situation, and performers playing traditional instruments in conjunction with taped sounds. This latter represents one of the most frequent current uses of tape music. Tape music has also stimulated new kinds of virtuosity in the performance of traditional instruments, as has been mentioned.[12]

A second, and more fundamentally crucial, area of increased control was that governing the myriad of choices the composer makes in writing the piece to begin with. In this century the greatest degree of predetermined control of choices has been that represented by the technique of *serial organization*. As first developed and practiced by the twentieth-century Viennese composers Arnold Schoenberg, Alban Berg, and Anton Webern, the principle of serial organization was applied only to the choice of pitches used throughout a composition; these appeared always in a certain serial order, as determined by one form or another of a basic predetermined series of the twelve tones of the tempered scale. This "classical" serial technique has been used by many American composers, including Ben Weber, George Rochberg, Ross Lee Finney, and in some works, Aaron Copland. We encountered it in the work of Wallingford Riegger in chapter 15.

The serial organization of pitches alone has a history of more than half a century. Ultimately, the more decisive and inevitable move towards subjecting the *total* aural result of a composition to the intellectual predetermination of serial procedures was taken. What has become popularly known as *total serialization* involves, ideally, a procedure by which the ordering of all the other measurable dimensions of sound—duration, intensity, timbre, and register—is serially determined.[13] This procedure results in a composition that has been called "the unpremeditated result of comprehensive premeditation."[14] The idea itself has become well known, although actual pieces in which all the so-called parameters of music (a significant borrowing of a term from mathematics) have been serially predetermined are relatively rare.

Serialism has provided the ultimate justification on purely rational grounds for every aspect of a composition, and as such has been useful to those who, for one reason or another, are committed to the goal of minimizing or eliminating the role of the composer's intuition(formerly called inspiration)—a goal paradoxically identical with that of many composers who have adopted procedures to *decrease* their control over their materials, as we shall see. More pragmatically, serialism has been useful in turning up, through its characteristic of unpredictability, new possibilities of sound relationships that might not occur to the composer relying on intuition and imagination alone. Having performed this function to a degree—that is, having suggested certain new sound characteristics and usages (some of which have already been described earlier in this chapter) —serialism has receded in importance as a practical procedure. As Ernst Krenek has said:

Such features as extended static complexes, improvisational and aleatoric passages, pointillistically scattered tones of widely contrasting dynamic levels, novel manners of articulation, and unusual sound qualities (many of which were inspired by experience in the electronic medium) are now available to composers without their having to repeat the serial operations which generated them.[15]

Many composers soon realized, in fact, the limitations of serialism. Of these, two became especially evident. The first of these stems from the basic premise of serialism that all the pitches, durations, intensities, and other properties comprising the predetermined series must be heard before any can be repeated. Thus the incessant change dictated by the constant and inexorable rotation through the series means that the whole gamut of sound material must be, in practical terms, nearly constantly present to the ear. But, as the proverb has it, the more things change, the more they are the same, and the aural result of this constant change is often actually a kind of *static* quality—a limitation difficult to overcome even in music using older procedures in which only pitch is serialized. As the German avant-gardist Stockhausen has put it: "If from one sound to the next, pitch, duration, timbre and intensity change . . . one is constantly traversing the entire realm of experience in a very short time, and thus one finds oneself in a state of suspended animation, the music 'stands still.' " [16]

A second limitation has already been hinted at, and this is the built-in tendency of serialism to defeat the avowed purpose of those adopting it as a means of achieving totally predetermined control; the music comes to resemble, to a remarkable degree, that generated by opposite procedures of purposeful randomness. As Krenek has said of serialism: "It is reasonable to assume that in pursuing this concept beyond certain limits one would reach a point of diminishing returns, for the internal organization of the final product would become so complicated that its outward appearance would be hardly distinguishable from that of organized chaos." [17]

The compositional approach of maximum rationalization and control (not necessarily always taking the form of total serialism) continues to be cultivated. The fact that the universities tend to be the centers for its cultivation, often pursued with the aid of foundation grants, has helped to foster the analogy of this type of composition to pure scientific research. There is created around this kind of music, and the theorizing that goes with it, a rarified atmosphere in which the layman is made to feel not only uncomfortable but unwelcome and inferior. The pronouncements of some composers are not calculated to dispel this. Charles Wuorinen has said: "Composers have always been 'intellectuals' and this stance is absolutely unavoidable today, for music has grown too rich and complex to be handled by the illiterate." [18]

Today it is not only the layman who might conceivably feel "illiterate"; the researches and writings of Milton Babbitt, for example, are largely a closed book to the musician, and even the composer, unless he or she has become familiar with the mathematical terms and concepts that have been adopted by this branch of composition. The role of the researcher who works without consideration of any broader "practical" applications— or any "public," for that matter—is claimed for the composer of advanced music. This view is cogently expressed by Milton Babbitt himself in a now-famous article significantly titled "Who Cares If You Listen?" [19] Written for a magazine with broad circulation (*High Fidelity*), and in this case in terms any intelligent layman can understand, it is recommended as one of the most lucid and unequivocal statements of the viewpoint of the composer-as-research-specialist.

Toward Minimum Rational Control by the Composer

The second path of new music has been that of progressive relinquishment of rational control by the composer. Here, as with its opposite, serialism, the musical result cannot be envisoned in full, but for a different reason—the composer has deliberately willed it so. Increasingly, aspects of the whole result are left either to the performer or to the operation, in some form or other, of chance.

IMPROVISATION

A certain degree of planned relinquishment of control to the performer (quite aside from the ever-present matters of interpretation) has existed from time to time, principally in the realm of improvisation. This specialized art (native in one particular form to jazz) virtually died out in European music in the early nineteenth century, but it has been revived in the new music of the last half of the twentieth, with new "rules of the game." The work of the Improvisation Chamber Ensemble, a small group founded by Lukas Foss in 1957, consisting of piano, clarinet, cello, and percussion, set high standards for this new improvisation. In the interludes to Foss's *Time Cycle*, and in various other pieces, we hear skilled and disciplined artists who, after long practice together, produce highly integrated compositions, the outlines of which are carefully planned, but the actual details of which are spontaneous and differ with each performance.[20] Of the methods of the Ensemble, Foss and Richard Dufallo, clarinetist and Ensemble member, have written:

A specific formal or textural musical vision is committed to paper. . . . The musicians, as they play, translate the symbols into sound. They do not stake their hope on the element of chance and its capacity for yielding interesting musical results,—they do not put their trust into the order, the system, which coordinates chance happenings. System and chance form the basis for ensemble improvisation, but the *performer holds the reins*. He does not passively translate his symbols into sound, he listens critically, and plays accordingly. . . . He corrects chance rather than surrenders to chance —chance controlled rather than chance in control.[21]

LIMITED INDETERMINACY

Improvisation is, of course, a form of indeterminacy, in that the details of the result are purposely not planned in advance. Improvisation in the strict sense, as exemplified in the work of the Ensemble, involves wide performer choices within a carefully planned structure, and the interaction of players who are highly skilled, experienced in this type of performance, and used to working together. It is therefore rare. Furthermore, as in the case of improvisation in jazz, the effective scope of improvisation is inversely proportional to the size of the group. Therefore composers, in view of the limitations of true improvisation, have found other related means of applying indeterminacy within controlled limits.

Indeterminate notation is one means used, supplying performers with a basic idea of the sound and certain guides and limitations to its production. Graph notation, for instance, an early idea that survives in various forms, was used by Morton Feldman in the early 1950s to produce such works as *Projection 4 for Violin and Piano* (1951) and *Intersection 3* (1953), the latter having been realized on both piano and pipe organ. Indeterminate notation has since evolved with varying degrees of distance from traditional notation, and more importantly, varying degrees of latitude given the player in interpreting it. While a certain degree of standardization is beginning to evolve, most indeterminate notation must continue to rely heavily upon explanatory directions, which are sometimes as lengthy as the notation itself.[22]

Closely related to indeterminate notation is the practice of giving the performers (including the conductor) certain choices in the performance—choices relating to the order of musical events (including how many of the total possible are to be performed at all) and to the duration of these events. Earl Brown's *Available Forms I* (1961) furnishes an example of this procedure. This is a work for chamber ensemble in which the conductor moves at will from one to another of six "events," the notations for all of which are available to the performers at all times. To such procedures Brown has given a name: "open form."

UNLIMITED INDETERMINACY

The progression towards a minimization of control by the composer may be thought of as a continuum, beginning with improvisation. Further along, in the limited indeterminacy we have described, certain freedoms of a somewhat different character have been given the performer, and no two realizations of a work can be the same. It is important to recognize, however, that this is still indeterminacy in the service of the composer's initial vision, or image, of a piece. As we move further along the continuum in the direction of ever-decreasing control over the realized sound itself, we become involved with significant changes in the esthetic concepts of what constitutes the essence and function of music, and of art in general. With Cage's "my purpose is to remove purpose," we encounter at once a fundamentally different attitude and a fundamentally different esthetic. The listener who brings some intellectual background to highly indeterminate music has already been warned of the nature of the realm he is entering, as he departs from the fairly uncomplicated stance of perceiving a work purely in terms of its sounds and steps into the maze of the composer's methods and rationale. As David Cope has pointed out, the listener's reactions and judgments are apt to be profoundly affected as he or she enters this maze:

> If the listener is unaware of the compositional process (in this case "chance") he will tend to judge the composition more or less as any other, depending upon background and experience. On the other hand, if he is aware of the act of indeterminacy his whole set of aesthetics is jarred and judgment is tied to a completely different set of aesthetics according to personal bias.[23]

He enters the realm of art as *process*, rather than finished product—a realm he glimpsed already in some of the ideas of Charles Ives. (Feldman: "Down with the masterpiece—up with art.")

Although the extramusical accident has always been *one factor* in the composition of music, the listener encounters here the almost surgical isolation of chance, and its elevation to a position in which it replaces altogther what has been called imagination, intuition, inspiration. In this he encounters once again (as he did with indeterminacy's complementary opposite, total organization) the goal of removing artistic decisions from the domain of human memory, experience, and intuition, the effects of which are to be expurgated much as (in another context) would be the consequences of "original sin."

John Cage's *Music of Changes* (a piano piece written in 1951, lasting forty-three minutes) furnishes a useful early example of this, having been arrived at through an elaborate process of using charts and coin tosses in accord with the Chinese oracular book of wisdom *I Ching* ("Book of Changes"). Cage described in some detail his method of making the piece, and summed it up with this statement:

> It is thus possible to make a musical composition the continuity of which is free of individual taste and memory (psychology) and also of the literature and "traditions" of the art. The sounds enter the time-space centered within themselves, unimpeded by service to any abstraction, their 360 degrees of circumference free for an infinite play of interpenetration.[24]

With this type of new music, the scope of the composer in determining the actual sounds decreased; his role became more and more circumscribed by the relinquishment of more and more parameters to chance or to the performer, until it was reduced to that of merely setting up systems, or arranging for the unpredictable to happen. As this occurred—as compositional possibilities became narrowed and exhausted—there was a corresponding and compensatory widening of the *arena* of composer involvement, into the visual, the spatial, the theatrical realm. Cage foresaw this when he said in 1957: "where do we go from here? Towards theatre."[25] (It is also true that staged, or multimedia, pieces were initiated partly through the necessity of having something visual going on during the performances of electronic music.) The extension of the new music into the domain of multimedia is actually a fairly complex subject, for there are many essentially different events that come under this heading.

The so-called theater pieces show the clearest relationship to the traditional cooperation of music and spectacle. They represent a considerable degree of coordination of the media involved. Some involve dance, an art which has been particularly hospitable in this century to new ideas in music (it will be recalled, for instance, that Cage's prepared piano was invented for use with the dance). Some pieces represent a "theatricalization" of the basic concert situation, in which the performers themselves become "actors." Partch's later works evolved along this line. Roger Reynold's setting of Wallace Stevens's poem *The Emperor of Ice Cream* (1962) epitomizes this form of the new music.

There are other multimedia events in which indeterminacy takes a much more decisive hand: The auditory and visual elements are combined with little or no attempt at coordination. Whether or not these elements are in themselves indeterminate, their relationship to each other is. One of the earliest examples of this was *La Poème électronique* of 1958, described in the previous chapter, in which Varèse's music was accompanied by multiple visual projections selected by Le Corbusier, who had designed the pavilion as the "vessel" for both. Neither artist knew what the content of the other's work was going to be.

With Cage and others, this multimedia indeterminacy becomes more complex. Cage's *Variations IV* (1964), for example, was "performed" in an art gallery in Los Angeles, and involved a collage of many sound sources (radio broadcasts, electronic sounds, street noises outside the gallery, and various sounds made by the "audience" itself as the people went through the gallery) combined with lights and other visual phenomena. HPSCHD, by Cage and Lejaren Hiller, was an even more complex effort. The sound alone was a dense overlaying of fifty-two electronic sound tapes and seven amplified harpsichords played by live performers. The basic source material for the harpsichordists was *Introduction to the Composition of Waltzes by Means of Dice*, attributed to Mozart (the witty diversion of a genius at play, which has been cited again and again with singular seriousness by theorists of twentieth-century indeterminacy in search of antecedents). The choice of nearly all the sound material, live and electronic, was controlled by chance—in this case, by a computerized version of *I Ching*. The whole performance (which took place in the huge Assembly Hall of the University of Illinois in 1969, and lasted four and a half hours) was accompanied by visual projections from sixty-four slide projectors and eight movie projectors going simultaneously, as well as miscellaneous light beams and the reflected light from spinning mirrored balls—a manufactured "kinetic environment," and the most complex embodiment up to that time of Cage's dictum that "the more things there are, as is said, the merrier." [26]

A composer of Cage's reputation (he functions as a kind of dean of the experimental school) was able to command the forces necessary to produce the kind of new-music extravaganza represented by *HPSCHD*. Otherwise, such theatrical pieces have languished of late, unable to compete in resources and excitement with the elaborately staged light shows that rock groups have mounted for their live performances.

The work of the Cagean wing of experimental music has suggested the concept of art as *therapy*—for the individual and for society. The silences in the works (by which is meant the lack of planned or intended sounds) condition us to listen carefully to the sounds of the environment wherever the concert may be taking place, much as the windows and other openings in modern architecture make the surroundings a part of the structure. Thus we are encouraged, through art, to listen more attentively to the sounds that surround us constantly. The same is true of theater; as Cage says: "Theatre takes place all the time wherever one is and art simply facilitates persuading one this is the case." This view certainly has contributions to make to the richness and variety of our perceptions in the last half of the twentieth century. The problem lies in the fact that while many are ready to grant that this increased awareness of sounds (and of sights, and of "theatre") is beneficial, and can have a considerable esthetic dimension, they are not so sure they want to pay for a slice of life, as it were, served up to them as art. For whether it is or is not art, it is something anyone can do for himself, and do-it-yourself art reduces the role of the specialist composer to zero and quickly puts him out of business. Cage himself, in a one-man dialogue, asked himself the ultimate question—"Why bother, since, as you have pointed out, sounds are continually happening whether you produce them or not?" [27]—but avoided answering it.

At various points along the continuum of indeterminacy we can distinguish various states of mind, as revealed in its manifestations. With John Cage we are in a state of genial, witty, and provocative questioning of assumptions about composing, performing, and listening. As we move along the continuum and into the next generations of composers, the basic "purpose . . . to remove purpose" sometimes takes on the dimensions of a deadly serious nihilism, often with overtones of social and political anarchy, and accompanied by occasional statements showing a genuine confusion between art and life. This manifests itself in anti-music (the real or symbolic destruction of works of art and of the *concept* of the art work), in minimal music (the expansion of minimal material—a single figure or sound—into dimensions of inordinate length), in danger music (the introduction into a performance of elements of real danger, mostly in terms of potential damage to hearing from very loud sounds—another manifestation of the confusion of art and life), and finally in compositions that could not possibly be actually performed, existing only as unrealizable concepts (a single piece of music taking several hundred years to perform, for example). Thus, liberated from purpose, the indeterminacy branch of the new music has pursued its ever-narrowing way, inexorably, to the vanishing point.[28]

BEYOND PROCEDURES AND RATIONALES: A NEW AUTONOMY

We have observed the twin centrifugal forces operating in the new music of the 1950s and 1960s: mathematical serialism, with its elitist, academic preciosity, and Dada-Zen experimentalism, with its philosophized, anti-art happenings. Divergent in method, both have been characterized by extremism. Yet they have been shown to be paradoxically similar in certain tendencies—the tendency to treat sounds as isolated entities, as ends in themselves, and the tendency to remove from the composition of music the operation of human imagination, intuition, and memory. Both approaches have been shown to have severe limitations. The anti-art, indeterminacy approach (one thing in art is as good as any other) has, by the logical extension of its premises, put its creative artists out of work or driven them into ludicrously untenable positions. The "scientific research" approach, on the other hand, has led to formidable intellectual accomplishments on the part of its composers and theorists, while isolating the composers from any real contact, as composers, with the day-to-day musical life of the country. Often characterized by ivory-tower exclusiveness, and kept going by the universities and the foundations, this approach deprives its practitioners of a sine qua non: the functioning of composers in relation to a significant public, even a small one.[29]

Yet the implications of both approaches have had to be worked through, not ignored. Both have left their discernible marks. (Serialism of pitch, flexible and subservient to ends beyond itself, is still found useful as a procedure; here and there indeterminacy persists; and a hint of the quixotic Cagean touch is to be encountered unexpectedly, even in the work of staunchly autonomous composers such as George Crumb.) But as vital and productive artistic movements they have made their points, and have reached the stage of diminishing returns.

We have treated the fringes; what of the center—the "new liberalism" of which composer Billy Jim Layton wrote over a decade ago?[30] We seem now to have reached the age in which the autonomous composer can come into his own, free to refuse to be committed to a single procedure or esthetic, free to put dogmatism aside and to use any of a vast number of techniques in the service of an essentially expressive and communicative purpose. As Billy Jim Layton has expressed it:

> There is not the slightest reason to reject any particular technical device—electronic means, chance methods, anything—merely because it was invented or employed for aesthetic ends with which we are not much in sympathy. The true liberal will accept whatever in his judgment is useful and necessary to him, whether of the past or the present. What really matters is whether he has a firm hold upon his aesthetic goal, consequently permitting these technical procedures to find their place in a total scheme which has flexibility and strength.[31]

The newer "new music," having survived the centrifugal movements described above, has emerged with certain characteristics that it would be helpful to note. In terms of its sound surface, it is less easy to describe in general terms than the earlier avant-garde and experimental music. True, much of it still does in fact exhibit many of the same characteristics: the preoccupation with unusual tone colors; the tendency to use extremes of dynamic level (with more of an emphasis now on extremely soft sounds); the frequent reliance on gestures expressed in rapid flurries of notes; and above all, in terms of moment-to-moment procedures, a continued use of pointillism and of a mosaic-like structure, resulting in a music of individual sounds—a succession of more or less isolated moments or events. But having assimilated the new tone colors, and the effects obtainable through serialism and indeterminacy, the newest music has tended to broaden its range and become less easily stereotyped—even to the extent, for example, of incorporating diatonic tonal or modal passages, not as quotations but as an integral resource of the musical language.[32]

There are three important trends to be pointed out in the most recent new music—trends that may have some significance for its future. The first is a resurgence of programmaticism; the second is the renewed importance of the performer; and the third is the reaffirmation of art itself, of its relation to life, and of the role of the artist.

A New Programmaticism

The attention to the "emancipation" of sound, and the concept of music as an unrelated series of pure sounds—a sequence of fortuitous moments—now seems to have called for a counterbalancing attention to form, continuity, and what may be described as "content." Both form and content are now often related to extramusical references. These references may take the form of understandable settings of understandable texts, such as George Rochberg's *Songs in Praise of Krishna* (1970) and Ralph Shapey's *Praise* (1971).

In the province of pure instrumental music, extramusical references create what is in effect a new program music, which is perhaps best exemplified in the work of George Crumb, whom we find using numerology (*Black Angels*, 1970) and the zodiac (*Makrokosmos I* and *II*, the latter completed in 1973) as form-generating agents. As referential ingredients of "content," he uses such devices as whispered or shouted fragments of text, or words and names in Morse code. He has introduced theatrical elements with distinct programmatic associations in *Voice of the Whale* (1971), to be performed in deep-blue stage lighting by musicians wearing half-masks, which, "by effacing the sense of human projection, are intended to represent, symbolically, the powerful forces of nature."

The pronounced tendency in much of the new music to make references extends even to the use of other music as "subject matter." Thus the quotation is nearly as much a part of the music of the late 1960s and the 1970s as it was with Ives three-quarters of a century earlier. In some extreme examples, representing possibly a late vestigial stage of Dadaist experimentalism, existing music forms the entire substance of the composition. (In *Baroque Variations* Lukas Foss merely makes certain arrangements concerning the disposition of pieces by Handel, Scarlatti, and Bach, and composes the "holes" in these pieces—portions that are to be "played" inaudibly.) But this type of collage art, created from "found objects" in the manner of Marcel Duchamp's "ready-mades," is not a significant part of the picture. Far more important is the limited referential quote. The broad acquaintanceship and increased sophistication of contemporary composers is shown in the wide field from which these quotes are chosen; thus Far Eastern music, the plainchant of the Roman Catholic Church (with its ample historical precedent for being used as "subject matter"), and the music of the fifteenth-century Josquin des Prez rub shoulders with Schubert, Richard Strauss, the Negro spiritual, and the popular tune.

The New Importance of the Performer

Pure electronic music continues to be cultivated, but hampered by its limitations, it seems to be losing what audience it had, as attendance at "performances" attests, even at festivals designed for the cognoscenti of contemporary music. There is a new emphasis on the performer, as has been noted, and new virtuosos have appeared on the scene, dedicated to the execution of the exacting new music. Consequently, the standards of performance of the new music have never been higher, and the difficulty of what is being written has never been greater. Even the once-new sound resources of electronic music have paled somewhat in interest compared to what the performers are able to do—singers such as Bethany Beardsley and Jan DeGaetani, pianists such as Robert Miller (equally skillful at the keyboard or inside the piano), woodwind players such as Harvey Sollberger (flutist) or William O. Smith (clarinetist), and percussionists such as Raymond Des Roches and Jan Williams. The composer-performer has reemerged, a more important figure in music than at any time since the nineteenth century and the days of Paganini, Chopin, and Liszt. Most of them (like Lukas Foss, Charles Wuorinen, David Burge, Yehudi Wyner, and Robert Helps) are pianists.

The new sounds (which have by no means lost their fascination for composers at this stage) now tend once more to be those made by live performers. The expanded resources explored by composers like George Crumb (in Crumb's case often wedded to the poetic imagery of Federico García Lorca) will certainly have their part to play in new music written in the 1970s and beyond.

The Reaffirmation of Art

Ralph Shapey, composer and conductor of new music, has offered this definition:

An Artist:
is perhaps the mirror of his times, on an heightened (hallucinatory) level, giving expressions to mankind's basic search for the meaning of its being, other than existence.[33]

Billy Jim Layton wrote, as long ago as 1965: "The best hope for the world today, the direction, I am fully confident, of the important, vital music to be written, is that of a responsive and enlightened liberalism. . . . Today there is need for a new, rich, meaningful, varied, understandable and vital music which maintains contact with the great central tradition of humanism in the West."[34]

At about the same time, after a personal crisis (the death of his son), George Rochberg wrote, in part:

It became crystal clear to me that I could not continue to write so-called "serial" music. . . . It was finished . . . hollow . . . meaningless. It also became clearer than ever before that the only justification for claiming one was engaged in the artistic act was to open one's art completely to life and its entire gamut of terror and joys (real and imagined); and to find, if one could, new ways to transmute these into whatever magic one was capable of. I rediscovered and reaffirmed with an intensity I had never known before the basic impulse which led me to want to compose music in the first place, a long time ago.[35]

The expressions and acts of artistic nihilism typical of the experimental music movement of the 1960s are heard and seen less frequently in this decade. We have apparently arrived at an era in which many of the proponents and practitioners of our new music are ready to reaffirm art, in its essential relation to humanity, and to reinstate the artist.

FURTHER READING

A Reference Work

VINTON, JOHN (ed.). *Dictionary of Contemporary Music*. New York: E. P. Dutton & Co., 1971.
> A most useful and comprehensive reference work, with an impressive list of contributors and board of advisors.

Anthologies of Articles, Essays, and Interviews

BORETZ, BENJAMIN, and CONE, EDWARD T. (eds.). *Perspectives on American Composers*. New York: W. W. Norton & Co., 1971.

* CHASE, GILBERT (ed.). *The American Composer Speaks*. See the reading list for chapter 16.

LANG, PAUL HENRY (ed.). *Problems of Modern Music*. New York: W. W. Norton & Co., 1960.
> Transcriptions from the proceedings of the 1959 Princeton Seminar in Advanced Musical Studies.

* SCHWARTZ, ELLIOTT, and CHILDS, BARNEY (eds.). *Contemporary Composers on Contemporary Music*. See the reading list for chapter 16.

Other Books

CAGE, JOHN. *Silence*. See the reading list for chapter 16.

—— (ed.). *Notations*. New York: Something Else Press, 1969.
> A rather large collection illustrating a great range of mid-twentieth-century notation, with brief quotations on the subject by composers.

John Cage. New York: C. F. Peters, 1962.
> A catalog of his works up to that time, including data on performances and an interview with Roger Reynolds.

CHASE, GILBERT. *America's Music*. 2nd rev. ed. New York: McGraw-Hill Book Co., 1966.
> Chapter 31, "The Scene in the Sixties."

COPE, DAVID. *New Directions in Music*. Dubuque, Iowa: Wm. C. Brown Co., 1971.
> A brief, useful introduction to the subject.

---

* Items thus marked are part of the suggested reference library to be available in connection with this book.

———. *New Music Composition*. New York: Schirmer Books (Macmillan), 1977.

    A textbook for the would-be composer, but with useful information for the general reader. Well organized; the "Works for Analysis" for each chapter constitute a useful list of examples of various procedures.

HILLER, LEJAREN A., JR., and ISAACSON, LEONARD M. *Experimental Music: Composition with an Electronic Computer*. New York: McGraw-Hill Book Co., 1959.

    A detailed account of experiments in the use of computers to compose music, carried out at the University of Illinois in the late 1950s.

NYMAN, MICHAEL. *Experimental Music: Cage and Beyond*. New York: Schirmer Books (Macmillan), 1974.

    A rather extensive treatment, essentially chronological, of the Cagean-indeterminacy school of the 1950s and 1960s.

SCHWARTZ, ELLIOTT. *Electronic Music: A Listener's Guide*. Rev. ed. New York: Praeger Publishers, 1975.

    A comprehensive introduction to the subject, dealing with far more than just the technological aspects (although these are amply covered, including a section on do-it-yourself tape music).

YATES, PETER. *Twentieth-Century Music: Its Evolution from the End of the Harmonic Era into the Present Era of Sound*. See the reading list for chapter 16.

Periodicals

Perspectives of New Music. Annandale-on-Hudson, N.Y. 12504.

    Semiannual, since 1962. The more or less official journal of the academic wing of the avant-garde, with highly prestigious contributors and editorial board.

Source: Music of the Avant-Garde. Composer/Performer Editions, 2101 22nd St., Sacramento, Calif. 95818

    An important publication during its five-year life span; its articles and scores are representative of the important trends and composers of the period, especially of the indeterminacy wing of the new music.

Electronic Music Review. Independent Electronic Music Center, Inc., Trumansburg, N.Y. 14886.

    A specialized journal, issued January 1967 to July 1968.

LISTENING

There is currently available a wide selection of new music on records, by major companies like Columbia as well as by the smaller and more specialized companies like Nonesuch, and especially Composers Recordings, Inc., the largest producer specializing in this music. It will therefore be appropriate merely to suggest a few albums that may be especially useful.

The Music of Paul Chihara, Chou Wen-Chung, Earl Kim, and Roger Reynolds. RAAM: NW-237.

New Music for Virtuosos. RAAM: NW-209. Works by Milton Babbitt, Leslie Bassett, William O. Smith, and Charles Wuorinen.

The Avant-Garde String Quartet in the U.S.A., by the Concord String Quartet (3 records, 9 composers). Vox: SVBX-5306.

New Music for the Piano, pianist Robert Helps (2 records, 24 composers, only some relevant to this chapter). RCA: LM-7042.

PROJECTS

1. After listening to a considerable amount of new music, both live and electronic, paying attention only to the sounds themselves, compile your own list of "sound effects" (characteristic sounds or sound gestures, such as are described under the heading "The Surface of the New Music" in this chapter) that you encounter frequently. Describe each as fully as you can, using such analogies as occur to you, and citing specific examples.

2. Luigi Russolo, leader of the Italian futurist movement of the early twentieth century, which used noise as the basis for musical composition, listed the following categories of noises as susceptible to being used to make music (as quoted in Schwartz, *Electronic Music*):

   1. Bangs, thunderclaps, explosions.
   2. Whistles, hisses, snorts.
   3. Whispers, murmurs, rustling, gurgling.
   4. Screams, buzzes, crackling, sounds produced by friction.
   5. Sounds produced by striking metal, wood, stone.
   6. Animal and human cries, such as roars, groans, sobs, laughter.

   After critical listening to a considerable amount of electronic music, determine to what extent this list would serve to categorize its sounds. Devise a revised category of sounds if you feel it necessary. Cite specific examples.

3. Cite at least five illustrations from live new music of passages you feel could have been influenced by electronic music; describe their characteristics and cite similar passages in electronic music.

4. Write a brief essay on the values or limitations, as you see them, of having electronic instruments reproduce music originally written for live performers—a trend associated with such commercially successful popularizations as the *Switched-On Bach* recordings.

5. Write a well-reasoned critique of Milton Babbitt's important

essay "Who Cares If You Listen?" (reprinted in both Chase, *The American Composer Speaks*, and Schwartz and Childs, *Contemporary Composers*). Deal with as many of its implications as you can fathom. For example, what do you think would happen if all "advanced" composers of "specialized" music withdrew in isolation from the "public life of unprofessional compromise and exhibitionism"? Or, related to this, what would be the ramifications of the "complete elimination of the public and social aspects of musical composition"?

6. If you have a fairly extensive background in mathematics, study a technical and mathematically oriented article on the new music, such as Milton Babbitt's "Twelve-Tone Invariants as Compositional Determinants," in Lang, *Problems of Modern Music*; or Babbitt's "Set Structure as a Compositional Determinant" or his "Twelve-Tone Rhythmic Structure and the Electronic Medium," both in *Perspectives on Contemporary Music Theory* (New York: W. W. Norton & Co., Inc., 1972). Interpret for the layman, in a lecture, as much of the mathematics involved as you can.

7. Interview a performer who has worked out a piece written in indeterminate notation: What are the problems, challenges, and rewards? (In addition to touring organizations performing new music, there are new-music groups at most colleges and universities that have a sizeable number of music students.) Recapitulate the essence of the interview—with comments, background, and illustrations of the notation, if possible—either orally or in a paper.

8. Assemble examples of at least five different methods of achieving indeterminacy in new music (either in composition or in performance). Describe the methods in detail. In the case of compositions indeterminate as to performance, compare if possible two (necessarily different) realizations of the same composition.

9. The most efficient piece of indeterminacy yet designed was a "composition" consisting of one word: LISTEN. (See Nyman, *Experimental Music*, p. 88, for a reference to this, and a description of how this "piece" was "realized" through field trips to sound environments such as power stations.) Write a brief essay describing several other experiments and stages of indeterminacy leading up to this ultimate renunciation of the function of the artist in selecting and transforming his material. Discuss the concept of art as a kind of therapy, to "make us conscious of the life and sounds outside the accepted musical-social environment" (*ibid.*, p. 88).

10. Taking a periodical such as *Time* magazine as a source, write a summary of, and commentary on, the pieces and programs of new music reviewed in any one-year period since 1970.

Notes

CHAPTER 1: ANGLO-AMERICAN FOLK TRADITION

1. A sample of recordings of *Barbara Allen:* in *Folk Songs of the Old World—The Roger Wagner Chorale* (Capitol: S-345; *Joan Baez*, vol. 2 (Vanguard: 2097); *Anglo-American Ballads*, in *Library of Congress Archive of American Folk Song* (recording L-1).

2. Available on *Library of Congress Archive of American Folk Song* (hereafter abbreviated AAFS) recording L-1 (cited above).

3. Jean Ritchie, *Singing Family of the Cumberlands* (New York: Oak Publications, 1963), p. 17.

4. Charles Seeger, notes to *Versions and Variants of Barbara Allen* (AAFS: L-54).

5. See Roger D. Abrahams and George Foss, *Anglo-American Folksong Style* (Englewood Cliffs, N.J.: Prentice-Hall, 1968), p. 29.

6. See Bertrand Harris Bronson, *The Traditional Tunes of the Child Ballads*, vol. 1 (Princeton, N.J.: Princeton University Press, 1959), pp. 9–33.

7. The word *antine* here invites an interesting study. There is no such word in English usage. Baring-Gould, collector of the first of these versions using it, postulates that it is a corruption of the French *antienne*, which means

"antiphon." Since an antiphon is a piece of liturgical music, the image of every grove ringing "with a merry antine" is a plausible and indeed a rather happy one. The second version, collected in California in 1938, shows a further step in the process of change through misunderstanding, since the sense of *antine* as music, even in the corrupted form of the word, has now been lost, and the refrain reverts once more to the "plant" motif, carrying with it the euphonious but by now completely meaningless word.

8. Evelyn Wells, *The Ballad Tree* (New York: Ronald Press Co., 1950), p. 97.

9. One example will illustrate this. *The Grey Cock* exists in a complete traditional text (only recently discovered) in which the lover, hurrying at night to the house of his beloved, has to cross a burning river. He finally arrives, is let in, and they spend the night together, in the course of which it is revealed that the lover is really a ghost, his earthly form having presumably perished in the fire. Knowing that the dead must return to the grave before the cock crows, the beloved offers bribes to the bird not to crow before daylight. The cock, however, crows prematurely, and the lovers must part forever. In most current versions the supernatural element has been eliminated, the lover remains an ordinary mortal, the crowing of the cock is simply a conventional announcement of the coming of day, and the whole ballad has become merely a commonplace tale of the night visitation of a lover. Five versions of this ballad appear in the excellent recorded collection, *The Long Harvest* (Argo: [Z] DA-66-75), complete with texts and notes. See the list of recordings at the end of this chapter.

10. Bronson, in his monumental *Traditional Tunes of the Child Ballads*, vol. 2, actually identifies 4 tune groups for this ballad, for which he prints 191 variants altogether, with 7 additional "sports." Not all 4 tune types have wide currency in America, however. Charles Seeger, in his article "Versions and Variants of the Tunes of Barbara Allen," treats extensively the two versions that he recognizes as current in America, which are here represented in our examples. This fascinating article was first printed in *Selected Reports*, vol. 1, no. 1 (Los Angeles: Institute of Ethnomusicology, University of California, 1966) and reprinted as notes to *Versions and Variants of Barbara Allen* (AAFS: L-54).

11. Seeger, "Versions and Variants," p. 122.

12. Bronson, *Traditional Tunes of the Child Ballads*, vol. 1, p. 3.

13. The reader with some musical background and a curiosity about the subject may wish to consult Bertrand Bronson, "Folk Song and the Modes," *Musical Quarterly* vol. 32, no. 1 (January 1946): 37–49.

14. For an interesting comparison of an older and a newer tune side by side, listen to two adjacent bands on a record entitled *Oh, My Little Darling: Folk Song Types* (NW-245), part of the *Recorded Anthology of American Music* (hereafter abbreviated RAAM). *Sweet William*, a Child ballad (Child 7), is sung unaccompanied to an old-type tune using the pentatonic scale. *The Lexington Murder* is sung to a more recent type of tune, with

a guitar accompaniment that uses the familiar three basic chords; the tune follows the chords.

15. As an illustration of this, compare the written version of *Barbara Allen* as given on page 11 with the performance from which it was derived, that of Mrs. Rebecca Tarwater, available on *Anglo-American Ballads* (AAFS: L-1).

16. For an interesting treatment of this whole question, see Alan Lomax, "Folk Song Style," *American Anthropologist*, vol. 61, no. 6 (December 1959), and also the introduction to *The Folk Songs of North America* by the same author (Garden City, N.Y.: Doubleday & Co., 1960).

17. Vance Randolph and Floyd C. Shoemaker have described the play-party as it existed in the Ozarks and reproduced some eighty play-party songs, with descriptions of the dances, in *Ozark Folksongs*, vol. 3 (Columbia, Mo.: The State Historical Society of Missouri, 1949). Some play-party games are also given in Cecil Sharp's *English Folk-Songs from the Southern Appalachians*, ed. Maude Karpeles, vol. 2 (London: Oxford University Press, 1932), pp. 367–383.

18. A representative selection of such songs may be heard on recordings such as *Old-Time Music at Clarence Ashley's*, Folkways: 2355, which includes *Sally Ann*, *The Old Man at the Mill*, and *Pretty Little Pink*; or *Mountain Music of Kentucky*, Folkways: 2317, which includes *Blackeyed Susie*.

19. These lines as found on Folkways records 2355 and 2317, cited above; used by permission.

20. Printed versions of these appear in most collections, including those in the reading list at the end of this chapter. For recorded versions, consult the list of recordings given there also. Because of the increased interest in fiddling, and the corresponding increase in fiddling contests and fiddlers' conventions, it is now much easier to hear live performances of this music —always much more satisfactory.

21. See Hans Nathan, *Dan Emmett and the Rise of Early Negro Minstrelsy* (Norman: University of Oklahoma Press, 1962) p. 92, and Mark Twain, *Life on the Mississippi*, chapter 3.

22. Marion Thede, *The Fiddle Book* (New York: Oak Publications, n.d.), p. 26.

23. See the endpaper of R. P. Christeson's excellently printed collection *The Old-Time Fiddler's Repertory* (Columbia, Mo.: University of Missouri Press, 1973).

CHAPTER 2: AFRO-AMERICAN FOLK TRADITION

1. An article with a title like "The Survival of African Music in America" would seem to belong to our own time. It was published in *Appleton's Popular Science Monthly* in September 1899. An important early study,

by Jeannette Robinson Murphy, it was reprinted in the notes to the Folkways album *Roots of Black Music in America*, FA-2694.

2. Marshall Stearns includes a treatment of this in his *The Story of Jazz* (New York: Oxford University Press, 1956).

3. Two permanently valuable documents to come out of this area are the *Slave Songs of the Georgia Sea Islands* by Lydia Parrish (New York, 1942; reprint, Hatboro, Pa., Folklore Associates, 1965), and the recordings of *Animal Tales Told in the Gullah Dialect* by Albert Stoddard (AAFS: L-44, 45, 46). The Gullah dialect has been found to contain a high percentage of West African words, as has been revealed in Lorenzo Turner's study *Africanisms in the Gullah Dialect* (Chicago: University of Chicago Press, 1949). A fine recording illustrating both the sacred and the secular music of the islands is included in RAAM as *Georgia Sea Island Songs* (NW-278), recorded in 1960–61 by Alan Lomax, who has also provided notes for the album.

4. Jazz, coming out of folk roots, is the American music most obviously expressing this trait, but the spiritual, especially in its folk phase, manifests it significantly. This may be heard in an example such as *Handwriting on the Wall*, from *Afro-American Spirituals, Work Songs, and Ballads* (AAFS: L-3), or *Sheep, Sheep, Don't You Know the Road*, from RAAM: NW-278 (cited above).

5. Any number of other examples might be substituted, of course, but of these the first may be found in *African Drums* (Folkways: FE-4502), band 6, and the second in AAFS: L-3, band A-7 (cited above). The entire album *Roots of Black Music in America* (Folkways: 2694) is relevant and instructive.

6. The following quotations are from Eileen Southern, *The Music of Black Americans* (New York: W. W. Norton & Co., 1971), pp. 36, 59, 68.

7. Among them James Miller McKim, as quoted in Miles Mark Fisher, *Negro Slave Songs in the United States* (Ithaca, N.Y.: Cornell University Press, 1953), pp. 12–13. See also Murphy, "The Survival of African Music in America," reprinted in notes to *Roots of Black Music in America* (Folkways: FA-2694).

8. William Francis Allen, in his preface to Allen et al., *Slave Songs of the United States* (New York: Oak Publications, 1965), pp. iv–vi.

9. For an early reference, see Allen et al., *Slave Songs of the United States*, p. viii. For later references, see John Lovell, Jr. *Black Song: The Forge and the Flame* (New York: Macmillan Co., 1972), especially pp. 65–67.

10. In no other known case has the question of the origin of a body of folk music been the subject of such vexatious, acrimonious, and altogether unfortunate controversy. Out of a multitude of writings, two books and their authors may be taken as representative of the opposing views in the matter: *White and Negro Spirituals* by George Pullen Jackson (Locust Valley, N.Y.: J. J. Augustin, 1943) and *Black Song: The Forge and the Flame*, by John Lovell, Jr. Aside from the fact that Jackson deals primarily

with the music and Lovell with the texts, both suffer from critical weaknesses, not the least being a basically biased and unsympathetic approach —the white man for the black man's music, and the black man for the white man's. It is a lack of willingness to try to understand divergent kinds of music that leads to the attempt to "elevate" one kind by demeaning another. Value judgments subservient to such biases are pernicious. Sound, objective study is what is sorely needed. If a scholar would come forward who could do for the texts of the spirituals what Child and others did for the texts of the Anglo-American ballads, and if another would do the work Bronson did for their music, then we should have a substantial and highly important corpus of scholarship. Unfortunately, it may be too late for this, as we get further and further away from the origins of this vast body of song and poetry.

11. As reprinted in Jackson, *White and Negro Spirituals*.

12. *Look How They Done My Lord*, from *Spirituals with Dock Reed and Vera Hall Ward* (Folkways: FA-2038); *Handwriting on the Wall*, from *Afro-American Spirituals, Work Songs, and Ballads* (AAFS: L-3). Both of these appear in printed versions in Johnson, *The Books of Negro Spirituals* (New York: Viking Press, 1940). Other selections on the same recordings are also illustrative, and valuable.

13. The neutral seventh is especially clear in *Low Down the Chariot and Let Me Ride*, on FA-2038, cited above.

14. Both are included in the album *Negro Folk Music of Africa and America* (Folkways: 4500). Excellent examples are also to be heard on *Georgia Sea Island Songs* (RAAM: NW-278).

15. The most ubiquitous of the preachers was Rev. J. M. Gates, whose sermons are included in the Riverside *History of Classic Jazz*; in the Folkways *History of Jazz* series, vol. 1, *The South* (2801); and in the *Anthology of American Folk Music*, vol. 2, *Social Music* (Folkways: 2952).

16. An interesting example is a variant of *Do Lord Remember Me*, recorded with banjo in 1936, found on *Negro Religious Songs and Services* (AAFS: L-10).

17. Recordings such as *He Got Better Things for You*, made in 1929 by the Memphis Sanctified Singers (*Anthology of American Folk Music*, Folkways: 2952), and *Precious Lord*, made by the Gospel Keys, probably in the early 1940s (*The Asch Recordings*, Folkways: AA-1), illustrate this.

18. Listen to his famous *Ain't No Grave Can Hold My Body Down*, recorded in 1942 (*Negro Religious Songs and Services*, AAFS: L-10); also *Since I Laid My Burden Down* (*Anthology of American Folk Music*, Folkways: 2952).

19. *Lift Up a Standard for My King* (related to a traditional spiritual) and *I'm a Soldier in the Army of the Lord* (*Negro Blues and Hollers*, AAFS: L-59) illustrate this, as does *I'm in the Battlefield for My Lord* by Rev. D. C. Rice and His Sanctified Congregation (*Anthology of American Folk Music*, Folkways: 2952). The first two are field recordings from the early 1940s; the last was recorded commercially in 1929.

20. Many contemporary examples illustrate this, but for one from the 1950s listen to *He's a Friend of Mine*, as performed by the Spirit of Memphis on *An Introduction to Gospel Song* (Folkways: RF-5).

21. Quoted in Harold Courlander, *Negro Folk Music, U.S.A.* (New York: Columbia University Press, 1963), pp. 81–82.

22. *Negro Work Songs and Calls* (AAFS: L-8); *Negro Folk Music of Alabama*, vol. 1 (Folkways: 4417). For transcriptions of some of the calls in this latter album, and an excellent treatment of the subject, see Courlander, *Negro Folk Music, U.S.A.*, chapter 4. Two rather extended street cries of Charleston are included on the first side of the Riverside *History of Classic Jazz* (see suggestions for listening, chapter 12); a few more meager examples from New Orleans are included on *The Music of New Orleans*, vol. 1 (Folkways: 2461).

23. Both may be heard on AAFS: L-8, cited above, side A. The first is band 7; the second, band 6. The importance of *hearing* the calls in conjunction with this exposition cannot be overemphasized; only in this way can the true musical "feel" of the blue notes be experienced. In the transcriptions, both have been transposed, for the sake of comparison.

24. This inflected dominant can be heard in the spiritual *Trouble So Hard* (*Afro-American Spirituals, Work Songs, and Ballads*, AAFS: L-3), and in a call recorded in *Negro Folk Music of Alabama*, vol. 1 (Folkways: 4417) and transcribed in Courlander, *Negro Folk Music, U.S.A.*, p. 84. The flattened dominant became important in the jazz of the 1950s.

25. *Afro-American Blues and Game Songs* (AAFS: L-4).

26. *Negro Blues and Hollers* (AAFS: L-59, band A-2).

27. *Afro-American Blues and Game Songs* (AAFS: L-4).

28. Paul Oliver, *The Meaning of the Blues* (New York: Macmillan Co., 1960. Paperback, Collier Books, 1963).

29. As quoted in Bruce Cook, *Listen to the Blues* (New York: Charles Scribner's Sons, 1973), p. 40.

30. Examples of these vocal styles have been conveniently assembled in *The Rural Blues*, ed. Samuel Charters (Folkways: RF-202).

31. *Levee Camp Moan*, performed by Texas Alexander (*The Country Blues*, vol. 2, Folkways: RF-9), and *Special Rider Blues*, performed by Son House (*Negro Blues and Hollers*, AAFS: L-59), illustrate this.

32. LeRoi Jones, *Blues People* (New York: William Morrow & Co., 1963), pp. 81–82.

33. Perhaps the richest recorded collection is *Negro Prison Songs from the Mississippi State Penitentiary*, collected and annotated by Alan Lomax (Tradition: TLP-1020). *Early in the Mornin'*, from this record, is particularly fine. *Long John* (from *Afro-American Spirituals, Work Songs, and Ballads*, AAFS: L-3) and *Hammer, Ring* (from *Negro Work Songs and Calls*, AAFS: L-8) are also good examples.

34. Printed versions appear in a great number of collections. As for recordings by traditional singers, there are greatly truncated versions sung by Lead-

belly (*History of Jazz*, vol. 1, Folkways: 2801) and the Williamson brothers (*Anthology of American Folk Music*, vol. 1, Folkways: 2951). A version in the manner of a work song is found on AAFS: L-3, cited above; and the derivative blues (*Spike Driver Blues*), as sung by Mississippi John Hurt, is in *Anthology of American Folk Music*, vol. 3 (Folkways: 2953).

35. This is splendidly illustrated in the ballad *The Titanic*, in *Georgia Sea Island Songs* (RAAM: NW-278).

CHAPTER 3: INDIAN, SPANISH, AND FRENCH MUSIC

1. Walter Collins O'Kane, *Sun in the Sky* (Norman: University of Oklahoma Press, 1950), pp. 186–191.

2. Frances Densmore, *The American Indians and Their Music* (New York: Women's Press, 1926), p. 63.

3. See *Songs of Love, Luck, Animals, and Magic* (RAAM: NW-297).

4. Densmore, *The American Indians and Their Music*, p. 63.

5. This may be heard as sung by Pigeon himself: *Pigeon's Dream Song*, on *Songs of the Menominee, Mandan, and Hidatsa* (AAFS: L-33, band A-5).

6. This may be heard on AAFS: L-33, cited above, band B-7.

7. This may be heard on *Music of the American Indian: Sioux* (AAFS: L-40, band A-7). A sung version of the song follows the flute performance.

8. A Chinook version of *Jesus Loves Me* can be heard on *Music of the American Indian: Northwest (Puget Sound)* (AAFS: L-34), and a Hopi version of *Dixie* on *Music of the American Indian: Pueblo: Taos, San Ildefonso, Zuni, Hopi* (AAFS: L-43).

9. This may be heard as performed by the Los Angeles Northern Singers on *Songs of Earth, Water, Fire and Sky*, RAAM NW 246. Willard Rhodes regards this category of songs as "a passing fad or fashion which flourished because of the element of novelty in uniting an Indian melody with English words." (Rhodes, "Acculturation in North American Indian Music," in *Acculturation in the Americas* [Chicago: University of Chicago Press, 1952]). But he may well not have grasped the significance of this special type of song.

10. Ghost Dance songs recorded among Great Basin and Plains tribes may be heard on *Songs of the Pawnee and Northern Ute* (AAFS: L-25), *Plains: Comanche, Cheyenne, Kiowa, Caddo, Wichita, Pawnee* (AAFS: L-39), *Kiowa* (AAFS: L-35), *Great Basin: Paiute, Washo, Ute, Bannock, Shoshone* (AAFS: L-38), and *Sioux* (AAFS: L-40).

11. There can be no doubt of the acculturational influence on the peyote cult and music. Peyotism has adopted superficially certain Christian words and symbols, and the words appear in many of the songs. An interesting example from the Sioux, in which JESUS ONLY is spelled out twice, can be heard on AAFS: L-40, cited above. Other peyote songs can be heard on

AAFS L-35 and 38, cited above, and on *Delaware, Cherokee, Choctaw, Creek* (L-37) and *Navajo* (L-41).

12. David P. McAllester, *Peyote Music* (New York: The Viking Fund Publications in Anthropology, no. 13, 1949), p. 85.

13. Alan Merriam, *Ethnomusicology of the Flathead Indians* (Chicago: Aldine Publishing Co., 1967), p. 147.

14. Robert Louis Stevenson, "The Old Pacific Capital," in *Across the Plains.*

15. For a book and some excellent recordings, see the lists at the end of this chapter.

16. As an example, a *Pedimento de las Posadas* was recorded in a small town in south Texas in 1934. It may be heard in its original version, as recorded by John A. and Alan Lomax, on *Bahaman Songs, French Ballads and Dance Tunes, Spanish Religious Songs and Game Songs* (AAFS: L-5). Printed excerpts from a New Mexico version of *Los Pastores,* including a different *Las Posadas,* may be found in John Donald Robb, *Hispanic Folk Songs of New Mexico* (Albuquerque: University of New Mexico Press, 1954).

17. This variant is transcribed from the earliest version to appear on phonograph records, about 1929. It may be heard on *Texas-Mexican Border Music,* vol. 2 (Folklyric: 9004), available from Arhoolie Records, 10341 San Pablo Ave., El Cerrito, Calif. 94530. The complete histories of the case and of the ballad are found in Americo Paredes, *"With his pistol in his hand."* (Austin: University of Texas Press, 1958).

18. Transcribed from Falcon: FLP-2091.

19. A recent illuminating and informative album documents this music very well. It is entitled *Caliente = Hot: Puerto Rican and Cuban Musical Expression in New York* (RAAM: NW-244).

20. This version found in Irène Thérèse Whitfield, *Louisiana French Folk Songs* (New York: Dover Publications, 1969).

21. They may be heard on *Bahaman Songs, French Tunes* (AAFS: L-5), as recorded in New Iberia, Louisiana, in 1934; transcriptions are printed in John A. and Alan Lomax, *Our Singing Country* (New York: Macmillan Co., 1949).

22. *Les clefs de la prison* may be heard on AAFS: L-5, cited above. *O chère 'tite fille,* on the same recording, was also used by Virgil Thomson, as was the Cajun song *Pas loin de chez moi,* to be found in Whitfield, *Louisiana French Folk Songs,* p. 108. *La femme qui jovait les cartes* has been reissued on *Louisiana Cajun Music: The Early 30's* (Old Timey: LP-109).

23. This song, under the title *Mon coeur t'appelle,* may be heard on Old Timey: LP-109, cited above. Its printed version as a folk song appears in Whitfield, *Louisiana Songs,* p. 88.

24. *Home, Sweet Home* may be heard on *Anthology of American Folk Music* (Folkways: 2952); the *Casey Jones* tune is found in Whitfield, *Louisiana Songs,* p. 114, as *Les filles de Mann Dugas.*

25. The term is said to have originated in the words of a traditional song, *Les haricots sont pas sales* ("Snap beans are not salty")—*les haricots* being rendered in Negro Cajun as *zydeco*.

26. "Creole," in *Encyclopaedia Britannica*, 1964 ed.

27. Originally appearing in The Century Magazine, these are both reprinted in Bernard Katz, ed., *The Social Implications of Early Negro Music in the United States* (New York: Arno Press, 1969). The articles, together with some of the writings of Lafcadio Hearn, make well-nigh indispensable background reading for anyone wishing to understand the Afro-American folk music heard in the multi-layered, colorful, cruel, and often violent society of postbellum Louisiana. Cable's earlier observations and study had led to the inclusion of seven Louisiana *patois* folk songs in the pioneer publication *Slave Songs of the United States* (1867), and his later collaborations with Lafcadio Hearn and Henry Krehbiel bore fruit in the sections devoted to this music in the latter's important study, *Afro-American Folksongs* (1914).

28. Quote and following musical example both from Cable, "The Dance in Place Congo," reprinted in Katz, *Social Implications of Early Negro Music*, pp. 38–40.

29. Cable, "The Dance in Place Congo," p. 42.

30. The Music is found in *ibid.*, p. 43; the story in Henry Edward Krehbiel, *Afro-American Folksongs* (New York: Frederick Ungar, 1914), p. 151.

31. The music example is from Whitfield, *Louisiana Songs*. An early commercial Cajun recording of it, with accordian, can be heard on *Anthology of American Folk Music* (Folkways: 2952).

32. In fact some of the best detailed treatment of black music in the pre-twentieth-century West Indies and New Orleans is found in Marshall Stearns, *The Story of Jazz* (New York: Oxford University Press, 1956). See especially chapters 3, 4, and 5.

33. *Songs of Slavic Americans* (RAAM: NW-283) is a valuable documentation of their music, as recorded in the 1920s. *Folk Music of Immigrants from Europe and the Near East* (NW-264) is a much broader collection.

34. This situation is now fortunately being remedied, by studies such as that of Dr. Cheryl Ho of California State University, Sacramento.

CHAPTER 4: FOLK MUSIC IN MODERN AMERICA

1. John Powell, in preface to George Pullen Jackson *Spiritual Folk-Songs of Early America* (New York: Dover Publications, 1964).

2. John Greenway, *American Folksongs of Protest* (Philadelphia: University of Pennsylvania Press, 1953; paperback, New York: A. S. Barnes & Co., 1960).

3. The complete version is printed and recorded in *The Birth of Liberty* (RAAM: NW-276).

4. D. K. Wilgus, *Anglo-American Folksong Scholarship Since 1898* (New Brunswick, N.J.: Rutgers University Press, 1959), p. 228.

5. R. Serge Denisoff, *Great Day Coming: Folk Music and the American Left* (Urbana: University of Illinois Press, 1971).

6. The entire text and the tune are in Greenway, *American Folksongs of Protest*, p. 249. They appear, with a tune variant, in *Hard-Hitting Songs for Hard-Hit People*, comp. and ed. Alan Lomax, Woody Guthrie, and Pete Seeger (New York: Oak Publications, 1967), p. 186. The ILD (International Labor Defense) sent lawyers into North Carolina to defend accused union leaders.

7. The complete text appears in Greenway, *Folksongs of Protest*, pp. 269–70, and the text and tune in Lomax et al., *Hard-Hitting Songs*, p. 142. Aunt Molly's rendition of it for the Library of Congress has been released on *Aunt Molly Jackson, Library of Congress Recordings* (Rounder: 1002).

8. Quoted in Denisoff, *Great Day Coming*, pp. 21–22.

9. Greenway, *Folksongs of Protest*, p. 259.

10. *Ibid.*, p. 115.

11. *Ibid.*, p. 275.

12. Charles Seeger, "The Folkness of the Non-Folk, vs. the Non-Folkness of the Folk," in Bruce Jackson, ed., *Folklore and Society* (Hatboro, Pa.: Folklore Associates, 1966).

13. For a sampling of the Almanac Singer's music, see *Hootenanny at Carnegie Hall* (Folkways: FH-2512) or *Talking Union* (Folkways: FH-5285). One song from the latter, *All I Want* (a propaganda song for the Farmer-Labor party recorded in 1941) is included in RAAM: NW-270.

14. Pete Seeger, quoted in Denisoff, *Great Day Coming*, p. 119.

15. Quoted in *Ibid.*, p. 82.

16. Quoted in *Ibid.*, p. 86.

17. In 1950 the *People's Song Bulletin* was reconstituted as *Sing Out!*, a periodical still being published. In 1962 a new periodical, *Broadside*, was founded, and it took over the publication and dissemination of the more narrowly topical and virulently propagandistic type of songs.

18. Josh Dunson, *Freedom in the Air: Song Movements of the Sixties* (New York: International Publishers, 1965).

19. Sam Hinton, quoted in Serge R. Denisoff, *Sing a Song of Social Significance* (Bowling Green, Ohio: Bowling Green University Popular Press, 1972), p. 13.

20. D. K. Wilgus, quoted in Denisoff, *Great Day Coming*, p. 120.

21. Local history records that Thomas Dula was hanged in 1868 for the murder of Laura Foster in Wilkes County, North Carolina. A ballad on the subject was picked up from oral tradition and published in a collection by Duke

University Press in 1952. It is said that the Kingston Trio got their version from traditional singer Frank Proffitt, however.

CHAPTER 5: RELIGIOUS MUSIC OF EARLY AMERICA

1. David McKay and Richard Crawford, *William Billings of Boston* (Princeton, N.J.: Princeton University Press, 1975), p. 8.
2. As found in Waldo Selden Pratt, *The Music of the Pilgrims* (Boston: Oliver Ditson, 1921).
3. Recordings of *Guide Me, O Thou Great Jehovah; Amazing Grace; Why Must I Wear This Shroud?;* and *When Jesus Christ Was Here on Earth* as sung in rural Baptist churches in Kentucky furnish an illustration from living tradition of a practice that must be virtually identical with the Usual Way of three hundred years ago, even to the lining out. These can be heard on *The Gospel Ship* (RAAM: NW-294). Hear also a similar rendition of *Amazing Grace* on *Mountain Music of Kentucky* (Folkways: FA-2317).
4. James Franklin, brother of Benjamin, indulged in some wild and humorous hyperbole on this point (which indeed must have had some basis in experience) when he wrote in the *New England Courant* in 1724: "I am credibly inform'd, that a certain Gentlewoman miscarry'd at the ungrateful and yelling Noise of a Deacon in reading the first line of a Psalm; and methinks if there were no other Argument against this Practice (unless there were an absolute necessity for it) the Consideration of it's being a Procurer of Abortion, might prevail with us to lay it aside." (Quoted in McKay and Crawford, *William Billings of Boston*, p. 14.)
5. There is evidence that singing masters sometimes took their pay in produce—Indian corn, for example. For this and many other interesting details of the New England singing school tradition, see Alan Buechner, "Yankee Singing Schools and the Golden Age of Choral Music in New England: 1760–1800" (Ph.D. dissertation, Harvard University, 1960), and based on this, his copious annotations to the recording *The New England Harmony* (Folkways: FA-2377).
6. McKay and Crawford, *William Billings of Boston*, p. 23.
7. Gilbert Chase, *America's Music*, 2d ed. (New York: McGraw-Hill Book Co., 1966), pp. 124–125.
8. Fortunately, several of these books are now available in facsimile reprint form, including Lyon's *Urania*, Belcher's *Harmony of Maine*, and Billings's *Continental Harmony* and *Psalm-Singer's Amusement*. Consult the reading list.
9. This may be heard in *The New England Harmony* (Folkways: FA-2377).
10. In spite of the new stirrings of cultural, as well as political, independence, the extent to which this flourishing of native activity built upon European traditions and sources, especially British, should be known and acknowl-

edged. There was a parallel, and earlier, tradition in England, and much of the pedagogical material for the introductions came from British books such as William Tans'ur's *Royal Melody Complete*. A lot of the music, both tunes and settings, came from British and continental sources, especially towards the end of the period; it should also be noted that the fuging tune itself (or, to be more exact, the "fuging psalm-tune") was developed in England in the mid-eighteenth century. There is no art (or art form) without forebears.

11. The most comprehensive recording available to date is *The New England Harmony*, cited above. See also the suggestions for listening at the end of this chapter.

12. In 1956 the Moravian Music Foundation, with headquarters in Winston-Salem, was founded, for the purpose of "research, publication, and education," having as its basic resource the Peter Memorial Library, with over ten thousand manuscripts of early Moravian music. Through the efforts of the foundation, much of this music is now available in modern editions. The sacred songs and choruses are eminently useful and rewarding for church as well as concert performances. A representative sampling is available on records. Consult the reading and listening lists at the end of this chapter.

13. Donald M. McCorkle, *The Moravian Contribution to American Music*, p. 9, as quoted in Chase, *America's Music*.

14. As a matter of fact, many of the musical practices of the Shakers (if not the music itself) bear some resemblance to those of the Indians: the origins of the songs in visions, the use of meaningless syllables, the concept of songs as "gifts," the use of song to accompany ritualistic movement.

15. This and the following Shaker song appear in Edward Deming Andrews, *The Gift to Be Simple: Songs, Dances and Rituals of the American Shakers* (Locust Valley, N.Y.: J. J. Augustin, 1940).

16. *Ibid.*, pp. 7–8.

CHAPTER 6: LATER NATIVE RELIGIOUS MUSIC

1. Quotes in this paragraph are from Robert Stevenson, *Protestant Church Music in America* (New York: W. W. Norton & Co., 1966; paperback reprint, 1970).

2. Stevenson, *ibid.*

3. Not long after the invention of the four-shape system, a system of seven shapes was devised, in 1832—one shape for each tone of the diatonic scale, and for each of the syllables used in continental European practice (do, re, mi, etc.). The seven-shape, seven-syllable system did become established in portions of the South. But although the seven-syllable system ultimately triumphed everywhere else in the English-speaking world, it did not succeed in dislodging the four-syllable (fa, sol, la, mi) practice from its stronghold in *Sacred Harp* circles—nor has it to this day.

4. George Pullen Jackson, *Down-East Spirituals and Others*, 2nd ed. (New York: J. J. Augustin, 1953), p. 176.

5. The solemn chorale that figures so prominently in Bach's St. Matthew Passion, *O Haupt voll Blut und Wunden* ("O head, now bloody and wounded") was originally a Renaissance love song, *Mein G'muth ist mir verwirret, das macht ein Jungfrau zart* ("My mind is all in disarray; this is what a tender young maid has done").

6. There are numerous recordings of this well-known folk hymn—renditions in both the white and the black tradition. One of the most interesting is a lined-out version on *The Gospel Ship* (RAAM: NW-294).

7. Recorded on *White Spirituals from "The Sacred Harp"* (RAAM: NW-205) and *Sacred Harp Singing* (AAFS: L-11).

8. From the autobiography of James B. Finley, quoted in Charles A. Johnson, *The Frontier Camp Meeting* (Dallas: Southern Methodist University Press, 1955), pp. 64–65.

9. Johnson, *The Frontier Camp Meeting*, vii.

10. From a letter written in Kentucky in 1803, printed in the *Methodist Magazine*, London, that year. Quoted in Johnson, *The Frontier Camp Meeting*, p. 57.

11. Samuel E. Asbury, quoted in Gilbert Chase, *America's Music*, 2nd rev. ed. (New York: McGraw-Hill Book Co., 1966), p. 223.

12. See Jackson, *White and Negro Spirituals*, (New York, 1944; reprint, New York: Da Capo Press, 1975), pp. 83–86, and the interesting collection of such wandering choruses and rhyme pairs in two appendices.

13. As reprinted in Jackson, *White and Negro Spirituals*, pp. 120, 181. As documentation for the parallel traditions, a comparative list of 116 tunes from both is included.

14. As an illustration, one of the more popular hymns in this collection is *Safe in the Arms of Jesus*, with words by Fanny Crosby. Fanny Jane Crosby (1820–1915), using hundreds of pen names in addition to her own, worked for years under a contract that called for the production of three songs a week. How far she exceeded even this is indicated in her own statement, "I have often composed as many as six or seven hymns in one day." It is no wonder that her total output has been estimated at more than eight thousand hymns.

15. A similar chorus may be heard in *My Lord Keeps a Record*, a gospel hymn rendered in traditional mountain style in Virginia, on *The Gospel Ship* (RAAM: NW-294).

16. Erik Routly, *The Music of Christian Hymnody*, quoted in Stevenson, *Protestant Church Music in America*, p. 112.

17. Eileen Southern, *The Music of Black Americans: A History* (New York: W. W. Norton & Co., 1971), p. 402.

18. For an interesting performance of this, see the suggestions for listening for this chapter.

19. For example, Blind Willie Johnson, and an early group called the Gospel

Keys. There are quite a few recordings of Johnson—e.g., in *Anthology of American Folk Music*, vol. 2 (Folkways: 2952), *The Country Blues*, vol. 1 (Folkways: RF-1), and *Country Gospel Song* (Folkways: RF-19)—and two of the Gospel Keys (*The Asch Recordings*, Folkways: AA 1/2).

20. See chapter 12; also the following recordings: *I'm Gonna Lift Up a Standard for My King* and *I'm a Soldier in the Army of the Lord*, in *Negro Blues and Hollers* (AAFS: L-59); *I'm in the Battlefield for My Lord* and *He Got Better Things for You* and *Since I Laid My Burden Down*, in Folkways: 2952, cited above; and *Urban Holiness Service* (Folkways: 8901).

CHAPTER 7: COUNTRY MUSIC

1. It is interesting to note that the term *hillbilly* itself (like so many labels which have stuck in art generally) was originally a somewhat uncomplimentary one. The first recorded use of the term appeared in a New York periodical in 1900, as follows: "A Hill-Billie is a free and untrammelled white citizen of Alabama, who lives in the hills, has no means to speak of, dresses as he can, talks as he pleases, drinks whiskey when he gets it, and fires off his revolver as the fancy takes him." (Quoted by Archie Green in "Hillbilly Music: Source and Symbol," *Journal of American Folklore* [July–September 1965].)

2. It would be interesting to speculate as to just what accounts for this popularity among those who feel strong ties to rural life and mores, wherever they may happen to live, as well as for the scorn with which this music is regarded among those who belong culturally to the city and its milieu. It is perhaps not too great an oversimplification to state that the line between those who appreciate country music and those who hold it in contempt may be drawn with fair accuracy on the basis of whether their background, attitudes, and values are basically rural or urban.

3. Bill Malone is of the opinion that this style of playing may well have been picked up from the instruction manuals that came with the instruments when they were purchased from the mail-order houses. (See his *Country Music, U.S.A.* [Austin, Tex., and London: University of Texas Press, 1968], p. 126.)

4. From the American practice, now familiar, of adopting a brand name (e.g., Kleenex, Xerox) as a generic name for a product in common use.

5. Dock Boggs's singing, especially in *Sugar Baby* (1928), illustrates this well. *Anthology of American Folk Music*, vol. 3, band 62 (Folkways: 2953).

6. This trait can be heard in examples ranging from authentic folk renditions of *Amazing Grace* and *Wayfaring Stranger* on *Mountain Music of Kentucky* (Folkways: 2317) to the singing of such country stars as Roy Acuff in *Great Speckle Bird*, included in *Roy Acuff's Greatest Hits* (Columbia: CS-1034), and Hank Williams in *I Saw the Light*, included in the album of the same title (MGM: SE-3331). For a study of singing styles as a

crucial element of folk music, see Alan Lomax, "Folk Song Style," *American Anthropologist*, vol. 61, no. 6 (December 1959), and also his introduction to *The Folk Songs of North America* (Garden City, N.Y.: Doubleday & Co., 1960).

7. Riley Puckett, 1924, singing *Rock All Our Babies to Sleep*, as noted in Malone, *Country Music, U.S.A.*, p. 95n.

8. Lomax, *The Folk Songs of North America*, p. 281.

9. Jimmie Rodgers's famous *Blue Yodel #1* (*T for Texas*) is illustrative—found on *The Best of the Legendary Jimmie Rodgers* (RCA: LSP-3315[e]). His *Blue Yodel No. 11* is found on *Country Music South and West* (RAAM: NW-287).

10. Quoted in Malone, *Country Music, U.S.A.*, pp. 236–237. For an ancedote on the relation between experience and sincerity see Maurice Zolotow, "Hillbilly Boom," *Saturday Evening Post*, quoted in Linnell Gentry, ed., *A History and Encyclopedia of Country, Western, and Gospel Music*, 2d ed. (Nashville: Clairmont Corp., 1969), pp. 60–61.

11. Clarence Ashley, an old-time musician, recorded almost as an afterthought during one session in 1930 his version of *The House Carpenter*, a venerable English and Scotch ballad from the Child canon. It turned out to be one of his most memorable recordings. It can be heard in *Anthology of American Folk Music*, vol. 1, band 3 (Folkways: 2951).

12. *Old-Time Music at Clarence Ashley's* (Folkways: 2355).

13. The same tune was later used by Woody Guthrie in his *Tom Joad*, one of his *Dust Bowl Ballads* based on John Steinbeck's *Grapes of Wrath*. Other Mixolydian tunes may be heard on RAAM: NW-236: *I Truly Understand You Love Another Man*; *Old Joe Clark*; and *Little Maggie*.

14. *Snow Dove*, also known as *The Butcher Boy*, in *Mountain Music Bluegrass Style* (Folkways: FA-2318).

15. *Wreck on the Highway* may be heard on *Roy Acuff's Greatest Hits*, Columbia CS 1034.

16. For a provocative discussion of sentimentality as a characteristic attitude of the South, and some speculation as to its origins, see Cash, *The Mind of the South*, especially pp. 82–87, 126–130.

17. *No Letter in the Mail*, as sung on *Mountain Music of Kentucky* (Folkways: FA-2317).

18. As sung on *Old Time Music by Mike Seeger* (Folkways: FA-2325).

19. *Katy Cline*, as sung on *Mountain Music Bluegrass Style* (Folkways: FA-2318).

20. *Little Black Train*, as sung by Dock Boggs, in *Dock Boggs*, vol. 2 (Folkways: FA-2392).

21. From *No Disappointment in Heaven*, as sung by Dock Boggs, Folkways: FA-2392, cited above.

22. *'Mid the Green Fields of Virginia*, sung by the Carter Family, on the album of the same name (RCA: ANL-1-1107[e]).

23. *New River Train*, in *Mountain Music Bluegrass Style* (Folkways: FA-2318).

24. *Rowan County Crew*, as sung by Dock Boggs in *Dock Boggs*, vol. 1 (Folkways: FA-2351).

25. Among these are *The Wagoner's Lad* in Cecil Sharp, *English Folk-Songs from the Southern Appalachians*, vol. 2 (London: Oxford University Press, 1932), p. 123—recorded in 1928 by Buell Kazee (*Anthology of American Folk Music*, #7 vol. 1, band 7, Folkways: 2951); and *Sally Ann* (Sharp, p. 351), recorded by Clarence Ashley on *Old-Time Music at Clarence Ashley's* (Folkways: 2355).

26. Sharp, p. 35; recorded in Folkways: 2951, cited above, band 17.

27. See Doron Antrim, "Whoop-and-Holler Opera," reprinted in Gentry, *A History and Encyclopedia*, pp. 65–70.

28. For Clarence Ashley's fascinating accounts of this primitive but influential form of traveling show-business, see the note of *Old-Time Music at Clarence Ashley's* (Folkways: FA-2355).

29. Malone, *Country Music, U.S.A.* p. 44.

30. *Ibid.*, p. 39. Eck Robertson and Henry Gilliland were the musicians. Later, during the subsequent boom period, Robertson again recorded.

31. For examples illustrative of this phase of "old-time" music, an excellent and representative selection of material from the early recordings by such artists as Clarence Ashley, Buell Kazee, Uncle Dave Macon, Dock Boggs, the Stoneman Family, and the Carter Family is available in the *Anthology of American Folk Music*, vols. 1–3 (Folkways: 2951–53).

32. RCA Victor's long-playing reissues of Rodgers's songs (see note 9) have continued to sell extremely well, demonstrating the popularity of his music with succeeding generations of listeners.

33. Nathan Howard Thorp, *Songs of the Cowboy* (Estancia, N.M.: News Print Shop, 1908), and John Alan Lomax, *Cowboy Songs and Other Frontier Ballads* (New York: Macmillan Co., 1910).

34. The work of Ernest Tubb furnishes the best examples of this style; see, for example, *The Ernest Tubb Story* (MCA: 2-4040) and one song on *Country Music in the Modern Era* (RAAM: NW-207).

35. Bluegrass takes its name, not from the bluegrass region of Kentucky, but from the Blue Grass Boys, the string band of Bill Monroe, who was largely responsible for the development of the style that has by now become very prevalent. The work of Bill Monroe's band furnishes probably the best examples of the style (e.g., *Bill Monroe's Country Music Hall of Fame*, MCA-140). The work of Lester Flatt and Earl Scruggs, both of whom played with Monroe earlier, is representative and important (e.g., *Flatt and Scruggs*, Columbia: GP-30). An excellent sampling is found in *Thirty Years of Bluegrass* (RAAM: NW-225).

CHAPTER 8: BLUES, FROM COUNTRY TO CITY

1. W. C. Handy, ed., *Blues: An Anthology* (New York, 1926; reprint, New York, Macmillan Co., 1972).

2. Paramount: 12384; reissued on *Ma Rainey*, vol. 2 (Biograph: BLP-12011).

3. Handy, *Blues: An Anthology.*

4. It was this kind of material (which even Bessie Smith had to record occasionally in the 1930s) that gave the blues a connotation of obscenity, and was a commercial debasement that should not be confused with the real blues, in which the frankness, however unacceptable in some contexts, is a genuine expression.

5. One example each of Ma Rainey's recordings is included in two of the jazz anthologies listed at the end of this chapter (Riverside and Folkways). Over 30 of her performances have been reissued by Biograph Records: BLP-12001, 12011, 12032.

6. Bessie Smith is well represented by single selections in most comprehensive jazz anthologies (including *The Smithsonian Collection of Classic Jazz* and the Riverside and Folkways anthologies). In addition, Columbia Records, which owns practically all the Bessie Smith recordings, has reissued all 160 available recordings, with sound carefully reprocessed to compensate for the weaknesses of early recording techniques.

7. *Countin' the Blues:* Ma Rainey, vocal; Louis Armstrong, cornet; Buster Bailey, clarinet; Charlie Green, trombone; Fletcher Henderson, piano, with banjo and drums (1924), on *Ma Rainey*, vol. 2 (Biograph: BLP-12011). Examples of Armstrong's work with other singers of the period may be heard on Columbia's imported *Rare Recordings of the Twenties*, in four volumes, CBS-64218, 65379, 65380, 65421. Single examples are included in most jazz anthologies.

8. *Dippermouth Blues*, King Oliver's Creole Jazz Band, *Smithsonian Collection of Classic Jazz* (hereafter abbreviated Sm.), side 1, band 6; or *Folkways History of Jazz Series* (hereafter FHJ), vol. 3, side 2, band 1. (References to volume when applicable, side, and band will be abbreviated III: 2:1) The typical blues harmonic pattern is outlined in chapter 2, p. 51.

9. *Ko-ko*, Duke Ellington, Sm. 7:2.

10. *Parker's Mood*, Charlie Parker, Sm. 8:3.

11. *Honky-Tonk Train*, Meade "Lux" Lewis, Sm. 4:2 or FHJ X:1:5.

12. *No. 29*, in *Riverside History of Classic Jazz*, 5:2. *Yancey Stomp*, FHJ X:1:7. *How Long Blues*, FHJ II:2:1.

13. Charles Keil, *Urban Blues* (Chicago: University of Chicago Press, 1966), appendix C.

14. It was from this same prison farm that the blues singer Robert Pete Williams was released twenty-five years later, again through the offices of a folklorist, Harry Oster.

15. LeRoi Jones, *Blues People* (New York: William Morrow & Co., 1963), p. 168.

16. *Ibid.*, pp. 171–172.

17. The best single collection documenting this phase is the recording *Blues Roots/Chicago—the 1930s* (Folkways: RBF-16).

18. Rhythm-and-blues, like the earlier race records, is a vast commercial category. Charlie Gillett has written: "As a market category . . . 'rhythm and blues' was simply a signal that the singer was black, and recording for a black audience," The RAAM album *Straighten Up and Fly Right: Rhythm and Blues from the Close of the Swing Era to the Dawn of Rock 'n' Roll* (NW-261) gives a broad sampling of styles from the 1940s and early 1950s, with excellent notes. For other sources see the suggestions for listening at the end of this chapter.

19. Keil, *Urban Blues*, especially chapter 7, "Soul and Solidarity." The quote above appears on p. 160.

20. These often consist of exaggeratedly "straight" music rendered with a satirical irony. Otis Redding's album *Try a Little Tenderness* (Atco: SD-33-261) is an example. The same thing can be observed in "new wave" jazz, discussed in chapter 12.

21. Keil, in his valuable *Urban Blues*, includes a rather detailed description and analysis of a complete stage appearance, in chapter 5, "Big Bobby Blue Bland on Stage."

22. Charles Seeger, "The Folkness of the Non-Folk vs. the Non-Folkness of the Folk," in *Folklore and Society*, ed. Bruce Jackson (Hatboro, Pa.: Folklore Associates, 1966).

23. Paul Oliver, *The Story of the Blues* (New York: Chilton Book Co., 1969), p. 168.

24. *Ibid.*

CHAPTER 9: ROCK

1. Carl Belz, *The Story of Rock*, 2nd ed. (New York: Oxford University Press, 1972; paperback ed., New York: Harper Colophon Books, 1973).

2. Charlie Gillett, *The Sound of the City* (New York: Dell Publishing Co., 1970).

3. The best-known representatives, from the mid-fifties, include Joe Turner, Hank Ballard and the Midnighters, LaVern Baker, and the Chords. For an interesting documentation of more regional sounds of the period, closer to the folk tradition, see *Roots: Rhythm and Blues* (Folkways: RBF-20) and *Roots: The Rock and Roll Sound of Louisiana and Mississippi* (Folkways: FJ-2865).

4. Belz, *The Story of Rock*.

5. For a more sociological interpretation of the death songs, or "coffin songs," see R. Serge Denisoff, *Sing a Song of Social Significance* (Bowling Green, Ohio: Bowling Green University Popular Press, 1972), pp. 171 ff.

6. It is symbolic, perhaps, that one of the most perceptive and readable histories of American pop music is *After the Ball*, by the young Britisher Ian

Whitcomb, (London: Penguin Press, 1972), written at the conclusion of his own brief career as a rock star both in England and America.

7. Belz, *The Story of Rock*.

8. See for example the interview of Frank Zappa by Frank Kofsky from *Jazz and Pop*, reprinted in Jonathan Eisen, ed., *The Age of Rock* (New York: Vintage Books, 1969).

9. We have already seen that from the mid-sixties on the British and American rock scenes are almost inextricably interwoven, with British developments often slightly in the lead. Commuting is commonplace, as illustrated by the fact that the album in which this piece appears ("Five Bridges") was recorded half in England and half in New York.

10. From liner notes, *Five Bridges* (Mercury: SR-61295).

11. Fine-art music, always in a somewhat precarious position economically, is vulnerable to the blandishments of the mass success (and money) of mass art. An interesting case in point was a 1977 concert by the Los Angeles Philharmonic, which drew a huge crowd to the Hollywood Bowl to hear music from a then-current science fiction film *Star Wars*, complete with a spectacular laser show. The event had nationwide media coverage.

12. Other San Francisco groups active at this time were the Grateful Dead, Moby Grape, Big Brother and the Holding Company, and Country Joe and the Fish.

CHAPTER 10: BROADWAY, HOLLYWOOD, AND TIN PAN ALLEY

1. James Maher evoked the extraordinarily rich mixture that went into the creation of a native idiom in a passage of eloquent fantasy (unfortunately too long to quote) cited in Alec Wilder, *American Popular Song: The Great Innovators, 1900–1950* (New York: Oxford University Press, 1972), pp. 7–8.

2. Wilder has documented this extensively in *American Popular Song*, which is organized along the lines of this stratification. George Gershwin noted the same thing early in his career; of his first acquaintance with the songs of Jerome Kern he wrote: "Kern was the first composer who made me conscious that most popular music was of inferior quality, and that musical-comedy music was made of better material."

3. The austerity resolution passed by the Continental Congress did not stifle all theatrical endeavor for the duration; a theatrical company formed in Baltimore gave two seasons of operas in that city (which was in American hands) and then moved, without hindrance from either side, to New York (which was in British hands), where they performed until the British were evacuated.

4. A single song, possibly borrowed from the repertory of the English music hall as an interpolation, is reprinted in Stanley Appelbaum, ed., *Show Songs from "The Black Crook" to "The Red Mill"* (New York: Dover Publications, 1974).

5. In order to confound too simple a picture of the tastes of the time, however, it is necessary to note that the works of Richard Genée and François Chassaigne were more popular at the time than those of their respective countrymen, Strauss and Offenbach. In any era, the siftings of public taste require time.

6. A sampling of five of Braham's songs from the Harrigan and Hart comedies is reprinted in Appelbaum, *Show Songs*.

7. Cohan's songs are almost too well known to call for sources for reference, but an assortment of the most familiar are available in *Ibid.* and in Robert Fremont, ed., *Favorite Songs of the Nineties* (New York: Dover Publications, 1973).

8. *I'm a Jonah Man*, a song not by Cook, interpolated into *In Dahomey* for black comedian Bert Williams, is reprinted in Appelbaum, *Show Songs*.

9. *Shuffle Along* (RAAM: NW-260).

10. Kern was to an extent ambivalent in this regard; and it must be said that Romberg, the most adaptable musically of our three adopted composers, could on occasion write a tune as American as any, as he showed for example in the lovely *Softly, as in a Morning Sunrise*).

11. The entire number is reprinted in Fremont, *Favorite Songs of the Nineties*.

12. An excellent sampling of this genre, with notes by George Oppenheimer, is *Follies, Scandals, and Other Diversions: From Ziegfeld to the Shuberts* (RAAM: NW-215).

13. For an interesting sampling of the music which accompanied the silent films, listen to *The Mighty Wurlitzer: Music for Movie-Palace Organs* (RAAM: NW-227).

14. Mark Evans, *Soundtrack: The Music of the Movies* (New York: Hopkinson & Blake, 1975), p. 194.

15. One producer is reputed to have retained or fired composers for his films based on the judgments of his twelve-year-old son.

16. Henry Mancini, quoted in Tony Thomas, *Music for the Movies* (New York: A. S. Barnes & Co., 1973), p. 195.

17. Quoted in Isaac Goldberg, *Tin Pan Alley: A Chronicle of American Popular Music* (Frederick Ungar Publishing Co., 1961), p. 207. An even more ingenious scheme for plugging a song called *Please Go 'Way and Let Me Sleep* is also recounted.

18. Quoted in *Ibid.*, pp. 197–201.

19. Quoted in Ian Whitcomb, *After the Ball* (London: Penguin Press, 1972), pp. 210–211.

CHAPTER 11: MINSTRELSY, RAGTIME, AND PRE-JAZZ

1. Lewis W. Paine, *Six Years in a Georgia Prison*, New York, 1851, quoted in Eileen Southern, ed., *Readings in Black American Music* (New York: W. W. Norton & Co., 1971), p. 91. Paine, a white man from Rhode

Island, went to the South for an extended stay on business and was sentenced to prison there for helping a slave to escape.

2. Mark Twain, incidentally, had enthusiastic praise for the minstrel show in its pure (that is, early) form, hailing it as a truly indigenous type of entertainment. At the same time he directed his barbed wit at the American penchant for lavishing money and attention on "foreign products"—a reference, presumably, to the Italian, German, and French opera being produced in New York and other cities during the latter part of the nineteenth century. He was not the first, or last, to sound this theme in his century or in ours, and call for an American Declaration of Independence in the arts.

3. W. C. Handy gives a vivid account of the last heyday of the touring minstrel companies around the turn of the century (most of them by this time consisted entirely of black performers) in his autobiography, *Father of the Blues* (New York: Macmillan Co., 1941), chapters 4 and 5.

4. Hans Nathan, *Dan Emmett and the Rise of Early Negro Minstrelsy* (Norman: University of Oklahoma Press, 1962), p. 128.

5. *Ibid.*, p. 276.

6. See Marshall Stearns, *The Story of Jazz* (New York: Oxford University Press, 1956), chapter 11.

7. Douglas Gilbert, *American Vaudeville: Its Life and Times* (New York, 1940. Reprint, New York: Dover Publications, Inc., 1963), pp. 78–79.

8. *Ibid.*, p. 284.

9. An archival re-creation of the 1921 production of *Shuffle Along* is included in the RAAM album of that title (NW-260). Of special interest here is the minstrel-like skit of side 2, band 2, *The Fight*.

10. The "Ethiopian songs" of minstrelsy thus antedated the popularity of the spirituals after the Civil War, which were also, for different reasons, somewhat diluted and adapted for popular consumption.

11. Quoted in Nathan, *Dan Emmett*, p. 340. An explanation of syncopation, and some further examples, are to be found in the following section on ragtime itself.

12. Nathan has made a useful start in reconstructing the score of a minstrel tune for voice and the four typical instruments much as it may have sounded in the 1840s. See *Ibid.*, pp. 403 ff.

13. These last three were written by the prolific black minstrel and songwriter James Bland.

14. Many banjo tunes from the time of the early minstrel show were called "jigs."

15. Available in the *Smithsonian Collection of Classic Jazz*, in which it can be compared with Joplin's own performance, from a piano roll, of the original.

16. As, for example, the rags of Joplin performed by Joshua Rifkin (Nonesuch-71248), or the album *Heliotrope Bouquet: Piano Rags 1900–1970*, performed by William Bolcom (Nonesuch: 71257).

17. A more genetic explanation of the syncopation of ragtime and jazz as survivals of the genuine polyrhythms of African music is put forward in Gunther Schuller's *Early Jazz: Its Roots and Musical Development* (New York: Oxford University Press, 1968), chapter one, based on the research of A. M. Jones. However plausible and interesting this theory, a consideration of it is beyond the scope of the present work. The explanation of syncopation (an undertaking always fraught with the greatest risks!) presented here is intended to instill a workable understanding of it from the standpoint of the Euro-American rhythmic basis (that of a single dominating pulse), which is the heritage and conditioning of most listeners.

18. The opening of this song is quoted in Eileen Southern's important work, *The Music of Black Americans* (New York: W. W. Norton & Co., 1971), p. 298.

19. *Ibid.*, p. 341.

20. Quoted in *Ibid.*, p. 348.

21. The sound of this orchestra may be heard on *A History of Jazz: The New York Scene 1914–1945* (Folkways: RBF-3).

22. An interesting account of the band's experiences is contained in *From Harlem to the Rhine*, by Arthur Little, a captain in the regiment. Excerpts are reprinted in Southern, *Readings in Black American Music*.

23. Quoted in Southern, *The Music of Black Americans*, p. 365.

24. Much of the foregoing is based on Bunk Johnson's description, as quoted in Stearns, *The Story of Jazz*, pp. 50–51.

25. *The Music of New Orleans*, vol. 2, *Music of the Eureka Brass Band* (Folkways: FA-2462).

26. From Foster's autobiography, quoted in Bruce Cook, *Listen to the Blues* (New York: Charles Scribner's Sons, 1973), p. 88.

CHAPTER 12: JAZZ: ITS TIMES AND STYLES

1. See André Hodeir, *Jazz: Its Evolution and Essence*, trans. David Noakes (New York: Grove Press, 1956), chapter 2.

2. *Dippermouth Blues*, from *The Smithsonian Collection of Classic Jazz* (henceforth abbreviated Sm.), side 1, band 6, or from *The Folkways History of Jazz Series* (henceforth FHJ), vol. 3, side 2, band 1. (References to volume when applicable, side, and band will be abbreviated III:2:1). *Snake Rag*, FHJ III:1:4. *Aunt Hagar's Blues*, from *The Encyclopedia of Jazz*, 1920s (henceforth Enc.), 1:1. *Grandpa's Spells*, Sm. 1:7. *Black Bottom Stomp*, Sm. 2:1. *Big Foot Ham*, from *The Riverside History of Classic Jazz* (henceforth Riv.), 4:3. *Froggie Moore*, Riv. 4:1. *Stockyard Strut* and *Society Blues*, from *Steppin' on the Gas: Rags to Jazz, 1913–1917* (RAAM: NW-269), 1:6 and 1:8. See the list of recordings at the end of the chapter for complete data on the anthologies referred to.

3. *Royal Garden Blues*, Riv. 7:2. *Jazz Me Blues*, FHJ VI:2:3. *There'll Be*

Some Changes Made, FHJ VI:2:7. These last two recordings are interesting to listen to in connection with a rather illuminating critique of both by one of the musicians involved, Mezz Mezzrow. The first appendix to his *Really the Blues* (New York: Random House, 1946) is a discussion of the whole relationship between the New Orleans and Chicago styles by a musician who speaks colorfully and lucidly from firsthand knowledge.

4. See the previous chapter. See also Eileen Southern, *The Music of Black Americans*, chapter 12, and Southern (ed.), *Readings in Black American Music*, chapter 8 (both New York: W. W. Norton & Co., 1971).

5. *Harlem Strut*, Riv. 8:1. *Carolina Shout*, Sm. 2:4. *You Can't Do What My Last Man Did*, FHJ VII:2:5. *You've Got to Be Modernistic*, Enc. (1920s) 2:2. *What Is This Thing Called Love?*, from *Jive at Five: The Style Makers of Jazz, 1920s–1940s* (RAAM: NW–274), 1:3.

6. Marshall Stearns, *The Story of Jazz* (New York: Oxford University Press, 1956), p. 122.

7. For a documentation of the development of the big bands elsewhere, notably in Chicago, St. Louis, Kansas City, and San Antonio, see *Big Bands and Territory Bands of the 1920s*, and *Sweet and Low Blues: Big Bands and Territory Bands of the 1930s* (RAAM: NW-256 and 217).

8. See the chart on pp. 330–331 for a graphic picture of the bands' makeup and growth.

9. *Dippermouth Blues*, Sm. 1:6 or FHJ III:2:1,*Sugar Foot Stomp*, FHJ VII: 2:2.

10. *The Stampede*, Sm. 3:6.

11. *East St. Louis Toodle-Oo*, Sm. 6:4 and 5; Enc. (1920s) 2:6. The Smithsonian collection presents an interesting juxtaposition of the 1927 version of this work with one made ten years later, showing clearly the evolution of Ellington's style during this period.

12. *Toby*, FHJ X:2:2 or from *Big Bands* (RAAM: NW-217), 2:1. *Moten Swing*, FHJ VIII:2:6 or Sm. 3:8. *Roseland Shuffle*, *Enc.* (1930s) 2:5. *Every Tub*, from *Jive At Five* (RAAM: NW-274), 1:1 *Dickie's Dream*, FHJ X: 2:7. An early example is *There's a Squabblin'*, by Walter Page's Blue Devils, with Count Basie on piano, from *Sweet and Low Blues* (RAAM: NW-256), 2:3.

13. *Ko-ko*, Sm. 7:2.

14. See Stearns, *The Story of Jazz*, pp. 149–150; Nat Shapiro and Nat Hentoff, eds., *Hear Me Talkin' to Ya* (New York: Dover Publications, 1966), pp. 313–321; Benny Goodman and Irving Kolodin, *The Kingdom of Swing* (Harrisburg, Pa.: Stackpole Sons, 1939).

15. *St. Louis Blues*, *Sugar Foot Stomp*, from *The King of Swing: Benny Goodman Complete 1937–38 Jazz Concert, no. 2* (Columbia: OSL-180). This album consists of actual broadcast performances of the Goodman band, trio, and quartet during 1937 and 1938.

16. *Tin Tin Deo*, from *Three Decades of Jazz: 1939–1949* (Bluenote: BST-89902), 4:6.

17. *I Found a New Baby*, Sm. 6:2 or from *Jive at Five* (RAAM: NW-274), 1:7.

18. The Smithsonian Collection includes several of these recordings. For a variety of small combos see *Little Club Jazz: Small Groups of the Thirties* (RAAM: NW-250).

19. *South Rampart Street Parade*, Enc. (1930s), 2:3. *Somebody Loves Me*, Enc. (1940s), 2:3.

20. *Down by the River*, FHJ III:1:6. *Make Me a Pallet on the Floor*, Riv. 10:2.

21. Ross Russell, from *The Record Changer*, as excerpted in Martin Williams, ed., *The Art of Jazz* (New York: Grove Press, 1960), p. 202. The entire article is worth reading.

22. *Shaw 'Nuff*, Sm. 7:6. *KoKo*, Sm. 7:7. Both are also included on *Bebop* (RAAM: NW-271), which is devoted entirely to this style, with excellent notes.

23. *Oop-Pap-a-Da*, from *The Bebop Era* (RCA Vintage: LPV-519), 2:5.

24. *Boplicity*, Sm. 9:1.

25. *Criss-Cross*, Sm. 9:5.

26. *Django*, Sm. 10:4. See also *Woody'n You*, from *Nica's Dream: Small Jazz Groups of the Fifties and Early Sixties* (RAAM: NW-242).

27. *So What*, Sm. 11:3.

28. *Blues for Eileen*, Feather (ed.), *Encyclopedia of Jazz (in the 60's)*: vol. 1, Verve V6-8677 2:2; *Dexterity*, Feather (ed.), *Encyclopedia of Jazz on Records*, vol. 5 MCA 2-4063 2:3.

29. *The Jitterbug Waltz*, as played by Fats Waller, was an early example. Later examples include *It's a Raggy Waltz*, and others, by Dave Brubeck, from *Adventures in Time* (Columbia: G-30625).

30. *Take Five*, from Brubeck, *Adventures in Time*.

31. *Unsquare Dance* from Brubeck, *Adventures in Time*. *Tears of Joy*, from Ellis, album of same name (Columbia: KG-30927).

32. From Brubeck, *Adventures in Time*.

33. *Alabama*, Sm. 12:4. For an explanation of the medieval modes surviving in folk music, see chapter 1.

34. Examples of this trend can be heard in albums such as *New Directions* by David Mack (SRS-12009).

35. Liebermann, *Concerto for Jazz Band and Symphony Orchestra* (RCA: LM-1888).

36. From *Jazz Abstractions* (Atlantic: 1365).

37. For an album which explores various interesting aspects of jazz seeking of new resources, see *Avant-Garde and Third-Stream Jazz*, with notes by Gunther Schuller (RAAM: NW-216).

38. *Back at the Chicken Shack*, from *Three Decades of Jazz: 1959–69* (Blue Note: BST-89904).

39. All from *The New Wave in Jazz* (Impulse: AS-90).

40. *Blood, Sweat and Tears* (Columbia: CS-9720) and *Chicago Transit Authority* (Columbia: GP-8). In a time when recorded performances are superseded nearly as rapidly as journalistic publication, these two albums have demonstrated noteworthy endurance for a decade.

41. *Chase* (Epic: 30472) and *Electric Bath* (Columbia: CS-9585).

42. *Blues in Orbit*, from *Gil Evans Svengali* (Atlantic: SD-1643).

CHAPTER 13: EIGHT PIONEERS

1. The *Bellarmonic*; see Oscar G. Sonneck, *Francis Hopkinson and James Lyon: Two Studies in Early American Music* (Washington, D.C., 1905; reprinted, New York: Da Capo Press, 1966), pp. 74–75.

2. Sonneck, *Hopkinson and Lyon*, pp. 78–79.

3. It is reproduced in *Ibid.*, p. 199. Recorded performances of it include one by Margaret Truman; the Trumans furnish another example, rare in our day, of a family representing a combination of interests in politics and the arts.

4. Available in a facsimile edition (Philadelphia: Musical Americana, 5458 Montgomery Ave., 1954). There are actually eight songs, since one was added after the title page was engraved.

5. Quoted in Arthur L. Rich, *Lowell Mason, "The Father of Singing Among the Children"* (Chapel Hill: University of North Carolina Press, 1946).

6. Louis Moreau Gottschalk *Notes of a Pianist* (New York: Alfred A. Knopf, 1964), pp. 300–303.

7. *Ibid.*, pp. 39–40.

8. *Ibid.*, p. 52.

9. *Ibid.*, pp. 102–103.

10. John Philip Sousa, *Marching Along* (Boston: Hale, Cushman & Flint, 1941), p. 132.

11. Dvořák was speaking in this context of Negro "plantation melodies," but the whole of his message was broader, at least as interpreted by those composers whose tendencies towards nationalism he stimulated.

12. Arthur Farwell, "A Letter to American Composers," *The Wa-Wan Press* (New York: Arno Press and The New York Times, 1970), vol. I, p. xvii.

13. Arthur Farwell, "An Affirmation of American Music" (1903), reprinted in Gilbert Chase, ed., *The American Composer Speaks* (Baton Rouge: Louisiana State University Press, 1966), pp. 91–93.

14. *A Guide to the Music of Arthur Farwell* has been privately printed; see the reading list for this chapter. In many cases the same work was adapted for various media (piano, chamber combination, chorus, orchestra).

15. See the record list for this chapter; this is one of the few Farwell compositions that have been recorded.

16. *A Guide to the Music of Arthur Farwell*, p. 85.

CHAPTER 14: FILM, DANCE, DRAMA, AND POETRY

1. Roger Sessions, *Reflections on the Music Life in the United States* (New York: Merlin Press, 1956), p. 16.
2. Sessions, *Reflections on Music Life*, p. 140. Paul Rosenfeld was an influential and controversial writer on the music of the time, enthusiastic about modern American music and active in its behalf. See the reading list for this chapter.
3. Aaron Copland, *Music and Imagination* (Cambridge: Harvard University Press, 1952), p. 104.
4. Aaron Copland, *The New Music* (New York: McGraw-Hill Book Co., 1941), pp. 161–162.
5. The complete text is included in the score of the orchestral suite, published by G. Schirmer, Inc.
6. It is currently obtainable from the Creative Film Society, 7237 Canby Ave., Reseda, Calif. 91335.
7. Kathleen Hoover and John Cage, *Virgil Thomson: His Life and Music* (Freeport, N.Y.: Books for Libraries Press, 1970), pp. 177–178.
8. See the reading list for chapter 1 for bibliographical references for all three of these collections. Both Thomson and Copland have consistently gone to the most prestigious sources for their folk material.
9. *The River* is currently obtainable from the Oregon Division of Continuing Education, 1633 S. W. Park Ave., Portland, Ore. 97207.
10. Extract from program note for the Kansas City Orchestra.
11. A selection of his reviews and articles for the period is collected in paperback as his *Music Reviewed, 1940–1954* (New York: Vintage Books, 1967).
12. The film is currently available from Budget Films, 4590 Santa Monica Blvd., Los Angeles, Calif. 90029.
13. *On the Waterfront* is currently available from McGraw-Hill Films, 1221 Ave. of the Americas, New York, N.Y. 10020, or from West Coast Films, 25 Lusk St., San Francisco, Calif. 94107.
14. All the cowboy songs used by Copland in *Billy the Kid* may be found in John and Alan Lomax's *Cowboy Songs and Other Frontier Ballads*, a basic collection first issued in 1910 by John Lomax (New York: The Macmillan Co.). All are reprinted by permission of The Macmillan Company.
15. Arthur Berger, *Aaron Copland*, (Westport, Conn.: Greenwood Press, 1971), p. 93.
16. Philip L. Miller's "Opera, the Story of an Immigrant," included in an otherwise excellent collection of essays edited by Paul Henry Lang, *One Hundred Years of Music in America* (New York: Grosset & Dunlap and G. Schirmer, 1961), is typical of this approach. Miller also seems to imply that opera, for the "sophisticated," should *remain* an alien immigrant; pass-

ing lightly over our American operas, the best that he can hold out as representative of the more genuine operatic treats in store for us is a revival of *Il Giuramento*, an opera written in 1837 by a sufficiently obscure Neapolitan composer named Giuseppe Saverio Rafaele Mercadante.

17. A complete recording of *The Mother of Us All*, together with complete text, is included in RAAM as NW: 288–289.

18. For one assessment of why this is so, which faults American composers themselves, see Charles Hamm, "Opera and the American Composer," in Gilbert Chase, ed., *The American Composer Speaks* (Baton Rouge: Louisiana State University Press, 1966).

19. An excellent sampling of American songs from this period is the album *When I Have Sung My Songs* (RAAM: NW-247), with comprehensive notes by Philip Miller.

20. This song is included in the album *But Yesterday Is Not Today* (RAAM: NW-243).

21. For an excellent brief study of Duke's songs, see Ruth Friedburg, "The Songs of John Duke," in the Bulletin of the National Association of Teachers of Singing, May 1963.

22. *Richard Cory*, Simon and Garfunkel, *Sounds of Silence* (Columbia: PC-9269).

23. Both may be heard in *The Art Song in America*, vol. 2, available from Duke University Press, Durham, N.C., and in *Songs by American Composers*, ST/AND 411/412, the latter album including also two additional mountain ballads, *Lonesome Man* and *Sugar in the Cane*.

24. Text as included in score published by G. Schirmer, Inc.

25. A recording of it is included in RAAM: NW-296.

26. The text is too long to quote, but is readily available in any edition of Whitman's works.

CHAPTER 15: MUSIC BY AND FOR ITSELF

1. Available in many recorded versions. Music published by New World Music, New York.

2. All four are included in the *Recorded Anthology of American Music* (RAAM), on *Aaron Copland: Works for Piano 1926–1948* (RAAM: NW-277). Music published by Boosey and Hawkes, New York.

3. Available in several recorded versions. Music published by G. Schirmer, New York.

4. Both these works are available in a most useful three-record album of nine quartets performed by the Kohon Quartet and issued as *American String Quartets, Volume II: 1900–1950* (Vox: SVBX-5305).

5. Recordings of all these quartets except the Harris are included in *American String Quartets*, cited above. The Harris quartet is included in *Cham-*

ber Works of Henry Cowell, Arthur Shepherd, and Roy Harris (RAAM: NW-218).

6. Several recordings. Score published by G. Schirmer, New York.

7. Several recordings. Score published by Associated Music Publishers, New York.

8. Numerous recordings. Score published by G. Schirmer, New York.

9. See for example his article "Problems of American Composers" (1933), reprinted in Gilbert Chase, ed., *The American Composer Speaks* (Baton Rouge: Louisiana State University Press, 1966).

10. Program notes, New York Philharmonic Symphony.

11. Available in RAAM: NW-286.

12. Recording included in *Winds of Change* (RAAM: NW-211).

13. Several recordings. Score published by Associated Music Publishers, New York.

14. Virgil Thomson, *American Music Since 1910* (New York: Holt, Rinehart and Winston, 1970), p. 130.

CHAPTER 16: NEW WAYS WITH OLD TOOLS

1. Cowell, Henry and Sidney, *Charles Ives and His Music* (New York: Oxford University Press, 1969, rev. ed.).

2. In *American Composers on American Music* (Stanford, 1933; republished, New York: Frederick Ungar, 1962).

3. For a famous and amusing anecdote concerning President Lincoln, General Grant, and George Ives's Brigade Band of the First Connecticut Heavy Artillery, see Cowell and Cowell, *Charles Ives and His Music*, p. 15.

4. For a rather full treatment of this theme, see Frank Rossiter, *Charles Ives and His America* (New York: Liveright Publishing Corp., 1975).

5. George Ives's copybook contains a version of *London Bridge* with the tune in G and the accompaniment in F-sharp. This was to prove a very seminal concept for Charles, as we shall see presently.

6. This description, together with other pregnant observations and speculations concerning the spatial element in music, is found in a rambling "Conductor's Note" published in 1929 with the Fourth Symphony (New York: Associated Music Publishers, 1965).

7. Included on *Old Songs Deranged: Charles Ives, Music for Theater Orchestra* (Columbia: M-32969).

8. Cowell and Cowell, *Charles Ives and His Music*, p. 121.

9. For the partial text of an interesting pencilled memo Ives wrote into the score concerning this plan of composing, see Charles Ives, *Charles E. Ives: Memos*, ed. John Kirkpatrick (New York: W. W. Norton & Co., 1972), p. 164.

10. Charles Ives, *Essays Before a Sonata, and Other Writings* (New York: 1961; paperback reprint, 1964), pp. 97–98.

11. Ives, *Memos*, pp. 87–88.

12. *Ibid.*, p. 104.

13. Cowell and Cowell, *Charles Ives and His Music*, pp. 176–177.

14. *Ibid.*, pp. 4–5.

15. *Memos*, p. 142.

16. Cited in Vivian Perlis, ed., *Charles Ives Remembered* (New Haven: Yale University Press, 1974), p. 160.

17. Ives *Essays Before a Sonata*, p. 84.

18. *Ibid.*, pp. 88, 92–93.

19. Quoted in Cowell and Cowell, *Charles Ives and His Music*, p. 97.

20. Audience reaction to an early performance of Ruggles's music provoked a famous outburst on the part of Charles Ives. He seldom went to concerts, but in 1931 he attended a Town Hall performance, under Slonimsky, which included *Men and Mountains*. In response to some hisses near him, Ives, according to his own account later, "jumped up and shouted 'You god damn sissy . . . when you hear strong masculine music like this, get up and use your ears like a man!' " (Ives, *Memos*, p. 141.)

21. Charles Seeger, "Carl Ruggles," in *Musical Quarterly*, reprinted in Cowell, *American Composers on American Music*.

22. Cowell's own performance of this and 19 other of his piano compositions may be heard on *The Piano Music of Henry Cowell* (Folkways: FM-3349).

23. These quartets were considered unplayable by Cowell himself at the time he wrote them (1915–1919). With today's more highly developed skills this is no longer the case; Cowell's two-minute *Quartet Euphometric* has been recorded, and is available in *Chamber Works of Henry Cowell, Arthur Shepherd, and Roy Harris* (RAAM: NW-218).

24. Most of these piano pieces are published (by Associated Music Publishers, New York), so that the notation is accessible for examination. All of this may be heard in a recording as played by the composer himself. (*The Piano Music of Henry Cowell*, Folkways: FM-3349). Cowell performed these for years on tour in the United States and abroad; his recorded renditions often vary widely from the printed score. Nevertheless, the recording is a fascinating and well-nigh indispensable document, and includes the composer's spoken annotations.

25. Recordings of most of the pieces mentioned are available; the RAAM includes a rather typical 10-minute chamber work, his *Suite for Violoncello and Harp*, on *Chamber Music by Lou Harrison, Ben Weber, Lukas Foss, and Ingolf Dahl* (NW-281).

26. As Partch added more instruments to his collection, he rescored earlier works; thus the version of *U.S. Highball* recorded in Illinois in the late 1950s and issued by Gate 5 Records includes many more instruments than were used in the original version.

27. Partch's instruments are pictured and described in detail in his *Genesis of*

a Music, 2nd ed. (New York: Da Capo Press, 1974); their sound is demonstrated, with commentary by Partch himself, on a record that is included with the recording of his last large work, *Delusion of the Fury* (Columbia: M2-30576).

28. Partch, *Genesis of a Music*, xi.

29. The Johnston String Quartet is available on Nonesuch: H-71224, and the Sonata for Microtonal Piano in the RAAM album *Sound Forms for Piano* (NW-203).

30. In a note to Odile Vivier, as quoted in Fernand Ouellette, *Edgard Varèse*, trans. Derek Coltman (New York: The Orion Press, 1968), p. 56.

31. Varèse, "Freedom for Music," in Gilbert Chase, ed., *The American Composer Speaks* (Baton Rouge: Louisiana State University Press, 1966), pp. 190–191.

32. Varèse, from a lecture given at Princeton University, 1959. In Elliott Schwartz and Barney Childs, eds., *Contemporary Composers on Contemporary Music* (New York: Holt, Rinehart and Winston, 1967), p. 202.

33. Varèse, from a lecture as reprinted in *Ibid.*, p. 197.

34. A first version of *Nocturnal* was performed in 1961, but he did not wish it performed again until he had revised it, a project he never completed.

35. Craft, jacket notes to Columbia: ML-5478, which includes *Intégrales*, *Octandre*, and three other compositions of Varèse.

36. Ouellette, *Edgard Varèse*, p. 181.

CHAPTER 17: TECHNOLOGY AND ESTHETIC CONCEPTS

1. Roger Sessions, "Problems and Issues Facing the Composer Today," in Paul Henry Lang, ed., *Problems of Modern Music* (New York: W. W. Norton & Co., 1960), p. 24.

2. John Cage, *Silence* (Middletown, Conn.: 1961. Paperback, Cambridge, Mass.: M.I.T. Press, 1966), p. 7.

3. This is illustrated in *Fancies for Clarinet Alone* by William O. Smith (both composer and performer), included in *New Music for Virtuosos* (RAAM: NW-209).

4. In this regard it is interesting to compare portions of an electronic piece such as *Touch*, by Morton Subotnick (Columbia: MS-7316), with portions of live pieces such as Morton Feldman's *Out of "Last Pieces"* (Columbia: ML-6133) or Earle Brown's *Available Forms I* (RCA VICS 1239).

5. Ralph Shapey, as quoted in notes to the recording of his *Evocation* (CRI: 141).

6. Morton Feldman, in an interview with Robert Ashley, in Elliott Schwartz and Barney Childs, eds., *Contemporary Composers on Contemporary Music* (New York: Holt, Rinehart & Winston, 1967), p. 365.

7. Ralph Shapey, in notes about his own works quoted on CRI: 232 and 141.

8. Brian O'Doherty on the music of Morton Feldman, quoted on CRI: 276.

9. Cage, *Silence*, p. 10. The notion of letting "sounds be themselves" is strikingly reminiscent of the Polish philosopher Wronsky's definition of music as "the corporealization of the intelligence that is in sounds"—a definition that greatly influenced Varèse.

10. Milton Babbitt, in *Musical America*, February 1961; quoted in Gilbert Chase, ed., *America's Music*, 2d rev. ed. (New York: McGraw-Hill Book Co., 1966).

11. In Schwartz and Childs, *Contemporary Composers on Contemporary Music*.

12. For the combination of tape music with live performance, see first *Déserts*, by Edgard Varèse (dealt with in the previous chapter); also Leon Kirchner's Quartet No. 3 for String Quartet and Electronic Tape (included in a highly useful album, *The Avant-Garde String Quartet in the U.S.A.*, SVBX: 5306); Roger Reynolds's *From Behind the Unreasoning Mask*, in *The Music of Paul Chihara, Chou Wen-chung, Earl Kim, and Roger Reynolds* (RAAM: NW-237); and two pieces by Milton Babbitt in *New Music for Virtuosos* (RAAM: NW-209). Examples of the new virtuosity in the performance of traditional instruments are also found in this latter album.

13. An example of such a piece is *Post-Partitions* (available in RAAM: NW-209, cited above) by Milton Babbitt, a composer long associated with such total procedural control, having pioneered in this direction in this country. Also by Babbitt are the similarly constructed *Composition for Four Instruments* and *Composition for Viola and Piano*, both on CRI: 138.

14. Ernst Krenek, "Serialism," in John Vinton, ed., *Dictionary of Contemporary Music* (New York: E. P. Dutton & Co., 1971), p. 673.

15. *Ibid.*

16. Karlheinz Stockhausen; quoted in Michael Nyman, *Experimental Music: Cage and Beyond* (New York: Schirmer Books [Macmillan], 1974), p. 23.

17. Krenek, "Serialism," p. 673.

18. Charles Wuorinen, in an interview with Barney Childs, in Schwartz and Childs, *Contemporary Composers on Contemporary Music*, p. 375.

19. Reprinted both in *Ibid.* and in Gilbert Chase, ed., *The Amerian Composer Speaks* (Baton Rouge: Louisiana State University Press, 1966).

20. *Time Cyle*, with improvised interludes, is available on Columbia Special Products: AMS-6280. *Studies in Improvisation* (RCA: LM-2558) is unfortunately currently out of print.

21. From notes to *Studies in Improvisation* (RCA: LM-2558).

22. John Cage, ed., *Notations* (New York: Something Else Press, 1969), reproduces a broad sampling of mid-twentieth-century notation.

23. David Cope, *New Music Composition* (New York: Schirmer Books [Macmillan], 1977), p. 116.

24. Cage, *Silence*, p. 59.

25. *Ibid.*, p. 12.

26. A recorded version, reduced in forces, cut to twenty minutes in length, and of course minus the excitement of the visual element, is available on Nonesuch: 71224.

27. Cage, *Silence*, p. 17.

28. This movement is particularly well documented in Nyman, *Experimental Music*. Nyman, in fact, applied the term "experimental music" specifically to the work of what might be called the Cagean school.

29. Milton Babbitt himself recommended this isolation in 1959. In "Who Cares If You Listen?" he wrote: "And so, I dare suggest that the composer would do himself and his music an immediate and eventual service by total, resolute, and voluntary withdrawal from this public world to one of the private performance and electronic media, with its very real possibility of complete elimination of the public and social aspects of musical composition." (Reprinted in Chase, *The American Composer Speaks*, and Schwartz and Childs, *Contemporary Composers on Contemporary Music*.)

30. Billy Jim Layton, "The New Liberalism," *Perspectives of New Music*, vol. 3 no. 2 (Spring–Summer 1965), pp. 137–142.

31. *Ibid.*

32. George Crumb's *Voice of the Whale*, 1971 (Columbia: M-32739), and Morton Feldman's *Rothko Chapel*, 1972 (Columbia: Y-34138), both illustrate this.

33. Ralph Shapey, from the notes to the recording of his *Praise*, CRI: 355.

34. Layton, "The New Liberalism."

35. George Rochberg, from notes to his *Contra Mortem et Tempus*, as quoted in notes to the recording, CRI: 231.

Index

WITHDRAW